MW01070343

Mastering Embedded Linux Programming

Third Edition

Create fast and reliable embedded solutions with Linux 5.4 and the Yocto Project 3.1 (Dunfell)

Frank Vasquez

Chris Simmonds

Packt

BIRMINGHAM—MUMBAI

Mastering Embedded Linux Programming

Third Edition

Group Product Manager: Wilson Dsouza
Publishing Product Manager: Sankalp Khattri
Senior Editor: Rahul Dsouza
Content Development Editor: Sayali Pingale
Technical Editor: Sarvesh Jaywant
Copy Editor: Safis Editing
Project Coordinator: Neil Dmello
Proofreader: Safis Editing
Indexer: Tejal Soni
Production Designer: Nilesh Mohite

First published: December 2015
Second edition: June 2017
Third edition: March 2021
Production reference: 0140421

Published by Packt Publishing Ltd.
Livery Place
35 Livery Street
Birmingham
B3 2PB, UK.

ISBN 978-1-78953-038-4

`www.packt.com`

To the open source software community (especially the Yocto Project) for welcoming me in wholeheartedly. And to my wife Deborah for putting up with the late-night hardware hacking. The world runs on Linux.

– Frank Vasquez

Contributors

About the authors

Frank Vasquez is an independent software consultant specializing in consumer electronics. He has over a decade of experience designing and building embedded Linux systems. During that time, he has shipped numerous devices including a rackmount DSP audio server, a diver-held sonar camcorder, and a consumer IoT hotspot. Before his career as an embedded Linux engineer, Frank was a database kernel developer at IBM, where he worked on DB2. He lives in Silicon Valley.

Chris Simmonds is a software consultant and trainer living in southern England. He has almost two decades of experience in designing and building open source embedded systems. He is the founder and chief consultant at 2net Ltd, which provides professional training and mentoring services in embedded Linux, Linux device drivers, and Android platform development. He has trained engineers at many of the biggest companies in the embedded world, including ARM, Qualcomm, Intel, Ericsson, and General Dynamics. He is a frequent presenter at open source and embedded conferences, including the Embedded Linux Conference and Embedded World.

About the reviewers

Ned Konz is an autodidact who believes in Sturgeon's law and tries to work on the other 10% of everything. His work experience over the last 45 years includes software and electronics design for industrial machines, and consumer and medical devices, as well as doing user interface research with Alan Kay's team at HP Labs. He has embedded Linux in devices including high-end SONAR systems, inspection cameras, and the Glowforge laser cutter. As a senior embedded systems programmer at Product Creation Studio in Seattle, he designs software and electronics for a variety of client products. In his spare time, he builds electronics gadgets and plays bass in a rock band. He has also done two solo bicycle tours of over 4,500 miles each.

I'd like to thank my wife Nancy for her support, and Frank Vasquez for recommending me as a technical reviewer.

Khem Raj holds a bachelor's degree (Hons) in electronics and communications engineering. In his career spanning 20 years in software systems, he has worked with organizations ranging from start-ups to Fortune 500 companies. During this time, he has worked on developing operating systems, compilers, computer programming languages, scalable build systems, and system software development and optimization. He is passionate about open source and is a prolific open source contributor, maintaining popular open source projects such as the Yocto Project. He is a frequent speaker at open source conferences. He is an avid reader and a lifelong learner.

Table of Contents

3

All about Bootloaders

4

Configuring and Building the Kernel

5
Building a Root Filesystem

6
Selecting a Build System

7
Developing with Yocto

8

Yocto Under the Hood

Section 2: System Architecture and Design Decisions

9

Creating a Storage Strategy

10

Updating Software in the Field

11
Interfacing with Device Drivers

12
Prototyping with Breakout Boards

13

Starting Up – The init Program

14

Starting with BusyBox runit

15

Managing Power

Section 3: Writing Embedded Applications

16
Packaging Python

17
Learning about Processes and Threads

18
Managing Memory

Section 4: Debugging and Optimizing Performance

19

Debugging with GDB

20

Profiling and Tracing

21

Real-Time Programming

Other Books You May Enjoy

Index

Preface

Linux has been the mainstay of embedded computing for many years. And yet, there are remarkably few books that cover the topic as a whole: this book is intended to fill that gap. The term "embedded Linux" is not well defined and can be applied to the operating system inside a wide range of devices ranging from thermostats to Wi-Fi routers to industrial control units. However, they are all built on the same basic open source software. Those are the technologies that I describe in this book, based on my experience as an engineer and the materials I have developed for my training courses.

Technology does not stand still. The industry based around embedded computing is just as susceptible to Moore's law as mainstream computing. The exponential growth that this implies has meant that a surprisingly large number of things have changed since the first edition of this book was published. This third edition is fully revised to use the latest versions of the major open source components, which include Linux 5.4, the Yocto Project 3.1 Dunfell, and Buildroot 2020.02 LTS. In addition to Autotools, the book now covers CMake, a modern build system that has seen increased adoption in recent years.

Mastering Embedded Linux Programming covers the topics in roughly the order that you will encounter them in a real-life project. The first eight chapters are concerned with the early stages of the project, covering basics such as selecting the toolchain, the bootloader, and the kernel. I introduce the idea of embedded build systems, using Buildroot and the Yocto Project as examples. The section ends with new in-depth coverage of the Yocto Project.

Section 2, Chapters 9 to *15*, looks at the various design decisions that need to be made before development can take place in earnest. It covers the topics of filesystems, software update, device drivers, the `init` program, and power management. *Chapter 12* demonstrates various techniques for rapid prototyping with a breakout board, including how to read schematics, solder headers, and troubleshoot signals using a logic analyzer. *Chapter 14* is a deep dive into Buildroot where you will learn how to partition your system software into separate services using BusyBox `runit`.

Section 3, *Chapters 16*, *17*, and *18*, will help you in the implementation phase of the project. We start with Python packaging and dependency management, a topic of growing importance as machine learning applications continue to take the world by storm. Next, we move on to various forms of inter-process communication and multithreaded programming. The section concludes with a careful examination of how Linux manages memory and demonstrates how to measure memory usage and detect memory leaks using the various tools that are available.

The fourth section, which includes *Chapters 19* and *20*, shows you how to make effective use of the many debug and profiling tools that Linux has to offer in order to detect problems and identify bottlenecks. *Chapter 19* now describes how to configure Visual Studio Code for remote debugging using GDB. *Chapter 20* now includes coverage of BPF, a new technology that enables advanced programmatic tracing inside the Linux kernel. The final chapter brings together several threads to explain how Linux can be used in real-time applications.

Each chapter introduces a major area of embedded Linux. It describes the background so that you can learn the general principles, but it also includes detailed working examples that illustrate each of these areas. You can treat this as a book of theory, or a book of examples. It works best if you do both: understand the theory and try it out in real life.

Who this book is for

This book is written for developers with an interest in embedded computing and Linux who want to extend their knowledge into the various branches of the subject. In writing the book, I assume a basic understanding of the Linux command line, and in the programming examples, a working knowledge of the C and Python languages. Several chapters focus on the hardware that goes into an embedded target board, and, so, familiarity with hardware and hardware interfaces will be a definite advantage in these cases.

What this book covers

Chapter 1, *Starting Out*, sets the scene by describing the embedded Linux ecosystem and the choices available to you as you start your project.

Chapter 2, *Learning about Toolchains*, describes the components of a toolchain and shows you how to create a toolchain for cross-compiling code for the target board. It describes where to get a toolchain and provides details on how to build one from the source code.

Chapter 3, All about Bootloaders, explains the role of the bootloader in loading the Linux kernel into memory, and uses U-Boot as an example. It also introduces device trees as the mechanism used to encode the details of the hardware in almost all embedded Linux systems.

Chapter 4, Configuring and Building the Kernel, provides information on how to select a Linux kernel for an embedded system and configure it for the hardware within the device. It also covers how to port Linux to the new hardware.

Chapter 5, Building a Root Filesystem, introduces the ideas behind the user space part of an embedded Linux implementation by means of a step-by-step guide on how to configure a root filesystem.

Chapter 6, Selecting a Build System, covers two commonly used embedded Linux build systems, Buildroot and the Yocto Project, which automate the steps described in the previous four chapters.

Chapter 7, Developing with Yocto, demonstrates how to build system images on top of an existing BSP layer, develop onboard software packages with Yocto's extensible SDK, and roll your own embedded Linux distribution complete with runtime package management.

Chapter 8, Yocto under the Hood, is a tour of Yocto's build workflow and architecture including an explanation of Yocto's unique multi-layer approach. It also breaks down the basics of BitBake syntax and semantics with examples from actual recipe files.

Chapter 9, Creating a Storage Strategy, discusses the challenges created by managing flash memory, including raw flash chips and **embedded MMC** (**eMMC**) packages. It describes the filesystems that are applicable to each type of technology.

Chapter 10, Updating Software in the Field, examines various ways of updating the software after the device has been deployed, and includes fully managed **Over-the-Air** (**OTA**) updates. The key topics under discussion are reliability and security.

Chapter 11, Interfacing with Device Drivers, describes how kernel device drivers interact with the hardware by implementing a simple driver. It also describes the various ways of calling device drivers from user space.

Chapter 12, Prototyping with Breakout Boards, demonstrates how to prototype hardware and software quickly using a pre-built Debian image for the BeagleBone Black together with a peripheral breakout board. You will learn how to read datasheets, wire up boards, mux device tree bindings, and analyze SPI signals.

Chapter 13, Starting Up – The init Program, explains how the first user space program–`init`–starts the rest of the system. It describes three versions of the `init` program, each suitable for a different group of embedded systems, ranging from the simplicity of the BusyBox `init`, through System V `init`, to the current state-of-the-art approach, `systemd`.

Chapter 14, Starting with BusyBox runit, shows you how to use Buildroot to divide your system up into separate BusyBox `runit` services each with its own dedicated process supervision and logging like that provided by `systemd`.

Chapter 15, Managing Power, considers the various ways that Linux can be tuned to reduce power consumption, including dynamic frequency and voltage scaling, selecting deeper idle states, and system suspend. The aim is to make devices that run for longer on a battery charge and also run cooler.

Chapter 16, Packaging Python, explains what choices are available for bundling Python modules together for deployment and when to use one method over another. It covers `pip`, virtual environments, `conda`, and Docker.

Chapter 17, Learning about Processes and Threads, describes embedded systems from the point of view of the application programmer. This chapter looks at processes and threads, inter-process communications, and scheduling policies.

Chapter 18, Managing Memory, introduces the ideas behind virtual memory and how the address space is divided into memory mappings. It also describes how to measure memory usage accurately and how to detect memory leaks.

Chapter 19, Debugging with GDB, shows you how to use the GNU debugger, GDB, together with the debug agent, `gdbserver`, to debug applications running remotely on the target device. It goes on to show how you can extend this model to debug kernel code, making use of the kernel debug stubs with KGDB.

Chapter 20, Profiling and Tracing, covers the techniques available to measure the system performance, starting from whole system profiles and then zeroing in on particular areas where bottlenecks are causing poor performance. It also describes how to use Valgrind to check the correctness of an application's use of thread synchronization and memory allocation.

Chapter 21, Real-Time Programming, provides a detailed guide to real-time programming on Linux, including the configuration of the kernel and the `PREEMPT_RT` real-time kernel patch. The kernel trace tool, Ftrace, is used to measure kernel latencies and show the effect of the various kernel configurations.

To get the most out of this book

The software used in this book is entirely open source. In almost all cases, I have used the latest stable versions available at the time of writing. While I have tried to describe the main features in a manner that is not version-specific, it is inevitable that some of the examples will need adaptation to work with later software.

Hardware/software covered in the book	OS requirements
BeagleBone Black	Not applicable
Raspberry Pi 4	Not applicable
QEMU (32-bit Arm)	Linux (Any)
Yocto Project 3.1 (Dunfell)	Compatible Linux distribution*
Buildroot 2020.02 LTS	Linux (Any)
Crosstool-NG 1.24.0	Linux (Any)
U-Boot v2021.01	Linux (Any)
Linux kernel 5.4	Linux (Any)

* See the *Compatible Linux Distribution* section of the *Yocto Project Quick Build* guide at `https://www.yoctoproject.org/docs/current/brief-yoctoprojectqs/brief-yoctoprojectqs.html` for more details.

Embedded development involves two systems: the host, which is used for developing the programs, and the target, which runs them. For the host system, I have used Ubuntu 20.04 LTS, but most Linux distributions will work with just a little modification. You may decide to run Linux as a guest in a virtual machine, but you should be aware that some tasks, such as building a distribution using the Yocto Project, are quite demanding and are better run on a native installation of Linux.

I chose three exemplar targets: the QEMU emulator, the BeagleBone Black, and the Raspberry Pi 4. Using QEMU means that you can try out most of the examples without having to invest in any additional hardware. On the other hand, some things work better if you do have real hardware, for which, I have chosen the BeagleBone Black because it is not expensive, it is widely available, and it has very good community support. The Raspberry Pi 4 was added in the third edition for its built-in Wi-Fi and Bluetooth. Of course, you are not limited to just these three targets. The idea behind the book is to provide you with general solutions to problems so that you can apply them to a wide range of target boards.

Download the example code files

You can download the example code files for this book from GitHub at `https://github.com/PacktPublishing/Mastering-Embedded-Linux-Programming-Third-Edition`.

In case there's an update to the code, it will be updated on the existing GitHub repository. We also have other code bundles from our rich catalog of books and videos available at `https://github.com/PacktPublishing/`. Check them out!

Download the color images

We also provide a PDF file that has color images of the screenshots/diagrams used in this book. You can download it here: `http://www.packtpub.com/sites/default/files/downloads/9781789530384_ColorImages.pdf`.

Conventions used

There are a number of text conventions used throughout this book.

`Code in text`: Indicates code words in text, database table names, folder names, filenames, file extensions, pathnames, dummy URLs, user input, and Twitter handles. Here is an example: "To configure the host side of the network, you need the `tunctl` command from the User Mode Linux (UML) project."

A block of code is set as follows:

```
#include <stdio.h>
#include <stdlib.h>
int main (int argc, char *argv[])
{
    printf ("Hello, world!\n");
    return 0;
}
```

Any command-line input or output is written as follows:

```
$ sudo tunctl -u $(whoami) -t tap0
```

Bold: Indicates a new term, an important word, or words that you see onscreen. For example, words in menus or dialog boxes appear in the text like this. Here is an example: "Click **Flash** from Etcher to write the image."

> **Tips or important notes**
> Appear like this.

Get in touch

Feedback from our readers is always welcome.

General feedback: If you have questions about any aspect of this book, mention the book title in the subject of your message and email us at `customercare@packtpub.com`.

Errata: Although we have taken every care to ensure the accuracy of our content, mistakes do happen. If you have found a mistake in this book, we would be grateful if you would report this to us. Please visit `www.packtpub.com/support/errata`, selecting your book, clicking on the Errata Submission Form link, and entering the details.

Piracy: If you come across any illegal copies of our works in any form on the Internet, we would be grateful if you would provide us with the location address or website name. Please contact us at `copyright@packt.com` with a link to the material.

If you are interested in becoming an author: If there is a topic that you have expertise in and you are interested in either writing or contributing to a book, please visit `authors.packtpub.com`.

Reviews

Please leave a review. Once you have read and used this book, why not leave a review on the site that you purchased it from? Potential readers can then see and use your unbiased opinion to make purchase decisions, we at Packt can understand what you think about our products, and our authors can see your feedback on their book. Thank you!

For more information about Packt, please visit `packt.com`.

Section 1: Elements of Embedded Linux

The objective of *Section 1* is to help the reader set up their development environment and create a working platform for the later phases. It is often referred to as the "board bring-up" phase.

This part of the book comprises the following chapters:

- *Chapter 1, Starting Out*
- *Chapter 2, Learning About Toolchains*
- *Chapter 3, All About Bootloaders*
- *Chapter 4, Configuring and Building the Kernel*
- *Chapter 5, Building a Root Filesystem*
- *Chapter 6, Selecting a Build System*
- *Chapter 7, Developing with Yocto*
- *Chapter 8, Yocto Under the Hood*

1
Starting Out

You are about to begin working on your next project, and this time it is going to be running Linux. What should you think about before you put finger to keyboard? Let's begin with a high-level look at embedded Linux and see why it is popular, what are the implications of open source licenses, and what kind of hardware you will need to run Linux.

Linux first became a viable choice for embedded devices around 1999. That was when Axis (`https://www.axis.com`) released their first Linux-powered network camera and TiVo (`https://business.tivo.com`) their first **Digital Video Recorder** (**DVR**). Since 1999, Linux has become ever more popular, to the point that today it is the operating system of choice for many classes of product. In 2021, there were over two billion devices running Linux. That includes a large number of smartphones running Android, which uses a Linux kernel, and hundreds of millions of set-top boxes, smart TVs, and Wi-Fi routers, not to mention a very diverse range of devices such as vehicle diagnostics, weighing scales, industrial devices, and medical monitoring units that ship in smaller volumes.

In this chapter, we will cover the following topics:

- Choosing Linux
- When not to choose Linux
- Meeting the players
- Moving through the project life cycle
- Navigating open source

- Selecting hardware for embedded Linux
- Obtaining the hardware for this book
- Provisioning your development environment

Choosing Linux

Why is Linux so pervasive? And why does something as simple as a TV need to run something as complex as Linux just to display streaming video on a screen?

The simple answer is Moore's Law: Gordon Moore, co-founder of Intel, observed in 1965 that the density of components on a chip will double approximately every 2 years. That applies to the devices that we design and use in our everyday lives just as much as it does to desktops, laptops, and servers. At the heart of most embedded devices is a highly integrated chip that contains one or more processor cores and interfaces with main memory, mass storage, and peripherals of many types. This is referred to as a **System on Chip**, or **SoC**, and SoCs are increasing in complexity in accordance with Moore's Law. A typical SoC has a technical reference manual that stretches to thousands of pages. Your TV is not simply displaying a video stream as the old analog sets used to do.

The stream is digital, possibly encrypted, and it needs processing to create an image. Your TV is (or soon will be) connected to the internet. It can receive content from smartphones, tablets, and home media servers. It can be (or soon will be) used to play games and so on. You need a full operating system to manage this degree of complexity.

Here are some points that drive the adoption of Linux:

- Linux has the necessary functionality. It has a good scheduler, a good network stack, support for USB, Wi-Fi, Bluetooth, many kinds of storage media, good support for multimedia devices, and so on. It ticks all the boxes.
- Linux has been ported to a wide range of processor architectures, including some that are very commonly found in SoC designs – Arm, MIPS, x86, and PowerPC.
- Linux is open source, so you have the freedom to get the source code and modify it to meet your needs. You, or someone working on your behalf, can create a board support package for your particular SoC board or device. You can add protocols, features, and technologies that may be missing from the mainline source code. You can remove features that you don't need to reduce memory and storage requirements. Linux is flexible.

- Linux has an active community; in the case of the Linux kernel, very active. There is a new release of the kernel every 8 to 10 weeks, and each release contains code from more than 1,000 developers. An active community means that Linux is up to date and supports current hardware, protocols, and standards.
- Open source licenses guarantee that you have access to the source code. There is no vendor tie-in.

For these reasons, Linux is an ideal choice for complex devices. But there are a few caveats I should mention here. Complexity makes it harder to understand. Coupled with the fast-moving development process and the decentralized structures of open source, you have to put some effort into learning how to use it and to keep on re-learning as it changes. I hope that this book will help in the process.

When not to choose Linux

Is Linux suitable for your project? Linux works well where the problem being solved justifies the complexity. It is especially good where connectivity, robustness, and complex user interfaces are required. However, it cannot solve every problem, so here are some things to consider before you jump in:

- Is your hardware up to the job? Compared to a traditional **real-time operating system** (**RTOS**) such as VxWorks or QNX, Linux requires a lot more resources. It needs at least a 32-bit processor and lots more memory. I will go into more detail in the section on typical hardware requirements.
- Do you have the right skill set? The early parts of a project, board bring-up, require detailed knowledge of Linux and how it relates to your hardware. Likewise, when debugging and tuning your application, you will need to be able to interpret the results. If you don't have the skills in-house, you may want to outsource some of the work. Of course, reading this book helps!
- Is your system real-time? Linux can handle many real-time activities so long as you pay attention to certain details, which I will cover in detail in *Chapter 21, Real-Time Programming*.
- Will your code require regulatory approval (medical, automotive, aerospace, and so on)? The burden of regulatory verification and validation might make another OS a better choice. Even if you do choose Linux for use in these environments, it may make sense to purchase a commercially available distribution from a company that has supplied Linux for existing products, like the one you are building.

Consider these points carefully. Probably the best indicator of success is to look around for similar products that run Linux and see how they have done it; follow best practice.

Meeting the players

Where does open source software come from? Who writes it? In particular, how does this relate to the key components of embedded development—the toolchain, bootloader, kernel, and basic utilities found in the root filesystem?

The main players are as follows:

- **The open source community**: This, after all, is the engine that generates the software you are going to be using. The community is a loose alliance of developers, many of whom are funded in some way, perhaps by a not-for-profit organization, an academic institution, or a commercial company. They work together to further the aims of the various projects. There are many of them—some small, some large. Some that we will be making use of in the remainder of this book are Linux itself, U-Boot, BusyBox, Buildroot, the Yocto Project, and the many projects under the GNU umbrella.
- **CPU architects**: These are the organizations that design the CPUs we use. The important ones here are Arm/Linaro (Arm Cortex-A), Intel (x86 and x86_64), SiFive (RISC-V), and IBM (PowerPC). They implement or, at the very least, influence support for the basic CPU architecture.
- **SoC vendors** (Broadcom, Intel, Microchip, NXP, Qualcomm, TI, and many others): They take the kernel and toolchain from the CPU architects and modify them to support their chips. They also create reference boards: designs that are used by the next level down to create development boards and working products.
- **Board vendors and OEMs**: These people take the reference designs from SoC vendors and build them in to specific products, for instance, set-top boxes or cameras, or create more general-purpose development boards, such as those from Advantech and Kontron. An important category are the cheap development boards such as BeagleBoard/BeagleBone and Raspberry Pi that have created their own ecosystems of software and hardware add-ons.
- **Commercial Linux vendors**: Companies such as Siemens (Mentor), Timesys, and Wind River offer commercial Linux distributions that have undergone strict regulatory verification and validation across multiple industries (medical, automotive, aerospace, and so on).

These form a chain, with your project usually at the end, which means that you do not have a free choice of components. You cannot simply take the latest kernel from `https://www.kernel.org/`, except in a few rare cases, because it does not have support for the chip or board that you are using.

This is an ongoing problem with embedded development. Ideally, the developers at each link in the chain would push their changes upstream, but they don't. It is not uncommon to find a kernel that has many thousands of patches that are not merged. In addition, SoC vendors tend to actively develop open source components only for their latest chips, meaning that support for any chip more than a couple of years old will be frozen and not receive any updates.

The consequence is that most embedded designs are based on old versions of software. They do not receive security fixes, performance enhancements, or features that are in newer versions. Problems such as Heartbleed (a bug in the OpenSSL libraries) and ShellShock (a bug in the bash shell) go unfixed. I will talk more about this later in this chapter under the topic of security.

What can you do about it? First, ask questions of your vendors (NXP, Texas Instruments, and Xilinx, to name just a few): what is their update policy, how often do they revise kernel versions, what is the current kernel version, what was the one before that, and what is their policy for merging changes upstream? Some vendors are making great strides in this way. You should prefer their chips.

Secondly, you can take steps to make yourself more self-sufficient. The chapters in *Section 1* explain the dependencies in more detail and show you where you can help yourself. Don't just take the package offered to you by the SoC or board vendor and use it blindly without considering the alternatives.

Moving through the project life cycle

This book is divided into four sections that reflect the phases of a project. The phases are not necessarily sequential. Usually, they overlap and you will need to jump back to revisit things that were done previously. However, they are representative of a developer's preoccupations as the project progresses:

- *Elements of Embedded Linux* (*Chapters 1* to *8*) will help you set up the development environment and create a working platform for the later phases. It is often referred to as the **board bring-up** phase.
- *System Architecture and Design Choices* (*Chapters 9* to *15*) will help you to look at some of the design decisions you will have to make concerning the storage of programs and data, how to divide work between kernel device drivers and applications, and how to initialize the system.
- *Writing Embedded Applications* (*Chapters 16* to *18*) shows how to package and deploy Python applications, make effective use of the Linux process and thread model, and how to manage memory in a resource-constrained device.

- *Debugging and Optimizing Performance* (*Chapters 19* to *21*) describes how to trace, profile, and debug your code in both the applications and the kernel. The last chapter explains how to design for real-time behavior when required.

Now, let's focus on the four basic elements of embedded Linux that comprise the first section of the book.

The four elements of embedded Linux

Every project begins by obtaining, customizing, and deploying these four elements: the toolchain, the bootloader, the kernel, and the root filesystem. This is the topic of the first section of this book.

- **Toolchain**: The compiler and other tools needed to create code for your target device.
- **Bootloader**: The program that initializes the board and loads the Linux kernel.
- **Kernel**: This is the heart of the system, managing system resources and interfacing with hardware.
- **Root filesystem**: Contains the libraries and programs that are run once the kernel has completed its initialization.

Of course, there is also a fifth element, not mentioned here. That is the collection of programs specific to your embedded application that make the device do whatever it is supposed to do, be it weigh groceries, display movies, control a robot, or fly a drone.

Typically, you will be offered some or all of these elements as a package when you buy your SoC or board. But, for the reasons mentioned in the preceding paragraph, they may not be the best choices for you. I will give you the background to make the right selections in the first eight chapters and I will introduce you to two tools that automate the whole process for you: Buildroot and the Yocto Project.

Navigating open source

The components of embedded Linux are *open source*, so now is a good time to consider what that means, why open sources work the way they do, and how this affects the often proprietary embedded device you will be creating from it.

Licenses

When talking about open source, the word *free* is often used. People new to the subject often take it to mean *nothing to pay*, and open source software licenses do indeed guarantee that you can use the software to develop and deploy systems for no charge. However, the more important meaning here is freedom, since you are free to obtain the source code, modify it in any way you see fit, and redeploy it in other systems. These licenses give you this right. Compare that with freeware licenses, which allow you to copy the binaries for no cost but do not give you the source code, or other licenses that allow you to use the software for free under certain circumstances, for example, for personal use, but not commercial. These are not open source.

I will provide the following comments in the interest of helping you understand the implications of working with open source licenses, but I would like to point out that I am an engineer and not a lawyer. What follows is my understanding of the licenses and the way they are interpreted.

Open source licenses fall broadly into two categories: *copyleft* licenses, such as the **GNU General Public License** (**GPL**), and permissive licenses, such as the **BSD** and **MIT** licenses.

The permissive licenses say, in essence, that you may modify the source code and use it in systems of your own choosing so long as you do not modify the terms of the license in any way. In other words, with that one restriction, you can do with it what you want, including building it into possibly proprietary systems.

The GPL licenses are similar but have clauses that compel you to pass the rights to obtain and modify the software on to your end users. In other words, you share your source code. One option is to make it completely public by putting it onto a public server. Another is to offer it only to your end users by means of a written offer to provide the code when requested. The GPL goes further to say that you cannot incorporate GPL code into proprietary programs. Any attempt to do so would make the GPL apply to the whole. In other words, you cannot combine a GPL and proprietary code in one program. Aside from the Linux kernel, the GNU Compiler Collection and GNU Debugger as well as many other freely available tools associated with the GNU project fall under the umbrella of the GPL.

So, what about libraries? If they are licensed with the GPL, any program linked with them becomes GPL also. However, most libraries are licensed under the **GNU Lesser General Public License** (**LGPL**). If this is the case, you are allowed to link with them from a proprietary program.

> **Important note**
>
> All of the preceding description relates specifically to GPL v2 and LGPL v2.1. I should mention the latest versions of GPL v3 and LGPL v3. These are controversial, and I will admit that I don't fully understand the implications. However, the intention is to ensure that the GPL v3 and LGPL v3 components in any system can be replaced by the end user, which is in the spirit of open source software for everyone.

The GPL v3 and LGPL v3 have their problems though. There are issues with security. If the owner of a device has access to the system code, then so might an unwelcome intruder. Often the defense is to have kernel images that are signed by an authority such as the vendor, so that unauthorized updates are not possible. Is that an infringement of my right to modify my device? Opinions differ.

> **Important note**
>
> The TiVo set-top box is an important part of this debate. It uses a Linux kernel, which is licensed under GPL v2. TiVo have released the source code of their version of the kernel and so comply with the license. TiVo also has a bootloader that will only load a kernel binary that is signed by them. Consequently, you can build a modified kernel for a TiVo box, but you cannot load it on the hardware. The **Free Software Foundation** (**FSF**) takes the position that this is not in the spirit of open source software and refers to this procedure as **Tivoization**. The GPL v3 and LGPL v3 were written to explicitly prevent this from happening. Some projects, the Linux kernel in particular, have been reluctant to adopt the GPL version 3 licenses because of the restrictions they would place on device manufacturers.

Selecting hardware for embedded Linux

If you are designing or selecting hardware for an embedded Linux project, what do you look out for?

First, a CPU architecture that is supported by the kernel—unless you plan to add a new architecture yourself, of course! Looking at the source code for Linux 5.4, there are 25 architectures, each represented by a sub-directory in the `arch/` directory. They are all 32- or 64-bit architectures, most with an MMU, but some without. The ones most often found in embedded devices are Arm, MIPS, PowerPC, and x86, each in 32 and 64-bit variants, all of which have **memory management units** (**MMUs**).

Most of this book is written with this class of processor in mind. There is another group that doesn't have an MMU and that runs a subset of Linux known as **microcontroller Linux** or **uClinux**. These processor architectures include ARC (Argonaut RISC Core), Blackfin, MicroBlaze, and Nios. I will mention uClinux from time to time, but I will not go into detail because it is a rather specialized topic.

Second, you will need a reasonable amount of RAM. 16 MiB is a good minimum, although it is quite possible to run Linux using half that. It is even possible to run Linux with 4 MiB if you are prepared to go to the trouble of optimizing every part of the system. It may even be possible to get lower, but there comes a point at which it is no longer Linux.

Third, there is non-volatile storage, usually flash memory. 8 MiB is enough for a simple device such as a webcam or a simple router. As with RAM, you can create a workable Linux system with less storage if you really want to, but the lower you go, the harder it becomes. Linux has extensive support for flash storage devices, including raw NOR and NAND flash chips, and managed flash in the form of SD cards, eMMC chips, USB flash memory, and so on.

Fourth, a serial port is very useful, preferably a UART-based serial port. It does not have to be fitted on production boards, but makes board bring-up, debugging, and development much easier.

Fifth, you need some means of loading software when starting from scratch. Many microcontroller boards are fitted with a **Joint Test Action Group** (**JTAG**) interface for this purpose. Modern SoCs also have the ability to load boot code directly from removable media, especially SD and micro SD cards, or serial interfaces such as UART or USB.

In addition to these basics, there are interfaces to the specific bits of hardware your device needs to get its job done. Mainline Linux comes with open source drivers for many thousands of different devices, and there are drivers (of variable quality) from the SoC manufacturer and from the OEMs of third-party chips that may be included in the design, but remember my comments on the commitment and ability of some manufacturers. As a developer of embedded devices, you will find that you spend quite a lot of time evaluating and adapting third-party code, if you have it, or liaising with the manufacturer if you don't. Finally, you will have to write the device support for interfaces that are unique to the device or find someone to do it for you.

Obtaining the hardware for this book

The examples in this book are intended to be generic, but to make them relevant and easy to follow, I have had to choose specific hardware. I have chosen three exemplar devices: the Raspberry Pi 4, the BeagleBone Black, and QEMU. The first is by far the most popular Arm-based single board computer on the market. The second is a widely available and cheap development board that can be used in serious embedded hardware. The third is a machine emulator that can be used to create a range of systems that are typical of embedded hardware. It was tempting to use QEMU exclusively, but, like all emulations, it is not quite the same as the real thing. Using the Raspberry Pi 4 and BeagleBone Black, you have the satisfaction of interacting with real hardware and seeing real LEDs flash. While the BeagleBone Black is several years old now, it remains *open source hardware* (unlike the Raspberry Pi). This means that the board design materials are freely available for anyone to build a BeagleBone Black or derivative into their products.

In any case, I encourage you to try out as many of the examples as you can, using either of these three platforms, or indeed any embedded hardware you may have to hand.

The Raspberry Pi 4

At the time of writing, the Raspberry Pi 4 Model B is the flagship tiny, dual-display, desktop computer produced by the Raspberry Pi Foundation. Their website is `https://raspberrypi.org/`. The Pi 4's technical specs include the following:

- A Broadcom BCM2711 1.5 GHz quad-core Cortex-A72 (Arm® v8) 64-bit SoC
- 2, 4, or 8 GiB DDR4 RAM
- 2.4 GHz and 5.0 GHz 802.11ac wireless, Bluetooth 5.0, BLE
- A serial port for debug and development
- A MicroSD slot, which can be used as the boot device
- A USB-C connector that is used to power the board
- 2 × full size USB 3.0 and 2 × full size USB 2.0 host ports
- A Gigabit Ethernet port
- 2 × micro-HDMI ports for video and audio output

In addition, there is a 40-pin expansion header for which there are a great variety of daughter boards, known as **HATs** (**Hardware Attached on Top**), that allow you to adapt the board to do many different things. However, you will not need any HATs for the examples in this book. Instead, you will make use of the Pi 4's built-in Wi-Fi and Bluetooth (which the BeagleBone Black lacks).

In addition to the board itself, you will require the following:

- A 5V USB-C power supply capable of delivering 3 A or more
- A USB to TTL serial cable with 3.3V logic-level pins like the Adafruit 954
- A MicroSD card and a means of writing to it from your development PC or laptop, which will be needed to load software onto the board
- An Ethernet cable and a router to connect it to, as some of the examples require network connectivity

Next is the BeagleBone Black.

The BeagleBone Black

The BeagleBone and the later BeagleBone Black are open hardware designs for a small, credit card-sized development board produced by CircuitCo LLC. The main repository of information is at `https://beagleboard.org/`. The main points of the specifications are as follows:

- A TI AM335x 1 GHz Arm® Cortex-A8 Sitara SoC
- 512 MiB DDR3 RAM
- 2 or 4 GiB 8-bit eMMC onboard flash storage
- A serial port for debug and development
- A MicroSD slot, which can be used as the boot device
- A Mini-USB OTG client/host port that can also be used to power the board
- A full size USB 2.0 host port
- A 10/100 Ethernet port
- An HDMI port for video and audio output

In addition, there are two 46-pin expansion headers for which there are a great variety of daughter boards, known as **capes**, which allow you to adapt the board to do many different things. However, you do not need to fit any capes for the examples in this book.

In addition to the board itself, you will require the following:

- A Mini-USB to USB-A cable (supplied with the board).
- A serial cable that can interface with the 6-pin 3.3V TTL level signals provided by the board. The BeagleBoard website has links to compatible cables.

- A MicroSD card and a means of writing to it from your development PC or laptop, which will be needed to load software onto the board.
- An Ethernet cable and a router to connect it to, as some of the examples require network connectivity.
- A 5V power supply capable of delivering 1 A or more.

In addition to the above, *Chapter 12, Prototyping with Breakout Boards*, also requires the following:

- A SparkFun model GPS-15193 Breakout board.
- A Saleae Logic 8 logic analyzer. This apparatus will be used to probe pins for SPI communications between the BeagleBone Black and NEO-M9N.

QEMU

QEMU is a machine emulator. It comes in a number of different flavors, each of which can emulate a processor architecture and a number of boards built using that architecture. For example, we have the following:

- `qemu-system-arm`: 32-bit Arm
- `qemu-system-mips`: MIPS
- `qemu-system-ppc`: PowerPC
- `qemu-system-x86`: x86 and x86_64

For each architecture, QEMU emulates a range of hardware, which you can see by using the `-machine help` option. Each machine emulates most of the hardware that would normally be found on that board. There are options to link hardware to local resources, such as using a local file for the emulated disk drive.

Here is a concrete example:

```
$ qemu-system-arm -machine vexpress-a9 -m 256M -drive
file=rootfs.ext4,sd -net nic -net use -kernel zImage -dtb
vexpress- v2p-ca9.dtb -append "console=ttyAMA0,115200 root=/
dev/mmcblk0" -serial stdio -net nic,model=lan9118 -net
tap,ifname=tap0
```

The options used in the preceding command line are as follows:

- `-machine vexpress-a9`: Creates an emulation of an Arm Versatile Express development board with a Cortex A-9 processor
- `-m 256M`: Populates it with 256 MiB of RAM
- `-drive file=rootfs.ext4,sd`: Connects the SD interface to the local file `rootfs.ext4` (which contains a filesystem image)
- `-kernel zImage`: Loads the Linux kernel from the local file named `zImage`
- `-dtb vexpress-v2p- ca9.dtb`: Loads the device tree from the local file `vexpress-v2p-ca9.dtb`
- `-append "..."`: Appends this string as the kernel command line
- `-serial stdio`: Connects the serial port to the terminal that launched QEMU, usually so that you can log on to the emulated machine via the serial console
- `-net nic,model=lan9118`: Creates a network interface
- `-net tap,ifname=tap0`: Connects the network interface to the virtual network interface, `tap0`

To configure the host side of the network, you need the `tunctl` command from the **User Mode Linux** (**UML**) project; on Debian and Ubuntu, the package is named `uml-utilites`:

```
$ sudo tunctl -u $(whoami) -t tap0
```

This creates a network interface named `tap0` that is connected to the network controller in the emulated QEMU machine. You configure `tap0` in exactly the same way as any other interface.

All of these options are described in detail in the following chapters. I will be using Versatile Express for most of my examples, but it should be easy to use a different machine or architecture.

Provisioning your development environment

I have only used open source software, both for the development tools and the target operating system and applications. I assume that you will be using Linux on your development system. I tested all the host commands using Ubuntu 20.04 LTS, and so there is a slight bias toward that particular version, but any modern Linux distribution is likely to work just fine.

Summary

Embedded hardware will continue to get more complex, following the trajectory set by Moore's Law. Linux has the power and the flexibility to make use of hardware in an efficient way. Together we will learn how to harness that power so we can build robust products that delight our users. This book will take you through the five phases of the embedded project's life cycle, beginning with the four elements of embedded Linux.

The sheer variety of embedded platforms and the fast pace of development lead to isolated pools of software. In many cases, you will become dependent on this software, especially the Linux kernel that is provided by your SoC or board vendor, and, to a lesser extent, the toolchain. Some SoC manufacturers are getting better at pushing their changes upstream and the maintenance of these changes is getting easier. Despite these improvements, selecting the right hardware for your embedded Linux project is still an exercise fraught with peril. Open source license compliance is another topic you need to be aware when building products atop the embedded Linux ecosystem.

In this chapter, you were introduced to the hardware and some of the software you will use throughout this book (namely QEMU). Later on, we will examine some powerful tools that can help you create and maintain the software for your device. We cover Buildroot and dig deep into the Yocto Project. Before I describe these build tools, I will describe the four elements of embedded Linux, which you can apply to all embedded Linux projects, however they are created.

The next chapter is all about the first of these, the toolchain, which you need in order to compile code for your target platform.

2
Learning about Toolchains

The toolchain is the first element of embedded Linux and the starting point of your project. You will use it to compile all the code that will run on your device. The choices you make at this early stage will have a profound impact on the final outcome. Your toolchain should be capable of making effective use of your hardware by using the optimum instruction set for your processor. It should support the languages that you require and have a solid implementation of the **Portable Operating System Interface** (**POSIX**) and other system interfaces.

Your toolchain should remain constant throughout the project. In other words, once you have chosen your toolchain, it is important to stick with it. Changing compilers and development libraries in an inconsistent way during a project will lead to subtle bugs. That being said, it is still best to update your toolchain when security flaws or bugs are found.

Obtaining a toolchain can be as simple as downloading and installing a TAR file, or it can be as complex as building the whole thing from source code. In this chapter, I take the latter approach, with the help of a tool called **crosstool-NG**, so that I can show you the details of creating a toolchain. Later on, in *Chapter 6, Selecting a Build System*, I will switch to using the toolchain generated by the build system, which is the more usual means of obtaining a toolchain. When we get to *Chapter 14, Starting with BusyBox runit*, we'll save ourselves some time by downloading a prebuilt Linaro toolchain to use with Buildroot.

In this chapter, we will cover the following topics:

- Introducing toolchains
- Finding a toolchain
- Building a toolchain using the crosstool-NG tool
- The anatomy of a toolchain
- Linking with libraries – static and dynamic linking
- The art of cross-compiling

Technical requirements

To follow along with the examples, make sure you have the following:

- A Linux-based host system with `autoconf`, `automake`, `bison`, `bzip2`, `cmake`, `flex`, `g++`, `gawk`, `gcc`, `gettext`, `git`, `gperf`, `help2man`, `libncurses5-dev`, `libstdc++6`, `libtool`, `libtool-bin`, `make`, `patch`, `python3-dev`, `rsync`, `texinfo`, `unzip`, `wget`, and `xz-utils` or their equivalents installed.

I recommend using Ubuntu 20.04 LTS or later since the exercises in this chapter were all tested against that Linux distribution at the time of writing. Here is the command to install all the required packages on Ubuntu 20.04 LTS:

```
$ sudo apt-get install autoconf automake bison bzip2 cmake \
flex g++ gawk gcc
gettext git gperf help2man libncurses5-dev libstdc++6 libtool \
libtool-bin make
patch python3-dev rsync texinfo unzip wget xz-utils
```

All of the code for this chapter can be found in the `Chapter02` folder from the book's GitHub repository: `https://github.com/PacktPublishing/Mastering-Embedded-Linux-Programming-Third-Edition`

Introducing toolchains

A toolchain is a set of tools that compiles source code into executables that can run on your target device and includes a compiler, a linker, and runtime libraries. Initially, you need one to build the other three elements of an embedded Linux system: the bootloader, the kernel, and the root filesystem. It has to be able to compile code written in assembly, C, and C++ since these are the languages used in the base open source packages.

Usually, toolchains for Linux are based on components from the GNU project (`http://www.gnu.org`), and that is still true in the majority of cases at the time of writing. However, over the past few years, the **Clang** compiler and the associated **Low Level Virtual Machine** (**LLVM**) project (`http://llvm.org`) have progressed to the point that it is now a viable alternative to a GNU toolchain. One major distinction between LLVM and GNU-based toolchains is the licensing; LLVM has a BSD license while GNU has the GPL.

There are some technical advantages to Clang as well, such as faster compilation and better diagnostics, but GNU GCC has the advantage of compatibility with the existing code base and support for a wide range of architectures and operating systems. While it took some years to get there, Clang can now compile all the components needed for embedded Linux and is a viable alternative to GNU. To learn more about that, see `https://www.kernel.org/doc/html/latest/kbuild/llvm.html`.

There is a good description of how to use Clang for cross-compilation at `https://clang.llvm.org/docs/CrossCompilation.html`. If you would like to use it as part of an embedded Linux build system, the EmbToolkit (`https://embtoolkit.org`) fully supports both GNU and LLVM/Clang toolchains, and various people are working on using Clang with Buildroot and the Yocto Project. I will cover embedded build systems in *Chapter 6, Selecting a Build System*. Meanwhile, this chapter focuses on the GNU toolchain as it is still the most popular and mature toolchain for Linux.

A standard GNU toolchain consists of three main components:

- **Binutils**: A set of binary utilities including the assembler and the linker. It is available at `http://gnu.org/software/binutils`.
- **GNU Compiler Collection** (**GCC**): These are the compilers for C and other languages, which, depending on the version of GCC, include C++, Objective-C, Objective-C++, Java, Fortran, Ada, and Go. They all use a common backend that produces assembler code, which is fed to the GNU assembler. It is available at `http://gcc.gnu.org/`.
- **C library**: A standardized **application program interface** (**API**) based on the POSIX specification, which is the main interface to the operating system kernel for applications. There are several C libraries to consider, as we shall see later on in this chapter.

Along with these, you will need a copy of the Linux kernel headers, which contain definitions and constants that are needed when accessing the kernel directly. Right now, you need them to be able to compile the C library, but you will also need them later when writing programs or compiling libraries that interact with particular Linux devices, for example, to display graphics via the Linux frame buffer driver. This is not simply a question of making a copy of the header files in the `include` directory of your kernel source code. Those headers are intended for use in the kernel only and contain definitions that will cause conflicts if used in their raw state to compile regular Linux applications.

Instead, you will need to generate a set of sanitized kernel headers, which I have illustrated in *Chapter 5, Building a Root Filesystem*.

It is not usually crucial whether the kernel headers are generated from the exact version of Linux you are going to be using or not. Since the kernel interfaces are always backward compatible, it is only necessary that the headers are from a kernel that is the same as, or older than, the one you are using on the target.

Most people would consider the **GNU Debugger** (**GDB**) to be part of the toolchain as well, and it is usual that it is built at this point. I will talk about GDB in *Chapter 19, Debugging with GDB*.

Now that we've talked about kernel headers and seen what the components of a toolchain are, let's look at the different types of toolchains.

Types of toolchains

For our purposes, there are two types of toolchain:

- **Native**: This toolchain runs on the same type of system (sometimes the same actual system) as the programs it generates. This is the usual case for desktops and servers, and it is becoming popular on certain classes of embedded devices. The Raspberry Pi running Debian for ARM, for example, has self-hosted native compilers.
- **Cross**: This toolchain runs on a different type of system than the target, allowing the development to be done on a fast desktop PC and then loaded onto the embedded target for testing.

Almost all embedded Linux development is done using a cross-development toolchain, partly because most embedded devices are not well suited to program development since they lack computing power, memory, and storage, but also because it keeps the host and target environments separate. The latter point is especially important when the host and the target are using the same architecture, `x86_64`, for example. In this case, it is tempting to compile natively on the host and simply copy the binaries to the target.

This works up to a point, but it is likely that the host distribution will receive updates more often than the target, or that different engineers building code for the target will have slightly different versions of the host development libraries. Over time, the development and target systems will diverge, and you will violate the principle that the toolchain should remain constant throughout the life of the project. You can make this approach work if you ensure that the host and the target build environments are in lockstep with each other. However, a much better approach is to keep the host and the target separate, and a cross toolchain is the way to do that.

However, there is a counter argument in favor of native development. Cross development creates the burden of cross compiling all the libraries and tools that you need for your target. We will see later in the section titled *The art of cross compiling* that cross development is not always simple because many open source packages are not designed to be built in this way. Integrated build tools, including Buildroot and the Yocto Project, help by encapsulating the rules to cross-compile a range of packages that you need in typical embedded systems, but if you want to compile a large number of additional packages, then it is better to natively compile them. For example, building a Debian distribution for the Raspberry Pi or BeagleBone using a cross compiler would be very hard. Instead, they are natively compiled.

Creating a native build environment from scratch is not easy. You would still need a cross compiler at first to create the native build environment on the target, which you then use to build the packages. Then, in order to perform the native build in a reasonable amount of time, you would need a build farm of well-provisioned target boards, or you may be able to use **Quick EMUlator** (**QEMU**) to emulate the target.

Meanwhile, in this chapter, I will focus on a more mainstream cross compiler environment, which is relatively easy to set up and administer. We will start by looking at what distinguishes one target CPU architecture from another.

CPU architectures

The toolchain has to be built according to the capabilities of the target CPU, which includes the following:

- **CPU architecture**: **ARM**, **Microprocessor without Interlocked Pipelined Stages** (**MIPS**), x86_64, and so on.
- **Big- or little-endian operation**: Some CPUs can operate in both modes, but the machine code is different for each.

- **Floating point support**: Not all versions of embedded processors implement a hardware floating-point unit, in which case the toolchain has to be configured to call a software floating-point library instead.
- **Application Binary Interface (ABI)**: The calling convention used for passing parameters between function calls.

With many architectures, the ABI is constant across the family of processors. One notable exception is ARM. The ARM architecture transitioned to the **Extended Application Binary Interface (EABI)** in the late 2000s, resulting in the previous ABI being named the **Old Application Binary Interface (OABI)**. While the OABI is now obsolete, you'll continue to see references to EABI. Since then, the EABI has split into two, based on the way the floating-point parameters are passed.

The original EABI uses general-purpose (integer) registers, while the newer **Extended Application Binary Interface Hard-Float (EABIHF)** uses floating point registers. The EABIHF is significantly faster at floating-point operations, since it removes the need for copying between integer and floating-point registers, but it is not compatible with CPUs that do not have a floating-point unit. The choice, then, is between two incompatible ABIs; you cannot mix and match the two, and so you have to decide at this stage.

GNU uses a prefix to the name of each tool in the toolchain, which identifies the various combinations that can be generated. It consists of a tuple of three or four components separated by dashes, as described here:

- **CPU**: This is the CPU architecture, such as ARM, MIPS, or x86_64. If the CPU has both endian modes, they may be differentiated by adding `el` for little-endian or `eb` for big-endian. Good examples are little-endian MIPS, `mipsel`, and big-endian ARM, `armeb`.
- **Vendor**: This identifies the provider of the toolchain. Examples include `buildroot`, `poky`, or just `unknown`. Sometimes it is left out altogether.
- **Kernel**: For our purposes, it is always `linux`.
- **Operating system**: A name for the user space component, which might be `gnu` or `musl`. The ABI may be appended here as well, so for ARM toolchains, you may see `gnueabi`, `gnueabihf`, `musleabi`, or `musleabihf`.

You can find the tuple used when building the toolchain by using the `-dumpmachine` option of `gcc`. For example, you may see the following on the host computer:

```
$ gcc -dumpmachine
x86_64-linux-gnu
```

This tuple indicates a CPU of `x86_64`, a kernel of `linux`, and a user space of `gnu`.

> **Important note**
>
> When a native compiler is installed on a machine, it is normal to create links to each of the tools in the toolchain with no prefixes, so that you can call the C compiler with the `gcc` command.

Here is an example using a cross compiler:

```
$ mipsel-unknown-linux-gnu-gcc -dumpmachine
mipsel-unknown-linux-gnu
```

This tuple indicates a CPU of little-endian MIPS, an `unknown` vendor, a kernel of `linux`, and a user space of `gnu`.

Choosing the C library

The programming interface to the Unix operating system is defined in the C language, which is now defined by the POSIX standards. The **C library** is the implementation of that interface; it is the gateway to the kernel for Linux programs, as shown in the following diagram. Even if you are writing programs in another language, maybe Java or Python, the respective runtime support libraries will have to call the C library eventually, as shown here:

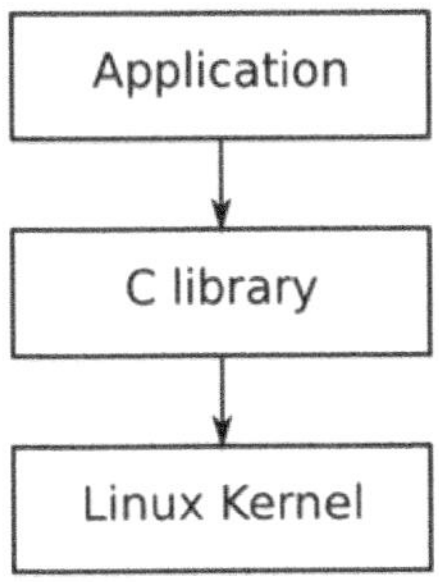

Figure 2.1 – C library

Whenever the C library needs the services of the kernel, it will use the kernel system call interface to transition between user space and kernel space. It is possible to bypass the C library by making the kernel system calls directly, but that is a lot of trouble and almost never necessary.

There are several C libraries to choose from. The main options are as follows:

- **glibc**: This is the standard GNU C library, available at `https://gnu.org/software/libc`. It is big and, until recently, not very configurable, but it is the most complete implementation of the POSIX API. The license is LGPL 2.1.
- **musl libc**: This is available at `https://musl.libc.org`. The `musl libc` library is comparatively new but has been gaining a lot of attention as a small and standards-compliant alternative to GNU `libc`. It is a good choice for systems with a limited amount of RAM and storage. It has an MIT license.
- **uClibc-ng**: This is available at `https://uclibc-ng.org`. `u` is really a Greek `mu` character, indicating that this is the microcontroller C library. It was first developed to work with uClinux (Linux for CPUs without memory management units) but has since been adapted to be used with full Linux. The `uClibc-ng` library is a fork of the original `uClibc` project (`https://uclibc.org`), which has unfortunately fallen into disrepair. Both are licensed with LGPL 2.1.
- **eglibc**: This is available at `http://www.eglibc.org/home`. Now obsolete, `eglibc` was a fork of `glibc` with changes to make it more suitable for embedded usage. Among other things, `eglibc` added configuration options and support for architectures not covered by `glibc`, in particular the PowerPC e500 CPU core. The code base from `eglibc` was merged back into `glibc` in version 2.20. The `eglibc` library is no longer maintained.

So, which to choose? My advice is to use `uClibc-ng` only if you are using uClinux. If you have a very limited amount of storage or RAM, then `musl libc` is a good choice, otherwise, use `glibc`, as shown in this flow chart:

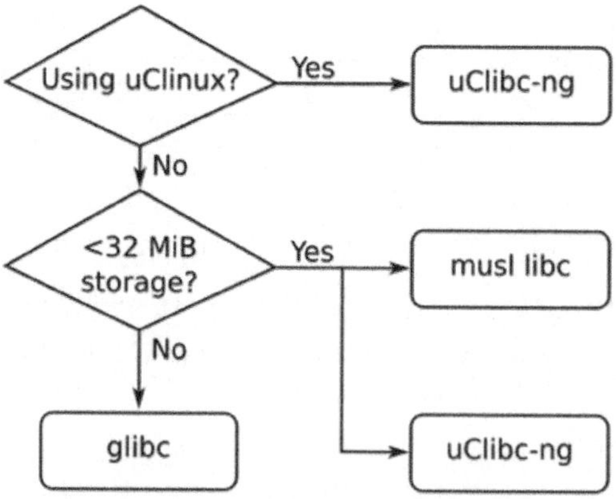

Figure 2.2 – Choosing a C library

Your choice of C library could limit your choice of toolchain since not all pre-built toolchains support all C libraries.

Finding a toolchain

You have three choices for your cross-development toolchain: you may find a ready-built toolchain that matches your needs; you can use one generated by an embedded build tool, which is covered in *Chapter 6, Selecting a Build System*; or you can create one yourself as described later in this chapter.

A pre-built cross toolchain is an attractive option, in that you only have to download and install it, but you are limited to the configuration of that particular toolchain and you are dependent on the person or organization you got it from.

Most likely, it will be one of these:

- An SoC or board vendor. Most vendors offer a Linux toolchain.
- A consortium dedicated to providing system-level support for a given architecture. For example, Linaro, (`https://www.linaro.org`) have pre-built toolchains for the ARM architecture.
- A third-party Linux tool vendor, such as Mentor Graphics, TimeSys, or MontaVista.
- The cross-tool packages for your desktop Linux distribution. For example, Debian-based distributions have packages for cross compiling for ARM, MIPS, and PowerPC targets.
- A binary SDK produced by one of the integrated embedded build tools. The Yocto Project has some examples at `http://downloads.yoctoproject.org/releases/yocto/yocto-[version]/toolchain`.
- A link from a forum that you can't find anymore.

In all of these cases, you have to decide whether the pre-built toolchain on offer meets your requirements. Does it use the C library you prefer? Will the provider give you updates for security fixes and bugs, bearing in mind my comments on support and updates from *Chapter 1, Starting Out*. If your answer is no to any of these, then you should consider creating your own.

Unfortunately, building a toolchain is no easy task. If you truly want to do the whole thing yourself, take a look at *Cross Linux From Scratch* (`https://trac.clfs.org`). There you will find step-by-step instructions on how to create each component.

A simpler alternative is to use crosstool-NG, which encapsulates the process into a set of scripts and has a menu-driven frontend. You still need a fair degree of knowledge, though, just to make the right choices.

It is simpler still to use a build system such as Buildroot or the Yocto Project, since they generate a toolchain as part of the build process. This is my preferred solution, as I have shown in *Chapter 6, Selecting a Build System*.

With the ascendance of crosstool-NG, building your own toolchain is certainly a valid and viable option. Let's look at how to do that next.

Building a toolchain using crosstool-NG

Some years ago, Dan Kegel wrote a set of scripts and makefiles for generating cross-development toolchains and called it crosstool (`http://kegel.com/crosstool/`). In 2007, Yann E. Morin used that base to create the next generation of crosstool, crosstool-NG (`https://crosstool-ng.github.io`). Today it is by far the most convenient way to create a standalone cross toolchain from source.

In this section, we will use crosstool-NG to build toolchains for the BeagleBone Black and QEMU.

Installing crosstool-NG

Before you can build crosstool-NG from source, you will first need to install a native toolchain and some build tools on your host machine. See the section on *Technical requirements* at the beginning of this chapter for crosstool-NG's complete list of build and runtime dependencies.

Next, get the current release from the crosstool-NG Git repository. In my examples, I have used version `1.24.0`. Extract it and create the frontend menu system, `ct-ng`, as shown in the following commands:

```
$ git clone https://github.com/crosstool-ng/crosstool-ng.git
$ cd crosstool-ng
$ git checkout crosstool-ng-1.24.0
$ ./bootstrap
$ ./configure --prefix=${PWD}
$ make
$ make install
```

The `--prefix=${PWD}` option means that the program will be installed into the current directory, which avoids the need for root permissions, as would be required if you were to install it in the default location `/usr/local/share`.

We now have a working installation of crosstool-NG that we can use to build cross toolchains with. Type `bin/ct-ng` to launch the crosstool menu.

Building a toolchain for BeagleBone Black

Crosstool-NG can build many different combinations of toolchains. To make the initial configuration easier, it comes with a set of samples that cover many of the common use cases. Use `bin/ct-ng list-samples` to generate the list.

The BeagleBone Black has a TI AM335x SoC, which contains an ARM Cortex A8 core and a VFPv3 floating-point unit. Since the BeagleBone Black has plenty of RAM and storage, we can use `glibc` as the C library. The closest sample is `arm-cortex_a8-linux-gnueabi`.

You can see the default configuration by prefixing the name with `show-`, as demonstrated here:

```
$ bin/ct-ng show-arm-cortex_a8-linux-gnueabi
[G...]    arm-cortex_a8-linux-gnueabi
    Languages       : C,C++
    OS              : linux-4.20.8
    Binutils        : binutils-2.32
    Compiler        : gcc-8.3.0
    C library       : glibc-2.29
    Debug tools     : duma-2_5_15 gdb-8.2.1 ltrace-0.7.3
strace-4.26
    Companion libs  : expat-2.2.6 gettext-0.19.8.1 gmp-6.1.2
isl-0.20 libelf-0.8.13 libiconv-1.15 mpc-1.1.0 mpfr-4.0.2
ncurses-6.1 zlib-1.2.11
    Companion tools :
```

This is a close match with our requirements, except that it uses the `eabi` binary interface, which passes floating-point arguments in integer registers. We would prefer to use hardware floating point registers for that purpose because it would speed up function calls that have `float` and `double` parameter types. You can change the configuration later, so for now you should select this target configuration:

```
$ bin/ct-ng arm-cortex_a8-linux-gnueabi
```

At this point, you can review the configuration and make changes using the configuration menu command `menuconfig`:

```
$ bin/ct-ng menuconfig
```

The menu system is based on the Linux kernel `menuconfig`, and so navigation of the user interface will be familiar to anyone who has configured a kernel. If not, refer to *Chapter 4, Configuring and Building the Kernel*, for a description of `menuconfig`.

There are three configuration changes that I would recommend you make at this point:

- In **Paths and misc options**, disable **Render the toolchain read-only** (`CT_PREFIX_DIR_RO`).
- In **Target options | Floating point**, select **hardware (FPU)** (`CT_ARCH_FLOAT_HW`).
- In **Target options**, enter `neon` for **Use specific FPU**.

The first is necessary if you want to add libraries to the toolchain after it has been installed, which I describe later, in the *Linking with libraries* section. The second selects the `eabihf` binary interface for the reasons discussed earlier. The third is needed to build the Linux kernel successfully. The names in parentheses are the configuration labels stored in the configuration file. When you have made the changes, exit the `menuconfig` menu and save the configuration as one does.

Now you can use crosstool-NG to get, configure, and build the components according to your specification, by typing the following command:

```
$ bin/ct-ng build
```

The build will take about half an hour, after which you will find your toolchain is present in `~/x-tools/arm-cortex_a8-linux-gnueabihf`.

Next, let's build a toolchain that targets QEMU.

Building a toolchain for QEMU

On the QEMU target, you will be emulating an ARM-versatile PB evaluation board that has an ARM926EJ-S processor core, which implements the ARMv5TE instruction set. You need to generate a crosstool-NG toolchain that matches the specification. The procedure is very similar to the one for the BeagleBone Black.

You begin by running bin/ct-ng list-samples to find a good base configuration to work from. There isn't an exact fit, so use a generic target, arm-unknown-linux-gnueabi. You select it as shown, running distclean first to make sure that there are no artifacts left over from a previous build:

```
$ bin/ct-ng distclean
$ bin/ct-ng arm-unknown-linux-gnueabi
```

As with the BeagleBone Black, you can review the configuration and make changes using the configuration menu command bin/ct-ng menuconfig. There is only one change necessary:

- In **Paths and misc options**, disable **Render the toolchain read-only** (CT_PREFIX_DIR_RO).

Now, build the toolchain with the command shown here:

```
$ bin/ct-ng build
```

As before, the build will take about half an hour. The toolchain will be installed in ~/x-tools/arm-unknown-linux-gnueabi.

You will need a working cross toolchain to complete the exercises in the next section.

Anatomy of a toolchain

To get an idea of what is in a typical toolchain, I want to examine the crosstool-NG toolchain you have just created. The examples use the ARM Cortex A8 toolchain created for the BeagleBone Black, which has the prefix arm-cortex_a8-linux-gnueabihf-. If you built the ARM926EJ-S toolchain for the QEMU target, then the prefix will be arm-unknown-linux-gnueabi instead.

The ARM Cortex A8 toolchain is in the directory ~/x-tools/arm-cortex_a8-linux-gnueabihf/bin. In there, you will find the cross compiler, arm-cortex_a8-linux-gnueabihf-gcc. To make use of it, you need to add the directory to your path using the following command:

```
$ PATH=~/x-tools/arm-cortex_a8-linux-gnueabihf/bin:$PATH
```

Now you can take a simple `helloworld` program, which in the C language looks like this:

```
#include <stdio.h>
#include <stdlib.h>

int main (int argc, char *argv[])
{
    printf ("Hello, world!\n");
    return 0;
}
```

You compile it like this:

```
$ arm-cortex_a8-linux-gnueabihf-gcc helloworld.c -o helloworld
```

You can confirm that it has been cross-compiled by using the `file` command to print the type of the file:

```
$ file helloworld
helloworld: ELF 32-bit LSB executable, ARM, EABI5 version 1
(SYSV), dynamically linked, interpreter /lib/ld-linux-armhf.
so.3, for GNU/Linux 4.20.8, with debug_info, not stripped
```

Now that you've verified that your cross compiler works, let's take a closer look at it.

Finding out about your cross compiler

Imagine that you have just received a toolchain and that you would like to know more about how it was configured. You can find out a lot by querying `gcc`. For example, to find the version, you use `--version`:

```
$ arm-cortex_a8-linux-gnueabihf-gcc --version
arm-cortex_a8-linux-gnueabihf-gcc (crosstool-NG 1.24.0) 8.3.0
Copyright (C) 2018 Free Software Foundation, Inc.
This is free software; see the source for copying conditions.
There is NO warranty; not even for MERCHANTABILITY or FITNESS
FOR A PARTICULAR PURPOSE.
```

To find how it was configured, use -v:

```
$ arm-cortex_a8-linux-gnueabihf-gcc -v
Using built-in specs.
COLLECT_GCC=arm-cortex_a8-linux-gnueabihf-gcc
COLLECT_LTO_WRAPPER=/home/frank/x-tools/arm-cortex_a8-linux-
gnueabihf/libexec/gcc/arm-cortex_a8-linux-gnueabihf/8.3.0/
lto-wrapper
Target: arm-cortex_a8-linux-gnueabihf
Configured with: /home/frank/crosstool-ng/.build/arm-cortex_
a8-linux-gnueabihf/src/gcc/configure --build=x86_64-build_
pc-linux-gnu --host=x86_64-build_pc-linux-gnu --target=arm-
cortex_a8-linux-gnueabihf --prefix=/home/frank/x-tools/
arm-cortex_a8-linux-gnueabihf --with-sysroot=/home/frank/x-
tools/arm-cortex_a8-linux-gnueabihf/arm-cortex_a8-linux-
gnueabihf/sysroot --enable-languages=c,c++ --with-cpu=cortex-a8
--with-float=hard --with-pkgversion='crosstool-NG 1.24.0'
--enable-__cxa_atexit --disable-libmudflap --disable-libgomp
--disable-libssp --disable-libquadmath --disable-libquadmath-
support --disable-libsanitizer --disable-libmpx --with-gmp=/
home/frank/crosstool-ng/.build/arm-cortex_a8-linux-gnueabihf/
buildtools --with-mpfr=/home/frank/crosstool-ng/.build/
arm-cortex_a8-linux-gnueabihf/buildtools --with-mpc=/home/
frank/crosstool-ng/.build/arm-cortex_a8-linux-gnueabihf/
buildtools --with-isl=/home/frank/crosstool-ng/.build/
arm-cortex_a8-linux-gnueabihf/buildtools --enable-lto --with-
host-libstdcxx='-static-libgcc -Wl,-Bstatic,-lstdc++,-Bdynamic
-lm' --enable-threads=posix --enable-target-optspace --enable-
plugin --enable-gold --disable-nls --disable-multilib --with-
local-prefix=/home/frank/x-tools/arm-cortex_a8-linux-gnueabihf/
arm-cortex_a8-linux-gnueabihf/sysroot --enable-long-long
Thread model: posix
gcc version 8.3.0 (crosstool-NG 1.24.0)
```

There is a lot of output there, but the interesting things to note are the following:

- `--with-sysroot=/home/frank/x-tools/arm-cortex_a8-linux-gnueabihf/arm-cortex_a8-linux-gnueabihf/sysroot`: This is the default `sysroot` directory; see the following section for an explanation.
- `--enable-languages=c,c++`: Using this, we have both C and C++ languages enabled.

- `--with-cpu=cortex-a8`: The code is generated for an ARM Cortex A8 core.
- `--with-float=hard`: Generates opcodes for the floating-point unit and uses the VFP registers for parameters.
- `--enable-threads=posix`: This enables the POSIX threads.

These are the default settings for the compiler. You can override most of them on the `gcc` command line. For example, if you want to compile for a different CPU, you can override the configured setting, `--with-cpu`, by adding `-mcpu` to the command line, as follows:

```
$ arm-cortex_a8-linux-gnueabihf-gcc -mcpu=cortex-a5 \
helloworld.c \
-o helloworld
```

You can print out the range of architecture-specific options available using `--target-help`, as follows:

```
$ arm-cortex_a8-linux-gnueabihf-gcc --target-help
```

You may be wondering whether it matters that you get the configuration exactly right at this point, since you can always change it as shown here. The answer depends on the way you anticipate using it. If you plan to create a new toolchain for each target, then it makes sense to set everything up at the beginning, because it will reduce the risk of getting it wrong later on. Jumping ahead a little to *Chapter 6, Selecting a Build System*, I call this the Buildroot philosophy. If, on the other hand, you want to build a toolchain that is generic and you are prepared to provide the correct settings when you build for a particular target, then you should make the base toolchain generic, which is the way the Yocto Project handles things. The preceding examples follow the Buildroot philosophy.

The sysroot, library, and header files

The toolchain `sysroot` is a directory that contains subdirectories for libraries, header files, and other configuration files. It can be set when the toolchain is configured through `--with-sysroot=`, or it can be set on the command line using `--sysroot=`. You can see the location of the default `sysroot` by using `-print-sysroot`:

```
$ arm-cortex_a8-linux-gnueabihf-gcc -print-sysroot
/home/frank/x-tools/arm-cortex_a8-linux-gnueabihf/arm-cortex_
a8-linux-gnueabihf/sysroot
```

You will find the following subdirectories in `sysroot`:

- `lib`: Contains the shared objects for the C library and the dynamic linker/loader, `ld-linux`
- `usr/lib`: The static library archive files for the C library, and any other libraries that may be installed subsequently
- `usr/include`: Contains the headers for all the libraries
- `usr/bin`: Contains the utility programs that run on the target, such as the `ldd` command
- `usr/share`: Used for localization and internationalization
- `sbin`: Provides the `ldconfig` utility, used to optimize library loading paths

Plainly, some of these are needed on the development host to compile programs, and others, for example, the shared libraries and `ld-linux`, are needed on the target at runtime.

Other tools in the toolchain

Below is a list of commands to invoke the various other components of a GNU toolchain, together with a brief description:

- `addr2line`: Converts program addresses into filenames and numbers by reading the debug symbol tables in an executable file. It is very useful when decoding addresses printed out in a system crash report.
- `ar`: The archive utility is used to create static libraries.
- `as`: This is the GNU assembler.
- `c++filt`: This is used to demangle C++ and Java symbols.
- `cpp`: This is the C preprocessor and is used to expand `#define`, `#include`, and other similar directives. You seldom need to use this by itself.
- `elfedit`: This is used to update the ELF header of the ELF files.
- `g++`: This is the GNU C++ frontend, which assumes that source files contain C++ code.
- `gcc`: This is the GNU C frontend, which assumes that source files contain C code.
- `gcov`: This is a code coverage tool.
- `gdb`: This is the GNU debugger.

- `gprof`: This is a program profiling tool.
- `ld`: This is the GNU linker.
- `nm`: This lists symbols from object files.
- `objcopy`: This is used to copy and translate object files.
- `objdump`: This is used to display information from object files.
- `ranlib`: This creates or modifies an index in a static library, making the linking stage faster.
- `readelf`: This displays information about files in ELF object format.
- `size`: This lists section sizes and the total size.
- `strings`: This displays strings of printable characters in files.
- `strip`: This is used to strip an object file of debug symbol tables, thus making it smaller. Typically, you would strip all the executable code that is put onto the target.

We will now switch gears from command-line tools and return to the topic of the C library.

Looking at the components of the C library

The C library is not a single library file. It is composed of four main parts that together implement the POSIX API:

- `libc`: The main C library that contains the well-known POSIX functions such as `printf`, `open`, `close`, `read`, `write`, and so on
- `libm`: Contains math functions such as `cos`, `exp`, and `log`
- `libpthread`: Contains all the POSIX thread functions with names beginning with `pthread_`
- `librt`: Has the real-time extensions to POSIX, including shared memory and asynchronous I/O

The first one, `libc`, is always linked in but the others have to be explicitly linked with the `-l` option. The parameter to `-l` is the library name with `lib` stripped off. For example, a program that calculates a sine function by calling `sin()` would be linked with `libm` using `-lm`:

```
$ arm-cortex_a8-linux-gnueabihf-gcc myprog.c -o myprog -lm
```

You can verify which libraries have been linked in this or any other program by using the `readelf` command:

```
$ arm-cortex_a8-linux-gnueabihf-readelf -a myprog | grep
"Shared library"
 0x00000001 (NEEDED)                     Shared library: [libm.so.6]
 0x00000001 (NEEDED)                     Shared library: [libc.so.6]
```

Shared libraries need a runtime linker, which you can expose using this:

```
$ arm-cortex_a8-linux-gnueabihf-readelf -a myprog | grep
"program interpreter"
      [Requesting program interpreter: /lib/ld-linux-armhf.so.3]
```

This is so useful that I have a script file named `list-libs`, which you will find in the book code archive in `MELP/list-libs`. It contains the following commands:

```
#!/bin/sh
${CROSS_COMPILE}readelf -a $1 | grep "program interpreter"
${CROSS_COMPILE}readelf -a $1 | grep "Shared library"
```

There are other library files we can link to other than the four components of the C library. We will look at how to do that in the next section.

Linking with libraries – static and dynamic linking

Any application you write for Linux, whether it be in C or C++, will be linked with the `libc` C library. This is so fundamental that you don't even have to tell `gcc` or `g++` to do it because it always links `libc`. Other libraries that you may want to link with have to be explicitly named through the `-l` option.

The library code can be linked in two different ways: statically, meaning that all the library functions your application calls and their dependencies are pulled from the library archive and bound into your executable; and dynamically, meaning that references to the library files and functions in those files are generated in the code but the actual linking is done dynamically at runtime. You will find the code for the examples that follow in the book code archive in `MELP/Chapter02/library`.

We'll start with static linking.

Static libraries

Static linking is useful in a few circumstances. For example, if you are building a small system that consists of only BusyBox and some script files, it is simpler to link BusyBox statically and avoid having to copy the runtime library files and linker. It will also be smaller because you only link in the code that your application uses rather than supplying the entire C library. Static linking is also useful if you need to run a program before the filesystem that holds the runtime libraries is available.

You can link all the libraries statically by adding `-static` to the command line:

```
$ arm-cortex_a8-linux-gnueabihf-gcc -static helloworld.c -o
helloworld-static
```

You will note that the size of the binary increases dramatically:

```
$ ls -l
total 4060
-rwxrwxr-x 1 frank frank   11816 Oct 23 15:45 helloworld
-rw-rw-r-- 1 frank frank     123 Oct 23 15:35 helloworld.c
-rwxrwxr-x 1 frank frank 4140860 Oct 23 16:00 helloworld-static
```

Static linking pulls code from a library archive, usually named `lib[name].a`. In the preceding case, it is `libc.a`, which is in `[sysroot]/usr/lib`:

```
$ export SYSROOT=$(arm-cortex_a8-linux-gnueabihf-gcc -print-
sysroot)
$ cd $SYSROOT
$ ls -l usr/lib/libc.a
-rw-r--r-- 1 frank frank 31871066 Oct 23 15:16 usr/lib/libc.a
```

Note that the syntax export `SYSROOT=$(arm-cortex_a8-linux-gnueabihf-gcc -print-sysroot)` places the path to the `sysroot` in the shell variable, `SYSROOT`, which makes the example a little clearer.

Creating a static library is as simple as creating an archive of object files using the `ar` command. If I have two source files named `test1.c` and `test2.c`, and I want to create a static library named `libtest.a`, then I would do the following:

```
$ arm-cortex_a8-linux-gnueabihf-gcc -c test1.c
$ arm-cortex_a8-linux-gnueabihf-gcc -c test2.c
$ arm-cortex_a8-linux-gnueabihf-ar rc libtest.a test1.o test2.o
$ ls -l
```

```
total 24
-rw-rw-r-- 1 frank frank 2392 Oct 9 09:28 libtest.a
-rw-rw-r-- 1 frank frank 116 Oct 9 09:26 test1.c
-rw-rw-r-- 1 frank frank 1080 Oct 9 09:27 test1.o
-rw-rw-r-- 1 frank frank 121 Oct 9 09:26 test2.c
-rw-rw-r-- 1 frank frank 1088 Oct 9 09:27 test2.o
```

Then I could link `libtest` into my `helloworld` program, using this:

```
$ arm-cortex_a8-linux-gnueabihf-gcc helloworld.c -ltest \
-L../libs -I../libs -o helloworld
```

Now let's rebuild the same program using dynamic linking.

Shared libraries

A more common way to deploy libraries is as shared objects that are linked at runtime, which makes more efficient use of storage and system memory, since only one copy of the code needs to be loaded. It also makes it easy to update the library files without having to relink all the programs that use them.

The object code for a shared library must be position-independent, so that the runtime linker is free to locate it in memory at the next free address. To do this, add the `-fPIC` parameter to `gcc`, and then link it using the `-shared` option:

```
$ arm-cortex_a8-linux-gnueabihf-gcc -fPIC -c test1.c
$ arm-cortex_a8-linux-gnueabihf-gcc -fPIC -c test2.c
$ arm-cortex_a8-linux-gnueabihf-gcc -shared -o libtest.so
test1.o test2.o
```

This creates the shared library, `libtest.so`. To link an application with this library, you add `-ltest`, exactly as in the static case mentioned in the preceding section, but this time the code is not included in the executable. Instead, there is a reference to the library that the runtime linker will have to resolve:

```
$ arm-cortex_a8-linux-gnueabihf-gcc helloworld.c -ltest \
-L../libs -I../libs -o helloworld
$ MELP/list-libs helloworld
    [Requesting program interpreter: /lib/ld-linux-armhf.so.3]
 0x00000001 (NEEDED)              Shared library: [libtest.so.6]
 0x00000001 (NEEDED)              Shared library: [libc.so.6]
```

The runtime linker for this program is `/lib/ld-linux-armhf.so.3`, which must be present in the target's filesystem. The linker will look for `libtest.so` in the default search path: `/lib` and `/usr/lib`. If you want it to look for libraries in other directories as well, you can place a colon-separated list of paths in the `LD_LIBRARY_PATH` shell variable:

```
$ export LD_LIBRARY_PATH=/opt/lib:/opt/usr/lib
```

Because shared libraries are separate from the executables they link to, we need to be aware of their versions when deploying them.

Understanding shared library version numbers

One of the benefits of shared libraries is that they can be updated independently of the programs that use them.

Library updates are of two types:

- Those that fix bugs or add new functions in a backward-compatible way
- Those that break compatibility with existing applications

GNU/Linux has a versioning scheme to handle both these cases.

Each library has a release version and an interface number. The release version is simply a string that is appended to the library name; for example, the JPEG image library `libjpeg` is currently at release `8.2.2` and so the library is named `libjpeg.so.8.2.2`. There is a symbolic link named `libjpeg.so` to `libjpeg.so.8.2.2`, so that when you compile a program with `-ljpeg`, you link with the current version. If you install version `8.2.3`, the link is updated, and you will link with that one instead.

Now suppose that version `9.0.0` comes along and that breaks the backward compatibility. The link from `libjpeg.so` now points to `libjpeg.so.9.0.0`, so that any new programs are linked with the new version, possibly throwing compile errors when the interface to `libjpeg` changes, which the developer can fix.

Any programs on the target that are not recompiled are going to fail in some way, because they are still using the old interface. This is where an object known as the **soname** helps. The soname encodes the interface number when the library was built and is used by the runtime linker when it loads the library. It is formatted as `<library name>.so.<interface number>`. For `libjpeg.so.8.2.2`, the soname is `libjpeg.so.8` because the interface number when that `libjpeg` shared library was built is `8`:

```
$ readelf -a /usr/lib/x86_64-linux-gnu/libjpeg.so.8.2.2 \
| grep SONAME
 0x000000000000000e (SONAME)     Library soname: [libjpeg.so.8]
```

Any program compiled with it will request `libjpeg.so.8` at runtime, which will be a symbolic link on the target to `libjpeg.so.8.2.2`. When version `9.0.0` of `libjpeg` is installed, it will have a soname of `libjpeg.so.9`, and so it is possible to have two incompatible versions of the same library installed on the same system. Programs that were linked with `libjpeg.so.8.*.*` will load `libjpeg.so.8`, and those linked with `libjpeg.so.9.*.*` will load `libjpeg.so.9`.

This is why, when you look at the directory listing of `/usr/lib/x86_64-linux-gnu/libjpeg*`, you find these four files:

- `libjpeg.a`: This is the library archive used for static linking.
- `libjpeg.so -> libjpeg.so.8.2.2`: This is a symbolic link, used for dynamic linking.
- `libjpeg.so.8 -> libjpeg.so.8.2.2`: This is a symbolic link, used when loading the library at runtime.
- `libjpeg.so.8.2.2`: This is the actual shared library, used at both compile time and runtime.

The first two are only needed on the host computer for building and the last two are needed on the target at runtime.

While you can invoke the various GNU cross-compilation tools directly from the command line, this technique does not scale beyond toy examples such as `helloworld`. To really be effective at cross-compiling, we need to combine a cross toolchain with a build system.

The art of cross-compiling

Having a working cross toolchain is the starting point of a journey, not the end of it. At some point, you will want to begin cross-compiling the various tools, applications, and libraries that you need on your target. Many of them will be open source packages, each of which has its own method of compiling and its own peculiarities.

There are some common build systems, including the following:

- Pure makefiles, where the toolchain is usually controlled by the `make` variable `CROSS_COMPILE`
- The GNU build system known as **Autotools**
- **CMake** (`https://cmake.org`)

Both Autotools and makefiles are needed to build even a basic embedded Linux system. CMake is cross-platform and has seen increased adoption over the years especially among the C++ community. In this section, we will cover all three build tools.

Simple makefiles

Some important packages are very simple to cross-compile, including the Linux kernel, the U-Boot bootloader, and BusyBox. For each of these, you only need to put the toolchain prefix in the make variable `CROSS_COMPILE`, for example, `arm-cortex_a8-linux-gnueabi-`. Note the trailing dash `-`.

So, to compile BusyBox, you would type this:

```
$ make CROSS_COMPILE=arm-cortex_a8-linux-gnueabihf-
```

Or, you can set it as a shell variable:

```
$ export CROSS_COMPILE=arm-cortex_a8-linux-gnueabihf-
$ make
```

In the case of U-Boot and Linux, you also have to set the make variable `ARCH` to one of the machine architectures they support, which I will cover in *Chapter 3, All About Bootloaders*, and *Chapter 4, Configuring and Building the Kernel.*

Both Autotools and CMake can generate makefiles. Autotools only generates makefiles whereas CMake supports other ways of building projects depending on which platform(s) we are targeting (strictly Linux in our case). Let's look at cross-compiling with Autotools first.

Autotools

The name Autotools refers to a group of tools that are used as the build system in many open source projects. The components, together with the appropriate project pages, are as follows:

- GNU Autoconf (`https://www.gnu.org/software/autoconf/autoconf.html`)
- GNU Automake (`https://www.gnu.org/savannah-checkouts/gnu/automake/`)
- GNU Libtool (`https://www.gnu.org/software/libtool/libtool.html`)
- Gnulib (`https://www.gnu.org/software/gnulib/`)

The role of Autotools is to smooth over the differences between the different types of systems that the package may be compiled for, accounting for different versions of compilers, different versions of libraries, different locations of header files, and dependencies with other packages.

Packages that use Autotools come with a script named `configure` that checks dependencies and generates makefiles according to what it finds. The `configure` script may also give you the opportunity to enable or disable certain features. You can find the options on offer by running `./configure --help`.

To configure, build and install a package for the native operating system, you would typically run the following three commands:

```
$ ./configure
$ make
$ sudo make install
```

Autotools is able to handle cross-development as well. You can influence the behavior of the configured script by setting these shell variables:

- `CC`: The C compiler command.
- `CFLAGS`: Additional C compiler flags.
- `CXX`: The C++ compiler command.
- `CXXFLAGS`: Additional C++ compiler flags.
- `LDFLAGS`: Additional linker flags; for example, if you have libraries in a non-standard directory `<lib dir>`, you would add it to the library search path by adding `-L<lib dir>`.
- `LIBS`: Contains a list of additional libraries to pass to the linker; for instance, `-lm` for the math library.
- `CPPFLAGS`: Contains C/C++ preprocessor flags; for example, you would add `-I<include dir>` to search for headers in a non-standard directory `<include dir>`.
- `CPP`: The C preprocessor to use.

Sometimes it is sufficient to set only the `CC` variable, as follows:

```
$ CC=arm-cortex_a8-linux-gnueabihf-gcc ./configure
```

At other times, that will result in an error like this:

```
[...]
checking for suffix of executables...
checking whether we are cross compiling... configure: error: in
'/home/frank/sqlite-autoconf-3330000':
configure: error: cannot run C compiled programs.
If you meant to cross compile, use '--host'.
See 'config.log' for more details
```

The reason for the failure is that `configure` often tries to discover the capabilities of the toolchain by compiling snippets of code and running them to see what happens, which cannot work if the program has been cross-compiled.

> **Important note**
>
> Pass `--host=<host>` to `configure` when you are cross-compiling so that `configure` searches your system for the cross-compiling toolchain targeting the specified `<host>` platform. That way, `configure` does not try to run snippets of non-native code as part of the configuration step.

Autotools understands three different types of machines that may be involved when compiling a package:

- **Build**: The computer that builds the package, which defaults to the current machine.
- **Host**: The computer the program will run on. For a native compile, this is left blank and it defaults to be the same computer as Build. When you are cross-compiling, set it to be the tuple of your toolchain.
- **Target**: The computer the program will generate code for. You would set this when building a cross compiler.

So, to cross-compile, you just need to override the host, as follows:

```
$ CC=arm-cortex_a8-linux-gnueabihf-gcc \
./configure --host=arm-cortex_a8-linux-gnueabihf
```

One final thing to note is that the default install directory is <sysroot>/usr/local/*. You would usually install it in <sysroot>/usr/* so that the header files and libraries would be picked up from their default locations.

The complete command to configure a typical Autotools package is as follows:

```
$ CC=arm-cortex_a8-linux-gnueabihf-gcc \
./configure --host=arm-cortex_a8-linux-gnueabihf --prefix=/usr
```

Let's dive deeper into Autotools and use it to cross-compile a popular library.

An example - SQLite

The SQLite library implements a simple relational database and is quite popular on embedded devices. You begin by getting a copy of SQLite:

```
$ wget http://www.sqlite.org/2020/sqlite-autoconf-3330000.tar.
gz
$ tar xf sqlite-autoconf-3330000.tar.gz
$ cd sqlite-autoconf-3330000
```

Next, run the configure script:

```
$ CC=arm-cortex_a8-linux-gnueabihf-gcc \
./configure --host=arm-cortex_a8-linux-gnueabihf --prefix=/usr
```

That seems to work! If it had failed, there would be error messages printed to the Terminal and recorded in config.log. Note that several makefiles have been created, so now you can build it:

```
$ make
```

Finally, you install it into the toolchain directory by setting the make variable DESTDIR. If you don't, it will try to install it into the host computer's /usr directory, which is not what you want:

```
$ make DESTDIR=$(arm-cortex_a8-linux-gnueabihf-gcc -print-
sysroot) install
```

You may find that the final command fails with a file permissions error. A crosstool-NG toolchain is read-only by default, which is why it is useful to set `CT_PREFIX_DIR_RO` to `y` when building it. Another common problem is that the toolchain is installed in a system directory, such as `/opt` or `/usr/local`. In that case, you will need `root` permissions when running the install.

After installing, you should find that various files have been added to your toolchain:

- `<sysroot>/usr/bin: sqlite3`: This is a command-line interface for SQLite that you can install and run on the target.
- `<sysroot>/usr/lib`: `libsqlite3.so.0.8.6`, `libsqlite3.so.0`, `libsqlite3.so`, `libsqlite3.la`, `libsqlite3.a`: These are the shared and static libraries.
- `<sysroot>/usr/lib/pkgconfig: sqlite3.pc`: This is the package configuration file, as described in the following section.
- `<sysroot>/usr/lib/include: sqlite3.h`, `sqlite3ext.h`: These are the header files.
- `<sysroot>/usr/share/man/man1: sqlite3.1`: This is the manual page.

Now you can compile programs that use `sqlite3` by adding `-lsqlite3` at the link stage:

```
$ arm-cortex_a8-linux-gnueabihf-gcc -lsqlite3 sqlite-test.c -o
sqlite-test
```

Here, `sqlite-test.c` is a hypothetical program that calls SQLite functions. Since `sqlite3` has been installed into the `sysroot`, the compiler will find the header and library files without any problem. If they had been installed elsewhere, you would have had to add `-L<lib dir>` and `-I<include dir>`.

Naturally, there will be runtime dependencies as well, and you will have to install the appropriate files into the target directory as described in *Chapter 5, Building a Root Filesystem*.

In order to cross-compile a library or package, its dependencies first need to be cross-compiled. Autotools relies on a utility called `pkg-config` to gather vital information about packages cross-compiled by Autotools.

Package configuration

Tracking package dependencies is quite complex. The package configuration utility `pkg-config` (`https://www.freedesktop.org/wiki/Software/pkg-config/`) helps track which packages are installed and which compile flags each package needs by keeping a database of Autotools packages in `[sysroot]/usr/lib/pkgconfig`. For instance, the one for SQLite3 is named `sqlite3.pc` and contains essential information needed by other packages that need to make use of it:

```
$ cat $(arm-cortex_a8-linux-gnueabihf-gcc -print-sysroot)/usr/
lib/pkgconfig/sqlite3.pc
# Package Information for pkg-config

prefix=/usr
exec_prefix=${prefix}
libdir=${exec_prefix}/lib
includedir=${prefix}/include

Name: SQLite
Description: SQL database engine
Version: 3.33.0
Libs: -L${libdir} -lsqlite3
Libs.private: -lm -ldl -lpthread
Cflags: -I${includedir}
```

You can use `pkg-config` to extract information in a form that you can feed straight to `gcc`. In the case of a library like `libsqlite3`, you want to know the library name (`--libs`) and any special C flags (`--cflags`):

```
$ pkg-config sqlite3 --libs --cflags
Package sqlite3 was not found in the pkg-config search path.
Perhaps you should add the directory containing 'sqlite3.pc'
to the PKG_CONFIG_PATH environment variable
No package 'sqlite3' found
```

Oops! That failed because it was looking in the host's `sysroot` and the development package for `libsqlite3` has not been installed on the host. You need to point it at the `sysroot` of the target toolchain by setting the `PKG_CONFIG_LIBDIR` shell variable:

```
$ export PKG_CONFIG_LIBDIR=$(arm-cortex_a8-linux-gnueabihf-gcc \
-print-sysroot)/usr/lib/pkgconfig
$ pkg-config sqlite3 --libs --cflags
-lsqlite3
```

Now the output is `-lsqlite3`. In this case, you knew that already, but generally you wouldn't, so this is a valuable technique. The final commands to compile would be the following:

```
$ export PKG_CONFIG_LIBDIR=$(arm-cortex_a8-linux-gnueabihf-gcc \
-print-sysroot)/usr/lib/pkgconfig
$ arm-cortex_a8-linux-gnueabihf-gcc $(pkg-config sqlite3
--cflags --libs) \
sqlite-test.c -o sqlite-test
```

Many configure scripts read the information generated by `pkg-config`. This can lead to errors when cross-compiling as we shall see next.

Problems with cross-compiling

`sqlite3` is a well-behaved package and cross-compiles nicely, but not all packages are the same. Typical pain points include the following:

- Home-grown build systems for libraries such as `zlib` that have a `configure` script that does not behave like the Autotools `configure` described in the previous section
- Configure scripts that read `pkg-config` information, headers, and other files from the host, disregarding the `--host` override
- Scripts that insist on trying to run cross-compiled code

Each case requires careful analysis of the error and additional parameters to the `configure` script to provide the correct information, or patches to the code to avoid the problem altogether. Bear in mind that one package may have many dependencies, especially with programs that have a graphical interface using GTK or Qt, or that handle multimedia content. As an example, `mplayer`, which is a popular tool for playing multimedia content, has dependencies on over 100 libraries. It would take weeks of effort to build them all.

Therefore, I would not recommend manually cross-compiling components for the target in this way, except when there is no alternative or the number of packages to build is small. A much better approach is to use a build tool such as Buildroot or the Yocto Project or avoid the problem altogether by setting up a native build environment for your target architecture. Now you can see why distributions such as Debian are always compiled natively.

CMake

CMake is more of a meta build system in the sense that it relies on an underlying platform's native tools to build software. On Windows, CMake can generate project files for Microsoft Visual Studio and on macOS, it can generate project files for Xcode. Integrating with the principal IDEs for each of the major platforms is no simple task and explains the success of CMake as the leading cross-platform build system solution. CMake also runs on Linux, where it can be used in conjunction with a cross-compiling toolchain of your choice.

To configure, build, and install a package for a native Linux operating system, run the following commands:

```
$ cmake .
$ make
$ sudo make install
```

On Linux, the native build tool is GNU `make` so CMake generates makefiles by default for us to build with. Oftentimes, we want to perform out-of-source builds so that object files and other build artifacts remain separate from source files.

To configure an out-of-source build in a subdirectory named `_build`, run the following commands:

```
$ mkdir _build
$ cd _build
$ cmake ..
```

This will generate the makefiles inside a `_build` subdirectory within the project directory where the `CMakeLists.txt` is located. The `CMakeLists.txt` file is the CMake equivalent of the `configure` script for Autotools-based projects.

We can then build the project out-of-source from inside the `_build` directory and install the package just as before:

```
$ make
$ sudo make install
```

CMake uses absolute paths so the `_build` subdirectory cannot be copied or moved once the makefiles have been generated or any subsequent `make` step will likely fail. Note that CMake defaults to installing packages into system directories such as `/usr/bin` even for out-of-source builds.

To generate the makefiles so that `make` installs the package in the `_build` subdirectory, replace the previous `cmake` command with the following:

```
$ cmake .. -D CMAKE_INSTALL_PREFIX=../_build
```

We no longer need to preface `make install` with `sudo` because we do not need elevated permissions to copy the package files into the `_build` directory.

Similarly, we can use another CMake command-line option to generate makefiles for cross-compilation:

```
$ cmake .. -D CMAKE_C_COMPILER="/usr/local/share/x-tools/
arm-cortex_a8-linux-gnueabihf-gcc"
```

But the best practice for cross-compiling with CMake is to create a toolchain file that sets `CMAKE_C_COMPILER` and `CMAKE_CXX_COMPILER` in addition to other relevant variables for targeting embedded Linux.

CMake works best when we design our software in a modular way by enforcing well-defined API boundaries between libraries and components.

Here are some key terms that come up time and time again in CMake:

- `target`: A software component such as a library or executable.
- `properties`: Include the source files, compiler options, and linked libraries needed to build a target.
- `package`: A CMake file that configures an external target for building just as if it was defined within your `CMakeLists.txt` itself.

For example, if we had a CMake-based executable named `dummy` that needed to take a dependency on SQLite, we could define the following `CMakeLists.txt`:

```
cmake_minimum_required (VERSION 3.0)
project (Dummy)
add_executable(dummy dummy.c)
find_package (SQLite3)
target_include_directories(dummy PRIVATE ${SQLITE3_INCLUDE_
DIRS})
target_link_libraries (dummy PRIVATE ${SQLITE3_LIBRARIES})
```

The `find_package` command searches for a package (`SQLite3` in this case) and imports it so that the external target can be added as a dependency to the `dummy` executable's list of `target_link_libraries` for linking.

CMake comes with numerous finders for popular C and C++ packages including OpenSSL, Boost, and protobuf, making native development much more productive than if we were to use just pure makefiles.

The `PRIVATE` qualifier prevents details such as headers and flags from leaking outside of the `dummy` target. Using `PRIVATE` makes more sense when the target being built is a library instead of an executable. Think of targets as modules and attempt to minimize their exposed surface areas when using CMake to define your own targets. Only employ the `PUBLIC` qualifier when absolutely necessary and utilize the `INTERFACE` qualifier for header-only libraries.

Model your application as a dependency graph with edges between targets. This graph should not only include the libraries that your application links to directly but any transitive dependencies as well. For best results, remove any cycles or other unnecessary independencies seen in the graph. It is often best to perform this exercise before you start coding. A little planning can make the difference between a clean, easily maintainable `CMakeLists.txt` and an inscrutable mess that nobody wants to touch.

Summary

The toolchain is always your starting point; everything that follows from that is dependent on having a working, reliable toolchain.

You may start with nothing but a toolchain—perhaps built using crosstool-NG or downloaded from Linaro—and use it to compile all the packages that you need on your target. Or you may obtain the toolchain as part of a distribution generated from source code using a build system such as Buildroot or the Yocto Project. Beware of toolchains or distributions that are offered to you for free as part of a hardware package; they are often poorly configured and not maintained.

Once you have a toolchain, you can use it to build the other components of your embedded Linux system. In the next chapter, you will learn about the bootloader, which brings your device to life and begins the boot process. We will use the toolchain we built in this chapter to build a working bootloader for the BeagleBone Black.

Further reading

Here are a couple of videos that capture the state of the art on cross toolchains and build systems at the time of writing:

- *A Fresh Look at Toolchains and Crosscompilers in 2020*, by Bernhard "Bero" Rosenkränzer: `https://www.youtube.com/watch?v=BHaXqXzAs0Y`
- *Modern CMake for modular design*, by Mathieu Ropert: `https://www.youtube.com/watch?v=eC9-iRN2b04`

3
All about Bootloaders

The bootloader is the second element of embedded Linux. It is the part that starts the system and loads the operating system kernel. In this chapter, we will look at the role of the bootloader and, in particular, how it passes control from itself to the kernel using a data structure called a **device tree**, also known as a **flattened device tree** or **FDT**. I will cover the basics of device trees, as this will help you follow the connections described in a device tree and relate it to real hardware.

I will look at the popular open source bootloader known as U-Boot and show you how to use it to boot a target device, as well as how to customize it so that it can run on a new device by using the BeagleBone Black as an example.

In this chapter, we will cover the following topics:

- What does a bootloader do?
- The boot sequence
- Moving from the bootloader to a kernel
- Introducing device trees
- U-Boot

Let's get started!

Technical requirements

To follow along with the examples in this chapter, make sure you have the following:

- A Linux-based host system with `device-tree-compiler`, `git`, `make`, `patch`, and `u-boot-tools` or their equivalents installed.
- The Crosstool-NG toolchain for BeagleBone Black from *Chapter 2, Learning About Toolchains.*
- A microSD card reader and card.
- A USB to TTL 3.3V serial cable
- BeagleBone Black
- A 5V 1A DC power supply

All the code that will be used in this chapter can be found in the `Chapter03` folder of this book's GitHub repository: `https://github.com/PacktPublishing/Mastering-Embedded-Linux-Programming-Third-Edition`.

What does a bootloader do?

In an embedded Linux system, the bootloader has two main jobs: to initialize the system to a basic level and to load the kernel. In fact, the first job is somewhat subsidiary to the second, in that it is only necessary to get as much of the system working as is needed to load the kernel.

When the first lines of the bootloader code are executed, following a power-on or a reset, the system is in a very minimal state. The DRAM controller is not set up, so the main memory is not accessible. Likewise, other interfaces are not configured, so storage that's accessed via NAND flash controllers, MMC controllers, and so on is unavailable. Typically, the only resources that are operational at the beginning are a single CPU core, some on-chip static memory, and the boot ROM.

System bootstrap consists of several phases of code, each bringing more of the system into operation. The final act of the bootloader is to load the kernel into RAM and create an execution environment for it. The details of the interface between the bootloader and the kernel are architecture-specific, but in each case, it has to do two things. First, the bootloader has to pass a pointer to a structure containing information about the hardware configuration. Second, it has to pass a pointer to the kernel command line.

The kernel command line is a text string that controls the behavior of Linux. Once the kernel has begun executing, the bootloader is no longer needed and all the memory it was using can be reclaimed.

A subsidiary job of the bootloader is to provide a maintenance mode for updating boot configurations, loading new boot images into memory, and, maybe, running diagnostics. This is usually controlled by a simple command-line user interface, commonly over a serial console.

The boot sequence

In simpler times, some years ago, it was only necessary to place the bootloader in non-volatile memory at the reset vector of the processor. **NOR flash** memory was common at that time and, since it can be mapped directly into the address space, it was the ideal method of storage. The following diagram shows such a configuration, with the **Reset vector** at `0xfffffffc` at the top end of an area of flash memory. The bootloader is linked so that there is a jump instruction at that location that points to the start of the bootloader code:

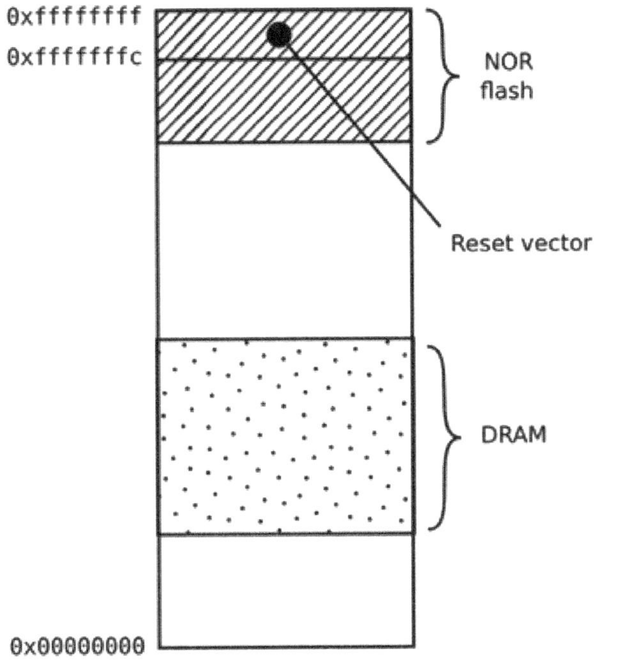

Figure 3.1 – NOR flash

From that point on, the bootloader code running in NOR flash memory can initialize the DRAM controller so that the main memory – the **DRAM** – becomes available and then copies itself into the DRAM. Once fully operational, the bootloader can load the kernel from flash memory into DRAM and transfer control to it.

However, once you move away from a simple linearly addressable storage medium such as NOR flash, the boot sequence becomes a complex, multi-stage procedure. The details are very specific to each SoC, but they generally follow each of the following phases.

Phase 1 – ROM code

In the absence of reliable external memory, the code that runs immediately after a reset or power-on has to be stored on-chip in the SoC; this is known as **ROM code**. It is loaded into the chip when it is manufactured, and hence the ROM code is proprietary and cannot be replaced by an open source equivalent. Usually, it does not include code to initialize the memory controller, since DRAM configurations are highly device-specific, and so it can only use **Static Random Access Memory (SRAM)**, which does not require a memory controller.

Most embedded SoC designs have a small amount of SRAM on-chip, varying in size from as little as 4 KB to several hundred KB:

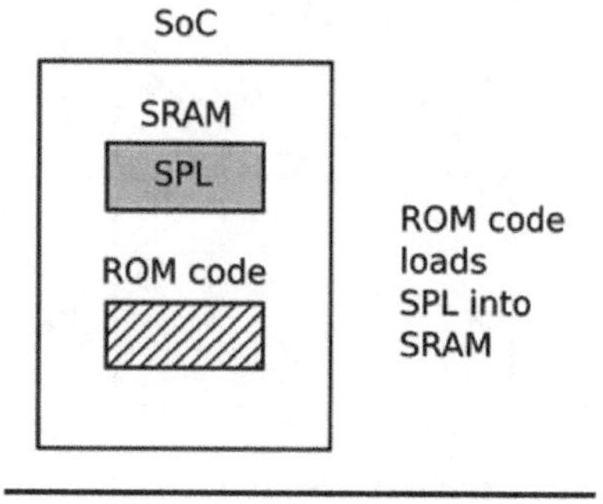

Figure 3.2 – Phase 1 – ROM code

The ROM code is capable of loading a small chunk of code from one of several pre-programmed locations into the SRAM. As an example, TI OMAP and Sitara chips try to load code from the first few pages of NAND flash memory, or from flash memory connected through a **Serial Peripheral Interface (SPI)**, or from the first sectors of an MMC device (which could be an eMMC chip or an SD card), or from a file named `MLO` on the first partition of an MMC device. If it's reading from all these memory devices fails, then it tries reading a byte stream from Ethernet, USB, or UART; the latter is provided mainly as a means of loading code into flash memory during production, rather than for use in normal operation. Most embedded SoCs have ROM code that works in a similar way. In SoCs, where the SRAM is not large enough to load a full bootloader such as U-Boot, there has to be an intermediate loader called the **secondary program loader (SPL)**.

At the end of the ROM code phase, the SPL is present in the SRAM and the ROM code jumps to the beginning of that code.

Phase 2 – secondary program loader

The SPL must set up the memory controller and other essential parts of the system in preparation for loading the **Tertiary Program Loader** (**TPL**) into DRAM. The functionality of the SPL is limited by the size of the SRAM. It can read a program from a list of storage devices, as can the ROM code, once again using pre-programmed offsets from the start of a flash device. If the SPL has filesystem drivers built in to it, it can read well-known filenames, such as `u-boot.img`, from a disk partition. The SPL usually doesn't allow for any user interaction, but it may print version information and progress messages, which you can see on the console. The following diagram explains the phase 2 architecture:

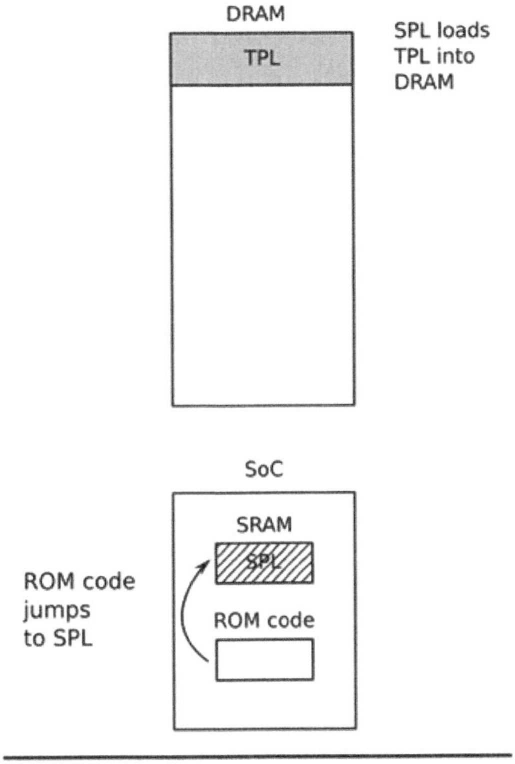

Figure 3.3 – Phase 2 – SPL

The preceding diagram shows the jump from ROM code to SPL. As the SPL executes within SRAM, it loads the TPL into DRAM. At the end of the second phase, the TPL is present in DRAM, and the SPL can make a jump to that area.

The SPL may be open source, as is the case with the TI x-loader and Atmel AT91Bootstrap, but it is quite common for it to contain proprietary code that is supplied by the manufacturer as a binary blob.

Phase 3 – TPL

At this point, we are running a full bootloader, such as U-Boot, which we will learn about a bit later in this chapter. Usually, there is a simple command-line user interface that lets you perform maintenance tasks, such as loading new boot and kernel images into flash storage, and loading and booting a kernel, and there is a way to load the kernel automatically without user intervention.

The following diagram explains the phase 3 architecture:

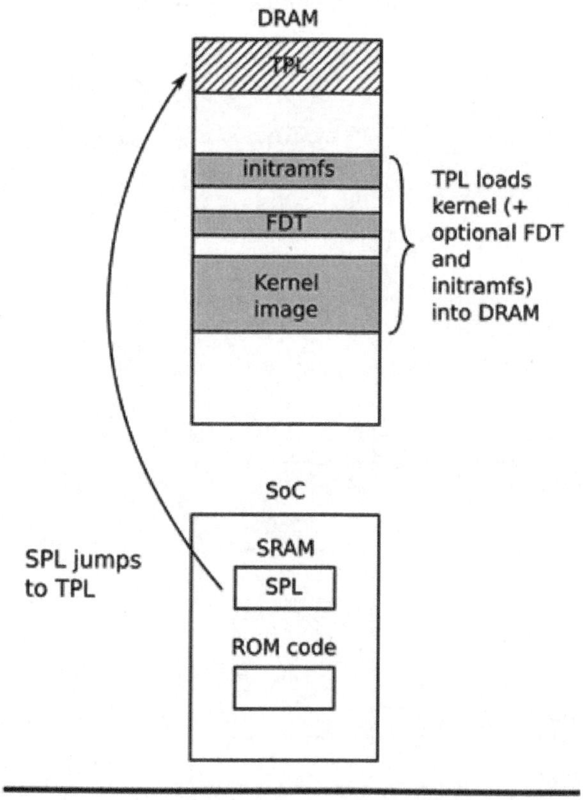

Figure 3.4 – Phase 3 – TPL

The preceding diagram shows the jump from SPL in SRAM to TPL in DRAM. As the TPL executes, it loads the kernel into DRAM. We also have the choice of appending an FDT and/or initial RAM disk to the image in DRAM if we want. Either way, at the end of the third phase, there is a kernel in memory, waiting to be started.

Embedded bootloaders usually disappear from memory once the kernel is running and have no further part in the operation of the system. Before that happens, the TPL needs to hand off control of the boot process to the kernel.

Moving from the bootloader to a kernel

When the bootloader passes control to the kernel, it has to pass some basic information, which includes the following:

- The *machine number*, which is used on PowerPC and Arm platforms without support for a device tree, to identify the type of the SoC.
- Basic details of the hardware that's been detected so far, including (at the very least) the size and location of the physical RAM and the CPU's clock speed.
- The kernel command line.
- Optionally, the location and size of a device tree binary.
- Optionally, the location and size of an initial RAM disk, called the **initial RAM file system (initramfs)**.

The kernel command line is a plain ASCII string that controls the behavior of Linux by giving, for example, the name of the device that contains the root filesystem. We will look at the details of this in the next chapter. It is common to provide the root filesystem as a RAM disk, in which case it is the responsibility of the bootloader to load the RAM disk image into memory. We will cover how create initial RAM disks in *Chapter 5, Building a Root Filesystem*.

The way this information is passed is dependent on the architecture and has changed in recent years. For instance, with PowerPC, the bootloader simply used to pass a pointer to a board information structure, whereas with Arm, it passed a pointer to a list of *A tags*. There is a good description of the format of A tags in the kernel source in `Documentation/arm/Booting`.

In both cases, the amount of information that was passed was very limited, leaving the bulk of it to be discovered at runtime or hard-coded into the kernel as **platform data**. The widespread use of platform data meant that each board had to have a kernel configured and modified for that platform. A better way was needed, and that way is the device tree. In the Arm world, the move away from A tags began in earnest in February 2013 with the release of Linux 3.8. Today, almost all Arm systems use device tree to gather information about the specifics of the hardware platform, allowing a single kernel binary to run on a wide range of those platforms.

Now that we've learned what a bootloader does, what the stages of the boot sequence are, and how it passes control to the kernel, let's learn how to configure a bootloader so that it runs on popular embedded SoCs.

Introducing device trees

If you are working with Arm or PowerPC SoCs, you are almost certainly going to encounter device trees at some point. This section aims to give you a quick overview of what they are and how they work. We will revisit the topic of device trees repeatedly throughout the course of this book.

A device tree is a flexible way of defining the hardware components of a computer system. Bear in mind that a device tree is just static data, not executable code. Usually, the device tree is loaded by the bootloader and passed to the kernel, although it is possible to bundle the device tree with the kernel image itself to cater for bootloaders that are not capable of loading them separately.

The format is derived from a Sun Microsystems bootloader known as **OpenBoot**, which was formalized as the Open Firmware specification, which is IEEE standard IEEE1275-1994. It was used in PowerPC-based Macintosh computers and so was a logical choice for the PowerPC Linux port. Since then, it has been adopted at a large scale by the many Arm Linux implementations and, to a lesser extent, by MIPS, MicroBlaze, ARC, and other architectures.

I would recommend visiting `https://www.devicetree.org` for more information.

Device tree basics

The Linux kernel contains a large number of device tree source files in `arch/$ARCH/boot/dts`, and this is a good starting point for learning about device trees. There are also a smaller number of sources in the U-boot source code in `arch/$ARCH/dts`. If you acquired your hardware from a third party, the `dts` file forms part of the board support package, so you should expect to receive one along with the other source files.

The device tree represents a computer system as a collection of components joined together in a hierarchy, such as a tree. The device tree begins with a root node, represented by a forward slash, /, which contains subsequent nodes representing the hardware of the system. Each node has a name and contains a number of properties in the form `name = "value"`. Here is a simple example:

```
/dts-v1/;
/{
    model = "TI AM335x BeagleBone";
    compatible = "ti,am33xx";
    #address-cells = <1>;
    #size-cells = <1>;
    cpus {
        #address-cells = <1>;
```

```
        #size-cells = <0>;
        cpu@0 {
            compatible = "arm,cortex-a8";
            device_type = "cpu";
            reg = <0>;
        };
    };
    memory@0x80000000 {
        device_type = "memory";
        reg = <0x80000000 0x20000000>; /* 512 MB */
    };
};
```

Here, we have a root node that contains a `cpus` node and a `memory` node. The `cpus` node contains a single CPU node named `cpu@0`. The names of these nodes often include an `@`, followed by an address that distinguishes the node from other nodes of the same type. `@` is required if the node has a `reg` property.

Both the root and CPU nodes have a `compatible` property. The Linux kernel uses this property to find a matching device driver by comparing it with the strings that are exported by each device driver in a `of_device_id` structure (more on this in *Chapter 11, Interfacing with Device Drivers*).

> **Important Note**
>
> It is a convention that the value of the `compatible` property is composed of a manufacturer name and a component name, to reduce confusion between similar devices made by different manufacturers; hence, `ti,am33xx` and `arm,cortex-a8`. It is also quite common to have more than one value for the `compatible` property where there is more than one driver that can handle this device. They are listed with the most suitable mentioned first.

The CPU node and the memory node have a `device_type` property, which describes the class of device. The node name is often derived from `device_type`.

The reg property

The `memory` and `cpu` nodes shown earlier have a `reg` property, which refers to a range of units in a register space. A `reg` property consists of two values representing the real physical address and the size (length) of the range. Both are written as zero or more 32-bit integers, called cells. Hence, the previous `memory` node refers to a single bank of memory that begins at `0x80000000` and is `0x20000000` bytes long.

Understanding reg properties becomes more complex when the address or size values cannot be represented in 32 bits. For example, on a device with 64-bit addressing, you need two cells for each:

```
/{
    #address-cells = <2>;
    #size-cells = <2>;
    memory@80000000 {
        device_type = "memory";
        reg = <0x00000000 0x80000000 0 0x80000000>;
    };
};
```

The information about the number of cells required is held in the #address-cells and #size_cells properties in an ancestor node. In other words, to understand a reg property, you have to look backward down the node hierarchy until you find #address-cells and #size_cells. If there are none, the default values are 1 for each – but it is bad practice for device tree writers to depend on defaults.

Now, let's return to the cpu and cpus nodes. CPUs have addresses as well; in a quad core device, they might be addressed as 0, 1, 2, and 3. That can be thought of as a one-dimensional array without any depth, so the size is zero. Therefore, you can see that we have #address-cells = <1> and #size-cells = <0> in the cpus node, and in the child node, cpu@0, we assign a single value to the reg property, reg = <0>.

Labels and interrupts

The structure of the device tree we've described so far assumes that there is a single hierarchy of components, whereas there are, in fact, several. As well as the obvious data connection between a component and other parts of the system, it might also be connected to an interrupt controller, to a clock source, and to a voltage regulator. To express these connections, we can add a label to a node and reference the label from other nodes. These labels are sometimes referred to as **phandles**, because when the device tree is compiled, nodes with a reference from another node are assigned a unique numerical value in a property called phandle. You can see them if you decompile the device tree binary.

Take, as an example, a system containing an LCD controller that can generate interrupts and an interrupt-controller:

```
/dts-v1/;
{
```

```
    intc: interrupt-controller@48200000 {
        compatible = "ti,am33xx-intc";
        interrupt-controller;
        #interrupt-cells = <1>;
        reg = <0x48200000 0x1000>;
    };
    lcdc: lcdc@4830e000 {
        compatible = "ti,am33xx-tilcdc";
        reg = <0x4830e000 0x1000>;
        interrupt-parent = <&intc>;
        interrupts = <36>;
        ti,hwmods = "lcdc";
        status = "disabled";
    };
};
```

Here, we have the `interrupt-controller@48200000` node with a label of `intc`. The `interrupt-controller` property identifies it as an interrupt controller. Like all interrupt controllers, it has an `#interrupt-cells` property, which tells us how many cells are needed to represent an interrupt source. In this case, there is only one that represents the **interrupt request** (**IRQ**) number. Other interrupt controllers may use additional cells to characterize the interrupt; for example, to indicate whether it is edge or level triggered. The number of interrupt cells and their meanings is described in the bindings for each interrupt controller. The device tree bindings can be found in the Linux kernel source, in the `Documentation/devicetree/bindings/` directory.

Looking at the `lcdc@4830e000` node, it has an `interrupt-parent` property, which references the interrupt controller it is connected to, using the label. It also has an `interrupts` property, which is `36` in this case. Note that this node has its own label, `lcdc`, which is used elsewhere: any node can have a label.

Device tree include files

A lot of hardware is common between SoCs of the same family and between boards using the same SoC. This is reflected in the device tree by splitting out common sections into include files, usually with the `.dtsi` extension. The Open Firmware standard defines `/include/` as the mechanism to be used, as in this snippet from `vexpress-v2p-ca9.dts`:

```
/include/ "vexpress-v2m.dtsi"
```

Look through the .dts files in the kernel, though, and you will find an alternative include statement that is borrowed from C; for example, in am335x-boneblack.dts:

```
#include "am33xx.dtsi"
#include "am335x-bone-common.dtsi"
```

Here is another example from am33xx.dtsi:

```
#include <dt-bindings/gpio/gpio.h>
#include <dt-bindings/pinctrl/am33xx.h>
#include <dt-bindings/clock/am3.h>
```

Lastly, include/dt-bindings/pinctrl/am33xx.h contains normal C macros:

```
#define PULL_DISABLE          (1 << 3)
#define INPUT_EN              (1 << 5)
#define SLEWCTRL_SLOW         (1 << 6)
#define SLEWCTRL_FAST          0
```

All of this is resolved if the device tree sources are built using the Kbuild system, which runs them through the C preprocessor, CPP, where the #include and #define statements are processed into text that is suitable for the device tree compiler. This motivation is illustrated in the previous example; it means that the device tree sources can use the same definitions of constants as the kernel code.

When we include files, using either syntax, the nodes are overlaid on top of one another to create a composite tree in which the outer layers extend or modify the inner ones. For example, am33xx.dtsi, which is general to all am33xx SoCs, defines the first MMC controller interface, like this:

```
mmc1: mmc@48060000 {
    compatible = "ti,omap4-hsmmc";
    ti,hwmods = "mmc1";
    ti,dual-volt;
    ti,needs-special-reset;
    ti,needs-special-hs-handling;
    dmas = <&edma_xbar 24 0 0
        &edma_xbar 25 0 0>;
    dma-names = "tx", "rx";
    interrupts = <64>;
```

```
    reg = <0x48060000 0x1000>;
    status = "disabled";
};
```

Note that status is disabled, meaning that no device driver should be bound to it, and also that it has a label of mmc1.

Both the BeagleBone and the BeagleBone Black have a microSD card interface attached to mmc1. This is why, in am335x-bone-common.dtsi, the same node is referenced by its label; that is, &mmc1:

```
&mmc1 {
    status = "okay";
    bus-width = <0x4>;
    pinctrl-names = "default";
    pinctrl-0 = <&mmc1_pins>;
    cd-gpios = <&gpio0 6 GPIO_ACTIVE_LOW>;
};
```

The status property is set to okay, which causes the MMC device driver to bind with this interface at runtime on both variants of the BeagleBone. Also, a reference to a label is added to the pin control configuration, mmc1_pins. Alas, there is not sufficient space here to describe pin control and pin multiplexing. You will find some information in the Linux kernel source in the Documentation/devicetree/bindings/pinctrl directory.

However, the mmc1 interface is connected to a different voltage regulator on the BeagleBone Black. This is expressed in am335x-boneblack.dts, where you will see another reference to mmc1, which associates it with the voltage regulator via the vmmcsd_fixed label:

```
&mmc1 {
    vmmc-supply = <&vmmcsd_fixed>;
};
```

So, layering the device tree source files like this gives us flexibility and reduces the need for duplicated code.

Compiling a device tree

The bootloader and kernel require a binary representation of the device tree, so it has to be compiled using the device tree compiler; that is, dtc. The result is a file ending with .dtb, which is referred to as a device tree binary or a device tree blob.

There is a copy of `dtc` in the Linux source, in `scripts/dtc/dtc`, and it is also available as a package on many Linux distributions. You can use it to compile a simple device tree (one that does not use `#include`) like this:

```
$ dtc simpledts-1.dts -o simpledts-1.dtb
DTC: dts->dts on file "simpledts-1.dts"
```

Be wary of the fact that `dtc` does not give helpful error messages and makes no checks other than on the basic syntax of the language, which means that debugging a typing error in a source file can be a lengthy process.

To build more complex examples, you will have to use the Kbuild kernel, as shown in *Chapter 4, Configuring and Building the Kernel.*

Like the kernel, the bootloader can use a device tree to initialize an embedded SoC and its peripherals. This device tree is critical when you're loading the kernel from a mass storage device such as a QSPI flash. While embedded Linux offers a choice of bootloaders, we will only cover one. We'll dig deep into that bootloader next.

U-Boot

We are going to focus on U-Boot exclusively because it supports a good number of processor architectures and a large number of individual boards and devices. It has been around for a long time and has a good community for support.

U-Boot, or to give its full name, **Das U-Boot**, began life as an open source bootloader for embedded PowerPC boards. Then, it was ported to Arm-based boards and later to other architectures, including MIPS and SH. It is hosted and maintained by Denx Software Engineering. There is plenty of information available on it, and a good place to start is `https://www.denx.de/wiki/U-Boot`. There is also a mailing list at `u-boot@lists.denx.de` that you can subscribe to by filling out and submitting the form provided at `https://lists.denx.de/listinfo/u-boot`.

Building U-Boot

Begin by getting the source code. As with most projects, the recommended way is to clone the `.git` archive and check out the tag you intend to use – which, in this case, is the version that was current at the time of writing:

```
$ git clone git://git.denx.de/u-boot.git
$ cd u-boot
$ git checkout v2021.01
```

Alternatively, you can get a tarball from ftp://ftp.denx.de/pub/u-boot.

There are more than 1,000 configuration files for common development boards and devices in the configs/ directory. In most cases, you can take a good guess regarding which to use, based on the filename, but you can get more detailed information by looking through the per-board README files in the board/ directory, or you can find information in an appropriate web tutorial or forum.

Taking the BeagleBone Black as an example, we will find that there is a likely configuration file named configs/am335x_evm_defconfig and the text **The binary produced by this board supports ... Beaglebone Black** in the board's README file for the am335x chip, board/ti/am335x/README. With this knowledge, building U-Boot for a BeagleBone Black is simple. You need to inform U-Boot of the prefix for your cross compiler by setting the CROSS_COMPILE make variable, and then selecting the configuration file using a command of the make [board]_defconfig type. Therefore, to build U-Boot using the Crosstool-NG compiler we created in *Chapter 2, Learning About Toolchains*, you would type in the following:

```
$ source ../MELP/Chapter02/set-path-arm-cortex_a8-linux-
gnueabihf
$ make am335x_evm_defconfig
$ make
```

The results of the compilation are as follows:

- u-boot: U-Boot in ELF object format, suitable for use with a debugger
- u-boot.map: The symbol table
- u-boot.bin: U-Boot in raw binary format, suitable for running on your device
- u-boot.img: This is u-boot.bin with a U-Boot header added, suitable for uploading to a running copy of U-Boot
- u-boot.srec: U-Boot in Motorola S-record (**SRECORD** or **SRE**) format, suitable for transferring over a serial connection

The BeagleBone Black also requires a **secondary program loader** (**SPL**), as described earlier. This is built at the same time and is named MLO:

```
$ ls -l MLO u-boot*
-rw-rw-r-- 1 frank frank  108260 Feb  8 15:24 MLO
-rwxrwxr-x 1 frank frank 6028304 Feb  8 15:24 u-boot
-rw-rw-r-- 1 frank frank  594076 Feb  8 15:24 u-boot.bin
```

```
-rw-rw-r-- 1 frank frank   20189 Feb  8 15:23 u-boot.cfg
-rw-rw-r-- 1 frank frank   10949 Feb  8 15:24 u-boot.cfg.
configs
-rw-rw-r-- 1 frank frank   54860 Feb  8 15:24 u-boot.dtb
-rw-rw-r-- 1 frank frank  594076 Feb  8 15:24 u-boot-dtb.bin
-rw-rw-r-- 1 frank frank  892064 Feb  8 15:24 u-boot-dtb.img
-rw-rw-r-- 1 frank frank  892064 Feb  8 15:24 u-boot.img
-rw-rw-r-- 1 frank frank    1722 Feb  8 15:24 u-boot.lds
-rw-rw-r-- 1 frank frank  802250 Feb  8 15:24 u-boot.map
-rwxrwxr-x 1 frank frank  539216 Feb  8 15:24 u-boot-nodtb.bin
-rwxrwxr-x 1 frank frank 1617810 Feb  8 15:24 u-boot.srec
-rw-rw-r-- 1 frank frank  211574 Feb  8 15:24 u-boot.sym
```

The procedure is similar for other targets.

Installing U-Boot

Installing a bootloader on a board for the first time requires some outside assistance. If the board has a hardware debug interface, such as **JTAG** (**Joint Test Action Group**), it is usually possible to load a copy of U-Boot directly into RAM and get it running. From that point, you can use U-Boot commands so that it copies itself into flash memory. The details of this are very board-specific and outside the scope of this book.

Many SoC designs have a boot ROM built in that can be used to read boot code from various external sources, such as SD cards, serial interfaces, or USB mass storage. This is the case with the `am335x` chip in the BeagleBone Black, which makes it easy to try out new software.

You will need an SD card reader to write the images to a card. There are two types: external readers that plug into a USB port, and the internal SD readers that are present on many laptops. A device name is assigned by Linux when a card is plugged into the reader. The `lsblk` command is a useful tool for finding out which device has been allocated. For example, this is what I see when I plug a nominal 8 GB microSD card into my card reader:

```
$ lsblk
NAME        MAJ:MIN RM   SIZE RO TYPE MOUNTPOINT
sda           8:0    1   7.4G  0 disk
└─sda1        8:1    1   7.4G  0 part /media/frank/6662-6262
nvme0n1     259:0    0 465.8G  0 disk
├─nvme0n1p1 259:1    0   512M  0 part /boot/efi
```

```
├─nvme0n1p2 259:2    0    16M  0 part
├─nvme0n1p3 259:3    0 232.9G  0 part
└─nvme0n1p4 259:4    0 232.4G  0 part /
```

In this case, `nvme0n1` is my 512 GB hard drive and `sda` is the microSD card. It has a single partition, `sda1`, which is mounted as the `/media/frank/6662-6262` directory.

> **Important Note**
>
> Although the microSD card had 8 GB printed on the outside, it was only 7.4 GB on the inside. In part, this is because of the different units being used. The advertised capacity is measured in gigabytes, 109, but the sizes reported by software are in gibibytes, 230. Gigabytes is abbreviated to GB, while gibibytes is abbreviated to GiB. The same applies for KB and KiB and MB and MiB. In this book, I have tried to use the right units. In the case of the SD card, it so happens that 8 GB is approximately 7.4 GiB.

If I use the built-in SD card slot, I see this:

```
$ lsblk
NAME          MAJ:MIN RM   SIZE RO TYPE MOUNTPOINT
mmcblk0       179:0    1   7.4G  0 disk
└─mmcblk0p1 179:1    1   7.4G  0 part /media/frank/6662-6262
nvme0n1       259:0    0 465.8G  0 disk
├─nvme0n1p1 259:1    0   512M  0 part /boot/efi
├─nvme0n1p2 259:2    0    16M  0 part
├─nvme0n1p3 259:3    0 232.9G  0 part
└─nvme0n1p4 259:4    0 232.4G  0 part /
```

In this case, the microSD card appears as `mmcblk0` and the partition is `mmcblk0p1`. Note that the microSD card you use may have been formatted differently to this one, so you may see a different number of partitions with different mount points. When formatting an SD card, it is very important to be sure of its device name. You really don't want to mistake your hard drive for an SD card and format that instead. This has happened to me more than once. So, I have provided a shell script in this book's code archive named `MELP/format-sdcard.sh`, which has a reasonable number of checks to prevent you (and me) from using the wrong device name. The parameter is the device name of the microSD card, which would be `sdb` in the first example and `mmcblk0` in the second. Here is an example of its use:

```
$ MELP/format-sdcard.sh mmcblk0
```

The script creates two partitions: the first is 64 MiB, formatted as `FAT32`, and will contain the bootloader, while the second is 1 GiB, formatted as `ext4`, which you will use in *Chapter 5, Building a Root Filesystem*. The script aborts when it's applied to any drive greater than 32 GiB, so be prepared to modify it if you are using larger microSD cards.

Once you have formatted the microSD card, remove it from the card reader and then re-insert it so that the partitions are auto mounted. On current versions of Ubuntu, the two partitions should be mounted as `/media/[user]/boot` and `/media/[user]/rootfs`. Now, you can copy the SPL and U-Boot to it, like this:

```
$ cp MLO u-boot.img /media/frank/boot
```

Finally, unmount it:

```
$ sudo umount /media/frank/boot
```

Now, with no power on the BeagleBone board, insert the microSD card into the reader. Plug in the serial cable. A serial port should appear on your PC as `/dev/ttyUSB0`. Start a suitable terminal program, such as `gtkterm`, `minicom`, or `picocom`, and attach to the port at `115200` bits per second (bps) with no flow control. `gtkterm` is probably the easiest to set up and use:

```
$ gtkterm -p /dev/ttyUSB0 -s 115200
```

If you get a permissions error, then you may need to add yourself to the `dialout` group and reboot to use this port.

Press and hold the Boot Switch button (nearest to the microSD slot) on the BeagleBone Black, power up the board using the external 5V power connector, and release the button after about 5 seconds. You should see some output, followed by a U-Boot prompt, on the serial console:

```
U-Boot SPL 2021.01 (Feb 08 2021 - 15:23:22 -0800)
Trying to boot from MMC1


U-Boot 2021.01 (Feb 08 2021 - 15:23:22 -0800)

CPU  : AM335X-GP rev 2.1
Model: TI AM335x BeagleBone Black
DRAM:  512 MiB
```

```
WDT:    Started with servicing (60s timeout)
NAND:   0 MiB
MMC:    OMAP SD/MMC: 0, OMAP SD/MMC: 1
Loading Environment from FAT... *** Warning - bad CRC, using
default environment

<ethaddr> not set. Validating first E-fuse MAC
Net:    eth2: ethernet@4a100000, eth3: usb_ether
Hit any key to stop autoboot:  0
=>
```

Hit any key on your keyboard to stop U-Boot from autobooting with the default environment. Now that we have a U-Boot prompt in front of us, let's put U-Boot through its paces.

Using U-Boot

In this section, I will describe some of the common tasks that you can use U-Boot to perform.

Usually, U-Boot offers a command-line interface over a serial port. It provides a command prompt that is customized for each board. In these examples, I will use `=>`. Typing `help` prints out all the commands that have been configured in this version of U-Boot; typing `help <command>` prints out more information about a particular command.

The default command interpreter for the BeagleBone Black is quite simple. You cannot do command-line editing by pressing the left or right keys; there is no command completion by pressing the *Tab* key; and there is no command history by pressing the up key. Pressing any of these keys will disrupt the command you are currently trying to type, and you will have to type *Ctrl* + *C* and start all over again. The only line editing key you can safely use is the backspace. As an option, you can configure a different command shell called **Hush**, which has more sophisticated interactive support, including command-line editing.

The default number format is hexadecimal. Consider the following command as an example:

```
=> nand read 82000000 400000 200000
```

This will read `0x200000` bytes from offset `0x400000` from the start of the NAND flash memory into RAM address `0x82000000`.

Environment variables

U-Boot uses environment variables extensively to store and pass information between functions and even to create scripts. Environment variables are simple `name=value` pairs that are stored in an area of memory. The initial population of variables may be coded in the board configuration header file, like this:

```
#define CONFIG_EXTRA_ENV_SETTINGS
"myvar1=value1"
"myvar2=value2"
[…]
```

You can create and modify variables from the U-Boot command line using `setenv`. For example, `setenv foo bar` creates the `foo` variable with the `bar` value. Note that there is no = sign between the variable name and the value. You can delete a variable by setting it to a `null` string, `setenv foo`. You can print all the variables to the console using `printenv`, or a single variable using `printenv foo`.

If U-Boot has been configured with space to store the environment, you can use the `saveenv` command to save it. If there is raw NAND or NOR flash, then an `erase` block can be reserved for this purpose, often with another being used as a redundant copy to guard against corruption. If there is eMMC or SD card storage, it can be stored in a reserved array of sectors, or in a file named `uboot.env` in a partition of the disk. Other options include storing it in a serial EEPROM connected via an I2C or SPI interface or non-volatile RAM.

Boot image format

U-Boot doesn't have a filesystem. Instead, it tags blocks of information with a 64-byte header so that it can track the contents. We prepare files for U-Boot using the `mkimage` command-line tool, which comes bundled with the `u-boot-tools` package on Ubuntu. You can also get `mkimage` by running `make tools` from within the U-Boot source tree, and then invoke it as `tools/mkimage`.

Here is a brief summary of the command's usage:

```
$ mkimage
Error: Missing output filename
Usage: mkimage -l image
          -l ==> list image header information
       mkimage [-x] -A arch -O os -T type -C comp -a addr -e ep
-n name -d data_file[:data_file...] image
```

```
        -A ==> set architecture to 'arch'
        -O ==> set operating system to 'os'
        -T ==> set image type to 'type'
        -C ==> set compression type 'comp'
        -a ==> set load address to 'addr' (hex)
        -e ==> set entry point to 'ep' (hex)
        -n ==> set image name to 'name'
        -d ==> use image data from 'datafile'
        -x ==> set XIP (execute in place)
    mkimage [-D dtc_options] [-f fit-image.its|-f auto|-F]
[-b <dtb> [-b <dtb>]] [-i <ramdisk.cpio.gz>] fit-image
         <dtb> file is used with -f auto, it may occur
multiple times.
        -D => set all options for device tree compiler
        -f => input filename for FIT source
        -i => input filename for ramdisk file
Signing / verified boot options: [-E] [-B size] [-k keydir] [-K
dtb] [ -c <comment>] [-p addr] [-r] [-N engine]
        -E => place data outside of the FIT structure
        -B => align size in hex for FIT structure and header
        -k => set directory containing private keys
        -K => write public keys to this .dtb file
        -c => add comment in signature node
        -F => re-sign existing FIT image
        -p => place external data at a static position
        -r => mark keys used as 'required' in dtb
        -N => openssl engine to use for signing
    mkimage -V ==> print version information and exit
Use '-T list' to see a list of available image types
```

For example, to prepare a kernel image for an Arm processor, you can use the following command:

```
$ mkimage -A arm -O linux -T kernel -C gzip -a 0x80008000 \
-e 0x80008000
-n 'Linux' -d zImage uImage
```

In this instance, the architecture is `arm`, the operating system is `linux`, and the image type is `kernel`. Additionally, the compression scheme is `gzip`, the load address is `0x80008000`, and the entry point is the same as the load address. Lastly, the image name is `Linux`, the image datafile is named `zImage`, and the image being generated is named `uImage`.

Loading images

Usually, you will load images from removable storage, such as an SD card or a network. SD cards are handled in U-Boot by the MMC driver. A typical sequence that's used to load an image into memory is as follows:

```
=> mmc rescan
=> fatload mmc 0:1 82000000 uimage
reading uimage
4605000 bytes read in 254 ms (17.3 MiB/s)
=> iminfo 82000000

## Checking Image at 82000000 ...
Legacy image found
Image Name: Linux-3.18.0
Created: 2014-12-23 21:08:07 UTC
Image Type: ARM Linux Kernel Image (uncompressed)
Data Size: 4604936 Bytes = 4.4 MiB
Load Address: 80008000
Entry Point: 80008000
Verifying Checksum ... OK
```

The `mmc rescan` command re-initializes the MMC driver, perhaps to detect that an SD card has recently been inserted. Next, `fatload` is used to read a file from a FAT-formatted partition on the SD card. The format is as follows:

```
fatload <interface> [<dev[:part]> [<addr> [<filename> [bytes
[pos]]]]]
```

If `<interface>` is `mmc`, as in our case, `<dev:part>` is the device number of the MMC interface counting from zero, and the partition number counting from one. Hence, `<0:1>` is the first partition on the first device, which is `mmc 0` for the microSD card (the onboard eMMC is `mmc 1`). The memory location, `0x82000000`, is chosen to be in an area of RAM that is not being used at this moment. If we intend to boot this kernel, we must make sure that this area of RAM will not be overwritten when the kernel image is decompressed and located at the runtime location, `0x80008000`.

To load image files over a network, you must use the **Trivial File Transfer Protocol (TFTP)**. This requires you to install a TFTP daemon, `tftpd`, on your development system and start running it. You must also configure any firewalls between your PC and the target board to allow the TFTP protocol on UDP port `69` to pass through. The default configuration of TFTP only allows access to the `/var/lib/tftpboot` directory. The next step is to copy the files you want to transfer to the target into that directory. Then, assuming that you are using a pair of static IP addresses, which removes the need for further network administration, the sequence of commands to load a set of kernel image files should look like this:

```
=> setenv ipaddr 192.168.159.42
=> setenv serverip 192.168.159.99
=> tftp 82000000 uImage
link up on port 0, speed 100, full duplex
Using cpsw device
TFTP from server 192.168.159.99; our IP address is
192.168.159.42
Filename 'uImage'.
Load address: 0x82000000
Loading:
###############################################################
###############################################################
###############################################################
###############################################################
############################################################
3 MiB/s
done
Bytes transferred = 4605000 (464448 hex)
```

Finally, let's look at how to program images into NAND flash memory and read them back, which is handled by the `nand` command. This example loads a kernel image via TFTP and programs it into flash:

```
=> tftpboot 82000000 uimage
=> nandecc hw
=> nand erase 280000 400000
NAND erase: device 0 offset 0x280000, size 0x400000
Erasing at 0x660000 -- 100% complete.
OK
=> nand write 82000000 280000 400000

NAND write: device 0 offset 0x280000, size 0x400000
4194304 bytes written: OK
```

Now, you can load the kernel from flash memory using the `nand read` command:

```
=> nand read 82000000 280000 400000
```

Once the kernel has been loaded into RAM, we can boot it.

Booting Linux

The `bootm` command starts a kernel image running. The syntax is as follows:

```
bootm [address of kernel] [address of ramdisk] [address of
dtb].
```

The address of the kernel image is necessary, but the addresses of `ramdisk` and `dtb` can be omitted if the kernel configuration does not need them. If there is `dtb` but no `initramfs`, the second address can be replaced with a dash (`-`). This would look like this:

```
=> bootm 82000000 - 83000000
```

Plainly, typing a long series of commands to boot your board each time it is powered up is not acceptable. Let's look at how to automate the boot process.

Automating the boot with U-Boot scripts

U-Boot stores a sequence of commands in environment variables. If the special variable named `bootcmd` contains a script, it is run at power-up after a delay of `bootdelay` seconds. If you watch this on the serial console, you will see the delay counting down to zero. You can press any key during this period to terminate the countdown and enter an interactive session with U-Boot.

The way that you create scripts is simple, though not easy to read. You simply append commands separated by semicolons, which must be preceded by a \ escape character. So, for example, to load a kernel image from an offset in flash memory and boot it, you might use the following command:

```
setenv bootcmd nand read 82000000 400000 200000\;bootm 82000000
```

We now know how to boot a kernel on a BeagleBone Black using U-Boot. But how do we port U-Boot to a new board that has no BSP? We'll cover that in the remainder of this chapter.

Porting U-Boot to a new board

Let's assume that your hardware department has created a new board called **Nova** that is based on the BeagleBone Black and that you need to port U-Boot to it. You will need to understand the layout of the U-Boot code and how the board configuration mechanism works. In this section, I will show you how to create a variant of an existing board – the BeagleBone Black – which you could go on to use as the basis for further customizations. There are quite a few files that need to be changed. I have put them together into a patch file in the code archive in `MELP/Chapter03/0001-BSP-for-Nova.patch`. You can simply apply that patch to a clean copy of U-Boot version 2021.01 like this:

```
$ cd u-boot
$ patch -p1 < MELP/Chapter03/0001-BSP-for-Nova.patch
```

If you want to use a different version of U-Boot, you will have to make some changes to the patch for it to apply cleanly.

The remainder of this section will describe how the patch was created. If you want to follow along step by step, you will need a clean copy of U-Boot 2021.01 without the Nova BSP patch. The main directories we will be dealing with are as follows:

- `arch`: Contains code that's specific to each supported architecture in the `arm`, `mips`, and `powerpc` directories. Within each architecture, there is a subdirectory for each member of the family; for example, in `arch/arm/cpu/`, there are directories for the architecture variants, including `amt926ejs`, `armv7`, and `armv8`.

- board: Contains code that's specific to a board. Where there are several boards from the same vendor, they can be collected together into a subdirectory. Hence, the support for the am335x EVM board, which the BeagleBone is based on, is in board/ti/am335x.
- common: Contains core functions, including the command shells and the commands that can be called from them, each in a file named cmd_[command name].c.
- doc: Contains several README files describing various aspects of U-Boot. If you are wondering how to proceed with your U-Boot port, this is a good place to start.
- include: In addition to many shared header files, this contains the very important include/configs/ subdirectory, where you will find the majority of the board configuration settings.

The way that Kconfig extracts configuration information from Kconfig files and stores the total system configuration in a file named .config will be described in some detail in *Chapter 4, Configuring and Building the Kernel*. Each board has a default configuration stored in configs/[board name]_defconfig. For the Nova board, we can begin by making a copy of the configuration for the EVM:

```
$ cp configs/am335x_evm_defconfig configs/nova_defconfig
```

Now, edit configs/nova_defconfig and insert CONFIG_TARGET_NOVA=y after CONFIG_AM33XX=y, as shown here:

```
CONFIG_ARM=y
CONFIG_ARCH_CPU_INIT=y
CONFIG_ARCH_OMAP2PLUS=y
CONFIG_TI_COMMON_CMD_OPTIONS=y
CONFIG_AM33XX=y
CONFIG_TARGET_NOVA=y
CONFIG_SPL=y
[...]
```

Note that CONFIG_ARM=y causes the contents of arch/arm/Kconfig to be included, and that CONFIG_AM33XX=y causes arch/arm/mach-omap2/am33xx/Kconfig to be included.

Next, insert CONFIG_SYS_CUSTOM_LDSCRIPT=y and CONFIG_SYS_LDSCRIPT=="board/ti/nova/u-boot.lds" into the same file after CONFIG_DISTRO_DEFAULTS=y, as shown here:

```
[...]
CONFIG_SPL=y
CONFIG_DEFAULT_DEVICE_TREE="am335x-evm"
CONFIG_DISTRO_DEFAULTS=y
CONFIG_SYS_CUSTOM_LDSCRIPT=y
CONFIG_SYS_LDSCRIPT="board/ti/nova/u-boot.lds"
CONFIG_SPL_LOAD_FIT=y
[...]
```

We are now done modifying configs/nova_defconfig.

Board-specific files

Each board has a subdirectory named board/[board name] or board/[vendor]/[board name], which should contain the following:

- Kconfig: Contains the configuration options for the board.
- MAINTAINERS: Contains a record of whether the board is currently maintained and, if so, by whom.
- Makefile: Used to build the board-specific code.
- README: Contains any useful information about this port of U-Boot; for example, which hardware variants are covered.

In addition, there may be source files for board-specific functions.

Our Nova board is based on a BeagleBone, which, in turn, is based on a TI am335x EVM. So, we should make copies of the am335x board files:

```
$ mkdir board/ti/nova
$ cp -a board/ti/am335x/* board/ti/nova
```

Next, edit `board/ti/nova/Kconfig` and set `SYS_BOARD` to `"nova"` so that it will build the files in `board/ti/nova`. Then, set `SYS_CONFIG_NAME` to `"nova"` as well so that it will use `include/configs/nova.h` as the configuration file:

```
if TARGET_NOVA

config SYS_BOARD
        default "nova"

config SYS_VENDOR
        default "ti"

config SYS_SOC
        default "am33xx"

config SYS_CONFIG_NAME
        default "nova"
[...]
```

There is one other file here that we need to change. The linker script, which has been placed at `board/ti/nova/u-boot.lds`, contains a hard-coded reference to `board/ti/am335x/built-in.o`. Change it, as shown here:

```
{
    *(.__image_copy_start)
    *(.vectors)
    CPUDIR/start.o (.text*)
    board/ti/nova/built-in.o (.text*)
}
```

Now, we need to link the `Kconfig` file for Nova into the chain of `Kconfig` files. First, edit `arch/arm/Kconfig` and insert `source "board/ti/nova/Kconfig"` after `source "board/tcl/sl50/Kconfig"`, as shown here:

```
[...]
source "board/st/stv0991/Kconfig"
source "board/tcl/sl50/Kconfig"
source "board/ti/nova/Kconfig"
```

```
source "board/toradex/colibri_pxa270/Kconfig"
source "board/variscite/dart_6ul/Kconfig"
[...]
```

Then, edit `arch/arm/mach-omap2/am33xx/Kconfig` and add a configuration option for `TARGET_NOVA` immediately after `TARGET_AM335X_EVM`, as shown here:

```
[...]
config TARGET_NOVA
        bool "Support the Nova! board"
        select DM
        select DM_GPIO
        select DM_SERIAL
        select TI_I2C_BOARD_DETECT
        imply CMD_DM
        imply SPL_DM
        imply SPL_DM_SEQ_ALIAS
        imply SPL_ENV_SUPPORT
        imply SPL_FS_EXT4
        imply SPL_FS_FAT
        imply SPL_GPIO_SUPPORT
        imply SPL_I2C_SUPPORT
        imply SPL_LIBCOMMON_SUPPORT
        imply SPL_LIBDISK_SUPPORT
        imply SPL_LIBGENERIC_SUPPORT
        imply SPL_MMC_SUPPORT
        imply SPL_NAND_SUPPORT
        imply SPL_OF_LIBFDT
        imply SPL_POWER_SUPPORT
        imply SPL_SEPARATE_BSS
        imply SPL_SERIAL_SUPPORT
        imply SPL_SYS_MALLOC_SIMPLE
        imply SPL_WATCHDOG_SUPPORT
        imply SPL_YMODEM_SUPPORT
        help
          The Nova target board
[...]
```

All the `imply SPL_` lines are necessary so that U-Boot builds cleanly without errors.

Now that we have copied and modified the board-specific files for our Nova board, let's move on to the header files.

Configuring header files

Each board has a header file in `include/configs/` that contains most of the configuration information. The file is named by the `SYS_CONFIG_NAME` identifier in the board's `Kconfig` file. The format of this file is described in detail in the `README` file, at the top level of the U-Boot source tree. For the purposes of our Nova board, simply copy `include/configs/am335x_evm.h` into `include/configs/nova.h` and make a few changes, as shown here:

```
[...]
#ifndef __CONFIG_NOVA_H
#define __CONFIG_NOVA_H

include <configs/ti_am335x_common.h>
#include <linux/sizes.h>

#undef CONFIG_SYS_PROMPT
#define CONFIG_SYS_PROMPT "nova!> "

#ifndef CONFIG_SPL_BUILD
# define CONFIG_TIMESTAMP
#endif
[...]
#endif  /* ! __CONFIG_NOVA_H */
```

Besides replacing `__CONFIG_AM335X_EVM_H` with `__CONFIG_NOVA_H`, the only change that needs to be made is to set a new command prompt so that we can identify this bootloader at runtime.

With the source tree fully modified, we are now ready to build U-Boot for our custom board.

Building and testing

To build U-Boot for the Nova board, select the configuration you have just created:

```
$ source ../MELP/Chapter02/set-path-arm-cortex_a8-linux-
gnueabihf
$ make distclean
$ make nova_defconfig
$ make
```

Copy `MLO` and `u-boot.img` to the boot partition of the microSD card you created earlier and boot the board. You should see an output like this (note the command prompt):

```
U-Boot SPL 2021.01-dirty (Feb 08 2021 - 21:30:41 -0800)
Trying to boot from MMC1


U-Boot 2021.01-dirty (Feb 08 2021 - 21:30:41 -0800)

CPU  : AM335X-GP rev 2.1
Model: TI AM335x BeagleBone Black
DRAM:  512 MiB
WDT:   Started with servicing (60s timeout)
NAND:  0 MiB
MMC:   OMAP SD/MMC: 0, OMAP SD/MMC: 1
Loading Environment from FAT... *** Warning - bad CRC, using
default environment

<ethaddr> not set. Validating first E-fuse MAC
Net:   eth2: ethernet@4a100000, eth3: usb_ether
Hit any key to stop autoboot:  0
nova!>
```

You can create a patch for all these changes by checking them into Git and using the `git format-patch` command:

```
$ git add .
$ git commit -m "BSP for Nova"
[detached HEAD 093ec472f6] BSP for Nova
```

```
12 files changed, 2379 insertions(+)
 create mode 100644 board/ti/nova/Kconfig
 create mode 100644 board/ti/nova/MAINTAINERS
 create mode 100644 board/ti/nova/Makefile
 create mode 100644 board/ti/nova/README
 create mode 100644 board/ti/nova/board.c
 create mode 100644 board/ti/nova/board.h
 create mode 100644 board/ti/nova/mux.c
 create mode 100644 board/ti/nova/u-boot.lds
 create mode 100644 configs/nova_defconfig
 create mode 100644 include/configs/nova.h
$ git format-patch -1
0001-BSP-for-Nova.patch
```

Generating this patch concludes our coverage of U-Boot as a TPL. U-Boot can also be configured to bypass the TPL stage of the boot process altogether. Next, let's examine this alternate approach to booting Linux.

Falcon mode

We are used to the idea that booting a modern embedded processor involves the CPU boot ROM loading an SPL, which loads `u-boot.bin`, which then loads a Linux kernel. You may be wondering if there is a way to reduce the number of steps, thereby simplifying and speeding up the boot process. The answer is U-Boot **Falcon mode**. The idea is simple: have the SPL load a kernel image directly, missing out `u-boot.bin`. There is no user interaction and there are no scripts. It just loads a kernel from a known location in flash or eMMC into memory, passes it a pre-prepared parameter block, and starts it running. The details of configuring Falcon mode are beyond the scope of this book. If you would like to find out more information, take a look at `doc/README.falcon`.

> **Important Note**
>
> Falcon mode is named after the peregrine falcon, which is the fastest bird of all, capable of reaching speeds of more than 200 miles per hour in a dive.

Summary

Every system needs a bootloader to bring the hardware to life and to load a kernel. U-Boot has found favor with many developers because it supports a useful range of hardware and it is fairly easy to port to a new device. In this chapter, we learned how to inspect and drive U-Boot interactively from the command line over a serial console. These command-line exercises included loading a kernel over a network using TFTP for rapid iteration. Lastly, we learned how to port U-Boot to a new device by generating a patch for our Nova board.

Over the last few years, the complexity and ever-increasing variety of embedded hardware has led to the introduction of the device tree as a way of describing hardware. The device tree is simply a textual representation of a system that is compiled into a **device tree binary** (**DTB**), and which is passed to the kernel when it loads. It is up to the kernel to interpret the device tree and to load and initialize drivers for the devices it finds there.

In use, U-Boot is very flexible, allowing images to be loaded from mass storage, flash memory, or a network, and then booted. Having covered some of the intricacies of booting Linux, in the next chapter, we will cover the next stage of the process as the third element of your embedded project – the kernel – comes into play.

4
Configuring and Building the Kernel

The kernel is the third element of embedded Linux. It is the component that is responsible for managing resources and interfacing with hardware, and so affects almost every aspect of your final software build. It is usually tailored to your particular hardware configuration, although, as we saw in *Chapter 3, All About Bootloaders*, device trees allow you to create a generic kernel that is tailored to particular hardware by the contents of the device tree.

In this chapter, we will look at how to get a kernel for a board, and how to configure and compile it. We will look again at Bootstrap, this time focusing on the part the kernel plays. We will also look at device drivers and how they pick up information from the device tree.

We will cover the following main topics:

- What does the kernel do?
- Choosing a kernel
- Building the kernel
- Booting the kernel
- Porting Linux to a new board

Technical requirements

To follow along with the examples, make sure you have the following:

- A Linux-based host system
- The crosstool-NG toolchains from *Chapter 2, Learning About Toolchains*
- A microSD card reader and card
- The microSD card with U-Boot installed from *Chapter 3, All About Bootloaders*
- A USB to TTL 3.3V serial cable
- Raspberry Pi 4
- A 5V 3A USB-C power supply
- BeagleBone Black
- A 5V 1A DC power supply

All of the code for this chapter can be found in the `Chapter04` folder from the book's GitHub repository: `https://github.com/PacktPublishing/Mastering-Embedded-Linux-Programming-Third-Edition`.

What does the kernel do?

Linux began in 1991 when Linus Torvalds started writing an operating system for Intel 386- and 486-based personal computers. He was inspired by the Minix operating system written by Andrew S. Tanenbaum 4 years earlier. Linux differed in many ways from Minix; the main difference being that it was a 32-bit virtual memory kernel and the code was open source, later released under the GPL v2 license. He announced it on August 25, 1991, on the `comp.os.minix` newsgroup in a famous post that began with the following:

> *Hello everybody out there using minix—I'm doing a (free) operating system (just a hobby, won't be big and professional like GNU) for 386(486) AT clones. This has been brewing since April, and is starting to get ready. I'd like any feedback on things people like/dislike in minix, as my OS resembles it somewhat (same physical layout of the filesystem (due to practical reasons) among other things).*

To be strictly accurate, Linus did not write an operating system, rather he wrote a kernel, which is only one component of an operating system. To create a complete operating system with user space commands and a shell command interpreter, he used components from the GNU project, especially the toolchain, the C library, and basic command-line tools. That distinction remains today and gives Linux a lot of flexibility in the way it is used.

The Linux kernel can be combined with a GNU user space to create a full Linux distribution that runs on desktops and servers, which is sometimes called GNU/Linux; it can be combined with an Android user space to create the well-known mobile operating system, or it can be combined with a small BusyBox-based user space to create a compact embedded system.

Contrast this with the BSD operating systems, FreeBSD, OpenBSD, and NetBSD, in which the kernel, the toolchain, and the user space are combined into a single code base. By removing the toolchain, you can deploy slimmer runtime images without a compiler or header files. By decoupling user space from the kernel, you gain options in terms of init systems (`runit` versus `systemd`), C libraries (`musl` versus `glibc`), and package formats (`.apk` versus `.deb`).

The kernel has three main jobs: to manage resources, to interface with hardware, and to provide an API that offers a useful level of abstraction to user space programs, as summarized in the following diagram:

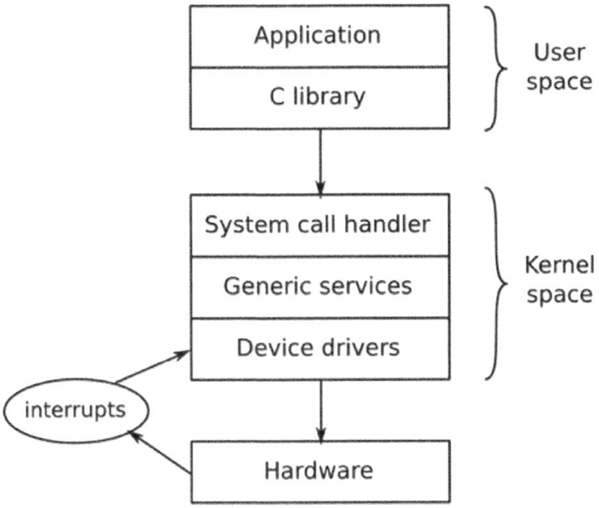

Figure 4.1 – User space, kernel space, and hardware

Applications running in **user space** run at a low CPU privilege level. They can do very little other than make library calls. The primary interface between the **user space** and the **kernel space** is the **C library**, which translates user-level functions, such as those defined by POSIX, into kernel system calls. The system call interface uses an architecture-specific method, such as a trap or a software interrupt, to switch the CPU from low-privilege user mode to high-privilege kernel mode, which allows access to all memory addresses and CPU registers.

The **system call handler** dispatches the call to the appropriate kernel subsystem: memory allocation calls go to the memory manager, filesystem calls to the filesystem code, and so on. Some of those calls require input from the underlying hardware and will be passed down to a device driver. In some cases, the hardware itself invokes a kernel function by raising an interrupt.

> **Important note**
>
> The preceding diagram shows that there is a second entry point into kernel code: hardware interrupts. Interrupts can only be handled in a device driver, never by a user space application.

In other words, all the useful things that your application does, it does them through the kernel. The kernel, then, is one of the most important elements in the system. So, it is important to understand how to choose one – let's do that next.

Choosing a kernel

The next step is to choose the kernel for your project, balancing the desire to always use the latest version of software against the need for vendor-specific additions and an interest in the long-term support of the code base.

Kernel development cycle

Linux is developed at a fast pace, with a new version being released every 8 to 12 weeks. The way that the version numbers are constructed has changed a bit in recent years. Before July 2011, there was a three-number version scheme with version numbers that looked like 2.6.39. The middle number indicated whether it was a developer or stable release; odd numbers (2.1.x, 2.3.x, 2.5.x) were for developers and even numbers were for end users.

From version 2.6 onward, the idea of a long-lived development branch (the odd numbers) was dropped, as it slowed down the rate at which new features were made available to the users. The change in numbering from 2.6.39 to 3.0 in July 2011 was purely because Linus felt that the numbers were becoming too large; there was no huge leap in the features or architecture of Linux between those two versions. He also took the opportunity to drop the middle number. Since then, in April 2015 and March 2019, he bumped the major from 3 to 4 and 4 to 5 respectively, again purely for neatness, not because of any large architectural shift.

Linus manages the development kernel tree. You can follow him by cloning the Git tree like so:

```
$ git clone git://git.kernel.org/pub/scm/linux/kernel/git/
torvalds/linux.git
```

This will check out into the subdirectory `linux`. You can keep up to date by running the `git pull` command in that directory from time to time.

Currently, a full cycle of kernel development begins with a merge window of 2 weeks, during which Linus accepts patches for new features. At the end of the merge window, a stabilization phase begins, during which Linus produces weekly release candidates with version numbers ending in `-rc1`, `-rc2`, and so on, usually up to `-rc7` or `-rc8`. During this time, people test the candidates and submit bug reports and fixes. When all significant bugs have been fixed, the kernel is released.

The code incorporated during the merge window has to be fairly mature already. Usually, it is pulled from the repositories of the many subsystem and architecture maintainers of the kernel. By keeping to a short development cycle, features can be merged when they are ready. If a feature is deemed not sufficiently stable or well developed by the kernel maintainers, it can simply be delayed until the next release.

Keeping a track of what has changed from release to release is not easy. You can read the commit log in Linus' Git repository but, with roughly 10,000 or more entries, it is not easy to get an overview. Thankfully, there is the Linux **KernelNewbies** website, `https://kernelnewbies.org`, where you will find a succinct overview of each version at `https://kernelnewbies.org/LinuxVersions`.

Stable and long-term support releases

The rapid rate of change of Linux is a good thing in that it brings new features into the mainline code base, but it does not fit very well with the longer life cycle of embedded projects. Kernel developers address this in two ways, with **stable** releases and **long-term** releases. After the release of a mainline kernel (maintained by Linus Torvalds), it is moved to the **stable** tree (maintained by Greg Kroah-Hartman). Bug fixes are applied to the stable kernel, while the mainline kernel begins the next development cycle. Point releases of the stable kernel are marked by a third number, 3.18.1, 3.18.2, and so on. Before version 3, there were four release numbers, 2.6.29.1, 2.6.39.2, and so on.

You can get the stable tree by using the following command:

```
$ git clone git://git.kernel.org/pub/scm/linux/kernel/git/
stable/linux-stable.git
```

You can use `git checkout` to get a particular version, for example, version 5.4.50:

```
$ cd linux-stable
$ git checkout v5.4.50
```

Usually, only the stable kernel is updated until the next mainline release (8 to 12 weeks later), so you will see that there is just one or sometimes two stable kernels at `https://www.kernel.org/`. To cater to those users who would like updates for a longer period of time and be assured that any bugs will be found and fixed, some kernels are labeled **long-term** and maintained for 2 or more years. There is at least one long-term kernel release each year.

Looking at `https://www.kernel.org/` at the time of writing, there are a total of five long-term kernels: 5.4, 4.19, 4.14, 4.9, and 4.4. The oldest has been maintained for nearly 5 years and is at version 4.4.256. If you are building a product that you will have to maintain for this length of time, then the latest long-term kernel (5.4 in this case) might well be a good choice.

Vendor support

In an ideal world, you would be able to download a kernel from `https://www.kernel.org/` and configure it for any device that claims to support Linux. However, that is not always possible; in fact, mainline Linux has solid support for only a small subset of the many devices that can run Linux. You may find support for your board or **System on Chip** (**SoC**) from independent open source projects such as Linaro or the Yocto Project, or from companies providing third-party support for embedded Linux, but in many cases, you will be obliged to look to the vendor of your SoC or board for a working kernel.

As we know, some vendors are better at supporting Linux than others. My advice at this point is to choose vendors who give good support or who, even better, take the trouble to get their kernel changes into the mainline. Search the Linux kernel mailing list or commit history for recent activity around a candidate SoC or board. When upstream changes are absent from the mainline kernel, the verdict as to whether a vendor offers good support is largely based on word of mouth. Some vendors are notorious for releasing only one kernel code drop before redirecting all their energies toward their newer SoCs.

Licensing

The Linux source code is licensed under GPL v2, which means that you must make the source code of your kernel available in one of the ways specified in the license.

The actual text of the license for the kernel is in the `COPYING` file. It begins with an addendum written by Linus that states that code calling the kernel from user space via the system call interface is not considered a derivative work of the kernel and so is not covered by the license. Hence, there is no problem with proprietary applications running on top of Linux.

However, there is one area of Linux licensing that causes endless confusion and debate: kernel modules. A **kernel module** is simply a piece of code that is dynamically linked with the kernel at runtime, thereby extending the functionality of the kernel. The GPL makes no distinction between static and dynamic linking, so it would appear that the source for kernel modules is covered by the GPL. But, in the early days of Linux, there were debates about exceptions to this rule, for example, in connection with the Andrew filesystem. This code predates Linux and therefore (it was argued) is not a derivative work, and so the license does not apply.

Similar discussions took place over the years with respect to other pieces of code, with the result that it is now accepted practice that the GPL does not necessarily apply to kernel modules. This is codified by the kernel `MODULE_LICENSE` macro, which may take the `Proprietary` value to indicate that it is not released under the GPL. If you plan to use the same arguments yourself, you may want to read through an oft-quoted email thread titled *Linux GPL and binary module exception clause?*, which is archived at `https://yarchive.net/comp/linux/gpl_modules.html`.

The GPL should be considered a good thing because it guarantees that when we are working on embedded projects, we can always get the source code for the kernel. Without it, embedded Linux would be much harder to use and more fragmented.

Building the kernel

Having decided which kernel to base your build on, the next step is to build it.

Getting the source

All three of the targets used in this book, the Raspberry Pi 4, BeagleBone Black, and the ARM Versatile PB, are well supported by the mainline kernel. Therefore, it makes sense to use the latest long-term kernel available from `https://www.kernel.org/`, which at the time of writing was 5.4.50. When you come to do this for yourself, you should check to see if there is a later version of the 5.4 kernel and use that instead since it will have fixes for bugs found after 5.4.50 was released.

> **Important note**
>
> If there is a later long-term release, you may want to consider using that one, but be aware that there may have been changes that mean that the following sequence of commands does not work exactly as given.

To fetch and extract a release tarball of the 5.4.50 Linux kernel, use the following:

```
$ wget https://cdn.kernel.org/pub/linux/kernel/v5.x/linux-5.4.50.tar.xz
$ tar xf linux-5.4.50.tar.xz
$ mv linux-5.4.50 linux-stable
```

To fetch a later version, replace `5.4.50` after `linux-` with the desired long-term release.

There is a lot of code here. There are over 57,000 files in the 5.4 kernel containing C source code, header files, and assembly code, amounting to a total of over 14 million lines of code, as measured by the SLOCCount utility. Nevertheless, it is worth knowing the basic layout of the code and to know, approximately, where to look for a particular component. The main directories of interest are the following:

- `arch`: Contains architecture-specific files. There is one subdirectory per architecture.
- `Documentation`: Contains kernel documentation. Always look here first if you want to find more information about an aspect of Linux.
- `drivers`: Contains device drivers – thousands of them. There is a subdirectory for each type of driver.
- `fs`: Contains filesystem code.
- `include`: Contains kernel header files, including those required when building the toolchain.
- `init`: Contains the kernel startup code.
- `kernel`: Contains core functions, including scheduling, locking, timers, power management, and debug/trace code.
- `mm`: Contains memory management.
- `net`: Contains network protocols.
- `scripts`: Contains many useful scripts, including the **device tree compiler** (**DTC**) which I described in *Chapter 3, All About Bootloaders*.
- `tools`: Contains many useful tools, including the Linux performance counters tool, `perf`, which I will describe in *Chapter 20, Profiling and Tracing*.

Over time, you will become familiar with this structure, and realize that if you are looking for the serial port code of a particular SoC, you will find it in `drivers/tty/serial` and not in `arch/$ARCH/mach-foo`, because it is a device driver and not something CPU architecture-specific.

Understanding kernel configuration - Kconfig

One of the strengths of Linux is the degree to which you can configure the kernel to suit different jobs, from a small, dedicated device such as a smart thermostat to a complex mobile handset. In current versions, there are many thousands of configuration options. Getting the configuration right is a task in itself, but before we get into that, I want to show you how it works so that you can better understand what is going on.

The configuration mechanism is called `Kconfig`, and the build system that it integrates with is called `Kbuild`. Both are documented in `Documentation/kbuild`. `Kconfig/Kbuild` is used in a number of other projects as well as the kernel, including crosstool-NG, U-Boot, Barebox, and BusyBox.

The configuration options are declared in a hierarchy of files named `Kconfig`, using a syntax described in `Documentation/kbuild/kconfig-language.rst`.

In Linux, the top-level `Kconfig` looks like this:

```
mainmenu "Linux/$(ARCH) $(KERNELVERSION) Kernel Configuration"

comment "Compiler: $(CC_VERSION_TEXT)"

source "scripts/Kconfig.include"
[...]
```

And the first line of `arch/Kconfig` is this:

```
source "arch/$(SRCARCH)/Kconfig"
```

That line includes the architecture-dependent configuration file, which sources other `Kconfig` files, depending on which options are enabled.

Having the architecture play such a prominent role has three implications:

- First, you must specify an architecture when configuring Linux by setting `ARCH=[architecture]`, otherwise, it will default to the local machine architecture.

- Second, the value you set for ARCH usually determines the value of SRCARCH so you rarely need to set SRCARCH explicitly.
- Third, the layout of the top-level menu is different for each architecture.

The value you put into ARCH is one of the subdirectories you find in the arch directory, with the oddity that ARCH=i386 and ARCH=x86_64 both source arch/x86/Kconfig.

The Kconfig files consist largely of menus, delineated by the menu and endmenu keywords. Menu items are marked by the config keyword.

Here is an example, taken from drivers/char/Kconfig:

```
menu "Character devices"
[...]
config DEVMEM
	bool "/dev/mem virtual device support"
	default y
	help
	  Say Y here if you want to support the /dev/mem device.
	  The /dev/mem device is used to access areas of physical
	  memory.
	  When in doubt, say "Y".
[...]
endmenu
```

The parameter following config names a variable that, in this case, is DEVMEM. Since this option is a bool (Boolean), it can only have two values: if it is enabled, it is assigned to y, if it is not enabled, the variable is not defined at all. The name of the menu item that is displayed on the screen is the string following the bool keyword.

This configuration item, along with all the others, is stored in a file named .config.

> **Tip**
>
> The leading dot (.) in .config means that it is a hidden file that will not be shown by the ls command unless you type ls -a to show all the files.

The line corresponding to this configuration item reads as follows:

```
CONFIG_DEVMEM=y
```

There are several other data types in addition to bool. Here is the complete list:

- bool: Either y or not defined.
- tristate: Used where a feature can be built as a kernel module or built into the main kernel image. The values are m for a module, y to be built in, and not defined if the feature is not enabled.
- int: An integer value using decimal notation.
- hex: An unsigned integer value using hexadecimal notation.
- string: A string value.

There may be dependencies between items, expressed by the depends on construct, as shown here:

```
config MTD_CMDLINE_PARTS
    tristate "Command line partition table parsing"
    depends on MTD
```

If CONFIG_MTD has not been enabled elsewhere, this menu option is not shown and so cannot be selected.

There are also reverse dependencies; the select keyword enables other options if this one is enabled. The Kconfig file in arch/$ARCH has a large number of select statements that enable features specific to the architecture, as can be seen here for ARM:

```
config ARM
    bool
    default y
    select ARCH_CLOCKSOURCE_DATA
    select ARCH_HAS_DEVMEM_IS_ALLOWED
[...]
```

By selecting ARCH_CLOCKSOURCE_DATA and ARCH_HAS_DEVMEM_IS_ALLOWED, we are assigning a value of y to these variables so that these features are built statically into the kernel.

There are several configuration utilities that can read the Kconfig files and produce a .config file. Some of them display the menus onscreen and allow you to make choices interactively. menuconfig is probably the one most people are familiar with, but there are also xconfig and gconfig.

To use `menuconfig`, you first need to have `ncurses`, `flex`, and `bison` installed. The following command installs all these prerequisites on Ubuntu:

```
$ sudo apt install libncurses5-dev flex bison
```

You launch `menuconfig` via the `make` command, remembering that, in the case of the kernel, you have to supply an architecture, as illustrated here:

```
$ make ARCH=arm menuconfig
```

Here, you can see `menuconfig` with the `DEVMEM` config option highlighted previously:

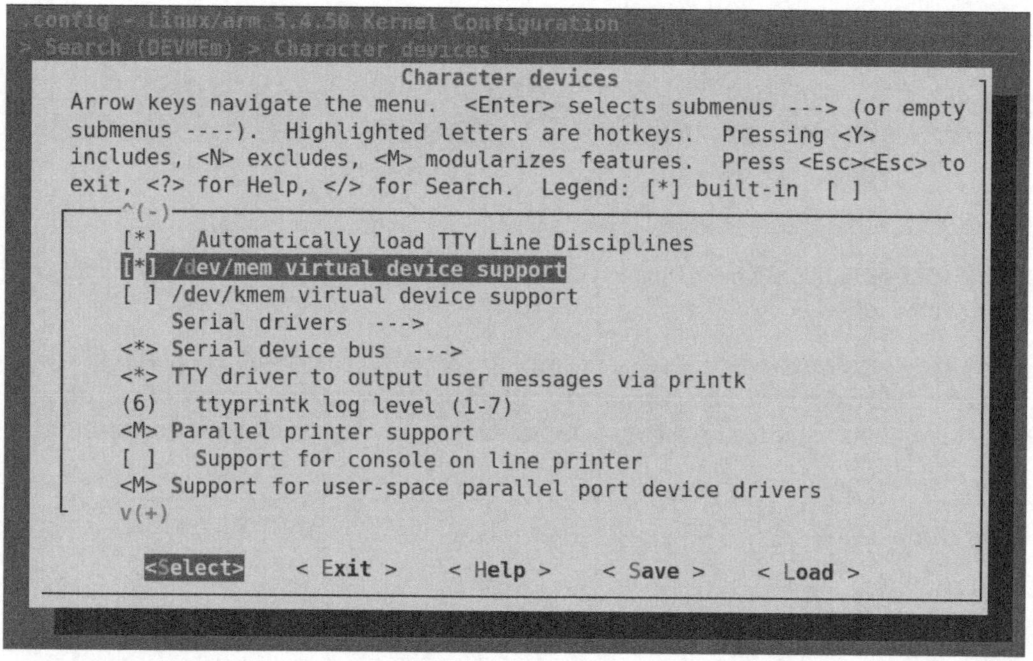

Figure 4.2 – Selecting DEVMEM

The star (`*`) to the left of an item means that the driver has been selected to be built statically into the kernel or, if it is an `M`, that it has been selected to be built as a kernel module for insertion into the kernel at runtime.

> **Tip**
>
> You often see instructions such as enable CONFIG_BLK_DEV_INITRD, but with so many menus to browse through, it can take a while to find the place where that configuration is set. All configuration editors have a search function. You can access it in menuconfig by pressing the forward slash key, /. In xconfig, it is in the **Edit** menu, but make sure you leave off the CONFIG_ part of the configuration item you are searching for.

With so many things to configure, it is unreasonable to start with a clean sheet each time you want to build a kernel, so there is a set of known working configuration files in arch/$ARCH/configs, each containing suitable configuration values for a single SoC or a group of SoCs.

You can select one with the make [configuration file name] command. For example, to configure Linux to run on a wide range of SoCs using the ARMv7-A architecture, you would type the following:

```
$ make ARCH=arm multi_v7_defconfig
```

This is a generic kernel that runs on various different boards. For a more specialized application, for example, when using a vendor-supplied kernel, the default configuration file is part of the board support package; you will need to find out which one to use before you can build the kernel.

There is another useful configuration target named oldconfig. You use it when moving a configuration to a newer kernel version. This target takes an existing .config file and prompts you with questions about new configuration options. Copy .config from the old kernel to the new source directory and run the make ARCH=arm oldconfig command to bring it up to date.

The oldconfig target can also be used to validate a .config file that you have edited manually (ignoring the text **Automatically generated file; DO NOT EDIT** that occurs at the top; sometimes it is OK to ignore warnings).

If you do make changes to the configuration, the modified .config file becomes part of your board support package and needs to be placed under source code control.

When you start the kernel build, a header file, include/generated/autoconf.h, is generated, which contains a #define for each configuration value so that it can be included in the kernel source.

Now that we've settled on a kernel and learned how to configure it, we will now go about identifying our kernel.

Using LOCALVERSION to identify your kernel

You can discover the kernel version and release that you have built using the `make kernelversion` and `make kernelrelease` targets:

```
$ make ARCH=arm kernelversion
5.4.50
$ make ARCH=arm kernelrelease
5.4.50
```

This is reported at runtime through the `uname` command and is also used in naming the directory where kernel modules are stored.

If you change the configuration from the default, it is advisable to append your own version information, which you can configure by setting `CONFIG_LOCALVERSION`. As an example, if I wanted to mark the kernel I am building with the `melp` identifier and version `1.0`, I would define the local version in `menuconfig` like this:

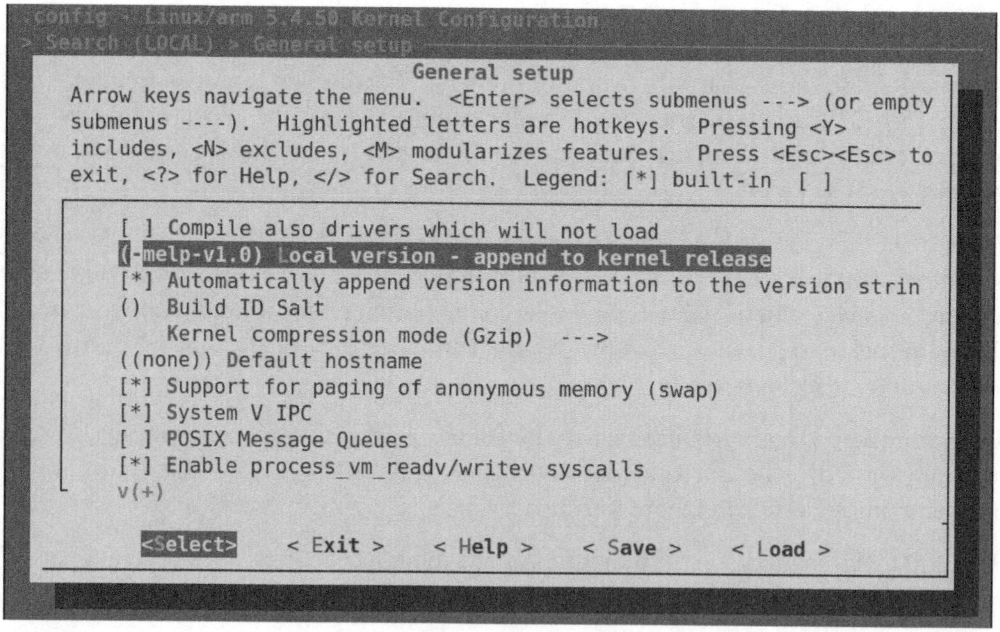

Figure 4.3 – Appending to kernel release version

Running `make kernelversion` produces the same output as before, but now if I run `make kernelrelease`, I see the following:

```
$ make ARCH=arm kernelrelease
5.4.50-melp-v1.0
```

That was a pleasant detour into kernel versioning, but now let's get back to the business of configuring our kernel for compilation.

When to use kernel modules

I have mentioned kernel modules several times already. Desktop Linux distributions use them extensively so that the correct device and kernel functions can be loaded at runtime, depending on the hardware detected and features required. Without them, every single driver and feature would have to be statically linked into the kernel, making it infeasibly large.

On the other hand, with embedded devices, the hardware and kernel configuration are usually known at the time the kernel is built, and therefore modules are not so useful. In fact, they cause a problem because they create a version dependency between the kernel and the root filesystem, which can cause boot failures if one is updated but not the other. Consequently, it is quite common for embedded kernels to be built without any modules at all.

Here are a few cases where kernel modules are a good idea in embedded systems:

- When you have proprietary modules, for the licensing reasons given in the preceding section.
- To reduce boot time by deferring the loading of non-essential drivers.
- When there are several drivers that could be loaded, and it would take up too much memory to compile them statically. For example, you have a USB interface that supports a range of devices. This is essentially the same argument as is used in desktop distributions.

Next, let's learn how to compile a kernel image with or without kernel modules using `Kbuild`.

Compiling – Kbuild

The kernel build system, `Kbuild`, is a set of `make` scripts that take the configuration information from the `.config` file, work out the dependencies, and compile everything that is necessary to produce a kernel image. This kernel image contains all the statically linked components, possibly a device tree binary, and possibly one or more kernel modules. The dependencies are expressed in makefiles that are in each directory with buildable components. For instance, the following two lines are taken from `drivers/char/Makefile`:

```
obj-y += mem.o random.o
obj-$(CONFIG_TTY_PRINTK) += ttyprintk.o
```

The `obj-y` rule unconditionally compiles a file to produce the target, so `mem.c` and `random.c` are always part of the kernel. In the second line, `ttyprintk.c` is dependent on a configuration parameter. If `CONFIG_TTY_PRINTK` is `y`, it is compiled as a built-in; if it is `m`, it is built as a module; and if the parameter is undefined, it is not compiled at all.

For most targets, just typing `make` (with the appropriate `ARCH` and `CROSS_COMPILE`) will do the job, but it is instructive to take it one step at a time. See the last section of *Chapter 2, Learning about Toolchains*, for the meaning of the `CROSS_COMPILE` `make` variable.

Finding out which kernel target to build

To build a kernel image, you need to know what your bootloader expects. This is a rough guide:

- **U-Boot**: Traditionally, U-Boot has required `uImage`, but newer versions can load a `zImage` file using the `bootz` command.
- **x86 targets**: Requires a `bzImage` file.
- **Most other bootloaders**: Require a `zImage` file.

Here is an example of building a `zImage` file:

```
$ make -j 4 ARCH=arm CROSS_COMPILE=arm-cortex_a8-linux-
gnueabihf- zImage
```

> Tip
>
> The `-j 4` option tells `make` how many jobs to run in parallel, which reduces the time taken to build. A rough guide is to run as many jobs as you have CPU cores.

There is a small issue with building a `uImage` file for ARM with multi-platform support, which is the norm for the current generation of ARM SoC kernels. Multi-platform support for ARM was introduced in Linux 3.7. It allows a single kernel binary to run on multiple platforms and is a step on the road toward having a small number of kernels for all ARM devices. The kernel selects the correct platform by reading the machine number or the device tree passed to it by the bootloader. The problem occurs because the location of physical memory might be different for each platform, and so the relocation address for the kernel (usually `0x8000` bytes from the start of physical RAM) might also be different.

The relocation address is coded into the uImage header by the mkimage command when the kernel is built, but it will fail if there is more than one relocation address to choose from. To put it another way, the uImage format is not compatible with multi-platform images. You can still create a uImage binary from a multi-platform build, so long as you give the LOADADDR of the particular SoC you are hoping to boot this kernel on. You can find the load address by looking in arch/$ARCH/mach-[your SoC]/Makefile.boot and noting the value of zreladdr-y:

```
$ make -j 4 ARCH=arm CROSS_COMPILE=arm-cortex_a8-linux-
gnueabihf- LOADADDR=0x80008000 uImage
```

Regardless of which kernel image format we target, the same two build artifacts are first created before the bootable image is generated.

Build artifacts

A kernel build generates two files in the top-level directory: vmlinux and System.map. The first, vmlinux, is the kernel as an ELF binary. If you have compiled your kernel with debug enabled (CONFIG_DEBUG_INFO=y), it will contain debug symbols that can be used with debuggers such as kgdb. You can also use other ELF binary tools, such as size to measure the length of each section (text, data, and bss) that comprises the vmlinux executable:

```
$ arm-cortex_a8-linux-gnueabihf-size vmlinux
   text      data       bss       dec       hex       filename
14005643   7154342   403160   21563145   1490709   vmlinux
```

The dec and hex values are the total file size in decimal and hexadecimal respectively.

System.map contains the symbol table in a human-readable form.

Most bootloaders cannot handle ELF code directly. There is a further stage of processing that takes vmlinux and places those binaries in arch/$ARCH/boot that are suitable for the various bootloaders:

- Image: vmlinux converted to raw binary format.
- zImage: For the PowerPC architecture, this is just a compressed version of Image, which implies that the bootloader must do the decompression. For all other architectures, the compressed Image is piggybacked onto a stub of code that decompresses and relocates it.
- uImage: zImage plus a 64-byte U-Boot header.

While the build is running, you will see a summary of the commands being executed:

```
$ make -j 4 ARCH=arm CROSS_COMPILE=arm-cortex_a8-linux-
gnueabihf- \
zImage
  CC      scripts/mod/empty.o
  CC      scripts/mod/devicetable-offsets.s
  MKELF   scripts/mod/elfconfig.h
  HOSTCC  scripts/mod/modpost.o
  HOSTCC  scripts/mod/sumversion.o
[...]
```

Sometimes, when the kernel build fails, it is useful to see the actual commands being executed. To do that, add `V=1` to the command line:

```
$ make -j 4 ARCH=arm CROSS_COMPILE=arm-cortex_a8-linux-
gnueabihf- \
V=1 zImage
[...]
arm-cortex_a8-linux-gnueabihf-gcc -Wp,-MD,drivers/tty/.
tty_baudrate.o.d  -nostdinc -isystem /home/frank/x-tools/
arm-cortex_a8-linux-gnueabihf/lib/gcc/arm-cortex_a8-linux-
gnueabihf/8.3.0/include -I./arch/arm/include -I./arch/arm/
include/generated  -I./include -I./arch/arm/include/uapi -I./
arch/arm/include/generated/uapi -I./include/uapi -I./include/
generated/uapi -include ./include/linux/kconfig.h -include
./include/linux/compiler_types.h -D__KERNEL__ -mlittle-
endian -Wall -Wundef -Werror=strict-prototypes -Wno-trigraphs
-fno-strict-aliasing -fno-common -fshort-wchar -fno-PIE
-Werror=implicit-function-declaration -Werror=implicit-int
-Wno-format-security -std=gnu89 -fno-dwarf2-cfi-asm -fno-ipa-
sra -mabi=aapcs-linux -mfpu=vfp -funwind-tables -marm -Wa,-mno-
warn-deprecated -D__LINUX_ARM_ARCH__=7 -march=armv7-a -msoft-
float -Uarm -fno-delete-null-pointer-checks -Wno-frame-address
-Wno-format-truncation -Wno-format-overflow -O2 --param=allow-
store-data-races=0 -Wframe-larger-than=1024 -fstack-protector-
strong -Wno-unused-but-set-variable -Wimplicit-fallthrough
-Wno-unused-const-variable -fomit-frame-pointer -fno-var-
tracking-assignments -Wdeclaration-after-statement -Wvla
-Wno-pointer-sign -Wno-stringop-truncation -Wno-array-bounds
-Wno-stringop-overflow -Wno-restrict -Wno-maybe-uninitialized
-fno-strict-overflow -fno-merge-all-constants -fmerge-
```

```
constants -fno-stack-check -fconserve-stack -Werror=date-time
-Werror=incompatible-pointer-types -Werror=designated-init
-fmacro-prefix-map=./= -Wno-packed-not-aligned    -DKBUILD_
BASENAME='"tty_baudrate"' -DKBUILD_MODNAME='"tty_baudrate"' -c
-o drivers/tty/tty_baudrate.o drivers/tty/tty_baudrate.c
[...]
```

In this section, we learned how `Kbuild` takes a precompiled `vmlinux` ELF binary and converts it into a bootable kernel image. Next, we will look at how we can compile device trees.

Compiling device trees

The next step is to build the device tree, or trees if you have a multi-platform build. The `dtbs` target builds device trees according to the rules in `arch/$ARCH/boot/dts/Makefile`, using the device tree source files in that directory. The following is a snippet from building the `dtbs` target for `multi_v7_defconfig`:

```
$ make ARCH=arm dtbs
[...]
  DTC     arch/arm/boot/dts/alpine-db.dtb
  DTC     arch/arm/boot/dts/artpec6-devboard.dtb
  DTC     arch/arm/boot/dts/at91-kizbox2.dtb
  DTC     arch/arm/boot/dts/at91-nattis-2-natte-2.dtb
  DTC     arch/arm/boot/dts/at91-sama5d27_som1_ek.dtb
[...]
```

The compiled `.dtb` files are generated in the same directory as the sources.

Compiling modules

If you have configured some features to be built as modules, you can build them separately using the `modules` target:

```
$ make -j 4 ARCH=arm CROSS_COMPILE=arm-cortex_a8-linux-
gnueabihf- \
modules
```

The compiled modules have a .ko suffix and are generated in the same directory as the source code, meaning that they are scattered all around the kernel source tree. Finding them is a little tricky, but you can use the modules_install make target to install them in the right place. The default location is /lib/modules in your development system, which is almost certainly not what you want. To install them in the staging area of your root filesystem (we will talk about root filesystems in the next chapter), provide the path using INSTALL_MOD_PATH:

```
$ make -j4 ARCH=arm CROSS_COMPILE=arm-cortex_a8-linux-gnueabihf- \
INSTALL_MOD_PATH=$HOME/rootfs modules_install
```

Kernel modules are put into the /lib/modules/[kernel version] directory, relative to the root of the filesystem.

Cleaning kernel sources

There are three make targets for cleaning the kernel source tree:

- clean: Removes object files and most intermediates.
- mrproper: Removes all intermediate files, including the .config file. Use this target to return the source tree to the state it was in immediately after cloning or extracting the source code. If you are curious about the name, Mr. Proper is a cleaning product common in some parts of the world. The meaning of make mrproper is to give the kernel sources a really good scrub.
- distclean: This is the same as mrproper, but also deletes editor backup files, patch files, and other artifacts of software development.

We've seen the kernel compilation steps and their resulting outputs. Now let's build some kernels for the boards we have on hand.

Building a 64-bit kernel for the Raspberry Pi 4

Even though there is already support for the Raspberry Pi 4 in the mainline kernel, I found the Raspberry Pi Foundation's fork of Linux (https://github.com/raspberrypi/linux) to be more stable at the time of writing. The 4.19.y branch of that fork is also more actively maintained than that same fork's rpi-5.4.y branch. This situation may change in the near future, but for now, let's stick with the 4.19.y branch.

Since the Raspberry Pi 4 has a 64-bit quad core ARM Cortex-A72 CPU, we will use a GNU toolchain from Arm that targets AArch64 GNU/Linux to cross-compile a 64-bit kernel for it. This prebuilt toolchain can be downloaded from `https://developer.arm.com/tools-and-software/open-source-software/developer-tools/gnu-toolchain/gnu-a/downloads`:

```
$ cd ~
$ wget https://developer.arm.com/-/media/Files/downloads/
gnu-a/10.2-2020.11/binrel/gcc-arm-10.2-2020.11-x86_64-aarch64-
none-linux-gnu.tar.xz
$ tar xf gcc-arm-10.2-2020.11-x86_64-aarch64-none-linux-gnu.
tar.xz
$ mv gcc-arm-10.2-2020.11-x86_64-aarch64-none-linux-gnu \
gcc-arm-aarch64-none-linux-gnu
```

`gcc-arm-10.2-2020.11-x86_64-aarch64-none-linux-gnu` was the current `x86_64` Linux-hosted cross compiler targeting AArch64 GNU/Linux at the time of writing. If downloading fails, replace `10.2-2020.11` in the preceding commands with whatever the current release version is now.

Next, install a couple of packages we need to fetch and build the kernel:

```
$ sudo apt install subversion libssl-dev
```

Now that you have the requisite toolchain and packages installed, clone the `4.19.y` kernel repo one level deep in a directory named `linux` and export some prebuilt binaries to a `boot` subdirectory:

```
$ git clone --depth=1 -b rpi-4.19.y https://github.com/
raspberrypi/linux.git
$ svn export https://github.com/raspberrypi/firmware/trunk/boot
$ rm boot/kernel*
$ rm boot/*.dtb
$ rm boot/overlays/*.dtbo
```

Navigate to the newly cloned `linux` directory and build the kernel:

```
$ PATH=~/gcc-arm-aarch64-none-linux-gnu/bin/:$PATH
$ cd linux
$ make ARCH=arm64 CROSS_COMPILE=aarch64-none-linux-gnu- \
bcm2711_defconfig
$ make -j4 ARCH=arm64 CROSS_COMPILE=aarch64-none-linux-gnu-
```

When the build finishes, copy the kernel image, device tree blobs, and boot parameters to the boot subdirectory:

```
$ cp arch/arm64/boot/Image ../boot/kernel8.img
$ cp arch/arm64/boot/dts/overlays/*.dtbo ../boot/overlays/
$ cp arch/arm64/boot/dts/broadcom/*.dtb ../boot/
$ cat << EOF > ../boot/config.txt
enable_uart=1
arm_64bit=1
EOF
$ cat << EOF > ../boot/cmdline.txt
console=serial0,115200 console=tty1 root=/dev/mmcblk0p2
rootwait
EOF
```

These preceding commands are all found in the script `MELP/Chapter04/build-linux-rpi4-64.sh`. Note that the kernel command line written to `cmdline.txt` must be all on one line. Let's break these steps down into stages:

1. Clone the `rpi-4.19.y` branch of the Raspberry Pi Foundation's kernel fork into a `linux` directory.
2. Export the contents of the `boot` subdirectory from the Raspberry Pi Foundation's `firmware` repo to a `boot` directory.
3. Delete the existing kernel image(s), device tree blobs, and device tree overlays from the `boot` directory.
4. From the `linux` directory, build the 64-bit kernel, modules, and device tree for the Raspberry Pi 4.
5. Copy the newly built kernel image, device tree blobs, and device tree overlays from `arch/arm64/boot/` to the `boot` directory.
6. Write `config.txt` and `cmdline.txt` files out to the boot directory for the Raspberry Pi 4's bootloader to read and pass to the kernel.

Let's look at the settings in `config.txt`. The `enable_uart=1` line enables the serial console during boot, which is disabled by default. The `arm_64bit=1` line instructs the Raspberry Pi 4's bootloader to start the CPU in 64-bit mode and load the kernel image from a file named `kernel8.img` instead of the default `kernel.img` file for 32-bit ARM.

Now, let's look at cmdline.txt. The console=serial0,115200 and console=tty1 kernel command-line parameters instruct the kernel to output log messages to the serial console as our kernel boots.

Building a kernel for the BeagleBone Black

In light of the information already given, here is the complete sequence of commands to build a kernel, the modules, and a device tree for the BeagleBone Black, using the crosstool-NG ARM Cortex A8 cross compiler:

```
$ cd linux-stable
$ make ARCH=arm CROSS_COMPILE=arm-cortex_a8-linux-gnueabihf-
mrproper
$ make ARCH=arm multi_v7_defconfig
$ make -j4 ARCH=arm CROSS_COMPILE=arm-cortex_a8-linux-
gnueabihf- zImage
$ make -j4 ARCH=arm CROSS_COMPILE=arm-cortex_a8-linux-
gnueabihf- modules
$ make ARCH=arm CROSS_COMPILE=arm-cortex_a8-linux-gnueabihf-
dtbs
```

These commands are in the MELP/Chapter04/build-linux-bbb.sh script.

Building a kernel for QEMU

Here is the sequence of commands to build Linux for the ARM Versatile PB that is emulated by QEMU, using the crosstool-NG v5TE compiler:

```
$ cd linux-stable
$ make ARCH=arm CROSS_COMPILE=arm-unknown-linux-gnueabi-
mrproper
$ make -j4 ARCH=arm CROSS_COMPILE=arm-unknown-linux-gnueabi-
zImage
$ make -j4 ARCH=arm CROSS_COMPILE=arm-unknown-linux-gnueabi-
modules
$ make ARCH=arm CROSS_COMPILE=arm-unknown-linux-gnueabi- dtbs
```

These commands are in the MELP/Chapter04/build-linux-versatilepb.sh script. In this section, we saw how to compile kernels for our targets using Kbuild. Now, we will learn about booting up the kernel.

Booting the kernel

Booting Linux is highly device-dependent. In this section, I will show you how it works for the Raspberry Pi 4, BeagleBone Black, and QEMU. For other target boards, you must consult the information from the vendor or from the community project, if there is one.

At this point, you should have the kernel image files and the device tree blobs for the Raspberry Pi 4, BeagleBone Black, and QEMU.

Booting the Raspberry Pi 4

Raspberry Pis use a proprietary bootloader provided by Broadcom instead of U-Boot. Unlike previous Raspberry Pi models, the Raspberry Pi 4's bootloader resides on an onboard SPI EEPROM rather than on a microSD card. We still need to put the kernel image and device tree blobs for the Raspberry Pi 4 on a microSD to boot our 64-bit kernel.

To begin, you need a microSD card with a FAT32 `boot` partition large enough to hold the necessary kernel build artifacts. The `boot` partition needs to be the first partition on the microSD card. A partition size of 1 GB is sufficient. Insert the microSD card into your card reader and copy the entire contents of the `boot` directory to the `boot` partition. Unmount the card and insert it into the Raspberry Pi 4. Connect your USB-to-TTL serial cable to the GND, TXD, and RXD pins on the 40-pin GPIO header (`https://learn.adafruit.com/adafruits-raspberry-pi-lesson-5-using-a-console-cable/connect-the-lead`). Next, start a terminal emulator such as `gtkterm`. Lastly, power on the Raspberry Pi 4 and you should see the following output on the serial console:

```
[    0.000000] Booting Linux on physical CPU 0x0000000000
[0x410fd083]
[    0.000000] Linux version 4.19.127-v8+ (frank@franktop)
(gcc version 10.2.1 20201103 (GNU Toolchain for the A-profile
Architecture 10.2-2020.11 (arm-10.16))) #1 SMP PREEMPT Sat Feb
6 16:19:37 PST 2021
[    0.000000] Machine model: Raspberry Pi 4 Model B Rev 1.1
[    0.000000] efi: Getting EFI parameters from FDT:
[    0.000000] efi: UEFI not found.
[    0.000000] cma: Reserved 64 MiB at 0x0000000037400000
[    0.000000] random: get_random_bytes called from start_
kernel+0xb0/0x480 with crng_init=0
[    0.000000] percpu: Embedded 24 pages/cpu s58840 r8192
d31272 u98304
[    0.000000] Detected PIPT I-cache on CPU0
[...]
```

The sequence will end in kernel panic because the kernel cannot locate a root filesystem on the microSD card. Kernel panic is explained later in this chapter.

Booting the BeagleBone Black

To begin, you need a microSD card with U-Boot installed, as described in the *Installing U-Boot* section from *Chapter 3, All About Bootloaders*. Insert the microSD card into your card reader and from the `linux-stable` directory, copy the `arch/arm/boot/zImage` and `arch/arm/boot/dts/am335x-boneblack.dtb` files to the `boot` partition. Unmount the card and insert it into the BeagleBone Black. Start a terminal emulator, such as `gtkterm`, and be prepared to press the spacebar as soon as you see the U-Boot messages appear. Next, power on the BeagleBone Black and press the space bar. You should get a U-Boot prompt. Now enter the following commands shown after the U-Boot# prompt to load Linux and the device tree binary:

```
U-Boot# fatload mmc 0:1 0x80200000 zImage
reading zImage
7062472 bytes read in 447 ms (15.1 MiB/s)
U-Boot# fatload mmc 0:1 0x80f00000 am335x-boneblack.dtb
reading am335x-boneblack.dtb
34184 bytes read in 10 ms (3.3 MiB/s)
U-Boot# setenv bootargs console=ttyO0
U-Boot# bootz 0x80200000 - 0x80f00000
## Flattened Device Tree blob at 80f00000
Booting using the fdt blob at 0x80f00000
Loading Device Tree to 8fff4000, end 8ffff587 ... OK
Starting kernel ...
[ 0.000000] Booting Linux on physical CPU 0x0
[...]
```

Note that we set the kernel command line to `console=ttyO0`. That tells Linux which device to use for console output, which in this case is the first UART on the board, device `ttyO0`. Without this, we would not see any messages after `Starting the kernel...`, and therefore would not know whether it was working or not. The sequence would end in a kernel panic, for reasons I will explain later on.

Booting QEMU

Assuming that you have already installed `qemu-system-arm`, you can launch it with the kernel and the `.dtb` file for the ARM Versatile PB, as follows:

```
$ QEMU_AUDIO_DRV=none \
qemu-system-arm -m 256M -nographic -M versatilepb -kernel \
zImage
-append "console=ttyAMA0,115200" -dtb versatile-pb.dtb
```

Note that setting `QEMU_AUDIO_DRV` to `none` is just to suppress error messages from QEMU about missing configurations for the audio drivers, which we do not use. As with the Raspberry Pi 4 and BeagleBone Black, this will end with kernel panic and the system will halt. To exit from QEMU, press *Ctrl* + *A* and then *x* (two separate keystrokes). Now, let's discuss what kernel panic is.

Kernel panic

While things started off well, they ended badly:

```
[ 1.886379] Kernel panic - not syncing: VFS: Unable to mount
root fs on unknown-block(0,0)
[ 1.895105] ---[ end Kernel panic - not syncing: VFS: Unable to
mount root fs on unknown-block(0, 0)
```

This is a good example of kernel panic. Kernel panic occurs when the kernel encounters an unrecoverable error. By default, it will print out a message to the console and then halt. You can set the `panic` command-line parameter to allow a few seconds before reboots following a panic. In this case, the unrecoverable error is no root filesystem, illustrating that a kernel is useless without a user space to control it. You can supply a user space by providing a root filesystem, either as a ramdisk or on a mountable mass storage device. We will talk about how to create a root filesystem in the next chapter, but first I want to describe the sequence of events that leads up to `panic`.

Early user space

In order to transition from kernel initialization to user space, the kernel has to mount a root filesystem and execute a program in that root filesystem. This can be achieved via a ramdisk or by mounting a real filesystem on a block device. The code for all of this is in `init/main.c`, starting with the `rest_init()` function, which creates the first thread with PID `1` and runs the code in `kernel_init()`. If there is a ramdisk, it will try to execute the program `/init`, which will take on the task of setting up the user space.

If the kernel fails to find and run /init, it tries to mount a filesystem by calling the prepare_namespace() function in init/do_mounts.c. This requires a root= command line to give the name of the block device to use for mounting, usually in this form:

```
root=/dev/<disk name><partition number>
```

Or, in this form for SD cards and eMMC:

```
root=/dev/<disk name>p<partition number>
```

For example, for the first partition on an SD card, that would be root=/dev/mmcblk0p1. If the mount succeeds, it will try to execute /sbin/init, followed by /etc/init, /bin/init, and then /bin/sh, stopping at the first one that works. The program can be overridden on the command line. For a ramdisk, use rdinit=, and for a filesystem, use init=.

Kernel messages

Kernel developers are fond of printing out useful information through liberal use of printk() and similar functions. The messages are categorized according to importance, with 0 being the highest:

Level	Value	Meaning
KERN_EMERG	0	The system is unusable.
KERN_ALERT	1	Action must be taken immediately.
KERN_CRIT	2	Critical conditions.
KERN_ERR	3	Error conditions.
KERN_WARNING	4	Warning conditions.
KERN_NOTICE	5	Normal but significant conditions.
KERN_INFO	6	Informational.
KERN_DEBUG	7	Debug-level messages.

They are first written to a buffer, __log_buf, the size of which is two to the power of CONFIG_LOG_BUF_SHIFT. For example, if CONFIG_LOG_BUF_SHIFT is 16, then __log_buf is 64 KiB. You can dump the entire buffer using the dmesg command.

If the level of a message is less than the console log level, it is displayed on the console as well as being placed in __log_buf. The default console log level is 7, meaning that messages of level 6 and lower are displayed, filtering out KERN_DEBUG, which is level 7. You can change the console log level in several ways, including by using the loglevel=<level> kernel parameter, or the dmesg -n <level> command.

The kernel command line

The kernel command line is a string that is passed to the kernel by the bootloader, via the `bootargs` variable in the case of U-Boot; it can also be defined in the device tree or set as part of the kernel configuration in `CONFIG_CMDLINE`.

We have seen some examples of the kernel command line already, but there are many more. There is a complete list in `Documentation/kernel-parameters.txt`. Here is a shorter list of the most useful ones:

- `debug`: Sets the console log level to the highest level, `8`, to ensure that you see all the kernel messages on the console.
- `init=`: The `init` program to run from a mounted root filesystem, which defaults to `/sbin/init`.
- `lpj=`: Sets `loops_per_jiffy` to a given constant. There is a description of the significance of this in the paragraph following this list.
- `panic=`: Behavior when the kernel panics: if it is greater than zero, it gives the number of seconds before rebooting; if it is zero, it waits forever (this is the default); or if it is less than zero, it reboots without any delay.
- `quiet`: Sets the console log level to silent, suppressing all but emergency messages. Since most devices have a serial console, it takes time to output all those strings. Consequently, reducing the number of messages using this option reduces boot time.
- `rdinit=`: The `init` program to run from a ramdisk. It defaults to `/init`.
- `ro`: Mounts the root device as read-only. Has no effect on a ramdisk, which is always read/write.
- `root=`: The device on which to mount the root filesystem.
- `rootdelay=`: The number of seconds to wait before trying to mount the root device; defaults to zero. Useful if the device takes time to probe the hardware, but also see `rootwait`.
- `rootfstype=`: The filesystem type for the root device. In many cases, it is auto-detected during mount, but it is required for `jffs2` filesystems.
- `rootwait`: Waits indefinitely for the root device to be detected. Usually necessary with MMC devices.
- `rw`: Mounts the root device as read-write (default).

The `lpj` parameter is often mentioned in connection with reducing the kernel boot time. During initialization, the kernel loops for approximately 250 ms to calibrate a delay loop. The value is stored in the `loops_per_jiffy` variable and is reported like this:

```
Calibrating delay loop... 996.14 BogoMIPS (lpj=4980736)
```

If the kernel always runs on the same hardware, it will always calculate the same value. You can shave 250 ms off the boot time by adding `lpj=4980736` to the command line.

In the next section, we will learn how to port Linux to a new board based on the BeagleBone Black, our hypothetical Nova board.

Porting Linux to a new board

Porting Linux to a new board can be easy or difficult, depending on how similar your board is to an existing development board. In *Chapter 3, All About Bootloaders*, we ported U-Boot to a new board, named Nova, which is based on the BeagleBone Black. Very few changes need to be made to the kernel code, so it is very easy. If you are porting to completely new and innovative hardware, there will be more to do. We will delve deeper into the topic of additional hardware peripherals in *Chapter 12, Prototyping with Breakout Boards*.

The organization of architecture-specific code in `arch/$ARCH` differs from one system to another. The x86 architecture is pretty clean because most hardware details are detected at runtime. The PowerPC architecture puts SoC and board-specific files into subdirectory platforms. The ARM architecture, on the other hand, is quite messy, in part because there is a lot of variability between the many ARM-based SoCs. Platform-dependent code is put in directories named `mach-*`, approximately one per SoC. There are other directories named `plat-*`, which contain code common to several versions of an SoC. In the case of the BeagleBone Black, the relevant directory is `arch/arm/mach-omap2`. Don't be fooled by the name though; it contains support for OMAP2, 3, and 4 chips as well as the AM33xx family of chips that the BeagleBone uses.

In the following sections, I am going to explain how to create a device tree for a new board and how to key that into the initialization code of Linux.

A new device tree

The first thing to do is create a device tree for the board and modify it to describe the additional or changed hardware of the Nova board. In this simple case, we will just copy `am335x-boneblack.dts` to `nova.dts` and change the model name to `Nova` as shown here:

```
/dts-v1/;

#include "am33xx.dtsi"
#include "am335x-bone-common.dtsi"
#include "am335x-boneblack-common.dtsi"

/ {
        model = "Nova";
        compatible = "ti,am335x-bone-black", "ti,am335x-bone",
"ti,am33xx";
};
[...]
```

We can build the Nova device tree binary explicitly like this:

```
$ make ARCH=arm nova.dtb
```

If we want the device tree for Nova to be compiled by `make ARCH=arm dtbs` whenever an AM33xx target is selected, we could add a dependency in `arch/arm/boot/dts/Makefile` as follows:

```
[...]
dtb-$(CONFIG_SOC_AM33XX) +=
    nova.dtb
[...]
```

We can see the effect of using the Nova device tree by booting the BeagleBone Black, following the same procedure as in the *Booting the BeagleBone Black* section, with the same `zImage` file as before, but loading `nova.dtb` in place of `am335x-boneblack.dtb`. The following highlighted output is the point at which the machine model is printed out:

```
Starting kernel ...
[ 0.000000] Booting Linux on physical CPU 0x0
```

```
[ 0.000000] Linux version 5.4.50-melp-v1.0-dirty (frank@
franktop) (gcc version 8.3.0 (crosstool-NG crosstool-ng-1.24.0)
) #2 SMP Sat Feb 6 17:19:36 PST 2021
[ 0.000000] CPU: ARMv7 Processor [413fc082] revision 2 (ARMv7),
cr=10c5387d
[ 0.000000] CPU: PIPT / VIPT nonaliasing data cache, VIPT
aliasing instruction cache
[ 0.000000] OF: fdt:Machine model: Nova
[…]
```

Now that we have a device tree specifically for the Nova board, we could modify it to describe the hardware differences between Nova and the BeagleBone Black. There are quite likely to be changes to the kernel configuration as well, in which case you would create a custom configuration file based on a copy of `arch/arm/configs/multi_v7_defconfig`.

Setting the board's compatible property

Creating a new device tree means that we can describe the hardware on the Nova board, selecting device drivers and setting properties to match. But suppose the Nova board needs different early initialization code than the BeagleBone Black, how can we link that in?

The board setup is controlled by the `compatible` property in the root node. This is what we have for the Nova board at the moment:

```
/ {
    model = "Nova";
    compatible = "ti,am335x-bone-black", "ti,am335x-bone",
"ti,am33xx";
};
```

When the kernel parses this node, it will search for a matching machine for each of the values of the compatible property, starting on the left and stopping with the first match found. Each machine is defined in a structure delimited by `DT_MACHINE_START` and `MACHINE_END` macros. In `arch/arm/mach-omap2/board-generic.c`, we find the following:

```
#ifdef CONFIG_SOC_AM33XX
static const char *const am33xx_boards_compat[] __initconst = {
    "ti,am33xx",
    NULL,
};
```

```
 DT_MACHINE_START(AM33XX_DT, "Generic AM33XX (Flattened Device
Tree)")
    .reserve = omap_reserve,
    .map_io = am33xx_map_io,
    .init_early = am33xx_init_early,
    .init_machine = omap_generic_init,
    .init_late = am33xx_init_late,
    .init_time = omap3_gptimer_timer_init,
    .dt_compat = am33xx_boards_compat,
    .restart = am33xx_restart,
MACHINE_END
#endif
```

Note that the string array `am33xx_boards_compat` contains `"ti,am33xx"`, which matches one of the machines listed in the `compatible` property. In fact, it is the only match possible, since there are none for `ti,am335x-bone-black` or `ti,am335x-bone`. The structure between `DT_MACHINE_START` and `MACHINE_END` contains a pointer to the string array, and function pointers for the board setup functions.

You may wonder why to bother with `ti,am335x-bone-black` and `ti,am335x-bone` if they never match anything? The answer is partly that they are placeholders for the future, but also that there are places in the kernel that contain runtime tests for the machine using the `of_machine_is_compatible()` function; for example, in `drivers/net/ethernet/ti/cpsw-common.c`:

```
int ti_cm_get_macid(struct device *dev, int slave, u8 *mac_
addr)
{
[...]
    if (of_machine_is_compatible("ti,am33xx"))
        return cpsw_am33xx_cm_get_macid(dev, 0x630, slave, mac_
addr);
[...]
```

Thus, we have to look through not just the `mach-*` directories but the entire kernel source code to get a list of all the places that depend on the `machine compatible` property. In the 5.4 kernel, you will find that there are still no checks for `ti,am335x-bone-black` and `ti,am335x-bone`, but there may be in the future.

Returning to the Nova board, if we want to add machine-specific setup, we can add a machine in `arch/arm/mach-omap2/board-generic.c`, like this:

```
#ifdef CONFIG_SOC_AM33XX
[...]
static const char *const nova_compat[] __initconst = {
    "ti,nova",
    NULL,
};
 DT_MACHINE_START(NOVA_DT, "Nova board (Flattened Device
Tree)")
     .reserve = omap_reserve,
     .map_io = am33xx_map_io,
     .init_early = am33xx_init_early,
     .init_machine = omap_generic_init,
     .init_late = am33xx_init_late,
     .init_time = omap3_gptimer_timer_init,
     .dt_compat = nova_compat,
     .restart = am33xx_restart,
MACHINE_END
#endif
```

Then we could change the device tree root node like this:

```
/ {
    model = "Nova";
    compatible = "ti,nova", "ti,am33xx";
};
```

Now, the machine will match `ti,nova` in `board-generic.c`. We keep `ti,am33xx` because we want the runtime tests, such as the one in `drivers/net/ethernet/ti/cpsw-common.c`, to continue to work.

Summary

What makes Linux so powerful is the ability to configure the kernel however we need to. The definitive place to get the kernel source code is `https://www.kernel.org/`, but you will probably need to get the source for a particular SoC or board from the vendor of that device or a third party that supports that device. The customization of the kernel for a particular target may consist of changes to the core kernel code, additional drivers for devices that are not in mainline Linux, a default kernel configuration file, and a device tree source file.

Normally, you start with the default configuration for your target board and then tweak it by running one of the configuration tools, such as `menuconfig`. One of the things you should consider at this point is whether the kernel features and drivers should be compiled as modules or built in. Kernel modules are usually no great advantage for embedded systems, where the feature set and hardware are usually well defined. However, modules are often used as a way to import proprietary code into the kernel, and also to reduce boot time by loading non-essential drivers after booting.

Building the kernel produces a compressed kernel image file named `zImage`, `bzImage`, or `uImage`, depending on the bootloader you will be using and the target architecture. A kernel build will also generate any kernel modules (as `.ko` files) that you have configured, and device tree binaries (as `.dtb` files) if your target requires them.

Porting Linux to a new target board can be quite simple or very difficult, depending on how different the hardware is from that in the mainline or vendor-supplied kernel. If your hardware is based on a well-known reference design, then it may be just a question of making changes to the device tree or to the platform data. You may well need to add device drivers, which we'll discuss in *Chapter 11, Interfacing with Device Drivers*. However, if the hardware is radically different from a reference design, you may need additional core support, which is outside the scope of this book.

The kernel is the core of a Linux-based system, but it cannot work by itself. It requires a root filesystem that contains the user space components. The root filesystem can be a ramdisk or a filesystem accessed via a block device, which will be the subject of the next chapter. As we have seen, booting a kernel without a root filesystem results in kernel panic.

Additional reading

The following resources have more information about the topics introduced in this chapter:

- *So You Want to Build an Embedded Linux System?* by Jay Carlson: `https://jaycarlson.net/embedded-linux/`
- *Linux Kernel Development, Third Edition*, by Robert Love
- *Linux Weekly News*: `https://lwn.net`
- *BeagleBone Forum*: `https://beagleboard.org/discuss#bone_forum_embed`
- *Raspberry Pi Forums*: `https://www.raspberrypi.org/forums/`

5
Building a Root Filesystem

The root filesystem is the fourth and final element of embedded Linux. Once you have read this chapter, you will be able to build, boot, and run a simple embedded Linux system.

The techniques I will describe here are broadly known as **roll your own** or **RYO**. Back in the early days of embedded Linux, this was the only way to create a root filesystem. There are still some use cases where an RYO root filesystem is applicable, for example, when the amount of RAM or storage is very limited, for quick demonstrations, or for any case in which your requirements are not (easily) covered by the standard build system tools. Nevertheless, these cases are quite rare. Let me emphasize that the purpose of this chapter is educational; it is not meant to be a recipe for building everyday embedded systems: use the tools described in the next chapter for this.

The first objective is to create a minimal root filesystem that will give us a shell prompt. Then, using this as a base, we will add scripts to start up other programs and configure a network interface and user permissions. There are worked examples for both the BeagleBone Black and QEMU targets. Knowing how to build the root filesystem from scratch is a useful skill, and it will help you to understand what is going on when we look at more complex examples in later chapters.

In this chapter, we will cover the following topics:

- What should be in the root filesystem?
- Transferring the root filesystem to the target
- Creating a boot `initramfs`
- The `init` program
- Configuring user accounts
- A better way of managing device nodes
- Configuring the network
- Creating filesystem images with device tables
- Mounting the root filesystem using NFS
- Using TFTP to load the kernel

Technical requirements

To follow along with the examples, make sure you have the following:

- A Linux-based host system
- A microSD card reader and card
- The microSD card prepared for the BeagleBone Black from *Chapter 4, Configuring and Building the Kernel*
- `zImage` and DTB for QEMU from *Chapter 4, Configuring and Building the Kernel*
- A USB to TTL 3.3V serial cable
- BeagleBone Black
- A 5V 1A DC power supply
- An Ethernet cable and port for NFS and TFTP

All of the code for this chapter can be found in the `Chapter05` folder from the book's GitHub repository: `https://github.com/PacktPublishing/Mastering-Embedded-Linux-Programming-Third-Edition`

What should be in the root filesystem?

The kernel will get a root filesystem, either as an `initramfs` passed as a pointer from the bootloader or by mounting the block device given on the kernel command line by the `root=` parameter. Once it has a root filesystem, the kernel will execute the first program, by default named `init`, as described in the *Early user space* section in *Chapter 4, Configuring and Building the Kernel.* Then, as far as the kernel is concerned, its job is complete. It is up to the `init` program to begin starting other programs and bring the system to life.

To make a minimal root filesystem, you need these components:

- **init**: This is the program that starts everything off, usually by running a series of scripts. I will describe how `init` works in much more detail in *Chapter 13, Starting Up – The init Program.*
- **Shell**: You need a shell to give you a command prompt but, more importantly, also to run the shell scripts called by `init` and other programs.
- **Daemons**: A daemon is a background program that provides a service to others. Good examples are the system log daemon (`syslogd`) and the secure shell daemon (`sshd`). The `init` program must start the initial population of daemons to support the main system applications. In fact, `init` is itself a daemon: it is the daemon that provides the service of launching other daemons.
- **Shared libraries**: Most programs are linked with shared libraries and so they must be present in the root filesystem.
- **Configuration files**: The configuration for `init` and other daemons is stored in a series of text files, usually in the `/etc` directory.
- **Device nodes**: These are the special files that give access to various device drivers.
- **proc and sys**: These two pseudo filesystems represent kernel data structures as a hierarchy of directories and files. Many programs and library functions depend on `/proc` and `/sys`.
- **Kernel modules**: If you have configured some parts of your kernel to be modules, they need to be installed in the root filesystem, usually in `/lib/modules/[kernel version]`.

In addition, there are the device-specific applications that make the device do the job it is intended for, and also the runtime data files that they generate.

> **Important note**
>
> In some cases, you could condense most of the preceding programs into a single, statically-linked program, and start the program instead of `init`. For example, if your program was named `/myprog`, you would add the following command to the kernel command line `init=/myprog`. I have come across such a configuration only once, in a secure system in which the `fork` system call had been disabled, thus making it impossible for any other program to be started. The downside of this approach is that you can't make use of the many tools that normally go into an embedded system. You have to do everything yourself.

The directory layout

Interestingly, the Linux kernel does not care about the layout of files and directories beyond the existence of the program named by `init=` or `rdinit=`, so you are free to put things wherever you like. As an example, compare the file layout of a device running Android to that of a desktop Linux distribution: they are almost completely different.

However, many programs expect certain files to be in certain places, and it helps us developers if devices use a similar layout, Android aside. The basic layout of most Linux systems is defined in the **Filesystem Hierarchy Standard** (**FHS**), which is available at `https://refspecs.linuxfoundation.org/fhs.shtml`. The FHS covers all the implementations of Linux operating systems, from the largest to the smallest. Embedded devices tend to use a subset based on their needs, but it usually includes the following:

- `/bin`: Programs essential for all users
- `/dev`: Device nodes and other special files
- `/etc`: System configuration files
- `/lib`: Essential shared libraries, for example, those that make up the C library
- `/proc`: Information about processes represented as virtual files
- `/sbin`: Programs essential to the system administrator
- `/sys`: Information about devices and their drivers represented as virtual files
- `/tmp`: A place to put temporary or volatile files
- `/usr`: Additional programs, libraries, and system administrator utilities, in the `/usr/bin`, `/usr/lib`, and `/usr/sbin` directories, respectively
- `/var`: A hierarchy of files and directories that may be modified at runtime, for example, log messages, some of which must be retained after boot

There are some subtle distinctions here. The difference between `/bin` and `/sbin` is simply that the latter need not be included in the search path for non-root users. Users of Red Hat-derived distributions will be familiar with this. The significance of `/usr` is that it may be in a separate partition from the root filesystem, so it cannot contain anything that is needed to boot the system up.

The staging directory

You should begin by creating a **staging** directory on your host computer where you can assemble the files that will eventually be transferred to the target. In the following examples, I have used `~/rootfs`. You need to create a *skeleton* directory structure in it, for example, take a look here:

```
$ mkdir ~/rootfs
$ cd ~/rootfs
$ mkdir bin dev etc home lib proc sbin sys tmp usr var
$ mkdir usr/bin usr/lib usr/sbin
$ mkdir -p var/log
```

To see the directory hierarchy more clearly, you can use the handy `tree` command used in the following example with the `-d` option to show only the directories:

```
$ tree -d
.
├── bin
├── dev
├── etc
├── home
├── lib
├── proc
├── sbin
├── sys
├── tmp
├── usr
│   ├── bin
│   ├── lib
│   └── sbin
└── var
    └── log
```

As we shall see, not all directories have the same file permissions and the individual files inside a directory can have stricter permissions than the directory itself.

POSIX file access permissions

Every process, which in the context of this discussion means every running program, belongs to a user and one or more groups. The user is represented by a 32-bit number called the **user ID** or **UID**. Information about users, including the mapping from a UID to a name, is kept in `/etc/passwd`. Likewise, groups are represented by a **group ID** or **GID** with information kept in `/etc/group`. There is always a `root` user with a UID of `0` and a root group with a GID of `0`. The `root` user is also called the **superuser** because, in a default configuration, it bypasses most permission checks and can access all the resources in the system. Security in Linux-based systems is mainly about restricting access to the **root** account.

Each file and directory also has an owner and belongs to exactly one group. The level of access a process has to a file or directory is controlled by a set of access permission flags, called the **mode** of the file. There are 3 collections of 3 bits: the first collection applies to the *owner* of the file, the second to the *members* of the same group as the file, and the last to *everyone else* – the rest of the world. The bits are for **read** (`r`), **write** (`w`), and **execute** (`x`) permissions on the file. Since 3 bits fit neatly into an octal digit, they are usually represented in octal, as shown in the following diagram:

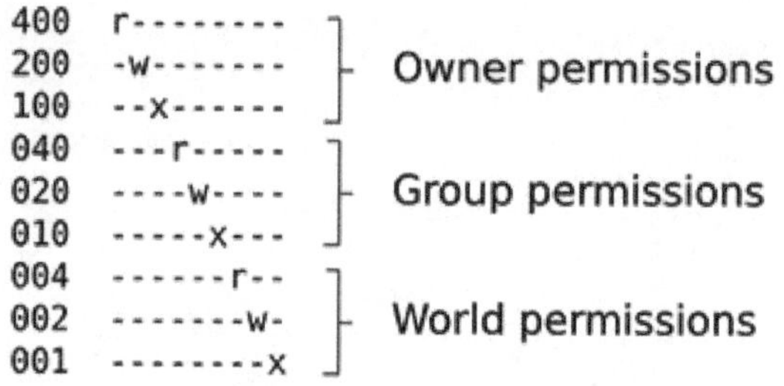

Figure 5.1 – File access permissions

There is a fourth preceding octal digit whose value has special significance:

- **SUID** (**4**): If the file is executable, it changes the effective UID of the process to that of the owner of the file when the program is run.
- **SGID** (**2**): Similar to SUID, this changes the effective GID of the process to that of the group of the file.
- **Sticky** (**1**): In a directory, this restricts deletion so that one user cannot delete files that are owned by another user. This is usually set on `/tmp` and `/var/tmp`.

The SUID bit is probably used most often. It gives non-root users a temporary privilege escalation to superuser to perform a task. A good example is the `ping` program: `ping` opens a raw socket, which is a privileged operation. In order for normal users to use `ping`, it is owned by the user `root` and has the SUID bit set so that when you run `ping`, it executes with UID `0` regardless of your UID.

To set this leading octal digit, use values of either 4, 2, or 1 with the `chmod` command. For example, to set SUID on `/bin/ping` in your staging `root` directory, you would prepend `4` to a mode of `755` like so:

```
$ cd ~/rootfs
$ ls -l bin/ping
-rwxr-xr-x 1 root root 35712 Feb 6 09:15 bin/ping
$ sudo chmod 4755 bin/ping
$ ls -l bin/ping
-rwsr-xr-x 1 root root 35712 Feb 6 09:15 bin/ping
```

Note that the second `ls` command shows the first 3 bits of the mode to be `rws`, whereas previously they had been `rwx`. That `s` indicates that the SUID bit is set.

File ownership permissions in the staging directory

For security and stability reasons, it is vitally important to pay attention to the ownership and permissions of the files that will be placed on the target device. Generally speaking, you want to restrict sensitive resources to be accessible only by the `root` user and run as few programs using non-root users as possible. It is best to run programs using non-root users so that if they are compromised by an outside attack, they offer as few system resources to the attacker as possible. For example, the device node called `/dev/mem` gives access to system memory, which is necessary in some programs. But, if it is readable and writeable by everyone, then there is no security because everyone can access everything in memory. So, `/dev/mem` should be owned by `root`, belong to the `root` group, and have a mode of `600`, which denies read and write access to all but the owner.

There is a problem with the staging directory though. The files you create there will be owned by you, but when they are installed on the device, they should belong to specific owners and groups, mostly the `root` user. An obvious fix is to change the ownership to `root` at this stage with the commands shown here:

```
$ cd ~/rootfs
$ sudo chown -R root:root *
```

The problem is that you need `root` privileges to run the `chown` command, and from that point onward, you will need to be `root` to modify any files in the staging directory. Before you know it, you are doing all your development logged on as `root`, which is not a good idea. This is a problem that we will come back to later.

Programs for the root filesystem

Now, it is time to start populating the `root` filesystem with the essential programs and the supporting libraries, configuration, and data files that they need to operate. I will begin with an overview of the types of programs you will need.

The init program

`init` is the first program to be run, and so it is an essential part of the root filesystem. In this chapter, we will be using the simple `init` program provided by BusyBox.

Shell

We need a shell to run scripts and to give us a command prompt so that we can interact with the system. An interactive shell is probably not necessary on a production device, but it is useful for development, debugging, and maintenance. There are various shells in common use in embedded systems:

- `bash`: This is the big beast that we all know and love from desktop Linux. It is a superset of the Unix Bourne shell with many extensions or *bashisms*.
- `ash`: Also based on the Bourne shell, it has a long history with the BSD variants of Unix. BusyBox has a version of `ash`, which has been extended to make it more compatible with `bash`. It is much smaller than `bash` and hence it is a very popular choice for embedded systems.
- `hush`: This is a very small shell that we briefly looked at in *Chapter 3, All about Bootloaders*. It is useful on devices with very little memory. There is a version of `hush` in BusyBox.

> **Tip**
>
> If you are using `ash` or `hush` as the shell on the target, make sure that you test your shell scripts on the target. It is very tempting to test them only on the host, using `bash`, and then be surprised that they don't work when you copy them to the target.

Next on the list is utilities.

Utilities

The shell is just a way of launching other programs, and a shell script is little more than a list of programs to run, with some flow control and a means of passing information between programs. To make a shell useful, you need the utility programs that the Unix command line is based on. Even for a basic root filesystem, you need approximately 50 utilities, which presents two problems. Firstly, tracking down the source code for each one and cross-compiling it would be quite a big job. Secondly, the resulting collection of programs would take up several tens of megabytes, which was a real problem in the early days of embedded Linux when a few megabytes was all you had. To solve this problem, BusyBox was born.

BusyBox to the rescue!

The genesis of **BusyBox** had nothing to do with embedded Linux. The project was instigated in 1996 by Bruce Perens for the Debian installer so that he could boot Linux from a 1.44 MB floppy disk. Coincidentally, this was about the size of the storage on contemporary devices, and so the embedded Linux community quickly took it up. BusyBox has been at the heart of embedded Linux ever since.

BusyBox was written from scratch to perform the essential functions of those essential Linux utilities. The developers took advantage of the 80:20 rule: the most useful 80% of a program is implemented in 20% of the code. Hence, BusyBox tools implement a subset of the functions of the desktop equivalents, but they do enough of it to be useful in the majority of cases.

Another trick BusyBox employs is to combine all the tools together into a single binary, making it easy to share code between them. It works like this: BusyBox is a collection of applets, each of which exports its `main` function in the form `[applet]_main`. For example, the `cat` command is implemented in `coreutils/cat.c` and exports `cat_main`. The `main` function of BusyBox itself dispatches the call to the correct applet, based on the command-line arguments.

So, to read a file, you can launch BusyBox with the name of the applet you want to run, followed by any arguments the applet expects, as shown here:

```
$ busybox cat my_file.txt
```

You can also run BusyBox with no arguments to get a list of all the applets that have been compiled.

Using BusyBox in this way is rather clumsy. A better way to get BusyBox to run the cat applet is to create a symbolic link from /bin/cat to /bin/busybox:

```
$ ls -l bin/cat bin/busybox
-rwxr-xr-x 1 root root 892868 Feb 2 11:01 bin/busybox
lrwxrwxrwx 1 root root 7      Feb 2 11:01 bin/cat -> busybox
```

When you type cat at the command line, BusyBox is the program that actually runs. BusyBox only has to check the path to the executable passed in via argv[0], which will be /bin/cat, extract the application name, cat, and do a table lookup to match cat with cat_main. All this is done in libbb/appletlib.c in this section of code (slightly simplified):

```
applet_name = argv[0];
applet_name = bb_basename(applet_name);
run_applet_and_exit(applet_name, argv);
```

BusyBox has over 300 applets, including an init program, several shells of varying levels of complexity, and utilities for most admin tasks. There is even a simple version of the vi editor so you can change text files on your device. A typical BusyBox binary will only enable several dozen applets.

To summarize, a typical installation of BusyBox consists of a single program with a symbolic link for each applet, but it behaves exactly as if it were a collection of individual applications.

Building BusyBox

BusyBox uses the same Kconfig and Kbuild system as the kernel, so cross-compiling is straightforward. You can get the source by cloning the BusyBox Git repo and checking out the version you want (1_31_1 was the latest at the time of writing), as follows:

```
$ git clone git://busybox.net/busybox.git
$ cd busybox
$ git checkout 1_31_1
```

You can also download the corresponding TAR file from https://busybox.net/downloads/.

Then, configure BusyBox by starting with the default configuration, which enables pretty much all of the features of BusyBox:

```
$ make distclean
$ make defconfig
```

At this point, you probably want to run `make menuconfig` to fine-tune the configuration. For example, you almost certainly want to set the install path in **Busybox Settings | Installation Options** (`CONFIG_PREFIX`) to point to the staging directory. Then, you can cross-compile in the usual way. If your intended target is the BeagleBone Black, use this command:

```
$ make ARCH=arm CROSS_COMPILE=arm-cortex_a8-linux-gnueabihf-
```

If your intended target is the QEMU emulation of a Versatile PB, use this command:

```
$ make ARCH=arm CROSS_COMPILE=arm-unknown-linux-gnueabi-
```

In either case, the result is the executable `busybox`. For a default configuration build like this, the size is about 900 KiB. If this is too big for you, you can slim it down by changing the configuration to leave out the utilities you don't need.

To install BusyBox into the staging area, use the following command:

```
$ make ARCH=arm CROSS_COMPILE=arm-cortex_a8-linux-gnueabihf-
install
```

This will copy the binary to the directory configured in `CONFIG_PREFIX` and create all the symbolic links to it.

Now we will look at an alternative to Busybox known as ToyBox.

ToyBox – an alternative to BusyBox

BusyBox is not the only game in town. In addition, there is **ToyBox**, which you can find at `http://landley.net/toybox/`. The project was started by Rob Landley, who was previously a maintainer of BusyBox. ToyBox has the same aim as BusyBox, but with more emphasis on complying with standards, especially POSIX-2008 and LSB 4.1, and less on compatibility with GNU extensions to those standards. ToyBox is smaller than BusyBox, partly because it implements fewer applets. And its license is BSD rather than GPL v2, making it compatible with operating systems that have a BSD-licensed user space, such as Android. Hence, ToyBox ships with all new Android devices. As of the recent 0.8.3 release, Toybox's `Makefile` can build a full Linux system that boots to a shell prompt given just the Linux and ToyBox sources.

Libraries for the root filesystem

Programs are linked with libraries. You could link them all statically, in which case, there would be no libraries on the target device. But, this takes up an unnecessarily large amount of storage if you have more than two or three programs. So, you need to copy shared libraries from the toolchain to the staging directory. How do you know which libraries?

One option is to copy all of the `.so` files from the `sysroot` directory of your toolchain. Instead of trying to predict which libraries to include, just assume that your image will eventually need them all. This is certainly logical and, if you are creating a platform to be used by others for a range of applications, it would be the correct approach. Be aware, though, that a full `glibc` is quite large. In the case of a crosstool-NG build of `glibc` 2.22, the libraries, locales, and other supporting files come to 33 MiB. Of course, you could cut down on that considerably using `musl libc` or `uClibc-ng`.

Another option is to cherry-pick only those libraries that you require, for which you need a means of discovering library dependencies. Using some of our knowledge from *Chapter 2, Learning about Toolchains*, we can use the `readelf` command for this task:

```
$ cd ~/rootfs
$ arm-cortex_a8-linux-gnueabihf-readelf -a bin/busybox | grep
"program interpreter"
[Requesting program interpreter: /lib/ld-linux-armhf.so.3]
$ arm-cortex_a8-linux-gnueabihf-readelf -a bin/busybox | grep
"Shared library"
0x00000001 (NEEDED) Shared library: [libm.so.6]
0x00000001 (NEEDED) Shared library: [libc.so.6]
```

The first `readelf` command searches the `busybox` binary for lines containing `program interpreter`. The second `readelf` command searches the `busybox` binary for lines containing `Shared library`. Now, you need to find these files in the toolchain `sysroot` directory and copy them to the staging directory. Remember that you can find `sysroot` like this:

```
$ arm-cortex_a8-linux-gnueabihf-gcc -print-sysroot
/home/chris/x-tools/arm-cortex_a8-linux-gnueabihf/arm-cortex_
a8-linux-gnueabihf/sysroot
```

To reduce the amount of typing, I am going to keep a copy of that in a shell variable:

```
$ export SYSROOT=$(arm-cortex_a8-linux-gnueabihf-gcc -print-sysroot)
```

If you look at `/lib/ld-linux-armhf.so.3` in `sysroot`, you will see that it is in fact a symbolic link:

```
$ cd $SYSROOT
$ ls -l lib/ld-linux-armhf.so.3
lrwxrwxrwx 1 chris chris 10 Mar 3 15:22 lib/ld-linux-armhf.so.3
-> ld-2.22.so
```

Repeat the exercise for `libc.so.6` and `libm.so.6`, and you will end up with a list of three files and three symbolic links. Now, you can copy each one using `cp -a`, which will preserve the symbolic link:

```
$ cd ~/rootfs
$ cp -a $SYSROOT/lib/ld-linux-armhf.so.3 lib
$ cp -a $SYSROOT/lib/ld-2.22.so lib
$ cp -a $SYSROOT/lib/libc.so.6 lib
$ cp -a $SYSROOT/lib/libc-2.22.so lib
$ cp -a $SYSROOT/lib/libm.so.6 lib
$ cp -a $SYSROOT/lib/libm-2.22.so lib
```

Repeat this procedure for each program.

> **Tip**
>
> It is only worth doing this to get the very smallest embedded footprint possible. There is a danger that you will miss libraries that are loaded through `dlopen(3)` calls – plugins mostly. We will look at an example with the **name service switch** (**NSS**) libraries when we come to configure network interfaces later on in this chapter.

Reducing the size by stripping

Libraries and programs are often compiled with some information stored in symbol tables to aid debugging and tracing. You seldom need these in a production system. A quick and easy way to save space is to strip the binaries of symbol tables. This example shows `libc` before stripping:

```
$ file rootfs/lib/libc-2.22.so
lib/libc-2.22.so: ELF 32-bit LSB shared object, ARM, EABI5
version 1 (GNU/Linux), dynamically linked (uses shared libs),
for GNU/Linux 4.3.0, not stripped
$ ls -og rootfs/lib/libc-2.22.so
-rwxr-xr-x 1 1542572 Mar 3 15:22 rootfs/lib/libc-2.22.so
```

Now, let's see the result of stripping the debug information:

```
$ arm-cortex_a8-linux-gnueabihf-strip rootfs/lib/libc-2.22.so
$ file rootfs/lib/libc-2.22.so
rootfs/lib/libc-2.22.so: ELF 32-bit LSB shared object, ARM,
EABI5 version 1 (GNU/Linux), dynamically linked (uses shared
libs), for GNU/Linux 4.3.0, stripped
$ ls -og rootfs/lib/libc-2.22.so
-rwxr-xr-x 1 1218200 Mar 22 19:57 rootfs/lib/libc-2.22.so
```

In this case, we saved 324,372 bytes, or about 20% of the size of the file before stripping.

> Tip
>
> Be careful about stripping kernel modules. Some symbols are required by the module loader to relocate the module code, and so the module will fail to load if they are stripped out. Use this command to remove debug symbols while keeping those used for relocation: `strip --strip-unneeded <module name>`.

Device nodes

Most devices in Linux are represented by device nodes, in accordance with the Unix philosophy that *everything is a file* (except network interfaces, which are sockets). A device node may refer to a block device or a character device. Block devices are mass storage devices, such as SD cards or hard drives. A character device is pretty much anything else, once again, with the exception of network interfaces. The conventional location for device nodes is the directory called `/dev`. For example, a serial port may be represented by the device node called `/dev/ttyS0`.

Device nodes are created using the program named mknod (short for *make node*):

```
mknod <name> <type> <major> <minor>
```

The parameters to mknod are as follows:

- name is the name of the device node that you want to create.
- type is either c for character devices or b for a block device.
- major and minor are a pair of numbers that are used by the kernel to route file requests to the appropriate device driver code. There is a list of standard major and minor numbers in the kernel source in the Documentation/devices.txt file.

You will need to create device nodes for all the devices you want to access on your system. You can do so manually using the mknod command as I will illustrate here or you can create them automatically at runtime using one of the device managers that I will mention later.

In a really minimal root filesystem, you need just two nodes to boot with BusyBox: console and null. The console only needs to be accessible to root, the owner of the device node, so the access permissions are 600 (rw-------). The null device should be readable and writable by everyone, so the mode is 666 (rw-rw-rw-). You can use the -m option for mknod to set the mode when creating the node. You need to be root to create device nodes, as shown here:

```
$ cd ~/rootfs
$ sudo mknod -m 666 dev/null c 1 3
$ sudo mknod -m 600 dev/console c 5 1
$ ls -l dev
total 0
crw------- 1 root root 5, 1 Mar 22 20:01 console
crw-rw-rw- 1 root root 1, 3 Mar 22 20:01 null
```

You can delete device nodes using the standard rm command. There is no rmnod command because, once created, they are just files.

The proc and sysfs filesystems

`proc` and `sysfs` are two pseudo filesystems that give a window into the inner workings of the kernel. They both represent kernel data as files in a hierarchy of directories: when you read one of the files, the contents you see do not come from disk storage; it has been formatted on the fly by a function in the kernel. Some files are also writable, meaning that a kernel function is called with the new data you have written and, if it is of the correct format and you have sufficient permissions, it will modify the value stored in the kernel's memory. In other words, `proc` and `sysfs` provide another way to interact with device drivers and other kernel code. The `proc` and `sysfs` filesystems should be mounted on the directories called `/proc` and `/sys`:

```
# mount -t proc proc /proc
# mount -t sysfs sysfs /sys
```

Although they are very similar in concept, they perform different functions. `proc` has been part of Linux since the early days. Its original purpose was to expose information about processes to the user space, hence the name. To this end, there is a directory for each process named `/proc/<PID>`, which contains information about its state. The process list command, `ps`, reads these files to generate its output. In addition, there are files that give information about other parts of the kernel, for example, `/proc/cpuinfo` tells you about the CPU, `/proc/interrupts` has information about interrupts, and so on.

Finally, in `/proc/sys`, there are files that display and control the state and behavior of kernel subsystems, especially scheduling, memory management, and networking. The manual page is the best reference for the files you will find in the `proc` directory, which you can see by typing `man 5 proc`.

On the other hand, the role of `sysfs` is to present the kernel **driver model** to the user space. It exports a hierarchy of files relating to devices and device drivers and the way they are connected to each other. I will go into more detail on the Linux driver model when I describe the interaction with device drivers in *Chapter 11, Interfacing with Device Drivers*.

Mounting filesystems

The `mount` command allows us to attach one filesystem to a directory within another, forming a hierarchy of filesystems. The one at the top, which was mounted by the kernel when it booted, is called the **root filesystem**. The format of the `mount` command is as follows:

```
mount [-t vfstype] [-o options] device directory
```

The parameters of mount are as follows:

- vfstype is the type of filesystem.
- options is a comma-separated list of mount options.
- device is the block device node the filesystem resides on.
- directory is the directory you want to mount the filesystem on.

There are various options you can give after -o; have a look at the manual page mount(8) for more information. As an example, if you wanted to mount an SD card containing an ext4 filesystem in the first partition onto the directory called /mnt, you would type the following code:

```
# mount -t ext4 /dev/mmcblk0p1 /mnt
```

Assuming the mount succeeds, you would be able to see the files stored on the SD card in the /mnt directory. In some cases, you can leave out the filesystem type and let the kernel probe the device to find out what is stored there. If mounting fails, you may first need to unmount the partition in case your Linux distro is configured to automount all the partitions on an SD card when it is inserted.

Looking at the example of mounting the proc filesystem, there is something odd: there is no device node, such as /dev/proc, since it is a pseudo filesystem and not a real one. But the mount command requires a device parameter. Consequently, we have to give a string where device should go, but it does not matter much what that string is. These two commands achieve exactly the same result:

```
# mount -t proc procfs /proc
# mount -t proc nodevice /proc
```

The procfs and nodevice strings are ignored by the mount command. It is fairly common to use the filesystem type in place of the device when mounting pseudo filesystems.

Kernel modules

If you have kernel modules, they need to be installed into the root filesystem, using the modules_install kernel make target, as we saw in *Chapter 4, Configuring and Building the Kernel*. This will copy them into the directory called /lib/modules/<kernel version> together with the configuration files needed by the modprobe command.

Be aware that you have just created a dependency between the kernel and the root filesystem. If you update one, you will have to update the other.

Now that we know how to mount a filesystem from an SD card, let's take a look at different options for mounting a root filesystem. The alternatives (ramdisk and NFS) may surprise you, especially if you are new to embedded Linux. A ramdisk protects the original source image from corruption and wear. We'll learn more about flash ware in *Chapter 9, Creating a Storage Strategy*. A network filesystem allows more rapid development because file changes can propagate instantly to the target(s).

Transferring the root filesystem to the target

After having created a skeleton root filesystem in your staging directory, the next task is to transfer it to the target. In the sections that follow, I will describe three possibilities:

- **initramfs**: Also known as a ramdisk, this is a filesystem image that is loaded into RAM by the bootloader. Ramdisks are easy to create and have no dependencies on mass storage drivers. They can be used in fallback maintenance mode when the main root filesystem needs updating. They can even be used as the main root filesystem in small embedded devices, and they are commonly used as the early user space in mainstream Linux distributions. Remember that the contents of the root filesystem are volatile, and any changes you make in the root filesystem at runtime will be lost when the system next boots. You would need another storage type to store permanent data such as configuration parameters.
- **Disk image**: This is a copy of the root filesystem formatted and ready to be loaded onto a mass storage device on the target. For example, it could be an image in the `ext4` format ready to be copied onto an SD card, or it could be in the `jffs2` format ready to be loaded into flash memory via the bootloader. Creating a disk image is probably the most common option. There is more information about the different types of mass storage in *Chapter 9, Creating a Storage Strategy*.
- **Network filesystem**: The staging directory can be exported to the network via an NFS server and mounted by the target at boot time. This is often done during the development phase, in preference to repeated cycles of creating a disk image and reloading it onto the mass storage device, which is quite a slow process.

I will start with ramdisk, and use it to illustrate a few refinements to the root filesystem, such as adding usernames and a device manager to create device nodes automatically. Then, I will show you how to create a disk image and how to use NFS to mount the root filesystem over a network.

Creating a boot initramfs

An initial RAM filesystem, or `initramfs`, is a compressed `cpio` archive. `cpio` is an old Unix archive format, similar to TAR and ZIP but easier to decode and so requiring less code in the kernel. You need to configure your kernel with `CONFIG_BLK_DEV_INITRD` to support `initramfs`.

As it happens, there are three different ways to create a boot ramdisk: as a standalone `cpio` archive, as a `cpio` archive embedded in the kernel image, and as a device table that the kernel build system processes as part of the build. The first option gives the most flexibility because we can mix and match kernels and ramdisks to our heart's content. However, it means that you have two files to deal with instead of one, and not all bootloaders have the facility to load a separate ramdisk. I will show you how to build one into the kernel later.

Standalone initramfs

The following sequence of instructions creates the archive, compresses it, and adds a U-Boot header ready for loading onto the target:

```
$ cd ~/rootfs
$ find . | cpio -H newc -ov --owner root:root >
../initramfs.cpio
$ cd ..
$ gzip initramfs.cpio
$ mkimage -A arm -O linux -T ramdisk -d initramfs.cpio.gz
uRamdisk
```

Note that we run `cpio` with the `--owner root:root` option. This is a quick fix for the file ownership problem mentioned earlier, in the *File ownership permissions in the staging directory* section. It makes everything in the `cpio` archive have a UID and GID of `0`.

The final size of the `uRamdisk` file is about 2.9 MB with no kernel modules. Add to that 4.4 MB for the kernel `zImage` file and 440 KB for U-Boot, and this gives a total of 7.7 MB of storage needed to boot this board. We are a little way off the 1.44 MB floppy that started it all off. If size was a real problem, you could use one of these options:

- Make the kernel smaller by leaving out drivers and functions you don't need.
- Make BusyBox smaller by leaving out utilities you don't need.
- Use `musl libc` or `uClibc-ng` in place of `glibc`.
- Compile BusyBox statically.

Now that we have assembled an `initramfs`, let's boot the archive.

Booting the initramfs

The simplest thing we can do is to run a shell on the console so that we can interact with the target. We can do that by adding `rdinit=/bin/sh` to the kernel command line. The next two sections show how to do that for both QEMU and the BeagleBone Black.

Booting with QEMU

QEMU has the option called `-initrd` to load `initramfs` into memory. You should already have, from *Chapter 4, Configuring and Building the Kernel*, a `zImage` compiled with the `arm-unknown-linux-gnueabi` toolchain and the device tree binary for the Versatile PB. From this chapter, you should have created an `initramfs`, which includes BusyBox compiled with the same toolchain. Now, you can launch QEMU using the script in `MELP/Chapter05/run-qemu-initramfs.sh` or using this command:

```
$ QEMU_AUDIO_DRV=none \
qemu-system-arm -m 256M -nographic -M versatilepb \
-kernel zImage
-append "console=ttyAMA0 rdinit=/bin/sh" \
-dtb versatile-pb.dtb
-initrd initramfs.cpio.gz
```

You should get a root shell with the prompt `/ #`.

Booting the BeagleBone Black

For the BeagleBone Black, we need the microSD card prepared in *Chapter 4, Configuring and Building the Kernel*, plus a root filesystem built using the `arm-cortex_a8-linux-gnueabihf` toolchain. Copy the `uRamdisk` you created earlier in this section to the boot partition on the microSD card, and then use it to boot the BeagleBone Black to the point where you get a U-Boot prompt. Then, enter these commands:

```
fatload mmc 0:1 0x80200000 zImage
fatload mmc 0:1 0x80f00000 am335x-boneblack.dtb fatload mmc 0:1
0x81000000 uRamdisk
setenv bootargs console=ttyO0,115200 rdinit=/bin/sh
bootz 0x80200000 0x81000000 0x80f00000
```

If all goes well, you will get a root shell with the prompt `/ #` on the serial console. After this is done, we will need to mount `proc` on both platforms.

Mounting proc

You will find that on both platforms the ps command doesn't work. This is because the proc filesystem has not been mounted yet. Try mounting it:

```
# mount -t proc proc /proc
```

Now, run ps again and you will see the process listing.

A refinement to this setup would be to write a shell script that mounts proc, and anything else that needs to be done at bootup. Then, you could run this script instead of /bin/sh at boot. The following snippet gives an idea of how it would work:

```
#!/bin/sh
/bin/mount -t proc proc /proc
# Other boot-time commands go here
/bin/sh
```

The last line, /bin/sh, launches a new shell that gives you an interactive root shell prompt. Using a shell as init in this way is very handy for quick hacks, for example, when you want to rescue a system with a broken init program. However, in most cases, you would use an init program, which we will cover later on in this chapter. But, before this, I want to look at two other ways to load initramfs.

Building an initramfs into the kernel image

So far, we have created a compressed initramfs as a separate file and used the bootloader to load it into memory. Some bootloaders do not have the ability to load an initramfs file in this way. To cope with these situations, Linux can be configured to incorporate initramfs into the kernel image. To do this, change the kernel configuration and set CONFIG_INITRAMFS_SOURCE to the full path of the cpio archive you created earlier. If you are using menuconfig, it is in **General setup | Initramfs source file(s)**. Note that it has to be the uncompressed cpio file ending in .cpio, not the gzipped version. Then, build the kernel.

Booting is the same as before, except that there is no ramdisk file. For QEMU, the command is like this:

```
$ QEMU_AUDIO_DRV=none \
qemu-system-arm -m 256M -nographic -M versatilepb \
-kernel zImage \
-append "console=ttyAMA0 rdinit=/bin/sh" \
-dtb versatile-pb.dtb
```

For the BeagleBone Black, enter these commands at the U-Boot prompt:

```
fatload mmc 0:1 0x80200000 zImage
fatload mmc 0:1 0x80f00000 am335x-boneblack.dtb
setenv bootargs console=ttyO0,115200 rdinit=/bin/sh
bootz 0x80200000 - 0x80f00000
```

Of course, you must remember to regenerate the `cpio` file each time you change the contents of the root filesystem and then rebuild the kernel.

Building an initramfs using a device table

A device table is a text file that lists the files, directories, device nodes, and links that go into an archive or filesystem image. The overwhelming advantage is that it allows you to create entries in the archive file that are owned by the `root` user, or any other UID, without having root privileges yourself. You can even create device nodes without needing root privileges. All this is possible because the archive is just a data file. It is only when it is expanded by Linux at boot time that real files and directories get created, using the attributes you have specified.

The kernel has a feature that allows us to use a device table when creating an `initramfs`. You write the device table file and then point `CONFIG_INITRAMFS_SOURCE` at it. Then, when you build the kernel, it creates the `cpio` archive from the instructions in the device table. At no point do you need `root` access.

Here is a device table for our simple `rootfs`, but missing most of the symbolic links to BusyBox to make it manageable:

```
dir /bin 775 0 0
dir /sys 775 0 0
dir /tmp 775 0 0
dir /dev 775 0 0
nod /dev/null 666 0 0 c 1 3
nod /dev/console 600 0 0 c 5 1
dir /home 775 0 0
dir /proc 775 0 0
dir /lib 775 0 0
slink /lib/libm.so.6 libm-2.22.so 777 0 0
slink /lib/libc.so.6 libc-2.22.so 777 0 0
slink /lib/ld-linux-armhf.so.3 ld-2.22.so 777 0 0
```

```
file /lib/libm-2.22.so /home/chris/rootfs/lib/libm-2.22.so 755
0 0
file /lib/libc-2.22.so /home/chris/rootfs/lib/libc-2.22.so 755
0 0
file /lib/ld-2.22.so /home/chris/rootfs/lib/ld-2.22.so 755 0 0
```

The syntax is fairly obvious:

- `dir <name> <mode> <uid> <gid>`
- `file <name> <location> <mode> <uid> <gid>`
- `nod <name> <mode> <uid> <gid> <dev_type> <maj> <min>`
- `slink <name> <target> <mode> <uid> <gid>`

The `dir`, `nod`, and `slink` commands create a filesystem object in the `initramfs` `cpio` archive with the name, mode, user ID, and group ID given. The `file` command copies the file from the source location into the archive and sets the mode, the user ID, and the group ID.

The task of creating an `initramfs` device table from scratch is made easier by a script in the kernel source code in `usr/gen_initramfs_list.sh`, which creates a device table from a given directory. For example, to create the `initramfs` device table for the `rootfs` directory, and to change the ownership of all files owned by user ID `1000` and group ID `1000` to user and group ID `0`, you would use this command:

```
$ bash linux-stable/scripts/gen_initramfs_list.sh -u 1000 \
-g 1000
rootfs > initramfs-device-table
```

Using this script's `-o` option lets you create a compressed `initramfs` file whose format depends on the file extension after `-o`.

Note that the script only works with a `bash` shell. If you have a system with a different default shell, as is the case with most Ubuntu configurations, you will find that the script fails. Hence, in the command given previously, I explicitly used `bash` to run the script.

The old initrd format

There is an older format for a Linux ramdisk, known as `initrd`. It was the only format available before Linux 2.6 and is still needed if you are using the MMU-less variant of Linux, uClinux. It is pretty obscure and I will not cover it here. There is more information in the kernel source in `Documentation/initrd.txt`.

Once our `initramfs` boots, then the system needs to start running programs. The first program that runs is the `init` program. Let's look at that next.

The init program

Running a shell, or even a shell script, at boot time is fine for simple cases, but really you need something more flexible. Normally, Unix systems run a program called `init` that starts up and monitors other programs. Over the years, there have been many `init` programs, some of which I will describe in *Chapter 13, Starting Up – The init Program*. For now, I will briefly introduce the `init` program from BusyBox.

The `init` program begins by reading the configuration file, `/etc/inittab`. Here is a simple example that is adequate for our needs:

```
::sysinit:/etc/init.d/rcS
::askfirst:-/bin/ash
```

The first line runs a shell script, `rcS`, when `init` is started. The second line prints the message **Please press Enter to activate this console** to the console and starts a shell when you press *Enter*. The leading - before `/bin/ash` means that it will become a login shell, which sources `/etc/profile` and `$HOME/.profile` before giving the shell prompt. One of the advantages of launching the shell like this is that job control is enabled. The most immediate effect is that you can use *Ctrl* + *C* to terminate the current program. Maybe you didn't notice it before, but wait until you run the `ping` program and find you can't stop it!

BusyBox `init` provides a default `inittab` if none is present in the root filesystem. It is a little more extensive than the preceding one.

The script called `/etc/init.d/rcS` is the place to put initialization commands that need to be performed at boot, for example, mounting the `proc` and `sysfs` filesystems:

```
#!/bin/sh
mount -t proc proc /proc
mount -t sysfs sysfs /sys
```

Make sure that you make `rcS` executable like this:

```
$ cd ~/rootfs
$ chmod +x etc/init.d/rcS
```

You can try `init` out on QEMU by changing the `-append` parameter like this:

```
-append "console=ttyAMA0 rdinit=/sbin/init"
```

For the BeagleBone Black, you need to set the `bootargs` variable in U-Boot as shown here:

```
setenv bootargs console=ttyO0,115200 rdinit=/sbin/init
```

Now, let's take a closer look at the `inittab` read by `init` during startup.

Starting a daemon process

Typically, you would want to run certain background processes at startup. Let's take the log daemon, `syslogd`, as an example. The purpose of `syslogd` is to accumulate log messages from other programs, mostly other daemons. Naturally, BusyBox has an applet for that!

Starting the daemon is as simple as adding a line like this to `etc/inittab`:

```
::respawn:/sbin/syslogd -n
```

`respawn` means that if the program terminates, it will be automatically restarted; `-n` means that it should run as a foreground process. The log is written to `/var/log/messages`.

> **Important note**
>
> You may also want to start `klogd` in the same way: `klogd` sends kernel log messages to `syslogd` so that they can be logged to permanent storage.

Next, we will learn how to configure user accounts.

Configuring user accounts

As I have hinted already, it is not good practice to run all programs as `root`, since if one program is compromised by an outside attack, then the whole system is at risk. It is preferable to create unprivileged user accounts and use them where full `root` is not necessary.

Usernames are configured in `/etc/passwd`. There is one line per user, with seven fields of information separated by colons, which are, in order, the following:

- The login name
- A hash code used to verify the password or, more usually, an `x` to indicate that the password is stored in `/etc/shadow`
- The user ID
- The group ID
- A comment field, often left blank
- The user's `home` directory
- The shell this user will use (optional)

Here is a simple example in which we have user `root` with UID `0` and user `daemon` with UID `1`:

```
root:x:0:0:root:/root:/bin/sh
daemon:x:1:1:daemon:/usr/sbin:/bin/false
```

Setting the shell for user `daemon` to `/bin/false` ensures that any attempt to log on with that name will fail.

Various programs have to read `/etc/passwd` in order to look up usernames and UIDs, and so the file has to be world-readable. This is a problem if the password hashes are stored in there as well, because a malicious program would be able to take a copy and discover the actual passwords using a variety of cracker programs. Therefore, to reduce the exposure of this sensitive information, the passwords are stored in `/etc/shadow` and `x` is placed in the password field to indicate that this is the case. The file called `/etc/shadow` only needs to be accessed by `root`, so as long as the `root` user is not compromised, the passwords are safe. The shadow password file consists of one entry per user, made up of nine fields. Here is an example that mirrors the password file shown in the preceding paragraph:

```
root::10933:0:99999:7:::
daemon:*:10933:0:99999:7:::
```

The first two fields are the username and the password hash. The remaining seven fields are related to password aging, which is not usually an issue on embedded devices. If you are curious about the full details, refer to the manual page for `shadow(5)`.

In the example, the password for `root` is empty, meaning that root can log on without giving a password. Having an empty password for `root` is useful during development but not for production. You can generate or change a password hash by running the `passwd` command on the target, which will write a new hash to `/etc/shadow`. If you want all subsequent root filesystems to have this same password, you could copy this file back to the staging directory.

Group names are stored in a similar way in `/etc/group`. There is one line per group consisting of four fields separated by colons. The fields are here:

- The name of the group
- The group password, usually an `x` character, indicating that there is no group password
- The GID or group ID
- An optional list of users who belong to this group, separated by commas

Here is an example:

```
root:x:0:
daemon:x:1:
```

Now that we have learned how to configure a user account, let's see how to add it to the root filesystem.

Adding user accounts to the root filesystem

Firstly, you have to add to your staging directory the files `etc/passwd`, `etc/shadow`, and `etc/group`, as shown in the preceding section. Make sure that the permissions of `etc/shadow` are `0600`. Next, you need to initiate the login procedure by starting a program called `getty`. There is a version of `getty` in BusyBox. You launch it from `inittab` using the `respawn` keyword, which restarts `getty` when a login shell is terminated. Your `inittab` should read like this:

```
::sysinit:/etc/init.d/rcS
::respawn:/sbin/getty 115200 console
```

Then, rebuild the ramdisk and try it out using QEMU or the BeagleBone Black as before.

Earlier in this chapter, we learned how to create device nodes using the `mknod` command. Now, let's take a look at some easier ways to create device nodes.

A better way of managing device nodes

Creating device nodes statically with mknod is quite hard work and inflexible. There are other ways to create device nodes automatically on demand:

- devtmpfs: This is a pseudo filesystem that you mount over /dev at boot time. The kernel populates it with device nodes for all the devices that the kernel currently knows about, and it creates nodes for new devices as they are detected at runtime. The nodes are owned by root and have default permissions of 0600. Some well-known device nodes, such as /dev/null and /dev/random, override the default to 0666. To see exactly how this is done, take a look at the Linux source file drivers/char/mem.c and see how struct memdev is initialized.
- mdev: This is a BusyBox applet that is used to populate a directory with device nodes and to create new nodes as needed. There is a configuration file, /etc/mdev.conf, which contains rules for ownership and the mode of the nodes.
- udev: This is the mainstream equivalent of mdev. You will find it on desktop Linux and in some embedded devices. It is very flexible and a good choice for higher-end embedded devices. It is now part of systemd.

> **Important note**
>
> Although both mdev and udev create the device nodes themselves, it is easier to just let devtmpfs do the job and use mdev/udev as a layer on top to implement the policy for setting ownership and permissions. The devtmpfs approach is the only maintainable way to generate device nodes prior to user space startup.

Let's look at some examples where we use these tools.

An example using devtmpfs

Support for the devtmpfs filesystem is controlled by the kernel configuration variable CONFIG_DEVTMPFS. It is not enabled in the default configuration of the ARM Versatile PB, so if you want to try out the following using this target, you will have to go back to your kernel configuration and enable this option. Trying out devtmpfs is as simple as entering this command:

```
# mount -t devtmpfs devtmpfs /dev
```

You will notice that afterward, there are many more device nodes in /dev. For a permanent fix, add this to /etc/init.d/rcS:

```
#!/bin/sh
mount -t proc proc /proc
mount -t sysfs sysfs /sys
mount -t devtmpfs devtmpfs /dev
```

If you enable CONFIG_DEVTMPFS_MOUNT in your kernel configuration, the kernel will automatically mount devtmpfs just after mounting the root filesystem. However, this option has no effect when booting initramfs, as we are doing here.

An example using mdev

While mdev is a bit more complex to set up, it does allow you to modify the permissions of device nodes as they are created. You begin by running mdev with the -s option, which causes it to scan the /sys directory looking for information about current devices. From this information, it populates the /dev directory with the corresponding nodes. If you want to keep track of new devices coming online and create nodes for them as well, you need to make mdev a hot plug client by writing to /proc/sys/kernel/hotplug. These additions to /etc/init.d/rcS will achieve all of this:

```
#!/bin/sh
mount -t proc proc /proc
mount -t sysfs sysfs /sys
mount -t devtmpfs devtmpfs /dev
echo /sbin/mdev > /proc/sys/kernel/hotplug
mdev -s
```

The default mode is 660 and the ownership is root:root. You can change this by adding rules in /etc/mdev.conf. For example, to give the null, random, and urandom devices their correct modes, you would add this to /etc/mdev.conf:

```
null root:root 666
random root:root 444
urandom root:root 444
```

The format is documented in the BusyBox source code in docs/mdev.txt, and there are more examples in the directory named examples.

Are static device nodes so bad after all?

Statically created device nodes do have one advantage over running a device manager: they don't take any time during boot to create. If minimizing boot time is a priority, using statically-created device nodes will save a measurable amount of time.

After devices are detected and their nodes are created, the next step in the startup sequence is usually configuring the network.

Configuring the network

Next, let's look at some basic network configurations so that we can communicate with the outside world. I am assuming that there is an Ethernet interface, `eth0`, and that we only need a simple IPv4 configuration.

These examples use the network utilities that are part of BusyBox, and they are sufficient for a simple use case, using the old-but-reliable `ifup` and `ifdown` programs. You can read the manual pages for both to get the details. The main network configuration is stored in `/etc/network/interfaces`. You will need to create these directories in the staging directory:

```
etc/network
etc/network/if-pre-up.d
etc/network/if-up.d
var/run
```

For a static IP address, `/etc/network/interfaces` would look like this:

```
auto lo
iface lo inet loopback

auto eth0
iface eth0 inet static
    address 192.168.1.101
    netmask 255.255.255.0
    network 192.168.1.0
```

For a dynamic IP address allocated using DHCP, `/etc/network/interfaces` would look like this:

```
auto lo
iface lo inet loopback

```

```
auto eth0
iface eth0 inet dhcp
```

You will also have to configure a DHCP client program. BusyBox has one named `udchpcd`. It needs a shell script that should go in `/usr/share/udhcpc/default.script`. There is a suitable default in the BusyBox source code in the `examples/udhcp/simple.script` directory.

Network components for glibc

`glibc` uses a mechanism known as the **name service switch** (**NSS**) to control the way that names are resolved to numbers for networking and users. Usernames, for example, may be resolved to UIDs via the file `/etc/passwd` and network services such as HTTP can be resolved to the service port number via `/etc/services`. All this is configured by `/etc/nsswitch.conf`; see the manual page, `nss(5)`, for full details. Here is a simple example that will suffice for most embedded Linux implementations:

```
passwd:    files
group:     files
shadow:    files
hosts:     files dns
networks:  files
protocols: files
services:  files
```

Everything is resolved by the correspondingly named file in `/etc`, except for the hostnames, which may additionally be resolved by a DNS lookup if they are not in `/etc/hosts`.

To make this work, you need to populate `/etc` with those files. Networks, protocols, and services are the same across all Linux systems, so they can be copied from `/etc` in your development PC. `/etc/hosts` should, at least, contain the loopback address:

```
127.0.0.1 localhost
```

The other files, `passwd`, `group`, and `shadow`, were described earlier, in the *Configuring user accounts* section.

The last piece of the jigsaw is the libraries that perform the name resolution. They are plugins that are loaded as needed based on the contents of `nsswitch.conf`, meaning that they do not show up as dependencies if you use `readelf` or `ldd`. You will simply have to copy them from the toolchain's `sysroot`:

```
$ cd ~/rootfs
$ cp -a $SYSROOT/lib/libnss* lib
$ cp -a $SYSROOT/lib/libresolv* lib
```

Our staging directory is now complete, so let's generate a filesystem from it.

Creating filesystem images with device tables

We saw earlier, in the *Creating a boot initramfs* section, that the kernel has an option to create `initramfs` using a device table. Device tables are really useful because they allow a non-root user to create device nodes and to allocate arbitrary UID and GID values to any file or directory. The same concept has been applied to tools that create other filesystem image formats, as shown in this mapping from filesystem format to tool:

- `jffs2`: `mkfs.jffs2`
- `ubifs`: `mkfs:ubifs`
- `ext2`: `genext2fs`

We will look at `jffs2` and `ubifs` in *Chapter 9, Creating a Storage Strategy*, when we look at filesystems for flash memory. The third, `ext2`, is a format commonly used for managed flash memory including SD cards. The example that follows uses `ext2` to create a disk image that can be copied to an SD card.

To begin with, you need to install the `genext2fs` tool on your host. On Ubuntu, the package to install is named `genext2fs`:

```
$ sudo apt install genext2fs
```

`genext2fs` takes a device table file with the format `<name> <type> <mode> <uid> <gid> <major> <minor> <start> <inc> <count>`, where the meanings of the fields are as follows:

- `name`:
- `type`: One of the following:

  `f`: A regular file

  `d`: A directory

c: A character special device file

b: A block special device file

p: A FIFO (named pipe)

- uid: The UID of the file
- gid: The GID of the file
- major and minor: The device numbers (device nodes only)
- start, inc, and count: Allow you to create a group of device nodes starting from the minor number in start (device nodes only)

You do not have to specify every file, as you do with the kernel initramfs table. You just have to point at a directory—the staging directory—and list the changes and exceptions you need to make in the final filesystem image.

A simple example that populates static device nodes for us is as follows:

```
/dev d 755 0 0 - - - - -
/dev/null c 666 0 0 1 3 0 0 -
/dev/console c 600 0 0 5 1 0 0 -
/dev/ttyO0 c 600 0 0 252 0 0 0 -
```

Then, you can use genext2fs to generate a filesystem image of 4 MB (that is 4,096 blocks of the default size, 1,024 bytes):

```
$ genext2fs -b 4096 -d rootfs -D device-table.txt -U rootfs.
ext2
```

Now, you can copy the resulting image, rootfs.ext2, to an SD card or similar, which we will do next.

Booting the BeagleBone Black

The script called MELP/format-sdcard.sh creates two partitions on the microSD card: one for the boot files and one for the root filesystem. Assuming that you have created the root filesystem image as shown in the previous section, you can use the dd command to write it to the second partition. As always, when copying files directly to storage devices like this, make absolutely sure that you know which is the microSD card. In this case, I am using a built-in card reader, which is the device called /dev/mmcblk0, so the command is as follows:

```
$ sudo dd if=rootfs.ext2 of=/dev/mmcblk0p2
```

Note that the card reader on your host system may have a different name.

Then, slot the micro SD card into the BeagleBone Black, and set the kernel command line to `root=/dev/mmcblk0p2`. The complete sequence of U-Boot commands is as follows:

```
fatload mmc 0:1 0x80200000 zImage
fatload mmc 0:1 0x80f00000 am335x-boneblack.dtb
setenv bootargs console=ttyO0,115200 root=/dev/mmcblk0p2
bootz 0x80200000 - 0x80f00000
```

This is an example of mounting a filesystem from a normal block device, such as an SD card. The same principles apply to other filesystem types and we will look at them in more detail in *Chapter 9, Creating a Storage Strategy*.

Mounting the root filesystem using NFS

If your device has a network interface, it is often useful to mount the root filesystem over the network during development. It gives you access to the almost unlimited storage on your host machine, so you can add in debug tools and executables with large symbol tables. As an added bonus, updates made to the root filesystem on the development machine are made available on the target immediately. You can also access all the target's log files from the host.

To begin with, you need to install and configure an NFS server on your host. On Ubuntu, the package to install is named `nfs-kernel-server`:

```
$ sudo apt install nfs-kernel-server
```

The NFS server needs to be told which directories are being exported to the network; this is controlled by `/etc/exports`. There is one line for each export. The format is described in the manual page `exports(5)`. As an example, to export the root filesystem on my host, I have this:

```
/home/chris/rootfs *(rw,sync,no_subtree_check,no_root_squash)
```

`*` exports the directory to any address on my local network. If you wish, you can give a single IP address or a range at this point. There follows a list of options enclosed in parentheses. There must not be any spaces between `*` and the opening parenthesis. The options are here:

- `rw`: This exports the directory as read-write.
- `sync`: This option selects the synchronous version of the NFS protocol, which is more robust but a little slower than the `async` option.

- `no_subtree_check`: This option disables subtree checking, which has mild security implications, but can improve reliability in some circumstances.
- `no_root_squash`: This option allows requests from user ID `0` to be processed without squashing to a different user ID. It is necessary to allow the target to correctly access the files owned by `root`.

Having made changes to `/etc/exports`, restart the NFS server to pick them up.

Now, you need to set up the target to mount the root filesystem over NFS. For this to work, your kernel has to be configured with `CONFIG_ROOT_NFS`. Then, you can configure Linux to do the mount at boot time by adding the following to the kernel command line:

```
root=/dev/nfs rw nfsroot=<host-ip>:<root-dir> ip=<target-ip>
```

The options are as follows:

- `rw`: This mounts the root filesystem read-write.
- `nfsroot`: This specifies the IP address of the host, followed by the path to the exported root filesystem.
- `ip`: This is the IP address to be assigned to the target. Usually, network addresses are assigned at runtime, as we have seen in the *Configuring the network* section. However, in this case, the interface has to be configured before the root filesystem is mounted and `init` has been started. Hence, it is configured on the kernel command line.

> **Important note**
>
> There is more information about NFS root mounts in the kernel source in `Documentation/filesystems/nfs/nfsroot.txt`.

Next, let's boot an image complete with a root filesystem on QEMU and a BeagleBone Black.

Testing with QEMU

The following script creates a virtual network between the network device called `tap0` on the host and `eth0` on the target using a pair of static IPv4 addresses and then launches QEMU with the parameters to use `tap0` as the emulated interface.

You will need to change the path to the root filesystem to be the full path to your staging directory and maybe the IP addresses if they conflict with your network configuration:

```
#!/bin/bash
KERNEL=zImage
DTB=versatile-pb.dtb
ROOTDIR=/home/chris/rootfs
HOST_IP=192.168.1.1
TARGET_IP=192.168.1.101
NET_NUMBER=192.168.1.0
NET_MASK=255.255.255.0

sudo tunctl -u $(whoami) -t tap0
sudo ifconfig tap0 ${HOST_IP}
sudo route add -net ${NET_NUMBER} netmask ${NET_MASK} dev tap0
sudo sh -c "echo 1 > /proc/sys/net/ipv4/ip_forward"

QEMU_AUDIO_DRV=none \
qemu-system-arm -m 256M -nographic -M versatilepb -kernel
${KERNEL} -append "console=ttyAMA0,115200 root=/dev/nfs rw
nfsroot=${HOST_IP}:${ROOTDIR} ip=${TARGET_IP}" -dtb ${DTB} -net
nic -net tap,ifname=tap0,script=no
```

The script is available in `MELP/Chapter05/run-qemu-nfsroot.sh`.

It should boot up as before, now using the staging directory directly via the NFS export. Any files that you create in that directory will be immediately visible to the target device, and any files created in the device will be visible to the development PC.

Testing with the BeagleBone Black

In a similar way, you can enter these commands at the U-Boot prompt of the BeagleBone Black:

```
setenv serverip 192.168.1.1
setenv ipaddr 192.168.1.101
setenv npath [path to staging directory]
setenv bootargs console=ttyO0,115200 root=/dev/nfs rw
nfsroot=${serverip}:${npath} ip=${ipaddr}
```

```
fatload mmc 0:1 0x80200000 zImage
fatload mmc 0:1 0x80f00000 am335x-boneblack.dtb
bootz 0x80200000 - 0x80f00000
```

There is a U-Boot environment file in `MELP/Chapter05/uEnv.txt`, which contains all these commands. Just copy it to the boot partition of the microSD card and U-Boot will do the rest.

Problems with file permissions

The files that you copied into the staging directory will be owned by the UID of the user you are logged on as, typically `1000`. However, the target has no knowledge of this user. What is more, any files created by the target will be owned by users configured by the target, often the `root` user. The whole thing is a mess. Unfortunately, there is no simple way out. The best solution is to make a copy of the staging directory and change ownership to UID and GID to `0`, using the `sudo chown -R 0:0 *` command. Then, export this directory as the NFS mount. It removes the convenience of having just one copy of the root filesystem shared between development and target systems, but at least the file ownership will be correct.

It's not uncommon in embedded Linux to link device drivers statically into the kernel rather than load them dynamically from the root filesystem as modules at runtime. So how do we reap the same benefits of rapid iteration provided by NFS when modifying the kernel source code or DTBs? The answer is TFTP.

Using TFTP to load the kernel

Now that we know how to mount the root filesystem over a network using NFS, you may be wondering if there is a way to load the kernel, device tree, and `initramfs` over the network as well. If we can do this, the only component that needs to be written to storage on the target is the bootloader. Everything else could be loaded from the host machine. It would save time since you would not need to keep reflashing the target, and you could even get work done while the flash storage drivers are still being developed (it happens).

The **Trivial File Transfer Protocol** (**TFTP**) is the answer to the problem. TFTP is a very simple file transfer protocol, designed to be easy to implement in bootloaders such as U-Boot.

To begin with, you need to install a TFTP daemon on your host. On Ubuntu, the package to install is named `tftpd-hpa`:

```
$ sudo apt install tftpd-hpa
```

By default, `tftpd-hpa` grants read-only access to files in the `/var/lib/tftpboot` directory. With `tftpd-hpa` installed and running, copy the files that you want to copy to the target into `/var/lib/tftpboot`, which for the BeagleBone Black, would be `zImage` and `am335x-boneblack.dtb`. Then enter these commands at the U-Boot command prompt:

```
setenv serverip 192.168.1.1
setenv ipaddr 192.168.1.101
tftpboot 0x80200000 zImage
tftpboot 0x80f00000 am335x-boneblack.dtb
setenv npath [path to staging]
setenv bootargs console=ttyO0,115200 root=/dev/nfs rw
nfsroot=${serverip}:${npath} ip=${ipaddr}
bootz 0x80200000 - 0x80f00000
```

You may find that the `tftpboot` command hangs, endlessly printing out the letter `T`, which means that the TFTP requests are timing out. There are a number of reasons why this happens, the most common ones being the following:

- There is an incorrect IP address for `serverip`.
- The TFTP daemon is not running on the server.
- There is a firewall on the server that is blocking the TFTP protocol. Most firewalls do indeed block the TFTP port, `69`, by default.

Once you have resolved the problem, U-Boot can load the files from the host machine and boot in the usual way. You can automate the process by putting the commands into a `uEnv.txt` file.

Summary

One of the strengths of Linux is that it can support a wide range of root filesystems, and so it can be tailored to suit a wide range of needs. We have seen that it is possible to construct a simple root filesystem manually with a small number of components and that BusyBox is especially useful in this regard. By going through the process one step at a time, it has given us insight into some of the basic workings of Linux systems, including network configuration and user accounts. However, the task rapidly becomes unmanageable as devices get more complex. And, there is the ever-present worry that there may be a security hole in the implementation that we have not noticed.

In the next chapter, I will show you how using an embedded build system can make the process of creating an embedded Linux system much easier and more reliable. I will start by looking at Buildroot, and then go onto look at the more complex, but powerful, Yocto Project.

Further reading

- *Filesystem Hierarchy Standard, Version 3.0* – `https://refspecs.linuxfoundation.org/fhs.shtml`
- *ramfs, rootfs and initramfs*, by Rob Landley, which is part of the Linux source in `Documentation/filesystems/ramfs-rootfs-initramfs.txt`

6
Selecting a Build System

In the preceding chapters, we covered the four elements of embedded Linux and showed you, step by step, how to build a toolchain, a bootloader, a kernel, and a root filesystem, before combining them into a basic embedded Linux system. And there are a lot of steps! Now, it is time to look at ways to simplify this process by automating it as much as possible. We will look at how embedded build systems can help and look at two of them in particular: Buildroot and the Yocto Project. Both are complex and flexible tools, and it would require an entire book to describe how they work in full. In this chapter, I only want to show you the general ideas behind build systems. I will show you how to build a simple device image to get an overall feel of the system, and then how to make some useful changes using the Nova board example from the previous chapters, as well as the Raspberry Pi 4.

In this chapter, we will cover the following topics:

- Comparing build systems
- Distributing binaries
- Introducing Buildroot
- Introducing the Yocto Project

Let's get started!

Technical requirements

To follow along with the examples in this chapter, make sure you have the following:

- A Linux-based host system with a minimum of 60 GB of available disk space
- Etcher for Linux
- A microSD card reader and card
- A USB to TTL 3.3V serial cable
- A Raspberry Pi 4
- A 5V 3A USB-C power supply
- An Ethernet cable and port for network connectivity
- A BeagleBone Black
- A 5V 1A DC power supply

All the code for this chapter can be found in the `Chapter06` folder of this book's GitHub repository: `https://github.com/PacktPublishing/Mastering-Embedded-Linux-Programming-Third-Edition`.

Comparing build systems

I described the process of creating a system manually in *Chapter 5, Building a Root Filesystem*, as the **Roll Your Own** (**RYO**) process. It has the advantage that you are in complete control of the software, and you can tailor it to do anything you like. If you want it to do something truly odd but innovative, or if you want to reduce the memory footprint to the smallest size possible, RYO is the way to go. But, in the vast majority of situations, building manually is a waste of time and produces inferior, unmaintainable systems.

The idea of a build system is to automate all the steps I have described up to this point. A build system should be able to build, from upstream source code, some or all of the following:

- A toolchain
- A bootloader
- A kernel
- A root filesystem

Building from upstream source code is important for a number of reasons. It means that you have the peace of mind that you can rebuild at any time, without external dependencies. It also means that you have the source code for debugging, and also that you can meet your license requirements to distribute the code to users where necessary.

Therefore, to do its job, a build system has to be able to do the following:

1. Download the source code from upstream, either directly from the source code control system or as an archive, and cache it locally.
2. Apply patches to enable cross compilation, fix architecture-dependent bugs, apply local configuration policies, and so on.
3. Build the various components.
4. Create a staging area and assemble a root filesystem.
5. Create image files in various formats, ready to be loaded onto the target.

Other things that are useful are as follows:

1. Add your own packages containing, for example, applications or kernel changes.
2. Select various root filesystem profiles: large or small, with and without graphics or other features.
3. Create a standalone SDK that you can distribute to other developers so that they don't have to install the complete build system.
4. Track which open source licenses are used by the various packages you have selected.
5. Have a user-friendly user interface.

In all cases, they encapsulate the components of a system into packages, some for the host and some for the target. Each package is defined by a set of rules to get the source, build it, and install the results in the correct location. There are dependencies between the packages and a build mechanism to resolve the dependencies and build the set of packages required.

Open source build systems have matured considerably over the last few years. There are many around, including the following:

- **Buildroot**: This is an easy-to-use system using GNU Make and Kconfig (`https://buildroot.org`).
- **EmbToolkit**: This is a simple system for generating root filesystems and toolchains, and is the only one so far that supports LLVM/Clang out of the box (`https://www.embtoolkit.org`).

- **OpenEmbedded**: This is a powerful system, which is also a core component of the Yocto Project and others (`https://openembedded.org`).
- **OpenWrt**: This is a build tool oriented toward building firmware for wireless routers (`https://openwrt.org`) that supports runtime package management out of the box.
- **PTXdist**: This is an open source build system sponsored by Pengutronix (`https://www.ptxdist.org`).
- **The Yocto Project**: This extends the OpenEmbedded core with metadata, tools, and documentation, and is probably the most popular system (`https://www.yoctoproject.org`).

I will concentrate on two of these: Buildroot and the Yocto Project. They approach the problem in different ways and have different objectives.

Buildroot has the primary aim of building root filesystem images, hence the name, although it can build bootloader and kernel images, as well as toolchains. It is easy to install and configure and generates target images quickly.

The Yocto Project, on the other hand, is more general in the way it defines the target system, and so it can build complex embedded devices. Every component is generated as a binary package, by default, using the RPM format, and then the packages are combined to make the filesystem image. Furthermore, you can install a package manager in the filesystem image, which allows you to update packages at runtime. In other words, when you build with the Yocto Project, you are, in effect, creating your own custom Linux distribution. Bear in mind that enabling runtime package management also means provisioning and running your own corresponding package repository.

Distributing binaries

Mainstream Linux distributions are, in most cases, constructed from collections of binary (precompiled) packages in either RPM or DEB format. **RPM** stands for the **Red Hat package manager** and is used in Red Hat, SUSE, Fedora, and other distributions based on them. Debian and Debian-derived distributions, including Ubuntu and Mint, use the Debian package manager format known as DEB. In addition, there is a lightweight format specific to embedded devices known as the Itsy package format or IPK, which is based on DEB.

The ability to include a package manager on the device is one of the big differentiators between build systems. Once you have a package manager on the target device, you have an easy path to deploy new packages to it and to update the existing ones. I will talk about the implications of this in *Chapter 10, Updating Software in the Field*.

Introducing Buildroot

The current versions of Buildroot are capable of building a toolchain, a bootloader, a kernel, and a root filesystem. It uses GNU `Make` as the principal build tool. There is good online documentation at `https://buildroot.org/docs.html`, including *The Buildroot user manual* at `https://buildroot.org/downloads/manual/manual.html`.

Background

Buildroot was one of the first build systems. It began as part of the uClinux and uClibc projects as a way of generating a small root filesystem for testing. It became a separate project in late 2001 and continued to evolve through to 2006, after which it went into a rather dormant phase. However, since 2009, when Peter Korsgaard took over stewardship, it has been developing rapidly, adding support for glibc-based toolchains and a greatly increased number of packages and target boards.

As a matter of interest, Buildroot is also the ancestor of another popular build system, OpenWrt (`http://wiki.openwrt.org`), which forked from Buildroot around 2004. The primary focus of OpenWrt is to produce software for wireless routers, and so the package mix is oriented toward the networking infrastructure. It also has a runtime package manager using the IPK format so that a device can be updated or upgraded without a complete reflash of the image. However, Buildroot and OpenWrt have diverged to such an extent that they are now almost completely different build systems. Packages built with one are not compatible with the other.

Stable releases and long-term support

The Buildroot developers produce stable releases four times a year, in February, May, August, and November. They are marked by Git tags of the form `<year>.02`, `<year>.05`, `<year>.08`, and `<year>.11`. From time to time, a release is marked for **long-term support** (**LTS**), which means that there will be point releases to fix security and other important bugs for 12 months after the initial release. The `2017.02` release was the first to receive the LTS label.

Installing

As usual, you can install Buildroot either by cloning the repository or downloading an archive. Here is an example of obtaining version `2020.02.9`, which was the latest stable version at the time of writing:

```
$ git clone git://git.buildroot.net/buildroot -b 2020.02.9
$ cd buildroot
```

The equivalent TAR archive is available at `https://buildroot.org/downloads`.

Next, you should read the *System requirements* section of *The Buildroot user manual*, available at `https://buildroot.org/downloads/manual/manual.html`, and make sure that you have installed all the packages listed there.

Configuring

Buildroot uses the kernel Kconfig/Kbuild mechanism, which I described in the *Understanding kernel configuration* section of *Chapter 4, Configuring and Building the Kernel*. You can configure Buildroot from scratch directly using `make menuconfig` (`xconfig` or `gconfig`), or you can choose one of the 100+ configurations for various development boards and the QEMU emulator, which you can find stored in the `configs/` directory. Typing `make list-defconfigs` lists all the default configurations.

Let's begin by building a default configuration that you can run on the Arm QEMU emulator:

```
$ cd buildroot
$ make qemu_arm_versatile_defconfig
$ make
```

> **Important note**
>
> You do not tell `make` how many parallel jobs to run with a `-j` option: Buildroot will make optimum use of your CPUs all by itself. If you want to limit the number of jobs, you can run `make menuconfig` and look under the Build options.

The build will take half an hour to an hour or more, depending on the capabilities of your host system and the speed of your link to the internet. It will download approximately 220 MiB of code and will consume about 3.5 GiB of disk space. When it is complete, you will find that two new directories have been created:

- `dl/`: This contains archives of the upstream projects that Buildroot has built.
- `output/`: This contains all the intermediate and final compiled resources.

You will see the following in `output/`:

- `build/`: Here, you will find the build directory for each component.
- `host/`: This contains various tools required by Buildroot that run on the host, including the executables of the toolchain (in `output/host/usr/bin`).

- `images/`: This is the most important of all since it contains the results of the build. Depending on what you selected when configuring, you will find a bootloader, a kernel, and one or more root filesystem images.
- `staging/`: This is a symbolic link to `sysroot` of the toolchain. The name of the link is a little confusing because it does not point to a staging area, as I defined it in *Chapter 5, Building a Root Filesystem*.
- `target/`: This is the staging area for the `root` directory. Note that you cannot use it as a root filesystem as it stands because the file ownership and the permissions are not set correctly. Buildroot uses a device table, as described in the previous chapter, to set ownership and permissions when the filesystem image is created in the `image/` directory.

Running

Some of the sample configurations have a corresponding entry in the `board/` directory, which contains custom configuration files and information about installing the results on the target. In the case of the system you have just built, the relevant file is `board/qemu/arm-versatile/readme.txt`, which tells you how to start QEMU with this target. Assuming that you have already installed `qemu-system-arm`, as described in *Chapter 1, Starting Out*, you can run it using this command:

```
$ qemu-system-arm -M versatilepb -m 256 \
-kernel output/images/zImage \
-dtb output/images/versatile-pb.dtb \
-drive file=output/images/rootfs.ext2,if=scsi,format=raw \
-append "root=/dev/sda console=ttyAMA0,115200" \
-serial stdio -net nic,model=rtl8139 -net user
```

There is a script named `MELP/Chapter06/run-qemu-buildroot.sh` in this book's code archive that includes that command. When QEMU boots up, you should see the kernel boot messages appear in the same Terminal window where you started QEMU, followed by a login prompt:

```
Booting Linux on physical CPU 0x0
Linux version 4.19.91 (frank@franktop) (gcc version 8.4.0
(Buildroot 2020.02.9)) #1 Sat Feb 13 11:54:41 PST 2021
CPU: ARM926EJ-S [41069265] revision 5 (ARMv5TEJ), cr=00093177
CPU: VIVT data cache, VIVT instruction cache
OF: fdt: Machine model: ARM Versatile PB
```

```
[...]
VFS: Mounted root (ext2 filesystem) readonly on device 8:0.
devtmpfs: mounted
Freeing unused kernel memory: 140K
This architecture does not have kernel memory protection.
Run /sbin/init as init process
EXT4-fs (sda): warning: mounting unchecked fs, running e2fsck is recommended
EXT4-fs (sda): re-mounted. Opts: (null)
Starting syslogd: OK
Starting klogd: OK
Running sysctl: OK
Initializing random number generator: OK
Saving random seed: random: dd: uninitialized urandom read (512 bytes read)
OK
Starting network: 8139cp 0000:00:0c.0 eth0: link up, 100Mbps, full-duplex, lpa 0x05E1
udhcpc: started, v1.31.1
random: mktemp: uninitialized urandom read (6 bytes read)
udhcpc: sending discover
udhcpc: sending select for 10.0.2.15
udhcpc: lease of 10.0.2.15 obtained, lease time 86400
deleting routers
random: mktemp: uninitialized urandom read (6 bytes read)
adding dns 10.0.2.3
OK

Welcome to Buildroot
buildroot login:
```

Log in as `root`, with no password.

You will see that QEMU launches a black window, in addition to the one with the kernel boot messages. It is there to display the graphics frame buffer of the target. In this case, the target never writes to the framebuffer, which is why it appears black. To close QEMU, either press *Ctrl* + *Alt* + *2* to get to the QEMU console and then type `quit`, or just close the framebuffer window.

Targeting real hardware

The steps for configuring and building a bootable image for the Raspberry Pi 4 are almost the same as for Arm QEMU:

```
$ cd buildroot
$ make clean
$ make raspberrypi4_64_defconfig
$ make
```

When the build finishes, the image is written to a file named `output/images/sdcard.img`. The `post-image.sh` script and the `genimage-raspberrypi4-64.cfg` configuration file used to write the image file are both located in the `board/raspberrypi/` directory. To write `sdcard.img` onto a microSD card and boot it on your Raspberry Pi 4, follow these steps:

1. Insert a microSD card into your Linux host machine.
2. Launch Etcher.
3. Click **Flash from file** from Etcher.
4. Locate the `sdcard.img` image that you built for the Raspberry Pi 4 and open it.
5. Click **Select target** from Etcher.
6. Select the microSD card that you inserted in *Step 1*.
7. Click **Flash** from Etcher to write the image.
8. Eject the microSD card when Etcher is done flashing.
9. Insert the microSD card into your Raspberry Pi 4.
10. Apply power to the Raspberry Pi 4 by way of the USB-C port.

Confirm that your Pi 4 booted successfully by plugging it into your Ethernet and observing that the network activity lights blink. In order to `ssh` into your Pi 4, you will need to add an SSH server such as `dropbear` or `openssh` to your Buildroot image configuration.

Creating a custom BSP

Next, let's use Buildroot to create a **Board Support Package (BSP)** for our Nova board using the same versions of U-Boot and Linux from earlier chapters. You can see the changes I made to Buildroot during this section in `MELP/Chapter06/buildroot`.

The recommended places to store your changes are as follows:

- `board/<organization>/<device>`: This contains any patches, binary blobs, extra build steps, configuration files for Linux, U-Boot, and other components.
- `configs/<device>_defconfig`: This contains the default configuration for the board.
- `package/<organization>/<package_name>`: This is the place where you can put any additional packages for this board.

Let's begin by creating a directory to store changes for the Nova board:

```
$ mkdir -p board/melp/nova
```

Next, clean the artifacts from any previous build, which you should always do when changing configurations:

```
$ make clean
```

Now, select the configuration for the BeagleBone, which we are going to use as the basis of the Nova configuration:

```
$ make beaglebone_defconfig
```

The `make beaglebone_defconfig` command configures Buildroot to build an image targeting the BeagleBone Black. This configuration is a good starting point, but we still need to customize it for our Nova board. Let's start by selecting the custom U-Boot patch we created for Nova.

U-Boot

In *Chapter 3, All about Bootloaders*, we created a custom bootloader for Nova based on the `2021.01` version of U-Boot and created a patch file for it, which you will find in `MELP/Chapter03/0001-BSP-for-Nova.patch`. We can configure Buildroot to select the same version and apply our patch. Begin by copying the patch file into `board/melp/nova`, and then use `make menuconfig` to set the U-Boot version to `2021.01`, the patch file to `board/melp/nova/0001-BSP-for-Nova.patch`, and the board name to Nova, as shown in the following screenshot:

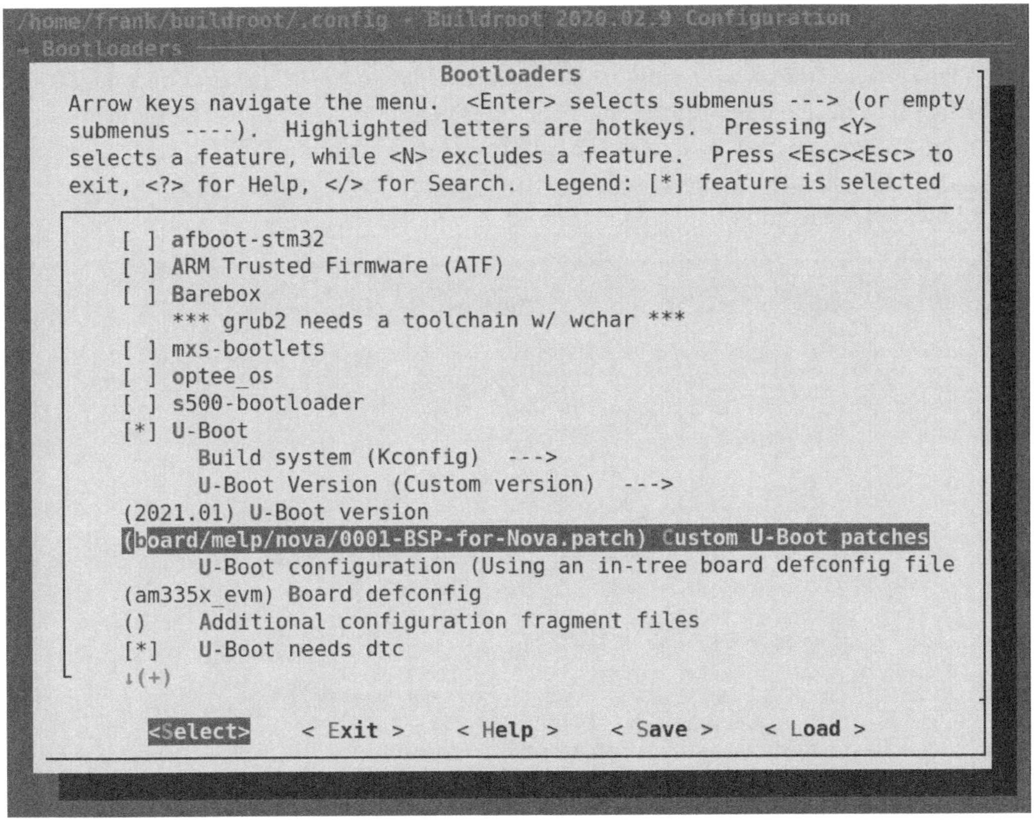

Figure 6.1 – Selecting custom U-Boot patches

We also need a U-Boot script to load the Nova device tree and the kernel from the SD card. We can put the file into `board/melp/nova/uEnv.txt`. It should contain these commands:

```
bootpart=0:1
bootdir=
bootargs=console=ttyO0,115200n8 root=/dev/mmcblk0p2 rw
rootfstype=ext4 rootwait
uenvcmd=fatload mmc 0:1 88000000 nova.dtb;fatload mmc 0:1
82000000 zImage;bootz 82000000 - 88000000
```

Note that despite the visible line wrapping, `bootargs` and `uenvcmd` are each defined on single lines. `rootfstype=ext4 rootwait` is part of `bootargs`, while `bootz 82000000 - 88000000` is part of `uenvcmd`.

Now that we've patched and configured U-Boot for our Nova board, the next step is patching and configuring the kernel.

Linux

In *Chapter 4*, *Configuring and Building the Kernel*, we based the kernel on Linux 5.4.50 and supplied a new device tree, which is in `MELP/Chapter04/nova.dts`. Copy the device tree to `board/melp/nova`, change the Buildroot kernel configuration to Linux version 5.4, and change the device tree source to `board/melp/nova/nova.dts`, as shown in the following screenshot:

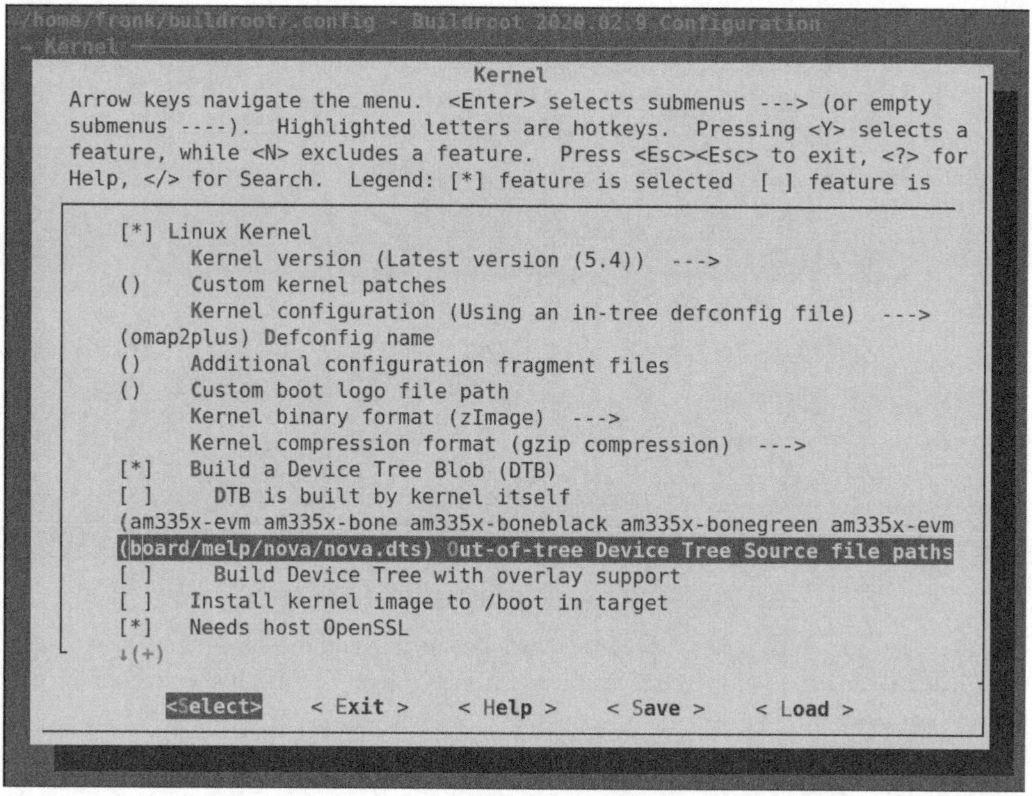

Figure 6.2 – Selecting the device tree source

We will also have to change the kernel series to be used for kernel headers so that they match the kernel being built:

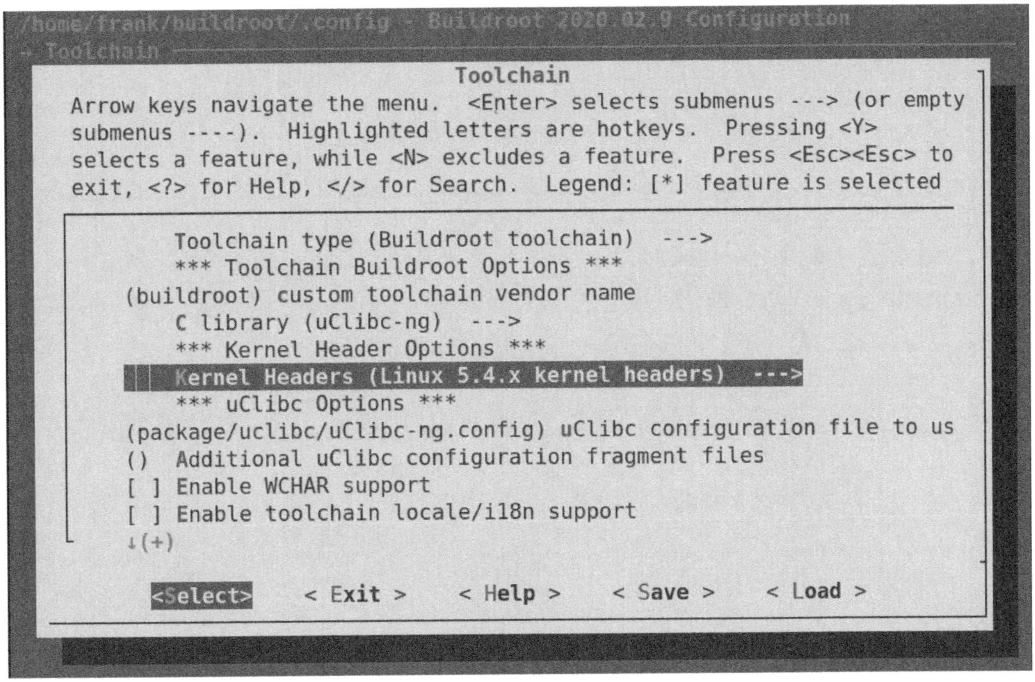

Figure 6.3 – Selecting custom kernel headers

Now that we've done this, let's build the system image, complete with the kernel and root filesystem.

Build

In the last stage of the build, Buildroot uses a tool named `genimage` to create an image for the SD card that we can copy directory to the card. We need a configuration file to lay out the image in the right way. We will name the file `board/melp/nova/genimage.cfg` and populate it, as shown here:

```
image boot.vfat {
    vfat {
        files = {
            "MLO",
            "u-boot.img",
            "zImage",
            "uEnv.txt",
            "nova.dtb",
        }
```

```
    }

    size = 16M
}

image sdcard.img {
    hdimage {
    }

    partition u-boot {
        partition-type = 0xC
        bootable = "true"
        image = "boot.vfat"
    }

    partition rootfs {
        partition-type = 0x83
        image = "rootfs.ext4"
        size = 512M
    }
}
```

This will create a file named `sdcard.img`, which contains two partitions named `u-boot` and `rootfs`. The first contains the boot files listed in `boot.vfat`, while the second contains the root filesystem image named `rootfs.ext4`, which will be generated by Buildroot.

Finally, we need to create a `post-image.sh` script that will call `genimage`, and thus create the SD card image. We will put it in `board/melp/nova/post-image.sh`:

```
#!/bin/sh
BOARD_DIR="$(dirname $0)"

cp ${BOARD_DIR}/uEnv.txt $BINARIES_DIR/uEnv.txt

GENIMAGE_CFG="${BOARD_DIR}/genimage.cfg"
GENIMAGE_TMP="${BUILD_DIR}/genimage.tmp"

```

```
rm -rf "${GENIMAGE_TMP}"

genimage \
    --rootpath "${TARGET_DIR}" \
    --tmppath "${GENIMAGE_TMP}" \
    --inputpath "${BINARIES_DIR}" \
    --outputpath "${BINARIES_DIR}" \
    --config "${GENIMAGE_CFG}"
```

This copies the `uEnv.txt` script into the `output/images` directory and runs `genimage` with our configuration file.

Note that `post-image.sh` needs to be executable; otherwise, the build will fail at the end:

```
$ chmod +x board/melp/nova/post-image.sh
```

Now, we can run `make menuconfig` again and drill down into the page. From that page, navigate down to **Custom scripts to run before creating filesystem images** and enter the path to our `post-image.sh` script, as shown in this screenshot:

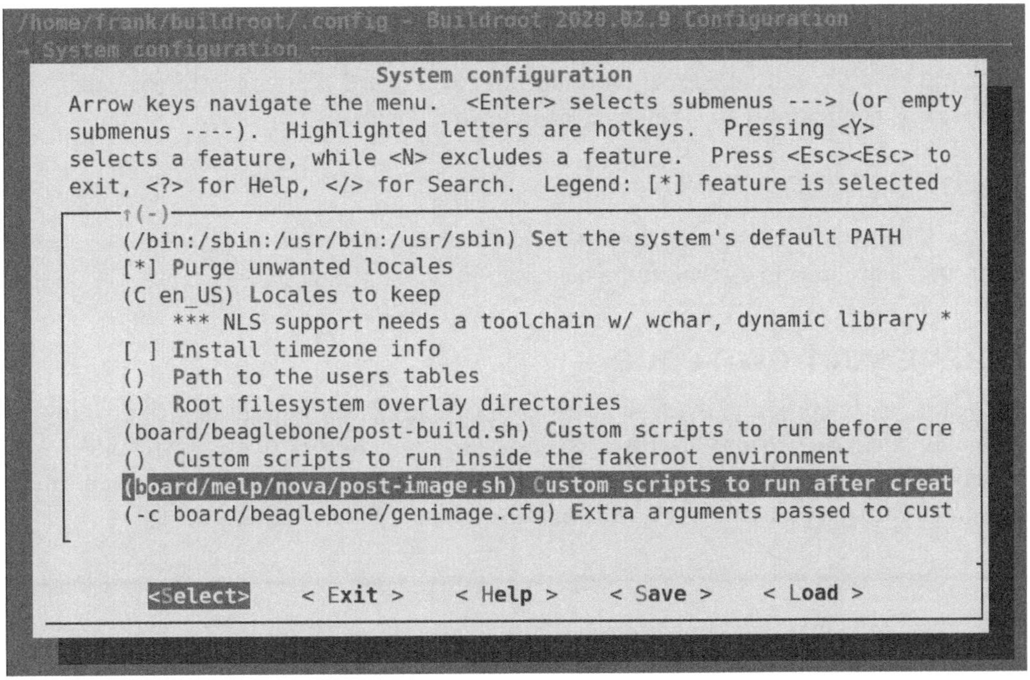

Figure 6.4 – Selecting custom scripts to run after creating filesystem images

Finally, you can build Linux for the Nova board just by typing `make`. When it has finished, you will see these files (and some additional DTBs) in the `output/images/` directory:

```
nova.dtb       sdcard.img      rootfs.ext2        u-boot.img
boot.vfat      rootfs.ext4     uEnv.txt           MLO
rootfs.tar     bzImage
```

To test it, insert a microSD card into your card reader and use Etcher to write `output/images/sdcard.img` out to an SD card, as we did for the Raspberry Pi 4. There is no need to format the microSD beforehand, as we did in the previous chapter, because `genimage` has created the exact disk layout required.

When Etcher finishes, insert the microSD card into the BeagleBone Black and power it on while pressing the Switch Boot button to force it to load from the SD card. You should see that it boots up with our selected versions of U-Boot, Linux, and with the Nova device tree.

Having shown that our custom configuration for the Nova board works, it would be nice to keep a copy of the configuration so that you and others can use it again, which you can do with this command:

```
$ make savedefconfig BR2_DEFCONFIG=configs/nova_defconfig
```

Now, you have a Buildroot configuration for the Nova board. Subsequently, you can retrieve this configuration by typing in the following command:

```
$ make nova_defconfig
```

We have successfully configured Buildroot. Now, what if you want to add your own code to it? We'll learn how to do that in the next section.

Adding your own code

Suppose there is a program that you have developed and that you want to include it in the build. You have two options: first, you can build it separately using its own build system, and then roll the binary into the final build as an overlay. Second, you can create a Buildroot package that can be selected from the menu and built like any other.

Overlays

An overlay is simply a directory structure that is copied over the top of the Buildroot root filesystem at a later stage in the build process. It can contain executables, libraries, and anything else you may want to include. Note that any compiled code must be compatible with the libraries that are deployed at runtime, which, in turn, means that it must be compiled with the same toolchain that Buildroot uses. Using the Buildroot toolchain is quite easy. Just add it to `PATH`:

```
$ PATH=<path_to_buildroot>/output/host/usr/bin:$PATH
```

The prefix for the toolchain is `<ARCH>-linux-`. So, to compile a simple program, you would do something like this:

```
$ PATH=/home/frank/buildroot/output/host/usr/bin:$PATH
$ arm-linux-gcc helloworld.c -o helloworld
```

Once you have compiled your program with the correct toolchain, you just need to install the executables and other supporting files into a staging area, and then mark it as an overlay for Buildroot. For the `helloworld` example, you might put it in the `board/melp/nova` directory:

```
$ mkdir -p board/melp/nova/overlay/usr/bin
$ cp helloworld board/melp/nova/overlay/usr/bin
```

Finally, you set `BR2_ROOTFS_OVERLAY` to the path pointing at the overlay. It can be configured in `menuconfig` with the **System configuration | Root filesystem overlay directories** option.

Adding a package

Buildroot packages (over 2,000 of them) are stored in the `package` directory, each in its own subdirectory. A package consists of at least two files: `Config.in`, containing the snippet of Kconfig code required to make the package visible in the configuration menu, and a Makefile named `<package_name>.mk`.

> **Important note**
>
> Note that a Buildroot package does not contain the code, just the instructions to get the code by downloading a tarball, doing `git pull` or whatever is necessary to obtain the upstream source.

The makefile is written in a format expected by Buildroot and contains directives that allow Buildroot to download, configure, compile, and install the program. Writing a new package makefile is a complex operation, and is covered in detail in *The Buildroot user manual*: `https://buildroot.org/downloads/manual/manual.html`. Here is an example that shows you how to create a package for a simple program stored locally, such as our `helloworld` program.

Begin by creating the `package/helloworld/` subdirectory with a configuration file, `Config.in`, which looks like this:

```
config BR2_PACKAGE_HELLOWORLD
    bool "helloworld"
    help
      A friendly program that prints Hello World! Every 10s
```

The first line must be of the `BR2_PACKAGE_<uppercase package name>` format. This is followed by a `bool` and the package name, as it will appear in the configuration menu, which will allow a user to select this package. The `help` section is optional but usually a good idea because it acts as self-documentation.

Next, link the new package to the **Target Packages** menu by editing `package/Config.in` and sourcing the configuration file, as shown here:

```
menu "My programs"
      source "package/helloworld/Config.in"
endmenu
```

You could append this new `helloworld` package to an existing submenu, but it's cleaner to create a new submenu, which only contains our package, and insert it before `menu "Audio and video applications"`.

After inserting `menu "My programs"` into `package/Config.in`, create a makefile, `package/helloworld/helloworld.mk`, to supply the data needed by Buildroot:

```
HELLOWORLD_VERSION = 1.0.0
HELLOWORLD_SITE = /home/frank/MELP/Chapter06/helloworld
HELLOWORLD_SITE_METHOD = local

define HELLOWORLD_BUILD_CMDS
    $(MAKE) CC="$(TARGET_CC)" LD="$(TARGET_LD)" -C $(@D) all
endef

```

```
define HELLOWORLD_INSTALL_TARGET_CMDS
    $(INSTALL) -D -m 0755 $(@D)/helloworld $(TARGET_DIR)/usr/
bin/helloworld
endef

$(eval $(generic-package))
```

You can find my `helloworld` package in this book's code archive in `MELP/Chapter06/buildroot/package/helloworld` and the source code for the program in `MELP/Chapter06/helloworld`. The location of the code is hardcoded to a local pathname. In a more realistic case, you would get the code from a source code system or from a central server of some kind: there are details on how to do this in *The Buildroot user manual*, and plenty of examples in other packages.

License compliance

Buildroot is based on a piece of open source software, as are the packages it compiles. At some point during the project, you should check the licenses, which you can do by running the following:

```
$ make legal-info
```

The information is gathered into `output/legal-info/`. There are summaries of the licenses used to compile the host tools in `host-manifest.csv` and, on the target, in `manifest.csv`. There is more information in the `README` file and in *The Buildroot user manual*.

We will revisit Buildroot again in *Chapter 14, Starting with BusyBox runit*. Now, let's switch build systems and start learning about the Yocto Project.

Introducing the Yocto Project

The Yocto Project is a more complex beast than Buildroot. Not only can it build toolchains, bootloaders, kernels, and root filesystems as Buildroot can, but it can generate an entire Linux distribution for you with binary packages that can be installed at runtime. The build process is structured around groups of recipes, similar to Buildroot packages but written using a combination of Python and shell script. The Yocto Project includes a task scheduler called **BitBake** that produces whatever you have configured, from the recipes. There is plenty of online documentation at `https://www.yoctoproject.org`.

Background

The structure of the Yocto Project makes more sense if you look at the background first. Its roots are in **OpenEmbedded** (`https://openembedded.org`), which, in turn, grew out of a number of projects to port Linux to various handheld computers, including the Sharp Zaurus and the Compaq iPaq. OpenEmbedded came to life in 2003 as the build system for those handheld computers. Soon after, other developers began to use it as a general build system for devices running embedded Linux. It was developed, and continues to be developed, by an enthusiastic community of programmers.

The OpenEmbedded project set out to create a set of binary packages using the compact IPK format, which could then be combined in various ways to create a target system and be installed on the target at runtime. It did this by creating recipes for each package and using BitBake as the task scheduler. It was, and is, very flexible. By supplying the right metadata, you can create an entire Linux distribution to your own specification. One that is fairly well-known is the **Ångström Distribution**, but there are many others as well.

At some time in 2005, Richard Purdie, then a developer at OpenedHand, created a fork of OpenEmbedded, which had a more conservative choice of packages, and created releases that were stable over a period of time. He named it **Poky** after the Japanese snack (if you are worried about these things, Poky is pronounced to rhyme with hockey). Although Poky was a fork, OpenEmbedded and Poky continued to run alongside each other, sharing updates and keeping the architectures more or less in step. Intel bought OpenedHand in 2008, and they transferred Poky Linux to the Linux Foundation in 2010 when they formed the Yocto Project.

Since 2010, the common components of OpenEmbedded and Poky have been combined into a separate project known as **OpenEmbedded Core**, or just **OE-Core**.

Therefore, the Yocto Project collects several components, the most important of which are as follows:

- **OE-Core**: This is the core metadata, and is shared with OpenEmbedded.
- **BitBake**: This is the task scheduler, and is shared with OpenEmbedded and other projects.
- **Poky**: This is the reference distribution.
- **Documentation**: This is the user's manuals and developer's guides for each component.
- **Toaster**: This is a web-based interface to BitBake and its metadata.

The Yocto Project provides a stable base, which can be used as-is or can be extended using **meta layers**, which I will discuss later in this chapter. Many SoC vendors provide BSPs for their devices in this way. Meta layers can also be used to create extended or just different build systems. Some are open source, such as the Ångström Distribution, while others are commercial, such as MontaVista Carrier Grade Edition, Mentor Embedded Linux, and Wind River Linux. The Yocto Project has a branding and compatibility testing scheme to ensure that there is interoperability between components. You will see statements such as "Yocto Project compatible" on various web pages.

Consequently, you should think of the Yocto Project as the foundation of a whole sector of embedded Linux, as well as being a complete build system in its own right.

> **Note**
>
> You may be wondering about the name, Yocto. *yocto* is the SI prefix for 10^{-24}, in the same way that *micro* is 10^{-6}. Why name the project Yocto? It was partly to indicate that it could build very small Linux systems (although, to be fair, so can other build systems), but also to steal a march on the Ångström Distribution, which is based on OpenEmbedded. An Ångström is 10^{-10}. That's huge, compared to a *yocto*!

Stable releases and supports

Usually, there is a release of the Yocto Project every 6 months: in April and October. They are principally known by their code names, but it is useful to know the version numbers of the Yocto Project and Poky as well. Here is a table of the six most recent releases at the time of writing:

Code name	Release date	Yocto version	Poky version
Gatesgarth	October 2020	3.2	24
Dunfell	April 2020	3.1	23
Zeus	October 2019	3.0	22
Warrior	April 2019	2.7	21
Thud	November 2018	2.6	20
Sumo	April 2018	2.5	19

The stable releases are supported with security and critical bug fixes for the current release cycle and the next cycle. In other words, each version is supported for approximately 12 months after the release. In addition, Dunfell is the first LTS release of Yocto. The LTS designation means that Dunfell will receive defect fixes and updates for an extended period of 2 years. Consequently, the plan going forward is to choose an LTS release of the Yocto Project every 2 years.

As with Buildroot, if you want continued support, you can update to the next stable release, or you can backport changes to your version. You also have the option of commercial support for periods of several years with the Yocto Project from operating system vendors, such as Mentor Graphics, Wind River, and many others. Now, let's learn how to install the Yocto Project.

Installing the Yocto Project

To get a copy of the Yocto Project, clone the repository, choosing the code name as the branch, which is `dunfell` in this case:

```
$ git clone -b dunfell git://git.yoctoproject.org/poky.git
```

It is good practice to run `git pull` periodically to grab the latest bug fixes and security patches from the remote branch.

Read the *Compatible Linux Distribution* and *Build Host Packages* sections of the *Yocto Project Quick Build* guide (`https://www.yoctoproject.org/docs/current/brief-yoctoprojectqs/brief-yoctoprojectqs.html`). Make sure that the essential packages for your Linux distribution are installed on your host computer. The next step is configuring.

Configuring

As with Buildroot, let's begin with a build for the QEMU Arm emulator. Begin by sourcing a script to set up the environment:

```
$ source poky/oe-init-build-env
```

This creates a working directory for you named `build/` and makes it the current directory. All of the configuration, as well as any intermediate and target image files, will be put in this directory. You must source this script each time you want to work on this project.

You can choose a different working directory by adding it as a parameter to `oe-init-build-env`; for example:

```
$ source poky/oe-init-build-env build-qemuarm
```

This will put you into the `build-qemuarm/` directory. This way, you can have several build directories, each for a different project: you choose which one you want to work with through the parameter that's passed to `oe-init-build-env`.

Initially, the build directory contains only one subdirectory named `conf/`, which contains the following configuration files for this project:

- `local.conf`: This contains a specification of the device you are going to build and the build environment.
- `bblayers.conf`: This contains the paths of the meta layers you are going to use. I will describe layers later on.

For now, we just need to set the `MACHINE` variable in `conf/local.conf` to `qemuarm` by removing the comment character (#) at the start of this line:

```
MACHINE ?= "qemuarm"
```

Now, we are ready to build our first image using Yocto.

Building

To actually perform the build, you need to run BitBake, telling it which root filesystem image you want to create. Some common images are as follows:

- `core-image-minimal`: This is a small console-based system that is useful for tests and as the basis for custom images.
- `core-image-minimal-initramfs`: This is similar to `core-image-minimal` but built as a ramdisk.
- `core-image-x11`: This is a basic image with support for graphics through an X11 server and the `xterminal` Terminal app.
- `core-image-full-cmdline`: This console-based system offers a standard CLI experience and full support for the target hardware.

By giving BitBake the final target, it will work backward and build all the dependencies first, beginning with the toolchain. For now, we just want to create a minimal image to see how it works:

```
$ bitbake core-image-minimal
```

The build is likely to take some time (probably more than an hour), even with several CPU cores and prodigious amounts of RAM. It will download about 10 GiB of source code, and it will consume about 40 GiB of disk space. When it is complete, you will find several new directories in the build directory, including `downloads/`, which contains all the source downloaded for the build, and `tmp/`, which contains most of the build artifacts. You should see the following in `tmp/`:

- `work/`: This contains the build directory and the staging area for the root filesystem.
- `deploy/`: This contains the final binaries to be deployed on the target:

  `deploy/images/[machine name]/`: Contains the bootloader, the kernel and the root filesystem images ready to be run on the target.

  `deploy/rpm/`: This contains the RPM packages that make up the images.

  `deploy/licenses/`: This contains the license files that are extracted from each package.

When the build is done, we can boot the finished image on QEMU.

Running the QEMU target

When you build a QEMU target, an internal version of QEMU is generated, which removes the need to install the QEMU package for your distribution, and thus avoids version dependencies. There is a wrapper script named `runqemu` we can use to run this version of QEMU.

To run the QEMU emulation, make sure that you have sourced `oe-init-build-env`, and then just type this:

```
$ runqemu qemuarm
```

In this case, QEMU has been configured with a graphic console so that the login prompt appears in a black framebuffer, as shown in the following screenshot:

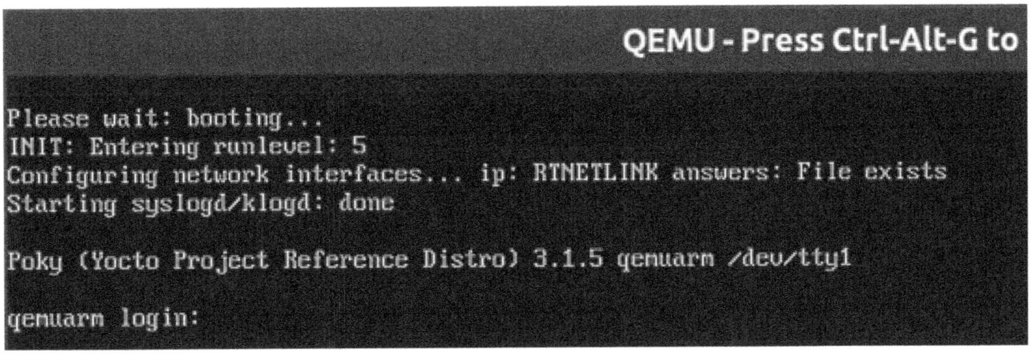
QEMU - Press Ctrl-Alt-G to
Please wait: booting...
INIT: Entering runlevel: 5
Configuring network interfaces... ip: RTNETLINK answers: File exists
Starting syslogd/klogd: done
Poky (Yocto Project Reference Distro) 3.1.5 qemuarm /dev/tty1
qemuarm login:

Figure 6.5 – QEMU graphic console

Log in as root, without a password. To close QEMU, close the framebuffer window.

To launch QEMU without the graphic window, add nographic to the command line:

```
$ runqemu qemuarm nographic
```

In this case, close QEMU using the key sequence *Ctrl* + *A* and then *x*.

The runqemu script has many other options. Type runqemu help for more information.

Layers

The metadata for the Yocto Project is structured into layers. By convention, each layer has a name beginning with meta. The core layers of the Yocto Project are as follows:

- meta: This is the OpenEmbedded core and contains some changes for Poky.
- meta-poky: This is the metadata specific to the Poky distribution.
- meta-yocto-bsp: This contains the board support packages for the machines that the Yocto Project supports.

The list of layers in which BitBake searches for recipes is stored in <your build directory>/conf/bblayers.conf and, by default, includes all three layers mentioned in the preceding list.

By structuring the recipes and other configuration data in this way, it is very easy to extend the Yocto Project by adding new layers. Additional layers are available from SoC manufacturers, the Yocto Project itself, and a wide range of people wishing to add value to the Yocto Project and OpenEmbedded. There is a useful list of layers at `http://layers.openembedded.org/layerindex/`. Here are some examples:

- `meta-qt5`: Qt 5 libraries and utilities
- `meta-intel`: BSPs for Intel CPUs and SoCs
- `meta-raspberrypi`: BSPs for the Raspberry Pi boards
- `meta-ti`: BSPs for TI Arm-based SoCs

Adding a layer is as simple as copying the `meta` directory to a suitable location and adding it to `bblayers.conf`. Make sure that you read the `REAMDE` file that should accompany each layer to see what dependencies it has on other layers, as well as which versions of the Yocto Project it is compatible with.

To illustrate the way layers work, let's create a layer for our Nova board, which we can use for the remainder of this chapter as we add features. You can view the complete implementation of the layer in the code archive in `MELP/Chapter06/meta-nova`.

Each meta layer has to have at least one configuration file, named `conf/layer.conf`, and it should also have the `README` file and a license.

To create our `meta-nova` layer, perform the following steps:

```
$ source poky/oe-init-build-env build-nova
$ bitbake-layers create-layer nova
$ mv nova ../meta-nova
```

This will put you in a working directory named `build-nova` and create a layer named `meta-nova` with a `conf/layer.conf`, an outline `README`, and an `MIT LICENSE` in `COPYING.MIT`. The `layer.conf` file looks like this:

```
# We have a conf and classes directory, add to BBPATH
BBPATH .= ":${LAYERDIR}"

# We have recipes-* directories, add to BBFILES
BBFILES += "${LAYERDIR}/recipes-*/*/*.bb \
            ${LAYERDIR}/recipes-*/*/*.bbappend"

BBFILE_COLLECTIONS += "nova"
```

```
BBFILE_PATTERN_nova = "^${LAYERDIR}/"
BBFILE_PRIORITY_nova = "6"

LAYERDEPENDS_nova = "core"
LAYERSERIES_COMPAT_nova = "dunfell"
```

It adds itself to `BBPATH` and the recipes it contains to `BBFILES`. From looking at the code, you can see that the recipes are found in the directories with names beginning with `recipes-` and have filenames ending in `.bb` (for normal BitBake recipes) or `.bbappend` (for recipes that extend existing recipes by overriding or adding to the instructions). This layer has the name `nova`, was added to the list of layers in `BBFILE_COLLECTIONS`, and has a priority of `6`. The layer's priority is used if the same recipe appears in several layers: the one in the layer with the highest priority wins.

Now, you need to add this layer to your build configuration using the following command:

```
$ bitbake-layers add-layer ../meta-nova
```

Make sure to run this command from your `build-nova` working directory after sourcing that environment.

You can confirm that your layer structure is set up correctly like this:

```
$ bitbake-layers show-layers
NOTE: Starting bitbake server...
layer                 path                                      priority
==========================================================================
meta                  /home/frank/poky/meta                            5
meta-poky             /home/frank/poky/meta-poky                       5
meta-yocto-bsp        /home/frank/poky/meta-yocto-bsp                  5
meta-nova             /home/frank/meta-nova                            6
```

Here, you can see the new layer. It has a priority of `6`, which means that we could override recipes in the other layers, which all have a lower priority.

At this point, it would be a good idea to run a build using this empty layer. The final target will be the Nova board but, for now, build for the BeagleBone Black by uncommenting `MACHINE ?= "beaglebone-yocto"` in `conf/local.conf`. Then, build a small image using `bitbake core-image-minimal`, as you did previously.

As well as recipes, layers may contain BitBake classes, configuration files for machines, distributions, and more. I will look at recipes next and show you how to create a customized image and how to create a package.

BitBake and recipes

BitBake processes metadata of several different types, including the following:

- **Recipes**: Files ending in `.bb`. These contain information about building a unit of software, including how to get a copy of the source code, the dependencies of other components, and how to build and install it.
- **Append**: Files ending in `.bbappend`. These allow some details of a recipe to be overridden or extended. A `bbappend` file simply appends its instructions to the end of a recipe (`.bb`) file of the same root name.
- **Include**: Files ending in `.inc`. These contain information that is common to several recipes, allowing information to be shared among them. The files may be included using the **include** or **require** keywords. The difference is that `require` produces an error if the file does not exist, whereas `include` does not.
- **Classes**: Files ending in `.bbclass`. These contain common build information; for example, how to build a kernel or how to build an autotools project. The classes are inherited and extended in recipes and other classes using the `inherit` keyword. The `classes/base.bbclass` class is implicitly inherited in every recipe.
- **Configuration**: Files ending in `.conf`. They define various configuration variables that govern the project's build process.

A recipe is a collection of tasks written in a combination of Python and shell script. The tasks have names such as `do_fetch`, `do_unpack`, `do_patch`, `do_configure`, `do_compile`, and `do_install`. You use BitBake to execute these tasks. The default task is `do_build`, which performs all the subtasks required to build the recipe. You can list the tasks available in a recipe using `bitbake -c listtasks [recipe]`. For example, you can list the tasks in `core-image-minimal` like this:

```
$ bitbake -c listtasks core-image-minimal
```

> **Important note**
>
> The `-c` option tells BitBake to run a specific task from a recipe without having to include the `do_` part at the beginning of the task's name.

The `do_listtasks` task is simply a special task that lists all the tasks defined within a recipe. Another example is the `fetch` task, which downloads the source code for a recipe:

```
$ bitbake -c fetch busybox
```

To get the code for a target and all its dependencies, which is useful when you want to make sure you have downloaded all the code for the image you are about to build, use the following command:

```
$ bitbake core-image-minimal --runall=fetch
```

The recipe files are usually named `<package-name>_<version>.bb`. They may have dependencies on other recipes, which would allow BitBake to work out all the subtasks that need to be executed to complete the top-level job.

As an example, to create a recipe for our `helloworld` program in `meta-nova`, you would create a directory structure like this:

```
meta-nova/recipes-local/helloworld
├── files
│   └── helloworld.c
└── helloworld_1.0.bb
```

The recipe is `helloworld_1.0.bb` and the source is local to the recipe directory in the `files/` subdirectory. The recipe contains these instructions:

```
DESCRIPTION = "A friendly program that prints Hello World!"
PRIORITY = "optional"
SECTION = "examples"

LICENSE = "GPLv2"
LIC_FILES_CHKSUM = "file://${COMMON_LICENSE_DIR}/GPL-2.0;md5=80
1f80980d171dd6425610833a22dbe6"

SRC_URI = "file://helloworld.c"

S = "${WORKDIR}"

do_compile() {
    ${CC} ${CFLAGS} ${LDFLAGS} helloworld.c -o helloworld
```

```
}

do_install() {
     install -d ${D}${bindir}
     install -m 0755 helloworld ${D}${bindir}
}
```

The location of the source code is set by SRC_URI. In this case, the file:// URI means that the code is local to the recipe directory. BitBake will search the files/, helloworld/, and helloworld-1.0/ directories, relative to the directory that contains the recipe. The tasks that need to be defined are do_compile and do_install, which compile the source file and install it into the target root filesystem: ${D} expands to the staging area of the recipe and ${bindir} to the default binary directory; that is, /usr/bin.

Every recipe has a license, defined by LICENSE, which is set to GPLv2 here. The file containing the text of the license and a checksum is defined by LIC_FILES_CHKSUM. BitBake will terminate the build if the checksum does not match, indicating that the license has changed in some way. Note that the MD5 checksum value and COMMON_LICENSE_DIR are on the same line, separated by a semicolon. The license file may be part of the package or it may point to one of the standard license texts in meta/files/common-licenses/, as is the case here.

By default, commercial licenses are disallowed, but it is easy to enable them. You need to specify the license in the recipe, as shown here:

```
LICENSE_FLAGS = "commercial"
```

Then, in your conf/local.conf file, you would explicitly allow this license, like so:

```
LICENSE_FLAGS_WHITELIST = "commercial"
```

Now, to make sure that our helloworld recipe compiles correctly, you can ask BitBake to build it, like so:

```
$ bitbake helloworld
```

If all goes well, you should see that it has created a working directory for it in tmp/work/cortexa8hf-neon-poky-linux-gnueabi/helloworld/. You should also see that there is an RPM package for it in tmp/deploy/rpm/cortexa8hf_neon/helloworld-1.0-r0.cortexa8hf_neon.rpm.

It is not part of the target image yet, though. The list of packages to be installed is held in a variable named IMAGE_INSTALL. You can append it to the end of that list by adding this line to conf/local.conf:

```
IMAGE_INSTALL_append = " helloworld"
```

Note that there has to be a space between the opening double quote and the first package name. Now, the package will be added to any image that you bitbake:

```
$ bitbake core-image-minimal
```

If you look in tmp/deploy/images/beaglebone-yocto/core-image-minimal-beaglebone-yocto.tar.bz2, you will see that /usr/bin/helloworld has indeed been installed.

Customizing images via local.conf

You may often want to add a package to an image during development or tweak it in other ways. As shown previously, you can simply append to the list of packages to be installed by adding a statement like this:

```
IMAGE_INSTALL_append = " strace helloworld"
```

You can make more sweeping changes via EXTRA_IMAGE_FEATURES. Here is a short list that should give you an idea of the features you can enable:

- dbg-pkgs: This installs debug symbol packages for all the packages installed in the image.
- debug-tweaks: This allows root logins without passwords and other changes that make development easier.
- package-management: This installs package management tools and preserves the package manager database.
- read-only-rootfs: This makes the root filesystem read-only. We will cover this in more detail in *Chapter 9, Creating a Storage Strategy*.
- x11: This installs the X server.
- x11-base: This installs the X server with a minimal environment.
- x11-sato: This installs the OpenedHand Sato environment.

There are many more features that you can add in this way. I recommend that you look at the *Image Features* section of the *Yocto Project Reference Manual* at `https://www.yoctoproject.org/docs/latest/ref-manual/ref-manual.html`, and also read through the code in `meta/classes/core-image.bbclass`.

Writing an image recipe

The problem with making changes to `local.conf` is that they are, well, local. If you want to create an image that is to be shared with other developers or to be loaded onto a production system, then you should put the changes into an **image recipe**.

An image recipe contains instructions about how to create the image files for a target, including the bootloader, the kernel, and the root filesystem images. By convention, image recipes are put into a directory named `images`, so you can get a list of all the images that are available by using this command:

```
$ ls meta*/recipes*/images/*.bb
```

You will find that the recipe for `core-image-minimal` is in `meta/recipes-core/images/core-image-minimal.bb`.

A simple approach is to take an existing image recipe and modify it using statements similar to those you used in `local.conf`.

For example, imagine that you want an image that is the same as `core-image-minimal` but includes your `helloworld` program and the `strace` utility. You can do that with a two-line recipe file, which includes (using the `require` keyword) the base image and adds the packages you want. It is conventional to put the image in a directory named `images`, so add the `nova-image.bb` recipe with the following content to `meta-nova/recipes-local/images`:

```
require recipes-core/images/core-image-minimal.bb
IMAGE_INSTALL += "helloworld strace"
```

Now, you can remove the `IMAGE_INSTALL_append` line from your `local.conf` and build it using this:

```
$ bitbake nova-image
```

This time, the build should proceed much more quickly because BitBake reuses the products left over from building `core-image-minimal`.

Not only does BitBake build images for running on a target device, but it can also build an SDK for developing on a host machine.

Creating an SDK

It is very useful to be able to create a standalone toolchain that other developers can install, avoiding the need for everyone in the team to have a full installation of the Yocto Project. Ideally, you want the toolchain to include development libraries and header files for all the libraries installed on the target. You can do that for any image using the `populate_sdk` task, as shown here:

```
$ bitbake -c populate_sdk nova-image
```

The result is a self-installing shell script in `tmp/deploy/sdk`:

```
poky-<c_library>-<host_machine>-<target_image><target_machine>-
toolchain-<version>.sh
```

For the SDK built with the `nova-image` recipe, it is this:

```
poky-glibc-x86_64-nova-image-cortexa8hf-neon-beaglebone-yocto-
toolchain-3.1.5.sh
```

If you only want a basic toolchain with just C and C++ cross compilers, the C library, and header files, you can run this instead:

```
$ bitbake meta-toolchain
```

To install the SDK, just run the shell script. The default install directory is `/opt/poky`, but the install script allows you to change this:

```
$ tmp/deploy/sdk/poky-glibc-x86_64-nova-image-cortexa8hf-neon-
beaglebone-yocto-toolchain-3.1.5.sh
Poky (Yocto Project Reference Distro) SDK installer version
3.1.5
================================================================
Enter target directory for SDK (default: /opt/poky/3.1.5):
You are about to install the SDK to "/opt/poky/3.1.5". Proceed
[Y/n]? Y
[sudo] password for frank:
Extracting SDK...........................................done
Setting it up...done
```

```
SDK has been successfully set up and is ready to be used.
Each time you wish to use the SDK in a new shell session, you need to source the environment setup script e.g.
$ . /opt/poky/3.1.5/environment-setup-cortexa8hf-neon-poky-linux-gnueabi
```

To make use of the toolchain, first, source the environment and set up the script:

```
$ source /opt/poky/3.1.5/environment-setup-cortexa8hf-neon-poky-linux-gnueabi
```

> **Tip**
>
> The `environment-setup-*` script that sets things up for the SDK is not compatible with the `oe-init-build-env` script that you source when working in the Yocto Project build directory. It is a good rule to always start a new Terminal session before you source either script.

The toolchain generated by the Yocto Project does not have a valid `sysroot` directory. We know this to be true because passing the `-print-sysroot` option to the toolchain's compiler returns `/not/exist`:

```
$ arm-poky-linux-gnueabi-gcc -print-sysroot
/not/exist
```

Consequently, if you try to cross compile, as I have shown in previous chapters, it will fail, like this:

```
$ arm-poky-linux-gnueabi-gcc helloworld.c -o helloworld
helloworld.c:1:10: fatal error: stdio.h: No such file or directory
    1 | #include <stdio.h>
      |          ^~~~~~~~~
compilation terminated.
```

This is because the compiler has been configured to work for a wide range of Arm processors, and the fine-tuning is done when you launch it using the right set of flags. Instead, you should use the shell variables that are created when you source the `environment-setup` script for cross compiling. It includes the following:

- `CC`: C compiler
- `CXX`: C++ compiler

- `CPP`: C preprocessor
- `AS`: Assembler
- `LD`: Linker

As an example, this is what we find that `CC` has been set to:

```
$ echo $CC
arm-poky-linux-gnueabi-gcc -mfpu=neon -mfloat-abi=hard
-mcpu=cortex-a8 -fstack-protector-strong -D_FORTIFY_SOURCE=2
-Wformat -Wformat-security -Werror=format-security --sysroot=/
opt/poky/3.1.5/sysroots/cortexa8hf-neon-poky-linux-gnueabi
```

So long as you use `$CC` to compile, everything should work fine:

```
$ $CC -O helloworld.c -o helloworld
```

Next, we will look at the license audit.

The license audit

The Yocto Project insists that each package has a license. A copy of the license is placed in `tmp/deploy/licenses/[package name]` for each package as it is built. In addition, a summary of the packages and licenses used in an image are put into the `<image name>-<machine name>-<date stamp>/` directory. For `nova-image`, which we just built, the directory would be named something like this:

```
tmp/deploy/licenses/nova-image-beaglebone-yocto-20210214072839/
```

This completes our survey of the two leading build systems for embedded Linux. Buildroot is simple and quick, making it a good choice for fairly simple single-purpose devices: traditional embedded Linux, as I like to think of them. The Yocto Project is more complex and flexible. Even though there is good support throughout the community and industry for the Yocto Project, the tool still has a very steep learning curve. You can expect it to take several months for you to become proficient with Yocto, and even then, it will sometimes do things that you don't expect.

Summary

In this chapter, you learned how to use both Buildroot and the Yocto Project to configure, customize, and build embedded Linux images. We used Buildroot to create a BSP with a custom U-Boot patch and device tree specification for a hypothetical board based on the BeagleBone Black. We then learned how to add our own code to an image in the form of a Buildroot package. You were also introduced to the Yocto Project, which we will cover in depth in the next two chapters. In particular, you learned some basic BitBake terminology, how to write an image recipe, and how to create an SDK.

Don't forget that any devices you create using these tools will need to be maintained in the field for a period of time, often over many years. Both the Yocto Project and Buildroot provide point releases for about 1 year after the initial release, and the Yocto Project now offers long term support for at least 2 years. In either case, you will find yourself having to maintain your release yourself; otherwise, you will be paying for commercial support. The third possibility, ignoring the problem, should not be considered as an option!

In the next chapter, we will look at file storage and filesystems, and at the ways that the choices you make there will affect the stability and maintainability of your embedded Linux system.

Further reading

The following resources contain more information about the topics that were introduced in this chapter:

- *The Buildroot user manual*, Buildroot Association: `http://buildroot.org/downloads/manual/manual.html`
- *Yocto Project documentation*, Yocto Project: `https://www.yoctoproject.org/documentation`
- *Embedded Linux Development Using the Yocto Project Cookbook*, by Alex González

7
Developing with Yocto

Bringing up Linux on unsupported hardware can be a painstaking process. Luckily, Yocto provides **Board Support Packages** (**BSPs**) to bootstrap embedded Linux development on popular single-board computers such as the BeagleBone Black and Raspberry Pi 4. Building on top of an existing BSP layer lets us quickly take advantage of complex built-in peripherals such as Bluetooth and Wi-Fi. In this chapter, we will create a custom application layer to do just that.

Next, we will look at the development workflow that's enabled by Yocto's extensible SDK. Modifying software running on a target device usually means swapping out the SD card. Since rebuilding and redeploying full images is too time-consuming, I will show you how to use `devtool` to quickly automate and iterate over your work. While doing so, you will learn how to save your work in your own layers so that it does not get lost.

Yocto not only builds Linux images but entire Linux distributions. We will discuss the reasons why you would do that before going through the motions of assembling our own Linux distribution. The many choices we will make include whether or not to add runtime package management for rapid application development on the target device. This comes at the cost of having to maintain a package database and remote package server, which I will touch on last.

In this chapter, we will cover the following topics:

- Building on top of an existing BSP
- Capturing changes with `devtool`
- Building your own distro
- Provisioning a remote package server

Let's get started!

Technical requirements

To follow along with the examples in this chapter, make sure you have the following:

- A Linux-based host system with a minimum of 60 GB available disk space
- Yocto 3.1 (Dunfell) LTS release
- Etcher for Linux
- A microSD card reader and card
- A Raspberry Pi 4
- A 5V 3A USB-C power supply
- An Ethernet cable and port for network connectivity
- A Wi-Fi router
- A smartphone with Bluetooth

You should have already built the 3.1 (Dunfell) LTS release of Yocto in *Chapter 6, Selecting a Build System*. If you have not, then please refer to the *Compatible Linux Distribution* and *Build Host Packages* sections of the *Yocto Project Quick Build* guide (`https://www.yoctoproject.org/docs/current/brief-yoctoprojectqs/brief-yoctoprojectqs.html`) before building Yocto on your Linux host according to the instructions in *Chapter 6*.

All the code for this chapter can be found in the `Chapter07` folder of this book's GitHub repository: `https://github.com/PacktPublishing/Mastering-Embedded-Linux-Programming-Third-Edition`.

Building on top of an existing BSP

A **Board Support Package** (**BSP**) layer adds support for a particular hardware device or family of devices to Yocto. This support usually includes the bootloader, device tree blobs, and additional kernel drivers needed to boot Linux on that specific hardware. A BSP may also include any additional user space software and peripheral firmware needed to fully enable and utilize all the features of the hardware. By convention, BSP layer names start with the `meta-` prefix, followed by the machine's name. Locating the best BSP for your target device is the first step toward building a bootable image for it using Yocto.

The OpenEmbedded layer index (`https://layers.openembedded.org/layerindex`) is the best place to start looking for quality BSPs. Your board's manufacturer or silicon vendor may also offer BSP layers. The Yocto Project provides a BSP for all variants of the Raspberry Pi. You can find the GitHub repository for that BSP layer and all the other layers endorsed by the Yocto project among the Yocto Project source repositories (`https://git.yoctoproject.org`).

Building an existing BSP

The following exercises assume you have already cloned or extracted the Dunfell release of Yocto to a directory named `poky` within your host environment. Before proceeding, we also need to clone the following dependency layers one level up from that `poky` directory so that the layer and `poky` directories sit next to each other:

```
$ git clone -b dunfell git://git.openembedded.org/meta-openembedded
$ git clone -b dunfell git://git.yoctoproject.org/meta-raspberrypi
```

Notice that the branch name of the dependency layers matches the Yocto release for compatibility. Keep all three clones up to date and in sync with their remotes using periodic `git pull` commands. The `meta-raspberrypi` layer is the BSP for all Raspberry Pis. Once these dependencies are in place, you can build an image that's been customized for the Raspberry Pi 4. But before we do that, let's explore the recipes for Yocto's generic images:

1. First, navigate to the directory where you cloned Yocto:

   ```
   $ cd poky
   ```

2. Next, move down into the directory where the recipes for the standard images are:

   ```
   $ cd meta/recipes-core/images
   ```

3. List the core image recipes:

```
$ ls -1 core*
core-image-base.bb
core-image-minimal.bb
core-image-minimal-dev.bb
core-image-minimal-initramfs.bb
core-image-minimal-mtdutils.bb
core-image-tiny-initramfs.bb
```

4. Display the `core-image-base` recipe:

```
$ cat core-image-base.bb
SUMMARY = "A console-only image that fully supports the target device \
hardware."

IMAGE_FEATURES += "splash"

LICENSE = "MIT"

inherit core-image
```

   Notice that this recipe inherits from `core-image`, so it's importing the contents of `core-image.bbclass`, which we will look at later.

5. Display the `core-image-minimal` recipe:

```
$ cat core-image-minimal.bb
SUMMARY = "A small image just capable of allowing a device to boot."

IMAGE_INSTALL = "packagegroup-core-boot ${CORE_IMAGE_EXTRA_INSTALL}"

IMAGE_LINGUAS = " "

LICENSE = "MIT"

```

```
inherit core-image

IMAGE_ROOTFS_SIZE ?= "8192"
IMAGE_ROOTFS_EXTRA_SPACE_append = "${@bb.utils.
contains("DISTRO_FEATURES", "systemd", " + 4096", ""
,d)}"
```

Like `core-image-base`, this recipe also inherits from the `core-image` class file.

6. Display the `core-image-minimal-dev` recipe:

```
$ cat core-image-minimal-dev.bb
require core-image-minimal.bb

DESCRIPTION = "A small image just capable of allowing a
device to boot and \
is suitable for development work."

IMAGE_FEATURES += "dev-pkgs"
```

Notice that this recipe requires the `core-image-minimal` recipe from the previous step. Recall that the `require` directive works much like `include`. Also, notice that `dev-pkgs` is appended to the list of `IMAGE_FEATURES`.

7. Navigate up to the `classes` directory under `poky/meta`:

```
$ cd ../../classes
```

8. Lastly, display the `core-image` class file:

```
$ cat core-image.bbclass
```

Notice the long list of available `IMAGE_FEATURES` at the top of this class file, including the aforementioned `dev-pkgs` feature.

Standard images such as `core-image-minimal` and `core-image-minimal-dev` are machine-agnostic. In *Chapter 6, Selecting a Build System*, we built `core-image-minimal` for both the QEMU Arm emulator and the BeagleBone Black. We could have just as easily built a `core-image-minimal` image for the Raspberry Pi 4. In contrast, a BSP layer includes image recipes intended for a specific board or series of boards.

Now, let's take a look at the `rpi-test-image` recipe inside the `meta-rasberrypi` BSP layer, to see how support for Wi-Fi and Bluetooth is added to `core-image-base` for the Raspberry Pi 4:

1. First, navigate one level above the directory where you cloned Yocto:

```
$ cd ../../..
```

2. Next, move down into the directory inside the `meta-raspberrypi` BSP layer, which is where the image recipes for the Raspberry Pis are:

```
$ cd meta-raspberrypi/recipes-core/images
```

3. List the Raspberry Pi image recipes:

```
$ ls -1
rpi-basic-image.bb
rpi-hwup-image.bb
rpi-test-image.bb
```

4. Display the `rpi-test-image` recipe:

```
$ cat rpi-test-image.bb
# Base this image on core-image-base
include recipes-core/images/core-image-base.bb

COMPATIBLE_MACHINE = "^rpi$"

IMAGE_INSTALL_append = " packagegroup-rpi-test"
```

   Notice that the `IMAGE_INSTALL` variable has been overridden so that it can append `packagegroup-rpi-test` and include those packages on the image.

5. Navigate to the neighboring `packagegroups` directory under `meta-raspberrypi/recipes-core`:

```
$ cd ../packagegroups
```

6. Lastly, display the `packagegroup-rpi-test` recipe:

```
$ cat packagegroup-rpi-test.bb
DESCRIPTION = "RaspberryPi Test Packagegroup"
LICENSE = "MIT"
```

```
LIC_FILES_CHKSUM = "file://${COMMON_LICENSE_DIR}/
MIT;md5=0835ade698e0bcf8506ecda2f7b4f302"

PACKAGE_ARCH = "${MACHINE_ARCH}"

inherit packagegroup

COMPATIBLE_MACHINE = "^rpi$"

OMXPLAYER  = "${@bb.utils.contains('MACHINE_FEATURES',
'vc4graphics', '', 'omxplayer', d)}"

RDEPENDS_${PN} = "\
    ${OMXPLAYER} \
    bcm2835-tests \
    rpio \
    rpi-gpio \
    pi-blaster \
    python3-rtimu \
    python3-sense-hat \
    connman \
    connman-client \
    wireless-regdb-static \
    bluez5 \
"
RRECOMMENDS_${PN} = "\
    ${@bb.utils.contains("BBFILE_COLLECTIONS", "meta-
multimedia", "bigbuckbunny-1080p bigbuckbunny-480p
bigbuckbunny-720p", "", d)} \
    ${MACHINE_EXTRA_RRECOMMENDS} \
"
```

Notice that the `connman`, `connman-client`, and `bluez5` packages are included in the list of runtime dependencies so that Wi-Fi and Bluetooth are fully enabled.

Finally, let's build `rpi-test-image` for the Raspberry Pi 4:

1. First, navigate one level above the directory where you cloned Yocto:

```
$ cd ../../..
```

2. Next, set up your BitBake work environment:

```
$ source poky/oe-init-build-env build-rpi
```

This sets up a bunch of environment variables and puts you in a newly created `build-rpi` directory.

3. Then, add the following layers to your image:

```
$ bitbake-layers add-layer ../meta-openembedded/meta-oe
$ bitbake-layers add-layer ../meta-openembedded/meta-python
$ bitbake-layers add-layer ../meta-openembedded/meta-networking
$ bitbake-layers add-layer ../meta-openembedded/meta-multimedia
$ bitbake-layers add-layer ../meta-raspberrypi
```

The order in which you add these layers matters because the `meta-networking` and `meta-multimedia` layers both depend on the `meta-python` layer. If `bitbake-layers add-layer` or `bitbake-layers show-layers` starts failing due to parse errors, then delete the `build-rpi` directory and restart this exercise from *Step 1*.

4. Verify that all the necessary layers have been added to the image:

```
$ bitbake-layers show-layers
```

There should be a total of eight layers in the list: `meta`, `meta-poky`, `meta-yocto-bsp`, `meta-oe`, `meta-python`, `meta-networking`, `meta-multimedia`, and `meta-raspberrypi`.

5. Observe the changes that the preceding `bitbake-layers add-layer` commands made to `bblayers.conf`:

```
$ cat conf/bblayers.conf
```

The same eight layers from the previous step should be assigned to the `BBLAYERS` variable.

6. List the machines supported by the meta-raspberrypi BSP layer:

```
$ ls ../meta-raspberrypi/conf/machine
```

   Notice that there are raspberrypi4 and raspberrypi4-64 machine configurations.

7. Add the following line to your conf/local.conf file:

```
MACHINE = "raspberrypi4-64"
```

   This overrides the following default in your conf/local.conf file:

```
MACHINE ??= "qemux86-64"
```

   Setting the MACHINE variable to raspberrypi4-64 ensures that the image we're about to build works for the Raspberry Pi 4.

8. Now, append ssh-server-openssh to the list of EXTRA_IMAGE_FEATURES in your conf/local.conf file:

```
EXTRA_IMAGE_FEATURES ?= "debug-tweaks ssh-server-openssh"
```

   This adds an SSH server to our image for local network access.

9. Lastly, build the image:

```
$ bitbake rpi-test-image
```

   The build could take anywhere from minutes to hours to complete the first time you run it, depending on how many CPU cores your host environment has available. TARGET_SYS should be aarch64-poky-linux, while MACHINE should be raspberrypi4-64, since this image is targeting 64-bit for the Arm Cortex-A72 cores in the Pi 4.

Once the image has finished building, there should be a file named rpi-test-image-raspberrypi4-64.rootfs.wic.bz2 in the tmp/deploy/images/raspberrypi4-64 directory:

```
$ ls -l tmp/deploy/images/raspberrypi4-64/rpi-test*wic.bz2
```

Notice that rpi-test-image-raspberrypi4-64.rootfs.wic.bz2 is a symbolic link pointing to the actual image file in the same directory. An integer denoting the date and time of the build is appended to the image filename before the wic.bz2 extension.

Now, write that image to a microSD card using Etcher and boot it on your Raspberry Pi 4:

1. Insert a microSD card into your host machine.
2. Launch Etcher.
3. Click **Flash from file** from Etcher.
4. Locate the `wic.bz2` image that you built for the Raspberry Pi 4 and open it.
5. Click **Select target** from Etcher.
6. Select the microSD card that you inserted in *Step 1*.
7. Click **Flash** from Etcher to write the image.
8. Eject the microSD card when Etcher is done flashing.
9. Insert the microSD card into your Raspberry Pi 4.
10. Apply power to the Raspberry Pi 4 by way of its USB-C port.

Confirm that your Pi 4 booted successfully by plugging it into your Ethernet and observing that the network activity lights blink.

Controlling Wi-Fi

In the previous exercise, we built a bootable image for the Raspberry Pi 4 that includes working Ethernet, Wi-Fi, and Bluetooth. Now that the device has booted and connected to your local network via Ethernet, let's connect to a nearby Wi-Fi network. We will use `connman` for this exercise since that is what the `meta-raspberrypi` layer ships with out of the box. Other BSP layers rely on different network interface configuration daemons such as `system-networkd` and `NetworkManager`. Follow these steps:

1. The image we built has a hostname of `raspberrypi4-64`, so you should be able to `ssh` into the device as `root`:

   ```
   $ ssh root@raspberrypi4-64.local
   ```

   Enter `yes` when you're asked if you want to continue connecting. You will not be prompted for a password. If no host is found at `raspberrypi4-64.local`, use a tool such as `arp-scan` to locate the IP address of your Raspberry Pi 4 and `ssh` into that instead of doing so by hostname.

2. Once you are in, verify that the Wi-Fi driver is on board:

```
root@raspberrypi4-64:~# lsmod | grep 80211
cfg80211              753664  1 brcmfmac
rfkill                 32768  6 nfc,bluetooth,cfg80211
```

3. Start `connman-client`:

```
root@raspberrypi4-64:~# connmanctl
connmanctl>
```

4. Turn on Wi-Fi:

```
connmanctl> enable wifi
Enabled wifi
```

Disregard `"Error wifi: Already enabled"` if the Wi-Fi is already on.

5. Register `connmanctl` as the connection agent:

```
connmanctl> agent on
Agent registered
```

6. Scan for Wi-Fi networks:

```
connmanctl> scan wifi
Scan completed for wifi
```

7. List all the available Wi-Fi networks:

```
connmanctl> services
*AO Wired                ethernet_dca6320a8ead_cable
    RT-AC66U_B1_38_2G    wifi_
dca6320a8eae_52542d41433636555f42315f33385f3247_managed_
psk
    RT-AC66U_B1_38_5G    wifi_
dca6320a8eae_52542d41433636555f42315f33385f3547_managed_
psk
```

`RT-AC66U_B1_38_2G` and `RT-AC66U_B1_38_5G` are Wi-Fi network SSIDs for an ASUS router. Your list will look different. The `*AO` part before `Wired` indicates that the device is currently online via Ethernet.

8. Connect to a Wi-Fi network:

```
connmanctl> connect wifi_
dca6320a8eae_52542d41433636555f42315f33385f3547_managed_
psk
Agent RequestInput wifi_
dca6320a8eae_52542d41433636555f42315f33385f3547_managed_
psk
  Passphrase = [ Type=psk, Requirement=mandatory ]
Passphrase? somepassword
Connected wifi_
dca6320a8eae_52542d41433636555f42315f33385f3547_managed_
psk
```

   Replace the service identifier after `connect` with your service identifier or target network from the previous step. Substitute your Wi-Fi passphrase for `somepassword`.

9. List the services again:

```
connmanctl> services
*AO Wired                ethernet_dca6320a8ead_cable
*AR RT-AC66U_B1_38_5G    wifi_
dca6320a8eae_52542d41433636555f42315f33385f3547_managed_
psk
    RT-AC66U_B1_38_2G    wifi_
dca6320a8eae_52542d41433636555f42315f33385f3247_managed_
psk
```

   This time, `*AR` appears before the SSID you just connected to, indicating that this network connection is ready. Ethernet takes precedence over Wi-Fi, so the device remains online over `Wired`.

10. Exit `connman-client`:

```
connmanctl> quit
```

11. Unplug your Raspberry Pi 4 from the Ethernet, thereby closing your `ssh` session:

```
root@raspberrypi4-64:~# client_loop: send disconnect:
Broken pipe
```

12. Reconnect to your Raspberry Pi 4:

```
$ ssh root@raspberrypi4-64.local
```

13. Start connman-client again:

```
root@raspberrypi4-64:~# connmanctl
connmanctl>
```

14. List the services again:

```
connmanctl> services
*AO RT-AC66U_B1_38_5G     wifi_
dca6320a8eae_52542d41433636555f42315f33385f3547_managed_
psk
```

Observe that the Wired connection is now gone and that the Wi-Fi SSID you connected to that was previously ready has now been promoted to online.

The connman daemon saves your Wi-Fi credentials to a network profile directory under /var/lib/connman, which persists on the microSD card. This means that connman will automatically reconnect to your Wi-Fi network when your Raspberry Pi 4 boots up. There is no need to go through these steps again after power cycling. You can leave your Ethernet unplugged if you like.

Controlling Bluetooth

In addition to the connman and connman-client packages, the meta-raspberrypi layer includes bluez5 for its Bluetooth stack. All of these packages, as well as the requisite Bluetooth drivers, are included in rpi-test-image, which we built for the Raspberry Pi 4. Let's get Bluetooth up and running and attempt to pair it with another device:

1. Power up your Raspberry Pi 4 and ssh in:

```
$ ssh root@raspberrypi4-64.local
```

2. Next, verify that the Bluetooth drivers are on board:

```
root@raspberrypi4-64:~# lsmod | grep bluetooth
bluetooth              438272  9 bnep
ecdh_generic            24576  1 bluetooth
rfkill                  32768  6 nfc,bluetooth,cfg80211
```

3. Initialize the HCI UART driver for Bluetooth connectivity:

```
root@raspberrypi4-64:~# btuart
bcm43xx_init
Flash firmware /lib/firmware/brcm/BCM4345C0.hcd
Set Controller UART speed to 3000000 bit/s
Device setup complete
```

4. Start `connman-client`:

```
root@raspberrypi4-64:~# connmanctl
connmanctl>
```

5. Turn on Bluetooth:

```
connmanctl> enable bluetooth
Enabled Bluetooth
```

   Disregard `"Error bluetooth: Already enabled"` if Bluetooth is already on.

6. Exit `connman-client`:

```
connmanctl> quit
```

7. Start the Bluetooth CLI:

```
root@raspberrypi4-64:~# bluetoothctl
Agent registered
[CHG] Controller DC:A6:32:0A:8E:AF Pairable: yes
```

8. Request the default agent:

```
[bluetooth]# default-agent
Default agent request successful
```

9. Power on the controller:

```
[bluetooth]# power on
Changing power on succeeded
```

10. Show information about the controller:

```
[bluetooth]# show
Controller DC:A6:32:0A:8E:AF (public)
Name: BlueZ 5.55
Alias: BlueZ 5.55
Class: 0x00200000
Powered: yes
Discoverable: no
DiscoverableTimeout: 0x000000b4
Pairable: yes
```

11. Start scanning for Bluetooth devices:

```
[bluetooth]# scan on
Discovery started
[CHG] Controller DC:A6:32:0A:8E:AF Discovering: yes
…
[NEW] Device DC:08:0F:03:52:CD Frank's iPhone
…
```

If your smartphone is nearby and has Bluetooth enabled, it should appear in the list as a `[NEW]` device. The `DC:08:0F:03:52:CD` part next to `Frank's iPhone` is the Bluetooth MAC address of my smartphone.

12. Stop scanning for Bluetooth devices:

```
[bluetooth]# scan off
…
[CHG] Controller DC:A6:32:0A:8E:AF Discovering: no
Discovery stopped
```

13. If you have an iPhone open, go to **Bluetooth** under **Settings** so that you can accept the pairing request from your Raspberry Pi 4.

14. Attempt to pair with your smartphone:

```
[bluetooth]# pair DC:08:0F:03:52:CD
Attempting to pair with DC:08:0F:03:52:CD
[CHG] Device DC:08:0F:03:52:CD Connected: yes
Request confirmation
[agent] Confirm passkey 936359 (yes/no):
```

Substitute your smartphone's Bluetooth MAC address for `DC:08:0F:03:52:CD`.

15. Before entering `yes`, accept the pairing request from your smartphone:

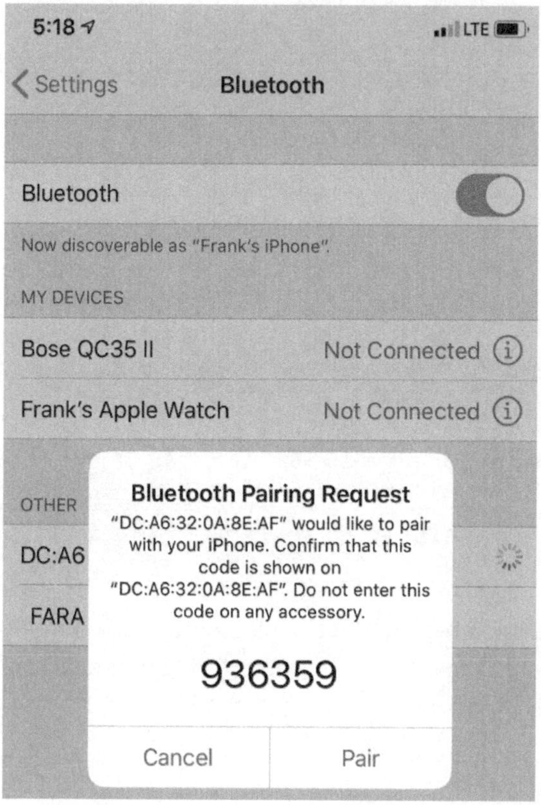

Figure 7.1 – Bluetooth pairing request

16. Enter `yes` to confirm the passkey:

```
[agent] Confirm passkey 936359 (yes/no): yes
[CHG] Device DC:08:0F:03:52:CD ServicesResolved: yes
[CHG] Device DC:08:0F:03:52:CD Paired: yes
Pairing successful
[CHG] Device DC:08:0F:03:52:CD ServicesResolved: no
[CHG] Device DC:08:0F:03:52:CD Connected: no
```

17. Connect to your smartphone:

```
[bluetooth]# connect DC:08:0F:03:52:CD
Attempting to connect to DC:08:0F:03:52:CD
[CHG] Device DC:08:0F:03:52:CD Connected: yes
Connection successful
[CHG] Device DC:08:0F:03:52:CD ServicesResolved: yes
Authorize service
```

   Again, substitute your smartphone's Bluetooth MAC address for `DC:08:0F:03:52:CD`.

18. When prompted to authorize the service, enter `yes`:

```
[agent] Authorize service 0000110e-0000-1000-8000-
00805f9b34fb (yes/no): yes
[Frank's iPhone]#
```

Your Raspberry Pi 4 is now paired and connected to your smartphone over Bluetooth. It should appear on your smartphone's list of Bluetooth devices as **BlueZ 5.55**. The `bluetoothctl` program has numerous commands and submenus. We've only just scratched the surface. I recommend entering `help` and perusing the self-documentation to get an idea of what you can do from the command line. Like `connman`, the **BlueZ** Bluetooth stack is a D-Bus service, so you can communicate with it programmatically over D-Bus from Python or other high-level programming languages using D-Bus bindings.

Adding a custom layer

If you are using a Raspberry Pi 4 to prototype a new product, then you can quickly generate your own custom images by adding packages to the list that's been assigned to the `IMAGE_INSTALL_append` variable in `conf/local.conf`. While this simple technique works, at some point, you are going to want to start developing your own embedded application. How do you build this additional software so that you can include it in your custom images? The answer is that you must create a custom layer with a new recipe to build your software. Let's get started:

1. First, navigate one level above the directory where you cloned Yocto.
2. Next, set up your BitBake work environment:

```
$ source poky/oe-init-build-env build-rpi
```

   This sets a bunch of environment variables and puts you back in the `build-rpi` directory.

3. Create a new layer for your application:

```
$ bitbake-layers create-layer ../meta-gattd
NOTE: Starting bitbake server...
Add your new layer with 'bitbake-layers add-layer ../
meta-gattd'
```

This layer is named `meta-gattd` for the GATT daemon. Name your layer whatever you like, but please adhere to the `meta-` prefix convention.

4. Navigate up to the new layer directory:

```
$ cd ../meta-gattd
```

5. Examine the layer's file structure:

```
$ tree
.
├── conf
│   └── layer.conf
├── COPYING.MIT
├── README
└── recipes-example
    └── example
        └── example_0.1.bb
```

6. Rename the `recipes-examples` directory:

```
$ mv recipes-example recipes-gattd
```

7. Rename the `example` directory:

```
$ cd recipes-gattd
$ mv example gattd
```

8. Rename the `example` recipe file:

```
$ cd gattd
$ mv example_0.1.bb gattd_0.1.bb
```

9. Display the renamed recipe file:

```
$ cat gattd_0.1.bb
```

You want to populate this recipe with the metadata that's needed to build your software, including `SRC_URI` and `md5` checksums.

10. For now, just replace `gattd_0.1.bb` with the finished recipe I have provided for you in `MELP/Chapter07/meta-gattd/recipes-gattd/gattd_0.1.bb`.
11. Create a Git repository for your new layer and push it to GitHub.

Now that we have a custom layer for our application, let's add it to your working image:

1. First, navigate one level above the directory where you cloned Yocto:

```
$ cd ../../..
```

2. Clone your layer or my `meta-gattd` layer from GitHub:

```
$ git clone https://github.com/fvasquez/meta-gattd.git
```

Replace `fvasquez` with your GitHub username and `meta-gattd` with your layer's repo name.

3. Next, set up your BitBake work environment:

```
$ source poky/oe-init-build-env build-rpi
```

This sets a bunch of environment variables and puts you back in the `build-rpi` directory.

4. Then, add the newly cloned layer to the image:

```
$ bitbake-layers add-layer ../meta-gattd
```

Replace `meta-gattd` with the name of your layer.

5. Verify that all the necessary layers have been added to the image:

```
$ bitbake-layers show-layers
```

There should be a total of nine layers in the list, including your new layer.

6. Now, add the extra package to your `conf/local.conf` file:

```
CORE_IMAGE_EXTRA_INSTALL += "gattd"
```

`CORE_IMAGE_EXTRA_INSTALL` is a convenience variable that's used to add extra packages to an image that inherits from the `core-image` class, like the `rpi-test-image` does. `IMAGE_INSTALL` is the variable that controls what packages are included in any image. We cannot use `IMAGE_INSTALL += "gattd"` in `conf/local.conf` because it replaces the default lazy assignment that's done in `core-image.bbclass`. Use `IMAGE_INSTALL_append = " gattd"` or `CORE_IMAGE_EXTRA_INSTALL += " gattd"` instead.

7. Lastly, rebuild the image:

```
$ bitbake rpi-test-image
```

If your software successfully builds and installs, it should be included on the finished `rpi-test-image-raspberrypi4-64.rootfs.wic.bz2` image. Write that image to a microSD card and boot it on your Raspberry Pi 4 to find out.

Adding packages to `conf/local.conf` makes sense during the earliest stages of development. When you are ready to share the fruits of your labor with the rest of your team, you should create an image recipe and put your packages there. At the end of the previous chapter, we went all the way and wrote a `nova-image` recipe to add a `helloworld` package to `core-image-minimal`.

Now that we've spent a good amount of time testing newly built images on actual hardware, it's time to turn our attention back to software. In the next section we'll look at a tool that was designed to streamline the tedious compile, test, and debug cycle we've grown accustomed to while developing embedded software.

Capturing changes with devtool

In the previous chapter, you learned how to create a recipe for a `helloworld` program from scratch. A copy-paste approach to packaging recipes may work initially, but it soon becomes very frustrating as your project grows and the number of recipes you need to maintain multiplies. I'm here to show you a better way of working with package recipes – both yours and those that are contributed to upstream by some third party. It is called `devtool` and it is the cornerstone of Yocto's extensible SDK.

Development workflows

Before you get started with `devtool`, you want to make sure that you're doing your work in a new layer instead of modifying recipes in-tree. Otherwise, you could easily overwrite and lose hours and hours of work:

1. First, navigate one level above the directory where you cloned Yocto.

2. Next, set up your BitBake work environment:

   ```
   $ source poky/oe-init-build-env build-mine
   ```

   This sets a bunch of environment variables and puts you in a new `build-mine` directory.

3. Set `MACHINE` in `conf/local.conf` for 64-bit Arm:

   ```
   MACHINE ?= "quemuarm64"
   ```

4. Create your new layer:

   ```
   $ bitbake-layers create-layer ../meta-mine
   ```

5. Now, add your new layer:

   ```
   $ bitbake-layers add-layer ../meta-mine
   ```

6. Check that your new layer was created where you want it to be:

   ```
   $ bitbake-layers show-layers
   ```

   There should be a total of four layers in the list; that is, `meta`, `meta-poky`, `meta-yocto-bsp`, and `meta-mine`.

To get some first-hand experience with development workflows, you are going to need a target to deploy to. That means building an image:

```
$ devtool build-image core-image-full-cmdline
```

Building a full image takes a few hours the first time you do so. When it's complete, go ahead and boot it:

```
$ runqemu qemuarm64 nographic
[...]
Poky (Yocto Project Reference Distro) 3.1.6 qemuarm64 ttyAMA0

qemuarm64 login: root
root@qemuarm64:~#
```

By specifying the `nographic` option, we can run QEMU directly in a separate shell. This makes typing easier than having to cope with the emulated graphics output. Log in as `root`. There is no password. To exit QEMU when running in `nographic` mode, enter *Ctrl* + *A*, followed by `x`, into the target shell. Leave QEMU running for now because we need it for the subsequent exercises. You can SSH into this VM with `ssh root@192.168.7.2`.

`devtool` supports three common development workflows:

- Add a new recipe.
- Patch the source built by an existing recipe.
- Upgrade a recipe to fetch a newer version of the upstream source.

When you initiate any of these workflows, `devtool` creates a temporary workspace for you to make your changes. This sandbox contains the recipe files and fetched source. When you are done with your work, `devtool` integrates your changes back into your layer so that the workspace can be destroyed.

Creating a new recipe

Let's say there is some open source software you want that no one has submitted a BitBake recipe for yet. And let's say that software in question is the lightweight `bubblewrap` container runtime. In this instance, you could download a source tarball release of `bubblewrap` from GitHub and create a recipe for it. That's exactly what `devtool add` does.

First, `devtool add` creates a workspace with its own local Git repository. Inside this new workspace directory, it creates a `recipes/bubblewrap` directory and extracts the tarball contents into a `sources/bubblewrap` directory. `devtool` knows about popular build systems such as Autotools and CMake and will do its best to figure out what kind of project this is (Autotools, in the case of `bubblewrap`). It then uses parsed metadata and built package data cached from previous BitBake builds to figure out the values of `DEPENDS` and `RDEPENDS`, as well as what files to inherit and require. Let's get started:

1. First, open another shell and navigate one level above the directory where you cloned Yocto.
2. Next, set up your BitBake environment:

   ```
   $ source poky/oe-init-build-env build-mine
   ```

   This sets a bunch of environment variables and puts you back in your `build-mine` working directory.

3. Then, run `devtool add` with the URL of the source tarball release:

```
$ devtool add https://github.com/containers/bubblewrap/
releases/download/v0.4.1/bubblewrap-0.4.1.tar.xz
```

   If everything goes according to plan, `devtool add` will generate a recipe that you can then build.

4. Before you build your new recipe, let's take a look at it:

```
$ devtool edit-recipe bubblewrap
```

   `devtool` will open `recipes/bubblewrap/bubblewrap_0.4.1.bb` in an editor. Notice that `devtool` has already filled in the `md5` checksums for you.

5. Add this line to the end of `bubblewrap_0.4.1.bb`:

```
FILES_${PN} += "/usr/share/*"
```

   Correct any obvious mistakes, save any changes, and exit your editor.

6. To build your new recipe, use the following command:

```
$ devtool build bubblewrap
```

7. Next, deploy the compiled `bwrap` executable to the target emulator:

```
$ devtool deploy-target bubblewrap root@192.168.7.2
```

   This installs the necessary build artifacts onto the target emulator.

8. From your QEMU shell, run the `bwrap` executable that you just built and deployed:

```
root@qemuarm64:~# bwrap --help
```

   If you see a bunch of `bubblewrap`-related self-documentation, then the build and deployment were successful. If you do not, then use `devtool` to repeat the edit, build, and deploy steps until you are convinced that `bubblewrap` works.

9. Once you are satisfied, clean up your target emulator:

```
$ devtool undeploy-target bubblewrap root@192.168.7.2
```

10. Merge all your work back into your layer:

```
$ devtool finish -f bubblewrap ../meta-mine
```

11. Delete the leftover sources from the workspace:

```
$ rm -rf workspace/sources/bubblewrap
```

If you think others might benefit from your new recipe, then submit a patch to Yocto.

Modifying the source built by a recipe

Let's say you find a bug in **jq**, a command-line JSON preprocessor. You search the Git repository at `https://github.com/stedolan/jq` and find that no one has reported the issue. Then, you look at the source code. It turns out that the fix requires just a few small code changes, so you decide to patch `jq` yourself. That's where `devtool modify` comes in.

This time, when `devtool` looks at Yocto's cached metadata, it sees that a recipe already exists for `jq`. Like `devtool add`, `devtool modify` creates a new temporary workspace with its own local Git repository, where it copies the recipe files and extracts the upstream sources. `jq` is written in C and located in an existing OpenEmbedded layer named `meta-oe`. We need to add this layer, as well as `jq`'s dependencies, to our working image before we can modify the package source:

1. First, delete a couple of layers from your `build-mine` environment:

```
$ bitbake-layers remove-layer workspace
$ bitbake-layers remove-layer meta-mine
```

2. Next, clone the `meta-openembedded` repository from GitHub:

```
$ git clone -b dunfell https://github.com/openembedded/
meta-openembedded.git ../meta-openembedded
```

3. Then, add the `meta-oe` and `meta-mine` layers to your image:

```
$ bitbake-layers add-layer ../meta-openembedded/meta-oe
$ bitbake-layers add-layer ../meta-mine
```

4. Verify that all the necessary layers have been added to the image:

```
$ bitbake-layers show-layers
```

There should be a total of five layers in the list; that is, `meta`, `meta-poky`, `meta-yocto-bsp`, `meta-oe`, and `meta-mine`.

5. Add the following line to `conf/local.conf` because the `onig` package is a runtime dependency of `jq`:

```
IMAGE_INSTALL_append = " onig"
```

6. Rebuild your image:

```
$ devtool build-image core-image-full-cmdline
```

7. Exit QEMU with *Ctrl* + *A* and `x` from your other shell and restart the emulator:

```
$ runqemu qemuarm64 nographic
```

Like many patching tools, `devtool modify` uses your commit messages to generate patch filenames, so keep your commit messages brief and meaningful. It also automatically generates the patch files themselves based on your Git history and creates a `.bbappend` file with the new patch filenames. Remember to prune and squash your Git commits so that `devtool` divides your work up into sensible patch files:

1. Run `devtool modify` with the name of the package you wish to modify:

```
$ devtool modify jq
```

2. Make your code changes using your preferred editor. Use the standard Git add and commit workflow to keep track of what you've done.
3. Build the modified sources using the following command:

```
$ devtool build jq
```

4. Next, deploy the compiled `jq` executable to the target emulator:

```
$ devtool deploy-target jq root@192.168.7.2
```

This installs the necessary build artifacts onto the target emulator.

If connecting fails, then delete the stale emulator's key, as shown here:

```
$ ssh-keygen -f "/home/frank/.ssh/known_hosts" \
-R "192.168.7.2"
```

Replace `frank` with your username in the path.

5. From your QEMU shell, run the `jq` executable that you just built and deployed. If you can no longer reproduce the bug, then your changes worked. Otherwise, repeat the edit, build, and deploy steps until you are satisfied.

6. Once you are satisfied, clean up your target emulator:

```
$ devtool undeploy-target jq root@192.168.7.2
```

7. Merge all your work back into your layer:

```
$ devtool finish jq ../meta-mine
```

   If the merge fails because the Git source tree is dirty, then remove or unstage any leftover `jq` build artifacts and try `devtool finish` again.

8. Delete the leftover sources from the workspace:

```
$ rm -rf workspace/sources/jq
```

If you think others might benefit from your patch(es), then submit them to the upstream project maintainers.

Upgrading a recipe to a newer version

Let's say you're running a Flask web server on your target device and a new version of Flask has just been released. This latest version of Flask has a new feature that you just can't wait to get your hands on. Instead of waiting for the Flask recipe maintainers to upgrade to the new release version, you decide to upgrade the recipe yourself. You would think that would be as easy as bumping a version number in a recipe file, but there are also `md5` checksums involved. Wouldn't it be great if the tedious process could be fully automated? Well, guess what `devtool upgrade` is for?

Flask is a Python 3 library, so your image needs to include Python 3, Flask, and Flask's dependencies before you can upgrade it. To obtain all those, follow these steps:

1. First, delete a couple of layers from your `build-mine` environment:

```
$ bitbake-layers remove-layer workspace
$ bitbake-layers remove-layer meta-mine
```

2. Next, add the `meta-python` and `meta-mine` layers to your image:

```
$ bitbake-layers add-layer ../meta-openembedded/meta-python
$ bitbake-layers add-layer ../meta-mine
```

3. Verify that all the necessary layers have been added to the image:

```
$ bitbake-layers show-layers
```

There should be a total of six layers in the list; that is, meta, meta-poky, meta-yocto-bsp, meta-oe, meta-python, and meta-mine.

4. Now, there should be lots of Python modules available for you to use:

```
$ bitbake -s | grep ^python3
```

One of those modules is python3-flask.

5. Make sure python3 and python3-flask are being built and installed on your image by searching for them both inside conf/local.conf. If they are not there, then you can include them both by adding the following line to your conf/local.conf:

```
IMAGE_INSTALL_append = " python3 python3-flask"
```

6. Rebuild your image:

```
$ devtool build-image core-image-full-cmdline
```

7. Exit QEMU with *Ctrl* + *A* and x from your other shell and restart the emulator:

```
$ runqemu qemuarm64 nographic
```

> **Important Note**
> At the time of writing, the version of Flask included with meta-python was 1.1.1 and the latest version of Flask available on PyPI was 1.1.2.

Now that all the pieces are in place, let's do the upgrade:

1. First, run devtool upgrade with the name of the package and the target version to upgrade to:

```
$ devtool upgrade python3-flask --version 1.1.2
```

2. Before you build your upgraded recipe, let's take a look at it:

```
$ devtool edit-recipe python3-flask
```

devtool will open recipes/python3/python3-flask_1.1.2.bb in an editor:

```
inherit pypi setuptools3
require python-flask.inc
```

There is nothing version-specific to change in this recipe, so save the new file and exit your editor.

3. To build your new recipe, use this command:

```
$ devtool build python3-flask
```

4. Next, deploy your new Flask module to the target emulator:

```
$ devtool deploy-target python3-flask root@192.168.7.2
```

This installs the necessary build artifacts onto the target emulator.

If connecting fails, then delete the stale emulator's key, as shown here:

```
$ ssh-keygen -f "/home/frank/.ssh/known_hosts" \
-R "192.168.7.2"
```

Replace `frank` with your username in the path.

5. From your QEMU shell, launch a `python3` REPL and check what version of Flask was deployed:

```
root@qemuarm64:~# python3
>>> import flask
>>> flask.__version__
'1.1.2'
>>>
```

If entering `flask.__version__` in the REPL returns `'1.1.2'`, then the upgrade worked. If it does not, then use `devtool` to repeat the edit, build, and deploy steps until you've figured out what went wrong.

6. Once you are satisfied, clean up your target emulator:

```
$ devtool undeploy-target python3-flask root@192.168.7.2
```

7. Merge all your work back into your layer:

```
$ devtool finish python3-flask ../meta-mine
```

If the merge fails because the Git source tree is dirty, then remove or unstage any leftover `python3-flask` build artifacts and try `devtool finish` again.

8. Delete the leftover sources from the workspace:

```
$ rm -rf workspace/sources/python3-flask
```

If you think others might also be anxious to upgrade their distros to the latest version of a package, then submit a patch to Yocto.

Finally, we've arrived at the topic of how to build our own distro. This feature is unique to Yocto and notably missing from Buildroot. A **distro layer** is a powerful abstraction that can be shared across multiple projects targeting different hardware.

Building your own distro

At the start of the previous chapter, I told you that Yocto gives you the ability to build your own custom Linux distribution. This is done by way of a distro layer like meta-poky. As we have seen, you don't need your own distro layer to build your own custom images. You can go a long way without ever having to modify any of Poky's distribution metadata. But if you want to alter distro policies (for example, features, C library implementations, choice of package manager, and so on), then you can choose to build your own distro.

Building your own distro is a three-step process:

1. Create a new distro layer.
2. Create a distro configuration file.
3. Add more recipes to your distro.

But before we get into the technical details of how to do that, let's consider when it's the right time to roll your own distro.

When and when not to

Distro settings define the package format (`rpm`, `deb`, or `ipk`), package feed, `init` system (`systemd` or `sysvinit`), and specific package versions. You could create your own distro in a new layer by inheriting from Poky and overriding what needs to change for your distro. However, if you find yourself adding a lot of values to your build directory's `local.conf` file aside from the obvious local settings (such as relative paths), then it is probably time to create your own distro from scratch.

Creating a new distro layer

You know how to create a layer. Creating a distro layer is no different. Let's get started:

1. First, navigate one level above the directory where you cloned Yocto.
2. Next, set up your BitBake work environment:

```
$ source poky/oe-init-build-env build-rpi
```

This sets a bunch of environment variables and puts you back in the `build-rpi` directory from earlier.

3. Delete the `meta-gattd` layer from your `build-rpi` environment:

```
$ bitbake-layers remove-layer meta-gattd
```

4. Comment out or delete `CORE_IMAGE_EXTRA_INSTALL` from `conf/local.conf`:

```
#CORE_IMAGE_EXTRA_INSTALL += "gattd"
```

5. Create a new layer for our distro:

```
$ bitbake-layers create-layer ../meta-mackerel
```

6. Now, add our new layer to the `build-rpi` configuration:

```
$ bitbake-layers add-layer ../meta-mackerel
```

The name of our distro is `mackerel`. Creating our own distro layer enables us to keep distro policies separate from package recipes (the implementation).

Configuring your distro

Create the distro configuration file in the `conf/distro` directory of your `meta-mackerel` distro layer. Give it the same name as your distro (for example, `mackerel.conf`).

Set the required `DISTRO_NAME` and `DISTRO_VERSSION` variables in `conf/distro/mackerel.conf`:

```
DISTRO_NAME = "Mackerel (Mackerel Embedded Linux Distro)"
DISTRO_VERSION = "0.1"
```

The following optional variables can also be set in `mackerel.conf`:

```
DISTRO_FEATURES: Add software support for these features.
DISTRO_EXTRA_RDEPENDS: Add these packages to all images.
DISTRO_EXTRA_RRECOMMENDS: Add these packages if they exist.
TCLIBC: Select this version of the C standard library.
```

Once you are done with those variables, you can define just about any variable in `conf/local.conf` that you want for your distro. Look at other distros' `conf/distro` directories, such as Poky's, to see how they organize things or copy and use `conf/distro/defaultsetup.conf` as a template. If you decide to break your distro configuration file up into multiple include files, make sure to place them in the `conf/distro/include` directory of your layer.

Adding more recipes to your distro

Add more distro-related metadata to your distro layer. You will want to add recipes for additional configuration files. These are configuration files that have yet to be installed by an existing recipe. More importantly, you will also want to add append files to customize existing recipes and add their configuration files to your distro.

Runtime package management

Including a package manager for your distro images is great for enabling secure over-the-air updates and rapid application development. When your team works on software that revs multiple times a day, frequent package updates is one way to keep everybody in sync and moving forward. Full image updates are unnecessary (only one package changes) and disruptive (reboot required). Being able to fetch packages from a remote server and install them on a target device is known as *runtime package management*.

Yocto has support for different package formats (`rpm` and `ipk`) and different package managers (`dnf` and `opkg`). The package format you select for your distro determines which package manager you can include on it.

To select a package format for our distro, you can set the `PACKAGE_CLASSES` variable in your distro's `conf` file. Add this line to `meta-mackerel/conf/distro/mackerel.conf`:

```
PACKAGE_CLASSES ?= "package_ipk"
```

Now, let's return to the `build-rpi` directory:

```
$ source poky/oe-init-build-env build-rpi
```

We are targeting the Raspberry Pi 4, so make sure `MACHINE` is still set accordingly in `conf/local.conf`:

```
MACHINE = "raspberrypi4-64"
```

Comment out PACKAGE_CLASSES in your build directory's conf/local.conf since our distro already selects package_ipk:

```
#PACKAGE_CLASSES ?= "package_rpm"
```

To enable runtime package management, append "package-management" to the list of EXTRA_IMAGE_FEATURES in your build directory's conf/local.conf:

```
EXTRA_IMAGE_FEATURES ?= "debug-tweaks ssh-server-openssh
package-management"
```

This will install a package database containing all the packages from your current build onto your distro image. A prepopulated package database is optional because you can always initialize a package database on the target after your distro image has been deployed.

Lastly, set the DISTRO variable in your build directory's conf/local.conf file to the name of our distro:

```
DISTRO = "mackerel"
```

This points your build directory's conf/local.conf file at our distro configuration file.

Finally, we are ready to build our distro:

```
$ bitbake -c clean rpi-test-image
$ bitbake rpi-test-image
```

We are rebuilding rpi-test-image with a different package format, so this will take a little while. The finished images are placed in a different directory this time around:

```
$ ls tmp-glibc/deploy/images/raspberrypi4-64/rpi-test-
image*wic.bz2
```

Write the image to a microSD card using Etcher and boot it on your Raspberry Pi 4. Plug it into your Ethernet and SSH in like you did previously:

```
$ ssh root@raspberrypi4-64.local
```

If connecting fails, then delete the Pi's stale key, as shown here:

```
$ ssh-keygen -f "/home/frank/.ssh/known_hosts" \
-R "raspberrypi4-64.local"
```

Replace frank with your username in the path.

Once you have logged in, verify that the opkg package manager has been installed:

```
root@raspberrypi4-64:~# which opkg
/usr/bin/opkg
```

A package manager isn't of much use without a remote package server to pull it from. Let's look at that next.

Provisioning a remote package server

Setting up an HTTP remote package server and pointing your target clients at it is easier than you might think. The client-side server address configuration varies between package managers. We will configure opkg manually on the Raspberry Pi 4.

Let's start with the package server:

1. First, navigate one level above the directory where you cloned Yocto.
2. Next, set up your BitBake work environment:

   ```
   $ source poky/oe-init-build-env build-rpi
   ```

   This sets a bunch of environment variables and puts you back in the build-rpi directory.
3. Build the curl package:

   ```
   $ bitbake curl
   ```

4. Populate the package index:

   ```
   $ bitbake package-index
   ```

5. Locate the package installer files:

   ```
   $ ls tmp-glibc/deploy/ipk
   ```

   There should be three directories named aarch64, all, and raspberrypi4_64 in ipk. The *architecture directory* is aarch64, while the *machine directory* is raspberrypi4_64. The names of these two directories will vary, depending on how your image has been configured for building.
6. Navigate to the ipk directory, which is where the package installer files are:

   ```
   $ cd tmp-glibc/deploy/ipk
   ```

7. Get the IP address of your Linux host machine.
8. Start the HTTP package server:

```
$ sudo python3 -m http.server --bind 192.168.1.69 80
[sudo] password for frank:
Serving HTTP on 192.168.1.69 port 80
(http://192.168.1.69:80/) ...
```

Replace `192.168.1.69` with your Linux host machine's IP address.

Now, let's configure the target client:

1. SSH back into your Raspberry Pi 4:

```
$ ssh root@raspberrypi4-64.local
```

2. Edit `/etc/opkg/opkg.conf` so that it looks like this:

```
src/gz all http://192.168.1.69/all
src/gz aarch64 http://192.168.1.69/aarch64
src/gz raspberrypi4_64 http://192.168.1.69/
raspberrypi4_64

dest root /
option lists_dir /var/lib/opkg/lists
```

Replace `192.168.1.69` with your Linux host machine's IP address.

3. Run `opkg update`:

```
root@raspberrypi4-64:~# opkg update
Downloading http://192.168.1.69/all/Packages.gz.
Updated source 'all'.
Downloading http://192.168.1.69/aarch64/Packages.gz.
Updated source 'aarch64'.
Downloading http://192.168.1.69/raspberrypi4_64/Packages.
gz.
Updated source 'raspberrypi4_64'.
```

4. Try to run `curl`:

```
root@raspberrypi4-64:~# curl
```

The command should fail because `curl` is not installed.

5. Install `curl`:

```
root@raspberrypi4-64:~# opkg install curl
Installing libcurl4 (7.69.1) on root
Downloading http://192.168.1.69/aarch64/
libcurl4_7.69.1-r0_aarch64.ipk.
Installing curl (7.69.1) on root
Downloading http://192.168.1.69/aarch64/curl_7.69.1-r0_
aarch64.ipk.
Configuring libcurl4.
Configuring curl.
```

6. Verify that `curl` was installed:

```
root@raspberrypi4-64:~# curl
curl: try 'curl --help' for more information
root@raspberrypi4-64:~# which curl
/usr/bin/curl
```

As you continue to work in the `build-rpi` directory from a Linux host machine, you can check for updates from your Raspberry Pi 4:

```
root@raspberrypi4-64:~# opkg list-upgradable
```

Then, you can apply them:

```
root@raspberrypi4-64:~# opkg upgrade
```

This is faster than rewriting an image, swapping out the microSD card, and rebooting.

Summary

I know that was a lot to absorb. And trust me – this is just the beginning. Yocto is a never-ending rabbit hole that you don't climb out of. The recipes and tools are constantly changing and much of the documentation, while there is lots of it, is sadly out of date. Luckily, there is `devtool`, which automates much of the tedium and mistakes of copy-paste development away. If you use the tools provided for you and continually save your work to your own layers, Yocto doesn't have to be painful. Before you know it, you'll be rolling your own distro layer and running your own remote package server.

A remote package server is just one way to deploy packages and applications. We will learn about a few others later in *Chapter 16, Packaging Python*. Despite the title, some of the techniques we'll look at in that chapter (for example, conda and Docker) apply to any programming language. While package managers are great for development, runtime package management is not commonly used on embedded systems running in production. We will look closely at full image and containerized over-the-air update mechanisms in *Chapter 10, Updating Software in the Field*.

Further reading

The following resources contain more information about the topics that were introduced in this chapter:

- *Transitioning to a Custom Environment*, Yocto Project: `https://www.yoctoproject.org/docs/transitioning-to-a-custom-environment`
- *Yocto Project Development Manual*, by Scott Rifenbark: `https://www.yoctoproject.org/docs/latest/dev-manual/dev-manual.html`
- *Using Devtool to Streamline Your Yocto Project Workflow*, by Tim Orling: `https://www.youtube.com/watch?v=CiD7rB35CRE`
- *Using a Yocto build workstation as a remote opkg repository*, Jumpnow Technologies: `https://jumpnowtek.com/yocto/Using-your-build-workstation-as-a-remote-package-repository.html`

8
Yocto Under the Hood

In this chapter, we'll dive deeper into **Yocto**, embedded Linux's premier build system. We will begin with a tour of Yocto's architecture, taking you through the entire build workflow step by step. Next, we'll look at Yocto's multi-layer approach and why it is a good idea to separate metadata into different layers. As more and more **BitBake** layers stack up inside your projects, problems will inevitably arise. We will examine a number of ways to debug Yocto build failures, including task logs, `devshell`, and dependency graphs.

After taking apart the build system, we'll revisit the topic of BitBake from the previous chapter. This time around, we'll cover more of the basic syntax and semantics so that you can write your own recipes from scratch. We'll look at real-world examples of BitBake shell and Python code from actual recipe, include, and configuration files so that you know what to expect when you begin to venture out into Yocto's ocean of metadata.

In this chapter, we will cover the following topics:

- Decomposing Yocto's architecture and workflow
- Separating metadata into layers
- Troubleshooting build failures
- Understanding BitBake syntax and semantics

Let's get started!

Technical requirements

To follow along with the examples in this chapter, make sure you have the following:

- A Linux-based system host system with a minimum of 60 GB available disk space
- Yocto 3.1 (Dunfell) LTS release

You should have already built the 3.1 (Dunfell) LTS release of Yocto in *Chapter 6, Selecting a Build System*. If you have not, then please refer to the *Compatible Linux Distribution* and *Build Host Packages* sections of the *Yocto Project Quick Build* guide (`https://www.yoctoproject.org/docs/current/brief-yoctoprojectqs/brief-yoctoprojectqs.html`) before building Yocto on your Linux host according to the instructions in *Chapter 6*.

Decomposing Yocto's architecture and workflow

Yocto is a complex beast. Taking it apart is the first step toward understanding it. The architecture of a build system can be organized in terms of its workflow. Yocto gets its workflow from the **OpenEmbbedded** project, which it is based on. Source materials feed into the system as inputs by way of metadata in the form of BitBake recipes. The build system uses this metadata to fetch, configure, and compile the source code into binary package feeds. These individual output packages are assembled inside a staging area before the finished Linux image and SDK are generated, complete with a manifest that includes a license for each package that's on board:

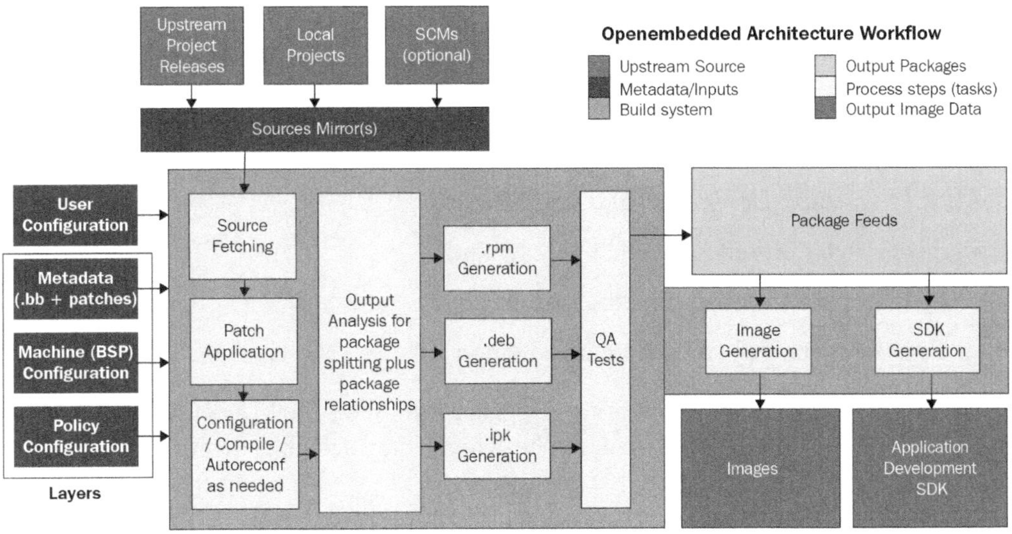

Figure 8.1 – OpenEmbedded architecture workflow

Here are the seven steps of Yocto's build system workflow, as shown in the preceding diagram:

1. Define layers for policy, machine, and software metadata.
2. Fetch sources from the source URI of a software project.
3. Extract the source code, apply any patches, and compile the software.
4. Install the build artifacts into a staging area for packaging.
5. Bundle the installed build artifacts into a package feed for the root filesystem.
6. Run QA checks on a binary package feed before submitting it.
7. Generate the finished Linux image and an SDK in parallel.

Except for the first and last steps, all of the steps in this workflow are performed on a per-recipe basis. Code linting, sanitizing, and other forms of static analysis may occur before or after compilation. Unit and integration tests can run directly on the build machine, on a QEMU instance acting as a stand-in for the target SoC, or on the target itself. When a build completes, the finished image can then be deployed to a group of dedicated devices for further testing. As the gold standard for embedded Linux build systems, Yocto is a vital component of the software CI/CD pipeline for many products.

The packages Yocto generates can be in either `rpm`, `deb`, or `ipk` format. In addition to the main binary package, the build system attempts to generate all of the following packages for a recipe by default:

- `dbg`: Binary files, including debug symbols
- `static-dev`: Header files and static libraries
- `dev`: Header files and shared library symlinks
- `doc`: Documentation, including man pages
- `locale`: Language translation information

Packages that would contain no files are not generated unless the `ALLOW_EMPTY` variable is enabled. The set of packages to be generated by default is determined by the `PACKAGES` variable. Both variables are defined in `meta/classes/packagegroup.bbclass`, but their values can be overridden by package group recipes that inherit from that `BitBake` class.

Building an SDK enables a whole other development workflow for manipulating individual package recipes. In the *Capturing changes with devtool* section of the previous chapter, we learned how to use `devtool` to add and modify SDK software packages so that we can integrate them back into an image.

Metadata

Metadata is the input that goes into the build system. It controls what gets built and how. Metadata is more than just recipes. BSPs, policies, patches, and other forms of configuration files are also metadata. Which version of a package to build and where to pull the source code from are certainly forms of metadata. A developer makes all these choices by naming files, setting variables, and running commands. These configuration actions, argument values, and their resulting artifacts are yet another form of metadata. Yocto parses all of these inputs and transforms them into a complete Linux image.

The first choice a developer makes with respect to building with Yocto is what machine architecture to target. You do this by setting the `MACHINE` variable in the `conf/local.conf` file for your project. When targeting QEMU, I like to use `MACHINE ?= "qemuarm64"` to specify `aarch64` as the machine architecture. Yocto ensures that the correct compiler flags propagate from a BSP down to the other build layers.

Architecture-specific settings are defined in files called *tunes*, which are located in Yocto's `meta/conf/machine/include` directory, and the individual BSP layers themselves. A number of BSP layers are included with every Yocto release. We worked extensively with the `meta-raspberrypi` BSP layer in the previous chapter. The source for each BSP resides inside its own Git repository.

To clone Xilinx's BSP layer, which contains support for their Zynq family of SoCs, use the following command:

```
$ git clone git://git.yoctoproject.org/meta-xilinx
```

This is just one example of the many BSP layers that accompany Yocto. You won't need this layer for any of the subsequent exercises, so feel free to discard it.

Metadata needs source code to act upon. BitBake's `do_fetch` task can obtain recipe source files in a number of different ways. Here are the two most prominent methods:

- When someone else develops some software that you need, the easiest way to get it is to tell BitBake to download a tarball release of the project.
- To extend someone else's open source software, simply fork the repository on GitHub. BitBake's `do_fetch` task can then use Git to clone the source files from a given `SRC_URI`.

If your team is responsible for the software, then you can choose to embed it into your work environment as a local project. You can do this either by nesting it as a subdirectory or defining it out-of-tree using the `externalsrc` class. Embedding means that the sources are tied to your layer repository and can't be easily used somewhere else. Out-of-tree projects that use `externalsrc` require identical paths on all building instances and sabotage reproducibility. Both of these techniques are merely tools used to expedite development. Neither should be used in production.

Policies are properties that are bundled together as a distribution layer. These include things such as which features (`systemd` for example), C library implementation (`glibc` or `musl`) and package manager are required by a Linux distribution. Each distro layer has its own `conf/distro` subdirectory. The `.conf` files inside that directory define the top-level policies for a distribution or image. See the `meta-poky` subdirectory for an example of a distro layer. This Poky reference distribution layer includes `.conf` files for building default, tiny, bleeding edge, and alternative flavors of Poky for your target device. We covered this in the previous chapter, in the *Building your own distro* section.

Build tasks

We already saw how BitBake's `do_fetch` task downloads and extracts the source for a recipe. The next steps in the build process are patching, configuring, and compiling said source code: `do_patch`, `do_configure`, and `do_compile`.

The `do_patch` task uses the `FILESPATH` variable and a recipe's `SRC_URI` variable to locate patch files and apply them to the intended source code. The `FILESPATH` variable, found in `meta/classes/base.bbclass`, defines the default set of directories that the build system uses to search for patch files (*Yocto Project Reference Manual*, `https://www.yoctoproject.org/docs/current/ref-manual/ref-manual.html#ref-tasks-patch`). By convention, patch files have names ending in `.diff` and `.patch` and reside in a subdirectory below where the corresponding recipe file is located. This default behavior can be extended and overridden by defining a `FILESEXTRAPATHS` variable and appending file pathnames to the recipe's `SRC_URI` variable. After patching the source code, the `do_configure` and `do_compile` tasks configure, compile, and link it:

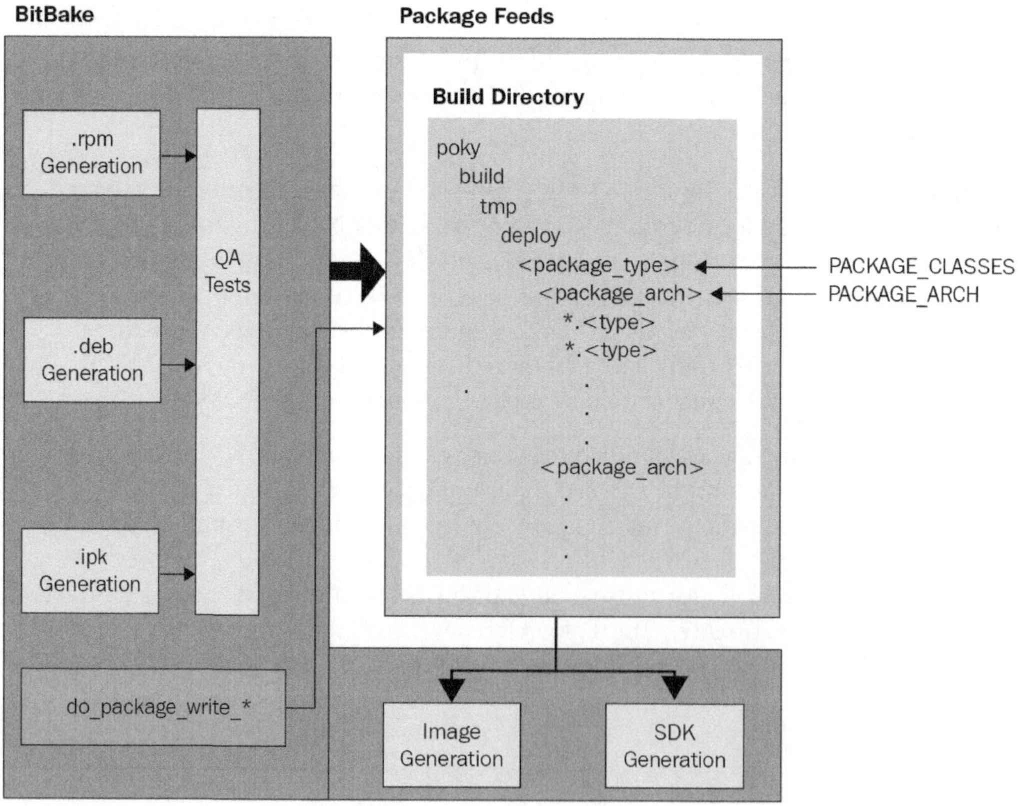

Figure 8.2 – Package feeds

When do_compile is done, the do_install task copies the resulting files to a staging area where they are readied for packaging. There, the do_package and do_package_data tasks work in tandem to process the build artifacts in the staging area and divide them up into packages. Before they are submitted to the package feeds area, the do_package_qa task subjects package artifacts to a battery of QA checks. These autogenerated QA checks are defined in meta/classes/insane.bbclass. Lastly, the do_package_write_* tasks create the individual packages and send them to the package feeds area. Once the package feeds area has been populated, BitBake is ready for image and SDK generation.

Image generation

Generating an image is a multi-stage process that relies on several variables to perform a series of tasks. The do_rootfs task creates the root filesystem for an image. These variables determine what packages get installed onto the image:

- IMAGE_INSTALL: Packages to install onto the image
- PACKAGE_EXCLUDE: Packages to omit from the image
- IMAGE_FEATURES: Additional packages to install onto the image
- PACKAGE_CLASSES: Package format (rpm, deb, or ipk) to use
- IMAGE_LINGUAS: Languages (cultures) to include support packages for

Recall that we added packages to the IMAGE_INSTALL variable back in *Chapter 6, Selecting a Build System*, as part of the *Writing an image recipe* section. The list of packages from the IMAGE_INSTALL variable is passed to a package manager (dnf, apt, or opkg) so that they can be installed on the image. Which package manager gets invoked depends on the format of the package feeds: do_package_write_rpm, do_package_write_deb, or do_package_write_ipk. Package installation happens regardless of whether a runtime package manager is included on the target. If there is no package manager onboard, then inessential files get deleted from the image at the end of this package installation phase for hygiene purposes and to save space.

Once package installation is complete, the package's post-installation scripts are run. These post-installation scripts come included with the packages. If all the post-installation scripts run successfully, a manifest is written to and optimizations are performed on the root filesystem image. This top-level .manifest file lists all the packages that have been installed on the image. The default library size and executable startup time optimizations are defined by the ROOTFS_POSTPROCESS_COMMAND variable.

Now that the root filesystem has been fully populated, the do_image task can begin image processing. First, all the pre-processing commands defined by the IMAGE_PREPROCESS_COMMAND variable get executed. Next, the process creates the final image output files. It does this by launching a do_image_* task for every image type (for example, cpio.lz4, ext4, and squashfs-lzo) specified in the IMAGE_FSTYPES variable. The build system then takes the contents of the IMAGE_ROOTFS directory and converts it into one or more image files. These output image files are compressed when the specified filesystem format allows for it. Lastly, the do_image_complete task finishes the image by executing every post-processing command defined by the IMAGE_POSTPROCESS_COMMAND variable.

Now that we have traced through Yocto's entire build workflow end-to-end, let's look at some best practices for structuring large projects.

Separating metadata into layers

Yocto metadata is organized around the following concepts:

- **distro**: OS features, including choice of C library, init system, and window manager
- **machine**: CPU architecture, kernel, drivers, and bootloader
- **recipe**: Application binaries and/or scripts
- **image**: Development, manufacturing, or production

These concepts map directly to actual byproducts of the build system, thus offering us guidance when designing our projects. We could rush to assemble everything inside a single layer, but that would likely result in a project that is inflexible and unmaintainable. Hardware inevitably gets revised, and one successful consumer device quickly multiplies into a series of products. For these reasons, it is better to adopt a multi-layered approach early on so that we end up with software components that we can easily modify, swap out, and reuse.

At a minimum, you should create individual distribution, BSP, and application layers for every major project that you start with Yocto. The distribution layer builds the target OS (Linux distro) that your application(s) will run on. Frame buffer and window manager configuration files belong in the distribution layer. The BSP layer specifies the bootloader, kernel, and device tree needed for the hardware to operate. The application layer contains the recipes needed to build all the packages that comprise your custom application(s).

We first encountered the MACHINE variable back in *Chapter 6, Selecting a Build System*, when we performed our first builds with Yocto. We looked at the DISTRO variable toward the end of the previous chapter, when we created our own distribution layer. The other Yocto exercises in this book rely on meta-poky for their distro layer. Layers are added to your build by inserting them into the BBLAYERS variable within the conf/bblayers.conf file in your active build directory. Here is an example of Poky's default BBLAYERS definition:

```
BBLAYERS ?= " \
  /home/frank/poky/meta \
  /home/frank/poky/meta-poky \
  /home/frank/poky/meta-yocto-bsp \
  "
```

Rather than edit bblayers.conf directly, use the bitbake-layers command-line tool to work with project layers. Resist the temptation to modify the Poky source tree directly. Always create your own layer (for example, meta-mine) above Poky and make your changes there. Here is what the BBLAYERS variable should look like within the conf/bblayers.conf file in your active build directory (for example, build-mine) during development:

```
BBLAYERS ?= " \
  /home/frank/poky/meta \
  /home/frank/poky/meta-poky \
  /home/frank/poky/meta-yocto-bsp \
  /home/frank/meta-mine \
  /home/frank/build-mine/workspace \
  "
```

workspace is a special temporary layer we encountered in the previous chapter when we experimented with devtool. Every BitBake layer has the same basic directory structure, regardless of what type of layer it is. Layer directory names typically start with the meta- prefix by convention. Take the following dummy layer, for example:

```
$ tree meta-example
meta-example
├── classes
│   ├── class-a.bbclass
│   ├── ...
│   └── class-z.bbclass
```

```
├── conf
│   └── layer.conf
├── COPYING.MIT
├── README
├── recipes-a
│   ├── package-a
│   │   └── package-a_0.1.bb
│   ├── ...
│   └── package-z
│       └── package-z_0.1.bb
├── recipes-b
│   └── ...
└── recipes-c
    └── ...
```

Every layer must have a `conf` directory with a `layer.conf` file so that BitBake can set up paths and search patterns for metadata files. We looked closely at the contents of `layer.conf` back in *Chapter 6, Selecting a Build System*, when we created a `meta-nova` layer for our Nova board. BSP and distribution layers may also have a `machine` or `distro` subdirectory under the `conf` directory with more `.conf` files. We examined the structure of the machine and distro layers in the previous chapter, when we built on top of the `meta-raspberrypi` layer and created our own `meta-mackerel` distro layer.

The `classes` subdirectory is only needed for layers that define their own BitBake classes. Recipes are organized by category, such as *connectivity*, so `recipes-a` is actually a placeholder for `recipes-connectivity` and so on. A category can contain one or more packages, each with its own set of BitBake recipe files (`.bb`). The recipe files are versioned by package release number. Again, names such as `package-a` and `package-z` are merely placeholders for real packages.

It's very easy to get lost in all these different layers. Even as you become more proficient with Yocto, there will be many times when you will find yourself asking how a particular file ended up on your image. Or, more likely, where are the recipe files you need to modify or extend to do what you need to do? Luckily, Yocto provides some command-line tools to help you answer these questions. I recommend that you explore `recipetool`, `oe-pkgdata-util`, and `oe-pkgdata-browser` and familiarize yourself with them. You could save yourself lots of hours.

Troubleshooting build failures

In the two preceding chapters, we learned how to build bootable images for QEMU, our Nova board, and the Raspberry Pi 4. But what happens when things go wrong? In this section, we will cover a number of useful debugging techniques that should make the prospect of wrangling Yocto build failures less intimidating.

To execute the commands in the subsequent exercises, you need to activate a BitBake environment, as follows:

1. First, navigate one level above the directory where you cloned Yocto.
2. Next, set up your BitBake work environment:

```
$ source poky/oe-init-build-env build-rpi
```

This sets a bunch of environment variables and puts you back in the `build-rpi` directory that we created in the previous chapter.

Isolating errors

So, your build failed, but where did it fail? You have an error message, but what does it mean and where did it come from? Do not despair. The first step in debugging is reproducing the bug. Once you can reproduce the bug, you can narrow the problem down to a series of known steps. Retracing those steps is how you spot the malfunction:

1. First, look at the BitBake build error message and see if you recognize any package or task names. If you're not sure what packages are in your workspace, you can use the following command to get a list of them:

    ```
    $ bitbake-layers show-recipes
    ```

2. Once you have identified which package failed to build, then search your current layers for any recipe or appends files related to that package, like so:

    ```
    $ find ../poky -name "*connman*.bb*"
    ```

    The package to search for is `connman` in this instance. The `../poky` argument in the preceding `find` command assumes your build directory is adjacent to `poky`, like `build-pi` from the previous chapter.

3. Next, list all the tasks available for the `connman` recipe:

    ```
    $ bitbake -c listtasks connman
    ```

4. To reproduce the error, you can rebuild `connman`, as follows:

```
$ bitbake -c clean connman && bitbake connman
```

Now that you know the recipe and task where your build failed, you are ready to move on to the next stage of debugging.

Dumping the environment

While you are debugging a build failure, you are going to want to see the current values of the variables within BitBake's environment. Let's start from the top and work our way down:

1. First, dump the global environment and search for the value of `DISTRO_FEATURES`:

   ```
   $ bitbake -e | less
   ```

   Enter `/DISTRO_FEATURES=` (note the leading forward slash); `less` should jump to a line that looks kind of like this:

   ```
   DISTRO_FEATURES="acl alsa argp bluetooth ext2 ipv4
   ipv6 largefile pcmcia usbgadget usbhost wifi xattr nfs
   zeroconf pci 3g nfc x11 vfat largefile opengl ptest
   multiarch wayland vulkan pulseaudio sysvinit gobject-
   introspection-data ldconfig"
   ```

2. To dump busybox's package environment and locate its source directory, use the following command:

   ```
   $ bitbake -e busybox | grep ^S=
   ```

3. To dump connman's package environment and locate its working directory, use the following command:

   ```
   $ bitbake -e connman | grep ^WORKDIR=
   ```

   A package's working directory is where its recipe task logs are saved during BitBake builds.

In *Step 1*, we could have piped the output from `bitbake -e` into `grep`, but `less` allows us to trace the evaluation of the variable more easily. Enter `/DISTRO_FEATURES` without the trailing equal sign in `less` to search for more occurrences of the variable. Hit *n* to jump forward to the next occurrence and *N* to jump back to the previous occurrence.

The same commands work for image as well as package recipes:

```
$ bitbake -e core-image-minimal | grep ^S=
```

In this case, the target environment to dump belongs to `core-image-minimal`.

Now that you know where the source and task log files are, let's look at some task logs.

Reading the task log

BitBake creates a log file for every shell task and saves it to a temp folder in the package's working directory. In the case of `connman`, the path to that temp folder looks sort of like this:

```
$ ./tmp/work/aarch64-poky-linux/connman/1.37-r0/temp
```

The format of the log filenames is `log.do_<task>.<pid>`. There are also `symlinks` with no `<pid>` at the end of their names, which point to the latest log files for each task. The log files contain the output of the task run, which in most cases is all the information you need to debug the problem. If not, guess what you can do?

Adding more logging

Logging from Python is different from logging from Shell in BitBake. To log from Python, you can use BitBake's `bb` module, which calls out to Python's standard `logger` module, as shown here:

```
bb.plain -> none; Output: logs console
bb.note -> logger.info; Output: logs
bb.warn -> logger.warning; Output: logs console
bb.error -> logger.error; Output: logs console
bb.fatal -> logger.critical; Output: logs console
bb.debug -> logger.debug; Output: logs console
```

To log from shell, you can use BitBake's `logging` class, whose source can be found at `meta/classes/logging.bbclass`. All recipes that inherit `base.bbclass` automatically inherit `logging.bbclass`. This means that all of the following logging functions should already be available to you from most shell recipe files:

```
bbplain -> Prints exactly what is passed in. Use sparingly.
bbnote -> Prints noteworthy conditions with the NOTE prefix.
bbwarn -> Prints a non-fatal warning with the WARNING prefix.
bberror -> Prints a non-fatal error with the ERROR prefix.
bbfatal -> Prints a fatal error and halts the build.
bbdebug -> Prints debug messages depending on log level.
```

According to the `logging.bbclass` source, the `bbdebug` function takes an integer debug log level as its first argument:

```
# Usage: bbdebug 1 "first level debug message"
#        bbdebug 2 "second level debug message
bbdebug () {
    USAGE = 'Usage: bbdebug [123] "message"'
    ...
}
```

Depending on the debug log level, a `bbdebug` message may or may not go to the console.

Running commands from devshell

BitBake provides a development shell so that you can run build commands manually in a more interactive environment. To get into a `devshell` for building `connman`, use the following command:

```
$ bitbake -c devshell connman
```

First, this command extracts and patches the source code for `connman`. Next, it opens a new Terminal in connman's source directory with the environment correctly set up for building. Once inside a `devshell`, you can run commands such as `./configure` and `make` or invoke the cross-compiler directly using `$CC`. `devshell` is perfect for experimenting with values such as `CFLAGS` or `LDFLAGS`, which get passed to tools such as CMake and Autotools as command-line arguments or environment variables. At the very least, you can increase the verbosity level of build commands if the error messages you are reading aren't meaningful.

Graphing dependencies

Sometimes, the cause of the build error cannot be located inside the package recipe files because the error actually occurred when building one of the package's dependencies. To get a list of dependencies for the `connman` package, use the following command:

```
$ bitbake -v connman
```

We can use BitBake's built-in task explorer to display and navigate dependencies:

```
$ bitbake -g connman -u taskexp
```

The preceding command launches the task explorer's graphical UI after analyzing `connman`:

> **Important Note**
> Some larger images, such as core-image-x11, have complex package dependency trees that will likely crash the task explorer.

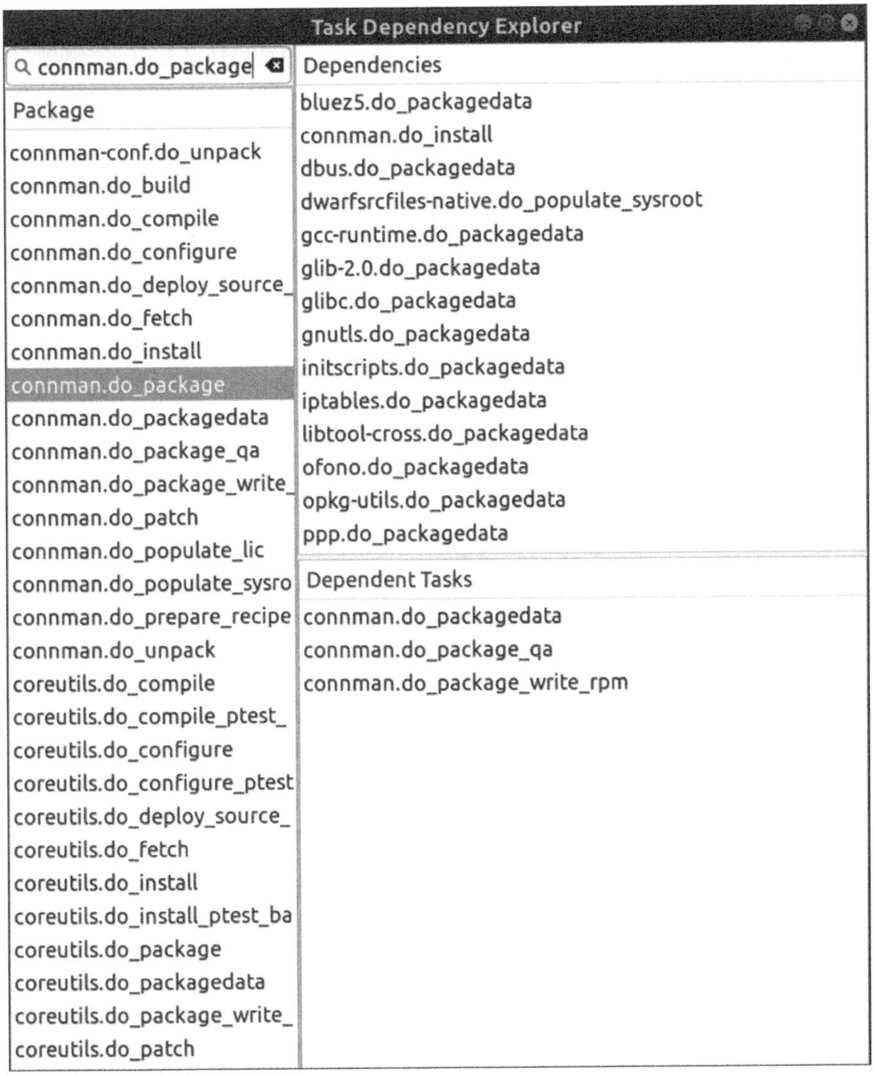

Figure 8.3 – Task explorer

Now, let's move away from the topic of builds and build failures and immerse ourselves in the raw materials of the Yocto Project; that is, BitBake metadata.

Understanding BitBake syntax and semantics

BitBake is a task runner. It is similar to GNU make in that respect, except that it operates on recipes instead of makefiles. The metadata in these recipes defines tasks in shell and Python. BitBake itself is written in Python. The OpenEmbedded project that Yocto is based on consists of BitBake and a large collection of recipes for building embedded Linux distributions. BitBake's power lies in its ability to run tasks in parallel while still satisfying inter-task dependencies. Its layered and inheritance-based approach to metadata enables Yocto to scale in ways Buildroot-based build systems simply cannot.

In *Chapter 6, Selecting a Build System*, we learned about the five types of BitBake metadata files; that is, .bb, .bbappend, .inc, .bbclass, and .conf. We also wrote BitBake recipes for building a basic helloworld program and nova-image image. Now, we will look more closely at the contents of BitBake metadata files. We know that tasks are written in a mix of shell and Python, but what goes where and why? What language constructs are available to us, and what can we do with them? How do we compose metadata to build our applications? Before you can harness the full power of Yocto, you need to learn to read and write BitBake.

Tasks

Tasks are functions that BitBake needs to run in sequence to execute a recipe. Recall that task names start with the do_ prefix. Here is a task from recipes-core/systemd:

```
do_deploy () {
    install ${B}/src/boot/efi/systemd-boot*.efi ${DEPLOYDIR}
}
addtask deploy before do_build after do_compile
```

In this example, a function named do_deploy is defined and immediately elevated to a task using the addtask command. The addtask command also specifies inter-task dependencies. For instance, this do_deploy task depends on the do_compile task completing, while the do_build task depends on the do_deploy task completing. The dependencies expressed by addtask can only be internal to the recipe file.

Tasks can also be deleted using the deltask command. This stops BitBake from executing the task as part of the recipe. To delete the preceding do_deploy task, use the following command:

```
deltask do_deploy
```

This deletes the task from the recipe, but the original do_deploy function definition remains and can still be called.

Dependencies

To ensure efficient parallel processing, BitBake handles dependencies at the task level. We saw just how `addtask` can be used to express dependencies between tasks within a single recipe file. Dependencies between tasks in different recipes also exist. In fact, these inter-task dependencies are what we usually think of when we consider build-time and runtime dependencies between packages.

Inter-task dependencies

Variable flags (**varflags**) are a means of attaching properties or attributes to variables. They behave like keys in a hash map in the sense that they let you set keys to values and retrieve values by their keys. BitBake defines a large set of varflags for use in recipes and classes. These varflags indicate what the components and dependencies of a task are. Here are some examples of varflags:

```
do_patch[postfuncs] += "copy_sources"
do_package_index[depends] += "signing-keys:do_deploy"
do_rootfs[recrdeptask] += "do_package_write_deb do_package_qa"
```

The value that's assigned to a varflag's key is often one or more other tasks. This means that BitBake varflags offer us another way to expresses inter-task dependencies, different from `addtask`. Most embedded Linux developers will probably never need to touch varflags in their day-to-day work. I introduce them here so that we can make sense of the following `DEPENDS` and `RDEPENDS` examples.

Build-time dependencies

BitBake uses the `DEPENDS` variable to manage build-time dependencies. The `deptask` varflag for a task signifies the task that must complete for each item in `DEPENDS` before that task can be executed (*BitBake User Manual*, `https://www.yoctoproject.org/docs/current/bitbake-user-manual/bitbake-user-manual.html#build-dependencies`):

```
do_package[deptask] += "do_packagedata"
```

In this example, the `do_packagedata` task of each item in `DEPENDS` must complete before `do_package` can execute.

Alternatively, you can bypass the `DEPENDS` variable and define your build-time dependencies explicitly using the `depends` flag:

```
do_patch[depends] += "quilt-native:do_populate_sysroot"
```

In this example, the do_populate_sysroot task belonging to the quilt-native namespace must complete before do_patch can execute. A recipe's tasks are often grouped together inside their own namespace to enable this sort of direct access.

Runtime dependencies

BitBake uses the PACKAGES and RDEPENDS variables to manage runtime dependencies. The PACKAGES variable lists all the runtime packages a recipe creates. Each of those packages can have RDEPENDS runtime dependencies. These are packages that must be installed for a given package to run. The rdeptask varflag for a task specifies which tasks must be completed for every runtime dependency before that task can be executed (*BitBake User Manual*, https://www.yoctoproject.org/docs/current/bitbake-user-manual/bitbake-user-manual.html#runtime-dependencies):

```
do_package_qa[rdeptask] = "do_packagedata"
```

In this example, the do_package_data task of each item in RDEPENDS must complete before do_package_qa can execute.

Similarly, the rdepends flag works much like the depends flag by allowing you to bypass the RDEPENDS variable. The only difference is that rdepends is enforced at runtime instead of build-time.

Variables

BitBake variable syntax resembles the make variable syntax. The scope of a variable in BitBake depends on the type of metadata file where a variable was defined. Every variable declared in a recipe file (.bb) is local. Every variable declared in a configuration file (.conf) is global. An image is just a recipe, so an image cannot affect what happens in another recipe.

Assignment and expansion

Variable assignment and expansion work like they do in shell. By default, assignment occurs as soon as the statement is parsed and is unconditional. The $ character triggers variable expansion. Enclosing braces are optional and serve to protect the variable to be expanded from characters immediately following it. Expanded variables are usually wrapped in double quotes to avoid accidental word splitting and globbing:

```
OLDPKGNAME = "dbus-x11"
PROVIDES_${PN} = "${OLDPKGNAME}"
```

Variables are mutable and normally evaluated at the time of reference, not assignment, like in `make`. This means that if a variable is referenced on the right-hand side of an assignment, then that referenced variable is not evaluated until the variable on the left-hand side is expanded. So, if a value on the right-hand side changes over time, then so does the value of the variable on the left-hand side.

Conditional assignment only defines a variable if it is undefined at the time of parsing. This prevents reassignment when you don't want that behavior:

```
PREFERRED_PROVIDER_virtual/kernel ?= "linux-yocto"
```

Conditional assignment is employed at the top of makefiles to prevent variables that may have already been set by the build system (for example, `CC`, `CFLAGS`, and `LDFLAGS`) from being overwritten. Conditional assignment ensures that we don't append or prepend to an undefined variable later on in a recipe.

Lazy assignment using `??=` behaves identically to `?=`, except that the assignment is made at the end of the parsing process rather than immediately (*BitBake User Manual*, `https://www.yoctoproject.org/docs/current/bitbake-user-manual/bitbake-user-manual.html#setting-a-weak-default-value`):

```
TOOLCHAIN_TEST_HOST ??= "localhost"
```

What that means is that if a variable name is on the left-hand side of multiple lazy assignments, then the last lazy assignment statement wins.

Another form of variable assignment forces the right-hand side of the assignment to be evaluated immediately at the time of parsing:

```
target_datadir := "${datadir}"
```

Note that the `:=` operator for immediate assignment comes from `make`, not shell.

Appending and prepending

Appending or prepending to variable or variable flags in BitBake is easy. The following two operators insert a single space in-between the value on the left-hand side and the value being appended or prepended from the right-hand side:

```
CXXFLAGS += "-std=c++11"
PACKAGES =+ "gdbserver"
```

Note that the `+=` operator means increment, not append, when applied to integer as opposed to string values.

If you wish to omit the single space, there are assignment operators that do that as well:

```
BBPATH .= ":${LAYERDIR}"
FILESEXTRAPATHS =. "${FILE_DIRNAME}/systemd:"
```

The single space versions of the appending and prepending assignment operators are used throughout BitBake metadata files.

Overrides

BitBake offers an alternative syntax for appending and prepending to variables. This style of concatenating is known as *override* syntax:

```
CFLAGS_append = " -DSQLITE_ENABLE_COLUMN_METADATA"
PROVIDES_prepend = "${PN} "
```

While it may not be obvious at first glance, the two preceding lines are not defining new variables. The `_append` and `_prepend` suffixes modify or *override* the values of existing variables. They function more like BitBake's `.=` and `=.` than the `+=` and `=+` operators in the sense that they omit the single space when combining strings. Unlike those operators, overrides are lazy, so assignment does not take place until all parsing completes.

Finally, let's look at a more advanced form of conditional assignment involving the `OVERRIDES` variable defined in `meta/conf/bitbake.conf`. The `OVERRIDES` variable is a colon-separated list of conditions that you want satisfied. This list is used to select between multiple versions of the same variable, each of which is distinguished by a different suffix. The various suffixes match the names of the conditions. Let's say the `OVERRIDES` list contains `${TRANSLATED_TARGET_ARCH}` as a condition. Now, you can define a version of a variable that is conditional on a target CPU architecture of `aarch64`, such as the `VALGRINDARCH_aarch64` variable:

```
VALGRINDARCH ?= "${TARGET_ARCH}"
VALGRINDARCH_aarch64 = "arm64"
VALGRINDARCH_x86-64 = "amd64"
```

When the `TRANSLATED_TARGET_ARCH` variable expands to `aarch64`, the `VALGRINDARCH_aarch64` version of the `VALGRINDARCH` variable is selected over all the other overrides. Selecting variable values based on `OVERRIDES` is cleaner and less brittle than other methods of conditional assignment, such as `#ifdef` directives in C.

BitBake also supports appending and prepending operations to variable values based on whether a specific item is listed in OVERRIDES (*BitBake User Manual*, https://www.yoctoproject.org/docs/current/bitbake-user-manual/bitbake-user-manual.html#conditional-metadata). Here are various real-world examples:

```
EXTRA_OEMAKE_prepend_task-compile = "${PARALLEL_MAKE} "
EXTRA_OEMAKE_prepend_task-install = "${PARALLEL_MAKEINST} "
DEPENDS = "attr libaio libcap acl openssl zip-native"
DEPENDS_append_libc-musl = " fts "
EXTRA_OECONF_append_libc-musl = " LIBS=-lfts "
EXTRA_OEMAKE_append_libc-musl = " LIBC=musl "
```

Notice how libc-musl is a condition for appending string values to the DEPENDS, EXTRA_OECONF, and EXTRA_OEMAKE variables. Like the earlier unconditional override syntax for appending and prepending to variables, this conditional syntax is also lazy. Assignment does not occur until after the recipes and configuration files have been parsed.

Conditionally appending and prepending to variables based on the contents of OVERRIDES is complicated and can result in unwanted surprises. I recommend getting lots of practice with conditional assignment based on OVERRIDES before adopting these even more advanced BitBake features.

Inline Python

The @ symbol in BitBake lets us inject and execute Python code inside variables. An inline Python expression gets evaluated each time the variable on the left-hand side of the = operator is expanded. An inline Python expression on the right-hand side of the := operator is evaluated only once at parse-time. Here are some examples of inline Python variable expansion:

```
PV = "${@bb.parse.vars_from_file(d.getVar('FILE', False),d)[1]
or '1.0'}"
BOOST_MAJ = "${@"_".join(d.getVar("PV").split(".")[0:2])}"
GO_PARALLEL_BUILD ?= "${@oe.utils.parallel_make_argument(d, '-p
%d')}"
```

Notice that bb and oe are aliases for BitBake and OpenEmbedded's Python modules. Also, notice that d.getVar("PV") is used to retrieve the value of the PV variable from the task's runtime environment. The d variable refers to a datastore object that BitBake saves a copy of the original execution environment to. This is largely how BitBake shell and Python code interoperate with one another.

Functions

Functions are the stuff that BitBake tasks are made of. They are written in either shell or Python and defined inside the `.bbclass`, `.bb`, and `.inc` files.

Shell

Functions written in shell are executed as functions or tasks. Functions that run as tasks usually have names that start with the `do_` prefix. Here is what a function looks like in shell:

```
meson_do_install() {
    DESTDIR='${D}' ninja -v ${PARALLEL_MAKEINST} install
}
```

Remember to remain shell-agnostic when writing your functions. BitBake executes shell snippets with `/bin/sh`, which may or may not be a Bash shell, depending on the host distro. Avoid bashisms by running the `scripts/verify-bashisms` linter against your shell scripts.

Python

BitBake understands three types of Python functions: pure, BitBake style, and anonymous.

Pure Python functions

A **pure Python function** is written in regular Python and called by other Python code. By *pure*, I mean that the function lives exclusively within the realm of the Python interpreter's execution environment, not *pure* in the functional programming sense. Here is an example from `meta/recipes-connectivity/bluez5/bluez5.inc`:

```
def get_noinst_tools_paths (d, bb, tools):
    s = list()
    bindir = d.getVar("bindir")
    for bdp in tools.split():
        f = os.path.basename(bdp)
        s.append("%s/%s" % (bindir, f))
    return "\n".join(s)
```

Notice that this function takes parameters just like a real Python function. There are a couple more noteworthy things I would also like to point out about this function. First, the datastore object is unavailable, so you need to pass it in as a function parameter (the `d` variable, in this instance). Second, the `os` module is automatically available, so there is no need to import or pass it in.

Pure Python functions can be called by inline Python assigned to shell variables using the @ symbol. In fact, that is precisely what happens on the next line of this include file:

```
FILES_${PN}-noinst-tools = \
"${@get_noinst_tools_paths(d, bb, d.getVar('NOINST_TOOLS'))}"
```

Notice that both the d datastore object and the bb module are automatically available inside the inline Python scope after the @ symbol.

BitBake style Python functions

A **BitBake style Python function** definition is denoted by the python keyword instead of Python's native def keyword. These functions are executed by invoking bb.build.exec_func() from other Python functions, including BitBake's own internal ones. Unlike pure Python functions, BitBake style functions do not take parameters. The absence of parameters isn't much of a problem since the datastore object is always available as a global variable; that is, d. While not as Pythonic, the BitBake style of defining functions is predominant throughout Yocto. Here is a BitBake style Python function definition from meta/classes/sign_rpm.bbclass:

```
python sign_rpm () {
    import glob
    from oe.gpg_sign import get_signer

    signer = get_signer(d, d.getVar('RPM_GPG_BACKEND'))
    rpms = glob.glob(d.getVar('RPM_PKGWRITEDIR') + '/*')

    signer.sign_rpms(rpms,
                     d.getVar('RPM_GPG_NAME'),
                     d.getVar('RPM_GPG_PASSPHRASE'),
                     d.getVar('RPM_FILE_CHECKSUM_DIGEST'),
                     int(d.getVar('RPM_GPG_SIGN_CHUNK')),
                     d.getVar('RPM_FSK_PATH'),
                     d.getVar('RPM_FSK_PASSWORD'))
}
```

Anonymous Python functions

An **anonymous Python function** looks much like a BitBake style Python function, but it executes during parsing. Because they run first, anonymous functions are good for operations that can be done at parse-time, such as initializing variables and other forms of setup. Anonymous function definitions can be written with or without the `__anonymous` function name:

```
python __anonymous () {
    systemd_packages = "${PN} ${PN}-wait-online"
    pkgconfig = d.getVar('PACKAGECONFIG')
    if ('openvpn' or 'vpnc' or 'l2tp' or 'pptp') in pkgconfig.
split():
        systemd_packages += " ${PN}-vpn"
    d.setVar('SYSTEMD_PACKAGES', systemd_packages)
}
python () {
    packages = d.getVar('PACKAGES').split()
    if d.getVar('PACKAGEGROUP_DISABLE_COMPLEMENTARY') != '1':
        types = ['', '-dbg', '-dev']
        if bb.utils.contains('DISTRO_FEATURES', 'ptest', True,
False, d):
            types.append('-ptest')
        packages = [pkg + suffix for pkg in packages
                    for suffix in types]
        d.setVar('PACKAGES', ' '.join(packages))
    for pkg in packages:
        d.setVar('ALLOW_EMPTY_%s' % pkg, '1')
}
```

The `d` variable within an anonymous Python function represents the datastore for the entire recipe (*BitBake User Manual*, `https://www.yoctoproject.org/docs/current/bitbake-user-manual/bitbake-user-manual.html#anonymous-python-functions`). So, when you set a variable inside an anonymous function scope, that value will be available to other functions by way of the global datastore object when they run.

RDEPENDS revisited

Let's return to the subject of runtime dependencies. These are packages that must be installed for a given package to run. This list is defined in the package's `RDEPENDS` variable. Here is an interesting excerpt from `populate_sdk_base.bbclass`:

```
do_sdk_depends[rdepends] = "${@get_sdk_ext_rdepends(d)}"
```

And here is the definition of the corresponding inline Python function:

```
def get_sdk_ext_rdepends(d):
    localdata = d.createCopy()
    localdata.appendVar('OVERRIDES', ':task-populate-sdk-ext')
    return localdata.getVarFlag('do_populate_sdk', 'rdepends')
```

There is quite a bit to unpack here. First, the function makes a copy of the datastore object so as not to modify the task runtime environment. Recall, that the `OVERRIDES` variable is a list of conditions used to select between multiple versions of a variable. The next line adds a condition of `task-populate-sdk-ext` to the `OVERRIDES` list in the local copy of the datastore. Lastly, the function returns the value of the `rdepends` varflag for the `do_populate_sdk` task. The difference now is that `rdepends` is evaluated using the `_task-populate-sdk-ext` versions of variables, such as the following:

```
SDK_EXT_task-populate-sdk-ext = "-ext"
SDK_DIR_task-populate-sdk-ext = "${WORKDIR}/sdk-ext"
```

I find this use of temporary `OVERRIDES` to be both clever and terrifying.

BitBake syntax and semantics can seem daunting. Combining shell and Python makes for an interesting mix of language features. Not only do we now know how to define variables and functions, but we can now also inherit from class files, override variables, and change conditions programmatically. These advanced concepts appear again and again in the `.bb`, `.bbappend`, `.inc`, `.bbclass`, and `.conf` files and will become increasingly recognizable over time. As we strive to achieve proficiency in BitBake and begin to stretch our newfound abilities, mistakes are bound to occur.

Summary

Even though you can build just about anything with Yocto, it's not always easy to tell what the build system is doing or how. There is hope for us, though. There are command-line tools to help us find where something came from and how to change it. There are task logs we can read from and write to. There is also `devshell`, which we can use to configure and compile individual things from the command line. And if we divide our projects into multiple layers from the outset, we are likely to get much more mileage out of the work we do.

BitBake's mix of shell and Python supports some powerful language constructs, such as inheritance, overrides, and conditional variable selection. That's both good and bad. It's good in the sense that layers and recipes are completely composable and customizable. It's bad in the sense that metadata in different recipe files and different layers can interact in strange and unexpected ways. Combine those powerful language features with the datastore object's ability to act as a portal between the shell and Python execution environments, and you have a recipe for countless hours of fun.

This concludes our in-depth exploration of the Yocto Project and the first section of this book on the *Elements of Embedded Linux*. In the next section of this book, we switch gears and examine *System Architecture and Design Decisions*, beginning with *Chapter 9, Creating a Storage Strategy*. We will get a chance to use Yocto again in *Chapter 10, Updating Software in the Field*, when we evaluate Mender.

Further reading

The following resources contain more information about the topics that were introduced in this chapter:

- *Yocto Projects Overview and Concepts Manual*, by Scott Rifenbark: `https://www.yoctoproject.org/docs/latest/overview-manual/overview-manual.html`
- *What I Wish I'd Known*, Yocto Project: `https://www.yoctoproject.org/docs/what-i-wish-id-known`
- *BitBake User Manual*, by Richard Purdie, Chris Larson, and Phil Blundell: `https://www.yoctoproject.org/docs/latest/bitbake-user-manual/bitbake-user-manual.html`
- *Embedded Linux Projects Using Yocto Project Cookbook*, by Alex Gonzalez

Section 2: System Architecture and Design Decisions

By the end of *Section 2*, we will be able to make informed decisions concerning the storage of programs and data, how to divide work between kernel device drivers and applications, and how to initialize the system.

This part of the book comprises the following chapters:

- *Chapter 9, Creating a Storage Strategy*
- *Chapter 10, Updating Software in the Field*
- *Chapter 11, Interfacing with Device Drivers*
- *Chapter 12, Prototyping with Breakout Boards*
- *Chapter 13, Starting Up – The init Program*
- *Chapter 14, Starting with BusyBox runit*
- *Chapter 15, Managing Power*

9
Creating a Storage Strategy

The mass storage options for embedded devices have a great impact on the rest of the system in terms of the robustness, speed, and methods used for in-field updates. Most devices employ flash memory in some form or another. Flash memory has become much less expensive over the past few years as storage capacities have increased from tens of megabytes to tens of gigabytes.

In this chapter, we will begin with a detailed look at the technology behind flash memory, as well as how different memory organization strategies affect the low-level driver software that has to manage it, including the Linux **memory technology device** (**MTD**) layer.

For each flash technology, there are different choices when it comes to the filesystem. I will describe those most commonly found on embedded devices and complete the survey by providing a summary of choices for each type of flash memory. Finally, we will consider some techniques that make the best use of flash memory and draw everything together into a coherent storage strategy.

In this chapter, we will cover the following topics:

- Storage options
- Accessing flash memory from the bootloader
- Accessing flash memory from Linux

- Filesystems for flash memory
- Filesystems for NOR and NAND flash memory
- Filesystems for managed flash
- Read-only compressed filesystems
- Temporary filesystems
- Making the root filesystem read-only
- Filesystem choices

Let's get started!

Technical requirements

To follow along with the examples in this chapter, make sure you have the following:

- A Linux-based host system with `e2fsprogs`, `genext2fs`, `mtd-utils`, `squashfs-tools`, and `util-linux` or their equivalents installed
- The U-Boot source tree from *Chapter 3, All About Bootloaders*
- A microSD card reader and card
- A USB to TTL 3.3V serial cable
- The Linux kernel source tree from *Chapter 4, Configuring and Building the Kernel*
- BeagleBone Black
- A 5V 1A DC power supply

You should have already downloaded and built U-Boot for the BeagleBone Black back in *Chapter 3, All About Bootloaders.* You should have obtained the Linux kernel source tree from *Chapter 4, Configuring and Building the Kernel.*

Ubuntu provides packages for most of the tools needed to create and format various filesystems. To install the tools on an Ubuntu 20.04 LTS system, use the following command:

```
$ sudo apt install e2fsprogs genext2fs mtd-utils squashfs-tools
util-linux
```

The `mtd-utils` package includes `mtdinfo`, `mkfs.jffs2`, `sumtool`, `nandwrite`, and the UBI command-line tools.

Storage options

Embedded devices need storage that takes little power and is physically compact, robust, and reliable over a lifetime of perhaps tens of years. In almost all cases, this means solid-state storage. Solid-state storage was introduced many years ago with **read-only memory (ROM)**, but for the past 20 years, it has been a flash memory of some kind. There have been several generations of flash memory in that time, progressing from NOR to NAND to managed flash such as eMMC.

NOR flash is expensive but reliable and can be mapped into the CPU address space, which allows you to execute code directly from flash. NOR flash chips are low capacity, ranging from a few megabytes to a gigabyte or so.

NAND flash memory is much cheaper than NOR and is available in higher capacities, in the range of tens of megabytes to tens of gigabytes. However, it needs a lot of hardware and software support to turn it into a useful storage medium.

Managed flash memory consists of one or more NAND flash chips, packaged with a controller that handles the complexities of flash memory and presents a hardware interface similar to that of a hard disk. The attraction is that it removes complexity from the driver software and insulates the system designer from the frequent changes in flash technology. SD cards, eMMC chips, and USB flash drives fit into this category. Almost all of the current generations of smartphones and tablets have eMMC storage, and this trend is likely to progress with other categories of embedded devices.

Hard drives are seldom found in embedded systems. One exception is digital video recording in set-top boxes and smart TVs, in which a large amount of storage is needed with fast write times.

In all cases, robustness is of prime importance: you want the device to boot and reach a functional state, despite power failures and unexpected resets. You should choose filesystems that behave well under such circumstances.

In this section, we will learn the difference between NOR and NAND flash and consider our options when choosing a managed flash technology.

NOR flash

The memory cells in NOR flash chips are arranged into erase blocks of, for example, 128 KiB. Erasing a block sets all the bits to 1. It can be programmed one word at a time (8, 16, or 32 bits, depending on the data bus width). Each erase cycle damages the memory cells slightly, and after a number of cycles, the erase block becomes unreliable and cannot be used anymore. The maximum number of erase cycles should be given in the data sheet for the chip but is usually in the range of 100K to 1M.

The data can be read word by word. The chip is usually mapped into the CPU address space, which means that you can execute code directly from NOR flash. This makes it a convenient place to put the bootloader code as it needs no initialization beyond hardwiring the address mapping. SoCs that support NOR flash in this way have configurations that provide a default memory mapping so that it encompasses the reset vector of the CPU.

The kernel, and even the root filesystem, can also be located in flash memory, avoiding the need for copying them into RAM, and thus creating devices with small memory footprints. This technique is known as **eXecute In Place**, or **XIP**. It is very specialized, and I will not examine it further here. I have included some references at the end of this chapter, in the *Further reading* section.

There is a standard register-level interface for NOR flash chips called the **Common Flash Interface** or **CFI**, which all modern chips support. The CFI is described in standard JESD68, which you can get from `https://www.jedec.org/`.

Now that we have learned what NOR flash is, let's look at NAND flash.

NAND flash

NAND flash is much cheaper than NOR flash and has a higher capacity. First-generation NAND chips stored one bit per memory cell in what is now known as a **single-level cell** (**SLC**) organization. Later generations moved on to two bits per cell in **multi-level cell** (**MLC**) chips and now to three bits per cell in **tri-level cell** (**TLC**) chips. As the number of bits per cell increased, the reliability of the storage decreased, requiring more complex controller hardware and software to compensate for this. Where reliability is a concern, you should make sure you are using SLC NAND flash chips.

As with NOR flash, NAND flash is organized into erase blocks ranging in size from 16 KiB to 512 KiB and, once again, erasing a block sets all the bits to 1. However, the number of erase cycles before the block becomes unreliable is lower, typically as few as 1K cycles for TLC chips and up to 100K for SLC. NAND flash can only be read and written in pages, usually of 2 or 4 KiB. Since they cannot be accessed byte by byte, they cannot be mapped into the address space, so code and data have to be copied into RAM before they can be accessed.

Data transfers to and from the chip are prone to bit flips, which can be detected and corrected using **error-correction codes** (**ECCs**). SLC chips generally use a simple **hamming code**, which can be implemented efficiently in software and can correct a single-bit error in a page read. MLC and TLC chips need more sophisticated codes, such as **Bose-Chaudhuri-Hocquenghem** (**BCH**), which can correct up to 8-bit errors per page. These need hardware support.

The ECCs have to be stored somewhere, and so there is an extra area of memory per page known as the **out-of-band (OOB)** area, or the spare area. SLC designs usually have 1 byte of OOB per 32 bytes of main storage, so for a 2 KiB page device, the OOB is 64 bytes per page, and for a 4 KiB page, it is 128 bytes. MLC and TLC chips have proportionally larger OOB areas, to accommodate for more complex ECCs. The following diagram shows the organization of a chip with a 128 KiB erase block and 2 KiB pages:

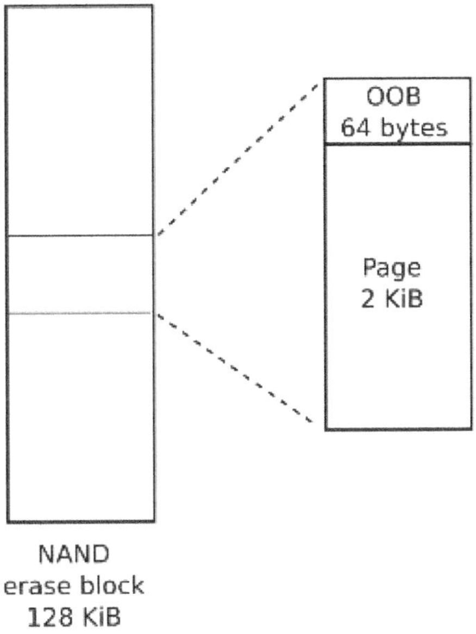

Figure 9.1 – OOB area

During production, the manufacturer tests all the blocks and marks any that fail by setting a flag in the OOB area of each page in the block. It is not uncommon to find that brand new chips have up to 2% of their blocks marked bad in this way. Saving the OOB information for analyzing before erasing the area can be useful when there is a problem. Furthermore, it is within the specification for a similar proportion of blocks to give errors on erase before the erase cycle limit is reached. The NAND flash driver should detect this and mark it as bad.

Once space has been made in the OOB area for a bad block flag and ECC bytes, there are still some bytes left. Some flash filesystems make use of these free bytes to store filesystem metadata. Consequently, many parts of the system are interested in the layout of the OOB area: the SoC ROM boot code, the bootloader, the kernel MTD driver, the filesystem code, and the tools to create filesystem images. There is not much standardization, so it is easy to get into a situation in which the bootloader writes data using an OOB format that cannot be read by the kernel MTD driver. It is up to you to make sure that they all agree.

Access to NAND flash chips requires a NAND flash controller, which is usually part of the SoC. You will need the corresponding driver in the bootloader and kernel. The NAND flash controller handles the hardware interface for the chip, transferring data to and from pages, and may include hardware for error correction.

There is a standard register-level interface for NAND flash chips known as the **Open NAND Flash Interface** or **ONFI**, which most modern chips adhere to. See `http://www.onfi.org/` for more information.

Modern NAND flash technology is complicated. Pairing NAND flash memory with a controller is no longer enough. We also need an interface to the hardware that abstracts most of the technical details, such as error correction, away.

Managed flash

The burden of supporting flash memory in the operating system – NAND in particular – becomes smaller if there is a well-defined hardware interface and a standard flash controller that hides the complexities of the memory. This is managed flash memory, and it is becoming more and more common. In essence, it means combining one or more flash chips with a microcontroller that offers an ideal storage device with a small sector size, and that is compatible with conventional filesystems. The most important types of chips for embedded systems are **Secure Digital** (**SD**) cards and the embedded variant known as **eMMC**.

MultiMediaCard and Secure Digital cards

The **MultiMediaCard** (**MMC**) was introduced in 1997 by SanDisk and Siemens as a form of packaged storage using flash memory. Shortly after, in 1999, SanDisk, Matsushita, and Toshiba created the **Secure Digital** (**SD**) card, which is based on MMC but adds encryption and DRM (the "secure" part of the name). Both were intended for consumer electronics such as digital cameras, music players, and similar devices. Currently, SD cards are the dominant form of managed flash for consumer and embedded electronics, even though the encryption features are seldom used. Newer versions of the SD specification allow smaller packaging (mini SD and microSD, which is often written as uSD) and larger capacities: high capacity SDHC up to 32 GB and extended capacity SDXC up to 2TB.

The hardware interface for MMC and SD cards is very similar, and it is possible to use full-sized MMC cards in full-sized SD card slots (but not the other way round). Early incarnations used a 1-bit **Serial Peripheral Interface** (**SPI**); more recent cards use a 4-bit interface.

There is a command set for reading and writing memory in sectors of 512 bytes. Inside the package is a microcontroller and one or more NAND flash chips, as shown in the following diagram:

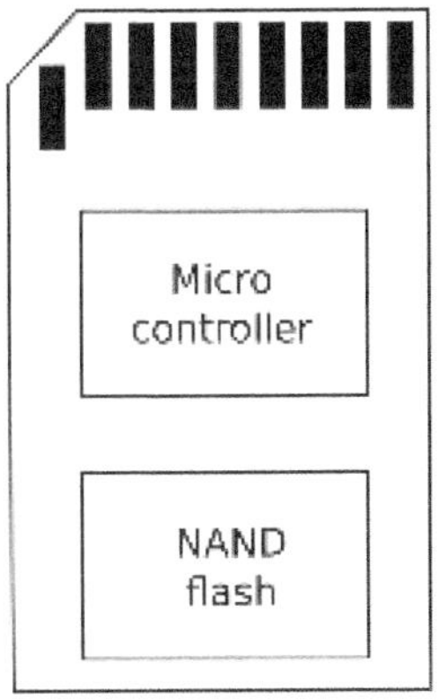

Figure 9.2 – SD card package

The microcontroller implements the command set and manages the flash memory, performing the function of a flash translation layer, as described later in this chapter. They are preformatted with a FAT filesystem: FAT16 on SDSC cards, FAT32 on SDHC, and exFAT on SDXC. The quality of the NAND flash chips and the software on the microcontroller varies greatly between cards. It is questionable whether any of them are sufficiently reliable for deep embedded use, and certainly not with a FAT filesystem, which is prone to file corruption. Remember that the prime use case for MMC and SD cards is for removable storage on cameras, tablets, and phones.

eMMC

Embedded MMC or **eMMC** is simply MMC memory that's been packaged so that it can be soldered on to the motherboard, using a 4- or 8-bit interface for data transfer. However, they are intended to be used as storage for an operating system, so the components are capable of performing that task. The chips are usually not preformatted with any filesystem.

Other types of managed flash

One of the first managed flash technologies was **CompactFlash** (**CF**), which uses a subset of the **Personal Computer Memory Card International Association** (**PCMCIA**) hardware interface. CF exposes memory through a parallel ATA interface and appears to the operating system as a standard hard disk. They were common in x86-based single board computers and professional video and camera equipment.

One other format that we use every day is the **USB flash drive**. In this case, memory is accessed through a USB interface and the controller implements the USB mass storage specification, as well as the flash translation layer and interface to the flash chip, or chips. The USB mass storage protocol, in turn, is based on the SCSI disk command set. As with MMC and SD cards, they are usually preformatted with a FAT filesystem. Their main use case in embedded systems is to exchange data with PCs.

A recent addition to the list of options for managed flash storage is **Universal Flash Storage** (**UFS**). Like eMMC, it is packaged in a chip that is mounted on the motherboard. It has a high-speed serial interface and can achieve data rates greater than eMMC. It supports a SCSI disk command set.

Now that we know what types of flash are available, let's learn how U-Boot loads a kernel image from each of them.

Accessing flash memory from the bootloader

In *Chapter 3, All About Bootloaders*, I mentioned the need for the bootloader to load kernel binaries and other images from various flash devices, and to perform system maintenance tasks such as erasing and reprogramming flash memory. It follows that the bootloader must have the drivers and infrastructure needed to support read, erase, and write operations on the type of memory you have, whether it be NOR, NAND, or managed. I will use U-Boot in the following examples; other bootloaders follow a similar pattern.

U-Boot and NOR flash

U-Boot has drivers for NOR CFI chips in `drivers/mtd` and utilizes various `erase` commands to erase memory and `cp.b` to copy data byte by byte, programming the flash cells. Suppose that you have NOR flash memory mapped from `0x40000000` to `0x48000000`, of which 4 MiB, starting at `0x40040000`, is a kernel image. Here, you would load a new kernel into flash using these U-Boot commands:

```
=> tftpboot 100000 uImage
=> erase 40040000 403fffff
=> cp.b 100000 40040000 $(filesize)
```

The `filesize` variable in the preceding example is set by the `tftpboot` command, to the size of the file just downloaded.

U-Boot and NAND flash

For NAND flash, you need a driver for the NAND flash controller on your SoC, which you can find in the U-Boot source code in the `drivers/mtd/nand` directory. You can use the `nand` command to manage memory using the `erase`, `write`, and `read` sub-commands. This example shows a kernel image being loaded into RAM at `0x82000000` and then placed into flash, starting at the `0x280000` offset:

```
=> tftpboot 82000000 uImage
=> nand erase 280000 400000
=> nand write 82000000 280000 $(filesize)
```

U-Boot can also read files stored in the JFFS2, YAFFS2, and UBIFS filesystems. `nand write` will skip blocks that are marked as bad. If the data you're writing is for a filesystem, make sure that the filesystem also skips bad blocks.

U-Boot and MMC, SD, and eMMC

U-Boot has drivers for several MMC controllers in `drivers/mmc`. You can access raw data using `mmc read` and `mmc write` at the user interface level, which allows you to handle raw kernel and filesystem images.

U-Boot can also read files from the FAT32 and ext4 filesystems on MMC storage.

U-Boot needs drivers to access NOR, NAND, and managed flash. Which driver you should use depends on your choice of NOR chip or the flash controller on your SoC. Accessing raw NOR and NAND flash from Linux involves additional layers of software.

Accessing flash memory from Linux

Raw NOR and NAND flash memory is handled by the **Memory Technology Device** subsystem, or **MTD**, which provides you with basic interfaces to read, erase, and write blocks of flash memory. In the case of NAND flash, there are also functions that handle the OOB area and are used to identify bad blocks.

For managed flash, you need drivers to handle a particular hardware interface. MMC/SD cards and eMMC use the `mmcblk` driver, while CompactFlash and hard drives use the SCSI disk driver, `sd`. USB flash drives use the `usb_storage` driver, together with the `sd` driver.

Memory technology devices

The MTD subsystem was started by David Woodhouse in 1999 and has been extensively developed over the intervening years. In this section, I will concentrate on the way it handles the two main technologies, NOR and NAND flash.

MTD consists of three layers: a core set of functions, a set of drivers for various types of chips, and user-level drivers that present the flash memory as a character device or a block device, as shown in the following diagram:

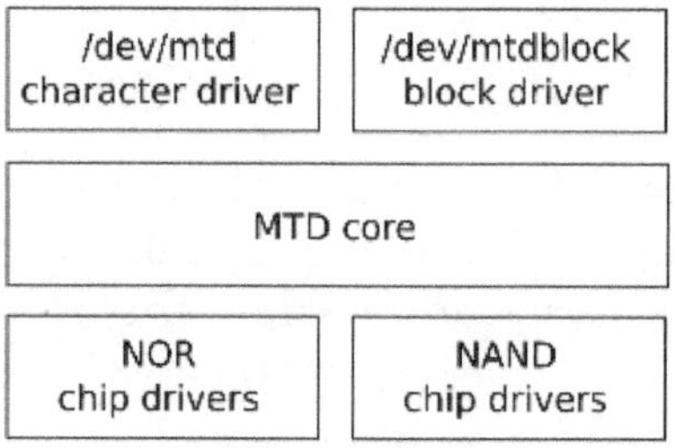

Figure 9.3 – MTD layers

The chip drivers are at the lowest level and interface with flash chips. Only a small number of drivers are needed for NOR flash chips, enough to cover the CFI standard and variations, plus a few non-compliant chips, which are now mostly obsolete. For NAND flash, you will need a driver for the NAND flash controller you are using; this is usually supplied as part of the board support package. There are drivers for about 40 of them in the current mainline kernel, in the `drivers/mtd/nand` directory.

MTD partitions

In most cases, you will want to partition the flash memory into a number of areas, for example, to provide space for a bootloader, a kernel image, or a root filesystem. In MTD, there are several ways to specify the size and location of partitions, with the main ones being as follows:

- Through the kernel command line using `CONFIG_MTD_CMDLINE_PARTS`
- Via the device tree using `CONFIG_MTD_OF_PARTS`
- With a platform-mapping driver

In the case of the first option, the kernel command-line option to use is `mtdparts`, which is defined as follows in the Linux source code in `drivers/mtd/cmdlinepart.c`:

```
mtdparts=<mtddef>[;<mtddef]
<mtddef> := <mtd-id>:<partdef>[,<partdef>]
```

```
<mtd-id> := unique name for the chip
<partdef> := <size>[@<offset>] [<name>] [ro] [lk]
<size> := size of partition OR "-" to denote all remaining
     space
<offset> := offset to the start of the partition; leave blank
     to follow the previous partition without any gap
<name> := '(' NAME ')'
```

Perhaps an example will help. Imagine that you have one flash chip of 128 MiB that is to be divided into five partitions. A typical command line would be this:

```
mtdparts=:512k(SPL)ro,780k(U-Boot)ro,128k(U-BootEnv),
4m(Kernel),-(Filesystem)
```

The first element, before the colon, is `mtd-id`, which identifies the flash chip, either by number or by the name assigned by the board support package. If there is only one chip, as there is here, it can be left empty. If there is more than one chip, the information for each is separated by a semicolon. Then, for each chip, there is a comma-separated list of partitions, each with a size in bytes, KiB (`k`) or MiB (`m`), and a name in parentheses. The `ro` suffix makes the partition read-only to MTD and is often used to prevent accidental overwriting of the bootloader. The size of the last partition for the chip may be replaced by a dash (`-`), indicating that it should take up all the remaining space.

You can see a summary of the configuration at runtime by reading `/proc/mtd`:

```
# cat /proc/mtd
dev: size erasesize name
mtd0: 00080000 00020000 "SPL"
mtd1: 000C3000 00020000 "U-Boot"
mtd2: 00020000 00020000 "U-BootEnv"
mtd3: 00400000 00020000 "Kernel"
mtd4: 07A9D000 00020000 "Filesystem"
```

There is more detailed information for each partition in `/sys/class/mtd`, including the erase block size and the page size, and it is nicely summarized using `mtdinfo`:

```
# mtdinfo /dev/mtd0
mtd0
Name:                SPL
Type:                nand
```

```
Eraseblock size:          131072 bytes, 128.0 KiB
Amount of eraseblocks:        4 (524288 bytes, 512.0 KiB)
Minimum input/output unit size: 2048 bytes
Sub-page size:          512 bytes
OOB size:          64 bytes
Character device major/minor:   90:0
Bad blocks are allowed:     true
Device is writable:    false
```

Another way of specifying MTD partitions is through the device tree. Here is an example that creates the same partitions as the command line example:

```
nand@0,0 {
 #address-cells = <1>;
 #size-cells = <1>;
 partition@0 {
  label = "SPL";
  reg = <0 0x80000>;
 };
 partition@80000 {
  label = "U-Boot";
  reg = <0x80000 0xc3000>;
 };
 partition@143000 {
  label = "U-BootEnv";
  reg = <0x143000 0x20000>;
 };
 partition@163000 {
  label = "Kernel";
  reg = <0x163000 0x400000>;
 };
 partition@563000 {
  label = "Filesystem";
  reg = <0x563000 0x7a9d000>;
 };
};
```

A third alternative is to code the partition information as platform data in an `mtd_partition` structure, as shown in this example taken from `arch/arm/mach-omap2/board-omap3beagle.c` (`NAND_BLOCK_SIZE` is defined elsewhere as `128 KiB`):

```
static struct mtd_partition omap3beagle_nand_partitions[] = {
  {
    .name = "X-Loader",
    .offset = 0,
    .size = 4 * NAND_BLOCK_SIZE,
    .mask_flags = MTD_WRITEABLE, /* force read-only */
  },
  {
    .name = "U-Boot",
    .offset = 0x80000;
    .size = 15 * NAND_BLOCK_SIZE,
    .mask_flags = MTD_WRITEABLE, /* force read-only */
  },
  {
    .name = "U-Boot Env",
    .offset = 0x260000;
    .size = 1 * NAND_BLOCK_SIZE,
  },
  {
    .name = "Kernel",
    .offset = 0x280000;
    .size = 32 * NAND_BLOCK_SIZE,
  },
  {
    .name = "File System",
    .offset = 0x680000;
    .size = MTDPART_SIZ_FULL,
  },
};
```

Platform data is deprecated: you will only find it used in BSPs for old SoCs that have not been updated to use a device tree.

MTD device drivers

The upper level of the MTD subsystem contains a pair of device drivers:

- A character device, with a major number of `90`. There are two device nodes per MTD partition number, N: `/dev/mtdN` (minor number=N*2) and `/dev/mtdNro` (minor number=(N*2 + 1)). The latter is just a read-only version of the former.
- A block device, with a major number of `31` and a minor number of N. The device nodes are in the form `/dev/mtdblockN`.

Let's look at the character device first since it is the most commonly used of the two.

The MTD character device, mtd

The character devices are the most important: they allow you to access the underlying flash memory as an array of bytes so that you can read and write (program) the flash. It also implements a number of `ioctl` functions that allow you to erase blocks and manage the OOB area on NAND chips. The following list has been taken from `include/uapi/mtd/mtd-abi.h`:

- `MEMGETINFO`: Gets basic MTD characteristic information.
- `MEMERASE`: Erases blocks in the MTD partition.
- `MEMWRITEOOB`: Writes out-of-band data for the page.
- `MEMREADOOB`: Reads out-of-band data for the page.
- `MEMLOCK`: Locks the chip (if supported).
- `MEMUNLOCK`: Unlocks the chip (if supported).
- `MEMGETREGIONCOUNT`: Gets the number of erase regions: non-zero if there are erase blocks of differing sizes in the partition, which is common for NOR flash, rare on NAND.
- `MEMGETREGIONINFO`: If `MEMGETREGIONCOUNT` is non-zero, this can be used to get the offset, size, and block count of each region.
- `MEMGETOOBSEL`: Deprecated.
- `MEMGETBADBLOCK`: This gets the bad block flag.
- `MEMSETBADBLOCK`: This sets the bad block flag.
- `OTPSELECT`: This sets OTP (one-time programmable) mode, if the chip supports it.
- `OTPGETREGIONCOUNT`: This gets the number of OTP regions.
- `OTPGETREGIONINFO`: This gets information about an OTP region.
- `ECCGETLAYOUT`: Deprecated.

There is a set of utility programs known as `mtd-utils` for manipulating flash memory that makes use of these `ioctl` functions. The source can be found at `git://git.infradead.org/mtd-utils.git` and is available as a package in the Yocto Project and Buildroot. The essential tools are shown in the following list. The package also contains utilities for the JFFS2 and UBI/UBIFS filesystems, which I will cover later. For each of these tools, the MTD character device is one of the following parameters:

- **flash_erase**: Erases a range of blocks.
- **flash_lock**: Locks a range of blocks.
- **flash_unlock**: Unlocks a range of blocks.
- **nanddump**: Dumps memory from NAND flash, optionally including the OOB area. Skips bad blocks.
- **nandtest**: Tests and performs diagnostics for NAND flash.
- **nandwrite**: Writes (programs) data from a file into NAND flash, skipping bad blocks.

> Tip
>
> You must always erase flash memory before writing new contents to it: `flash_erase` is the command that does this.

To program NOR flash, you simply copy bytes to the MTD device node using a file copy command such as `cp`.

Unfortunately, this doesn't work with NAND memory as the copy will fail at the first bad block. Instead, use `nandwrite`, which skips over any bad blocks. To read back NAND memory, you should use `nanddump`, which also skips bad blocks.

The MTD block device, mtdblock

The `mtdblock` driver isn't used often. Its purpose is to present flash memory as a block device you can use to format and mount a filesystem. However, it has severe limitations because it does not handle bad blocks in NAND flash, it does not do wear leveling, and it does not handle the mismatch in size between filesystem blocks and flash erase blocks. In other words, it does not have a flash translation layer, which is essential for reliable file storage. The only case where the `mtdblock` device is useful is for mounting read-only file systems such as SquashFS on top of reliable flash memory such as NOR.

> **Tip**
> If you want a read-only filesystem on NAND flash, you should use the UBI driver, as described later in this chapter.

Logging kernel oops to MTD

A kernel error, or oops, is normally logged via the klogd and syslogd daemons to a circular memory buffer or a file. Following a reboot, the log will be lost in the case of a ring buffer, and even in the case of a file, it may not have been properly written to before the system crashed. A more reliable method is to write oops and kernel panics to an MTD partition as a circular log buffer. You can enable it with `CONFIG_MTD_OOPS` and add `console=ttyMTDN` to the kernel command line, with `N` being the MTD device number to write the messages to.

Simulating NAND memory

The NAND simulator emulates a NAND chip using system RAM. The main use is for testing code that has to be NAND-aware without access to physical NAND memory. In particular, the ability to simulate bad blocks, bit flips, and other errors allows you to test code paths that are difficult to exercise using real flash memory. For more information, the best place to look is in the code itself, which provides a comprehensive description of the ways you can configure the driver. The code is in `drivers/mtd/nand/nandsim.c`. Enable it with the `CONFIG_MTD_NAND_NANDSIM` kernel configuration.

The MMC block driver

MMC/SD cards and eMMC chips are accessed using the `mmcblk` block driver. You need a host controller to match the MMC adapter you are using, which is part of the board support package. The drivers are located in the Linux source code in `drivers/mmc/host`.

MMC storage is partitioned using a partition table in exactly the same way you would for hard disks; that is, by using `fdisk` or a similar utility.

We now know how Linux accesses each type of flash. Next, we will look at the problems intrinsic to flash memory and how Linux deals with them, either by way of the filesystem or the block device driver.

Filesystems for flash memory

There are several challenges when it comes to making efficient use of flash memory for mass storage: the mismatch between the size of an erase block and a disk sector, the limited number of erase cycles per erase block, and the need for bad block handling on NAND chips. These differences are resolved by a **flash translation layer**, or **FTL**.

Flash translation layers

A flash translation layer has the following features:

- **Sub allocation**: Filesystems work best with a small allocation unit, traditionally a 512-byte sector. This is much smaller than a flash erase block of 128 KiB or more. Therefore, erase blocks have to be subdivided into smaller units to avoid wasting large amounts of space.
- **Garbage collection**: A consequence of suballocation is that an erase block will contain a mixture of good data and stale data once the filesystem has been in use for a while. Since we can only free up whole erase blocks, the only way to reclaim this free space is to coalesce the good data into one place, and then return the now empty erase block to the free list. This is known as garbage collection, and it is usually implemented as a background thread.
- **Wear leveling**: There is a limit on the number of erase cycles for each block. To maximize the lifespan of a chip, it is important to move data around so that each block is erased roughly the same number of times.
- **Bad block handling**: On NAND flash chips, you have to avoid using any block marked bad and also mark good blocks as bad if they cannot be erased.
- **Robustness**: Embedded devices may be powered off or reset without warning, so any filesystem should be able to cope without corruption, usually by incorporating a journal or a log of transactions.

There are several ways to deploy the flash translation layer:

- **In the filesystem**: As with JFFS2, YAFFS2, and UBIFS.
- **In the block device driver**: The UBI driver, which UBIFS depends on, implements some aspects of a flash translation layer.
- **In the device controller**: As with managed flash devices.

When the flash translation layer is in the filesystem or the block driver, the code is part of the kernel and so it is open source, meaning that we can see how it works and we can expect that it will be improved over time. On the other hand, if the FTL is inside a managed flash device, it is hidden from view and we cannot verify whether it works as we would want. Not only that, but putting the FTL into the disk controller means that it misses out on information that is held at the filesystem layer, such as which sectors belong to files that have been deleted and so do not contain useful data anymore. The latter problem is solved by adding commands that pass this information between the filesystem and the device. I will describe how this works in the section on the TRIM command later on. However, the question of code visibility remains. If you are using managed flash, you just have to choose a manufacturer you can trust.

Now that we know the motivation behind filesystems, let's look at which filesystems are best suited for which types of flash.

Filesystems for NOR and NAND flash memory

To use raw flash chips for mass storage, you have to use a filesystem that understands the peculiarities of the underlying technology. There are three such filesystems:

- **JFFS2 (Journaling Flash File System 2)**: This was the first flash filesystem for Linux and is still in use today. It works for NOR and NAND memory, but is notoriously slow during mount.
- **YAFFS2 (Yet Another Flash File System 2)**: This is similar to JFFS2, but specifically for NAND flash memory. It was adopted by Google as the preferred raw flash filesystem on Android devices.
- **UBIFS (Unsorted Block Image File System)**: This works in conjunction with the UBI block driver to create a reliable flash filesystem. It works well with both NOR and NAND memory, and since it generally offers better performance than JFFS2 or YAFFS2, it should be the preferred solution for new designs.

All of these use MTD as the common interface to flash memory.

JFFS2

The **Journaling Flash File System** had its beginnings in the software for the Axis 2100 network camera in 1999. For many years, it was the only flash filesystem for Linux and has been deployed on many thousands of different types of devices. Today, it is not the best choice, but I will cover it first because it shows the beginning of the evolutionary path.

JFFS2 is a log-structured filesystem that uses MTD to access flash memory. In a log-structured filesystem, changes are written sequentially as nodes to flash memory. A node may contain changes to a directory, such as the names of files created and deleted, or it may contain changes to file data. After a while, a node may be superseded by information contained in subsequent nodes and becomes an obsolete node. Both NOR and NAND flash are organized as erase blocks. Erasing a block sets all its bits to 1.

JFFS2 categorizes erase blocks into three types:

- **Free**: This contains no nodes at all.
- **Clean**: This only contains valid nodes.
- **Dirty**: This contains at least one obsolete node.

At any one time, there is one block receiving updates, which is called the open block. If power is lost or the system is reset, the only data that can be lost is the last write to the open block. In addition, nodes are compressed as they are written, increasing the effective storage capacity of the flash chip, which is important if you are using expensive NOR flash memory.

When the number of free blocks falls below a certain threshold, a garbage collector kernel thread is started, which scans for dirty blocks, copies the valid nodes into the open block, and then frees up the dirty block.

At the same time, the garbage collector provides a crude form of wear leveling because it cycles valid data from one block to another. The way that the open block is chosen means that each block is erased roughly the same number of times, as long as it contains data that changes from time to time. Sometimes, a clean block is chosen for garbage collection to make sure that blocks containing static data that is seldom written are also wear-leveled.

JFFS2 filesystems have a write-through cache, meaning that writes are written to the flash memory synchronously as if they have been mounted with the `-o` sync option. While improving reliability, it does increase the time to write data. There is a further problem with small writes: if the length of a write is comparable to the size of the node header (40 bytes), the overhead becomes high. A well-known corner case is log files, produced, for example, by `syslogd`.

Summary nodes

There is one overriding disadvantage to JFFS2: since there is no on-chip index, the directory's structure has to be deduced at mount-time by reading the log from start to finish. At the end of the scan, you have a complete picture of the directory structure of the valid nodes, but the time taken is proportional to the size of the partition. It is not uncommon to see mount times of the order of one second per megabyte, leading to total mount times of tens or hundreds of seconds.

Summary nodes became an option in Linux 2.6.15 for reducing the time to scan during a mount. A summary node is written at the end of the open erase block, just before it is closed. The summary node contains all of the information needed for the mount-time scan, thereby reducing the amount of data to process during the scan. Summary nodes can reduce mount times by a factor of between two and five, at the expense of an overhead of about 5% of the storage space. They are enabled with the `CONFIG_JFFS2_SUMMARY` kernel configuration.

Clean markers

An erased block with all its bits set to 1 is indistinguishable from a block that has been written with 1s, but the latter has not had its memory cells refreshed and cannot be programmed again until it is erased. JFFS2 uses a mechanism called **clean markers** to distinguish between these two situations. After a successful block erase, a clean marker is written, either to the beginning of the block or to the OOB area of the first page of the block. If the clean marker exists, then it must be a clean block.

Creating a JFFS2 filesystem

Creating an empty JFFS2 filesystem at runtime is as simple as erasing an MTD partition with clean markers and then mounting it. There is no formatting step because a blank JFFS2 filesystem consists entirely of free blocks. For example, to format MTD partition 6, you would enter these commands on the device:

```
# flash_erase -j /dev/mtd6 0 0
# mount -t jffs2 mtd6 /mnt
```

The `-j` option to `flash_erase` adds the clean markers, and mounting with the `jffs2` type presents the partition as an empty filesystem. Note that the device to be mounted is given as `mtd6`, not `/dev/mtd6`. Alternatively, you can give the block the `/dev/mtdblock6` device node. This is just a peculiarity of JFFS2. Once mounted, you can treat it like any other filesystem.

You can create a filesystem image directly from the staging area of your development system using `mkfs.jffs2` to write out the files in JFFS2 format, and `sumtool` to add the summary nodes. Both of these are part of the `mtd-utils` package.

As an example, to create an image of the files in `rootfs` for a NAND flash device with an erase block size of 128 KiB (`0x20000`) and with summary nodes, you would use these two commands:

```
$ mkfs.jffs2 -n -e 0x20000 -p -d ~/rootfs -o ~/rootfs.jffs2
$ sumtool -n -e 0x20000 -p -i ~/rootfs.jffs2 -o ~/rootfs-sum.
jffs2
```

The `-p` option adds padding at the end of the image file to make it a whole number of erase blocks. The `-n` option suppresses the creation of clean markers in the image, which is normal for NAND devices, as the clean marker is in the OOB area. For NOR devices, you would leave out the `-n` option. You can use a device table with `mkfs.jffs2` to set the permissions and the ownership of files by adding `-D [device table]`. Of course, Buildroot and the Yocto Project will do all this for you.

You can program the image into flash memory from your bootloader. For example, if you have loaded a filesystem image into RAM at address `0x82000000` and you want to load it into a flash partition that begins at `0x163000` bytes from the start of the flash chip and is `0x7a9d000` bytes long, the U-Boot commands for this would be as follows:

```
nand erase clean 163000 7a9d000
nand write 82000000 163000 7a9d000
```

You can do the same thing from Linux using the `mtd` driver, like this:

```
# flash_erase -j /dev/mtd6 0 0
# nandwrite /dev/mtd6 rootfs-sum.jffs2
```

To boot with a JFFS2 root filesystem, you need to pass the `mtdblock` device on the kernel command line for the partition and a `rootfstype` since JFFS2 cannot be auto-detected:

```
root=/dev/mtdblock6 rootfstype=jffs2
```

Shortly after JFFS2 was introduced, another log-structured filesystem appeared.

YAFFS2

The YAFFS filesystem was written by Charles Manning, beginning in 2001, specifically to handle NAND flash chips at a time when JFFS2 did not. Subsequent changes to handle larger (2 KiB) page sizes resulted in YAFFS2. The website for YAFFS is `https://www.yaffs.net`.

YAFFS is also a log-structured filesystem that follows the same design principles as JFFS2. The different design decisions mean that it has a faster mount-time scan, simpler and faster garbage collection, and has no compression, which speeds up reads and writes at the expense of less efficient use of storage.

YAFFS is not limited to Linux; it has been ported to a wide range of operating systems. It has a dual license: GPLv2, in order to be compatible with Linux, and a commercial license for other operating systems. Unfortunately, the YAFFS code has never been merged into mainline Linux, so you will have to patch your kernel.

To get YAFFS2 and patch a kernel, you would use the following:

```
$ git clone git://www.aleph1.co.uk/yaffs2
$ cd yaffs2
$ ./patch-ker.sh c m <path to your link source>
```

Then, you can configure the kernel with `CONFIG_YAFFS_YAFFS2`.

Creating a YAFFS2 filesystem

As with JFFS2, to create a YAFFS2 filesystem at runtime, you only need to erase the partition and mount it, but note that in this case, you do not enable clean markers:

```
# flash_erase /dev/mtd/mtd6 0 0
# mount -t yaffs2 /dev/mtdblock6 /mnt
```

To create a filesystem image, the simplest thing to do is use the `mkyaffs2` tool from `https://code.google.com/p/yaffs2utils` using the following command:

```
$ mkyaffs2 -c 2048 -s 64 rootfs rootfs.yaffs2
```

Here, `-c` is the page size and `-s` the OOB size. There is a tool named `mkyaffs2image` that is part of the YAFFS code, but it has a couple of drawbacks. Firstly, the page and OOB size are hard coded in the source: you will have to edit and recompile if you have memory that does not match the defaults of 2,048 and 64. Secondly, the OOB layout is incompatible with MTD, which uses the first two bytes as a bad block marker, whereas `mkyaffs2image` uses those bytes to store part of the YAFFS metadata.

To copy the image to the MTD partition from a Linux shell prompt on the target, follow these steps:

```
# flash_erase /dev/mtd6 0 0
# nandwrite -a /dev/mtd6 rootfs.yaffs2
```

To boot with a YAFFS2 root filesystem, add the following to the kernel command line:

```
root=/dev/mtdblock6 rootfstype=yaffs2
```

While we are on the topic of filesystems for raw NOR and NAND flash, let's look at one of the more modern options. This filesystem runs on top of the UBI driver.

UBI and UBIFS

The **Unsorted Block Image** (**UBI**) driver is a volume manager for flash memory that takes care of bad block handling and wear leveling. It was implemented by Artem Bityutskiy and first appeared in Linux 2.6.22. In parallel with that, engineers at Nokia were working on a filesystem that would take advantage of the features of UBI, which they called **UBIFS**; it appeared in Linux 2.6.27. Splitting the flash translation layer in this way makes the code more modular and also allows other filesystems to take advantage of the UBI driver, as we shall see later on.

UBI

UBI provides an idealized, reliable view of a flash chip by mapping **physical erase blocks** (**PEB**) to **logical erase blocks** (**LEB**). Bad blocks are not mapped to LEBs and so are never used. If a block cannot be erased, it is marked as bad and dropped from the mapping. UBI keeps a count of the number of times each PEB has been erased in the header of the LEB, and then changes the mapping to ensure that each PEB is erased the same number of times.

UBI accesses the flash memory through the MTD layer. As an extra feature, it can divide an MTD partition into a number of UBI volumes, which improves wear leveling in the following way: imagine that you have two filesystems, one containing fairly static data, such as a root filesystem, and the other containing data that is constantly changing.

If they are stored in separate MTD partitions, the wear leveling only has an effect on the second one, whereas if you choose to store them in two UBI volumes in a single MTD partition, the wear leveling takes place over both areas of the storage, and the lifetime of the flash memory is increased. The following diagram illustrates this situation:

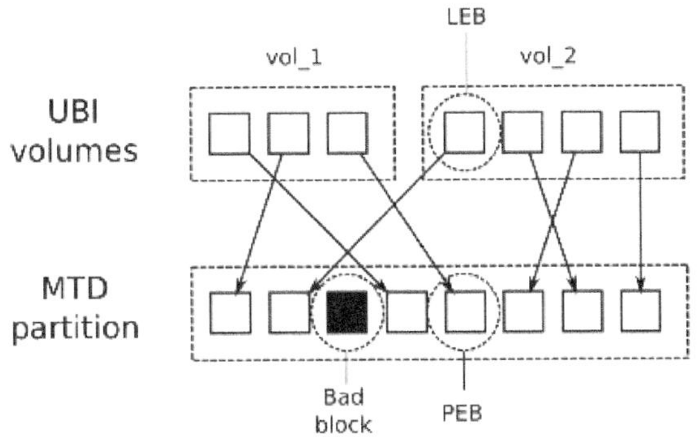

Figure 9.4 – UBI volumes

In this way, UBI fulfills two of the requirements of a flash translation layer: wear leveling and bad-block handling.

To prepare an MTD partition for UBI, you don't use `flash_erase` as with JFFS2 and YAFFS2. Instead, you use the `ubiformat` utility, which preserves the erase counts that are stored in the PEB headers. `ubiformat` needs to know the minimum unit of I/O, which for most NAND flash chips is the page size, but some chips allow reading and writing in subpages that are a half or a quarter of the page size. Consult the chip data sheet for details and, if in doubt, use the page size. This example prepares `mtd6` using a page size of `2048` bytes:

```
# ubiformat /dev/mtd6 -s 2048
ubiformat: mtd0 (nand), size 134217728 bytes (128.0 MiB),
1024 eraseblocks of 131072 bytes (128.0 KiB),
min. I/O size 2048 bytes
```

Then, you can use the `ubiattach` command to load the UBI driver on an MTD partition that has been prepared in this way:

```
# ubiattach -p /dev/mtd6 -O 2048
UBI device number 0, total 1024 LEBs (130023424 bytes, 124.0
MiB),
available 998 LEBs (126722048 bytes, 120.9 MiB),
LEB size 126976 bytes (124.0 KiB)
```

This creates the `/dev/ubi0` device node, through which you can access the UBI volumes. You can use `ubiattach` on several MTD partitions, in which case they can be accessed through `/dev/ubi1`, `/dev/ubi2`, and so on. Note that since each LEB has a header containing the meta information used by UBI, the LEB is smaller than the PEB by two pages. For example, a chip with a PEB size of 128 KiB and 2 KiB pages would have an LEB of 124 KiB. This is important information that you will need when creating a UBIFS image.

The PEB-to-LEB mapping is loaded into memory during the attach phase, a process that takes time proportional to the number of PEBs, typically a few seconds. A new feature was added in Linux 3.7 called the UBI fastmap, which checkpoints the mapping to flash from time to time and so reduces the attach time. The kernel configuration option for this is `CONFIG_MTD_UBI_FASTMAP`.

The first time you attach to an MTD partition after a `ubiformat`, there will be no volumes. You can create volumes using `ubimkvol`. For example, suppose you have a 128 MiB MTD partition and you want to split it into two volumes; the first is to be 32 MiB in size and the second will take up the remaining space:

```
# ubimkvol /dev/ubi0 -N vol_1 -s 32MiB
Volume ID 0, size 265 LEBs (33648640 bytes, 32.1 MiB),
LEB size 126976 bytes (124.0 KiB), dynamic, name "vol_1",
alignment 1
# ubimkvol /dev/ubi0 -N vol_2 -m
Volume ID 1, size 733 LEBs (93073408 bytes, 88.8 MiB),
LEB size 126976 bytes (124.0 KiB), dynamic, name "vol_2",
alignment 1
```

Now, you have a device with two nodes: `/dev/ubi0_0` and `/dev/ubi0_1`. You can confirm this using `ubinfo`:

```
# ubinfo -a /dev/ubi0
ubi0
Volumes count: 2
Logical eraseblock size: 126976 bytes, 124.0 KiB
Total amount of logical eraseblocks: 1024 (130023424 bytes,
124.0 MiB)
Amount of available logical eraseblocks: 0 (0 bytes)
Maximum count of volumes 128
Count of bad physical eraseblocks: 0
Count of reserved physical eraseblocks: 20
Current maximum erase counter value: 1
Minimum input/output unit size: 2048 bytes
Character device major/minor: 250:0
Present volumes: 0, 1

Volume ID: 0 (on ubi0)
Type: dynamic
Alignment: 1
Size: 265 LEBs (33648640 bytes, 32.1 MiB)
State: OK
Name: vol_1
```

```
Character device major/minor: 250:1
-----------------------------------
Volume ID: 1 (on ubi0)
Type: dynamic
Alignment: 1
Size: 733 LEBs (93073408 bytes, 88.8 MiB)
State: OK
Name: vol_2
Character device major/minor: 250:2
```

At this point, you have a 128 MiB MTD partition containing two UBI volumes of sizes 32 MiB and 88.8 MiB. The total storage available is 32 MiB plus 88.8 MiB, which equals 120.8 MiB. The remaining space, 7.2 MiB, is taken up by the UBI headers at the start of each PEB, and space is reserved for mapping out blocks that go bad during the lifetime of the chip.

UBIFS

UBIFS uses a UBI volume to create a robust filesystem. It adds sub-allocation and garbage collection to create a complete flash translation layer. Unlike JFFS2 and YAFFS2, it stores index information on-chip, so mounting is fast, although don't forget that attaching the UBI volume beforehand may take a significant amount of time. It also allows write-back caching as in a normal disk filesystem, which means that writes are much faster, but with the usual problem of potential loss of data that has not been flushed from the cache to flash memory in the event of power down. You can resolve this problem by making careful use of the `fsync(2)` and `fdatasync(2)` functions to force a flush of file data at crucial points.

UBIFS has a journal for fast recovery in the event of power down. The minimum size of the journal is 4 MiB, so UBIFS is not suitable for very small flash devices.

Once you have created the UBI volumes, you can mount them using the device node for the volume, such as `/dev/ubi0_0`, or by using the device node for the whole partition plus the volume name, as shown here:

```
# mount -t ubifs ubi0:vol_1 /mnt
```

Creating a filesystem image for UBIFS is a two-stage process: first, you create a UBIFS image using `mkfs.ubifs`, and then embed it into a UBI volume using `ubinize`.

For the first stage, `mkfs.ubifs` needs to be informed of the page size with `-m`, the size of the UBI LEB with `-e`, and the maximum number of erase blocks in the volume with `-c`. If the first volume is 32 MiB and an erase block is 128 KiB, then the number of erase blocks is 256. So, to take the contents of the `rootfs` directory and create a UBIFS image named `rootfs.ubi`, you would type the following:

```
$ mkfs.ubifs -r rootfs -m 2048 -e 124KiB -c 256 -o rootfs.ubi
```

The second stage requires you to create a configuration file for `ubinize`, which describes the characteristics of each volume in the image. The help page (`ubinize -h`) provides details about the format. This example creates two volumes, `vol_1` and `vol_2`:

```
[ubifsi_vol_1]
mode=ubi
image=rootfs.ubi
vol_id=0
vol_name=vol_1
vol_size=32MiB
vol_type=dynamic

[ubifsi_vol_2]
mode=ubi
image=data.ubi
vol_id=1
vol_name=vol_2
vol_type=dynamic
vol_flags=autoresize
```

The second volume has an `auto-resize` flag and so will expand to fill the remaining space on the MTD partition. Only one volume can have this flag. From this information, `ubinize` will create an image file named by the `-o` parameter, with the PEB size as `-p`, the page size as `-m`, and the sub-page size as `-s`:

```
$ ubinize -o ~/ubi.img -p 128KiB -m 2048 -s 512 ubinize.cfg
```

To install this image on the target, you would enter these commands on the target:

```
# ubiformat /dev/mtd6 -s 2048
# nandwrite /dev/mtd6 /ubi.img
# ubiattach -p /dev/mtd6 -O 2048
```

If you want to boot with a UBIFS root filesystem, you will need to provide these kernel command-line parameters:

```
ubi.mtd=6 root=ubi0:vol_1 rootfstype=ubifs
```

UBIFS completes our survey of filesystems for raw NOR and NAND flash memory. Next, we'll look at filesystems for managed flash.

Filesystems for managed flash

As the trend toward managed flash technologies continues, particularly eMMC, we need to consider how to use it effectively. While they appear to have the same characteristics as hard disk drives, the underlying NAND flash chips have the limitations of large erase blocks with limited erase cycles and bad block handling. And, of course, we need robustness in the event of losing power.

It is possible to use any of the normal disk filesystems, but we should try to choose one that reduces disk writes and has a fast restart after an unscheduled shutdown.

Flashbench

To make optimum use of the underlying flash memory, you need to know the erase block size and page size. Manufacturers do not publish these numbers as a rule, but it is possible to deduce them by observing the behavior of the chip or card.

Flashbench is one such tool. It was initially written by Arnd Bergman, as described in the LWN article available at `https://lwn.net/Articles/428584`. You can get the code from `https://github.com/bradfa/flashbench`.

Here is a typical run on a SanDisk 4 GB SDHC card:

```
$ sudo ./flashbench -a /dev/mmcblk0 --blocksize=1024
align 536870912 pre 4.38ms on 4.48ms post 3.92ms diff 332µs
align 268435456 pre 4.86ms on 4.9ms post 4.48ms diff 227µs
align 134217728 pre 4.57ms on 5.99ms post 5.12ms diff 1.15ms
align 67108864 pre 4.95ms on 5.03ms post 4.54ms diff 292µs
align 33554432 pre 5.46ms on 5.48ms post 4.58ms diff 462µs
align 16777216 pre 3.16ms on 3.28ms post 2.52ms diff 446µs
align 8388608 pre 3.89ms on 4.1ms post 3.07ms diff 622µs
align 4194304 pre 4.01ms on 4.89ms post 3.9ms diff 940µs
```

```
align 2097152 pre 3.55ms on 4.42ms post 3.46ms diff 917µs
align 1048576 pre 4.19ms on 5.02ms post 4.09ms diff 876µs
align 524288 pre 3.83ms on 4.55ms post 3.65ms diff 805µs
align 262144 pre 3.95ms on 4.25ms post 3.57ms diff 485µs
align 131072 pre 4.2ms on 4.25ms post 3.58ms diff 362µs
align 65536 pre 3.89ms on 4.24ms post 3.57ms diff 511µs
align 32768 pre 3.94ms on 4.28ms post 3.6ms diff 502µs
align 16384 pre 4.82ms on 4.86ms post 4.17ms diff 372µs
align 8192 pre 4.81ms on 4.83ms post 4.16ms diff 349µs
align 4096 pre 4.16ms on 4.21ms post 4.16ms diff 52.4µs
align 2048 pre 4.16ms on 4.16ms post 4.17ms diff 9ns
```

`flashbench` reads blocks of, in this case, 1,024 bytes just before and just after various power-of-two boundaries. As you cross a page or erase a block boundary, the reads after the boundary take longer. The rightmost column shows the difference and is the one that is most interesting. Reading from the bottom, there is a big jump at 4 KiB, which is the most likely size of a page. There is a second jump from 52.4µs to 349µs at 8 KiB. This is fairly common and indicates that the card can use multi-plane access to read two 4 KiB pages at the same time. Beyond that, the differences are less well marked, but there is a clear jump from 485µs to 805µs at 512 KiB, which is probably the erase block's size. Given that the card being tested is quite old, these are the sort of numbers you would expect.

Discard and TRIM

Usually, when you delete a file, only the modified directory node is written to storage, while the sectors containing the file's contents remain unchanged. When the flash translation layer is in the disk controller, as with managed flash, it does not know that this group of disk sectors no longer contains useful data and so it ends up copying stale data.

In the last few years, the addition of transactions that pass information about deleted sectors down to the disk controller has improved this situation. The SCSI and SATA specifications have a `TRIM` command, and MMC has a similar command named `ERASE`. In Linux, this feature is known as **discard**.

To make use of discard, you need a storage device that supports it – most current eMMC chips do – and a Linux device driver to match. You can check this by looking at the block system queue parameters in `/sys/block/<block device>/queue/`.

The ones of interest are as follows:

- `discard_granularity`: The size of the internal allocation unit of the device.
- `discard_max_bytes`: The maximum number of bytes that can be discarded in one go.
- `discard_zeroes_data`: If `1`, discarded data will be set to `0`.

If the device or the device driver do not support discard, these values will all be set to `0`. As an example, these are the parameters you will see from the 2 GiB eMMC chip on my BeagleBone Black:

```
# grep -s "" /sys/block/mmcblk0/queue/discard_*
/sys/block/mmcblk0/queue/discard_granularity:2097152
/sys/block/mmcblk0/queue/discard_max_bytes:2199023255040
/sys/block/mmcblk0/queue/discard_zeroes_data:1
```

More information can be found in the kernel documentation file; that is, `Documentation/block/queue-sysfs.txt`.

You can enable discard when mounting a filesystem by adding the `-o discard` option to the `mount` command. Both ext4 and F2FS support it.

> **Tip**
>
> Make sure that the storage device supports discard before using the `-o discard` mount option, as data loss can occur.

It is also possible to force discard from the command line independently of how the partition is mounted using the `fstrim` command, which is part of the `util-linux` package. Typically, you would run this command periodically to free up unused space. `fstrim` operates on a mounted filesystem, so to trim the root filesystem, `/`, you would type the following:

```
# fstrim -v /
/: 2061000704 bytes were trimmed
```

The preceding example uses the verbose option, `-v`, so that it prints out the number of bytes that have been potentially freed up. In this case, 2,061,000,704 is the approximate amount of free space in the filesystem, so it is the maximum amount of storage that could have been trimmed.

Ext4

The **extended filesystem**, **ext**, has been the main filesystem for Linux desktops since 1992. The current version, **ext4**, is very stable and well-tested, and has a journal that makes recovering from an unscheduled shutdown fast and mostly painless. It is a good choice for managed flash devices, and you will find that it is the preferred filesystem for Android devices that have eMMC storage. If the device supports discard, you can mount with the `-o discard` option.

To format and create an ext4 filesystem at runtime, you would type the following:

```
# mkfs.ext4 /dev/mmcblk0p2
# mount -t ext4 -o discard /dev/mmcblk0p1 /mnt
```

To create a filesystem image at build time, you can use the `genext2fs` utility, available from `http://genext2fs.sourceforge.net`. In this example, I have specified the block size with `-B` and the number of blocks in the image with `-b`:

```
$ genext2fs -B 1024 -b 10000 -d rootfs rootfs.ext4
```

`genext2fs` can make use of a device table to set the file permissions and ownership, as described in *Chapter 5, Building a Root Filesystem*, with `-D [file table]`.

As the name implies, this will actually generate an image in `Ext2` format. You can upgrade to `Ext4` using `tune2fs` as follows (details of the command's options can be found in the `tune2fs(8)` manual page):

```
$ tune2fs -j -J size=1 -O filetype,extents,uninit_bg,dir_index
\
rootfs.ext4
$ e2fsck -pDf rootfs.ext4
```

Both the Yocto Project and Buildroot use exactly these steps when creating images in `Ext4` format.

While a journal is an asset for devices that may power down without warning, it does add extra write cycles to each write transaction, wearing out the flash memory. If the device is battery powered, especially if the battery is not removable, the chances of an unscheduled power down are small, so you may want to leave the journal out.

Even with journaling, filesystem corruption can occur on unexpected power loss. In many devices, holding down the power button, unplugging the power cord, or pulling out the battery can result in immediate shutdown. Due to the nature of buffered I/O, data being written out to flash may be lost if the power goes out before the write is done flushing to storage. For these reasons, it is good to run `fsck` non-interactively on a user partition to check for and repair any filesystem corruption before mounting. Otherwise, the corruption can compound over time until it becomes a serious issue.

F2FS

The **Flash-Friendly File System**, known as **F2FS**, is a log-structured filesystem designed for managed flash devices, especially eMMC chips and SD cards. It was written by Samsung and was merged into mainline Linux in 3.8. It is marked as experimental, indicating that it has not been extensively deployed yet, but it seems that some Android devices are using it.

F2FS takes into account the page and erase block sizes, and then tries to align data on these boundaries. The log format provides resilience in the face of power down and also provides good write performance, in some tests showing a twofold improvement over ext4. There is a good description of the design of F2FS in the kernel documentation in `Documentation/filesystems/f2fs.txt`, and there are references at the end of this chapter, in the *Further reading* section.

The `mkfs.f2fs` utility creates an empty F2FS filesystem with the `-l` label:

```
# mkfs.f2fs -l rootfs /dev/mmcblock0p1
# mount -t f2fs /dev/mmcblock0p1 /mnt
```

There isn't (yet) a tool you can use to create F2FS filesystem images offline.

FAT16/32

The old Microsoft filesystems, FAT16 and FAT32, continue to be important as a common format understood by most operating systems. When you buy an SD card or USB flash drive, it is almost certain to be formatted as FAT32 and, in some cases, the on-card microcontroller is optimized for FAT32 access patterns. Also, some boot ROMs require a FAT partition for the second-stage bootloader – the TI OMAP-based chips, for example. However, FAT formats are definitely not suitable for storing critical files because they are prone to corruption and make poor use of the storage space.

Linux supports FAT16 through the `msdos` filesystem and both FAT32 and FAT16 through the `vfat` filesystem. To mount a device, say an SD card, on the second MMC hardware adapter, you would type this:

```
# mount -t vfat /dev/mmcblock1p1 /mnt
```

> **Important note**
>
> In the past, there have been licensing issues with the vfat driver, which may (or may not) infringe a patent held by Microsoft.

FAT32 has a limitation of 32 GiB on the device's size. Devices of a larger capacity may be formatted using the Microsoft exFAT format, and it is a requirement for SDXC cards. There is no kernel driver for exFAT, but it can be supported by means of a user space FUSE driver. Since exFAT is proprietary to Microsoft, there are bound to be licensing implications if you support this format on your device.

That does it for read-write filesystems geared toward managed flash. What about space-saving read-only filesystems? The choice is simple: SquashFS.

Read-only compressed filesystems

Compressing data is useful if you don't have quite enough storage to fit everything in. Both JFFS2 and UBIFS do on-the-fly data compression by default. However, if the files are never going to be written, as is usually the case with the root filesystem, you can achieve better compression ratios by using a read-only compressed filesystem. Linux supports several of these: `romfs`, `cramfs`, and `squashfs`. The first two are obsolete now, so I will only describe SquashFS.

SquashFS

The SquashFS filesystem was written by Phillip Lougher in 2002 as a replacement for cramfs. It existed as a kernel patch for a long time, eventually being merged into mainline Linux in version 2.6.29 in 2009. It is very easy to use: you create a filesystem image using `mksquashfs` and install it to the flash memory:

```
$ mksquashfs rootfs rootfs.squashfs
```

The resulting filesystem is read-only, so there is no mechanism for modifying any of the files at runtime. The only way to update a SquashFS filesystem is to erase the whole partition and program in a new image.

SquashFS is not bad-block aware and so must be used with reliable flash memory such as NOR flash. However, it can be used on NAND flash as long as you use UBI to create an emulated, reliable MTD. You have to enable the `CONFIG_MTD_UBI_BLOCK` kernel configuration, which will create a read-only MTD block device for each UBI volume. The following diagram shows two MTD partitions, each with accompanying `mtdblock` devices. The second partition is also used to create a UBI volume that is exposed as a third, reliable `mtdblock` device, which you can use for any read-only filesystem that is not bad-block aware:

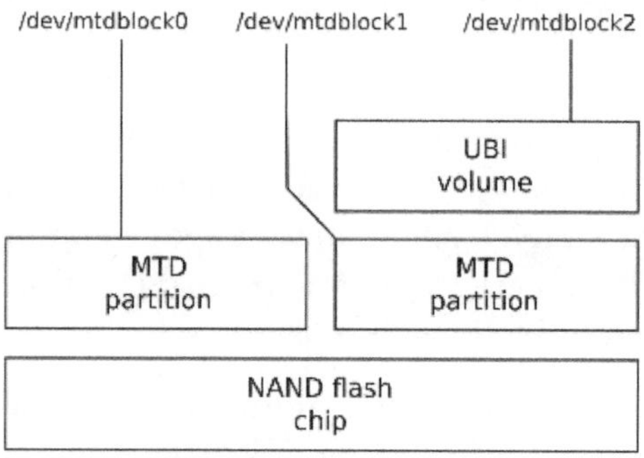

Figure 9.5 – UBI volume

A read-only filesystem is great for immutable contents, but what about temporary files that don't need to persist across reboots? This is where a RAM disk comes in handy.

Temporary filesystems

There are always some files that have a short lifetime or have no significance after a reboot. Many such files are put into `/tmp`, and so it makes sense to keep these files from reaching permanent storage.

The temporary filesystem, `tmpfs`, is ideal for this purpose. You can create a temporary RAM-based filesystem by simply mounting tmpfs:

```
# mount -t tmpfs tmp_files /tmp
```

As with `procfs` and `sysfs`, there is no device node associated with `tmpfs`, so you have to supply a placekeeper string, which is `tmp_files` in the preceding example.

The amount of memory used will grow and shrink as files are created and deleted. The default maximum size is half the physical RAM. In most cases, it would be a disaster if `tmpfs` grew to be that large, so it is a very good idea to cap it with the `-o` size parameter. The parameter can be given in bytes, KiB (`k`), MiB (`m`), or GiB (`g`), like this, for example:

```
# mount -t tmpfs -o size=1m tmp_files /tmp
```

In addition to /tmp, some subdirectories of /var contain volatile data, and it is good practice to use tmpfs for them as well, either by creating a separate filesystem for each or, more economically, using symbolic links. Buildroot does this like so:

```
/var/cache -> /tmp
/var/lock -> /tmp
/var/log -> /tmp
/var/run -> /tmp
/var/spool -> /tmp
/var/tmp -> /tmp
```

In the Yocto Project, /run and /var/volatile are tmpfs mounts with symbolic links pointing to them, as shown here:

```
/tmp -> /var/tmp
/var/lock -> /run/lock
/var/log -> /var/volatile/log
/var/run -> /run
/var/tmp -> /var/volatile/tmp
```

It is not uncommon to load the root filesystem into RAM on embedded Linux systems. That way, any damage to its contents that may occur at runtime is not permanent. The root filesystem does not need to reside on SquashFS or tmpfs to be protected, though; you just need to make the root filesystem is read-only.

Making the root filesystem read-only

You need to make your target device able to survive unexpected events, including file corruption, and still be able to boot and achieve at least a minimum level of functionality. Making the root filesystem read-only is a key part of achieving this ambition because it eliminates accidental overwrites. Making it read-only is easy: replace rw with ro on the kernel command line or use an inherently read-only filesystem such as SquashFS. However, you will find that there are a few files and directories that are traditionally writable:

- /etc/resolv.conf: This file is written by network configuration scripts to record the addresses of DNS name servers. The information is volatile, so you simply have to make it a symlink to a temporary directory; for example, /etc/resolv.conf -> /var/run/resolv.conf.

- /etc/passwd: This file, along with /etc/group, /etc/shadow, and /etc/gshadow, stores user and group names and passwords. They need to be symbolically linked to an area of persistent storage.
- /var/lib: Many applications expect to be able to write to this directory and to keep permanent data here as well. One solution is to copy a base set of files to a tmpfs filesystem at boot time and then bind mount /var/lib to the new location. You can do this by putting a sequence of commands such as these into one of the boot scripts:

```
$ mkdir -p /var/volatile/lib
$ cp -a /var/lib/* /var/volatile/lib
$ mount --bind /var/volatile/lib /var/lib
```

- /var/log: This is the place where syslog and other daemons keep their logs. Generally, logging to flash memory is not desirable because of the many small write cycles it generates. A simple solution is to mount /var/log using tmpfs, making all log messages volatile. In the case of syslogd, BusyBox has a version that can log to a circular ring buffer.

If you are using the Yocto Project, you can create a read-only root filesystem by adding IMAGE_FEATURES = "read-only-rootfs" to conf/local.conf or to your image recipe.

Filesystem choices

So far, we have looked at the technology behind solid-state memory and at the many types of filesystems. Now, it is time to summarize the options that are available. In most cases, you will be able to divide your storage requirements into these three categories:

- **Permanent, read-write data**: Runtime configuration, network parameters, passwords, data logs, and user data
- **Permanent, read-only data**: Programs, libraries, and configurations files that are constant; for example, the root filesystem
- **Volatile data**: Temporary storage; for example, /tmp

The choices for read-write storage are as follows:

- NOR: UBIFS or JFFS2
- NAND: UBIFS, JFFS2, or YAFFS2
- eMMC: ext4 or F2FS

For read-only storage, you can use any of these, mounted with the `ro` attribute. Additionally, if you want to save space, you could use SquashFS. Finally, for volatile storage, there is only one choice: `tmpfs`.

Summary

Flash memory has been the storage technology of choice for embedded Linux from the beginning, and over the years, Linux has gained very good support, from low-level drivers up to flash-aware filesystems, with the latest being UBIFS.

As the rate at which new flash technologies are introduced increases, it is becoming harder to keep pace with the changes at the high end. System designers are increasingly turning to managed flash in the form of eMMC, to provide a stable hardware and software interface that is independent of the memory chips inside. Embedded Linux developers are beginning to get to grips with these new chips. Support for TRIM in ext4 and F2FS is well-established, and it is slowly finding its way into the chips themselves. Also, the appearance of new filesystems that have been optimized to manage flash, such as F2FS, is a welcome step forward.

However, the fact remains that flash memory is not the same as a hard disk drive. You have to be careful when you're minimizing the number of filesystem writes – especially as the higher density TLC chips may be able to support as few as 1,000 erase cycles.

In the next chapter, I will continue on the theme of storage options, as I consider different ways to keep the software up to date on devices that may be deployed to remote locations.

Further reading

The following resources contain further information about the topics that were introduced in this chapter:

- *XIP: The past, the present... the future?*, by Vitaly Wool: `https://archive.fosdem.org/2007/slides/devrooms/embedded/Vitaly_Wool_XIP.pdf`
- *General MTD documentation*: `http://www.linux-mtd.infradead.org/doc/general.html`
- *Optimizing Linux with cheap flash drives*, by Arnd Bergmann: `https://lwn.net/Articles/428584/`

- *eMMC/SSD File System Tuning Methodology*, Cogent Embedded, Inc.: `https://elinux.org/images/b/b6/EMMC-SSD_File_System_Tuning_Methodology_v1.0.pdf`
- *Flash-Friendly File System (F2FS)*, by Joo-Young Hwang: `https://elinux.org/images/1/12/Elc2013_Hwang.pdf`
- *An F2FS teardown*, by Neil Brown: `https://lwn.net/Articles/518988/`

10
Updating Software in the Field

In previous chapters, we discussed various ways to build the software for a Linux device and also how to create system images for various types of mass storage. When you go into production, you just need to copy the system image to the flash memory, and it is ready to be deployed. Now, I want to consider the life of the device beyond the first shipment.

As we move into the era of the *Internet of Things*, the devices that we create are very likely to be connected together by the internet. At the same time, software is becoming exponentially more complex. More software means more bugs. Connection to the internet means those bugs can be exploited from afar. Consequentially, we have a common requirement to be able to update software *in the field*. Software updates bring more advantages than fixing bugs, however. They open the door to adding value to existing hardware by improving system performance over time or enabling features.

In this chapter, we will cover the following topics:

- From where do updates originate?
- What to update
- The basics of software updates
- Types of update mechanism
- OTA updates

- Using Mender for local updates
- Using Mender for OTA updates
- Using balena for local updates

Technical requirements

To follow along with the examples, make sure you have the following:

- A Linux-based host system with a minimum of 60 GB of available disk space
- Yocto 3.1 (Dunfell) LTS release
- Etcher for Linux
- A microSD card reader and card
- A Raspberry Pi 4
- A 5V 3A USB-C power supply
- A Wi-Fi router

Yocto is required for the *Using Mender for local updates* and *Using Mender for OTA updates* sections of this chapter.

You should have already built the 3.1 (Dunfell) LTS release of Yocto for *Chapter 6, Selecting a Build System*. If you have not, then refer to the *Compatible Linux Distribution* and *Build Host Packages* sections of the *Yocto Project Quick Build* guide (`https://www.yoctoproject.org/docs/current/brief-yoctoprojectqs/brief-yoctoprojectqs.html`) before building Yocto on your Linux host according to the instructions from *Chapter 6*.

All of the code for this chapter can be found in the `Chapter10` folder of the book's GitHub repository: `https://github.com/PacktPublishing/Mastering-Embedded-Linux-Programming-Third-Edition`.

From where do updates originate?

There are many approaches to software updates. Broadly, I characterize them as the following:

- Local updates, often performed by a technician who carries the update on a portable medium such as a USB flash drive or an SD card and has to access each system individually

- Remote updates, where the update is initiated by the user or a technician locally, but it is downloaded from a remote server
- **Over-the-air** (**OTA**) updates, where the update is pushed and managed entirely remotely, without any need for local input

I will begin by describing several approaches to software updates, and then I will show an example using Mender (`https://mender.io`).

What to update

Embedded Linux devices are very diverse in their design and implementation. However, they all have these basic components:

- Bootloader
- Kernel
- Root filesystem
- System applications
- Device-specific data

Some components are harder to update than others, as summarized in this diagram:

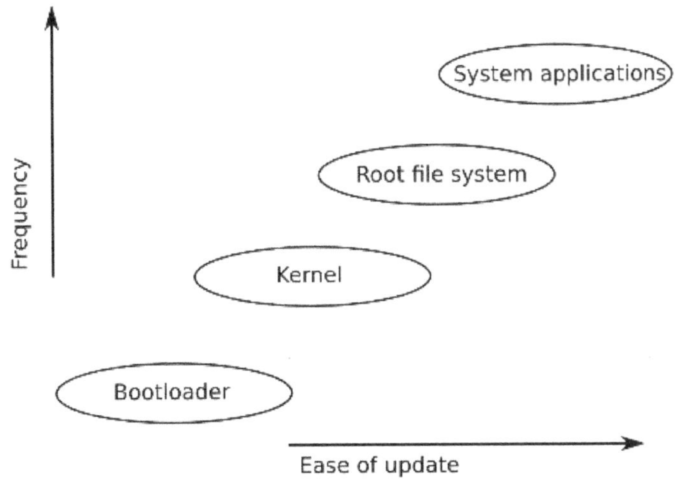

Figure 10.1 – Components of an update

Let's look at each component in turn.

Bootloader

The bootloader is the first piece of code to run when the processor is powered up. The way the processor locates the bootloader is very device-specific, but in most cases, there is only one such location, and so there can only be one bootloader. If there is no backup, updating the bootloader is risky: what happens if the system powers down midway? Consequently, most update solutions leave the bootloader alone. This is not a big problem, because the bootloader only runs for a short time at power-on and is not normally a great source of runtime bugs.

Kernel

The Linux kernel is a critical component that will certainly need updating from time to time.

There are several parts to the kernel:

- A binary image loaded by the bootloader, often stored in the root filesystem.
- Many devices also have a **Device Tree Binary** (**DTB**) that describes hardware to the kernel, and so has to be updated in tandem. The DTB is usually stored alongside the kernel binary.
- There may be kernel modules in the root filesystem.

The kernel and DTB may be stored in the root filesystem, so long as the bootloader has the ability to read that filesystem format, or it may be in a dedicated partition. In either case, it is possible and safer to have redundant copies.

Root filesystem

The root filesystem contains the essential system libraries, utilities, and scripts needed to make the system work. It is very desirable to be able to replace and upgrade all of these. The mechanism depends on the filesystem implementation.

Common formats for embedded root file systems are the following:

- Ramdisk, loaded from raw flash memory or a disk image at boot. To update it, you just need to overwrite the ramdisk image and reboot.
- Read-only compressed filesystems, such as `squashfs`, stored in a flash partition. Since these types of filesystem do not implement a write function, the only way to update them is to write a complete filesystem image to the partition.
- Normal filesystem types: For raw flash memory, JFFS2 and UBIFS formats are common, and for managed flash memory, such as eMMC and SD cards, the format is likely to be ext4 or F2FS. Since these are writable at runtime, it is possible to update them file by file.

System applications

The system applications are the main payload of the device; they implement its primary function. As such, they are likely to be updated frequently to fix bugs and to add features. They may be bundled with the root filesystem, but it is also common for them to be placed in a separate filesystem to make updating easier and to maintain separation between the system files, which are usually open source, and the application files, which are often proprietary.

Device-specific data

This is the combination of files that are modified at runtime and includes configuration settings, logs, user-supplied data, and the like. It is not often that they need to be updated, but they do need to be preserved during an update. Such data needs to be stored in a partition of its own.

Components that need to be updated

In summary, then, an update may include new versions of the kernel, root filesystem, and system applications. The device will have other partitions that should not be disturbed by an update, as is the case with the device runtime data.

The cost of software updates failing can be catastrophic. Secure software updates are also a major concern within both enterprise and home internet environments. Before we can ship any hardware, we need to be able to update the software with confidence.

The basics of software updates

Updating software seems, at first sight, to be a simple task: you just need to overwrite some files with new copies. But then your engineer's training kicks in as you begin to realize all the things that could go wrong. What if the power goes down during the update? What if a bug, not seen while testing the update, renders a percentage of the devices unbootable? What if a third party sends a fake update that enlists your device as part of a botnet? At the very least, the software update mechanism must be:

- Robust, so that an update does not render the device unusable
- Fail-safe, so that there is a fallback mode if all else fails
- Secure, to prevent the device from being hijacked by people installing unauthorized updates

In other words, we need a system that is not susceptible to Murphy's law, which states that if something can go wrong, then it will go wrong, eventually. Some of these problems are non-trivial, however. Deploying software to a device in the field is different from deploying software to the cloud. Embedded Linux systems need to detect and respond to mishaps like kernel panics or boot loops without any human intervention.

Making updates robust

You might think that the problem of updating Linux systems was solved a long time ago – we all have Linux desktops that we update regularly (don't we?). Also, there are vast numbers of Linux servers running in data centers that are similarly kept up to date. However, there is a difference between a server and a device. The former operates in a protected environment. It is unlikely to suffer a sudden loss of power or network connectivity. In the unlikely event that an update does fail, it is always possible to get access to the server and use external mechanisms to repeat the install.

Devices, on the other hand, are often deployed at remote sites with intermittent power and a poor network connection, which makes it much more likely that an update will be interrupted. Then, consider that it may be very expensive to get access to a device to take remedial action over a failed update if, for example, the device is an environmental monitoring station at the top of a mountain or controlling the valves of an oil well at the bottom of the sea. In consequence, it is much more important for embedded devices to have a robust update mechanism that will not result in the system becoming unusable.

The key word here is **atomicity**. The update as a whole must be atomic: there should be no stage at which part of the system is updated but no other parts. There must be a single, uninterruptible change to the system that switches to the new version of the software.

This removes the most obvious update mechanism from consideration: that of simply updating individual files, for example, by extracting an archive over parts of the filesystem. There is just no way to ensure that there will be a consistent set of files if the system is reset during the update. Even using a package manager such as `apt`, `yum`, or `zypper` does not help. If you look at the internals of all these package managers, you will see that they do indeed work by extracting an archive over the filesystem and running scripts to configure the package both before and after the update. Package managers are fine for the protected world of the data center, or even your desktop, but not for a device.

To achieve atomicity, the update must be installed alongside the running system, and then a switch is thrown to move from the old to the new. In later sections, we will describe two different approaches to achieving atomicity. The first is to have two copies of the root filesystem and other major components. One is live, while the other can receive updates. When the update is complete, the switch is thrown so that on reboot, the bootloader selects the updated copy. This is known as a **symmetric image update**, or an **A/B image update**. A variant of this theme is to use a special **recovery mode** operating system that is responsible for updating the main operating system. The guarantee of atomicity is shared between the bootloader and the recovery operating system. This is known as an **asymmetric image update**. It is the approach taken in Android prior to the Nougat 7.x version.

The second approach is to have two or more copies of the root filesystem in different subdirectories of the system partition, and then use `chroot(8)` at boot time to select one of them. Once Linux is running, the update client can install updates into the other root filesystem, and then when everything is complete and checked, it can throw the switch and reboot. This is known as an **atomic file update** and is exemplified by **OSTree**.

Making updates fail-safe

The next problem to consider is that of recovering from an update that was installed correctly but that contains code that stops the system from booting. Ideally, we want the system to detect this case and to revert to a previous working image.

There are several failure modes that can lead to a non-operational system. The first is a kernel panic, caused, for example, by a bug in a kernel device driver, or being unable to run the `init` program. A sensible place to start is by configuring the kernel to reboot a number of seconds after a panic. You can do this either when you build the kernel by setting `CONFIG_PANIC_TIMEOUT` or by setting the kernel command line to panic. For example, to reboot 5 seconds after a panic, you would add `panic=5` to the kernel command line.

You may want to go further and configure the kernel to panic on an Oops. Remember that an Oops is generated when the kernel encounters a fatal error. In some cases, it will be able to recover from the error, in other cases not, but in all cases, something has gone wrong and the system is not working as it should. To enable panic on Oops in the kernel configuration, set `CONFIG_PANIC_ON_OOPS=y` or, on the kernel command line, `oops=panic`.

A second failure mode occurs when the kernel launches `init` successfully but for some reason, the main application fails to run. For this, you need a watchdog. A **watchdog** is a hardware or software timer that restarts the system if the timer is not reset before it expires. If you are using `systemd`, you can use the built-in watchdog function, which I'll describe in *Chapter 13, Starting Up – The init Program*. If not, you may want to enable the watchdog support built into Linux, as described in the kernel source code in `Documentation/watchdog`.

Both failures result in **boot loops**: either a kernel panic or a watchdog timeout causes the system to reboot. If the problem is persistent, the system will reboot continually. To break out of the boot loop, we need some code in the bootloader to detect the case and to revert to the previous, known good, version. A typical approach is to use a **boot count** that is incremented by the bootloader on each boot, and that is reset to zero in user space once the system is up and running. If the system enters a boot loop, the counter is not reset and so continues to increase. Then, the bootloader is configured to take remedial action if the counter exceeds a threshold.

In U-Boot, this is handled by three variables:

- `bootcount`: This variable is incremented each time the processor boots.
- `bootlimit`: If `bootcount` exceeds the `bootlimit`, U-Boot runs the commands in `altbootcmd` instead of `bootcmd`.
- `altbootcmd`: This contains the alternative boot commands, for example, to roll back to a previous version of the software or to start the recovery-mode operating system.

For this to work, there must be a way for a user space program to reset the boot count. We can do that using U-Boot utilities that allow the U-Boot environment to be accessed at runtime:

- `fw_printenv`: Prints the value of a U-Boot variable
- `fw_setenv`: Sets the value of a U-Boot variable

These two commands need to know where the U-Boot environment block is stored, for which there is a configuration file in `/etc/fw_env.config`. For example, if the U-Boot environment is stored at offset `0x800000` from the start of the eMMC memory, with a backup copy at `0x1000000`, then the configuration would look like this:

```
# cat /etc/fw_env.config
/dev/mmcblk0 0x800000 0x40000
/dev/mmcblk0 0x1000000 0x40000
```

There is one final thing to cover in this section. Incrementing the boot count on each boot and then resetting it when the application begins to run leads to unnecessary writes to the environment block, wearing out the flash memory and slowing down system initialization. To prevent having to do this on all reboots, U-Boot has a further variable named `upgrade_available`. If `upgrade_available` is `0`, then `bootcount` is not incremented. `upgrade_available` is set to `1` after an update has been installed so that the boot count protection is in use only when it is needed.

Making updates secure

The final problem relates to the potential misuse of the update mechanism itself. Your prime intention when implementing an update mechanism is to provide a reliable automated or semi-automated method to install security patches and new features. However, others may use the same mechanism to install unauthorized versions of software and so *hijack* the device. We need to look at how we can ensure that this cannot happen.

The biggest vulnerability is that of a fake remote update. To prevent this, we need to authenticate the update server before starting the download. We also need a secure transfer channel, such as HTTPS, to guard against tampering with the download stream. I will return to this when describing OTA updates later on.

There is also the question of the authenticity of updates supplied locally. One way to detect a bogus update is to use a secure boot protocol in the bootloader. If the kernel image is signed at the factory with a digital key, the bootloader can check the key before it loads the kernel and refuses to load it if the keys do not match. So long as the keys are kept private by the manufacturer, it will not be possible to load a kernel that is not authorized. U-Boot implements such a mechanism, which is described in the U-Boot source code in `doc/uImage.FIT/verified-boot.txt`.

> **Important note**
>
> Secure boot: good or bad?
>
> If I have purchased a device that has a software update feature, then I am trusting the vendor of that device to deliver useful updates. I definitely do not want a malicious third party to install software without my knowledge. But should I be allowed to install software myself? If I own the device outright, should I not be entitled to modify it, including loading new software? Recall the TiVo set-top box, which ultimately led to the creation of the GPL v3 license. Remember also the Linksys WRT54G Wi-Fi router: when access to the hardware became easy, it spawned a whole new industry, including the OpenWrt project. See, for example, `https://www.wi-fiplanet.com/tutorials/article.php/3562391` for more details. This is a complex issue that sits at the crossroads between freedom and control. It is my opinion that some device manufacturers use security as an excuse to protect their, sometimes shoddy, software.

Now that we know what is required, how do we go about updating software on embedded Linux systems?

Types of update mechanism

In this section, I will describe three approaches to applying software updates: symmetric, or A/B, image update; asymmetric image update, also known as *recovery mode update*; and finally, atomic file update.

Symmetric image update

In this scheme, there are two copies of the operating system, each comprising the Linux kernel, root filesystem, and system applications. They are labeled as A and B in the following diagram:

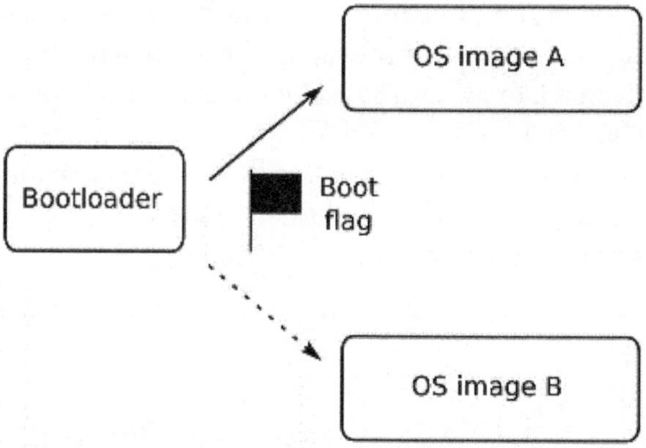

Figure 10.2 – symmetric image update

Symmetric image updates work as follows:

1. The bootloader has a flag that indicates which image it should load. Initially, the flag is set to A, so the bootloader loads OS image A.
2. To install an update, the updater application, which is part of the operating system, overwrites OS image B.
3. When complete, the updater changes the boot flag to B and reboots.
4. Now the bootloader will load the new operating system.
5. When a further update is installed, the updater overwrites image A and changes the boot flag to A, and so you ping-pong between the two copies.
6. If an update fails before the boot flag is changed, the bootloader continues to load the good operating system.

There are several open source projects that implement symmetric image update. One is the **Mender** client operating in standalone mode, which I will describe later, in the section on *Using Mender for local updates*. Another is **SWUpdate** (`https://github.com/sbabic/swupdate`). SWUpdate can receive multiple image updates in a CPIO format package and then deploy those updates to different parts of the system. It allows you to write plugins in the Lua language to do custom processing. It has filesystem support for raw flash memory that is accessed as MTD flash partitions, for storage organized into UBI volumes, and for SD/eMMC storage with a disk partition table. A third example is **RAUC**, the **Robust Auto-Update Controller**, (`https://github.com/rauc/rauc`). It too has support for raw flash storage, UBI volumes, and SD/eMMC devices. The images can be signed and verified using OpenSSL keys. A fourth example is **fwup** (`https://github.com/fwup-home/fwup`) by long-time Buildroot contributor Frank Hunleth.

There are some drawbacks to this scheme. One is that by updating an entire filesystem image, the size of the update package is large, which can put a strain on the network infrastructure connecting the devices. This can be mitigated by sending only the filesystem blocks that have changed by performing a binary `diff` of the new filesystem with the previous version. The commercial edition of Mender has support for such delta updates and delta updates are still a beta feature in RAUC and fwup at the time of writing.

A second drawback is the need to keep storage space for a redundant copy of the root filesystem and other components. If the root filesystem is the largest component, it comes close to doubling the amount of flash memory you need to fit. It is for this reason that the asymmetric update scheme is used, which I describe next.

Asymmetric image update

You can reduce storage requirements by keeping a minimal recovery operating system purely for updating the main one, as shown here:

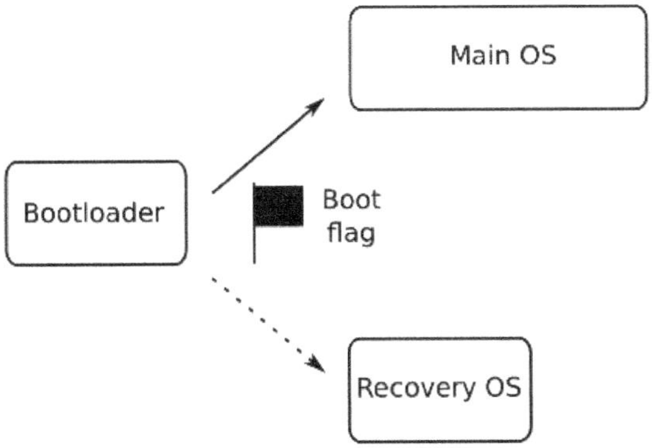

Figure 10.3 – Asymmetric image update

To install an asymmetric update, do the following:

1. Set the boot flag to point to the recovery OS and reboot.
2. Once the recovery OS is running, it can stream updates to the main operating system image.
3. If the update is interrupted, the bootloader will again boot into the recovery OS, which can resume the update.
4. Only when the update is complete and verified will the recovery OS clear the boot flag and reboot again, this time loading the new main operating system.
5. The fallback in the case of a correct but buggy update is to drop the system back into recovery mode, which can attempt remedial actions, possibly by requesting an earlier update version.

The recovery OS is usually a lot smaller than the main operating system, maybe only a few megabytes, and so the storage overhead is not great. As a matter of interest, this is the scheme that was adopted by Android prior to the Nougat release. For open source implementations of asymmetric image update, you could consider SWUpdate or RAUC, both of which I mentioned in the previous section.

A major drawback of this scheme is that while the recovery OS is running, the device is not operational. Such a scheme also does not allow for updates of the recovery OS itself. That would require something like A/B image updates, thus defeating the whole purpose.

Atomic file updates

Another approach is to have redundant copies of a root filesystem present in multiple directories of a single filesystem and then use the `chroot(8)` command to choose one of them at boot time. This allows one directory tree to be updated while another is mounted as the `root` directory. Furthermore, rather than making copies of files that have not changed between versions of the root filesystem, you could use links. That would save a lot of disk space and reduce the amount of data to be downloaded in an update package. These are the basic ideas behind atomic file update.

> **Important note**
>
> The `chroot` command runs a program in an existing directory. The program sees this directory as its `root` directory, and so cannot access any files or directories at a higher level. It is often used to run a program in a constrained environment, which is sometimes referred to as **chroot jail**.

The OSTree project (`https://ostree.readthedocs.org/en/latest/`), now renamed **libOSTree**, is the most popular implementation of this idea. OSTree started around 2011 as a means of deploying updates to the GNOME desktop developers, and to improve their continuous integration testing (`https://wiki.gnome.org/Projects/GnomeContinuous`). It has since been adopted as an update solution for embedded devices. It is one of the update methods available in **Automotive Grade Linux** (**AGL**), and it is available in the Yocto Project through the `meta-update` layer, which is supported by **Advanced Telematic Systems** (**ATS**).

With OSTree, the files are stored on the target in the `/ostree/repo/objects` directory. They are given names such that several versions of the same file can exist in the repository. Then, a given set of files are linked into a deployment directory, which has a name such as `/ostree/deploy/os/29ff9.../`. This is referred to as *checking out*, since it has some similarities to the way a branch is checked out of a Git repository. Each deploy directory contains the files that make up a root filesystem. There can be any number of them, but by default, there are only two. For example, here are two `deploy` directories, each with links back into the `repo` directory:

```
/ostree/repo/objects/...
/ostree/deploy/os/a3c83.../
  /usr/bin/bash
  /usr/bin/echo
/ostree/deploy/os/29ff9.../
  /usr/bin/bash
  /usr/bin/echo
```

To boot from an OSTree directory:

1. The bootloader boots the kernel with an `initramfs`, passing on the kernel command line the path of the deployment to use:

   ```
   bootargs=ostree=/ostree/deploy/os/deploy/29ff9...
   ```

2. The `initramfs` contains an `init` program, `ostree-init`, which reads the command line and executes the `chroot` to the path given.
3. When a system update is installed, the files that have changed are downloaded into the `repo` directory by the OSTree install agent.
4. When complete, a new `deploy` directory is created, with links to the collection of files that will make up the new root filesystem. Some of these will be new files, some will be the same as before.

5. Finally, the OSTree install agent will change the bootloader's boot flag so that on the next reboot, it will `chroot` to the new `deploy` directory.
6. The bootloader implements the check on the boot count and falls back to the previous root if a boot loop is detected.

Even though a developer can operate the updater or install the client manually on a target device, eventually, software updates need to happen automatically over the air.

OTA updates

Updating **over-the-air (OTA)** means having the ability to push software to a device or group of devices via a network, usually without any end user interaction with the device. For this to happen, we need a central server to control the update process and a protocol for downloading the update to the update client. In a typical implementation, the client polls the update server from time to time to check if there are any updates pending. The polling interval needs to be long enough that the poll traffic does not take a significant portion of the network bandwidth, but short enough that the updates can be delivered in a timely fashion. An interval of tens of minutes to several hours is often a good compromise. The poll messages from the device contain some sort of unique identifier, such as a serial number or MAC address, and the current software version. From this, the update server can see if an update is needed. The poll messages may also contain other status information, such as uptime, environmental parameters, or anything that would be useful for central management of the devices.

The update server is usually linked to a management system that will assign new versions of software to the various populations of devices under its control. If the device population is large, it may send updates in batches to avoid overloading the network. There will be some sort of status display where the current state of the devices can be shown, and problems highlighted.

Of course, the update mechanism must be secure so that fake updates cannot be sent to the end devices. This involves the client and server being able to authenticate each other by an exchange of certificates. Then the client can validate that the packages downloaded are signed by the key that is expected.

Here are three examples of open source projects that you can use for OTA updates:

- Mender in managed mode
- balena
- Eclipse hawkBit (`https://github.com/eclipse/hawkbit`) in conjunction with an updater client such as SWUpdate or RAUC

We will walk through the first two projects in detail, starting with **Mender**.

Using Mender for local updates

So much for the theory. In the next two sections of this chapter, I want to demonstrate how the principles I have talked about so far work in practice. For these examples, I will use Mender. Mender uses a symmetric A/B image update mechanism, with a fallback in the event of a failed update. It can operate in *standalone mode* for local updates, or in *managed mode* for OTA updates. I will begin with standalone mode.

Mender is written and supported by mender.io (`https://mender.io`). There is much more information about the software in the documentation section of the website. I will not delve deeply into the configuration of the software here since my aim is to illustrate the principles of software updates. Let's begin with the Mender client.

Building the Mender client

The Mender client is available as a Yocto meta layer. These examples use the Dunfell release of the Yocto Project, which is the same one that we used in *Chapter 6, Selecting a Build System*.

Start by fetching the `meta-mender` layer as follows:

```
$ git clone -b dunfell git://github.com/mendersoftware/meta-
mender
```

You want to navigate one level above the `poky` directory before cloning the `meta-mender` layer so that the two directories are located next to each other at the same level.

The Mender client requires some changes to the configuration of U-Boot to handle the boot flag and boot count variables. The stock Mender client layer has sub-layers for sample implementations of this U-Boot integration that we can use straight out of the box, such as `metameta-mender-qemu` and `meta-mender-raspberrypi`. We will use QEMU.

The next step is to create a build directory and add the layers for this configuration:

```
$ source poky/oe-init-build-env build-mender-qemu
$ bitbake-layers add-layer ../meta-openembedded/meta-oe
$ bitbake-layers add-layer ../meta-mender/meta-mender-core
$ bitbake-layers add-layer ../meta-mender/meta-mender-demo
$ bitbake-layers add-layer ../meta-mender/meta-mender-qemu
```

Then, we need to set up the environment by adding some settings to `conf/local.conf`:

```
1 MENDER_ARTIFACT_NAME = "release-1"
2 INHERIT += "mender-full"
3 MACHINE = "vexpress-qemu"
4 INIT_MANAGER = "systemd"
5 IMAGE_FSTYPES = "ext4"
```

Line 2 includes a BitBake class, named `mender-full`, which is responsible for the special processing of the image required to create the A/B image format. Line 3 selects a machine named `vexpress-qemu`, which uses QEMU to emulate an Arm Versatile Express board, rather than the Versatile PB that is the default in the Yocto Project. Line 4 selects `systemd` as the `init` daemon in place of the default System V `init`. I describe `init` daemons in more detail in *Chapter 13, Starting Up – The init Program*. Line 5 causes the root filesystem images to be generated in `ext4` format.

Now we can build an image:

```
$ bitbake core-image-full-cmdline
```

As usual, the results of the build are in `tmp/deploy/images/vexpress-qemu`. You will notice some new things in here compared to the Yocto Project builds we have done in the past. There is a file named `core-image-full-cmdline-vexpress-qemu-grub-[timestamp].mender`, and another similarly named file that ends with `.uefiimg`. The `.mender` file is required for the next subsection: *Installing an update*. The `.uefiimg` file is created using a tool from the Yocto Project known as `wic`. The output is an image that contains a partition table and that is ready to be copied directly to an SD card or eMMC chip.

We can run the QEMU target using the script provided by the Mender layer, which will first boot U-Boot and then load the Linux kernel:

```
$ ../meta-mender/meta-mender-qemu/scripts/mender-qemu
[...]
[  OK  ] Started Mender OTA update service.
[  OK  ] Started Mender Connect service.
[  OK  ] Started NFS status monitor for NFSv2/3 locking..
[  OK  ] Started Respond to IPv6 Node Information Queries.
[  OK  ] Started Network Router Discovery Daemon.
[  OK  ] Reached target Multi-User System.
```

```
        Starting Update UTMP about System Runlevel Changes...

Poky (Yocto Project Reference Distro) 3.1.6 vexpress-qemu
ttyAMA0

vexpress-qemu login:
```

If instead of a login prompt you see an error like:

```
mender-qemu: 117: qemu-system-arm: not found
```

Then install `qemu-system-arm` on your system and rerun the script:

```
$ sudo apt install qemu-system-arm
```

Log on as `root` with no password. Looking at the layout of the partitions on the target, we can see this:

```
# fdisk -l /dev/mmcblk0
Disk /dev/mmcblk0: 608 MiB, 637534208 bytes, 1245184 sectors
Units: sectors of 1 * 512 = 512 bytes
Sector size (logical/physical): 512 bytes / 512 bytes
I/O size (minimum/optimal): 512 bytes / 512 bytes
Disklabel type: gpt
Disk identifier: 15F2C2E6-D574-4A14-A5F4-4D571185EE9D

Device           Start     End Sectors  Size Type
/dev/mmcblk0p1   16384   49151   32768   16M EFI System
/dev/mmcblk0p2   49152  507903  458752  224M Linux filesystem
/dev/mmcblk0p3 507904  966655  458752  224M Linux filesystem
/dev/mmcblk0p4 966656 1245150  278495  136M Linux filesystem
```

There are four partitions in all:

- **Partition 1**: This contains the U-Boot boot files.
- **Partitions 2 and 3**: These contain the A/B root filesystems: at this stage, they are identical.
- **Partition 4**: This is just an extension partition that contains the remaining partitions.

Running the mount command shows that the second partition is being used as the root filesystem, leaving the third to receive updates:

```
# mount
/dev/mmcblk0p2 on / type ext4 (rw,relatime)
[...]
```

With the Mender client now on board, we can begin installing updates.

Installing an update

Now we want to make a change to the root filesystem and then install it as an update:

1. Open another shell and put yourself back in the working build directory:

    ```
    $ source poky/oe-init-build-env build-mender-qemu
    ```

2. Make a copy of the image we just built. This will be the live image that we are going to update:

    ```
    $ cd tmp/deploy/images/vexpress-qemu
    $ cp core-image-full-cmdline-vexpress-qemu-grub.uefiimg \
    core-image-live-vexpress-qemu-grub.uefiimg
    $ cd -
    ```

    If we don't do this, the QEMU script will just load the latest image generated by BitBake, including updates, which defeats the object of the demonstration.

3. Next, change the hostname of the target, which will be easy to see when it is installed. To do this, edit `conf/local.conf` and add this line:

    ```
    hostname_pn-base-files = "vexpress-qemu-release2"
    ```

4. Now we can build the image in the same way as before:

    ```
    $ bitbake core-image-full-cmdline
    ```

    This time we are not interested in the `.uefiimg` file, which contains a complete new image. Instead, we want to take only the new root filesystem, which is in `core-image-full-cmdline-vexpress-qemu-grub.mender`. The `.mender` file is in a format that is recognized by the Mender client. The `.mender` file format consists of version information, a header, and the root filesystem image put together in a compressed `.tar` archive.

5. The next step is to deploy the new artifact to the target, initiating the update locally on the device, but receiving the update from a server. Stop the emulator you started in the previous terminal session by entering *Ctrl* + *A* then *x* to terminate it. Then boot QEMU again with the newly copied image:

```
$ ../meta-mender/meta-mender-qemu/scripts/mender-qemu \
core-image-live
```

6. Check that the network is configured, with QEMU at `10.0.2.15`, and the host at `10.0.2.2`:

```
# ping 10.0.2.2
PING 10.0.2.2 (10.0.2.2) 56(84) bytes of data.
64 bytes from 10.0.2.2: icmp_seq=1 ttl=255 time=0.286 ms
^C
--- 10.0.2.2 ping statistics ---
1 packets transmitted, 1 received, 0% packet loss, time
0ms
rtt min/avg/max/mdev = 0.286/0.286/0.286/0.000 ms
```

7. Now, in another terminal session, start a web server on the host that can serve up the update:

```
$ cd tmp/deploy/images/vexpress-qemu
$ python3 -m http.server
Serving HTTP on 0.0.0.0 port 8000 (http://0.0.0.0:8000/)
...
```

It is listening on port `8000`. When you are done with the web server, type *Ctrl* + *C* to terminate it.

8. Back on the target, issue this command to get the update:

```
# mender --log-level info install \
> http://10.0.2.2:8000/core-image-full-cmdline-vexpress-
qemu-grub.mender
INFO[0751] Wrote 234881024/234881024 bytes to the
inactive partition
INFO[0751] Enabling partition with new image installed to
be a boot candidate: 3
```

The update was written to the third partition, `/dev/mmcblk0p3`, while our root filesystem is still on partition 2, `mmcblk0p2`.

9. Reboot QEMU by entering *reboot* from the QEMU command line. Note that now the root filesystem is mounted on partition 3, and that the hostname has changed:

```
# mount
/dev/mmcblk0p3 on / type ext4 (rw,relatime)
[...]
# hostname
vexpress-qemu-release2
```

Success!

10. There is one more thing to do. We need to consider the issue of boot loops. Using `fw_printenv` to look at the U-Boot variables, we see the following:

```
# fw_printenv upgrade_available
upgrade_available=1
# fw_printenv bootcount
bootcount=1
```

If the system reboots without clearing `bootcount`, U-Boot should detect it and fall back to the previous installation.

Let's test U-Boot's fallback behavior:

1. Reboot the target right away.
2. When the target comes up again, we see that U-Boot has reverted to the previous installation:

```
# mount
/dev/mmcblk0p2 on / type ext4 (rw,relatime)
[...]
# hostname
vexpress-qemu
```

3. Now, let's repeat the update procedure:

```
# mender --log-level info install \
> http://10.0.2.2:8000/core-image-full-cmdline-vexpress-qemu-grub.mender
# reboot
```

4. But this time, after the reboot, `commit` the change:

```
# mender commit
[...]
# fw_printenv upgrade_available
upgrade_available=0
# fw_printenv bootcount
bootcount=1
```

5. Once `upgrade_available` is cleared, U-Boot will no longer check `bootcount`, and so the device will continue to mount this updated root filesystem. When a further update is loaded, the Mender client will clear `bootcount` and set `upgrade_available` once again.

This example uses the Mender client from the command line to initiate an update locally. The update itself came from a server but could just as easily have been provided on a USB flash drive or an SD card. In place of Mender, we could have used the other image update clients mentioned: SWUpdate or RAUC. They each have their advantages, but the basic technique is the same.

The next stage is to see how OTA updates work in practice.

Using Mender for OTA updates

Once again, we will be using the Mender client on the device, but this time operating it in *managed mode*, and in addition, we will be configuring a server to deploy the update so that no local interaction is needed. Mender provides an open source server for this. For documentation on how to set up this demo server, see `https://docs.mender.io/2.4/getting-started/on-premise-installation`.

The installation requires Docker Engine version 19.03 or later to be installed. Refer to the Docker website at `https://docs.docker.com/engine/installation`. It also requires Docker Compose version 1.25 or later as described here: `https://docs.docker.com/compose/install/`.

To verify which versions of Docker and Docker Compose you have on your system, use these commands:

```
$ docker --version
Docker version 19.03.8, build afacb8b7f0
$ docker-compose --version
docker-compose version 1.25.0, build unknown
```

The Mender server also requires a command-line JSON parser called `jq`:

```
$ sudo apt install jq
```

Once all three are installed, then install the Mender integration environment as shown:

```
$ curl -L \
https://github.com/mendersoftware/integration/
archive/2.5.1.tar.gz | tar xz
$ cd integration-2.5.1
$ ./demo up
Starting the Mender demo environment...
[...]
Creating a new user...
****************************************

Username: mender-demo@example.com
Login password: D53444451DB6

****************************************
Please keep the password available, it will not be cached by
the login script.
Mender demo server ready and running in the background. Copy
credentials above and log in at https://localhost
Press Enter to show the logs.
Press Ctrl-C to stop the backend and quit.
```

When you run the `./demo up` script, you will see that it downloads several hundreds of megabytes of Docker images, which may take some time, depending on your internet connection speed. After a while, you will see that it creates a new demo user and password. This means that the server is up and running.

With the Mender web interface now running on `https://localhost/`, point a web browser at that URL and accept the certificate warning that pops up. The warning appears because the web service is using a self-signed certificate that the browser will not recognize. Enter the username and password generated by the Mender server into the login page.

We now need to make a change to the configuration of the target so that it will poll our local server for updates. For this demonstration, we map the `docker.mender.io` and `s3.docker.mender.io` server URLs to the address `localhost` by appending a line to the `hosts` file. To make this change with the Yocto Project, do the following:

1. First, navigate one level above the directory where you cloned Yocto.
2. Next, create a layer with a file that appends to the recipe that creates the `hosts` file, which is `recipes-core/base-files/base-files_3.0.14.bbappend`. There is already a suitable layer in `MELP/Chapter10/meta-ota` that you can copy:

   ```
   $ cp -a melp3/Chapter10/meta-ota .
   ```

3. Source the working build directory:

   ```
   $ source poky/oe-init-build-env build-mender-qemu
   ```

4. Add the `meta-ota` layer:

   ```
   $ bitbake-layers add-layer ../meta-ota
   ```

   Your layer structure should now contain eight layers including `meta-oe`, `meta-mender-core`, `meta-mender-demo`, `meta-mender-qemu`, and `meta-ota`.
5. Build the new image using the following command:

   ```
   $ bitbake core-image-full-cmdline
   ```

6. Then make a copy. This will become our live image for this section:

   ```
   $ cd tmp/deploy/images/vexpress-qemu
   $ cp core-image-full-cmdline-vexpress-qemu-grub.uefiimg \
   core-image-live-ota-vexpress-qemu-grub.uefiimg
   $ cd -
   ```

7. Boot up the live image:

   ```
   $ ../meta-mender/meta-mender-qemu/scripts/mender-qemu \
   core-image-live-ota
   ```

   After a few seconds, you will see a new device appear on the **Dashboard** of the web interface. This happens so quickly because, for the purposes of demonstrating the system, the Mender client has been configured to poll the server every 5 seconds. A much longer polling interval would be used in production: 30 minutes is suggested.

8. See how this polling interval is configured by looking at the `/etc/mender/mender.conf` file on the target:

```
# cat /etc/mender/mender.conf
{
    "InventoryPollIntervalSeconds": 5,
    "RetryPollIntervalSeconds": 30,
    "ServerURL": "https://docker.mender.io",
    "TenantToken": "dummy",
    "UpdatePollIntervalSeconds": 5
}
```

Notice the server URL in there as well.

9. Back in the web UI, click on the green check mark to authorize the new device:

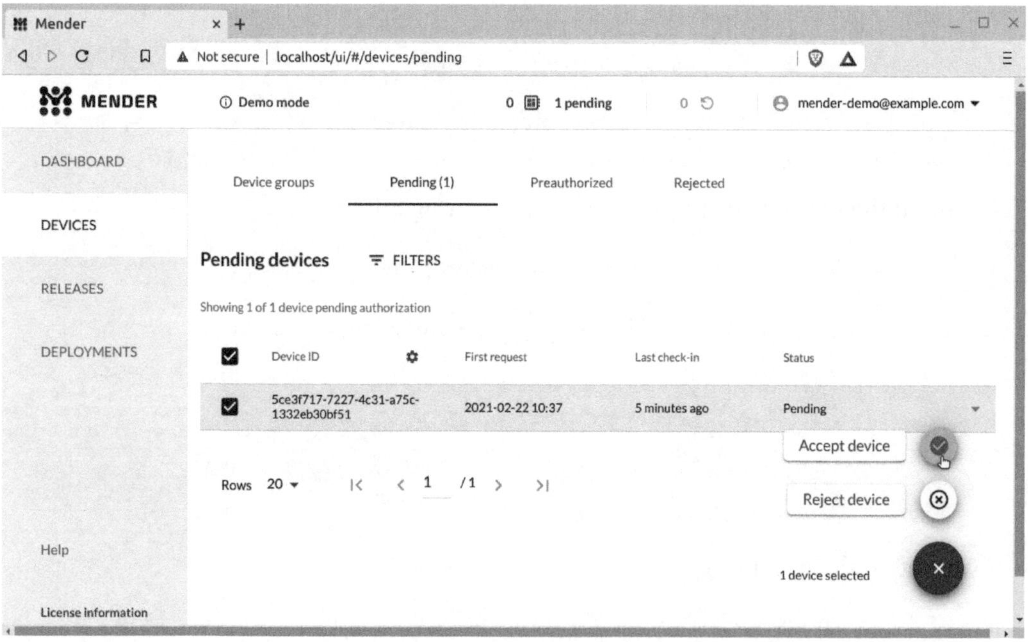

Figure 10.4 – Accept device

10. Then click on the entry for the device to see the details.

Now, we can once again create an update and deploy it – this time, OTA:

1. Update the following line in `conf/local.conf` as shown:

```
MENDER_ARTIFACT_NAME = "OTA-update1"
```

2. Build the image once again:

```
$ bitbake core-image-full-cmdline
```

   This will produce a new `core-image-full-cmdline-vexpress-qemu-grub.mender` file in `tmp/deploy/images/vexpress-qemu`.

3. Import this into the web interface by opening the **Releases** tab and clicking on the purple **Upload** button in the lower-left corner.

4. Browse for the `core-image-full-cmdline-vexpress-qemu-grub.mender` file in `tmp/deploy/images/vexpress-qemu` and upload it:

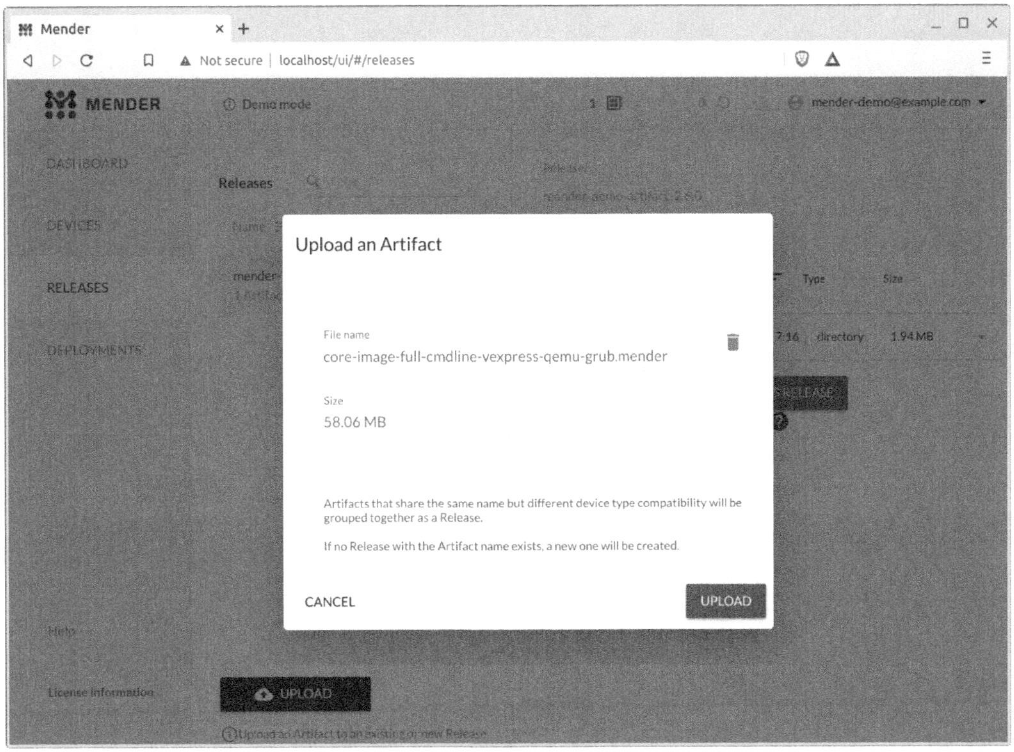

Figure 10.5 – Upload an Artifact

The Mender server should copy the file into the server data store, and a new artifact with the name **OTA-update1** should appear under **Releases**.

To deploy the update to our QEMU device, do the following:

1. Click on the **Devices** tab and select the device.
2. Click on the **Create a Deployment for this Device** option at the bottom right of the device information.
3. Select the **OTA-update1** artifact from the **Releases** page and click on the **Create Deployment with this Release** button:

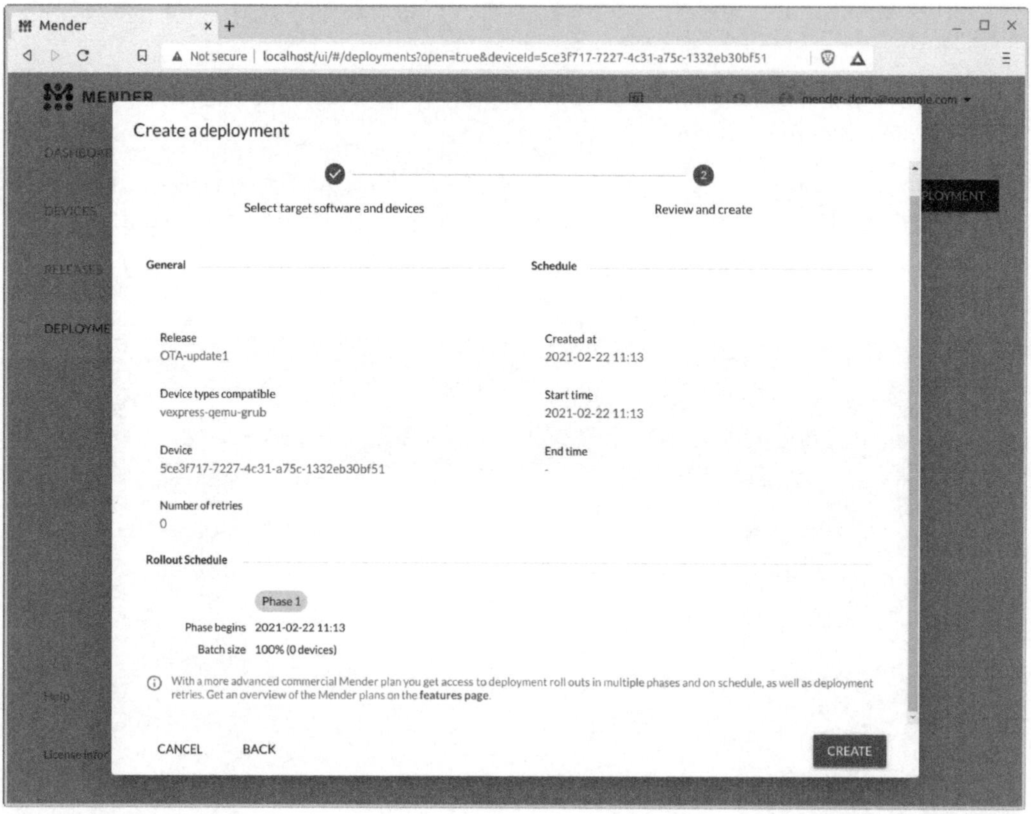

Figure 10.6 – Create a deployment

4. Click on the **Next** button in the **Select target software and devices** step of **Create a deployment**.
5. Click on the **Create** button in the **Review and create** step of **Create a deployment** to start the deployment.
6. The deployment should shortly transition from **Pending** to **In progress**:

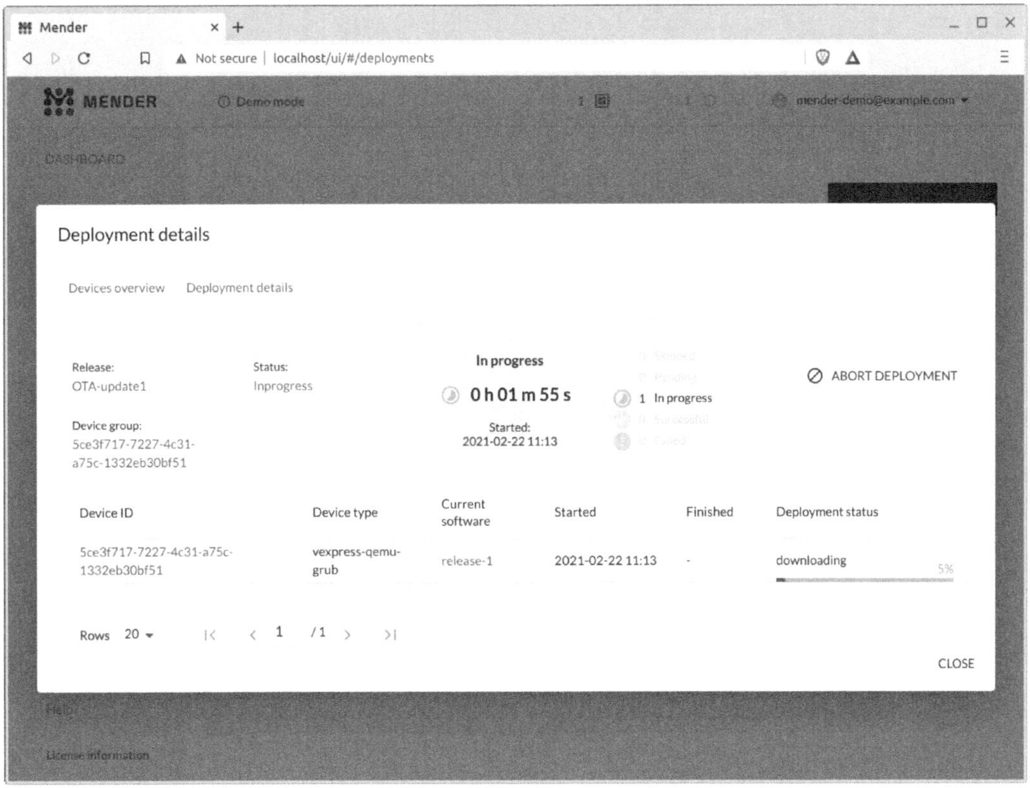

Figure 10.7 – In progress

7. After about 13 minutes, the Mender client should have written the update to the spare filesystem image, and then QEMU will reboot and commit the update. The web UI should then report **Finished**, and now the client is running **OTA-update1**:

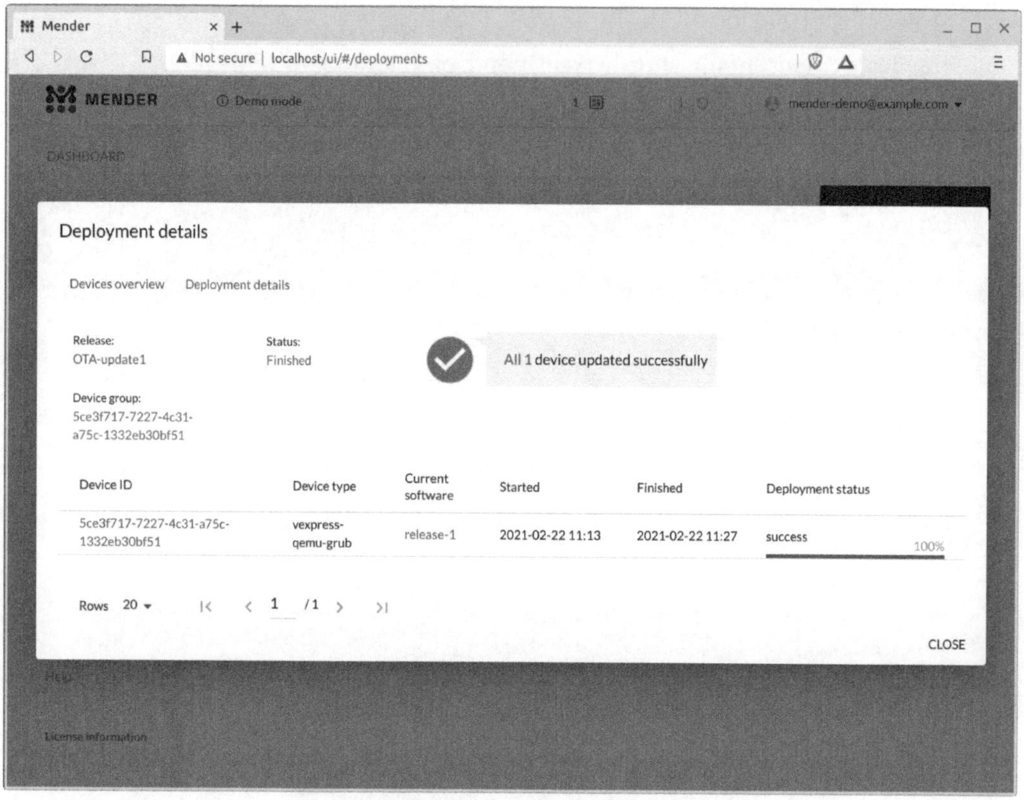

Figure 10.8 – Device updated successfully

Mender is neat and is used in many commercial products, but sometimes we just want to deploy a software project to a small fleet of popular dev boards as quickly as possible.

> **Tip**
>
> After a few experiments with the Mender server, you may want to clear the state and start all over again. You can do that with these two commands, entered in the `integration2.5.1/` directory:
>
> ```
> ./demo down
> ./demo up
> ```

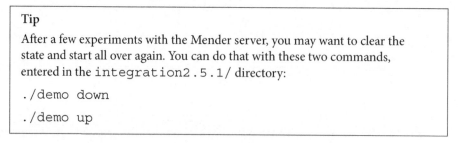

Rapid application development is where **balena** shines. We will spend the rest of this chapter using balena to deploy a simple Python application to a Raspberry Pi 4.

Using balena for local updates

Balena uses Docker containers to deploy software updates. Devices run balenaOS, a Yocto-based Linux distribution that comes with balenaEngine, balena's Docker-compatible container engine. OTA updates occur automatically by way of releases pushed from balenaCloud, a hosted service for managing fleets of devices. Balena can also operate in *local mode* so that updates originate from a server running on your local host machine rather than the cloud. We will stick to local mode for the following exercises.

Balena is written and supported by balena.io (`https://balena.io`). There is much more information about the software in the *Reference* section of the online *Docs* at `balena.io`. We won't dig into how balena works since our goal is to deploy and automatically update software on a small fleet of devices for fast development.

Balena provides prebuilt balenaOS images for popular dev boards such as the Raspberry Pi 4 and BeagleBone Black. Downloading these images requires a balenaCloud account.

Creating an account

The first thing you need to do even if you only intend to operate in local mode is to sign up for a balenaCloud account. You do this by visiting `https://dashboard.balena-cloud.com/signup` and entering your email address and a password, as shown:

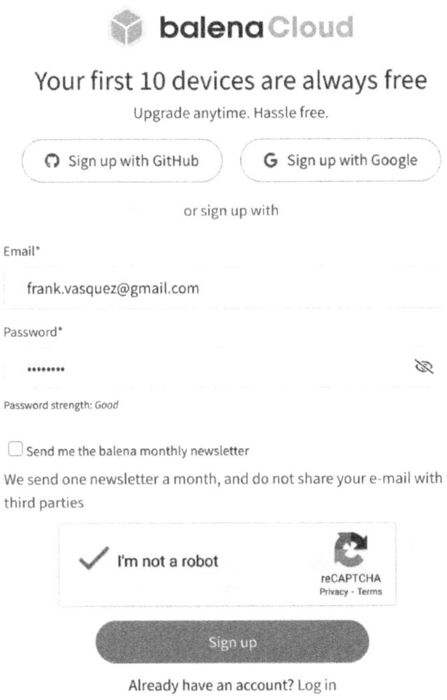

Figure 10.9 – balenaCloud signup

Click the **Sign up** button to submit the form and once it is done processing, you will be prompted to enter your profile details. You may choose to skip this form, at which point you will enter the balenaCloud dashboard under your new account.

If you sign out or your session expires, you can log back into the dashboard by navigating to `https://dashboard.balena-cloud.com/login` and entering the email address and password you signed up with.

Creating an application

Before we can add a Raspberry Pi 4 to a balenaCloud account, we first need to create an application.

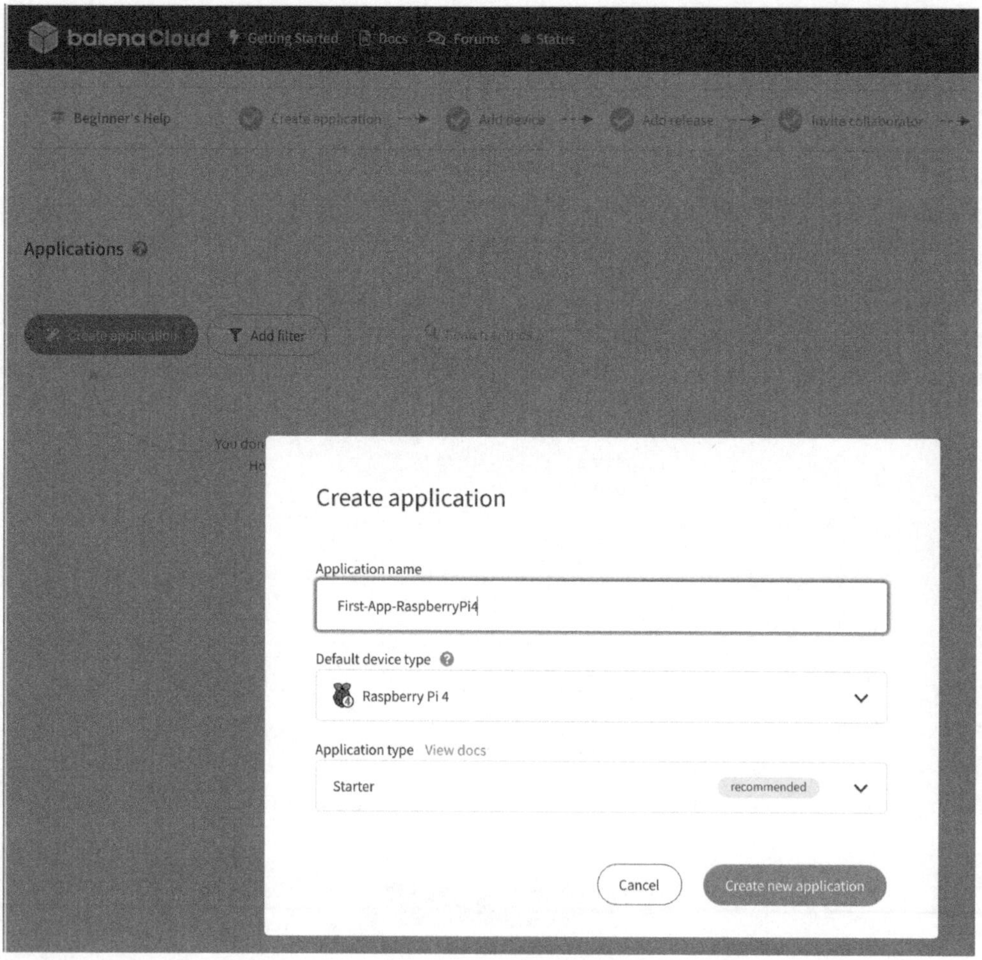

Figure 10.10 – Create application

Here are the steps for creating an application for the Raspberry Pi 4 on balenaCloud:

1. Log in to the balenaCloud dashboard with your email address and password.
2. Click on the **Create application** button in the upper-left corner, under **Applications**, to open the **Create application** dialog.
3. Enter a name for your new application and select **Raspberry Pi 4** for **Default device type**.
4. Click on the **Create new application** button in the **Create application** dialog to submit the form.

The **Application type** defaults to **Starter**, which is fine for these exercises. Your new application should appear in the balenaCloud dashboard under **Applications**.

Adding a device

Now that we have an application on balenaCloud, let's add a Raspberry Pi 4 to it:

1. Log in to the balenaCloud dashboard with your email address and password.
2. Click on the new application we created.
3. Click on the **Add device** button from the **Devices** page:

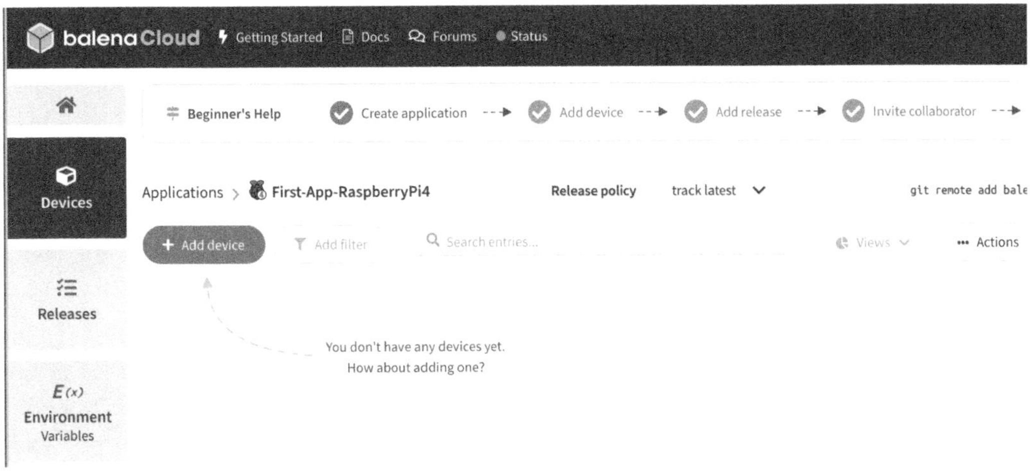

Figure 10.11 – Add device

4. Clicking on the button will bring up the **Add new device** dialog.
5. Ensure that **Raspberry Pi 4** is the selected device type. That option should already be selected since you created the application with **Raspberry Pi 4** as the **Default device type**.

6. Ensure that **balenaOS** is the selected OS.
7. Ensure that the selected version of balenaOS is the latest. That option should already be selected since **Add new device** defaults to the latest available version of balenaOS, which it designates as **recommended**.
8. Select **Development** as the edition of balenaOS. A development image is required to enable local mode for better testing and troubleshooting.
9. Select **Wifi + Ethernet** for **Network Connection**. You could choose **Ethernet only** but auto-connecting to Wi-Fi is a very convenient feature.
10. Enter your Wi-Fi router's SSID and passphrase in their respective fields. Replace `RT-AC66U_B1_38_2G` in the following screenshot with your Wi-Fi router's SSID:

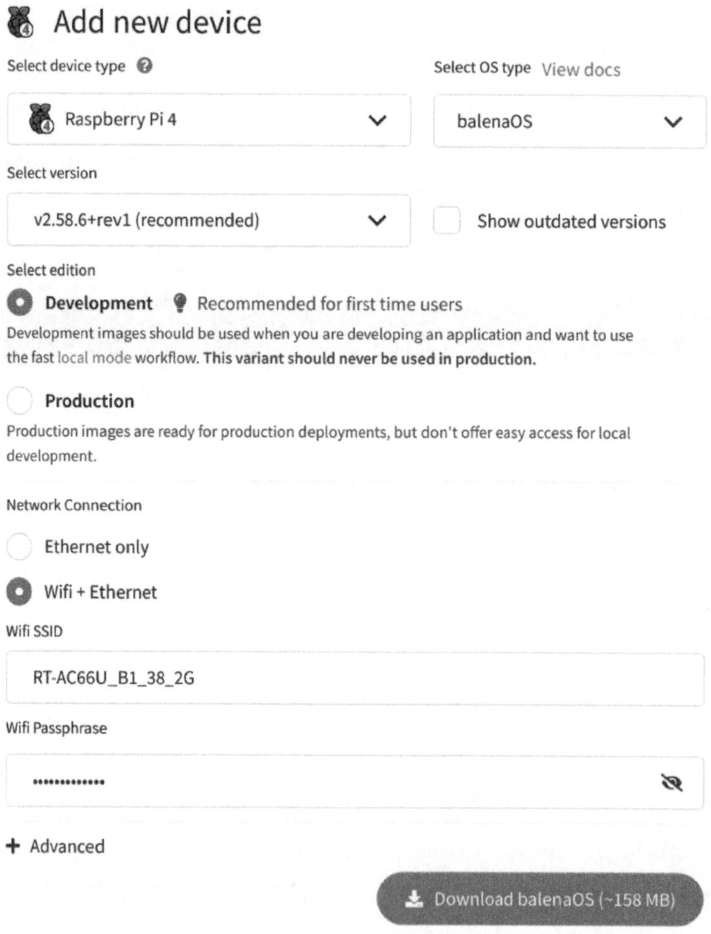

Figure 10.12 – Add new device

11. Click the **Download balenaOS** button.
12. Save the zipped image file to your host machine.

We now have a microSD card image we can use to provision any number of Raspberry Pi 4s for your application's test fleet.

The steps for provisioning a Raspberry Pi 4 from your host machine should be familiar to you by now. Locate the balenaOS `img.zip` file that you downloaded from balenaCloud and use Etcher to write it to a microSD card. Insert the microSD card into your Raspberry Pi 4 and power it up by way of the USB-C port.

It will take a minute or two for the Raspberry Pi 4 to appear on the **Devices** page of your balenaCloud dashboard:

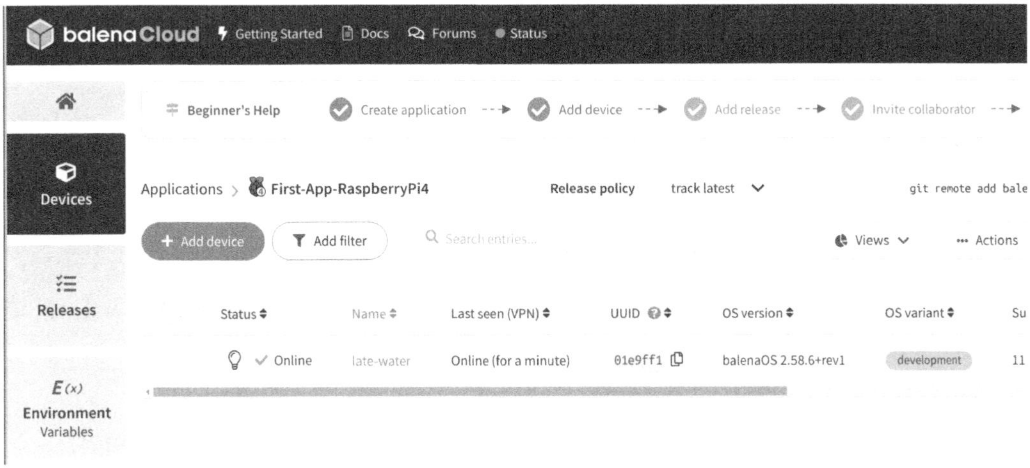

Figure 10.13 – Devices

Now that we have connected a Raspberry Pi 4 to a balena application, we need to enable local mode so that we can deploy OTA updates to it from a nearby host machine rather than the cloud:

1. Click on your target Raspberry Pi 4 from the **Devices** page of your balenaCloud dashboard. My device is named **late-water**. Yours will have a different name.
2. Click on the down arrow next to the light bulb on the device dashboard for your Raspberry Pi 4.

3. Select **Enable local mode** from the drop-down menu:

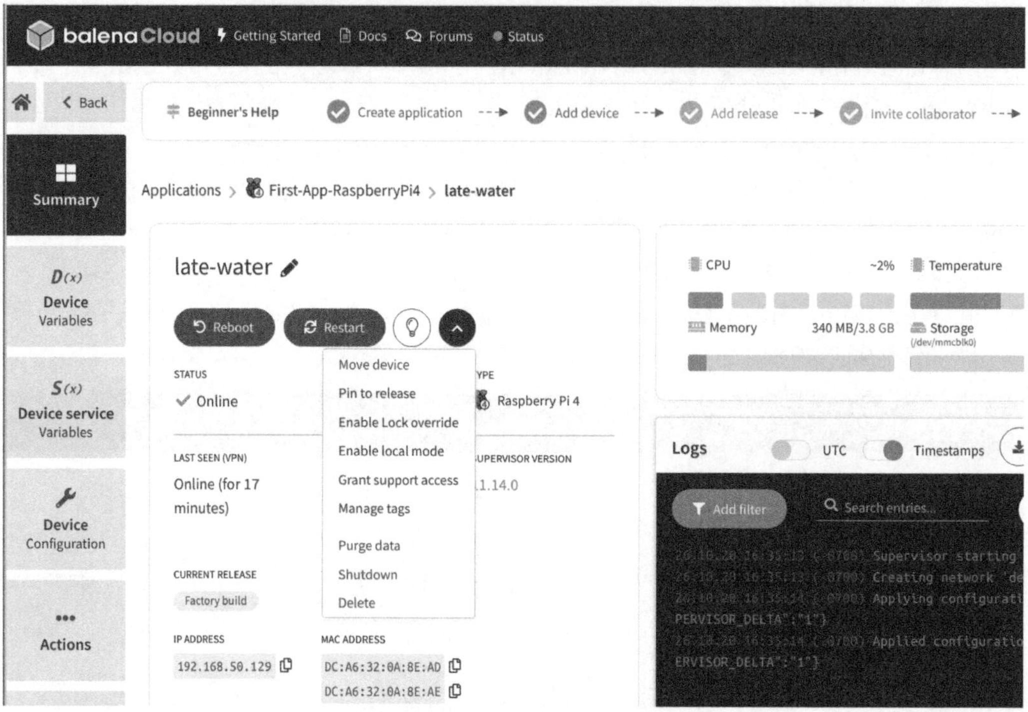

Figure 10.14 – Enable local mode

Once local mode is enabled, the **Logs** and **Terminal** panels are no longer available in the device dashboard. The status of the device changes from **Online (for N minutes)** to **Online (local mode)**.

With local mode now enabled on our target device, we are almost ready to deploy some code to it. Before we can do that, we need to install the balena CLI.

Installing the CLI

Here are the instructions for installing the balena CLI on a Linux host machine:

1. Open a web browser and navigate to the latest balena CLI release page at `https://github.com/balena-io/balena-cli/releases/latest`.
2. Click on the latest ZIP file for Linux to download it. Look for a filename of the form `balena-cli-vX.Y.Z-linux-x64-standalone.zip`, substituting major, minor, and patch version numbers for `X`, `Y`, and `Z`.

3. Extract the zip file contents to your home directory:

```
$ cd ~
$ unzip Downloads/balena-cli-v12.25.4-linux-x64-
standalone.zip
```

   The extracted contents are enclosed in a `balena-cli` directory.

4. Add the `balena-cli` directory to your `PATH` environment variable:

```
$ export PATH=$PATH:~/balena-cli
```

   Add a line like this to the `.bashrc` file in your home directory if you want these changes to your `PATH` variable to persist.

5. Verify that the installation was successful:

```
$ balena version
12.25.4
```

   The latest version of the balena CLI at the time of writing was 12.25.4.

Now that we have a working balena CLI, let's scan the local network for the Raspberry Pi 4 we provisioned:

```
$ sudo env "PATH=$PATH" balena scan
Reporting scan results
-
  host:          01e9ff1.local
  address:       192.168.50.129
  dockerInfo:
    Containers:         1
    ContainersRunning:  1
    ContainersPaused:   0
    ContainersStopped:  0
    Images:             2
    Driver:             overlay2
    SystemTime:         2020-10-26T23:44:44.37360414Z
    KernelVersion:      5.4.58
    OperatingSystem:    balenaOS 2.58.6+rev1
    Architecture:       aarch64
  dockerVersion:
    Version:    19.03.13-dev
    ApiVersion: 1.40
```

Notice the hostname of `01e9ff1.local` and IP address of `192.168.50.129` in the scan output. The hostname and IP address of your Raspberry Pi 4 will vary. Record these two pieces of information because we will need them for the remaining exercises.

Pushing a project

Let's push a Python project to the Raspberry Pi over the local network:

1. Clone a project for a simple "Hello World!" Python web server:

```
$ git clone https://github.com/balena-io-examples/balena-python-hello-world.git
```

2. Navigate into the project directory:

```
$ cd balena-python-hello-world
```

3. Push the code to your Raspberry Pi 4:

```
$ balena push 01e9ff1.local
```

   Substitute your device's hostname for the `01e9ff1.local` argument.

4. Wait for the Docker image to finish building and starting and let the application run in the foreground so that it logs to `stdout`.

5. Issue a request to the web server at `https://192.168.50.129` from a web browser. Substitute your device's IP address for `192.168.50.129`.

The web server running on the Raspberry Pi 4 should respond with "Hello World!" and a line like the following should appear in the live output from `balena push`:

```
[Logs]    [10/26/2020, 5:26:35 PM] [main] 192.168.50.146 - -
[27/Oct/2020 00:26:35] "GET / HTTP/1.1" 200 -
```

The IP address in the log entry should be that of the machine from which you issued the web request. A new log entry should appear every time you refresh the web page. To stop tailing the logs and return to the shell, enter *Ctrl* + *C*. The container will continue running on the target device and the "Hello World!" web server will continue to service requests.

We can restart tailing the logs at any time by issuing the following command:

```
$ balena logs 01e9ff1.local
```

Substitute your device's hostname for the `01e9ff1.local` argument.

The source code for this simple web server can be found in a file named `main.py` within the project directory:

```
tree
.
├── Dockerfile.template
├── img
│   ├── enable-public-URLs.png
│   └── log-output.png
├── README.md
├── requirements.txt
└── src
    └── main.py
```

Now let's make a slight modification to the project source code and redeploy:

1. Open `src/main.py` in your favorite editor.
2. Replace `'Hello World!'` with `'Hello from Pi 4!'` and save your changes. The following `git diff` output captures the changes:

```
$ git diff
diff --git a/src/main.py b/src/main.py
index 940b2df..26321a1 100644
--- a/src/main.py
+++ b/src/main.py
@@ -3,7 +3,7 @@ app = Flask(__name__)

 @app.route('/')
 def hello_world():
-    return 'Hello World!'
+    return 'Hello from Pi 4!'

 if __name__ == '__main__':
     app.run(host='0.0.0.0', port=80)
```

3. Push the new code to your Raspberry Pi 4:

```
$ balena push 01e9ff1.local
```

Substitute your device's hostname for the `01e9ff1.local` argument.

4. Wait for the Docker image to update. The process should be much quicker this time around because of an intelligent caching feature called **Livepush** that is unique to local mode.
5. Issue a request to the web server at `https://192.168.50.129` from a web browser. Substitute your device's IP address for `192.168.50.129`.

The web server running on the Raspberry Pi 4 should respond with "Hello from Pi 4!"

We can SSH into a local target device by IP address:

```
$ balena ssh 192.168.50.129
Last login: Tue Oct 27 00:32:04 2020 from 192.168.50.146
root@01e9ff1:~#
```

Substitute your device's IP address for `192.168.50.129`. This is not especially useful because the application is running inside a Docker container.

To SSH into the container where the Python web server is running and observe what it's doing, we need to include the service name in the `balena ssh` command:

```
$ balena ssh 192.168.50.129 main
root@01e9ff1:/usr/src/app# ls
Dockerfile  Dockerfile.template  README.md  requirements.txt
src
root@01e9ff1:/usr/src/app# ps -ef
UID        PID  PPID  C STIME TTY          TIME CMD
root         1     0  0 00:26 pts/0    00:00:01 /usr/local/bin/
python -u src/main.py
root        30     1  0 00:26 ?        00:00:00 /lib/systemd/
systemd-udevd --daemon
root        80     0  2 00:48 pts/1    00:00:00 /bin/bash
root        88    80  0 00:48 pts/1    00:00:00 ps -ef
#
```

The service name for this starter application is `main` as seen in the live logs output.

Congratulations! You have successfully created a balenaOS image and host development environment that you and your team can use to iterate on project code and quickly redeploy to a target device. This is no small feat. Pushing code changes in the form of a Docker container is a common development workflow that full-stack engineers are very accustomed to. With balena, they can now use the techniques they are familiar with to develop embedded Linux applications on actual hardware.

Summary

Being able to update the software on devices in the field is at the very least a useful attribute, and if the device is connected to the internet, it becomes an absolute must. And yet, all too often it is a feature that is left until the last part of a project, on the assumption that it is not a hard problem to solve. In this chapter, I hope that I have illustrated the problems that are associated with designing an effective and robust update mechanism, and also that there are several open source options readily available. You do not have to reinvent the wheel anymore.

The approach used most often, and also the one with the most real-world testing, is the symmetric image (A/B) update, or its cousin, the asymmetric (recovery) image update. Here, you have the choice of SWUpdate, RAUC, Mender, and fwup. A more recent innovation is the atomic file update, in the form of OSTree. This has good characteristics in reducing the amount of data that needs to be downloaded and the amount of redundant storage that needs to be fitted on the target. Lastly, with the proliferation of Docker came the desire for containerized software updates. This is the approach that balena takes.

It is quite common to deploy updates on a small scale by visiting each site and applying the update from a USB memory stick or SD card. But, if you want to deploy to remote locations, or deploy at scale, an **over-the-air** (**OTA**) update option will be needed.

The next chapter describes how you control the hardware components of your system through the use of device drivers, both in the conventional sense of drivers that are part of the kernel, and also the extent to which you can control hardware from the user space.

11 Interfacing with Device Drivers

Kernel device drivers are the mechanism through which the underlying hardware is exposed to the rest of the system. As a developer of embedded systems, you need to know how these device drivers fit into the overall architecture and how to access them from user space programs. Your system will probably have some novel pieces of hardware, and you will have to work out a way of accessing them. In many cases, you will find that there are device drivers provided for you, and you can achieve everything you want without writing any kernel code. For example, you can manipulate GPIO pins and LEDs using files in `sysfs`, and there are libraries you can use to access serial buses, including **SPI** (**Serial Peripheral Interface**) and **I2C** (**Inter-Integrated Circuit**).

There are many places to find out how to write a device driver, but few tell you why you would want to and the choices you have in doing so. This is what I want to cover here. However, remember that this is not a book dedicated to writing kernel device drivers, and that the information given here is to help you navigate the territory but not necessarily set up home there. There are many good books and articles that will help you to write device drivers, some of which are listed at the end of this chapter in the *Further reading* section.

In this chapter, we will cover the following topics:

- The role of device drivers
- Character devices
- Block devices
- Network devices
- Finding out about drivers at runtime
- Finding the right device driver
- Device drivers in user space
- Writing a kernel device driver
- Discovering the hardware configuration

Let's get started!

Technical requirements

To follow along with the examples in this chapter, make sure you have the following:

- A Linux-based host system
- A microSD card reader and card
- A BeagleBone Black
- A 5V 1A DC power supply
- An Ethernet cable and port for network connectivity

All the code for this chapter can be found in the `Chapter11` folder of this book's GitHub repository: `https://github.com/PacktPublishing/Mastering-Embedded-Linux-Programming-Third-Edition`.

The role of device drivers

As I mentioned in *Chapter 4, Configuring and Building the Kernel*, one of the functions of the kernel is to encapsulate the many hardware interfaces of a computer system and present them in a consistent manner to user space programs. The kernel has frameworks designed to make it easy to write a device driver, which is the piece of code that mediates between the kernel above and the hardware below. A device driver may be written to control physical devices such as a UART or an MMC controller, or it may represent a virtual device such as the null device (`/dev/null`) or a ramdisk. One driver may control multiple devices of the same kind.

Kernel device driver code runs at a high privilege level, as does the rest of the kernel. It has full access to the processor address space and hardware registers. It can handle interrupts and DMA transfers. It can also make use of the sophisticated kernel infrastructure for synchronization and memory management. However, you should be aware that there is a downside to this; if something goes wrong in a buggy driver, it can go really wrong and bring the system down. Consequently, there is a principle that device drivers should be as simple as possible by just providing information to applications where the real decisions are made. You often hear this being expressed as *no policy in the kernel*. It is the responsibility of user space to set the policy that governs the overall behavior of the system. For example, loading kernel modules in response to external events, such as plugging in a new USB device, is the responsibility of the user space program, `udev`, not the kernel. The kernel just supplies a means of loading a kernel module.

In Linux, there are three main types of device driver:

- **Character**: This is for an unbuffered I/O with a rich range of functions and a thin layer between the application code and the driver. It is the first choice when implementing custom device drivers.
- **Block**: This has an interface tailored for block I/O to and from mass storage devices. There is a thick layer of buffering designed to make disk reads and writes as fast as possible, which makes it unsuitable for anything else.
- **Network**: This is similar to a block device but is used for transmitting and receiving network packets rather than disk blocks.

There is also a fourth type that presents itself as a group of files in one of the pseudo filesystems. For example, you might access the GPIO driver through a group of files in `/sys/class/gpio`, as I will describe later on in this chapter. Let's begin by looking in at these three basic device types in more detail.

Character devices

Character devices are identified in the user space by a special file called a **device node**. This filename is mapped to a device driver using the major and minor numbers associated with it. Broadly speaking, the **major number** maps the device node to a particular device driver, while the **minor number** tells the driver which interface is being accessed. For example, the device node of the first serial port on the Arm Versatile PB is named `/dev/ttyAMA0`, and it has major number of `204` and minor number of `64`. The device node for the second serial port has the same major number, since it is handled by the same device driver, but the minor number is `65`. We can see the numbers for all four serial ports from the directory listing here:

```
# ls -l /dev/ttyAMA*
crw-rw---- 1 root root 204, 64 Jan 1 1970 /dev/ttyAMA0
crw-rw---- 1 root root 204, 65 Jan 1 1970 /dev/ttyAMA1
crw-rw---- 1 root root 204, 66 Jan 1 1970 /dev/ttyAMA2
crw-rw---- 1 root root 204, 67 Jan 1 1970 /dev/ttyAMA3
```

The list of standard major and minor numbers can be found in the kernel documentation in `Documentation/devices.txt`. The list does not get updated very often and does not include the `ttyAMA` device described in the preceding paragraph. Nevertheless, if you look at the kernel source code in `drivers/tty/serial/amba-pl011.c`, you will see where the major and minor numbers are declared:

```
#define SERIAL_AMBA_MAJOR 204
#define SERIAL_AMBA_MINOR 64
```

Where there is more than one instance of a device, as with the `ttyAMA` driver, the convention for forming the name of the device node is to take a base name, `ttyAMA`, and append the instance number from `0` to `3` in this example.

As I mentioned in *Chapter 5, Building a Root Filesystem*, the device nodes can be created in several ways:

- `devtmpfs`: The device node is created when the device driver registers a new device interface using a base name supplied by the driver (`ttyAMA`) and an instance number.
- `udev` or `mdev` (without `devtmpfs`): Essentially the same as with `devtmpfs`, except that a user space daemon program has to extract the device name from `sysfs` and create the node. I will talk about `sysfs` later.
- `mknod`: If you are using static device nodes, they are created manually using `mknod`.

You may have the impression from the numbers I have used here that both major and minor numbers are 8-bit numbers in the range 0 to 255. In fact, from Linux 2.6 onward, the major number is 12 bits long, which gives valid numbers from 1 to 4,095, and the minor number is 20 bits, from 0 to 1,048,575.

When you open a character device node, the kernel checks whether the major and minor numbers fall into a range registered by a character device driver. If so, it passes the call to the driver; otherwise, the open call fails. The device driver can extract the minor number to find out which hardware interface to use.

To write a program that accesses a device driver, you have to have some knowledge of how it works. In other words, a device driver is not the same as a file: the things you do with it change the state of the device. A simple example is the pseudorandom number generator, `urandom`, which returns bytes of random data every time you read it. Here is a program that does just this (you will find the code in `MELP/Chapter11/read-urandom`):

```
#include <stdio.h>
#include <sys/types.h>
#include <sys/stat.h>
#include <fcntl.h>
#include <unistd.h>

int main(void)
{
    int f;
    unsigned int rnd;
    int n;
    f = open("/dev/urandom", O_RDONLY);
    if (f < 0) {
        perror("Failed to open urandom");
        return 1;
    }
    n = read(f, &rnd, sizeof(rnd));
    if (n != sizeof(rnd)) {
        perror("Problem reading urandom");
        return 1;
    }
    printf("Random number = 0x%x\n", rnd);
```

```
    close(f);
    return 0;
}
```

The nice thing about the Unix driver model is that once we know that there is a device named `urandom`, every time we read from it, it returns a fresh set of pseudorandom data, so we don't need to know anything else about it. We can just use standard functions such as `open(2)`, `read(2)`, and `close(2)`.

> **Tip**
>
> You could use the stream I/O functions known as `fopen(3)`, `fread(3)`, and `fclose(3)` instead, but the buffering implicit in these functions often causes unexpected behavior. For example, `fwrite(3)` usually only writes to the user space buffer, not to the device. You would need to call `fflush(3)` to force the buffer to be written out. Therefore, it is best to not use stream I/O functions when calling device drivers.

Most device drivers employ a character interface. Mass storage devices are a notable exception. Reading and writing to disk requires a block interface for maximum speed.

Block devices

Block devices are also associated with a device node, which also has major and minor numbers.

> **Tip**
>
> Although character and block devices are identified using major and minor numbers, they are in different namespaces. A character driver with a major number of `4` is in no way related to a block driver with a major number of `4`.

With block devices, the major number is used to identify the device driver and the minor number is used to identify the partition. Let's look at the MMC driver on the BeagleBone Black as an example:

```
# ls -l /dev/mmcblk*
brw-rw---- 1 root disk 179, 0 Jan 1 2000 /dev/mmcblk0
brw-rw---- 1 root disk 179, 1 Jan 1 2000 /dev/mmcblk0p1
brw-rw---- 1 root disk 179, 2 Jan 1 2000 /dev/mmcblk0p2
```

```
brw-rw---- 1 root disk 179, 8 Jan 1 2000 /dev/mmcblk1
brw-rw---- 1 root disk 179, 16 Jan 1 2000 /dev/mmcblk1boot0
brw-rw---- 1 root disk 179, 24 Jan 1 2000 /dev/mmcblk1boot1
brw-rw---- 1 root disk 179, 9 Jan 1 2000 /dev/mmcblk1p1
brw-rw---- 1 root disk 179, 10 Jan 1 2000 /dev/mmcblk1p2
```

Here, `mmcblk0` is the microSD card slot, which has a card that has two partitions, and `mmcblk1` is the eMMC chip, which also has two partitions. The major number for the MMC block driver is `179` (you can look it up in `devices.txt`). The minor numbers are used in ranges to identify different physical MMC devices, and the partitions of the storage medium that are on that device. In the case of the MMC driver, the ranges are eight minor numbers per device: the minor numbers from `0` to `7` are for the first device, the numbers from `8` to `15` are for the second, and so on. Within each range, the first minor number represents the entire device as raw sectors, and the others represent up to seven partitions. On eMMC chips, there are two 128 KiB areas of memory reserved for use by a bootloader. These are represented as two devices known as `mmcblk1boot0` and `mmcblk1boot1`, and they have minor numbers of `16` and `24`, respectively.

As another example, you are probably aware of the SCSI disk driver, known as `sd`, which is used to control a range of disks that use the SCSI command set, which includes SCSI, SATA, USB mass storage, and **Universal Flash Storage (UFS)**. It has the major number `8` and ranges of 16 minor numbers per interface (or disk). The minor numbers from `0` to `15` are for the first interface with device nodes named `sda` up to `sda15`, the numbers from `16` to `31` are for the second disk with device nodes `sdb` up to `sdb15`, and so on. This continues up to the 16th disk from `240` to `255` with the node name `sdp`. There are other major numbers reserved for them because SCSI disks are so popular, but we needn't worry about that here.

Both the MMC and SCSI block drivers expect to find a partition table at the start of the disk. The partition table is created using utilities such as `fdisk`, `sfidsk`, and `parted`.

A user space program can open and interact with a block device directly via the device node. This is not a common thing to do, though, and is usually only done to perform administrative operations such as creating partitions, formatting a partition with a filesystem, and mounting. Once the filesystem has been mounted, you interact with the block device indirectly through the files in that filesystem.

Most block devices will have a kernel driver that works, so we rarely need to write our own. The same goes for network devices. Just like a filesystem abstracts the details of a block device, the network stack eliminates the need to interact directly with a network device.

Network devices

Network devices are not accessed through device nodes, and they do not have major and minor numbers. Instead, a network device is allocated a name by the kernel, based on a string and an instance number. Here is an example of the way a network driver registers an interface:

```
my_netdev = alloc_netdev(0, "net%d", NET_NAME_UNKNOWN, netdev_
setup);
ret = register_netdev(my_netdev);
```

This creates a network device named `net0` the first time it is called, `net1` the second time, and so on. More common names include `lo`, `eth0`, and `wlan0`. Note that this is the name it starts off with; device managers, such as `udev`, may change it to something different later on.

Usually, the network interface name is only used when configuring the network using utilities, such as `ip` and `ifconfig`, to establish a network address and route. Thereafter, you interact with the network driver indirectly by opening sockets and letting the network layer decide how to route them to the right interface.

However, it is possible to access network devices directly from the user space by creating a socket and using the `ioctl` commands listed in `include/linux/sockios.h`. For example, this program uses `SIOCGIFHWADDR` to query the driver for the hardware (MAC) address (the code is in `MELP/Chapter11/show-mac-addresses`):

```
#include <stdio.h>
#include <stdlib.h>
#include <string.h>
#include <unistd.h>
#include <sys/ioctl.h>
#include <linux/sockios.h>
#include <net/if.h>

int main(int argc, char *argv[])
{
    int s;
    int ret;
    struct ifreq ifr;
    int i;
```

```
    if (argc != 2) {
        printf("Usage %s [network interface]\n", argv[0]);
        return 1;
    }
    s = socket(PF_INET, SOCK_DGRAM, 0);
    if (s < 0) {
        perror("socket");
        return 1;
    }
    strcpy(ifr.ifr_name, argv[1]);
    ret = ioctl(s, SIOCGIFHWADDR, &ifr);
    if (ret < 0) {
        perror("ioctl");
        return 1;
    }
    for (i = 0; i < 6; i++)
        printf("%02x:", (unsigned char)ifr.ifr_hwaddr.sa_
data[i]);
    printf("\n");
    close(s);
    return 0;
}
```

This program takes a network interface name as an argument. After opening a socket, we copy the interface name to a struct and pass that struct in to the `ioctl` call on the socket, before printing out the resulting MAC address.

Now that we know what the three categories of device drivers are, how do we list the different drivers that are in use on our system?

Finding out about drivers at runtime

Once you have a running Linux system, it is useful to know which device drivers have been loaded and what state they are in. You can find out a lot by reading the files in `/proc` and `/sys`.

First of all, you can list the character and block device drivers that are currently loaded and active by reading `/proc/devices`:

```
# cat /proc/devices
Character devices:
  1 mem
  2 pty
  3 ttyp
  4 /dev/vc/0
  4 tty
  4 ttyS
  5 /dev/tty
  5 /dev/console
  5 /dev/ptmx
  7 vcs
 10 misc
 13 input
 29 fb
 81 video4linux
 89 i2c
 90 mtd
116 alsa
128 ptm
136 pts
153 spi
180 usb
189 usb_device
204 ttySC
204 ttyAMA
207 ttymxc
226 drm
239 ttyLP
240 ttyTHS
241 ttySiRF
242 ttyPS
243 ttyWMT
```

```
244 ttyAS
245 ttyO
246 ttyMSM
247 ttyAML
248 bsg
249 iio
250 watchdog
251 ptp
252 pps
253 media
254 rtc

Block devices:
259 blkext
  7 loop
  8 sd
 11 sr
 31 mtdblock
 65 sd
 66 sd
 67 sd
 68 sd
 69 sd
 70 sd
 71 sd
128 sd
129 sd
130 sd
131 sd
132 sd
133 sd
134 sd
135 sd
179 mmc
```

For each driver, you can see the major number and the base name. However, this does not tell you how many devices each driver is attached to. It only shows `ttyAMA` but it gives you no clue as to whether it is attached to four real serial ports. I will come back to that later when we look at `sysfs`.

Of course, network devices do not appear in this list, because they do not have device nodes. Instead, you can use tools such as `ifconfig` or `ip` to get a list of network devices:

```
# ip link show
1: lo: <LOOPBACK,UP,LOWER_UP> mtu 65536 qdisc noqueue state
UNKNOWN mode DEFAULT
 link/loopback 00:00:00:00:00:00 brd 00:00:00:00:00:00
2: eth0: <NO-CARRIER,BROADCAST,MULTICAST,UP> mtu 1500 qdisc
pfifo_fast state DOWN mode DEFAULT qlen 1000
 link/ether 54:4a:16:bb:b7:03 brd ff:ff:ff:ff:ff:ff
3: usb0: <BROADCAST,MULTICAST,UP,LOWER_UP> mtu 1500 qdisc
pfifo_fast state UP mode DEFAULT qlen 1000
 link/ether aa:fb:7f:5e:a8:d5 brd ff:ff:ff:ff:ff:ff
```

You can also find out about devices attached to USB or PCI buses using the well-known `lsusb` and `lspci` commands. There is information about them in the respective manual pages and plenty of online guides, so I will not describe them any further here.

The really interesting information is in `sysfs`, which is the next topic we'll cover.

Getting information from sysfs

You can define `sysfs` in a pedantic way as a representation of kernel objects, attributes, and relationships. A kernel object is a **directory**, an attribute is a **file**, and a relationship is a **symbolic link** from one object to another. From a more practical point of view, since the Linux device driver model represents all devices and drivers as kernel objects, you can see the kernel's view of the system laid out before you by looking in `/sys`, as shown here:

```
# ls /sys
block class devices fs module
bus dev firmware kernel power
```

In the context of discovering information about devices and drivers, I will look at three of these directories: `devices`, `class`, and `block`.

The devices - /sys/devices

This is the kernel's view of the devices that have been discovered since boot and how they are connected to each other. It is organized at the top level by the system bus, so what you see varies from one system to another. This is the QEMU emulation of the Arm Versatile:

```
# ls /sys/devices
platform software system tracepoint virtual
```

There are three directories that are present on all systems:

- `system/`: This contains devices at the heart of the system, including CPUs and clocks.
- `virtual/`: This contains devices that are memory-based. You will find the memory devices that appear as `/dev/null`, `/dev/random`, and `/dev/zero` in `virtual/mem`. You will find the loopback device, `lo`, in `virtual/net`.
- `platform/`: This is a catch-all for devices that are not connected via a conventional hardware bus. This may be almost everything on an embedded device.

The other devices appear in directories that correspond to actual system buses. For example, the PCI root bus, if there is one, appears as `pci0000:00`.

Navigating this hierarchy is quite hard, because it requires some knowledge of the topology of your system, and the pathnames become quite long and hard to remember. To make life easier, `/sys/class` and `/sys/block` offer two different views of the devices.

The drivers - /sys/class

This is a view of the device drivers presented by their type. In other words, it is a software view rather than a hardware view. Each of the subdirectories represents a class of driver and is implemented by a component of the driver framework. For example, UART devices are managed by the `tty` layer, and you will find them in `/sys/class/tty`. Likewise, you will find network devices in `/sys/class/net`, input devices such as the keyboard, the touchscreen, and the mouse in `/sys/class/input`, and so on.

There is a symbolic link in each subdirectory for each instance of that type of device pointing to its representation in `/sys/device`.

To take a concrete example, let's look at the serial ports on the Versatile PB. First of all, we can see that there are four of them:

```
# ls -d /sys/class/tty/ttyAMA*
/sys/class/tty/ttyAMA0 /sys/class/tty/ttyAMA2
/sys/class/tty/ttyAMA1 /sys/class/tty/ttyAMA3
```

Each directory is a representation of the kernel object that is associated with an instance of a device interface. Looking within one of these directories, we can see the attributes of the object, represented as files, and the relationships with other objects, represented by links:

```
# ls /sys/class/tty/ttyAMA0
close_delay flags line uartclk
closing_wait io_type port uevent
custom_divisor iomem_base power xmit_fifo_size
dev iomem_reg_shift subsystem
device irq type
```

The link called `device` points to the hardware object for the device. The link called `subsystem` points back to the parent subsystem, `/sys/class/tty`. The remaining directory entries are attributes. Some are specific to a serial port, such as `xmit_fifo_size`, while others apply to many types of device, such as the interrupt number, `irq`, and the device number, `dev`. Some attribute files are writable and allow you to tune parameters in the driver at runtime.

The `dev` attribute is particularly interesting. If you look at its value, you will find the following:

```
# cat /sys/class/tty/ttyAMA0/dev
204:64
```

These are the major and minor numbers of this device. This attribute is created when the driver registers this interface. It is from this file that `udev` and `mdev` find the major and minor numbers of the device driver.

The block drivers – /sys/block

There is one more view of the device model that is important to this discussion: the block driver view that you will find in `/sys/block`. There is a subdirectory for each block device. This example has been taken from a BeagleBone Black:

```
# ls /sys/block
loop0 loop4 mmcblk0 ram0 ram12 ram2 ram6
loop1 loop5 mmcblk1 ram1 ram13 ram3 ram7
loop2 loop6 mmcblk1boot0 ram10 ram14 ram4 ram8
loop3 loop7 mmcblk1boot1 ram11 ram15 ram5 ram9
```

If you look into `mmcblk1`, which is the eMMC chip on this board, you will see the attributes of the interface and the partitions within it:

```
# ls /sys/block/mmcblk1
alignment_offset ext_range mmcblk1p1 ro
bdi force_ro mmcblk1p2 size
capability holders power slaves
dev inflight queue stat
device mmcblk1boot0 range subsystem
discard_alignment mmcblk1boot1 removable uevent
```

The conclusion, then, is that you can learn a lot about the devices (the hardware) and the drivers (the software) that are present on a system by reading `sysfs`.

Finding the right device driver

A typical embedded board is based on a reference design from the manufacturer with changes to make it suitable for a particular application. The BSP that comes with the reference board should support all of the peripherals on that board. But, then you customize the design, perhaps by adding a temperature sensor attached via I2C, some lights and buttons connected via GPIO pins, a display panel via a MIPI interface, or many other things. Your job is to create a custom kernel to control all of these, but where do you start looking for device drivers that support all these peripherals?

The most obvious place to look is the driver support page on the manufacturer's website, or you could ask them directly. In my experience, this seldom gets the result you want; hardware manufacturers are not particularly Linux-savvy, and they often give you misleading information. They may have proprietary drivers as binary blobs, or they may have source code but for a different version of the kernel than the one you have. So, by all means try this route. Personally, I will always try to find an open source driver for the task in hand.

There may be support in your kernel already: there are many thousands of drivers in mainline Linux and there are many vendor-specific drivers in the vendor kernels. Begin by running `make menuconfig` (or `xconfig`) and search for the product name or number. If you do not find an exact match, try more generic searches, allowing for the fact that most drivers handle a range of products from the same family. Next, try searching through the code in the `drivers` directory (`grep` is you friend here).

If you still don't have a driver, you can try searching online and asking in the relevant forums to see if there is a driver for a later version of Linux. If you find one, you should seriously consider updating the BSP to use the later kernel. Sometimes, this is not practical, and so it may have to think of backporting the driver to your kernel. If the kernel versions are similar, it may be easy, but if they are more than 12 to 18 months apart, then chances are that the code will have changed to the extent that you will have to rewrite a chunk of the driver to integrate it with your kernel. If all of these options fail, you will have to find a solution yourself by writing the missing kernel driver. However, this is not always necessary. We will look at this in the next section.

Device drivers in user space

Before you start writing a device driver, pause for a moment to consider whether it is really necessary. There are generic device drivers for many common types of devices that allow you to interact with hardware directly from user space, without having to write a line of kernel code. User space code is certainly easier to write and debug. It is also not covered by the GPL, although I don't feel that is a good reason in itself to do it this way.

These drivers fall into two broad categories: those that you control through files in `sysfs`, including GPIO and LEDs, and serial buses that expose a generic interface through a device node, such as I2C.

GPIO

General-Purpose Input/Output (**GPIO**) is the simplest form of digital interface since it gives you direct access to individual hardware pins, each of which can be in one of two states: either high or low. In most cases, you can configure the GPIO pin to be either an input or an output. You can even use a group of GPIO pins to create higher level interfaces such as I2C or SPI by manipulating each bit in software, a technique that is called **bit banging**. The main limitation is the speed and accuracy of the software loops and the number of CPU cycles you want to dedicate to them. Generally speaking, it is hard to achieve timer accuracy better than a millisecond unless you configure a real-time kernel, as we shall see in *Chapter 21, Real-Time Programming*. More common use cases for GPIO are for reading push buttons and digital sensors and controlling LEDs, motors, and relays.

Most SoCs have a lot of GPIO bits, which are grouped together in GPIO registers, usually 32 bits per register. On-chip GPIO bits are routed through to GPIO pins on the chip package via a multiplexer, known as a **pin mux**. There may be additional GPIO pins available off-chip in the power management chip, and in dedicated GPIO extenders, connected through I2C or SPI buses. All this diversity is handled by a kernel subsystem known as `gpiolib`, which is not actually a library but the infrastructure GPIO drivers used to expose I/O in a consistent way. There are details about the implementation of `gpiolib` in the kernel source in `Documentation/gpio`, and the code for the drivers themselves is in `drivers/gpio`.

Applications can interact with `gpiolib` through files in the `/sys/class/gpio` directory. Here is an example of what you will see in there on a typical embedded board (a BeagleBone Black):

```
# ls /sys/class/gpio
export gpiochip0 gpiochip32 gpiochip64 gpiochip96 unexport
```

The directories named `gpiochip0` through to `gpiochip96` represent four GPIO registers, each with 32 GPIO bits. If you look in one of the `gpiochip` directories, you will see the following:

```
# ls /sys/class/gpio/gpiochip96
base label ngpio power subsystem uevent
```

The file named `base` contains the number of the first GPIO pin in the register, while `ngpio` contains the number of bits in the register. In this case, `gpiochip96/base` is 96 and `gpiochip96/ngpio` is 32, which tells you that it contains GPIO bits 96 to 127. It is possible for there to be a gap between the last GPIO in one register and the first GPIO in the next.

To control a GPIO bit from user space, you first have to export it from kernel space, which you can do by writing the GPIO number to `/sys/class/gpio/export`. This example shows the process for GPIO 53, which is wired to user LED 0 on the BeagleBone Black:

```
# echo 53 > /sys/class/gpio/export
# ls /sys/class/gpio
export gpio53 gpiochip0 gpiochip32 gpiochip64 gpiochip96
unexport
```

Now, there is a new directory, `gpio53`, which contains the files you need to control the pin.

> **Important note**
>
> If the GPIO bit is already claimed by the kernel, you will not be able to export it in this way.

The `gpio53` directory contains these files:

```
# ls /sys/class/gpio/gpio53
active_low direction power uevent
device edge subsystem value
```

The pin begins as an input. To change it to an output, write `out` to the `direction` file. The file value contains the current state of the pin, which is `0` for low and `1` for high. If it is an output, you can change the state by writing `0` or `1` to `value`. Sometimes, the meaning of low and high is reversed in hardware (hardware engineers enjoy doing that sort of thing), so writing `1` to `active_low` inverts the meaning of `value` so that a low voltage is reported as `1` and a high voltage is reported as `0`.

You can remove a GPIO from user space control by writing the GPIO number to `/sys/class/gpio/unexport`.

Handling interrupts from GPIO

In many cases, a GPIO input can be configured to generate an interrupt when it changes state, which allows you to wait for the interrupt rather than polling in an inefficient software loop. If the GPIO bit can generate interrupts, a file called `edge` exists. Initially, it has the value called `none`, meaning that it does not generate interrupts. To enable interrupts, you can set it to one of these values:

- `rising`: Interrupt on rising edge
- `falling`: Interrupt on falling edge
- `both`: Interrupt on both rising and falling edges
- `none`: No interrupts (default)

If you want to wait for a falling edge on GPIO 48, you must first enable the interrupts:

```
# echo 48 > /sys/class/gpio/export
# echo falling > /sys/class/gpio/gpio48/edge
```

To wait for an interrupt from the GPIO, follow these steps:

1. First, call `epoll_create` to create the `epoll` notification facility:

```
int ep;
ep = epoll_create(1);
```

2. Next, `open` the GPIO and `read` out its initial value:

```
int f;
int n;
char value[4];

f = open("/sys/class/gpio/gpio48/value", O_RDONLY | O_
NONBLOCK);
[...]
n = read(f, &value, sizeof(value));
if (n > 0) {
        printf("Initial value value=%c\n",
                value[0]);
        lseek(f, 0, SEEK_SET);
}
```

3. Call `epoll_ctl` to register the GPIO's file descriptor with `POLLPRI` as the event:

```
struct epoll_event ev, events;
ev.events = EPOLLPRI;
ev.data.fd = f;
int ret;

ret = epoll_ctl(ep, EPOLL_CTL_ADD, f, &ev);
```

4. Lastly, wait for an interrupt using the `epoll_wait` function:

```
while (1) {
        printf("Waiting\n");
        ret = epoll_wait(ep, &events, 1, -1);
        if (ret > 0) {
                n = read(f, &value, sizeof(value));
```

```
            printf("Button pressed: value=%c\n",
value[0]);
            lseek(f, 0, SEEK_SET);
      }
}
```

The complete source code for this program, as well as a `Makefile` and GPIO configuration script, can be found inside the `MELP/Chapter11/gpio-int/` directory that's included with this book's code archive.

While we could have used `select` and `poll` to handle interrupts, unlike those other two system calls, the performance of `epoll` does not degrade rapidly as the number of file descriptors being monitored increases.

Like GPIOs, LEDs are accessible from `sysfs`. The interface, however, is noticeably different.

LEDs

LEDs are often controlled though a GPIO pin, but there is another kernel subsystem that offers more specialized control that's specific for this purpose. The `leds` kernel subsystem adds the ability to set brightness, should the LED have that ability, and it can handle LEDs connected in other ways than a simple GPIO pin. It can be configured to trigger the LED on an event, such as block device access or just a heartbeat, to show that the device is working. You will have to configure your kernel with the `CONFIG_LEDS_CLASS` option and with the LED trigger actions that are appropriate to you. There is more information on `Documentation/leds/`, and the drivers are in `drivers/leds/`.

As with GPIOs, LEDs are controlled through an interface in `sysfs` in the `/sys/class/leds` directory. In the case of the BeagleBone Black, the names of the LEDs are encoded in the device tree in the form of `devicename:colour:function`, as shown here:

```
# ls /sys/class/leds
beaglebone:green:heartbeat beaglebone:green:usr2
beaglebone:green:mmc0 beaglebone:green:usr3
```

Now, we can look at the attributes of one of the LEDs:

```
# cd /sys/class/leds/beaglebone\:green\:usr2
# ls
brightness max_brightness subsystem uevent
device power trigger
```

Note that leading backslashes are required by the shell to escape the colons in the path.

The `brightness` file controls the brightness of the LED and can be a number between `0` (off) and `max_brightness` (fully on). If the LED doesn't support intermediate brightness, any non-zero value turns it on. The file called `trigger` lists the events that trigger the LED to turn on. The list of triggers is implementation-dependent. Here is an example:

```
# cat trigger
none mmc0 mmc1 timer oneshot heartbeat backlight gpio [cpu0]
default-on
```

The trigger currently selected is shown in square brackets. You can change it by writing one of the other triggers to the file. If you want to control the LED entirely through `brightness`, select `none`. If you set `trigger` to `timer`, two extra files will appear that allow you to set the on and off times in milliseconds:

```
# echo timer > trigger
# ls
brightness delay_on max_brightness subsystem uevent
delay_off device power trigger
# cat delay_on
500
# cat /sys/class/leds/beaglebone:green:heartbeat/delay_off
500
```

If the LED has on-chip timer hardware, the blinking takes place without interrupting the CPU.

I2C

I2C is a simple low speed 2-wire bus that is common on embedded boards, typically used to access peripherals that are not on the SoC, such as display controllers, camera sensors, GPIO extenders, and so on. There is a related standard known as **system management bus** (**SMBus**) that is found on PCs, which is used to access temperature and voltage sensors. SMBus is a subset of I2C.

I2C is a master-slave protocol, with the master being one or more host controllers on the SoC. Slaves have a 7-bit address assigned by the manufacturer (read the data sheet), allowing up to 128 nodes per bus, but 16 are reserved, so only 112 nodes are allowed in practice. The master may initiate read or write transactions with one of the slaves. Frequently, the first byte is used to specify a register on the slave, while the remaining bytes are the data that's read from or written to that register.

There is one device node for each host controller; for example, this SoC has four:

```
# ls -l /dev/i2c*
crw-rw---- 1 root i2c 89, 0 Jan 1 00:18 /dev/i2c-0
crw-rw---- 1 root i2c 89, 1 Jan 1 00:18 /dev/i2c-1
crw-rw---- 1 root i2c 89, 2 Jan 1 00:18 /dev/i2c-2
crw-rw---- 1 root i2c 89, 3 Jan 1 00:18 /dev/i2c-3
```

The device interface provides a series of `ioctl` commands that query the host controller and send the `read` and `write` commands to I2C slaves. There is a package named `i2c-tools`, which uses this interface to provide basic command-line tools to interact with I2C devices. The tools are as follows:

- `i2cdetect`: This lists the I2C adapters and probes the bus.
- `i2cdump`: This dumps data from all the registers of an I2C peripheral.
- `i2cget`: This reads data from an I2C slave.
- `i2cset`: This writes data to an I2C slave.

The `i2c-tools` package is available in Buildroot and the Yocto Project, as well as most mainstream distributions. So, as long as you know the address and protocol of the slave, writing a user space program to talk to the device is straightforward. The example that follows shows how to read the first four bytes from the AT24C512B EEPROM, which is mounted on the BeagleBone Black on I2C bus 0. It has a slave address of `0x50` (the code for this is in `MELP/Chapter11/i2c-example`):

```
#include <stdio.h>
#include <unistd.h>
#include <fcntl.h>
#include <sys/ioctl.h>
#include <linux/i2c-dev.h>

#define I2C_ADDRESS 0x50

```

```
int main(void)
{
    int f;
    int n;
    char buf[10];

    f = open("/dev/i2c-0", O_RDWR);

    /* Set the address of the i2c slave device */
    ioctl(f, I2C_SLAVE, I2C_ADDRESS);

    /* Set the 16-bit address to read from to 0 */
    buf[0] = 0; /* address byte 1 */
    buf[1] = 0; /* address byte 2 */
    n = write(f, buf, 2);

    /* Now read 4 bytes from that address */
    n = read(f, buf, 4);
    printf("0x%x 0x%x0 0x%x 0x%x\n",
    buf[0], buf[1], buf[2], buf[3]);

    close(f);
    return 0;
}
```

This program is like `i2cget` except that the address and register bytes being read from are both hardcoded rather than passed in as arguments. We can use `i2cdetect` to discover the addresses of any peripherals on an I2C bus. `i2cdetect` can leave I2C peripherals in a bad state or lock up the bus, so it's good practice to reboot after using it. A peripheral's data sheet tells us what the registers map to. With that information, we can then use `i2cset` to write to its registers over I2C. These I2C commands can easily be converted into a library of C functions for interfacing with the peripheral.

> **Important Note**
>
> There is more information about the Linux implementation of I2C in `Documentation/i2c/dev-interface`. The host controller drivers are in `drivers/i2c/busses`.

Another popular communication protocol is the **Serial Peripheral Interface (SPI)**, which utilizes a 4-wire bus.

SPI

The SPI bus is similar to I2C but is a lot faster by up to tens of MHz. The interface uses four wires with separate send and receive lines, which allow it to operate in full duplex. Each chip on the bus is selected with a dedicated chip select line. It is commonly used to connect to touchscreen sensors, display controllers, and serial NOR flash devices.

As with I2C, it is a master-slave protocol, with most SoCs implementing one or more master host controllers. There is a generic SPI device driver, which you can enable through the `CONFIG_SPI_SPIDEV` kernel configuration. It creates a device node for each SPI controller, which allows you to access SPI chips from the user space. The device nodes are named `spidev[bus].[chip select]`:

```
# ls -l /dev/spi*
crw-rw---- 1 root root 153, 0 Jan 1 00:29 /dev/spidev1.0
```

For examples of using the `spidev` interface, please refer to the example code in `Documentation/spi`.

So far, the device drivers we've seen all have longstanding upstream support within the Linux kernel. Because these device drivers are all generic (GPIO, LEDs, I2C, and SPI), accessing them from the user space is straightforward. At some point, you will encounter a piece of hardware that lacks a compatible kernel device driver. That hardware may be the centerpiece of your product (for example, Lidar, SDR, and so on). There may also be an FPGA in-between the SoC and this hardware. Under these circumstances, you may have no other recourse than to write your own kernel module(s).

Writing a kernel device driver

Eventually, when you have exhausted all the previous user space options, you will find yourself having to write a device driver to access a piece of hardware attached to your device. Character drivers are the most flexible and should cover 90% of all your needs; network drivers apply if you are working with a network interface and block drivers are for mass storage. The task of writing a kernel driver is complex and beyond the scope of this book. There are some references at the end that will help you on your way. In this section, I want to outline the options available for interacting with a driver – a topic not normally covered – and show you the bare bones of a character device driver.

Designing a character driver interface

The main character driver interface is based on a stream of bytes, as you would have with a serial port. However, many devices don't fit this description: a controller for a robot arm needs functions to move and rotate each joint, for example. Luckily, there are other ways to communicate with device drivers than just `read` and `write`:

- `ioctl`: The `ioctl` function allows you to pass two arguments to your driver, and these can have any meaning you like. By convention, the first argument is a command, which selects one of several functions in your driver, while the second is a pointer to a structure, which serves as a container for the input and output parameters. This is a blank canvas that allows you to design any program interface you like. It is pretty common when the driver and application are closely linked and written by the same team. However, `ioctl` is deprecated in the kernel, and you will find it hard to get any drivers with new uses of `ioctl` accepted upstream. The kernel maintainers dislike `ioctl` because it makes kernel code and application code too interdependent, and it is hard to keep both of them in step across kernel versions and architectures.
- `sysfs`: This is the preferred way to do things now, with a good example being the GPIO interface described earlier. The advantages are that it is somewhat self-documenting, so long as you choose descriptive names for the files. It is also scriptable because the file's content is usually text strings. On the other hand, the requirement for each file to contain a single value makes it hard to achieve atomicity if you need to change more than one value at a time. Conversely, `ioctl` passes all its arguments in a structure, in a single function call.
- `mmap`: You can get direct access to kernel buffers and hardware registers by mapping kernel memory into user space, thus bypassing the kernel. You may still need some kernel code to handle interrupts and DMA. There is a subsystem that encapsulates this idea, known as `uio`, which is short for **user I/O**. There is more documentation in `Documentation/DocBook/uio-howto`, and there are example drivers in `drivers/uio`.
- `sigio`: You can send a signal from a driver using the kernel function named `kill_fasync()` to notify applications of an event, such as input becoming ready or an interrupt being received. By convention, the signal called `SIGIO` is used, but it could be any. You can see some examples in the UIO driver, `drivers/uio/uio.c`, and in the RTC driver, `drivers/char/rtc.c`. The main problem is that it is difficult to write reliable signal handlers in the user space, and so it remains a little-used facility.

- `debugfs`: This is another pseudo filesystem that represents kernel data as files and directories, similar to `proc` and `sysfs`. The main distinction is that `debugfs` must not contain information that is needed for the normal operation of the system; it is for debug and trace information only. It is mounted as `mount -t debugfs debug /sys/kernel/debug`. There is a good description of `debugfs` in the `Documentation/filesystems/debugfs.txt` kernel documentation.
- `proc`: The `proc` filesystem is deprecated for all new code unless it relates to processes, which was the original intended purpose for the filesystem. However, you can use `proc` to publish any information you choose. And, unlike `sysfs` and `debugfs`, it is available to non-GPL modules.
- `netlink`: This is a socket protocol family. `AF_NETLINK` creates a socket that links the kernel space to the user space. It was originally created so that network tools could communicate with the Linux network code to access the routing tables and other details. It is also used by `udev` to pass events from the kernel to the `udev` daemon. It is very rarely used in general device drivers.

There are many examples of all of the preceding filesystems in the kernel source code, and you can design really interesting interfaces to your driver code. The only universal rule is the *principle of least astonishment*. In other words, application writers who are using your driver should find that everything works in a logical way, without any quirks or oddities.

The anatomy of a device driver

It's time to draw some threads together by looking at the code for a simple device driver.

Here is the start of a device driver named `dummy`, which creates four devices that can be accessed through `/dev/dummy0` to `/dev/dummy3`:

```
#include <linux/kernel.h>
#include <linux/module.h>
#include <linux/init.h>
#include <linux/fs.h>
#include <linux/device.h>

#define DEVICE_NAME "dummy"
#define MAJOR_NUM 42
#define NUM_DEVICES 4

static struct class *dummy_class;
```

Next, we will define the dummy_open(), dummy_release(), dummy_read(), and dummy_write() functions for the character device interface:

```
static int dummy_open(struct inode *inode, struct file *file)
{
    pr_info("%s\n", __func__);
    return 0;
}

static int dummy_release(struct inode *inode, struct file
*file)
{
    pr_info("%s\n", __func__);
    return 0;
}

static ssize_t dummy_read(struct file *file,
 char *buffer, size_t length, loff_t * offset)
{
    pr_info("%s %u\n", __func__, length);
    return 0;
}

static ssize_t dummy_write(struct file *file,
 const char *buffer, size_t length, loff_t * offset)
{
    pr_info("%s %u\n", __func__, length);
    return length;
}
```

After that, we need to initialize a file_operations structure and define the dummy_init() and dummy_exit() functions, which are called when the driver is loaded and unloaded:

```
struct file_operations dummy_fops = {
    .owner = THIS_MODULE,
    .open = dummy_open,
    .release = dummy_release,
```

```
    .read = dummy_read,
    .write = dummy_write,
};

int __init dummy_init(void)
{
    int ret;
    int i;
    printk("Dummy loaded\n");
    ret = register_chrdev(MAJOR_NUM, DEVICE_NAME, &dummy_fops);
    if (ret != 0)
        return ret;
    dummy_class = class_create(THIS_MODULE, DEVICE_NAME);
    for (i = 0; i < NUM_DEVICES; i++) {
        device_create(dummy_class, NULL,
                      MKDEV(MAJOR_NUM, i), NULL, "dummy%d", i);
    }
    return 0;
}

void __exit dummy_exit(void)
{
    int i;
    for (i = 0; i < NUM_DEVICES; i++) {
        device_destroy(dummy_class, MKDEV(MAJOR_NUM, i));
    }
    class_destroy(dummy_class);
    unregister_chrdev(MAJOR_NUM, DEVICE_NAME);
    printk("Dummy unloaded\n");
}
```

At the end of the code, the macros called `module_init` and `module_exit` specify the functions to be called when the module is loaded and unloaded:

```
module_init(dummy_init);
module_exit(dummy_exit);
```

The closing three macros named MODULE_* add some basic information about the module:

```
MODULE_LICENSE("GPL");
MODULE_AUTHOR("Chris Simmonds");
MODULE_DESCRIPTION("A dummy driver");
```

This information can be retrieved from the compiled kernel module using the modinfo command. The complete source code for the driver can be found in the MELP/Chapter11/dummy-driver directory, which is included with this book's code archive.

When the module is loaded, the dummy_init() function is called. You can see the point at which it becomes a character device when is makes the call to register_chrdev, passing a pointer to struct file_operations, which contains pointers to the four functions that the driver implements. While register_chrdev tells the kernel that there is a driver with a major number of 42, it doesn't say anything about the class of driver, and so it will not create an entry in /sys/class.

Without an entry in /sys/class, the device manager cannot create device nodes. So, the next few lines of code create a device class, dummy, and four devices of that class called dummy0 to dummy3. The result is that the /sys/class/dummy directory is created when the driver is initialized, containing subdirectories dummy0 to dummy3. Each of the subdirectories contains a file, dev, that contains the major and minor numbers of the device. This is all that a device manager needs to create device nodes: /dev/dummy0 to /dev/dummy3.

The dummy_exit() function has to release the resources claimed by dummy_init(), which here means freeing up the device class and major number.

The file operations for this driver are implemented by dummy_open(), dummy_read(), dummy_write(), and dummy_release(), and they are called when a user space program calls open(2), read(2), write(2), and close(2), respectively. They just print a kernel message so that you can see that they were called. You can demonstrate this from the command line using the echo command:

```
# echo hello > /dev/dummy0
dummy_open
dummy_write 6
dummy_release
```

In this case, the messages appear because I was logged onto the console, and kernel messages are printed to the console by default. If you are not logged onto the console, you can still see the kernel messages by using the dmesg command.

The full source code for this driver is less than 100 lines, but it is enough to illustrate how the linkage between a device node and driver code works; how the device class is created, allowing a device manager to create device nodes automatically when the driver is loaded; and how the data is moved between the user and kernel spaces. Next, you need to build it.

Compiling kernel modules

At this point, you have some driver code that you want to compile and test on your target system. You can copy it into the kernel source tree and modify makefiles to build it, or you can compile it as a module out of tree. Let's start by building out of tree.

You will need a simple makefile that uses the kernel build system to do all the hard work:

```
LINUXDIR := $(HOME)/MELP/build/linux

obj-m := dummy.o
all:
	make ARCH=arm CROSS_COMPILE=arm-cortex_a8-linux-gnueabihf-
\
	-C $(LINUXDIR) M=$(shell pwd)
clean:
	make -C $(LINUXDIR) M=$(shell pwd) clean
```

Set `LINUXDIR` to the directory of the kernel for your target device that you will be running the module on. The `obj-m := dummy.o` code will invoke the kernel build rule to take the source file, `dummy.c`, and create a kernel module, `dummy.ko`. I will show you how to load kernel modules in the next section.

> **Important Note**
> Kernel modules are not binary compatible between kernel releases and configurations: the module will only load on the kernel it was compiled with.

If you want to build a driver in the kernel source tree, the procedure is quite simple. Choose a directory appropriate to the type of driver you have. The driver is a basic character device, so I would put `dummy.c` in `drivers/char`. Then, edit the makefile in the directory, and add a line to build the driver unconditionally as a module, as follows:

```
obj-m += dummy.o
```

Alternatively, you can add the following line to build it unconditionally as a builtin:

```
obj-y += dummy.o
```

If you want to make the driver optional, you can add a `menu` option to the `Kconfig` file and make the compilation conditional on the configuration option, as I described in *Chapter 4, Configuring and Building the Kernel*, in the *Understanding kernel configuration* section.

Loading kernel modules

You can load, unload, and list modules using the simple `insmod`, `lsmod`, and `rmmod` commands, respectively. Here, they are loading the `dummy` driver:

```
# insmod /lib/modules/4.8.12-yocto-standard/kernel/drivers/dummy.ko
# lsmod
 Tainted: G
dummy 2062 0 - Live 0xbf004000 (O)
# rmmod dummy
```

If the module is placed in a subdirectory in `/lib/modules/<kernel release>`, you can create a **modules dependency database** using the `depmod -a` command, like so:

```
# depmod -a
# ls /lib/modules/4.8.12-yocto-standard
kernel    modules.alias    modules.dep    modules.symbols
```

The information in the `modules.*` files is used by the `modprobe` command to locate a module by name rather than its full path. `modprobe` has many other features, all of which are described on the `modprobe(8)` manual page.

Now that we have written and loaded our dummy kernel module, how do we get it to talk to some real piece of hardware? We need to bind our driver to that hardware either by way of the device tree or platform data. Discovering hardware and linking that hardware to a device driver is the topic of the next section.

Discovering the hardware configuration

The dummy driver demonstrates the structure of a device driver, but it lacks interaction with real hardware since it only manipulates memory structures. Device drivers are usually written to interact with hardware. Part of that is being able to discover the hardware in the first place, bearing in mind that it may be at different addresses in different configurations.

In some cases, the hardware provides the information itself. Devices on a discoverable bus such as PCI or USB have a query mode, which returns resource requirements and a unique identifier. The kernel matches the identifier and possibly other characteristics with the device drivers and marries them up.

However, most of the hardware blocks on an embedded board do not have such identifiers. You have to provide the information yourself in the form of a **device tree** or as C structures known as **platform data**.

In the standard driver model for Linux, device drivers register themselves with the appropriate subsystem: PCI, USB, open firmware (device tree), platform device, and so on. The registration includes an identifier and a callback function, called a `probe` function, that is called if there is a match between the ID of the hardware and the ID of the driver. For PCI and USB, the ID is based on the vendor and the product IDs of the devices; for device trees and platform devices, it is a name (a text string).

Device trees

I gave you an introduction to device trees in *Chapter 3, All About Bootloaders*. Here, I want to show you how the Linux device drivers hook up with this information.

As an example, I will use the Arm Versatile board, `arch/arm/boot/dts/versatile-ab.dts`, for which the Ethernet adapter is defined here:

```
net@10010000 {
    compatible = "smsc,lan91c111";
    reg = <0x10010000 0x10000>;
    interrupts = <25>;
};
```

Pay special attention to the `compatible` property of this node. This string value will reappear later in the source code for the Ethernet adapter. We will learn more about device trees in *Chapter 12, Prototyping with Breakout Boards*.

The platform data

In the absence of device tree support, there is a fallback method of describing hardware using C structures, known as the platform data.

Each piece of hardware is described by `struct platform_device`, which has a name and a pointer to an array of resources. The resource's type is determined by flags, which include the following:

- `IORESOURCE_MEM`: This is the physical address of a region of memory.
- `IORESOURCE_IO`: This is the physical address or port number of I/O registers.
- `IORESOURCE_IRQ`: This is the interrupt number.

Here is an example of the platform data for an Ethernet controller taken from `arch/arm/machversatile/core.c`, which has been edited for clarity:

```
#define VERSATILE_ETH_BASE 0x10010000
#define IRQ_ETH 25
static struct resource smc91x_resources[] = {
 [0] = {
   .start = VERSATILE_ETH_BASE,
   .end = VERSATILE_ETH_BASE + SZ_64K - 1,
   .flags = IORESOURCE_MEM,
},
 [1] = {
   .start = IRQ_ETH,
   .end = IRQ_ETH,
   .flags = IORESOURCE_IRQ,
},
};
static struct platform_device smc91x_device = {
  .name = "smc91x",
  .id = 0,
  .num_resources = ARRAY_SIZE(smc91x_resources),
  .resource = smc91x_resources,
};
```

It has a memory area of 64 KB and an interrupt. The platform data has to be registered with the kernel, usually when the board is initialized:

```
void __init versatile_init(void)
{
    platform_device_register(&versatile_flash_device);
    platform_device_register(&versatile_i2c_device);
    platform_device_register(&smc91x_device);
    [...]
```

The platform data shown here is functionally equivalent to the previous device tree source, except for the `name` field, which takes the place of the `compatible` property.

Linking hardware with device drivers

In the preceding section, you saw how an Ethernet adapter is described using a device tree and using platform data. The corresponding driver code is in `drivers/net/ethernet/smsc/smc91x.c`, and it works with both the device tree and platform data. Here is the initialization code, once again edited for clarity:

```
static const struct of_device_id smc91x_match[] = {
    { .compatible = "smsc,lan91c94", },
    { .compatible = "smsc,lan91c111", },
    {},
};
MODULE_DEVICE_TABLE(of, smc91x_match);
static struct platform_driver smc_driver = {
    .probe = smc_drv_probe,
    .remove = smc_drv_remove,
    .driver = {
        .name = "smc91x",
        .of_match_table = of_match_ptr(smc91x_match),
    },
};
static int __init smc_driver_init(void)
{
    return platform_driver_register(&smc_driver);
}
```

```
static void __exit smc_driver_exit(void)
{
    platform_driver_unregister(&smc_driver);
}
module_init(smc_driver_init);
module_exit(smc_driver_exit);
```

When the driver is initialized, it calls `platform_driver_register()`, pointing to `struct platform_driver`, in which there is a callback to a `probe` function, a driver name, `smc91x`, and a pointer to `struct of_device_id`.

If this driver has been configured by the device tree, the kernel will look for a match between the `compatible` property in the device tree node and the string being pointed to by the compatible structure element. For each match, it calls the `probe` function.

On the other hand, if it was configured through platform data, the `probe` function will be called for each match on the string pointed to by `driver.name`.

The `probe` function extracts information about the interface:

```
static int smc_drv_probe(struct platform_device *pdev)
{
    struct smc91x_platdata *pd = dev_get_platdata(&pdev->dev);
    const struct of_device_id *match = NULL;
    struct resource *res, *ires;
    int irq;

    res = platform_get_resource(pdev, IORESOURCE_MEM, 0);
    ires platform_get_resource(pdev, IORESOURCE_IRQ, 0);
    [...]
    addr = ioremap(res->start, SMC_IO_EXTENT);
    irq = ires->start;
    [...]
}
```

The calls to `platform_get_resource()` extract the memory and `irq` information from either the device tree or the platform data. It is up to the driver to map the memory and install the interrupt handler. The third parameter, which is zero in both of the previous cases, comes into play if there is more than one resource of that particular type.

Device trees allow you to configure more than just basic memory ranges and interrupts. There is a section of code in the `probe` function that extracts optional parameters from the device tree. In this snippet, it gets the `register-io-width` property:

```
match = of_match_device(of_match_ptr(smc91x_match), &pdev-
>dev);
if (match) {
    struct device_node *np = pdev->dev.of_node;
    u32 val;
    [...]
    of_property_read_u32(np, "reg-io-width", &val);
    [...]
}
```

For most drivers, specific bindings are documented in `Documentation/devicetree/bindings`. For this particular driver, the information is in `Documentation/devicetree/bindings/net/smsc911x.txt`.

The main thing to remember here is that drivers should register a `probe` function and enough information for the kernel to call `probe`, as it finds matches with the hardware it knows about. The linkage between the hardware described by the device tree and the device driver is done through the `compatible` property. The linkage between platform data and a driver is done through the name.

Summary

Device drivers have the job of handling devices, usually physical hardware but sometimes virtual interfaces, and presenting them to the user space in a consistent and useful way. Linux device drivers fall into three broad categories: character, block, and network. Of the three, the character driver interface is the most flexible and therefore, the most common. Linux drivers fit into a framework known as the driver model, which is exposed through `sysfs`. Pretty much the entire state of the devices and drivers is visible in `/sys`.

Each embedded system has its own unique set of hardware interfaces and requirements. Linux provides drivers for most standard interfaces, and by selecting the right kernel configuration, you can get a working target board very quickly. This leaves you with the non-standard components, for which you will have to add your own device support.

In some cases, you can sidestep the issue by using generic drivers for GPIO, I2C, and so on, and write user space code to do the work. I recommend this as a starting point, as it gives you the chance to become familiar with the hardware without writing kernel code. Writing kernel drivers is not particularly difficult, but you do you need to code carefully so as not to compromise the stability of the system.

So far, I have talked about writing the kernel driver code; if you go down this route, you will inevitably want to know how to check whether it is working correctly and detect any bugs. I will cover that topic in *Chapter 19, Debugging with GDB*.

The next chapter is all about user space initialization and the different options you have for the `init` program, from the simple BusyBox to more complex systems.

Further reading

The following resources contain further information about the topics that were introduced in this chapter:

- *Linux Kernel Development, 3rd Edition*, by Robert Love
- *Linux Weekly News*: `https://lwn.net/Kernel`
- *Async IO on Linux: select, poll, and epoll*, by Julia Evans: `https://jvns.ca/blog/2017/06/03/async-io-on-linux--select--poll--and-epoll`
- *Essential Linux Device Drivers, 1st Edition*, by Sreekrishnan Venkateswaran

12
Prototyping with Breakout Boards

Custom board bring-up is what embedded Linux engineers are called on to do time and time again. A consumer electronics manufacturer wants to build a new device and, more often than not, that device needs to run Linux. The process of assembling the Linux image typically starts before the hardware is ready, and is done using prototypes that are wired together from development and breakout boards. Peripheral I/O pins need to be muxed into device tree bindings for working communications. Only then can the task of coding middleware for an application begin.

Our goal in this chapter is to add a u-blox GPS module to the BeagleBone Black. This requires reading schematics and data sheets so that necessary modifications to the device tree source can be generated using Texas Instruments' **SysConfig** tool. Next, we will wire up a SparkFun GPS Breakout board to the BeagleBone Black and probe the connected SPI pins with a logic analyzer. Lastly, we will compile and run test code on the BeagleBone Black so that we can receive NMEA sentences from the ZOE-M8Q GPS module over SPI.

Rapid prototyping with real hardware involves lots of trial and error. In this chapter, we will get hands-on experience with soldering and assemble a test bench to study and debug digital signals. We will also revisit device tree source, but this time, we will pay special attention to the pin control configurations and how to utilize them to enable external or onboard peripherals. With a full Debian Linux distribution at our disposal, we can use tools such as `git`, `gcc`, `pip3`, and `python3` to develop software directly on the BeagleBone Black.

In this chapter, we will cover the following topics:

- Mapping schematics to the device tree's source
- Prototyping with breakout boards
- Probing SPI signals with a logic analyzer
- Receiving NMEA messages over SPI

Let's get started!

Technical requirements

To follow along with the examples in this chapter, make sure you have the following:

- A Linux-based host system
- A Buildroot 2020.02.9 LTS release
- Etcher for Linux
- A microSD card reader and card
- A USB to TTL 3.3V serial cable
- A BeagleBone Black
- A 5V 1A DC power supply
- An Ethernet cable and port for network connectivity
- A SparkFun model GPS-15193 Breakout
- A row (12 or more pins) of straight breakaway headers
- A soldering iron kit
- Six male to female jumper wires
- A U.FL GNSS antenna

You should have already installed the 2020.02.9 release of Buildroot in *Chapter 6, Selecting a Build System*. If you have not, then refer to the *System requirements* section of the *The Buildroot user manual* (`https://buildroot.org/downloads/manual/manual.html`) before installing Buildroot on your Linux host according to the instructions from *Chapter 6*.

A **logic analyzer** helps with troubleshooting and understanding SPI communications. I will be using the Saleae Logic 8 for demonstration purposes. I realize Saleae products are prohibitively expensive ($399 and up), so if you do not already own a Saleae logic analyzer, you can still get through this chapter without one. There are more affordable low-speed alternatives (`http://dangerousprototypes.com/docs/Bus_Pirate`) that are sufficient for SPI and I2C debugging, but I won't cover them in this book.

All the code for this chapter can be found in the `Chapter12` folder of this book's GitHub repository: `https://github.com/PacktPublishing/Mastering-Embedded-Linux-Programming-Third-Edition`.

Mapping schematics to the device tree's source

Because the BeagleBone Black's **Bill Of Materials** (**BOM**), PCB design files, and schematics are all open source, anyone can manufacture a BeagleBone Black as part of their consumer product. Since the BeagleBone Black is intended for development, it contains several components that may not be needed for production, such as an Ethernet cable, a USB port, and a microSD slot. As a dev board, the BeagleBone Black may also be missing one or more peripherals needed for your application such as sensors, an LTE modem, or an OLED display.

The BeagleBone Black is built around Texas Instruments' AM335x, a single core 32-bit ARM Cortex-A8 SoC with dual **Programmable Real-Time Units** (**PRU**). There is a more expensive Wireless variant of the BeagleBone Black made by Octavo Systems that swaps out Ethernet with a Wi-Fi and Bluetooth module. The BeagleBone Black Wireless is also open source hardware, but at some point, you may want to design your own custom PCB around the AM335x. Designing a daughterboard (known as a *"cape"*) for the BeagleBone Black is also an option.

For our purposes, we will integrate a u-blox ZOE-M8Q GPS module into a networked device. If you need to transfer lots of packets from a local network to and from the cloud, then running Linux is a sensible choice since it has an extremely mature TCP/IP network stack. The BeagleBone Black's ARM Cortex-A8 CPU meets the requirements (enough addressable RAM and a memory management unit) for running mainstream Linux. This means our product can benefit from security and bug fixes that have been made to the Linux kernel.

In *Chapter 11, Interfacing with Device Drivers*, we looked at an example of how to bind an Ethernet adapter to a Linux device driver. Binding peripherals is done with device tree source or C structs known as platform data. Over the years, using device tree source has become the preferred means of binding to Linux device drivers, especially on ARM SoCs. For these reasons, the examples in this chapter only involve device tree source. Like U-Boot, compiling device tree source into DTBs is also part of the Linux kernel build process.

Before we can start modifying the device tree source, we need to get acquainted with the schematics for the BeagleBone Black and SparkFun ZOE-M8Q GPS Breakout.

Reading schematics and data sheets

The BeagleBone Black has 2 x 46 pin expansion headers for I/O. These headers include UART, I2C, and SPI communications ports, in addition to numerous GPIOs. Most GPS modules, including ours, can send NMEA data over serial UARTs or I2C. Even though many user space GPS tools, such as `gpsd`, only work with modules connected via serial, I chose a GPS module with an SPI interface for this project. The BeagleBone Black has two SPI buses available. We only need one of these SPI buses to connect the u-blox ZOE-M8Q.

I chose SPI over UART and I2C for two reasons: UARTs are scarce on many SoCs and needed for things such as Bluetooth and/or a serial console; I2C drivers and hardware can have serious bugs. Some I2C kernel drivers are so poorly implemented that the bus locks up when there are too many connected peripherals talking. The I2C controllers found in Broadcom SoCs, such as the one in the Raspberry Pi 4, are notorious for glitching when peripherals attempt to perform clock stretching.

Here is a map of the pins on the BeagleBone Black's P9 expansion header:

P9
DGND 1 2 DGND
VDD_3V3 3 4 VDD_3V3
VDD_5V 5 6 VDD_5V
SYS_5V 7 8 SYS_5V
PWR_BUT 9 10 SYS_RESETN
GPIO_30 11 12 GPIO_60
GPIO_31 13 14 GPIO_40
GPIO_48 15 16 GPIO_51
SPI0_CS0 17 18 SPI0_D1
SPI1_CS1 19 20 SPI1_CS0
SPI0_D0 21 22 SPI0_SCLK
GPIO_49 23 24 GPIO_15
GPIO_117 25 26 GPIO_14
GPIO_125 27 28 SPI1_CS0
SPI1_D0 29 30 SPI1_D1
SPI1_SCLK 31 32 VDD_ADC
AIN4 33 34 GNDA_ADC
AIN6 35 36 AIN5
AIN2 37 38 AIN3
AIN0 39 40 AIN1
GPIO_20 41 42 SPI1_CS1
DGND 43 44 DGND
DGND 45 46 DGND

Figure 12.1 – P9 expansion header SPI ports

Pins 17, 18, 21, and 22 are assigned to the SPI0 bus. Pins 19, 20, 28, 29, 30, 31, and 42 are assigned to the SPI1 bus. Notice that pins 42 and 28 duplicate the functionality of pins 19 and 20 for SPI1. We can only utilize one pin for either SPI1_CS1 and SPI1_CS0. Any duplicate pins should be disabled or repurposed. Also, notice that SPI1 has CS0 and CS1 pins, whereas SPI0 only has a CS0 pin. **CS** stands for **chip select**. Since each SPI bus is a master-slave interface, pulling a CS signal line low typically selects which peripheral to transmit to on the bus. This kind of negative logic is known as *"active low"*.

Here is a block diagram of the BeagleBone Black's SPI1 bus with two peripherals attached:

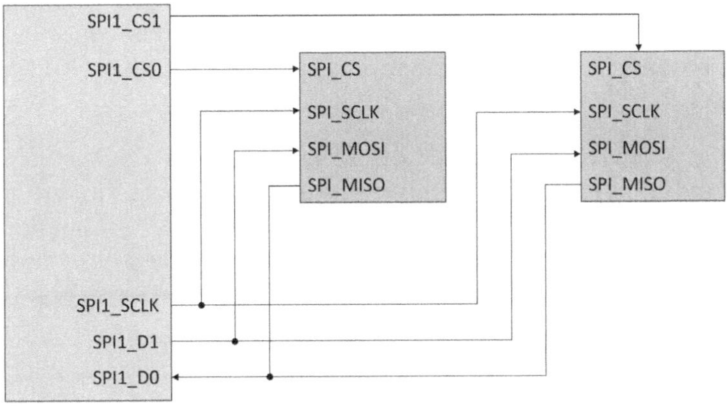

Figure 12.2 – SPI1 bus

If we look at the Beagle Bone Black's schematic (`https://github.com/beagleboard/beaglebone-black/blob/master/BBB_SCH.pdf`), we will see that four pins (28 to 31) on the P9 expansion header are labeled for SPI1:

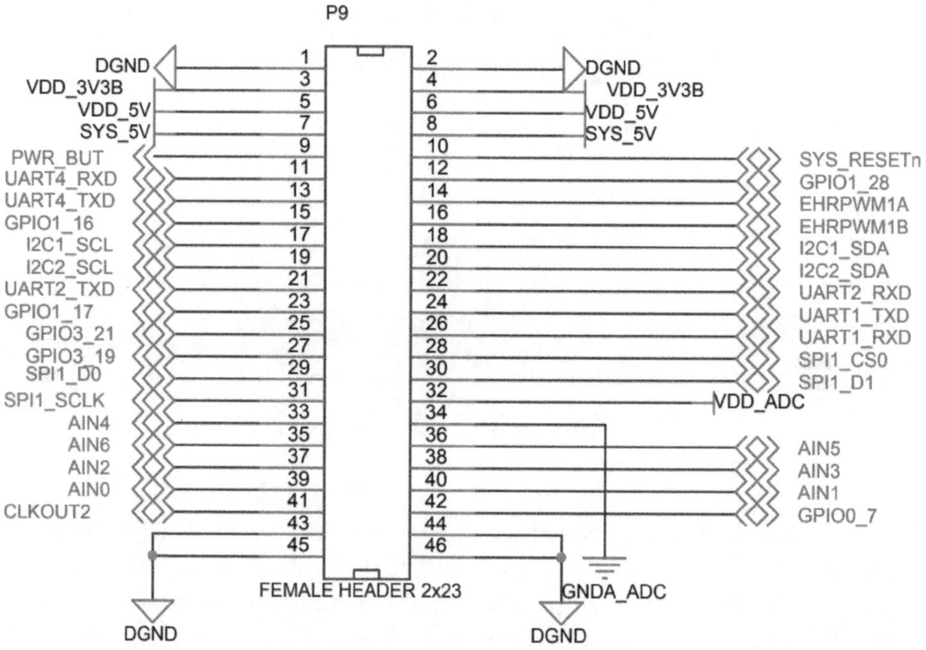

Figure 12.3 – P9 expansion header schematic

The extra SPI1 pins (19, 20, and 42) and all of the SPI0 pins (17, 18, 21, and 22) have been repurposed for I2C1, I2C2, and UART2 on the schematic. This alternate mapping is the result of pin mux configurations defined within the device tree source files. To route the missing SPI signal lines from the AM335x to their respective target pins on the expansion header, the proper pin mux configurations must be applied. Pin muxing can be done at runtime for prototyping but should transition to compile time before the finished hardware arrives.

In addition to CS0, you will notice that the SPI0 bus also has SCLK, D0, and D1 lines. **SCLK** stands for **SPI clock** and is always generated by the bus master, which is the AM335x in this case. Data transmitted over the SPI bus is synchronized to this SCLK signal. SPI supports much higher clock frequencies than I2C. The D0 data line corresponds to **master in, slave out** (**MISO**). The D1 data line corresponds to **master out, slave in** (**MOSI**). While both D0 and D1 can be assigned to either MISO or MOSI in software, we will stick with these default mappings. SPI is a **full-duplex** interface, which means that both the master and selected slave can send data at the same time.

Here is a block diagram showing the directions of all four SPI signals:

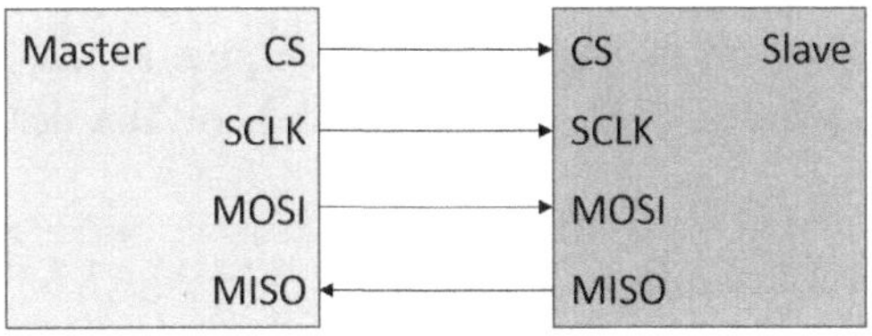

Figure 12.4 – SPI signals

Now, let's turn our attention away from the BeagleBone Black to the ZOE-M8Q. We'll start with the ZOE-M8 series data sheet, which can be downloaded from u-blox's product page at `https://www.u-blox.com/en/product/zoe-m8-series`. Jump to the section describing SPI. It says that SPI is disabled by default because its pins are shared with the UART and DDC interfaces. To enable SPI on the ZOE-M8Q, we must connect the D_SEL pin to the ground. Pulling down D_SEL converts the two UART and two DDC pins into four SPI pins.

Locate the schematic for the SparkFun ZOE-M8Q GPS Breakout by selecting the "**Documents**" tab from the product page at `https://www.sparkfun.com/products/15193`. Searching for the D_SEL pin reveals that it is on the left-hand side of the jumper labeled JP1. Closing the jumper connects D_SEL to GND, thereby enabling SPI:

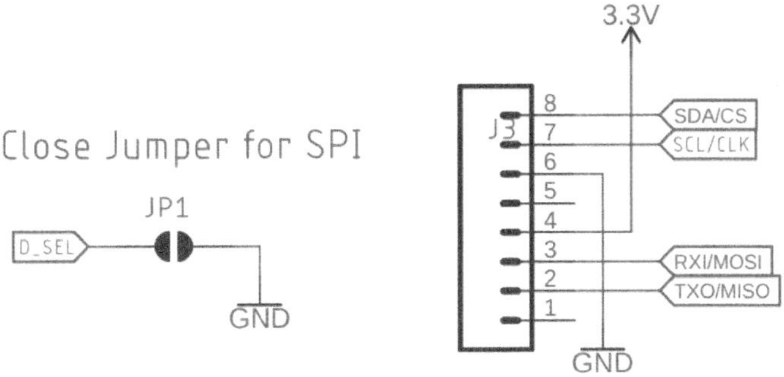

Figure 12.5 – D_SEL jumper and SPI connectors on the GPS breakout

The connectors for the CS, CLK, MOSI, and MISO pins are co-located with 3.3V and GND. Closing the jumper and attaching the headers to the six pins will require some soldering.

Always check the pin ratings when interconnecting chips or modules. The JP2 jumper on the GPS Breakout connects the SCL/CLK and SDA/CS pins to 2.2kΩ pull up resistors. The AM335x data sheet says these output pins are 6mA drivers, so enabling their weak internal pull ups adds 100μA of pull up current. The ZOE-M8Q has an 11kΩ pull up on the same pins, adding 300μA at 3.3V. The 2.2kΩ I2C pull ups on the GPS Breakout add another 1.5mA for a total of 1.9mA of pull up current, which is okay.

Returning to *Figure 12.1*, notice that the BeagleBone Black supplies 3.3V from pins 3 and 4 of its P9 expansion header. Pins 1 and 2 and 43 to 46 are tied to GND. In addition to connecting the four SPI lines on the GPS Breakout to pins 17, 18, 21, and 22, we will also wire the GPS module's 3.3V and GND to pins 3 and 43 on the BeagleBone Black's P9 expansion header.

Now that we have some idea of how to connect the ZOE-M8Q, let's enable the SPI0 bus on Linux, which is running on the BeagleBone Black. The quickest way to do this is to install a prebuilt Debian image from `BeagleBoard.org`.

Installing Debian on the BeagleBone Black

`BeagleBoard.org` provides Debian images for their various dev boards. Debian is a popular Linux distribution that includes a comprehensive set of open source software packages. It is a massive effort with contributors from all over the world. Building Debian for the various BeagleBoards is unconventional by embedded Linux standards because the process does not rely on cross-compilation. Rather than attempting to build Debian for the BeagleBone Black yourself, simply download a finished image directly from `BeagleBoard.org`.

To download the Debian Buster IoT microSD card image for the BeagleBone Black, issue the following command:

```
$ wget https://debian.BeagleBoard.org/images/bone-debian-10.3-iot-armhf-2020-04-06-4gb.img.xz
```

10.3 was the latest Debian image for AM335x-based BeagleBone boards at the time of writing. The major version number of 10 indicates that 10.3 is a Buster LTS release of Debian. Since Debian 10.0 was originally released on July 6, 2019, it should receive updates for up to 5 years from that date.

> **Important note**
>
> If possible, download version 10.3 (also known as Buster) rather than the latest Debian image from `BeagleBoard.org` for the exercises in this chapter. The BeagleBone bootloader, kernel, DTBs, and command-line tools are in constant flux, so the instructions may not work with a later Debian release.

Now that we have a Debian image for the BeagleBone Black, let's write it out to a microSD card and boot it. Locate the `bone-debian-10.3-iot-armhf-2020-04-06-4gb.img.xz` file that you downloaded from `BeagleBoard.org` from Etcher and write it out to a microSD card. Insert the microSD card into your BeagleBone Black and power it up with a 5V power supply. Next, plug the Ethernet cable from the BeagleBone Black into a free port on your router with an Ethernet cable. When the onboard Ethernet lights start blinking, your BeagleBone Black should be online. Internet access allows us to install packages and fetch code from Git repos from within Debian.

To `ssh` into the BeagleBone Black from your Linux host, use the following code:

```
$ ssh debian@beaglebone.local
```

Enter `temppwd` at the `debian` user's password prompt.

> **Important note**
>
> Many BeagleBone Blacks come with Debian already installed on the onboard flash, so they will still boot, even without a microSD card inserted. If the `BeagleBoard.org Debian Buster IoT Image 2020-04-06` message is displayed before the password prompt, then the BeagleBone Black was booted from the Debian 10.3 image on the microSD. If a different Debian release message is displayed before the password prompt, then verify whether or not the microSD card is properly inserted.

Now that we're on the BeagleBone Black, let's look at what SPI interfaces are available.

Enabling spidev

Linux comes with a user space API that provides `read()` and `write()` access to SPI devices. This user space API is known as `spidev` and is included in the Debian Buster image for the BeagleBone Black. We can confirm this by searching for the `spidev` kernel module:

```
debian@beaglebone:~$ lsmod | grep spi
spidev                  20480  0
```

Now, list the available SPI peripheral addresses:

```
$ ls /dev/spidev*
/dev/spidev0.0  /dev/spidev0.1  /dev/spidev1.0  /dev/spidev1.1
```

The /dev/spidev0.0 and /dev/spidev0.1 nodes are on the SPI0 bus, while the /dev/spidev1.0 and /dev/spidev1.1 nodes are on the SPI1 bus. We only need the SPI0 bus for this project.

U-Boot loads overlays on top of the device tree for the BeagleBone Black. We can select which device tree overlays to load by editing U-Boot's uEnv.txt configuration file:

```
$ cat /boot/uEnv.txt
#Docs: http://elinux.org/Beagleboard:U-boot_partitioning_
layout_2.0

uname_r=4.19.94-ti-r42
.
.
.
###U-Boot Overlays###
###Documentation: http://elinux.org/
Beagleboard:BeagleBoneBlack_Debian#U-Boot_Overlays
###Master Enable
enable_uboot_overlays=1
###
.
.
.
###Disable auto loading of virtual capes (emmc/video/wireless/
adc)
#disable_uboot_overlay_emmc=1
#disable_uboot_overlay_video=1
#disable_uboot_overlay_audio=1
#disable_uboot_overlay_wireless=1
#disable_uboot_overlay_adc=1
.
.
.
###Cape Universal Enable
enable_uboot_cape_universal=1
```

Confirm that the `enable_uboot_overlays` and `enable_uboot_cape_universal` environment variables are both set to `1`. A leading # means that anything after that character in the line is commented out. For this reason, U-Boot ignores all the `disable_uboot_overlay_<device>=1` statements shown in the preceding code. This configuration file is applied to U-Boot's environment, so any changes that are saved to `/boot/uEnv.txt` require a reboot to take effect.

> **Important note**
>
> The audio overlay conflicts with the SPI1 bus on the BeagleBone Black. Uncomment `disable_uboot_overlay_audio=1` in `/boot/uEnv.txt` if you wish to enable communications over SPI1.

To list the device tree overlays U-Boot has loaded, use the following commands:

```
$ cd /opt/scripts/tools
$ sudo ./version.sh | grep UBOOT
UBOOT: Booted Device-Tree:[am335x-boneblack-uboot-univ.dts]
UBOOT: Loaded Overlay:[AM335X-PRU-RPROC-4-19-TI-00A0]
UBOOT: Loaded Overlay:[BB-ADC-00A0]
UBOOT: Loaded Overlay:[BB-BONE-eMMC1-01-00A0]
UBOOT: Loaded Overlay:[BB-NHDMI-TDA998x-00A0]
```

The cape universal feature (`https://github.com/cdsteinkuehler/beaglebone-universal-io`) is unique to the AM3358 version of Debian. It provides access to nearly all of the BeagleBone Black's hardware I/O without us having to modify the device tree source or rebuild the kernel. Different pin mux configurations are activated at runtime using the `config-pin` command-line tool.

To view all the available pingroups, use the following code:

```
$ cat /sys/kernel/debug/pinctrl/*pinmux*/pingroups
```

To view just the SPI pingroups, use the following code:

```
$ cat /sys/kernel/debug/pinctrl/*pinmux*/pingroups | grep spi
group: pinmux_P9_19_spi_cs_pin
group: pinmux_P9_20_spi_cs_pin
group: pinmux_P9_17_spi_cs_pin
group: pinmux_P9_18_spi_pin
group: pinmux_P9_21_spi_pin
```

```
group: pinmux_P9_22_spi_sclk_pin
group: pinmux_P9_30_spi_pin
group: pinmux_P9_42_spi_cs_pin
group: pinmux_P9_42_spi_sclk_pin
```

Assigning only one pin to a pingroup is unusual. Normally, all the SPI pins (CS, SCLK, D0, and D1) for a bus are muxed together in the same pingroup. We can confirm this strange one-to-one pin to group relationship by looking at the device tree source, which is located inside the `/opt/source/dtb-4.19-ti/src/arm` directory on the Debian image.

The `am335x-boneblack-uboot-univ.dts` file in that source directory contains the following includes:

```
#include "am33xx.dtsi"
#include "am335x-bone-common.dtsi"
#include "am335x-bone-common-univ.dtsi"
```

That `.dts` file, together with the three included `.dtsi` files, define the device tree source. The `dtc` tool compiles these four source files into a `am335x-boneblack-uboot-univ.dtb` file. U-Boot also loads device tree overlays on top of this cape universal device tree. These device tree overlays have `.dtbo` as their file extension.

Here is the pingroup definition for `pinmux_P9_17_spi_cs_pin`:

```
P9_17_spi_cs_pin: pinmux_P9_17_spi_cs_pin { pinctrl-single,pins
= <
     AM33XX_IOPAD(0x095c, PIN_OUTPUT_PULLUP | INPUT_EN | MUX_
MODE0) >; };
```

The `pinmux_P9_17_spi_cs_pin` group configures pin 17 on the P9 expansion header to act as a CS pin for the SPI0 bus.

Here is the `P9_17_pinmux` definition, where `pinmux_P9_17_spi_cs_pin` is referenced:

```
/* P9_17 (ZCZ ball A16) */
P9_17_pinmux {
     compatible = "bone-pinmux-helper";
     status = "okay";
     pinctrl-names = "default", "gpio", "gpio_pu", "gpio_pd",
"gpio_input", "spi_cs", "i2c", "pwm", "pru_uart";
     pinctrl-0 = <&P9_17_default_pin>;
```

```
        pinctrl-1 = <&P9_17_gpio_pin>;
        pinctrl-2 = <&P9_17_gpio_pu_pin>;
        pinctrl-3 = <&P9_17_gpio_pd_pin>;
        pinctrl-4 = <&P9_17_gpio_input_pin>;
        pinctrl-5 = <&P9_17_spi_cs_pin>;
        pinctrl-6 = <&P9_17_i2c_pin>;
        pinctrl-7 = <&P9_17_pwm_pin>;
        pinctrl-8 = <&P9_17_pru_uart_pin>;
};
```

Notice that the `pinmux_P9_17_spi_cs_pin` group is one of nine different ways `P9_17_pinmux` can be configured. Since `spi_cs` is not the default configuration for that pin, the SPI0 bus is initially disabled.

To enable `/dev/spidev0.0`, run the following `config-pin` commands:

```
$ config-pin p9.17 spi_cs
Current mode for P9_17 is:     spi_cs
$ config-pin p9.18 spi
Current mode for P9_18 is:     spi
$ config-pin p9.21 spi
Current mode for P9_21 is:     spi
$ config-pin p9.22 spi_sclk
Current mode for P9_22 is:     spi_sclk
```

Rerun the `config-pin` commands and prefix them with `sudo` if you encounter permissions errors. Enter `temppwd` as `password` for the `debian` user. There is a `config-spi0.sh` script containing these four `config-pin` commands under `MELP/Chapter12` in the book code archive.

Debian comes with Git installed, so you can clone this book's repository to fetch the archive:

```
$ git clone https://github.com/PacktPublishing/Mastering-
Embedded-Linux-Programming-Third-Edition.git MELP
```

To enable `/dev/spidev0.0` upon booting your BeagleBone Black, use the following command:

```
$ MELP/Chapter12/config-spi0.sh
```

The sudo password is the same as the debian login prompt.

The Linux kernel source comes with a spidev_test program. I have included a copy of this spidev_test.c source file, which I obtained from https://github.com/rm-hull/spidev-test, in this book's code archive, under MELP/Chapter12/spidev-test.

To compile the spidev_test program, use the following commands:

```
$ cd MELP/Chapter12/spidev-test
$ gcc spidev_test.c -o spidev_test
```

Now, run the spidev_test program:

```
$ ./spidev_test -v
spi mode: 0x0
bits per word: 8
max speed: 500000 Hz (500 KHz)
TX | FF FF FF FF FF FF 40 00 00 00 00 95 FF FF FF FF FF FF FF
FF FF FF FF FF FF FF FF FF FF FF F0 0D  | ......@....?.........
........?.
RX | 00 00 00 00 00 00 00 00 00 00 00 00 00 00 00 00 00 00 00
00 00 00 00 00 00 00 00 00 00 00 00 00  | ....................
..........
```

The -v flag is short for --verbose and displays the contents of the TX buffer. This version of the spidev_test program defaults to using the /dev/spidev0.0 device, so no --device argument needs to be passed in to select the SPI0 bus. The full-duplex nature of SPI means that the bus master receives data while transmitting. In this case, the RX buffer contains all zeros, implying that no data was received. In fact, there is no assurance that any of the data in the TX buffer was even sent.

Use a jumper wire to connect pin 18 (SPI0_D1) to pin 21 (SPI0_D0) on the BeagleBone Black's P9 expansion header, as shown here:

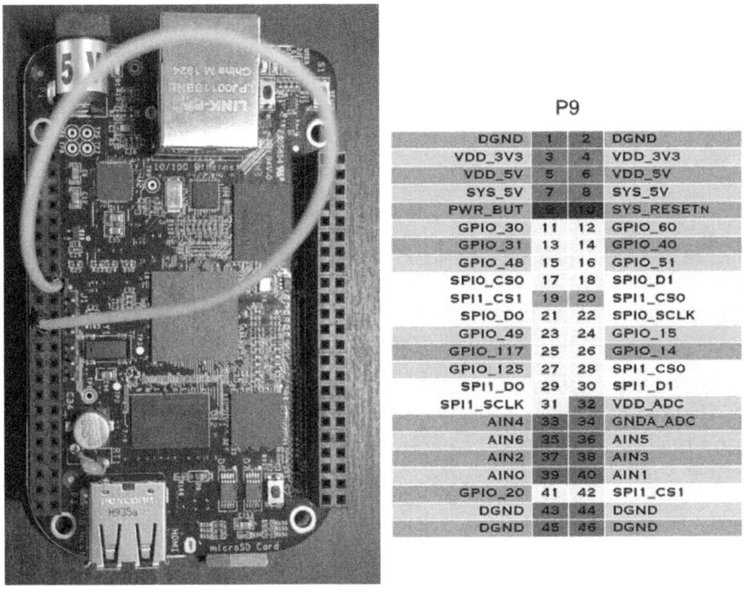

Figure 12.6 – SPI0 loopback

The map of the P9 expansion header is oriented so that the header is on the left-hand side of the BeagleBone Black when the USB port is at the bottom. The jumper wire from SPI0_D1 to SPI0_D0 forms a loopback connection by feeding MOSI (master out) into MISO (master in).

> **Important note**
>
> Don't forget to rerun the `config-spi0.sh` script after rebooting or power cycling your BeagleBone Black to re-enable the `/dev/spidev0.0` interface.

Rerun the `spidev_test` program with your loopback connection in place:

```
$ ./spidev_test -v
spi mode: 0x0
bits per word: 8
max speed: 500000 Hz (500 KHz)
TX | FF FF FF FF FF FF 40 00 00 00 00 95 FF FF FF FF
FF FF FF FF FF FF FF FF FF FF FF FF FF FF F0 0D  |
......@.......................
RX | FF FF FF FF FF FF 40 00 00 00 00 95 FF FF FF FF
FF FF FF FF FF FF FF FF FF FF FF FF FF FF F0 0D  |
......@.......................
```

The contents of the RX buffer should now match the contents of the TX buffer. We have verified that the `/dev/spidev0.0` interface is fully functional. For more on runtime pin muxing, including the origins of the BeagleBone Black's device tree and overlays, I recommend reading `https://cdn-learn.adafruit.com/downloads/pdf/introduction-to-the-beaglebone-black-device-tree.pdf`.

Customizing the device tree

`BeagleBoard.org`'s cape universal device tree is great for prototyping, but a tool such as `config-pin` is not suitable for production. When we ship a consumer device, we know what peripherals are included. There should be no hardware discovery involved in the boot process aside from reading a model and revision number from an EEPROM. U-Boot can then decide what device tree and overlays to load based on that. Like choosing kernel modules, the contents of the device tree are decisions best made at compile time, not runtime.

Eventually, we will need to customize the device tree source for our custom AM335x board. Most SoC vendors, including Texas Instruments, provide interactive pin mux tools for generating device tree source. We will use Texas Instruments online SysConfig tool to add a `spidev` interface to our Nova board. We already customized the device tree for the Nova back in the *Porting Linux to a new board* section of *Chapter 4, Configuring and Building the Kernel*, and again in *Chapter 6, Selecting a Build System,* when we learned how to create a custom BSP for Buildroot. This time, we will add to the `am335x-boneblack.dts` file instead of just copying it verbatim.

Visit `https://dev.ti.com` and create an account if you do not already have one. You will need a myTI account to access the online SysConfig tool.

To create a myTI account, follow these steps:

1. Click the **Login / Register** button in the top-right corner of the landing page.
2. Fill out the **New user** form.
3. Click the **Create account** button.

To launch the SysConfig tool, follow these steps:

1. Click the **Login / Register** button in the top-right corner of the landing page.
2. Log in by entering your email address and password under **Existing myTI user**.
3. Click on the SysConfig **Launch** button under **Cloud tools**.

The **Launch** button will take you to the SysConfig start page at `https://dev.ti.com/sysconfig/#/start`, which you can bookmark for quicker access. SysConfig lets us save our working designs to the cloud so that we can revisit them later.

To generate a SPI0 pinmux configuration for the AM335x, follow these steps:

1. Select **AM335x** from the **Device** menu under **Start a new Design**.
2. Leave the default **Part** and **Package** menu selections of **Default** and **ZCE** for the AM335x as-is.
3. Click the **Start** button.
4. Select **SPI** from the left sidebar.
5. Click the **ADD** button to add an SPI to your design:

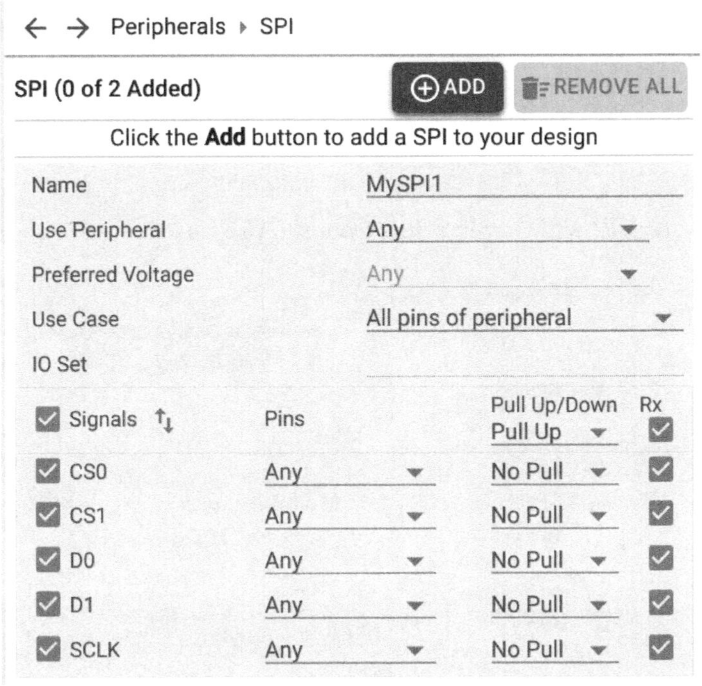

Figure 12.7 – Adding an SPI peripheral

6. Rename **MySP1** to `SPI0` by typing that into the **Name** field.

7. Select **SPI0** from the **Use Peripheral** menu:

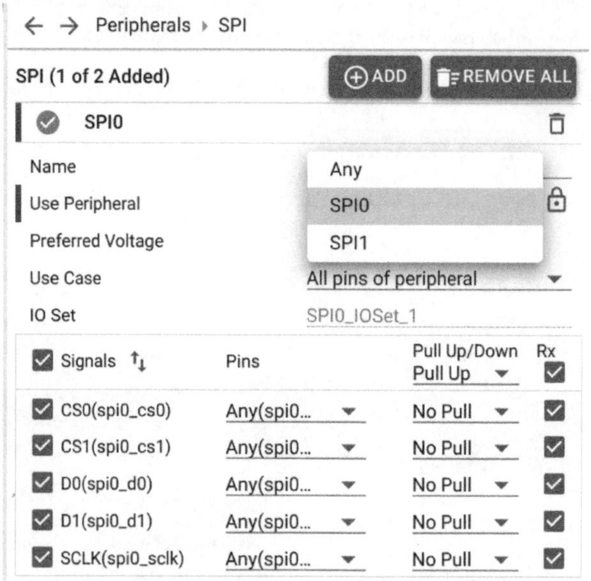

Figure 12.8 – Selecting SPI0

8. Select **Master SPI with 1 chip select** from the **Use Case** menu:

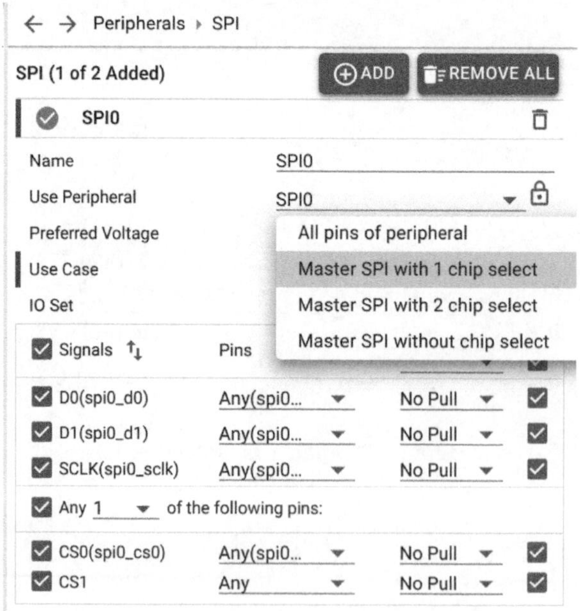

Figure 12.9 – Master SPI with 1 chip select

9. Uncheck the **CS1** checkbox to remove that item.
10. Click on `devicetree.dtsi` under **Generated Files** to view the device tree source.
11. Select **Pull Up** from the **Pull Up/Down** menu for **Signals**:

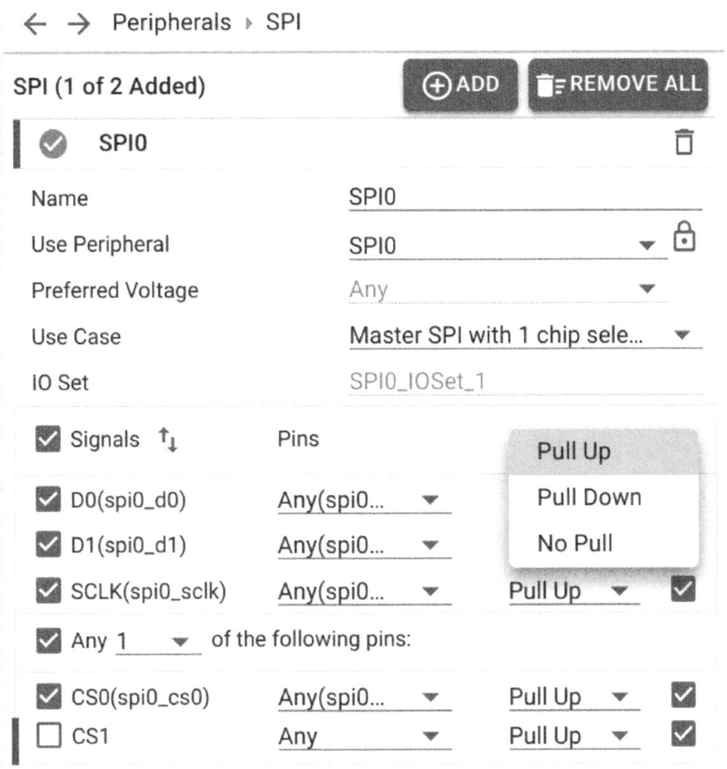

Figure 12.10 – Pull up signals

Notice what this did to the displayed device tree source. All instances of `PIN_INPUT` have been replaced with `PIN_INPUT_PULLUP`.

12. Uncheck the **Rx** checkboxes for **D1**, **SCLK**, and **CS0** since those pins are outputs from the AM335x master, not inputs:

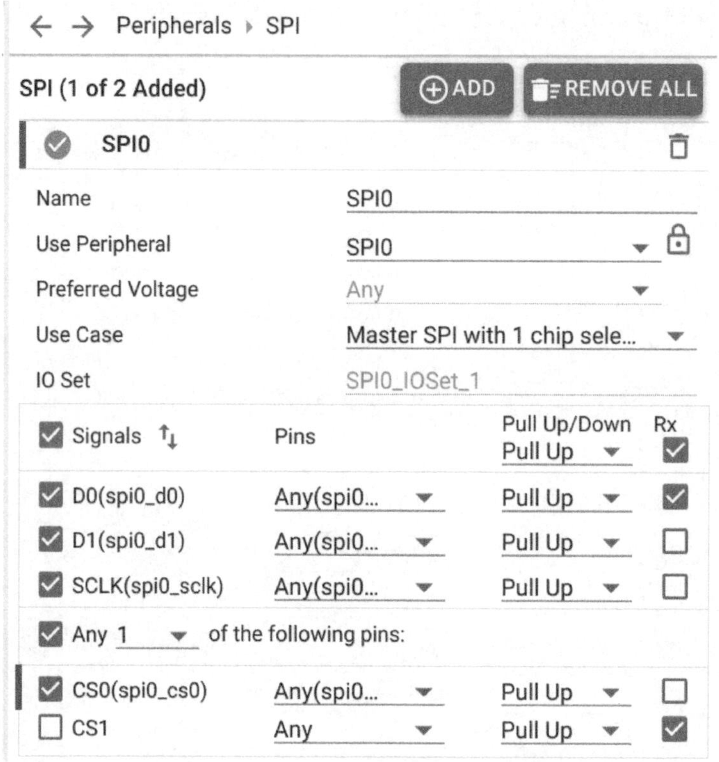

Figure 12.11 – Unchecking the Rx boxes

The **D0** pin corresponds to MISO (master in, slave out), so leave **Rx** checked for that pin. The `spi0_sclk`, `spi0_d1`, and `spi0_cs0` pins should now be configured as `PIN_OUTPUT_PULLUP` in the device tree source. Recall that SPI CS signals are usually active low, so a pullup is required to keep that line from floating.

13. Click on the floppy icon for `devicetree.dtsi` to save the device tree source file to your machine.
14. Click **Save As** from the **File** menu in the top-left corner to save your design.
15. Give your design file a descriptive name such as `nova.syscfg` and click **SAVE**.

16. The contents of the `.dtsi` file you saved to your machine should look like this:

```
&am33xx_pinmux {
        spi0_pins_default: spi0_pins_default {
                pinctrl-single,pins = <
                        AM33XX_IOPAD(0x950, PIN_OUTPUT_PULLUP | MUX_
MODE0) /* (A18) spi0_sclk.spi0_sclk */
                        AM33XX_IOPAD(0x954, PIN_INPUT_PULLUP | MUX_
MODE0) /* (B18) spi0_d0.spi0_d0 */
                        AM33XX_IOPAD(0x958, PIN_OUTPUT_PULLUP | MUX_
MODE0) /* (B17) spi0_d1.spi0_d1 */
                        AM33XX_IOPAD(0x95c, PIN_OUTPUT_PULLUP | MUX_
MODE0) /* (A17) spi0_cs0.spi0_cs0 */
                >;
        };
        [...]
};
```

I omitted the optional sleep pin settings because we won't need them. If we compare the hexadecimal pin addresses shown in the preceding code with the addresses of those same SPI0 pins in `am335x-bone-common-univ.dtsi`, we'll see that they match exactly.

The SPI0 pins in `am335x-bone-common-univ.dtsi` were all configured as follows:

```
AM33XX_IOPAD(0x095x, PIN_OUTPUT_PULLUP | INPUT_EN | MUX_MODE0)
```

Use of the `INPUT_EN` bitmask suggests that all four SPI0 pins in the cape universal device tree are configured as inputs, as well as outputs, when in fact only `spi0_ds0` at `0x954` needs to function as an input.

The `INPUT_EN` bitmask is one of many macros defined in the `/opt/source/dtb-4.19-ti/include/dt-bindings/pinctrl/am33xx.h` header file, which can be found on the Debian Buster IoT image:

```
#define PULL_DISABLE                (1 << 3)
#define INPUT_EN                    (1 << 5)
[...]
#define PIN_OUTPUT                  (PULL_DISABLE)
#define PIN_OUTPUT_PULLUP           (PULL_UP)
#define PIN_OUTPUT_PULLDOWN         0
```

```
#define PIN_INPUT                    (INPUT_EN | PULL_DISABLE)
#define PIN_INPUT_PULLUP             (INPUT_EN | PULL_UP)
#define PIN_INPUT_PULLDOWN           (INPUT_EN)
```

More TI device tree source macros are defined in the `/opt/source/dtb-4.19-ti include/dt-bindings/pinctrl/omap.h` header file:

```
#define OMAP_IOPAD_OFFSET(pa, offset)    (((pa) & 0xffff) - (offset))
[...]
#define AM33XX_IOPAD(pa, val)            OMAP_IOPAD_OFFSET((pa), 0x0800) (val)
```

Now that we have properly muxed the SPI0 pins, copy and paste the generated device tree source into our `nova.dts` file. Once this new `spi0_pins_default` pingroup has been defined, we can associate that pingroup with the `spi0` device node by overriding it, as follows:

```
&spi0 {
        status = "okay";
        pinctrl-names = "default";
        pinctrl-0 = <&spi0_pins_default>;
        [...]
}
```

The `&` symbol before the device node name means we are referring to, and thereby modifying, an existing node in the device tree rather than defining a new one.

I have included the finished `nova.dts` file in this book's code archive, inside the `MELP/Chapter12/buildroot/board/melp/nova` directory.

To build a custom Linux image with this device tree for our Nova board, follow these steps:

1. Copy `MELP/Chapter12/buildroot` over your Buildroot installation:

   ```
   $ cp -a MELP/Chapter12/buildroot/* buildroot
   ```

   This will either add a `nova_defconfig` file and `board/melp/nova` directory or replace the ones from `MELP/Chapter06/buildroot`.

2. `cd` to the directory where you installed Buildroot:

```
$ cd buildroot
```

3. Delete all the previous build artifacts:

```
$ make clean
```

4. Get ready to build an image for our Nova board:

```
$ make nova_defconfig
```

5. Build the image:

```
$ make
```

Once the build has finished, the image is written to a file named `output/images/sdcard.img`. Use Etcher to write that image to a microSD card. See the *Targeting real hardware* section of *Introducing Buildroot* in *Chapter 6, Selecting a Build System*, to learn how to do this. When Etcher is done flashing, insert the microSD into your BeagleBone Black. There is no SSH daemon included with the root filesystem, so you will need to attach a serial cable to log in.

To log into the BeagleBone Black via a serial console, follow these steps:

1. Plug the USB to TTL 3.3V serial cable from your Linux host to the J1 header on the BeagleBone Black. Make sure the black wire on the FTDI end of the cable connects to pin 1 on J1. A serial port should appear on your Linux host as `/dev/ttyUSB0`.
2. Start a suitable terminal program, such as `gtkterm`, `minicom`, or `picocom`, and attach it to the port at `115200` **bits per second (bps)** with no flow control. `gtkterm` is probably the easiest to set up and use:

```
$ gtkterm -p /dev/ttyUSB0 -s 115200
```

3. Apply power to the BeagleBone Black via the 5V barrel connector. You should see U-Boot output, kernel log output, and eventually a login prompt on the serial console.
4. Log in as `root` with no password.

Scroll up or enter `dmesg` to view the kernel messages during boot. Kernel messages like the following confirm that the `spidev0.0` interface was successfully probed via the binding we defined in `nova.dts`:

```
[    1.368869] omap2_mcspi 48030000.spi: registered master spi0
[    1.369813] spi spi0.0: setup: speed 16000000, sample
trailing edge, clk normal
[    1.369876] spi spi0.0: setup mode 1, 8 bits/w, 16000000 Hz
max --> 0
[    1.372589] omap2_mcspi 48030000.spi: registered child
spi0.0
```

The `spi-tools` package was included with the root filesystem for testing purposes. The package consists of the `spi-config` and `spi-pipe` command-line tools.

Here is the usage for `spi-config`:

```
# spi-config -h
usage: spi-config options...
  options:
    -d --device=<dev>  use the given spi-dev character device.
    -q --query         print the current configuration.
    -m --mode=[0-3]    use the selected spi mode:
             0: low idle level, sample on leading edge,
             1: low idle level, sample on trailing edge,
             2: high idle level, sample on leading edge,
             3: high idle level, sample on trailing edge.
    -l --lsb={0,1}     LSB first (1) or MSB first (0).
    -b --bits=[7...]   bits per word.
    -s --speed=<int>   set the speed in Hz.
    -r --spirdy={0,1}  consider SPI_RDY signal (1) or ignore it
(0).
    -w --wait          block keeping the file descriptor open
to avoid speed reset.
    -h --help          this screen.
    -v --version       display the version number.
```

And here is the usage for `spi-pipe`:

```
# spi-pipe -h
usage: spi-pipe options...
  options:
    -d --device=<dev>     use the given spi-dev character
device.
    -s --speed=<speed>    Maximum SPI clock rate (in Hz).
    -b --blocksize=<int> transfer block size in byte.
    -n --number=<int>     number of blocks to transfer (-1 =
infinite).
    -h --help             this screen.
    -v --version          display the version number.
```

I won't utilize `spi-tools` in this chapter, relying instead on `spidev-test` and a modified version of that same program that I call `spidev-read`.

We have now gone as far with the device tree source as we are going to go in this book. While DTS is extremely versatile, it can also be very frustrating. The `dtc` compiler is not very smart, so a lot of device tree source debugging happens at runtime using `modprobe` and `dmesg`. Forgetting a pullup or misconfiguring an input as an output when pin muxing can be enough to prevent a device from probing. Wi-Fi/Bluetooth modules with SDIO interfaces are especially challenging to bring up.

With SPI out of the way, it is now time to get up close and personal with the GPS module. We will return to the topic of the generic `spidev` interface when we have finished wiring up the SparkFun ZOE-M8Q GPS Breakout.

Prototyping with breakout boards

Now that we have SPI working on the BeagleBone Black, let's turn our attention back to the GPS module. Before we can wire up the SparkFun ZOE-M8Q GPS Breakout, we need to do some soldering. Soldering requires desk space, materials, and a considerable time investment.

To perform the soldering for this project, you will need the following items:

- A soldering iron (adjustable temperature) with a conical tip
- Any one of the following: a silicone car dashboard anti-slip mat, a silicone baking mat, or a ceramic tile
- A fine (0.031-inch gauge) electrical rosin core solder

- A soldering iron stand
- A wet sponge
- A wire cutter
- Safety glasses
- A Helping Hands tool, along with a magnifying glass and an LED light
- An X-Acto #2 knife with a #2 blade or #1 knife with a #11 blade

These items are nice to have but not necessary:

- An insulated silicone soldering mat
- solder wick
- A brass sponge
- Sticky tack or some similar putty-like adhesive
- Dental tools kit
- Needle nose pliers
- Tweezers

Most of these items come bundled together with the SparkFun Beginner Tool Kit, but they can be purchased elsewhere at a lower cost. If you are new to soldering, I also recommend obtaining some scrap PCBs to practice on before operating on the ZOE-M8Q. The holes on the SparkFun GPS Breakout are small and require a steady, delicate touch. A Helping Hands tool with a magnifying glass and alligator clips helps tremendously. Some sticky tack can also hold a breakout board in place on a hard, flat surface while you apply solder. When done, use an X-Acto knife to scrape off any excess sticky tack on or near the contacts.

Even if you are new to electronics, I encourage you to take the plunge and learn to solder. It might take a couple of days of frustration before you get the hang of it, but the satisfaction you get from building your own circuits is well worth it. I recommend reading MightyOhm's free *Soldering is Easy* comic book by Mitch Altman and Andie Nordgren to get started.

Here are some of my own helpful soldering tips. Wiping your soldering tip with a brass sponge keeps it free from troublesome oxidation. Use an X-Acto knife to scrape off any stray blobs of solder from PCBs. Use a hot iron to melt and play with some solder on your silicone mat to get accustomed to its properties. Lastly, always wear safety glasses when handling hot solder so none gets in your eyes.

Closing the SPI jumper

We located the D_SEL pin on the SparkFun GPS Breakout schematic on the left-hand side of a jumper named JP1. Tying the D_SEL pin to GND on the right-hand side of the jumper switches the ZOE-M8Q from I2C to SPI mode. The two SPI jumper pads already have some solder on them. We need to heat the pads so that we can move that solder around.

Flip the breakout board over to see the jumpers. Notice that the JP1 jumper is labeled SPI on the center left of the board:

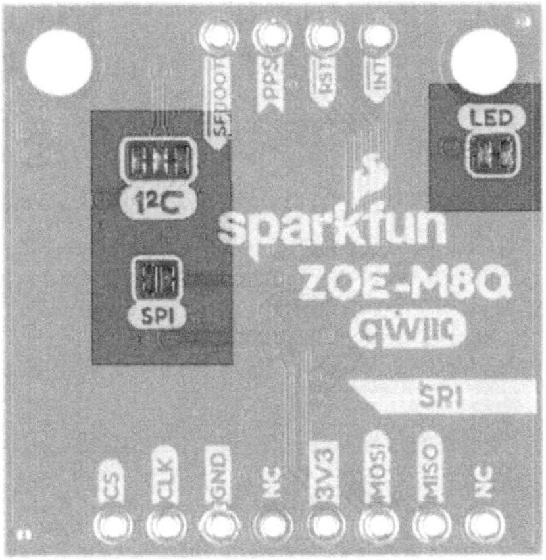

Figure 12.12 – Jumpers

To close the SPI jumper, do the following:

1. Plug in and heat your soldering iron to 600 °F.
2. Hold the GPS Breakout in place with the alligator clips from your Helping Hands.
3. Position your Helping Hands magnifying glass and LED light so that you can clearly see the SPI jumper.
4. Place the soldering tip on the left and right pads of the SPI jumper until the solder melts, forming a bridge between the two pads.
5. Feel free to add some more solder if necessary.
6. Use the tip of your soldering iron to melt and lift off any excess solder from the jumper pads.

Very little solder is needed to close the jumper. If the solder starts to smoke, turn down the temperature of your iron. Once the SPI jumper is closed, serial and I2C communications are disabled on the ZOE-M8Q. The FTDI and I2C pin labels on the top side of the breakout board no longer apply. Use the SPI pin labels on the underside of the board.

> **Tip**
>
> Use the side of the tip (also known as "the sweet spot"), not the very tip of the iron, for best results.

We don't need to repeat this same soldering procedure for the JP2 because the pads are already bridged on that jumper. JP2 has a separate pad for each of the two 2.2kΩ I2C pull up resistors. Notice that the JP2 is directly above JP1 and labeled I2C on the breakout board.

Now that the SPI jumper is closed, let's attach the GNSS antenna.

Attaching the GNSS antenna

A ceramic or Molex adhesive GNSS antenna helps the ZOE-M8Q obtain a GPS fix. U.FL connectors are fragile and should be handled with care. Lay the breakout board flat on a hard surface and use a magnifying glass to ensure proper placement of the antenna.

To attach the GNSS antenna to the U.FL connector, follow these steps:

1. Align the cable so that the female connector and the end rests evenly across the surface of the male connector on the board.
2. Place your finger lightly on top of the stacked connectors to make sure the female connector is not teetering.
3. Examine the two stacked connectors from above to make sure they are centered on top of one another.
4. Use the center of your finger to press down firmly on the center of the connector, until you feel the two connectors lock together in place.

Now that the antenna is attached, we are ready to attach the SPI header.

Attaching the SPI header

We will use six male to female jumper wires to connect the SparkFun GPS Breakout to the BeagleBoard Black. The male ends of the jumper wires plug into the P9 expansion header on the BeagleBone Black. The female ends plug into a row of straight breakaway headers that we will solder onto the breakout board. Through-hole soldering with the header pins in place can be difficult, because the pins leave little room in the holes for the solder and tip to slide in. That is why I recommend fine gauge (0.031 inches or smaller) solder for this project.

If you are inexperienced with handling small electronic components, you should first practice soldering some straight breakaway headers onto a scrap PCB. A little extra preparation could save you from damaging and having to replace your expensive ZOE-M8Q GPS module. A proper solder joint should flow around the header pin and fill the hole, forming a volcano-shaped mound. The solder joint needs to touch the metal ring around the hole. Any gaps between the pin and the metal ring will likely result in a bad connection.

To ready the SparkFun GPS Breakout so that you can attach the SPI header, follow these steps:

1. Break off a row of eight header pins.
2. Break off a row of four header pins.
3. Insert the row of eight through the SPI holes on the underside of the breakout board.
4. Insert the row of four through the holes opposite the SPI row on the underside of the breakout board. This header only serves to keep the board stable while you're soldering.
5. Hold the GPS Breakout in place with the alligator clips from your Helping Hands.
6. Position your Helping Hands magnifying glass and LED light so that you can clearly see the row of eight FTDI and I2C holes on the top side of the breakout board.
7. Plug in and heat your soldering iron to 600 to 650 °F for lead-based solder or 650 to 700 °F for lead-free solder.

Perform the following steps for the six holes on the top side of the breakout board labeled SDA, SCL, GND, 3V3, RXI, and TXO:

1. Apply a very small ball of solder to the tip of the hot iron to help prep the joint.
2. Heat the header pin and the edge of the metal ring around the hole by touching them with the tip of the iron.
3. With the tip of the iron still in place, feed solder into the joint until the hole is filled.
4. Pull the melted solder up slowly with the tip of the iron to form a mound.
5. Scrape any stray blobs of solder off with an X-Acto knife and use solder wick to remove any accidental solder bridges between holes.
6. Clean off any black oxidation that forms on the tip of the iron with either a wet or brass sponge.

Repeat these steps until all six pins have been soldered into their holes. When finished, the top side of the breakout board should look like this:

Figure 12.13 – Solder joints

Note that the jumper wires have already been attached in this photo, even though we haven't gotten to them yet. The two holes labeled NC in the row of eight do not require soldering because they are not connected to anything.

Connecting the SPI jumper wires

Flip the breakout board so that the underside is visible again. By doing this, we can attach the jumper wires. Use a black or gray wire for GND and a red or orange wire for 3V3 to avoid mixing them up and damaging your breakout board. It also helps to use different colors for the other wires so that we don't get the SPI lines confused.

Here are what the female ends of my six jumper wires look like when inserted into the header pins on the underside of the breakout board:

Figure 12.14 – Female ends of the SPI jumper wires

To connect the male ends of the SPI jumper wires to the P9 expansion header on the BeagleBone Black, follow these steps:

1. Disconnect the power from the BeagleBone Black.
2. Connect the GND wire from the GPS to pin 1 on P9.
3. Connect the CS wire from the GPS to pin 17 on P9.
4. Connect the CLK wire from the GPS to pin 22 on P9.
5. Connect the 3V3 wire from the GPS to pin 3 on P9.
6. Connect the MOSI wire from the GPS to pin 18 on P9.
7. Connect the MISO wire from the GPS to pin 21 on P9.

As a rule, it is best to connect the GND wire first before any of the other wires. This protects the BeagleBone's I/O lines from any electrostatic discharge that may have built up on the GPS Breakout.

The male ends of the six jumper wires should look like this when connected:

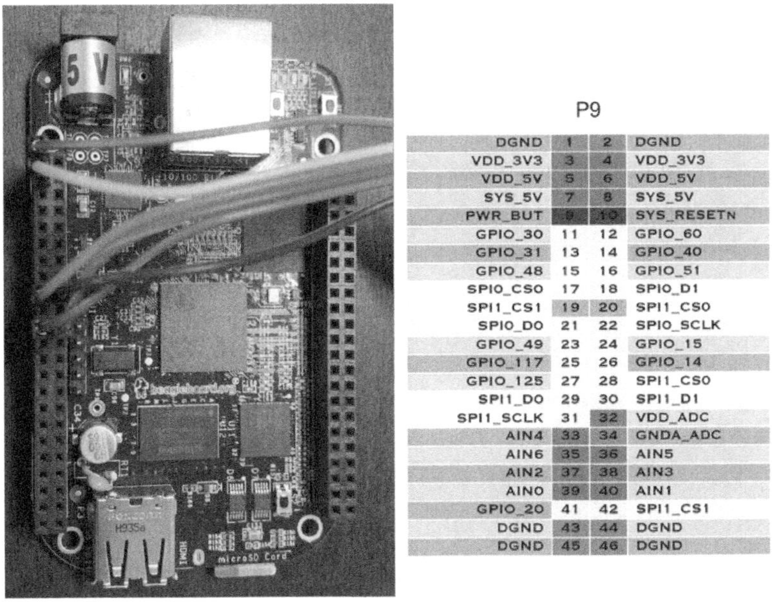

Figure 12.15 – Male ends of the SPI jumper wires

The gray wire connected to pin 1 is GND and the yellow wire connected to pin 3 is 3V3 in my case. The blue wire connected to pin 18 is MOSI on my GPS Breakout. Be careful not to plug the 3V3 wire into either of the VDD_5V pins that are just below the VDD_3V3 pins on P9, as you could destroy your breakout board.

To enable the SPI0 bus on the BeagleBone Black and power up the GPS Breakout, follow these steps:

1. Insert the Debian Buster IoT microSD card into your BeagleBone Black.
2. Apply power the BeagleBone Black by connecting the 5V power supply.
3. Connect your BeagleBone Black to the internet by plugging the board into a port on your router with an Ethernet cable.
4. SSH into your BeagleBone Black as `debian`:

   ```
   $ ssh debian@beaglebone.local
   ```

5. The password is `temppwd`.
6. Navigate to the directory for this chapter, which can be found in this book's archive:

   ```
   $ cd MELP/Chapter12
   ```

7. Enable the `/dev/spidev0.0` interface:

   ```
   $ sudo ./config-spi0.sh
   ```

Navigate to the `spidev-test` source directory and run the `spidev_test` program back-to-back a few times:

```
debian@beaglebone:~$ cd MELP/Chapter12/spidev-test
$ ./spidev_test
$ ./spidev_test
```

Pressing the *up arrow* key saves us from having to retype the previous command. On the second attempt, you should see an NMEA string starting with `$GNRMC` in the RX buffer:

```
$ ./spidev_test
spi mode: 0x0
bits per word: 8
max speed: 500000 Hz (500 KHz)
RX | 24 47 4E 52 4D 43 2C 2C 56 2C 2C 2C 2C 2C 2C 2C
2C 2C 2C 4E 2A 34 44 0D 0A 24 47 4E 56 54 47 2C  |
$GNRMC,,V,,,,,,,,,,N*4D..$GNVTG,
```

If you see an NMEA sentence in your RX buffer like the one shown here, then everything has gone according to plan. Congratulations! The hardest parts of this project are now over. The rest is "just software", as we like to say in the industry.

If no NMEA sentences (`https://en.wikipedia.org/wiki/NMEA_0183`) are being received by `spidev_test` from the GPS module, here are some questions we should ask ourselves:

1. Is the cape universal device tree loaded?

   Run the `version.sh` script under `/opt/scripts/tools` with `sudo` to verify this.

2. Did we run the `config-spi0` script without errors?

   Rerun `config-spi0` with `sudo` if you encounter permissions errors. Any subsequent `No such file or directory` errors imply that U-Boot failed to load the cape universal tree.

3. Is the power LED on the breakout board lighting up red?

   If not, then 3V3 is not connected, so the GPS Breakout is not powering on. If you have a multimeter, then you can use that to determine whether the GPS Breakout is indeed receiving 3.3 V from the BeagleBone Black.

4. Is the GND jumper wire from the GPS Breakout connected to pin 1 or 2 on P9?

   The GPS Breakout will not operate with proper grounding.

5. Are there any loose jumper wires on either end?

   All four of the remaining wires (CS, SCLK, MISO, and MOSI) are essential for a working SPI interface.

6. Are the MOSI and MISO jumper wires swapped on either end?

   Like swapping the TX and RX lines on a UART, this mistake is notoriously easy to make. Color coding our jumper wires helps but labeling them with their names using tape is even better.

7. Are the CS and SCLK jumper wires swapped on either end?

   Choosing distinct colors for our jumper wires helps us avoid mistakes like these.

If the answers to all these questions check out, then we are now ready to attach the logic analyzer. If you do not have a logic analyzer, then I suggest you reinspect the JP1 jumper and all six solder joints. Make sure the JP1 jumper pads are properly joined. Fill in any gaps between header pins and their surrounding metal rings. Remove any excess solder that could be shorting two adjacent pins together. Add some solder to joints where it may be lacking. Once you are satisfied with this rework, reconnect the jumper wires and reattempt this exercise. With some luck, the results will be better or different this time.

Successful completion of this exercise concludes all the soldering and wiring required for this project. If you are anxious to see the finished product in action, you can skip the next section and jump straight to the *Receiving NMEA messages over SPI* section. Once you have NMEA data streaming from the GPS module to a terminal window, we can pick up where we left off here and continue learning about SPI signals and digital logic.

Probing SPI signals with a logic analyzer

Even if you succeeded in receiving NMEA from your GPS module, you should attach a logic analyzer such as the Saleae Logic 8 if you have one. Probing the SPI signals helps us understand how the SPI protocol works and acts as a powerful debugging aid when things go wrong. In this section, we will use a Saleae Logic 8 to sample the SPI signals between the BeagleBone Black and ZOE-M8Q. If something is noticeably off with any of the four SPI signals, then a logic analyzer should make that mistake readily apparent.

The Saleae Logic 8 requires a laptop or desktop computer with a USB 2.0 port. The Saleae Logic 1 software is available for Linux, Mac OS X, and Windows. There is an `installdriver.sh` script that comes with the Linux version of Logic that grants the software permission to access the device. Find that script in the Logic installation's `Drivers` directory and run it from the command line so that you do not need to launch Logic with `sudo` every time. Create a shortcut to the `Logic` executable in the installation folder and place it on your desktop or launch bar for quicker access.

Once the Logic 1 software has been installed on your system, connect to the device with the high-speed USB cable that came with it. Launch the `Logic` application and wait a moment for the software to connect to and configure the device. When the Logic window says it is **Connected** at the top, then we are ready to start wiring up our test bench. Press down on the wide end of each test clip with your thumb to extend the grabbers and let go to clasp the pin. Use magnification to read the labels next to the through-holes and ensure the test clips are firmly wrapped around their respective pins.

To assemble a SPI test bench with the Saleae Logic 8, follow these steps:

1. Connect the nine-pin cable harness to the logic analyzer. Align the cable harness so that the gray lead points at the ground symbol and the black lead points at the **1** are on the underside of the logic analyzer, as shown here:

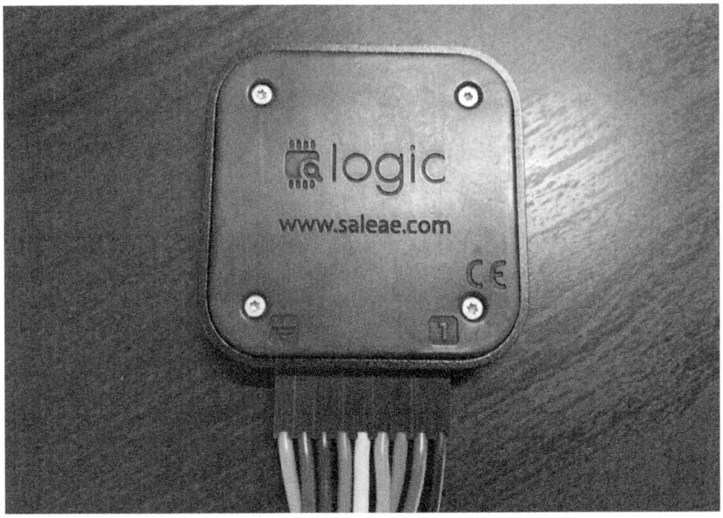

Figure 12.16 – Saleae Logic 8

2. Attach test clips to the ends of the gray, orange, red, brown, and black leads. Each test clip has two metal pins that can be inserted into the connector at the end of a lead. Only connect one of these pins to a lead. The black, brown, red, and orange leads correspond to the first four channels in the logic analyzer. The gray lead always connects to GND.
3. Disconnect your BeagleBone Black from the 5V power supply so that it is off.
4. Pull the female ends of all the jumper wires except for 3V3 from the header pins we soldered onto the GPS Breakout.
5. Grab the CS pin on the GPS Breakout with the clip on the orange lead.
6. Grab the SCLK pin on the GPS Breakout with the clip on the red lead.
7. Grab the GND pin on the GPS Breakout with the clip on the gray lead.
8. Skip the NC and 3V3 pins because we are not probing those.
9. Grab the MOSI pin on the GPS Breakout with the clip on the black lead.
10. Grab the MISO pin on the GPS Breakout with the clip on the brown lead.

11. Reconnect the female ends of the jumper wires to the header pins we soldered onto the GPS Breakout. If the jumper wires are already connected, then just slide the female ends up the header pins a bit and attach the test clips. Push the female ends down onto the pins so that they do not slip off easily. The finished assembly should look something like this:

Figure 12.17 – Test clips attached for probing

The yellow jumper wire is 3V3 in my case, so no test clip is attached to it. The blue jumper wire is MOSI, which is probed by the black lead from the logic analyzer.

12. Reconnect your BeagleBone Black to the 5V power supply. The GPS Breakout should power up and the onboard power LED should light up red.

To configure the Logic 8 so that it samples on four SPI channels, follow these steps:

1. Launch the Logic application and wait for it to connect to the logic analyzer over the USB port.

2. Click on the + sign in the **Analyzers** pane to add an analyzer:

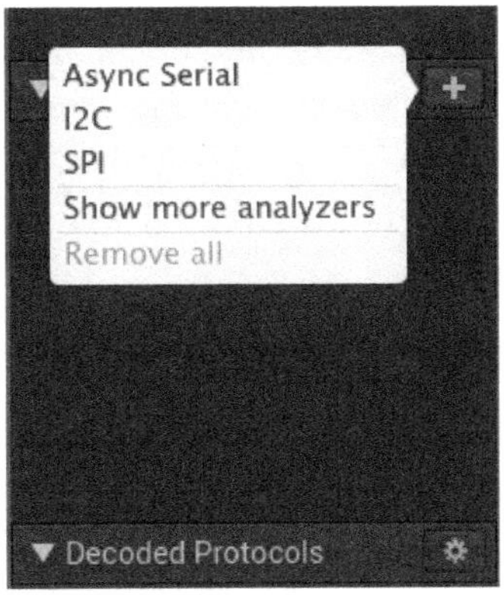

Figure 12.18 – Add Analyzer

3. Select **SPI** from the **Add Analyzer** pop-up menu.
4. Click the **Save** button in the **Analyzer Settings** dialog:

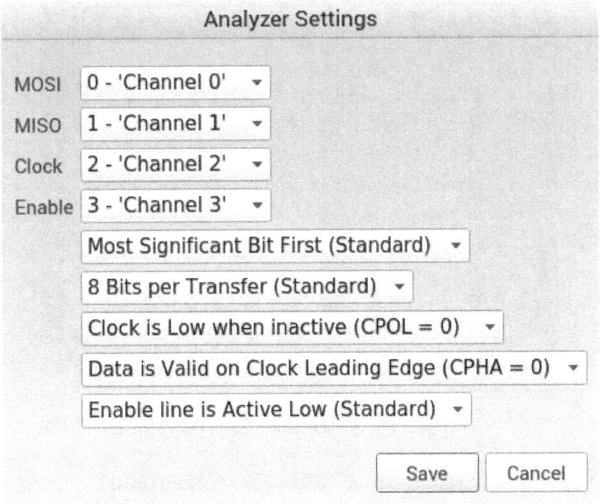

Figure 12.19 – Analyzer Settings

CPOL and **CPHA** stand for clock polarity and clock phase. A CPOL of 0 means the clock is low when inactive, while a CPOL of 1 means the clock is high when inactive. A CPHA of 0 means data is valid on a clock leading edge, while a CPHA of 1 means data is valid on a clock trailing edge. Four different SPI modes are available: mode 0 (CPOL = 0, CPHA = 0), mode 1 (CPOL = 0, CPHA = 1), mode 2 (CPOL = 1, CPHA = 1), and mode 3 (CPOL = 1, CPHA = 0). The ZOE-M8Q defaults to SPI mode 0.

5. Click on the cog button next to **Channel 4** on the left sidebar to bring up the **Channel Settings** pop-up menu:

Figure 12.20 – Hide This Channel

6. Select **Hide This Channel** from the **Channel Settings** menu.
7. Repeat *steps* 5 and 6 for Channels 5, 6, and 7 so that only Channels 0 to 3 are visible.
8. Click on the cog button next to Channel 0 (MOSI) on the left sidebar to bring up the **Channel Settings** pop-up menu.

9. Select **4x** from the **Channel Settings** menu:

Figure 12.21 – Enlarging the channel

10. Repeat *steps 8* and *9* for Channels 1 to 3 (MISO, CLOCK, and ENABLE) to make those signal graphs larger.
11. Click on the button to the right of the cog button for Channel 3 (ENABLE) on the left sidebar to bring up the **Trigger Settings** pop-up menu. ENABLE corresponds to SPI CS, so we want sampling to start upon receipt of an event from that channel.
12. Select the falling edge symbol as the trigger from the **Trigger Settings** menu:

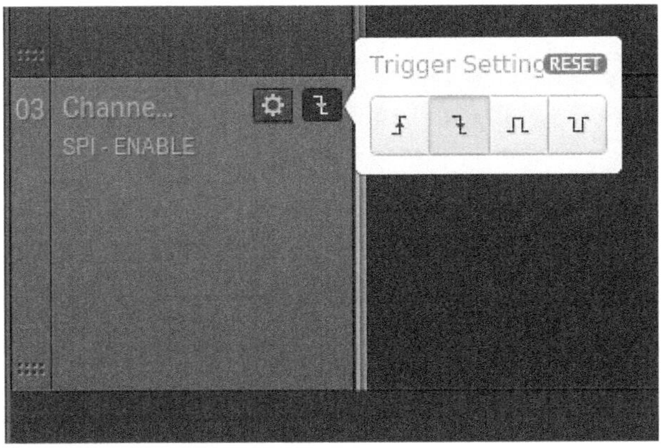

Figure 12.22 – Selecting the falling edge trigger

13. Click on the up/down arrow symbol on the **Start** button in the top-left corner to set the speed and duration of the sampling.
14. Lower the speed to **2 MS/s** and set the duration to **50 Milliseconds**:

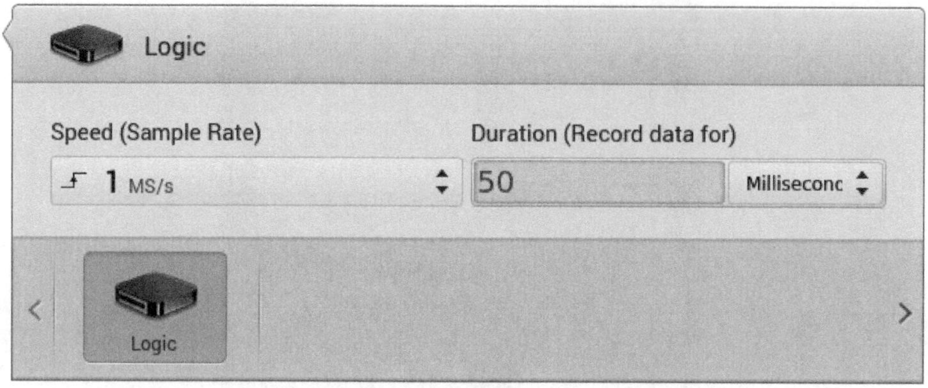

Figure 12.23 – Lowering the speed and duration

As a rule of thumb, the sample rate should be at least as four times as fast as the bandwidth. By this measure, a 1 MHz SPI port requires a minimum sample rate of 4 MS/s. Since `spidev_test` sets the speed of the SPI port to 500 kHz, then a sample rate of 2 MS/s should be just enough to keep up. Undersampling results in an irregular CLOCK signal. The SPI ports on the BeagleBone Black can operate as fast as 16 MHz. In fact, 16 MHz is the speed `spi0.0` defaults to in our custom `nova.dts`, as shown by `dmesg`.

To capture an SPI transmission from the BeagleBone Black, hit the **Start** button in the top-left corner. If the CS signal is behaving correctly, your capture should not start until you run the `spidev_test` program.

Upon executing `spidev_test` from the `debian@bealglebone` terminal, sampling should trigger and a graph similar to the following should appear in the **Logic** window:

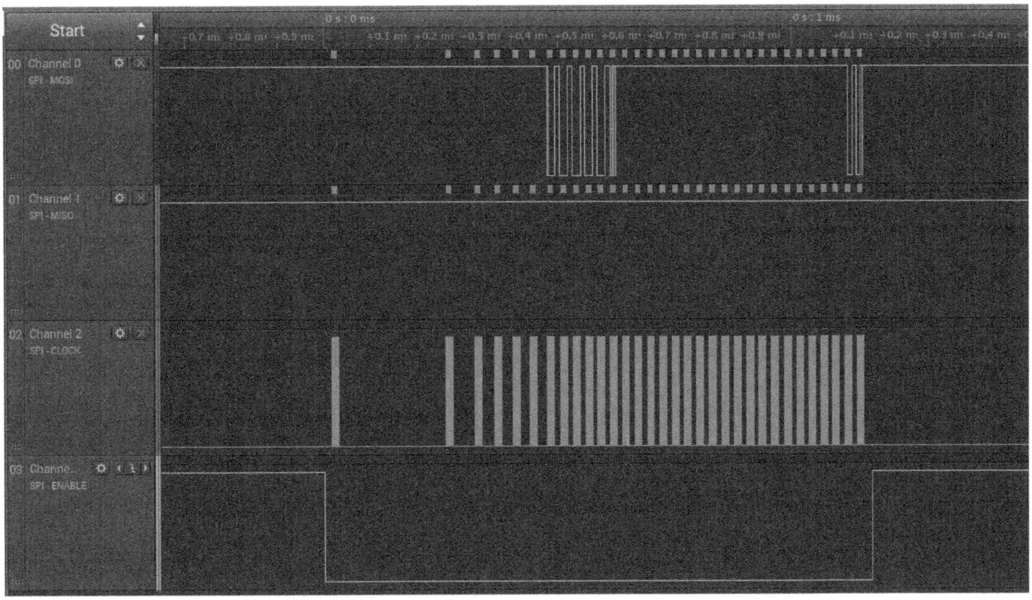

Figure 12.24 – spidev_test transmission

Use the scroll wheel on your mouse to zoom in and out of any interesting segments of the signal graphs. Notice that the ENABLE graph on Channel 3 drops low whenever data is sent by the BeagleBone Black on Channel 0 (MOSI). The CS signal for SPI is normally **active low**, so the ENABLE graph jumps high when no data is being transferred. If the ENABLE graph stays high, then no more data is sent to the GPS module because that peripheral never gets enabled on the SPI bus.

Here is a closeup of an interesting segment of the MOSI graph on Channel 0:

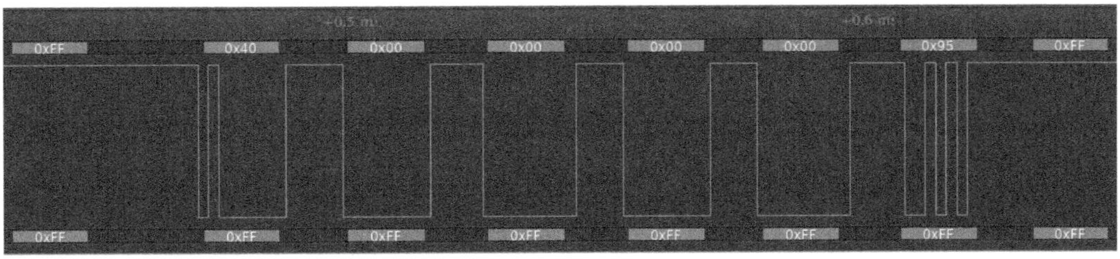

Figure 12.25 – MOSI segment

Notice that the recorded **0x40 0x00 0x00 0x00 0x00 0x95** byte sequence matches the contents of the default TX buffer for `spidev_test`. If you see this same byte sequence on Channel 1 instead, then the MOSI and MISO wires could be swapped somewhere in your circuit.

Here is the tail end of the SPI transfer:

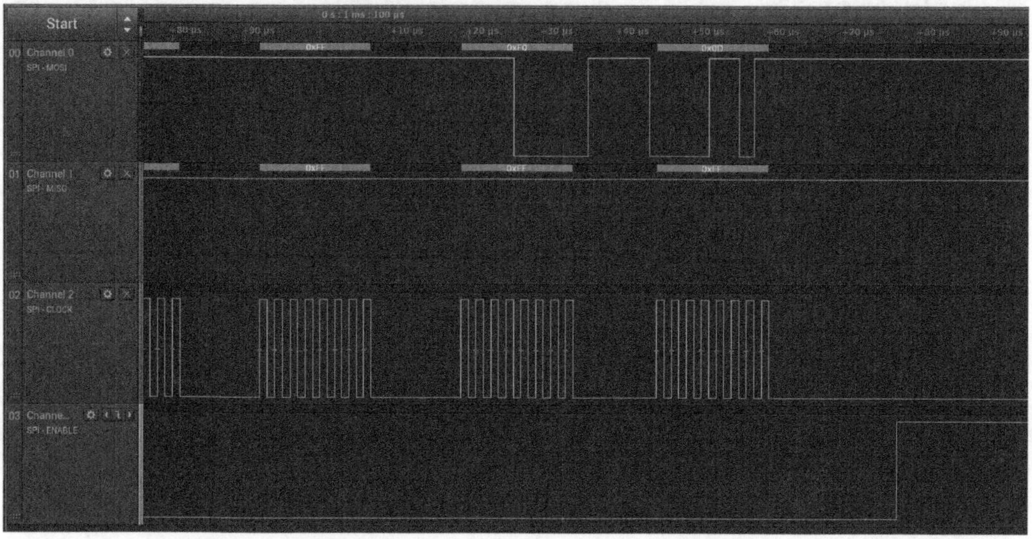

Figure 12.26 – End of spidev_test transmission

Notice that the last two bytes on Channel 0 (MOSI) of this segment are 0xF0 and 0x0D, just like in the default TX buffer. Also, notice that the CLOCK signal on Channel 2 oscillates for a regular number of cycles whenever a byte is transferred. If the CLOCK signal looks irregular, then either the data being sent is getting dropped or garbled or your sample rate isn't fast enough. The signal graph for Channel 1 (MISO) remains high throughout this session since no NMEA message is received from the GPS module on the first SPI transfer.

If the signal on Channel 3 (ENABLE) settles on the logic 0 state, this suggests that the pin being probed was muxed without the `PULL_UP` bit being set. The `PULL_UP` bit acts like a pull up resistor holding the line high when the CS signal is inactive, hence the term "active low". If you see what looks like a CLOCK signal on a channel other than 2, then either we probed the wrong pin or swapped SCLK with another wire somewhere. If the signal graphs match the images in the last three figures, then we have succeeded in verifying that SPI is operating as intended.

We now have another powerful tool in our embedded arsenal. Besides SPI, the Logic 8 can also be used to probe and analyze I2C signals. We will use it again in the next section to examine NMEA messages that are received from the GPS module.

Receiving NMEA messages over SPI

NMEA is a data message format supported by most GPS receivers. The ZOE-M8Q outputs NMEA sentences by default. These sentences are ASCII text, starting with the `$` character, followed by comma-separated fields. Raw NMEA messages are not always easy to read, so we will use a parser to add helpful annotations to the data fields.

What we want to do is read the stream of NMEA sentences from the ZOE-M8Q out of the `/dev/spidev0.0` interface. Since SPI is full-duplex, this also means writing to `/dev/spidev0.0`, although we can simply write the same 0xFF value over and over again. There is a program called `spi-pipe` that is designed to do this sort of thing. It is part of the `spi-tools` package, along with `spi-config`. Rather than relying on `spi-pipe`, I chose to modify `spidev-test` so that it streams the ASCII input from the GPS module to stdout. The source for my `spidev-read` program can be found in this book's code archive, inside the `MELP/Chapter12/spidev-read` directory.

To compile the `spidev_read` program, use the following commands:

```
debian@beaglebone:~$ cd MELP/Chapter12/spidev-read
$ gcc spidev_read.c -o spidev_read
```

Now, run the `spidev_read` program:

```
$ ./spidev_read
spi mode: 0x0
bits per word: 8
max speed: 500000 Hz (500 KHz)
$GNRMC,,V,,,,,,,,,,N*4D
$GNVTG,,,,,,,,,N*2E
$GNGGA,,,,,,0,00,99.99,,,,,,*56
$GNGSA,A,1,,,,,,,,,,,,,99.99,99.99,99.99*2E
$GNGSA,A,1,,,,,,,,,,,,,99.99,99.99,99.99*2E
$GPGSV,1,1,00*79
$GLGSV,1,1,00*65
$GNGLL,,,,,,V,N*7A
[...]
^C
```

You should see a spurt of NMEA sentences once every second. Hit *Ctrl* + *C* to cancel the stream and return to the command-line prompt.

Let's capture these SPI transfers with the Logic 8:

1. Click on the up/down arrow symbol on the **Start** button in the top-left corner to change the duration of the sampling.
2. Set the new duration to `3` seconds.
3. Click the **Start** button in the top-left corner.
4. Run the `spidev_read` program again.

The Logic software should stop capturing after 3 seconds and a graph similar to the following should appear in the **Logic** window:

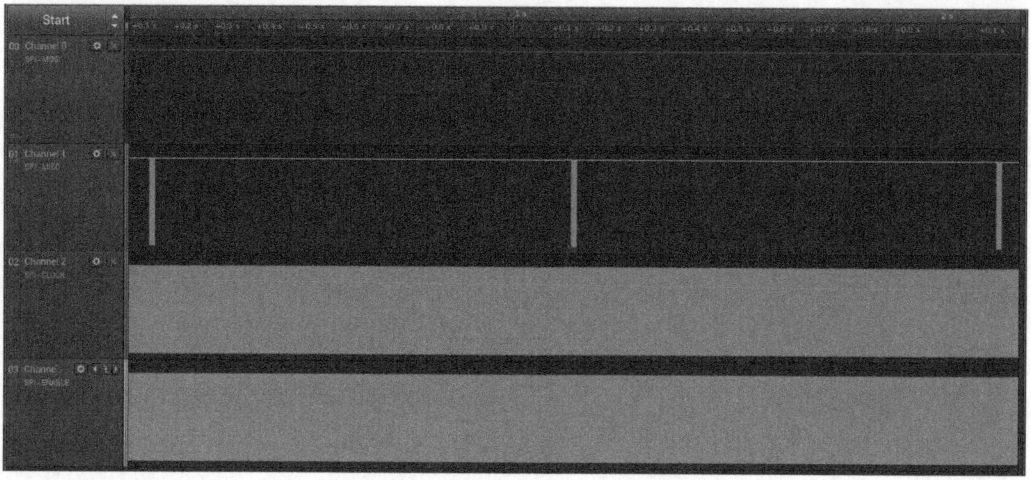

Figure 12.27 – spidev_read transmissions

We can clearly see the three spurts of the NMEA sentences on Channel 1 (MISO) precisely 1 second apart from each other.

Zoom in to get a closer look at one of these NMEA sentences:

Figure 12.28 – NMEA sentence segment

Notice that the data on MISO channel now coincides with drops in the ENABLE signal and oscillations on the CLOCK signal. The `spidev_read` program only writes `0xFF` bytes out to MOSI, so there is no activity on Channel 0.

I have included a NMEA parser script written in Python, along with the `spidev_read` source code. That `parse_nmea.py` script depends on the `pynmea2` library.

To install `pynmea2` on the BeagleBone Black, use the following command:

```
$ pip3 install pynmea2
Looking in indexes: https://pypi.org/simple, https://www.piwheels.org/simple
Collecting pynmea2
  Downloading https://files.pythonhosted.org/packages/88/5f/a3d09471582e710b4871e41b0b7792be836d6396a2630dee4c6ef44830e5/pynmea2-1.15.0-py3-none-any.whl
Installing collected packages: pynmea2
Successfully installed pynmea2-1.15.0
```

To pipe the output of `spidev_read` into the NMEA parser, use the following command:

```
$ cd MELP/Chapter12/spidev-read
$ ./spidev_read | ./parse_nmea.py
```

The parsed NMEA output looks as follows:

```
<RMC(timestamp=None, status='V', lat='', lat_dir='',
lon='', lon_dir='', spd_over_grnd=None, true_course=None,
datestamp=None, mag_variation='', mag_var_dir='') data=['N']>
<VTG(true_track=None, true_track_sym='', mag_track=None, mag_
track_sym='', spd_over_grnd_kts=None, spd_over_grnd_kts_sym='',
spd_over_grnd_kmph=None, spd_over_grnd_kmph_sym='', faa_
mode='N')>
<GGA(timestamp=None, lat='', lat_dir='', lon='', lon_
dir='', gps_qual=0, num_sats='00', horizontal_dil='99.99',
altitude=None, altitude_units='', geo_sep='', geo_sep_units='',
age_gps_data='', ref_station_id='')>
<GSA(mode='A', mode_fix_type='1', sv_id01='', sv_id02='',
sv_id03='', sv_id04='', sv_id05='', sv_id06='', sv_id07='',
sv_id08='', sv_id09='', sv_id10='', sv_id11='', sv_id12='',
pdop='99.99', hdop='99.99', vdop='99.99')>
<GSA(mode='A', mode_fix_type='1', sv_id01='', sv_id02='',
sv_id03='', sv_id04='', sv_id05='', sv_id06='', sv_id07='',
sv_id08='', sv_id09='', sv_id10='', sv_id11='', sv_id12='',
pdop='99.99', hdop='99.99', vdop='99.99')>
<GSV(num_messages='1', msg_num='1', num_sv_in_view='00')>
<GSV(num_messages='1', msg_num='1', num_sv_in_view='00')>
<GLL(lat='', lat_dir='', lon='', lon_dir='', timestamp=None,
status='V', faa_mode='N')>
[...]
```

My GPS module was unable to see any satellites or acquire a fixed position. This could be due to any number of reasons, such as choosing the wrong GPS antenna or no clear line-of-sight to the sky. If you are experiencing similar failures, that is okay. RF is complicated and the goal of this chapter was only to prove we could get SPI communications with the GPS module working. Now that we've done that, we can begin to experiment with alternate GPS antennas and more of the ZOE-M8Q's advanced features, such as its support for the much richer UBX message protocol.

With NMEA data now streaming out to the terminal, our project is finished. We succeeded in verifying that the BeagleBone Black can communicate with the ZOE-M8Q over SPI. If you skipped over the *Probing SPI signals with a logic analyzer* section, now is a good time to resume with that exercise. Like I2C, SPI is supported by most SoCs, so it is worth getting familiar with, especially if your application requires high-speed peripherals.

Summary

In this chapter, we learned how to integrate a peripheral with a popular SoC. To do that, we had to mux pins and modify the device tree source using knowledge gleaned from data sheets and schematics. Without finished hardware in hand, we had to rely on a breakout board and do some soldering so that the part could be wired together with a dev board. Lastly, we learned how to use a logic analyzer to verify and troubleshoot electrical signals. Now that we have working hardware, we can begin to develop our embedded application.

The next two chapters are all about system startup and the different options you have for the `init` program, from the simple BusyBox `init` to more complex systems such as System V `init`, `systemd`, and BusyBox's `runit`. Your choice of `init` program can have a big impact on the user experience of your product, both in terms of boot times and fault tolerance.

Further reading

The following resources provide more information about the topics that were introduced in this chapter:

- *Introduction to SPI Interface*, by Piyu Dhaker: `https://www.analog.com/en/analog-dialogue/articles/introduction-to-spi-interface.html`
- *Soldering is Easy*, by Mitch Altman, Andie Nordgren, and Jeff Keyzer: `https://mightyohm.com/blog/2011/04/soldering-is-easy-comic-book`
- *SparkFun GPS Breakout (ZOE-M8Q and SAM-M8Q) Hookup Guide*, by Elias the Sparkiest: `https://learn.sparkfun.com/tutorials/sparkfun-gps-breakout-zoe-m8q-and-sam-m8q-hookup-guide`

13
Starting Up – The init Program

We looked at how the kernel boots up to the point where it launches the first program, `init`, in *Chapter 4, Configuring and Building the Kernel*. In *Chapter 5, Building a Root Filesystem*, and *Chapter 6, Selecting a Build System*, we looked at creating root filesystems of varying complexity, all of which contained an `init` program. Now, it is time to look at the `init` program in more detail and discover why it is so important to the rest of the system.

There are many possible implementations of `init`. I will describe the three main ones in this chapter: BusyBox `init`, System V `init`, and `systemd`. For each one, I will give an overview of how it works and the types of systems it suits best. Part of this is balancing the trade-off between size, complexity, and flexibility. We will learn how to launch a daemon using both BusyBox `init` and System V `init`. We will also learn how to add a service to `systemd` that does the same.

In this chapter, we will cover the following topics:

- After the kernel has booted
- Introducing the `init` programs

- BusyBox `init`
- System V `init`
- `systemd`

Technical requirements

To follow along with the examples, make sure you have the following:

- A Linux-based host system
- Buildroot 2020.02.9 LTS release
- Yocto 3.1 (Dunfell) LTS release

You should have already installed the 2020.02.9 LTS release of Buildroot for *Chapter 6, Selecting a Build System*. If you have not, then refer to the *System requirements* section of *The Buildroot user manual* (`https://buildroot.org/downloads/manual/manual.html`) before installing Buildroot on your Linux host according to the instructions from *Chapter 6*.

You should have already built the 3.1 (Dunfell) LTS release of Yocto for *Chapter 6, Selecting a Build System*. If you have not, then refer to the *Compatible Linux Distribution* and *Build Host Packages* sections of the *Yocto Project Quick Build* guide (`https://www.yoctoproject.org/docs/current/brief-yoctoprojectqs/brief-yoctoprojectqs.html`) before building Yocto on your Linux host according to the instructions from *Chapter 6*.

All of the code for this chapter can be found in the `Chapter13` folder from the book's GitHub repository: `https://github.com/PacktPublishing/Mastering-Embedded-Linux-Programming-Third-Edition`.

After the kernel has booted

We saw in *Chapter 4, Configuring and Building the Kernel*, how the kernel bootstrap code seeks to find a root filesystem, either `initramfs` or a filesystem specified by `root=` on the kernel command line, and then executes a program that, by default, is `/init` for `initramfs` and `/sbin/init` for a regular filesystem. The `init` program has `root` privilege, and since it is the first process to run, it has a **process ID** (**PID**) of `1`. If, for some reason, `init` cannot be started, the kernel will panic.

The `init` program is the ancestor of all other processes, as shown here by the `pstree` command running on a simple embedded Linux system:

```
# pstree -gn
init(1)-+-syslogd(63)
        |-klogd(66)
        |-dropbear(99)
        `-sh(100)---pstree(109)
```

The job of the `init` program is to take control of the boot process in user space and set it running. It may be as simple as a `shell` command running a shell script—there is an example of this at the start of *Chapter 5, Building a Root Filesystem*—but in the majority of cases, you will be using a dedicated `init` daemon to perform the following tasks:

- During boot, after the kernel transfers control, the `init` program starts other daemon programs and configures system parameters and other things needed to get the system into a working state.
- Optionally, it launches a login daemon, such as `getty`, on terminals that allow a login shell.
- It adopts processes that become orphaned as a result of their immediate parent terminating and there being no other processes in the thread group.
- It responds to any of the `init`'s immediate children terminating by catching the `SIGCHLD` signal and collecting the return value to prevent them from becoming zombie processes. I will talk more about zombies in *Chapter 17, Learning About Processes and Threads*.
- Optionally, it restarts those daemons that have terminated.
- It handles the system shutdown.

In other words, `init` manages the life cycle of the system from bootup to shutdown. There is a school of thought that says `init` is well placed to handle other runtime events, such as new hardware and the loading and unloading of modules. This is what `systemd` does.

Introducing the init programs

The three init programs that you are most likely to encounter in embedded devices are BusyBox init, System V init, and systemd. Buildroot has options to build all three with BusyBox init as the default. The Yocto Project allows you to easily choose between System V init and systemd with System V init as the default. While Yocto's Poky-tiny distribution ships with BusyBox init, most other distribution layers do not.

The following table gives some metrics to compare the three:

Metric	BusyBox init	System V init	systemd
Complexity	Low	Medium	High
Boot-up speed	Fast	Slow	Medium
Required shell	ash	ash or bash	None
Number of executables	1	4	50(*)
libc	Any	Any	glibc
Size (MiB)	< 0.1(*)	0.1	34(**)

(*) BusyBox init is part of BusyBox's single executable, which is optimized for size on disk.

(**) Based on the Buildroot configuration of systemd.

Broadly speaking, there is an increase in flexibility and complexity as you go from BusyBox init to systemd.

BusyBox init

BusyBox has a minimal init program that uses a configuration file, /etc/inittab, to define rules to start programs at bootup and to stop them at shutdown. Usually, the actual work is done by shell scripts, which, by convention, are placed in the /etc/init.d directory.

init begins by reading /etc/inittab. This contains a list of programs to run, one per line, with this format:

```
<id>::<action>:<program>
```

The role of these parameters is as follows:

- `id`: This is the controlling terminal for the command.
- `action`: This includes the conditions to run this command, as shown in the following list.
- `program`: This is the program to run.

The actions are as follows:

- `sysinit`: Runs the program when `init` starts before any of the other types of actions.
- `respawn`: Runs the program and restarts it if it terminates. It is typically used to run a program as a daemon.
- `askfirst`: This is the same as `respawn`, but it prints the message `Please press Enter to activate this console` to the console, and it runs the program after *Enter* has been pressed. It is used to start an interactive shell on a terminal without prompting for a username or password.
- `once`: Runs the program once but does not attempt to restart it if it terminates.
- `wait`: Runs the program and waits for it to complete.
- `restart`: Runs the program when `init` receives the `SIGHUP` signal, indicating that it should reload the `inittab` file.
- `ctrlaltdel`: Runs the program when `init` receives the `SIGINT` signal, usually as a result of pressing *Ctrl* + *Alt* + *Del* on the console.
- `shutdown`: Runs the program when `init` shuts down.

Here is a small example that mounts `proc` and `sysfs` and runs a shell on a serial interface:

```
null::sysinit:/bin/mount -t proc proc /proc
null::sysinit:/bin/mount -t sysfs sysfs /sys
console::askfirst:-/bin/sh
```

For simple projects in which you want to launch a small number of daemons, and perhaps start a login shell on a serial terminal, it is easy to write the scripts manually. This would be appropriate if you are creating a **roll your own** (**RYO**) embedded Linux. However, you will find that handwritten `init` scripts rapidly become unmaintainable as the number of things to be configured increases. They are not very modular and so need updating each time a new component is added or removed.

Buildroot init scripts

Buildroot has been making effective use of BusyBox `init` for many years. Buildroot has two scripts in `/etc/init.d/` named `rcS` and `rcK`. The first one runs at bootup and iterates over all the scripts in `/etc/init.d/` with names that begin with a capital `S` followed by two digits, and runs them in numerical order. These are the start scripts. The `rcK` script is run at shutdown and iterates over all the scripts beginning with a capital `K` followed by two digits and runs them in numerical order. These are the kill scripts.

With this in place, it becomes easy for Buildroot packages to supply their own start and kill scripts, using the two-digit number to impose the order in which they should be run, and so the system becomes extensible. If you are using Buildroot, this is transparent. If not, you could use it as a model for writing your own BusyBox `init` scripts.

Like BusyBox `init`, System V `init` relies on shell scripts inside `/etc/init.d` and an `/etc/inittab` configuration file. While the two `init` systems are similar in many ways, System V `init` has more features and a much longer history.

System V init

This `init` program was inspired by the one from Unix System V and so dates back to the mid-1980s. The version most often found in Linux distributions was written initially by Miquel van Smoorenburg. Until recently, it was the `init` daemon for almost all desktop and server distributions and a fair number of embedded systems as well. However, in recent years, it has been replaced by `systemd`, which I will describe in the next section.

The BusyBox `init` daemon I have just described is just a trimmed-down version of System V `init`. Compared to BusyBox `init`, System V `init` has two advantages:

- Firstly, the boot scripts are written in a well-known, modular format, making it easy to add new packages at build time or runtime.
- Secondly, it has the concept of **runlevels**, which allow a collection of programs to be started or stopped in one go when switching from one runlevel to another.

There are eight runlevels, numbered from `0` to `6`, plus `S`:

- `S`: Runs startup tasks
- `0`: Halts the system
- `1` to `5`: Available for general use
- `6`: Reboots the system

Levels 1 to 5 can be used as you please. On desktop Linux distributions, they are conventionally assigned as follows:

- 1: Single user
- 2: Multi-user without network configuration
- 3: Multi-user with network configuration
- 4: Not used
- 5: Multi-user with graphical login

The init program starts the default runlevel given by the initdefault line in /etc/inittab as follows:

```
id:3:initdefault:
```

You can change the runlevel at runtime using the telinit [runlevel] command, which sends a message to init. You can find the current runlevel and the previous one using the runlevel command. Here is an example:

```
# runlevel
N 5
# telinit 3
INIT: Switching to runlevel: 3
# runlevel
5 3
```

Initially, the output from the runlevel command is N 5, indicating that there is no previous runlevel, because the runlevel has not changed since booting and the current runlevel is 5. After changing the runlevel, the output is 5 3, showing that there has been a transition from 5 to 3.

The halt and reboot commands switch to runlevels 0 and 6, respectively. You can override the default runlevel by giving a different one on the kernel command line as a single digit from 0 to 6. For example, to force the runlevel to be single user, you would append 1 to the kernel command line, and it would look something like this:

```
console=ttyAMA0 root=/dev/mmcblk1p2 1
```

Each runlevel has a number of scripts that stop things, called kill scripts, and another group that starts things, the start scripts. When entering a new runlevel, `init` first runs the kill scripts in the new level, and then the start scripts in the new level. Daemons that are currently running and that have neither a start script nor a kill script in the new runlevel are sent a `SIGTERM` signal. In other words, the default action on the switching runlevel is to terminate daemons unless told to do otherwise.

In truth, runlevels are not used that much in embedded Linux: most devices simply boot to the default runlevel and stay there. I have a feeling that it is partly because most people are not aware of them.

> **Tip**
>
> Runlevels are a simple and convenient way to switch between modes, for example, from production to maintenance mode.

System V `init` is an option in Buildroot and the Yocto Project. In both cases, the `init` scripts have been stripped of any `bash` shell specifics, so they will work with the BusyBox `ash` shell. However, Buildroot cheats somewhat by replacing the BusyBox `init` program with System V `init` and adding an `inittab` that mimics the behavior of BusyBox. Buildroot does not implement runlevels, except that switching to levels `0` or `6` halts or reboots the system.

Next, let's look at some of the details. The following examples are taken from the Yocto Project 3.1 release. Other distributions may implement the `init` scripts a little differently.

inittab

The `init` program begins by reading `/etc/inttab`, which contains entries that define what happens at each runlevel. The format is an extended version of the BusyBox `inittab` that I described in the preceding section, which is not surprising because BusyBox borrowed it from System V in the first place.

The format of each line in `inittab` is as follows:

```
id:runlevels:action:process
```

The fields are shown here:

- `id`: A unique identifier of up to four characters.
- `runlevels`: The runlevels for which this entry should be executed. This was left blank in the BusyBox `inittab`.

- `action`: One of the keywords given in the following paragraph.
- `process`: The command to run.

The actions are the same as for BusyBox `init`: `sysinit`, `respawn`, `once`, `wait`, `restart`, `ctrlaltdel`, and `shutdown`. However, System V `init` does not have `askfirst`, which is specific to BusyBox.

As an example, this is the complete `inittab` supplied by the Yocto Project target `core-image-minimal` for the `qemuarm` machine:

```
# /etc/inittab: init(8) configuration.
# $Id: inittab,v 1.91 2002/01/25 13:35:21 miquels Exp $

# The default runlevel.
id:5:initdefault:

# Boot-time system configuration/initialization script.
# This is run first except when booting in emergency (-b) mode.
si::sysinit:/etc/init.d/rcS

# What to do in single-user mode.
~~:S:wait:/sbin/sulogin
# /etc/init.d executes the S and K scripts upon change
# of runlevel.
#
# Runlevel 0 is halt.
# Runlevel 1 is single-user.
# Runlevels 2-5 are multi-user.
# Runlevel 6 is reboot.

l0:0:wait:/etc/init.d/rc 0
l1:1:wait:/etc/init.d/rc 1
l2:2:wait:/etc/init.d/rc 2
l3:3:wait:/etc/init.d/rc 3
l4:4:wait:/etc/init.d/rc 4
l5:5:wait:/etc/init.d/rc 5
l6:6:wait:/etc/init.d/rc 6

```

```
# Normally not reached, but fallthrough in case of emergency.
z6:6:respawn:/sbin/sulogin
AMA0:12345:respawn:/sbin/getty 115200 ttyAMA0
# /sbin/getty invocations for the runlevels
#
# The "id" field MUST be the same as the last
# characters of the device (after "tty").
#
# Format:
# <id>:<runlevels>:<action>:<process>
#

1:2345:respawn:/sbin/getty 38400 tty1
```

The first entry, `id:5:initdefault`, sets the default `runlevel` to `5`. The next entry, `si::sysinit:/etc/init.d/rcS`, runs the `rcS` script at bootup. There will be more about this later. A little further on, there is a group of six entries beginning with `l0:0:wait:/etc/init.d/rc 0`. They run the `/etc/init.d/rc` script each time there is a change in the runlevel. This script is responsible for processing the start and kill scripts.

Toward the end of `inittab`, there is an entry that runs a `getty` daemon to generate a login prompt on `/dev/ttyAMA0` when entering runlevels `1` through `5`, thereby allowing you to log on and get an interactive shell:

```
AMA0:12345:respawn:/sbin/getty 115200 ttyAMA0
```

The `ttyAMA0` device is the serial console on the Arm Versatile board we are emulating with QEMU; it will be different for other development boards. There is also an entry to run `getty` on `tty1`, which is triggered when entering runlevels `2` through `5`. This is a virtual console, which is often mapped to a graphical screen if you have built your kernel with `CONFIG_FRAMEBUFFER_CONSOLE` or `VGA_CONSOLE`. Desktop Linux distributions usually spawn six `getty` daemons on virtual terminals `1` to `6`, which you can select with the key combination *Ctrl* + *Alt* + *F1* through *Ctrl* + *Alt* + *F6*, with virtual terminal `7` reserved for the graphical screen. Ubuntu and Arch Linux are notable exceptions since they use virtual terminal `1` for graphics. Virtual terminals are seldom used on embedded devices.

The `/etc/init.d/rcS` script that is run by the `sysinit` entry does little more than entering the runlevel, `S`:

```
#!/bin/sh
[...]
exec /etc/init.d/rc S
```

Hence, the first runlevel entered is `S`, followed by the default runlevel of `5`. Note that runlevel `S` is not recorded and is never displayed as a prior runlevel by the `runlevel` command.

The init.d scripts

Each component that needs to respond to a runlevel change has a script in `/etc/init.d` to perform the change. The script should expect two parameters: `start` and `stop`. I will give an example of this later.

The runlevel-handling script, `/etc/init.d/rc`, takes the runlevel it is switching to as a parameter. For each runlevel, there is a directory named `rc<runlevel>.d`:

```
# ls -d /etc/rc*
/etc/rc0.d /etc/rc2.d /etc/rc4.d /etc/rc6.d
/etc/rc1.d /etc/rc3.d /etc/rc5.d /etc/rcS.d
```

There you will find a set of scripts beginning with a capital `S` followed by two digits, and you may also find scripts beginning with a capital `K`. These are the start and kill scripts, respectively. Here is an example of the scripts for runlevel `5`:

```
# ls /etc/rc5.d
S01networking S20hwclock.sh S99rmnologin.sh S99stop-bootlogd
S15mountnfs.sh S20syslog
```

These are in fact symbolic links back to the appropriate script in `init.d`. The `rc` script runs all the scripts beginning with a `K` first, adding the `stop` parameter, and then runs those beginning with an `S`, adding the `start` parameter. Once again, the two-digit code is there to impart the order in which the scripts should run.

Adding a new daemon

Imagine that you have a program named `simpleserver` that is written as a traditional Unix daemon; in other words, it forks and runs in the background. The code for such a program is in `MELP/Chapter13/simpleserver`. You will need an `init.d` script such as this, which you will find in `MELP/Chapter13/simpleserver-sysvinit`:

```
#! /bin/sh

case "$1" in
      start)
            echo "Starting simpelserver"
            start-stop-daemon -S -n simpleserver -a /usr/bin/
simpleserver
            ;;
     stop)
            echo "Stopping simpleserver"
            start-stop-daemon -K -n simpleserver
            ;;
     *)
            echo "Usage: $0 {start|stop}"
            exit 1
esac

exit 0
```

`start-stop-daemon` is a helper function that makes it easier to manipulate background processes such as this. It originally came from the Debian installer package, `dpkg`, but most embedded systems use the one from BusyBox. It starts the daemon with the `-S` parameter, making sure that there is never more than one instance running at any one time. To stop a daemon, you use the `-K` parameter, which causes it to send a signal, `SIGTERM` by default, to indicate to the daemon that it is time to terminate.

To make `simpleserver` operational, copy the script to the target directory called `/etc/init.d/simpleserver` and make it executable. Then, add links from each of the runlevels that you want to run this program from; in this case, only the default runlevel of `5`:

```
# cd /etc/init.d/rc5.d
# ln -s ../init.d/simpleserver S99simpleserver
```

The number 99 means that this will be one of the last programs to be started. Bear in mind that there may be other links beginning with S99, in which case the rc script will just run them in lexical order.

It is rare in embedded devices to have to worry too much about shutdown operations, but if there is something that needs to be done, add kill links to levels 0 and 6:

```
# cd /etc/init.d/rc0.d
# ln -s ../init.d/simpleserver K01simpleserver
# cd /etc/init.d/rc6.d
# ln -s ../init.d/simpleserver K01simpleserver
```

We can circumvent runlevels and ordering for more immediate testing and debugging of init.d scripts.

Starting and stopping services

You can interact with the scripts in /etc/init.d by calling them directly. Here is an example using the syslog script, which controls the syslogd and klogd daemons:

```
# /etc/init.d/syslog --help
Usage: syslog { start | stop | restart }

# /etc/init.d/syslog stop
Stopping syslogd/klogd: stopped syslogd (pid 198)
stopped klogd (pid 201)
done

# /etc/init.d/syslog start
Starting syslogd/klogd: done
```

All scripts implement start and stop, and they should also implement help. Some implement status as well, which will tell you whether the service is running or not. Mainstream distributions that still use System V init have a command named service to start and stop services, which hides the details of calling the scripts directly.

System V init is a simple init daemon that has served Linux admins for decades. While runlevels offer a greater degree of sophistication than BusyBox init, System V init still lacks the ability to monitor services and restart them if needed. As System V init starts to show its age, most popular Linux distributions have moved on to systemd.

systemd

systemd, https://www.freedesktop.org/wiki/Software/systemd/, defines itself as a *system and service manager*. The project was initiated in 2010 by Lennart Poettering and Kay Sievers to create an integrated set of tools for managing a Linux system based around an init daemon. It also includes device management (udev) and logging, among other things. systemd is state of the art and is still evolving rapidly. It is common on desktop and server Linux distributions and is becoming popular on embedded Linux systems too, especially on more complex devices. So, how is it better than System V init for embedded systems?

- The configuration is simpler and more logical (once you understand it). Rather than the sometimes convoluted shell scripts of System V init, systemd has unit configuration files that are written in a well-defined format.
- There are explicit dependencies between services, rather than a two-digit code that merely sets the sequence in which the scripts are run.
- It is easy to set the permissions and resource limits for each service, which is important for security.
- It can monitor services and restart them if needed.
- Services are started in parallel, potentially reducing boot time.

A complete description of systemd is neither possible nor appropriate here. As with System V init, I will focus on the embedded use cases with examples based on the configuration produced by the Yocto Project 3.1 release, with systemd version 244. I will give a quick overview, and then show you some specific examples.

Building systemd with the Yocto Project and Buildroot

The default init daemon in the Yocto Project is System V. To select systemd, add this line to your conf/local.conf:

```
INIT_MANAGER = "systemd"
```

Buildroot uses BusyBox init by default. You can select systemd though menuconfig by looking in the **System configuration | Init system** menu. You will also have to configure the toolchain to use glibc for the C library, since systemd does not support uClibc-ng or musl. In addition, there are restrictions on the version and configuration of the kernel. There is a complete list of library and kernel dependencies in the README file in the top level of the systemd source code.

Introducing targets, services, and units

Before I describe how systemd works, I need to introduce these three key concepts:

- **unit**: A configuration file that describes a target, a service, and several other things. Units are text files that contain properties and values.
- **service**: A daemon that can be started and stopped, very much like a System V init service.
- **target**: A group of services, similar to, but more general than, a System V init runlevel. There is a default target that is the group of services that are started at boot time.

You can change states and find out what is going on using the systemctl command.

Units

The basic item of configuration is the unit file. Unit files are found in three different places:

- /etc/systemd/system: Local configuration
- /run/systemd/system: Runtime configuration
- /lib/systemd/system: Distribution-wide configuration

When looking for a unit, systemd searches the directories in that order, stopping as soon as it finds a match, and allowing you to override the behavior of a distribution-wide unit by placing a unit of the same name in /etc/systemd/system. You can disable a unit completely by creating a local file that is empty or linked to /dev/null.

All unit files begin with a section marked [Unit], which contains basic information and dependencies. As an example, here is the Unit section of the D-Bus service, /lib/systemd/system/dbus.service:

```
[Unit]
Description=D-Bus System Message Bus
Documentation=man:dbus-daemon(1)
Requires=dbus.socket
```

In addition to the description and a reference to the documentation, there is a dependency on the dbus.socket unit expressed through the Requires keyword. This tells systemd to create a local socket when the D-Bus service is started.

Dependencies in the `Unit` section are expressed through the `Requires`, `Wants`, and `Conflicts` keywords:

- `Requires`: A list of units that this unit depends on that are started when this unit is started.
- `Wants`: A weaker form of `Requires`; the units listed are started but the current unit is not stopped if any of them fail.
- `Conflicts`: A negative dependency; the units listed are stopped when this one is started and, conversely, if one of them is started, this one is stopped.

These three keywords define **outgoing dependencies**. They are used mostly to create dependencies between targets. There is another set of dependencies called **incoming dependencies**, which are used to create links between *services* and *targets*. In other words, outgoing dependencies are used to create the list of targets that need to be started as the system goes from one state to another, and incoming dependencies are used to determine the services that should be started or stopped in any particular state. Incoming dependencies are created by the `WantedBy` keyword, which I will describe in the upcoming section on *Adding your own service*.

Processing the dependencies produces a list of units that should be started or stopped. The `Before` and `After` keywords determine the order in which they are started. The order of stopping is just the reverse of the start order:

- `Before`: Start this unit before the units listed.
- `After`: Start this unit after the units listed.

In the following example, the `After` directive makes sure that the web server is started after the network subsystem is started:

```
[Unit]
Description=Lighttpd Web Server
After=network.target
```

In the absence of the `Before` or `After` directive, the units will be started or stopped in parallel with no particular ordering.

Services

A **service** is a daemon that can be started and stopped, equivalent to a System V `init` service. A service is a type of unit file with a name ending in `.service`, for example, `lighttpd.service`.

A service unit has a `[Service]` section that describes how it should be run. Here is the relevant section from `lighttpd.service`:

```
[Service]
ExecStart=/usr/sbin/lighttpd -f /etc/lighttpd/lighttpd.conf -D
ExecReload=/bin/kill -HUP $MAINPID
```

These are the commands to run when starting the service and restarting it. There are many more configuration points you can add here, so refer to the manual page for `systemd.service(5)`.

Targets

A **target** is another type of unit that groups services (or other types of units). A target is a metaservice in that respect and also serves as a synchronization point. A target only has dependencies. Targets have names ending in `.target`, for example, `multi-user.target`. A target is a desired state that performs the same role as System V `init` runlevels. For example, this is the complete unit for `multi-user.target`:

```
[Unit]
Description=Multi-User System
Documentation=man:systemd.special(7)
Requires=basic.target
Conflicts=rescue.service rescue.target
After=basic.target rescue.service rescue.target
AllowIsolate=yes
```

This says that the basic target must be started before the multi-user target. It also says that since it conflicts with the rescue target, starting the rescue target will cause the multi-user target to be stopped first.

How systemd boots the system

Now, we can see how `systemd` implements the bootstrap. `systemd` is run by the kernel as a result of `/sbin/init` being symbolically linked to `/lib/systemd/systemd`. It runs the default target, `default.target`, which is always a link to the desired target, such as `multi-user.target` for a text login or `graphical.target` for a graphical environment. For example, if the default target is `multi-user.target`, you will find this symbolic link:

```
/etc/systemd/system/default.target -> /lib/systemd/system/
multi-user.target
```

The default target may be overridden by passing `system.unit=<new target>` on the kernel command line. You can use `systemctl` to find out the default target, as shown here:

```
# systemctl get-default
multi-user.target
```

Starting a target such as `multi-user.target` creates a tree of dependencies that bring the system into a working state. In a typical system, `multi-user.target` depends on `basic.target`, which depends on `sysinit.target`, which depends on the services that need to be started early. You can print a text graph using `systemctl list-dependencies`.

You can also list all the services and their current state using the following:

```
# systemctl list-units --type service
```

You can do the same for targets using the following:

```
# systemctl list-units --type target
```

Now that we've seen the dependency tree for the system, how do we insert an additional service into this tree?

Adding your own service

Using the same `simpleserver` example as before, here is a service unit, which you will find in `MELP/Chapter13/simpleserver-systemd`:

```
[Unit]
Description=Simple server

```

```
[Service]
Type=forking
ExecStart=/usr/bin/simpleserver

[Install]
WantedBy=multi-user.target
```

The [Unit] section only contains a description so that it shows up correctly when listed using systemctl and other commands. There are no dependencies; as I said, it is very simple.

The [Service] section points to the executable and has a flag to indicate that it forks. If it were even simpler and ran in the foreground, systemd would do the daemonizing for us and Type=forking would not be needed.

The [Install] section creates an incoming dependency on multi-user.target so that our server is started when the system goes into the multi-user mode.

Once the unit is saved in /etc/systemd/system/simpleserver.service, you can start and stop it using the systemctl start simpleserver and sytemctl stop simpleserver commands. You can also use systemctl to find its current status:

```
# systemctl status simpleserver
simpleserver.service - Simple server
  Loaded: loaded (/etc/systemd/system/simpleserver.service;
disabled)
  Active: active (running) since Thu 1970-01-01 02:20:50 UTC;
8s ago
Main PID: 180 (simpleserver)
  CGroup: /system.slice/simpleserver.service
          └─180 /usr/bin/simpleserver -n

Jan 01 02:20:50 qemuarm systemd[1]: Started Simple server.
```

At this point, it will only start and stop on command, as shown here. To make it persistent, you need to add a permanent dependency to a target. This is the purpose of the [Install] section in the unit; it says that when this service is enabled, it will become dependent on multi-user.target, and so will be started at boot time. You enable it using systemctl enable, like this:

```
# systemctl enable simpleserver
Created symlink from /etc/systemd/system/multiuser.target.
wants/simpleserver.service to /etc/systemd/system/simpleserver.
service.
```

Now, you can see how services add dependencies without having to keep on editing target unit files. A target can have a directory named <target_name>.target.wants, which can contain links to services. This is exactly the same as adding the dependent unit to the [Wants] list in the target. In this case, you will find that this link has been created:

```
/etc/systemd/system/multi-user.target.wants/simpleserver.
service -> /etc/systemd/system/simpleserver.service
```

If this is an important service, you might want to restart it if it fails. You can accomplish that by adding this flag to the [Service] section:

```
Restart=on-abort
```

Other options for Restart are on-success, on-failure, on-abnormal, on-watchdog, on-abort, or always.

Adding a watchdog

Watchdogs are a common requirement in embedded devices: you need to take action if a critical service stops working, usually by resetting the system. On most embedded SoCs, there is a hardware watchdog, which can be accessed via the /dev/watchdog device node. The **watchdog** is initialized with a timeout at boot, and then must be reset within that period, otherwise the watchdog will be triggered, and the system will reboot. The interface with the watchdog driver is described in the kernel source in Documentation/watchdog and the code for the drivers is in drivers/watchdog.

A problem arises if there are two or more critical services that need to be protected by a watchdog. systemd has a useful feature that distributes the watchdog between multiple services.

systemd can be configured to expect a regular keepalive call from a service and take action if it is not received, creating a per-service software watchdog. For this to work, you have to add code to the daemon to send the keepalive messages. It needs to check for a non-zero value in the WATCHDOG_USEC environment variable, and then call sd_notify(false, "WATCHDOG=1") within this time (a period of half of the watchdog timeout is recommended). There are examples in the systemd source code.

To enable the watchdog in the service unit, add something like this to the [Service] section:

```
WatchdogSec=30s
Restart=on-watchdog
StartLimitInterval=5min
StartLimitBurst=4
StartLimitAction=reboot-force
```

In this example, the service expects a keepalive call every 30 seconds. If it fails to be delivered, the service will be restarted, but if it is restarted more than four times in 5 minutes, systemd will force an immediate reboot. Once again, there is a full description of these settings in the systemd.service(5) manual page.

A watchdog like this takes care of individual services, but what if systemd itself fails, the kernel crashes, or the hardware locks up? In those cases, we need to tell systemd to use the watchdog driver: just add RuntimeWatchdogSec=NN to /etc/systemd/system.conf.systemd, which will reset the watchdog within that period, and so the system will reset if systemd fails for some reason.

Implications for embedded Linux

systemd has a lot of features that are useful in embedded Linux, including many that I have not mentioned in this brief description, such as resource control using slices (which are described in the manual pages for systemd.slice(5) and systemd.resource-control(5)), device management (udev(7)), and system logging facilities (journald(5)).

You have to balance that with its size: even with a minimal build of just the core components, systemd, udevd, and journald, it is approaching 10 MiB of storage, including the shared libraries.

You also have to keep in mind that systemd development follows the kernel and glibc closely, so it will not work on a kernel and glibc more than a year or two older than the release of systemd.

Summary

Every Linux device needs an `init` program of some kind. If you are designing a system that only has to launch a small number of daemons at startup and remains fairly static after that, then BusyBox `init` is sufficient for your needs. It is usually a good choice if you are using Buildroot as the build system.

If, on the other hand, you have a system that has complex dependencies between services at boot time or runtime, and you have the storage space, then `systemd` would be the best choice. Even without the complexity, `systemd` has some useful features in the way it handles watchdogs, remote logging, and so on, so you should certainly give it serious thought.

Meanwhile, System V `init` lives on. It is well understood, and there are `init` scripts already in existence for every component that is important to us. It remains the default `init` for the Yocto Project reference distribution (Poky).

In terms of reducing boot time, `systemd` is faster than System V `init` for a similar workload. However, if you are looking for a very fast boot, neither beats the simple BusyBox `init` with minimal boot scripts.

In the next chapter, we will look closely at a lesser-known `init` system that is well suited for embedded Linux systems. BusyBox `runit` offers the power and flexibility of `systemd` without the added complexity and overhead. If Buildroot is your choice of build system and BusyBox `init` does not meet your needs, then there are many good reasons to consider BusyBox `runit` instead. We will learn what those reasons are and get more hands-on experience with Buildroot in the process.

Further reading

- *systemd System and Service Manager*: `https://www.freedesktop.org/wiki/Software/systemd/`

  There are a lot of useful links at the bottom of the page at the preceding URL.

14
Starting with BusyBox runit

In the previous chapter, we looked at the classic System V `init` and state-of-the-art `systemd` programs. We also touched on BusyBox's minimal `init` program. Now, it is time to look at BusyBox's implementation of the `runit` program. BusyBox `runit` strikes a sensible balance between the simplicity of System V `init` and the flexibility of `systemd`. For this reason, the full version of `runit` is used in popular modern Linux distributions like Void. While `systemd` may dominate the cloud, it is usually overkill for many embedded Linux systems. BusyBox `runit` offers advanced features such as service supervision and dedicated service logging without the complexity and overhead of `systemd`.

In this chapter, I will show you how to divide your system up into separate BusyBox `runit` services, each with its own directory and `run` script. Next, we will see how `check` scripts can be used to force some services to wait for other services to start. Then, we will add dedicated logging to a service and learn how to configure log rotation. Finally, we close with an example of one service sending a signal to another by writing to a named pipe. Unlike System V `init`, BusyBox `runit` services start concurrently rather than sequentially, which can speed up boot times dramatically. Your choice of `init` program has a noticeable impact on the behavior and user experience of your product.

In this chapter, we will cover the following topics:

- Getting BusyBox `runit`
- Creating service directories and files
- Service supervision
- Depending on other services
- Dedicated service logging
- Signaling a service

Technical requirements

To follow along with the examples, make sure you have the following:

- A Linux-based host system
- Etcher for Linux
- A microSD card reader and card
- A USB to TTL 3.3V serial cable
- A Raspberry Pi 4
- A 5V 3A USB-C power supply

You should have already installed the 2020.02.9 LTS release of Buildroot for *Chapter 6, Selecting a Build System*. If you have not, then refer to the *System requirements* section of *The Buildroot user manual* (`https://buildroot.org/downloads/manual/manual.html`) before installing Buildroot on your Linux host according to the instructions from *Chapter 6*.

All of the code for this chapter can be found in the `Chapter14` folder of the book's GitHub repository: `https://github.com/PacktPublishing/Mastering-Embedded-Linux-Programming-Third-Edition`.

Getting BusyBox runit

To prepare the system for this chapter, we need to do the following:

1. Navigate to the directory where you cloned Buildroot for *Chapter 6, Selecting a Build System*:

```
$ cd buildroot
```

2. Check to see if `runit` is provided by BusyBox:

```
$ grep Runit package/busybox/busybox.config
# Runit Utilities
```

   BusyBox `runit` was still an available option in the Buildroot 2020.02.9 LTS release at the time of writing. Revert to that tag if you can no longer find BusyBox `runit` in a later release.

3. Undo any changes and delete any untracked files or directories:

```
$ make clean
$ git checkout .
$ git clean --force -d
```

   Note that `git clean --force` will delete the Nova U-Boot patch and any other files that we added to Buildroot in previous exercises.

4. Create a new branch named `busybox-runit` to capture your work:

```
$ git checkout -b busybox-runit
```

5. Add BusyBox `runit` to a default configuration for the Raspberry Pi 4:

```
$ cd configs
$ cp raspberrypi4_64_defconfig rpi4_runit_defconfig
$ cd ..
$ cp package/busybox/busybox.config \
board/raspberrypi/busybox-runit.config
$ make rpi4_runit_defconfig
$ make menuconfig
```

6. From the main menu, drill down into the **Toolchain | Toolchain type** submenu and select **External toolchain**:

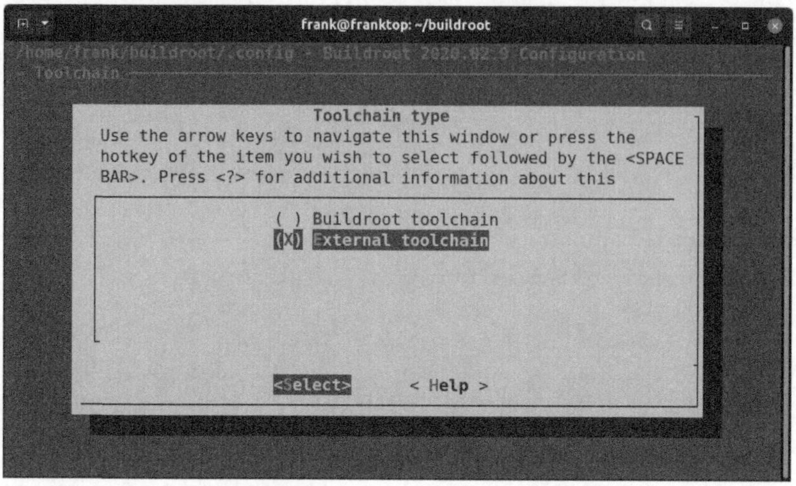

Figure 14.1 – Selecting External toolchain

7. Back out one level and drill down into the **Toolchain** submenu. Select the **Linaro AArch64** toolchain, then back out another level to return to the main menu:

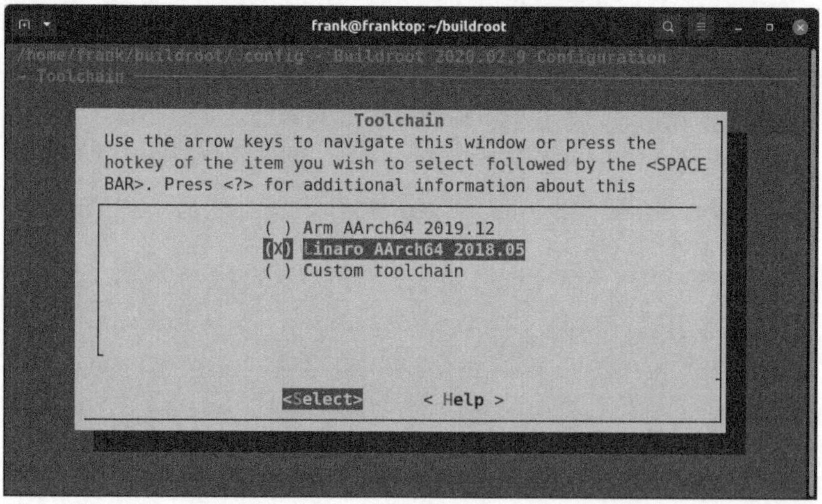

Figure 14.2 – Selecting the Linaro AArch64 toolchain

8. BusyBox should already be selected as the `init` system but you can confirm that by navigating to the **System configuration | Init system** submenu and observing that **BusyBox** is selected instead of **systemV** or **systemd**. Back out of the **Init system** submenu up to the main menu.

9. From the main menu, drill down into the **Target packages | BusyBox configuration file to use?** text field under **BusyBox**:

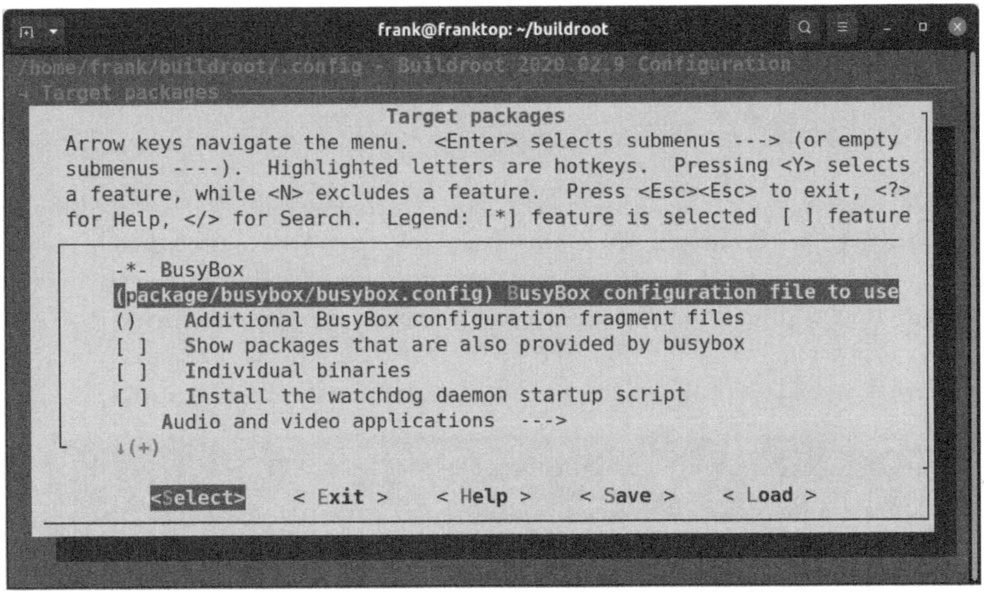

Figure 14.3 – Selecting a BusyBox configuration file to use

10. Replace the `package/busybox/busybox.config` string value in that text field with `board/raspberrypi/busybox-runit.config`:

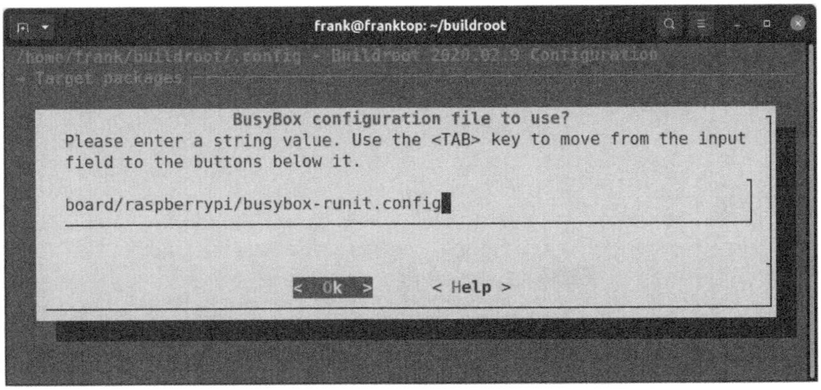

Figure 14.4 – BusyBox configuration file to use?

11. Exit out of `menuconfig` and choose **Yes** if asked to save your new configuration. Buildroot saves the new configuration to a file named `.config` by default.

12. Update `configs/rpi4_runit_defconfig` with the new location of the BusyBox configuration:

```
$ make savedefconfig
```

13. Now let's start configuring BusyBox for `runit`:

```
$ make busybox-menuconfig
```

14. Once inside `busybox-menuconfig`, you should notice a submenu called **Runit Utilities**. Drill down into that submenu and select all of the options on that menu page. The `chpst`, `setuidgid`, `envuidgid`, `envdir`, and `softlimit` utilities are command-line tools that are frequently referenced by service `run` scripts, so it is best to include them all. The `svc` and `svok` utilities are holdovers from `daemontools` so you can choose to opt out of them if you feel so inclined:

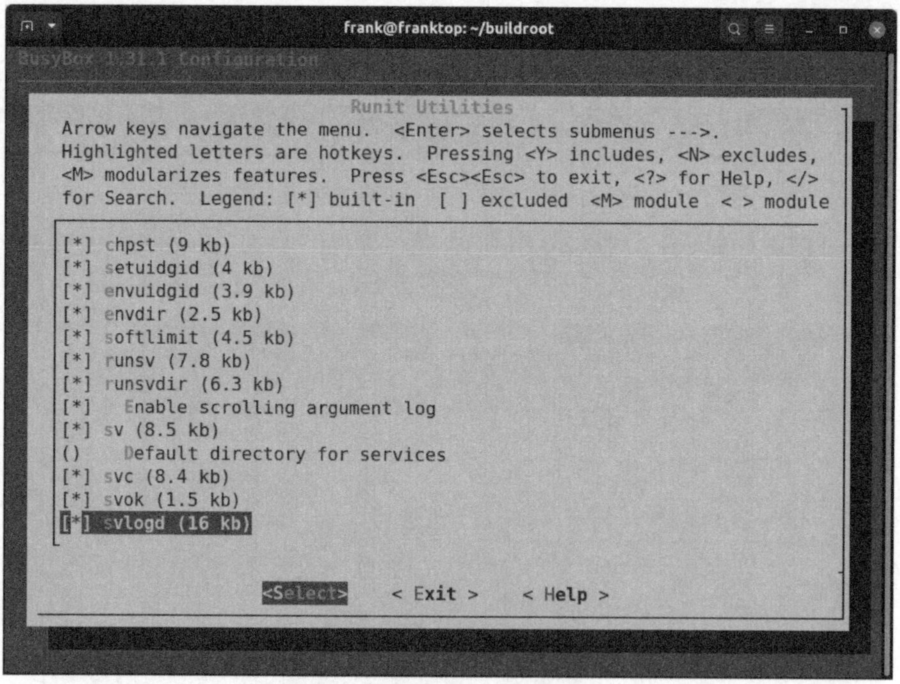

Figure 14.5 – Runit Utilities

15. From the **Runit Utilities** submenu, drill down into the **Default directory for services** text field.

16. Enter `/etc/sv` in the **Default directory for services** text field:

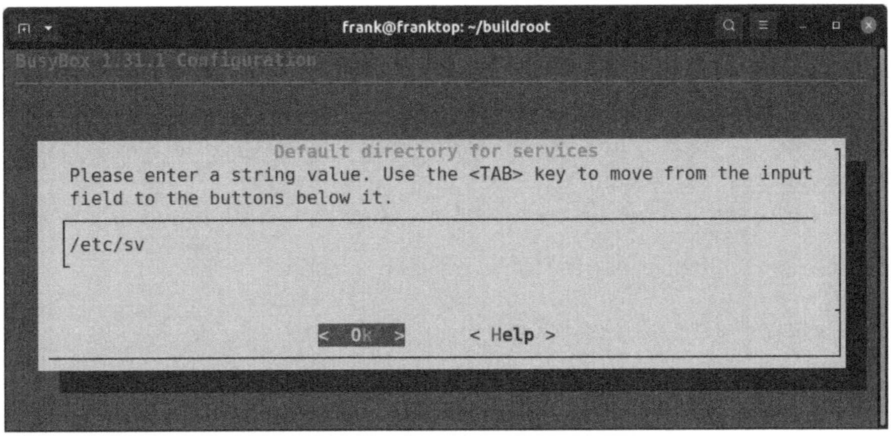

Figure 14.6 – Default directory for services

17. Exit out of `busybox-menuconfig` and choose **Yes** when asked to save your new configuration. Like the `menuconfig` option, `busybox-menuconfig` only saves your new BusyBox configuration to a `.config` file in an output directory. By default, the BusyBox output directory is `output/build/busybox-1.31.1` in the 2020.02.9 LTS version of Buildroot.
18. Save your changes to `board/raspberrypi/busybox-runit.config`:

```
$ make busybox-update-config
```

19. BusyBox includes an `inittab` file for its `init` program in Buildroot's `package/busybox` directory. This configuration file instructs BusyBox `init` to start user space by mounting various filesystems and linking file descriptors to `stdin`, `stdout`, and `stderr` device nodes. In order for BusyBox `init` to transfer control to BusyBox `runit`, we need to replace the following lines in `package/busybox/inittab`:

```
# now run any rc scripts
::sysinit:/etc/init.d/rcS
```

These lines need to be replaced with their BusyBox `runit` equivalents:

```
# now switch over to runit
null::respawn:runsvdir /etc/sv
```

20. We also need to remove the following lines from BusyBox's `inittab`:

```
# Stuff to do before rebooting
::shutdown:/etc/init.d/rcK
```

No replacement line is needed for the deleted `::shutdown` command since BusyBox `runit` automatically terminates the processes it supervises prior to reboot.

You now have new `configs/rpi4_runit_defconfig` and `board/raspberrypi/busybox-runit.config` files as well as a modified `package/busybox/inittab` file that you can use to enable BusyBox `runit` on a custom Linux image for the Raspberry Pi 4. Commit those three files to Git so that your work is not lost.

To build your custom image, use the following commands:

```
$ make rpi4_runit_defconfig
$ make
```

When the build is complete, a bootable image is written to an `output/images/sdcard.img` file. Flash this image onto a microSD card using Etcher, insert it into your Raspberry Pi 4, and power it up. The system won't do much besides boot because there are no services in `/etc/sv` for `runsvdir` to start yet.

To play around with BusyBox `runit`, attach a serial cable to your Raspberry Pi 4 and log in as `root` with no password. We did not add `connman` to this image so enter `/sbin/ifup -a` to bring up the Ethernet interface:

```
# /sbin/ifup -a
[  187.076662] bcmgenet: Skipping UMAC reset
[  187.151919] bcmgenet fd580000.genet: configuring instance for external RGMII (no delay)
udhcpc: started, v1.31.1
udhcpc: sending discover
[  188.191465] bcmgenet fd580000.genet eth0: Link is Down
udhcpc: sending discover
[  192.287490] bcmgenet fd580000.genet eth0: Link is Up - 1Gbps/Full - flow control rx/tx
udhcpc: sending discover
udhcpc: sending select for 192.168.1.130
udhcpc: lease of 192.168.1.130 obtained, lease time 86400
deleting routers
adding dns 192.168.1.254
```

We will examine the structure and layout of `runit` service directories in the next section.

Creating service directories and files

runit is a reimplementation of the daemontools process supervision kit. It was created by Gerrit Pape as a replacement for System V init and other Unix init schemes. At the time of writing, the two best sources of information on runit were Pape's website (http://smarden.org/runit/) and Void Linux's online documentation.

BusyBox's implementation of runit differs from standard runit mostly in terms of self-documentation. For example, sv --help makes no mention of the sv utility's start and check options, which are in fact supported by BusyBox's implementation. The source code for BusyBox runit can be found in BusyBox's output/build/busybox-1.31.1/runit directory. You can also browse the latest version of the BusyBox runit source code online at https://git.busybox.net/busybox/tree/runit. If there are any bugs in, or features missing from, BusyBox's implementation of runit, you can fix or add them by patching Buildroot's busybox package.

The Arch Linux distribution supports using BusyBox runit alongside systemd for simple process supervision. You can read more about how to do that on the Arch Linux Wiki. BusyBox defaults to init and the steps for replacing BusyBox init with runit are not documented. For these reasons, rather than replacing BusyBox init with runit, I will instead show you how to use BusyBox runit to add service supervision to BusyBox init.

Service directory layout

The following is a quote from the Void Linux distribution's original documentation (now deprecated) on runit:

> *"A service directory requires only one file, an executable named* run *which is expected to* exec *a process in the foreground."*

In addition to the requisite run script, a runit service directory can also contain a finish script, a check script, and a conf file. A finish script is run on service shutdown or process stop. The run script sources a conf file to set any environment variables prior to their use inside run.

The /etc/sv directory, like the BusyBox init /etc/init.d directory, is conventionally where runit services are stored. Here is a list of BusyBox init scripts for a simple embedded Linux system:

```
$ ls output/target/etc/init.d
S01syslogd  S02sysctl   S21haveged  S45connman  S50sshd  rcS
S02klogd    S20urandom  S30dbus     S49ntp      rcK
```

Buildroot supplies these BusyBox `init` scripts as part of the packages for various daemons. In the case of BusyBox `runit`, we have to produce these start scripts ourselves.

Here is the list of BusyBox `runit` services for the same system:

```
$ ls -D output/target/etc/sv
bluetoothd  dbus   haveged  ntpd  syslogd
connmand    dcron  klogd    sshd  watchdog
```

Each BusyBox `runit` service has its own directory with an executable `run` script inside of it. The BusyBox `init` scripts that are also on the target image will not run on startup because we removed `::sysinit:/etc/init.d/rcS` from `inittab`. Unlike `init` scripts, `run` scripts need to run in the foreground not the background in order to work with `runit`.

The Void Linux distribution is a treasure trove of `runit` service files. Here is a Void `run` script for `sshd`:

```
#!/bin/sh
# Will generate host keys if they don't already exist
ssh-keygen -A >/dev/null 2>&1
[ -r conf ] && . ./conf
exec /usr/sbin/sshd -D $OPTS 2>&1
```

The `runsvdir` utility starts and monitors the collection of services defined under the `/etc/sv` directory. For that reason, the `run` script for `sshd` needs to be installed as `/etc/sv/sshd/run` so that `runsvdir` can find it on startup. It also must be made executable or BusyBox `runit` won't be able to start it.

Contrast the contents of `/etc/sv/sshd/run` with this excerpt from Buildroot's `/etc/init.d/S50sshd`:

```
start() {
        # Create any missing keys
        /usr/bin/ssh-keygen -A

        printf "Starting sshd: "
        /usr/sbin/sshd
        touch /var/lock/sshd
        echo "OK"
}
```

sshd runs in the background by default. The -D option forces sshd to run in the foreground. runit expects you to preface foregrounded commands with exec in your run scripts. The exec command replaces the current program in the current process. The end result is that the ./run process started from /etc/sv/sshd becomes the /usr/sbin/sshd -D process without forking:

```
# ps aux | grep "[s]shd"
  201 root      runsv sshd
  209 root      /usr/sbin/sshd -D
```

Notice that the sshd run script sources a conf file for the $OPTS environment variable. If no conf file exists inside /etc/sv/sshd, then $OPTS is undefined and empty, which in this case happens to be fine. Like most runit services, sshd does not need a finish script to release any resources prior to system shutdown or reboot.

Service configuration

The init scripts that Buildroot includes in its packages are BusyBox init scripts. These init scripts need to be ported to BusyBox runit and installed to different directories under output/target/etc/sv. Rather than patch each package individually, I find it easier to bundle all the service files in a rootfs overlay or umbrella package outside of the Buildroot tree. Buildroot enables out-of-tree customizations by way of the BR2_EXTERNAL make variable, which points to a directory containing the customizations.

The most common way to get Buildroot into a br2-external tree is to embed it in the top level of a Git repo as a submodule:

```
$ cat .gitmodules
[submodule "buildroot"]
      path = buildroot
      url = git://git.buildroot.net/buildroot
      ignore = dirty
      branch = 15a05e6d5a875759d217d61b3c7b31ec87ea4eb5
```

Embedding Buildroot as a submodule simplifies the maintenance of any packages that you add or patches that you apply to Buildroot. The submodule is pinned to a tag so that any out-of-tree customizations remain stable until Buildroot is purposely upgraded. Notice that commit hash for the above `buildroot` submodule is pinned to the `2020.02.9` tag for that Buildroot LTS release:

```
$ cd buildroot
$ git show --summary
commit 15a05e6d5a875759d217d61b3c7b31ec87ea4eb5 (HEAD ->
busybox-runit, tag: 2020.02.9)
Author: Peter Korsgaard <peter@korsgaard.com>
Date:   Sun Dec 27 17:55:12 2020 +0100

    Update for 2020.02.9

    Signed-off-by: Peter Korsgaard <peter@korsgaard.com>
```

To run `make` when `buildroot` is a subdirectory of the parent `BR2_EXTERNAL` directory we need to pass some additional arguments:

```
$ make -C $(pwd)/buildroot BR2_EXTERNAL=$(pwd) O=$(pwd)/output
```

Here is the directory structure Buildroot recommends for a `br2-external` tree:

```
+-- board/
|   +-- <company>/
|       +-- <boardname>/
|           +-- linux.config
|           +-- busybox.config
|           +-- <other configuration files>
|           +-- post_build.sh
|           +-- post_image.sh
|           +-- rootfs_overlay/
|           |   +-- etc/
|           |   +-- <some file>
|           +-- patches/
|               +-- foo/
```

```
|                 |    +-- <some patch>
|                 +-- libbar/
|                      +-- <some other patches>
+-- configs/
|    +-- <boardname>_defconfig
+-- package/
|    +-- <company>/
|         +-- package1/
|         |    +-- Config.in
|         |    +-- package1.mk
|         +-- package2/
|              +-- Config.in
|              +-- package2.mk
+-- Config.in
+-- external.mk
+-- external.desc
```

Notice where the custom `rpi4_runit_defconfig` and `busybox-runit.config` files you created in the previous section would be inserted into this tree. According to Buildroot's guidelines, those two configs are supposed to be board-specific files. `<boardname>_defconfig` is prefixed with the name of the board the image is being configured for. `busybox.config` goes in a corresponding `board/<company>/<boardname>` directory. Also notice that the `rootfs_overlay/etc` directory where your custom BusyBox `inittab` would go is board-specific as well.

Since all the service configuration files for BusyBox `runit` reside in `/etc/sv`, it might seem reasonable to commit them all to a board-specific `rootfs` overlay. In my experience, this solution quickly becomes too inflexible. Oftentimes there is a need to configure more than one image for the same board. For instance, a consumer device may have separate development, production, and manufacturing images. Each image contains distinct services, so configuration needs to vary between images. For these reasons, service configuration is best done at the package level, not the board level. I use out-of-tree umbrella packages (one package for each type of image) to configure services for BusyBox `runit`.

At the top-level, a br2-external tree must contain external.desc, external.mk, and Config.in files. An external.desc file contains some basic metadata describing the br2-external tree:

```
$ cat external.desc
name: ACME
desc: Acme's external Buildroot tree
```

Buildroot sets the BR2_EXTERNAL_<name>_PATH variable to the absolute path of the br2-external tree so that variable can be referenced in Kconfig and makefiles. The desc field is an optional description made available as the BR2_EXTERNAL_<name>_DESC variable. Substitute <name> with ACME according to this external.desc.
An external.mk file typically only contains a single line referencing the BR2_EXTERNAL_<name>_PATH variable defined in external.desc:

```
$ cat external.mk
include $(sort $(wildcard $(BR2_EXTERNAL_ACME_PATH)/package/
acme/*/*.mk))
```

That include line tells Buildroot where to search for external package .mk files. The locations of the corresponding Config.in files for the external packages are defined in the top-level Config.in file for the br2-external tree:

```
$ cat Config.in
source "$BR2_EXTERNAL_ACME_PATH/package/acme/development/
Config.in"
source "$BR2_EXTERNAL_ACME_PATH/package/acme/manufacturing/
Config.in"
source "$BR2_EXTERNAL_ACME_PATH/package/acme/production/Config.
in"
```

Buildroot reads the br2-external tree's Config.in file and adds the package recipes contained therein to the top-level configuration menu. Let's fill in the rest of Buildroot's br2-external tree structure with the development, manufacturing, and production umbrella packages:

```
├── configs
│   ├── supergizmo_development_defconfig
│   ├── supergizmo_manufacturing_defconfig
│   └── supergizmo_production_defconfig
└── package
```

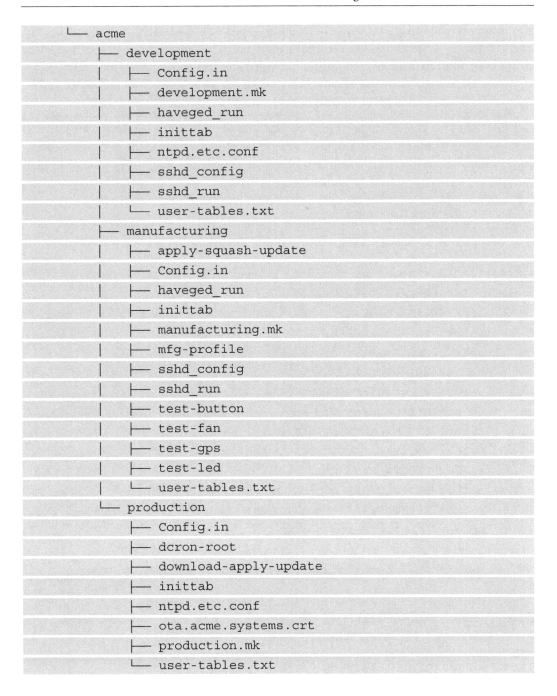

```
└── acme
    ├── development
    │   ├── Config.in
    │   ├── development.mk
    │   ├── haveged_run
    │   ├── inittab
    │   ├── ntpd.etc.conf
    │   ├── sshd_config
    │   ├── sshd_run
    │   └── user-tables.txt
    ├── manufacturing
    │   ├── apply-squash-update
    │   ├── Config.in
    │   ├── haveged_run
    │   ├── inittab
    │   ├── manufacturing.mk
    │   ├── mfg-profile
    │   ├── sshd_config
    │   ├── sshd_run
    │   ├── test-button
    │   ├── test-fan
    │   ├── test-gps
    │   ├── test-led
    │   └── user-tables.txt
    └── production
        ├── Config.in
        ├── dcron-root
        ├── download-apply-update
        ├── inittab
        ├── ntpd.etc.conf
        ├── ota.acme.systems.crt
        ├── production.mk
        └── user-tables.txt
```

If you compare this directory tree with Buildroot's previous one, you can see that `<boardname>` has been replaced with `supergizmo` and `<company>` has been replaced with `acme`. You can think of an umbrella package as an image overlay on top of some common base image. That way, all three images can share the same U-Boot, kernel, and drivers so that their changes only apply to user space.

Consider what packages need to be included on a device's development image for it to be effective. At a minimum, developers expect to be able to `ssh` into the device, execute commands with `sudo`, and edit onboard files with `vim`. Additionally, they want to be able to trace, debug, and profile their programs using tools such as `strace`, `gdb`, and `perf`. None of that software belongs on a device's production image for security reasons.

`Config.in` for the `development` umbrella package selects packages that should only be deployed to an in-house developer's preproduction hardware:

```
$ cat package/acme/development/Config.in
config BR2_PACKAGE_DEVELOPMENT
	bool "development"
	select BR2_PACKAGE_HAVEGED
	select BR2_PACKAGE_OPENSSH
	select BR2_PACKAGE_SUDO
	select BR2_PACKAGE_TMUX
	select BR2_PACKAGE_VIM
	select BR2_PACKAGE_STRACE
	select BR2_PACKAGE_LINUX_TOOLS_PERF
	select BR2_PACKAGE_GDB
	select BR2_PACKAGE_GDB_SERVER
	select BR2_PACKAGE_GDB_DEBUGGER
	select BR2_PACKAGE_GDB_TUI
	help
	  The development image overlay for Acme's SuperGizmo.
```

The different service scripts and configuration files get written to the `output/target` directory during the install step of the package build process. Here is the relevant excerpt from `package/acme/development/development.mk`:

```
define DEVELOPMENT_INSTALL_TARGET_CMDS
	$(INSTALL) -D -m 0644 $(@D)/inittab $(TARGET_DIR)/etc/
inittab
	$(INSTALL) -D -m 0755 $(@D)/haveged_run $(TARGET_DIR)/etc/
```

```
sv/haveged/run
	$(INSTALL) -D -m 0755 $(@D)/sshd_run $(TARGET_DIR)/etc/sv/
sshd/run
	$(INSTALL) -D -m 0644 $(@D)/sshd_config $(TARGET_DIR)/etc/
ssh/sshd_config
endef
```

Buildroot `<package>.mk` files contain `<package>_BUILD_CMDS` and `<package>_INSTALL_TARGET_CMDS` sections. This umbrella package is named `development` so the install macro for it is defined as `DEVELOPMENT_INSTALL_TARGET_CMDS`. The `<package>` prefix needs to match the `<package>` suffix in the `config BR2_<package>` line of the package's `Config.in` file or the macro names will result in package build errors.

The `haveged/run` and `sshd/run` scripts are installed to the `/etc/sv` directory on the target. The custom `inittab` needed to start `runsvdir` is installed to `/etc` on the target. Unless these files are installed in their right place with their intended permissions, BusyBox `runit` cannot start the `haveged` or `sshd` services.

`haveged` is a software random number generator meant to alleviate low-entropy conditions in the Linux `/dev/random` device. Low-entropy conditions can block `sshd` from starting because the SSH protocol relies heavily on random numbers. Some newer SoCs may not yet have kernel support for their hardware random number generators. Without also running `haveged` on these systems, `sshd` can take several minutes to begin accepting connections after booting.

Running `haveged` under BusyBox `runit` is quite simple:

```
$ cat package/acme/development/haveged_run
#!/bin/sh
exec /usr/sbin/haveged -w 1024 -r 0 -F
```

The `production` and `manufacturing` umbrella packages superimpose different sets of packages and services onto the image. The `production` image includes tools for downloading and applying software updates. The `manufacturing` image includes tools that factory technicians would use to provision and test the hardware. BusyBox `runit` is also a good fit for both of those use cases.

`Config.in` for the `production` umbrella package selects packages that are needed for periodic over-the-air software updates:

```
$ cat package/acme/production/Config.in
config BR2_PACKAGE_PRODUCTION
```

```
        bool "production"
        select BR2_PACKAGE_DCRON
        select BR2_PACKAGE_LIBCURL
        select BR2_PACKAGE_LIBCURL_CURL
        select BR2_PACKAGE_LIBCURL_VERBOSE
        select BR2_PACKAGE_JQ
        help
          The production image overlay for Acme's SuperGizmo.
```

Forced OTA updates are often undesirable in development and manufacturing environments, so these packages are excluded from those images. The `production` image includes a `download-apply-update` script that uses `curl` to query an OTA server for a newly available software update. A public SSL certificate is also included onboard so `curl` can verify the authenticity of the OTA server. The `dcron` daemon is configured to run `download-apply-update` every 10 to 20 minutes with some noise to avoid the stampeding herd. If a newer update is available, the script then downloads the image, verifies it, and applies it to the microSD card before rebooting. Here is the relevant excerpt from `package/acme/production/production.mk`:

```
define PRODUCTION_INSTALL_TARGET_CMDS
      $(INSTALL) -D -m 0644 $(@D)/inittab $(TARGET_DIR)/etc/
inittab
      $(INSTALL) -D -m 0644 $(@D)/dcron-root $(TARGET_DIR)/etc/
cron.d/root
      $(INSTALL) -D -m 0775 $(@D)/download-apply-update
$(TARGET_DIR)/usr/sbin/download-apply-update
      $(INSTALL) -D -m 0644 $(@D)/ota.acme.com.crt $(TARGET_
DIR)/etc/ssl/certs/ota.acme.com.crt
      $(INSTALL) -D -m 0644 $(@D)/ntpd.etc.conf $(TARGET_DIR)/
etc/ntp.conf
endef
```

Build the `production` image `cd` to the root of the `br2-external` tree and issue the following commands:

```
$ make clean
$ make supergizmo_production_defconfig
$ make
```

The steps for building the development and manufacturing images for the Acme SuperGizmo differ only in the choice of defconfig. The three defconfigs are almost identical except for the last line, which is either BR2_PACKAGE_DEVELOPMENT=y, BR2_PACKAGE_PRODUCTION=y, or BR2_PACKAGE_MANUFACTURING=y depending on the choice of image. The three umbrella packages are meant to be mutually exclusive so do not select more than one umbrella package for inclusion in the same image or you are likely to encounter unexpected results.

Service supervision

Once we have created service directories with run scripts under /etc/sv and ensured that BusyBox init starts runsvdir, BusyBox runit handles all the rest. That includes starting, stopping, monitoring, and restarting all the services under its control. The runsvdir utility starts a runsv process for each service directory and restarts a runsv process if it terminates. Because run scripts run their respective daemons in the foreground, runsv expects run to block so that when run exits, runsv will restart it automatically.

Service auto-restart is desirable during system startup because run scripts can crash. This is especially true under BusyBox runit where services start virtually simultaneously instead of one after the other. For instance, a service may fail to start when a dependent service or essential system resource (such as a GPIO or device driver) is not yet available. In the next section, I will show you how to express dependencies between services so that your system startup sequence remains deterministic.

Here are the runsv processes running on our simple embedded Linux system:

```
# ps aux | grep "[r]unsv"
  177 root      runsvdir /etc/sv
  179 root      runsv ntpd
  180 root      runsv haveged
  181 root      runsv syslogd
  182 root      runsv dcron
  185 root      runsv dbus
  187 root      runsv bluetoothd
  192 root      runsv watchdog
  195 root      runsv connmand
  199 root      runsv sshd
  202 root      runsv klogd
```

Notice that the `runsvdir /etc/sv` command in the `inittab` does not execute until PID 177. The process with PID 1 is `/sbin/init`, which is just a symbolic link pointing to `/bin/busybox`. PIDs 2 to 176 (not shown) are all kernel threads and system services so their commands appear inside square brackets when displayed by `ps`. Square brackets mean that a process does not have an actual command line associated with it. Since `connmand` and `bluetoothd` both depend on D-Bus to start, `runsv` may have restarted either service multiple times before D-Bus is up and running:

```
# pstree -a
init
  |-getty -L 115200 ttyS0
  |-hciattach /dev/ttyAMA0 bcm43xx 921600 flow -
60:81:f9:b0:8a:02
  |-runsvdir /etc/sv
  |   |-runsv ntpd
  |   |   `-ntpd -u ntp -c /etc/ntp.conf -U 60 -g -n
  |   |       `-{ntpd}
  |   |-runsv haveged
  |   |   `-haveged -w 1024 -r 0 -F
  |   |-runsv syslogd
  |   |   `-syslogd -n -O /var/data/log/messages -b 99 -s 1000
  |   |-runsv dcron
  |   |-runsv dbus
  |   |   `-dbus-daemon --system --nofork --nopidfile --syslog-
only
  |   |-runsv bluetoothd
  |   |   `-bluetoothd -E --noplugin=* -n
  |   |-runsv watchdog
  |   |   `-watchdog -T 10 -F /dev/watchdog
  |   |-runsv connmand
  |   |   `-connmand -n
  |   |-runsv sshd
  |   |   `-sshd -D
  |   `-runsv klogd
  |       `-klogd -n
  `-wpa_supplicant -u
```

Some services require a connection to the internet before they can start. This can delay service start by several seconds due to the asynchronous nature of DHCP. Since connmand manages all the network interfaces on this system, these services in turn depend on connmand. If the IP address of the device changes due to switching between networks or renewal of the DHCP lease, many of these same services may need to be restarted. Fortunately, BusyBox runit offers a way to restart services easily from the command line.

Controlling services

BusyBox runit provides an sv command-line tool for managing and inspecting services:

```
# sv --help
BusyBox v1.31.1 () multi-call binary.

Usage: sv [-v] [-w SEC] CMD SERVICE_DIR...

Control services monitored by runsv supervisor.
Commands (only first character is enough):

status: query service status
up: if service isn't running, start it. If service stops, 
restart it
once: like 'up', but if service stops, don't restart it
down: send TERM and CONT signals. If ./run exits, start ./
finish
     if it exists. After it stops, don't restart service
exit: send TERM and CONT signals to service and log service. If 
they exit,
     runsv exits too
pause, cont, hup, alarm, interrupt, quit, 1, 2, term, kill: 
send
STOP, CONT, HUP, ALRM, INT, QUIT, USR1, USR2, TERM, KILL signal 
to service
```

The help message for sv explains what the up, once, down, and exit commands do. It also illustrates how the pause, cont, hup, alarm, interrupt, quit, 1, 2, term, and kill commands map directly to POSIX signals. Notice that the first character of each command is enough to invoke it.

Let's experiment with various `sv` commands using `ntpd` as our target service. Your status times will vary from mine depending on how long you wait between commands:

1. Restart the `ntpd` service:

```
# sv t /etc/sv/ntpd
# sv s /etc/sv/ntpd
run: /etc/sv/ntpd: (pid 1669) 6s
```

   The `sv t` command restarts a service and the `sv s` command gets its status. The `t` is short for `term` so `sv t` sends a service the `TERM` signal before restarting it. The status message says that `ntpd` has been running for 6 seconds since restarting.

2. Now let's see what happens to the status when we use `sv d` to stop the `ntpd` service:

```
# sv d /etc/sv/ntpd
# sv s /etc/sv/ntpd
down: /etc/sv/ntpd: 7s, normally up
```

   This time, the status message says that `ntpd` has been down for 7 seconds since it was stopped.

3. Start the `ntpd` service back up:

```
# sv u /etc/sv/ntpd
# sv s /etc/sv/ntpd
run: /etc/sv/ntpd: (pid 2756) 5s
```

   The status message now says that `ntpd` has been running for 5 seconds since starting. Notice that the PID is higher than before because the system has been running for some time since `ntpd` was restarted.

4. Do a one-off start of `ntpd`:

```
# sv o /etc/sv/ntpd
# sv s /etc/sv/ntpd
run: /etc/sv/ntpd: (pid 3795) 3s, want down
```

   The `sv o` command is like `sv u` except that the target service does not restart again if it stops. You can confirm that by sending a `KILL` signal to the `ntpd` service using `sv k /etc/sv/ntpd` and observing that the `ntpd` service goes down and stays down.

Here are the long forms of the sv commands we covered:

```
# sv term /etc/sv/ntpd
# sv status /etc/sv/ntpd
# sv down /etc/sv/ntpd
# sv up /etc/sv/ntpd
# sv once /etc/sv/ntpd
```

If a service needs conditional error or signal handling, you can define that logic inside a `finish` script. A service `finish` script is optional and executes whenever `run` exits. A `finish` script takes two arguments: `$1`, an exit code from `run`, and `$2`, the least significant byte of the exit status as determined by the `waitpid` system call. The exit code from `run` is 0 when `run` exits normally and -1 when `run` exits abnormally. The status byte is 0 when `run` exits normally and the signal number when `run` is terminated by a signal. If `runsv` is unable to start `run`, then the exit code is 1 and the status byte is 0.

A service that detects IP address changes could restart network services by shelling out to `sv t`. This is similar to what `ifplugd` does except that `ifplugd` triggers on Ethernet link state instead of IP address changes. Such a service could be as simple as a shell script comprised of a single `while` loop that continuously polls all the network interfaces. You can also issue `sv` commands from a `run` or `finish` script as a way to communicate between services. I will show you how to do that in the next section.

Depending on other services

I mentioned how some services like `connmand` and `bluetoothd` require D-Bus. D-Bus is a message system bus that enables publish-subscribe interprocess communication. The Buildroot package for D-Bus provides a system `dbus-daemon` and a reference `libdbus` library. The `libdbus` library implements the low-level D-Bus C API but higher-level bindings to `libdbus` exist for other languages like Python. Some languages also offer alternative implementations of the D-Bus protocol that do not depend on `libdbus` at all. D-Bus services such as `connmand` and `bluetoothd` expect the system `dbus-daemon` to already be running before they can start.

Start dependencies

The official runit documentation recommends using sv start to express dependencies on other services under the control of runit. To make sure D-Bus is available before connmand starts, you should define your /etc/sv/connmand/run accordingly:

```
#!/bin/sh
/bin/sv start /etc/sv/dbus > /dev/null || exit 1
exec /usr/sbin/connmand -n
```

sv start /etc/sv/dbus attempts to start the system dbus-daemon if it is not already running. The sv start command is like sv up except that it will wait up to however many seconds are specified by the -w argument or SVWAIT environment variable for the service to start. The default maximum wait time when no -w argument or SVWAIT environment variable is defined is 7 seconds. If the service is already up, it returns an exit code of 0 for success. An exit code of 1 indicates failure causing /etc/sv/connmand/run to exit prematurely without starting connmand. The runsv process that monitors connmand will continue trying to start the service until it eventually succeeds.

Here is our corresponding /etc/sv/dbus/run, which I derived from Void's:

```
#!/bin/sh
[ ! -d /var/run/dbus ] && /bin/install -m755 -g 22 -o 22 -d /
var/run/dbus
[ -d /tmp/dbus ] || /bin/mkdir -p /tmp/dbus
exec /bin/dbus-daemon --system --nofork --nopidfile --syslog-
only
```

Contrast that with the following excerpt from Buildroot's /etc/init.d/S30dbus:

```
# Create needed directories.
[ -d /var/run/dbus ] || mkdir -p /var/run/dbus
[ -d /var/lock/subsys ] || mkdir -p /var/lock/subsys
[ -d /tmp/dbus ] || mkdir -p /tmp/dbus
RETVAL = 0
start() {
    printf "Starting system message bus: "
    dbus-uuidgen --ensure
    dbus-daemon --system
    RETVAL=$?
```

```
    echo "done"
    [ $RETVAL -eq 0 ] && touch /var/lock/subsys/dbus-daemon
}

stop() {
    printf "Stopping system message bus: "
    ## we don't want to kill all the per-user $processname, we
want
    ## to use the pid file *only*; because we use the fake
nonexistent
    ## program name "$servicename" that should be safe-ish
    killall dbus-daemon
    RETVAL=$?
    echo "done"
    if [ $RETVAL -eq 0 ]; then
        rm -f /var/lock/subsys/dbus-daemon
        rm -f /var/run/messagebus.pid
    fi
}
```

Notice how much more complex Buildroot's version of the D-Bus service script is. Because `runit` runs the `dbus-daemon` in the foreground, there is no need for `lock` or `pid` files and all the ceremony associated with those. You might presume that the preceding `stop()` function makes for a good `finish` script except that in the case of `runit`, there is no `dbus-daemon` to kill or `pid` or `lock` files to delete. Service `finish` scripts are optional in `runit` so they should only be reserved for meaningful work.

Custom start dependencies

If a `check` exists in the `/etc/sv/dbus` directory, `sv` runs this script to check whether or not the service is available. A service is considered to be available if `check` exits with 0. The `check` mechanism enables you to express additional postconditions for a service being available besides a running process. For example, just because `connmand` has started does not mean that a connection to the internet has necessarily been established. `check` scripts ensure that a service completes what it was intended to do before other services can start.

To verify whether Wi-Fi is up or not, you could define the following check:

```
#!/bin/sh
WIFI_STATE=$(cat /sys/class/net/wlan0/operstate)
"$WIFI_STATE" = "up" || exit 1
exit 0
```

By installing the preceding script to /etc/sv/connmand/check, you make Wi-Fi a requirement for the connmand service to start. That way, when you issue sv start /etc/sv/connmand, the command only returns an exit code of 0 if the Wi-Fi interface is up even if connmand is running.

You can execute check scripts without starting a service using the sv check command. Like sv start, if check exists in the service directory, sv runs this script to determine whether or not the service is available. A service is considered available if check exits with 0. sv will wait up to 7 seconds for check to return with an exit code of 0. Unlike sv start, if check returns a nonzero exit code, sv does not attempt to start the service.

Putting it all together

We have seen how the sv start and check mechanisms enable us to express start dependencies between services. Combining these features with finish scripts enables us to construct process supervision trees. For example, a service that acts as a parent process could call sv down to bring down its dependent child services when it stops. This advanced level of customization is what I believe makes BusyBox runit so powerful. You can tailor your system to behave just how you want it to using only simple, well-defined shell scripts. To learn more about supervision trees, I recommend the literature on Erlang fault tolerance.

Dedicated service logging

A dedicated service logger only logs the output coming from a single daemon. Dedicated logging is nice because diagnostic data for different services is distributed across separate log files. The monolithic log files generated by centralized system loggers such as syslogd are often hard to untangle. Both forms of logging have their purpose: dedicated logging excels at readability and centralized logging offers context. Your services can each have their own dedicated loggers and still write to syslog so you sacrifice neither.

How does it work?

Because service `run` scripts run in the foreground, adding a dedicated logger to a service only involves redirecting standard output from a service's `run` to a log file. You enable dedicated service logging by creating a `log` subdirectory inside the target service directory with another `run` script inside of it. This additional `run` is for the service's logger, not the service itself. When this `log` directory exists, a pipe is opened from the output of the `run` process in the service directory to the input of the `run` process in the `log` directory.

Here is a possible service directory layout for `sshd`:

```
# tree etc/sv/sshd
etc/sv/sshd
|-- finish
|-- log
|   `-- run
`-- run
```

More precisely, when the BusyBox `runit` `runsv` process encounters this service directory layout, it does several things in addition to starting `sshd/run` and `sshd/finish` if and when necessary:

1. Creates a pipe
2. Redirects standard out from `run` and `finish` to the pipe
3. Switches to the `log` directory
4. Starts `log/run`
5. Redirects the standard input of `log/run` to read from the pipe

`runsv` starts and monitors `sshd/log/run` just like it starts and monitors `sshd/run`. Once you add a logger for `sshd`, you'll notice that `sv d /etc/sv/sshd` only stops `sshd`. To stop the logger, you must enter `sv d /etc/sv/sshd/log` unless you add that command to the `/etc/sv/sshd/finish` script.

Adding dedicated logging to a service

BusyBox `runit` provides an `svlogd` logging daemon for use in your `log/run` scripts:

```
# svlogd --help
BusyBox v1.31.1 () multi-call binary.

```

```
Usage: svlogd [-tttv] [-r C] [-R CHARS] [-l MATCHLEN] [-b
BUFLEN] DIR...

Read log data from stdin and write to rotated log files in DIRs

-r C        Replace non-printable characters with C
-R CHARS    Also replace CHARS with C (default _)
-t          Timestamp with @tai64n
-tt         Timestamp with yyyy-mm-dd_hh:mm:ss.sssss
-ttt        Timestamp with yyyy-mm-ddThh:mm:ss.sssss
-v          Verbose
```

Notice that `svlogd` requires one or more `DIR` output directory paths as arguments.

To add dedicated logging to an existing BusyBox `runit` service, do the following:

1. Create a `log` subdirectory inside the service directory.
2. Create a `run` script inside the `log` subdirectory.
3. Make that `run` script executable.
4. Use `exec` to run `svlogd` inside `run`.

Here is an `/etc/sv/sshd/log/run` script from Void:

```
#!/bin/sh
[ -d /var/log/sshd ] || mkdir -p /var/log/sshd
exec chpst -u root:adm svlogd -t /var/log/sshd
```

Since `svlogd` will write `sshd` log files to `/var/log/sshd`, we first need to create that directory if it does not already exist. For `sshd` log files to persist, you may need to modify your `inittab` to mount `/var` to a writable flash partition on boot up before starting `runsvdir`. The `chpst -u root:adm` portion of the `exec` ensures that `svlogd` runs with `root` user and `adm` group privileges and permissions.

The `-t` option prefixes each line written to the log file with a TAI64N-formatted timestamp. While TAI64N timestamps are precise, they are not the most human-readable. The other timestamp options `svlogd` provides are `-tt` and `-ttt`. Some daemons write their own timestamps to standard out. To avoid writing lines with confusing double timestamps, simply omit `-t` or any of its variants from your `log/run svlogd` command.

You may be tempted to add a dedicated logger to the `klogd` and `syslogd` services. Resist that temptation. `klogd` and `syslogd` are system-wide logging daemons and they are both very good at what they do. There is really no point in logging what a logger is doing unless it is malfunctioning and you need to debug it. If you develop a service that logs to both `stdout` and `syslog`, make sure to exclude timestamps from the `syslog` message text. The `syslog` protocol includes a `timestamp` field for you to embed timestamps.

Each dedicated logger runs in its own separate process. The extra overhead needed to support these additional logger processes is something to consider when designing your embedded system. If you intend to use BusyBox `runit` to supervise numerous services on a resource-constrained system, be selective about which services to add dedicated logging to, otherwise responsiveness may suffer.

Log rotation

`svlogd` rotates log files automatically using a default of 10 log files each up to 1 million bytes in size. Recall that these rotated log files are written out to one or more `DIR` output directories paths passed into `svlogd` as arguments. Of course, these rotation settings are configurable, but before I get into that, let me explain how log rotation works.

Let's assume that `svlogd` somehow knows about two values named `NUM` and `SIZE`. `NUM` is the number of log files to retain. `SIZE` is the maximum size of a log file. `svlogd` appends log messages to a log file named `current`. When the size of `current` reaches `SIZE` bytes, then `svlogd` rotates `current`.

To rotate the `current` file, `svlogd` will do the following:

1. Close the `current` log file.
2. Make `current` read-only.
3. Rename `current` to `@<timestamp>.s`.
4. Create a new `current` log file and start writing to it.
5. Count the number of existing log files besides `current`.
6. Delete the oldest log file if `count` is equal to or exceeds `NUM`.

`<timestamp>` used to rename the `current` log file that is being rotated out is the timestamp at the time of file rotation, not creation.

Now observe the descriptions of SIZE, NUM, and PATTERN here:

```
# svlogd --help
BusyBox v1.31.1 () multi-call binary.
[Usage not shown]
DIR/config file modifies behavior:
sSIZE - when to rotate logs (default 1000000, 0 disables)
nNUM - number of files to retain
!PROG - process rotated log with PROG
+,-PATTERN - (de)select line for logging
E,ePATTERN - (de)select line for stderr
```

These settings are read from a DIR/config file if it exists. Notice that a SIZE of 0 disables log rotation and is not the default. Here is a DIR/config file that causes svlogd to keep up to 100 log files each up to 9,999,999 bytes in size for a total of roughly 1 GB in rotating logs written to one output directory:

```
s9999999
n100
```

If multiple DIR output directories are passed to svlogd, then svlogd logs to all of them. Why would you want to log the same messages to more than one directory? The answer is that you *don't* log the same messages to multiple directories. Since every output directory has its own config file, you use pattern matching to select which messages to log to which output directory.

Assuming PATTERN of length N, if a line in DIR/config starts with +, -, E, or e, svlogd matches the first N characters of each log message against PATTERN accordingly. The + and - prefixes apply to current and the E and e prefixes apply to standard error. +PATTERN selects and -PATTERN filters out matching lines for logging to current. EPATTERN selects and ePATTERN filters out matching lines for alerting to standard error.

Signaling a service

Earlier, in the *Start dependencies* section, I showed how the sv command-line tool can be used to control a service. Later on, I demonstrated how the sv start and sv down commands can be used inside run and finish scripts to communicate between services. You may have already guessed that runsv is sending POSIX signals to the run processes that it supervises when an sv command executes. But what you may not have known is that the sv tool controls its target runsv process over a named pipe. The named pipes supervise/control and optionally log/supervise/control are opened so that other processes can send commands to runsv. Signaling a service is easy with sv commands, but if you want to, you can bypass sv entirely and write control characters directly to the control pipe(s).

The runtime directory layout of a service with no dedicated logging looks like this:

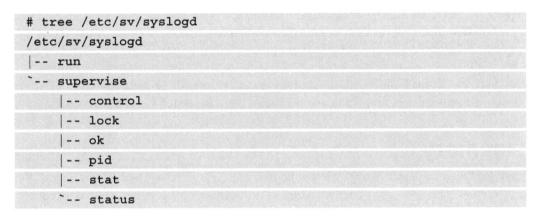

```
# tree /etc/sv/syslogd
/etc/sv/syslogd
|-- run
`-- supervise
    |-- control
    |-- lock
    |-- ok
    |-- pid
    |-- stat
    `-- status
```

The control file under /etc/sv/syslogd is the service's named pipe. The pid and stat files contain the live PID and status values (run or down) of the service. The supervise subdirectory and all of its contents are created and populated by runsv syslogd when the system starts up. If a service includes a dedicated logger, runsv will generate a supervise subdirectory for that as well.

The following control characters (`t`, `d`, `u`, and `o`) map directly to short forms of `sv` commands (`term`, `down`, `up`, and `once`) we have already encountered:

- `t term`: Sends the process a `TERM` signal before restarting the service.
- `d down`: Sends the process a `TERM` signal followed by a `CONT` signal and does not restart it.
- `u up`: Starts a service and restarts it if process exits.
- `o once`: Tries to start a service for up to 7 seconds and does not restart it afterward.
- `1`: Sends the process a `USR1` signal.
- `2`: Sends the process a `USR2` signal.

Control characters `1` and `2` are of special interest because they correspond to user-defined signals. It is up to the service on the receiving end to decide how to respond to `USR1` and `USR2` signals. If you are the developer tasked with extending a service, you can do that by implementing signal handlers. Two user-defined signals may not seem like much to work with, but if you combine these distinct events with updates written to a configuration file(s) you can achieve a lot. User-defined signals have the added advantage of not needing to stop or terminate a running process like the `STOP`, `TERM`, and `KILL` signals do.

Summary

This chapter was a deep dive into a lesser-known `init` system that I feel is largely underappreciated. Like `systemd`, BusyBox `runit` can enforce complex dependencies between services both during boot and at runtime. It just does it in a much simpler and I would argue more Unix-like way than `systemd` does. Plus, nothing beats BusyBox `runit` when it comes to boot times. If you are already using Buildroot as your build system, then I strongly encourage you to consider BusyBox `runit` for your device's `init` system.

We covered a lot of ground in our exploration. First, you learned how to get BusyBox `runit` onto your device and start it using Buildroot. Then I showed you how you can assemble and configure services together in different ways using out-of-tree umbrella packages. Next, we experimented with a live process supervision tree before delving into service dependencies and ways to express them. After that, I showed you how to add a dedicated logger and configure log rotation for a service. Lastly, I described how services can write to existing named pipes as a way to send signals to each other.

In the next chapter, I will turn my attention to the power management of Linux systems with the aim of showing how to reduce energy consumption. This will be especially useful if you are designing devices that run on battery power.

Further reading

Here are the various resources mentioned throughout the chapter:

- *The Buildroot user manual*: `http://nightly.buildroot.org/manual.html#customize`
- *runit documentation* by Gerrit Pape: `http://smarden.org/runit/`
- *Void Handbook*: `https://docs.voidlinux.org/config/services`
- *Adopting Erlang* by Tristan Sloughter, Fred Hebert, and Evan Vigil-McClanahan: `https://adoptingerlang.org/docs/development/supervision_trees`

15
Managing Power

For devices operating on battery power, power management is critical: anything we can do to reduce power usage will increase battery life. Even for devices running on mains power, reducing power usage has benefits in reducing the need for cooling and energy costs. In this chapter, I will introduce the four principles of power management:

- Don't rush if you don't have to.
- Don't be ashamed of being idle.
- Turn off things you are not using.
- Sleep when there is nothing else to do.

Putting these into more technical terms, the principles mean that the power management system should endeavor to reduce the CPU clock frequency. During idle periods, it should choose the deepest sleep state possible; it should reduce the load by powering down unused peripherals and it should be able to put the whole system into a suspended state while ensuring power state transitions are quick.

Linux has features that address each of these points. I will describe each one in turn, with examples and advice on how to apply them to an embedded system in order to make optimum use of power.

Some of the terminologies of system power management are taken from the **Advanced Configuration and Power Interface** (**ACPI**) specification: terms such as **C-states** and **P-states**. I will describe these as we get to them. The full reference to the specification is given in the *Further reading* section.

In this chapter, we will specifically cover the following topics:

- Measuring power usage
- Scaling the clock frequency
- Selecting the best idle state
- Powering down peripherals
- Putting the system to sleep

Technical requirements

To follow along with the examples, make sure you have the following:

- A Linux-based system
- Etcher for Linux
- A microSD card reader and card
- A USB to TTL 3.3V serial cable
- A BeagleBone Black
- A 5V 1A DC power supply
- An Ethernet cable and port for network connectivity

All of the code for this chapter can be found in the `Chapter15` folder from the book's GitHub repository: `https://github.com/PacktPublishing/Mastering-Embedded-Linux-Programming-Third-Edition`.

Measuring power usage

For the examples in this chapter, we need to use real hardware rather than virtual. This means that we need a BeagleBone Black with working power management. Unfortunately, the BSP for the BeagleBone that comes with the `meta-yocto-bsp` layer does not include the necessary firmware for the **Power Management IC** (**PMIC**), so we will use a pre-built Debian image instead. The missing firmware might exist in the `meta-ti` layer, but I did not investigate that. The procedure for installing Debian on the BeagleBone Black is the same as what we covered in *Chapter 12, Prototyping with Breakout Boards*, except for the Debian version.

To download the Debian Stretch IoT microSD card image for the BeagleBone Black, issue the following command:

```
$ wget https://debian.beagleboard.org/images/bone-debian-9.9-
iot-armhf-2019-08-03-4gb.img.xz
```

10.3 (aka Buster) was the latest Debian image for AM335x-based BeagleBones at the time of writing. We will use Debian 9.9 for the exercises in this chapter because the Linux kernel included with Debian 10.3 is missing some power management features. When the Debian Stretch IoT image to a microSD card is done downloading, use Etcher to write it to a microSD card.

> **Important note**
>
> If possible, download version 9.9 (aka Stretch) of Debian rather than the latest Debian image from `BeagleBoard.org` for the exercises in this chapter. The CPUIdle driver is missing from version 10.3 of Debian so the `menu` and `ladder` CPUIdle governors are missing from that version of the distribution. If version 9.9 is no longer available or supported, then download and try a newer version of Debian than 10.3 from `BeagleBoard.org`.

Now, with no power on the BeagleBone board, insert the microSD card into the reader. Plug in the serial cable. A serial port should appear on your PC as `/dev/ttyUSB0`. Start a suitable terminal program, such as `gtkterm`, `minicom`, or `picocom`, and attach to the port at `115200` bps (bits per second) with no flow control. `gtkterm` is probably the easiest to set up and use:

```
$ gtkterm -p /dev/ttyUSB0 -s 115200
```

If you get a permissions error, then you may need to add yourself to the `dialout` group and reboot to use this port.

Press and hold the Boot Switch button (nearest to the microSD slot) on the BeagleBone Black, power up the board using the external 5V power connector, and release the button after about 5 seconds. You should see U-Boot output, kernel log output, and eventually a login prompt on the serial console:

```
Debian GNU/Linux 9 beaglebone ttyS0

BeagleBoard.org Debian Image 2019-08-03

Support/FAQ: http://elinux.org/Beagleboard:BeagleBoneBlack_
Debian

default username:password is [debian:temppwd]

beaglebone login: debian
Password:
```

Log in as the `debian` user. The password is `temppwd` as shown in the preceding screenshot.

> **Important note**
>
> Many BeagleBone Blacks come with Debian already installed on the onboard flash so they will still boot even without a microSD card inserted. If the `BeagleBoard.org Debian Image 2019-08-03` message is displayed before the password prompt, then the BeagleBone Black probably booted from the Debian 9.9 image on the microSD. If a different Debian release message is displayed before the password prompt, then verify whether or not the microSD card is properly inserted.

To check which version of Debian is running, run the following:

```
debian@beaglebone:~$ cat /etc/os-release
PRETTY_NAME="Debian GNU/Linux 9 (stretch)"
NAME="Debian GNU/Linux"
VERSION_ID="9"
VERSION="9 (stretch)"
ID=debian
```

```
HOME_URL="https://www.debian.org/"
SUPPORT_URL="https://www.debian.org/support"
BUG_REPORT_URL="https://bugs.debian.org/"
```

Now check whether the power management is working:

```
debian@beaglebone:~$ cat /sys/power/state
freeze standby mem disk
```

If you see all four states, everything is working fine. If you see only `freeze`, the power management subsystem is not working. Go back and double-check the previous steps.

Now we can move on to measuring power usage. There are two approaches: *external* and *internal*. Measuring power externally, from outside the system, we just need an ammeter to measure the current and a voltmeter to measure the voltage, and then multiply the two together to get the wattage. You can use basic meters that give a readout, which you then note down. Or they can be much more sophisticated and combine data logging so that you can see the change in power as the load changes millisecond by millisecond. For the purposes of this chapter, I powered the BeagleBone from the Mini USB port and used a cheap USB power monitor of the type that costs a few dollars.

The other approach is to use the monitoring systems that are built into Linux. You will find that plenty of information is reported to you via `sysfs`. There is also a very useful program called **PowerTOP**, which gathers information together from various sources and presents it in a single place. PowerTOP is a package for both the Yocto Project and Buildroot. It is also available for installation on Debian.

To install PowerTop on the BeagleBone Black from Debian Stretch IoT, run the following:

```
debian@beaglebone:~$ sudo apt update
[…]
debian@beaglebone:~$ sudo apt install powertop
Reading package lists... Done
Building dependency tree
Reading state information... Done
Suggested packages:
  laptop-mode-tools
The following NEW packages will be installed:
  powertop
0 upgraded, 1 newly installed, 0 to remove and 151 not
upgraded.
```

```
Need to get 177 kB of archives.
After this operation, 441 kB of additional disk space will be used.
Get:1 http://deb.debian.org/debian stretch/main armhf powertop armhf 2.8-1+b1 [177 kB]
Fetched 177 kB in 0s (526 kB/s)
```

Don't forget to plug your BeagleBone Black into Ethernet and update the list of available packages before installing PowerTOP.

Here is an example of PowerTOP running on the BeagleBone Black:

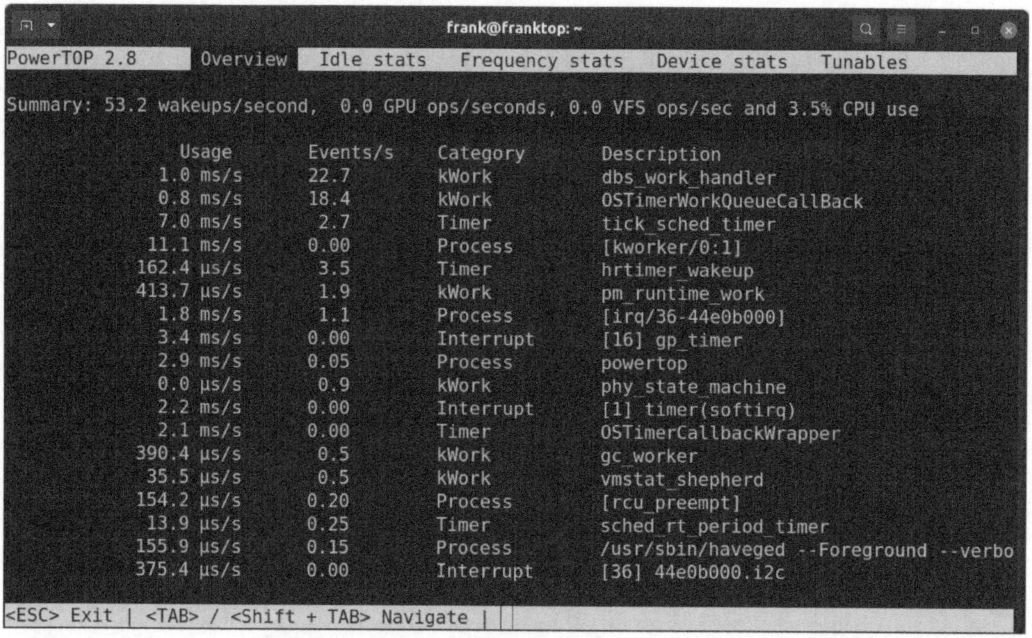
frank@franktop: ~
PowerTOP 2.8
Overview
Idle stats
Frequency stats
Device stats
Tunables
Summary: 53.2 wakeups/second, 0.0 GPU ops/seconds, 0.0 VFS ops/sec and 3.5% CPU use
Usage Events/s Category Description
1.0 ms/s 22.7 kWork dbs_work_handler
0.8 ms/s 18.4 kWork OSTimerWorkQueueCallBack
7.0 ms/s 2.7 Timer tick_sched_timer
11.1 ms/s 0.00 Process [kworker/0:1]
162.4 µs/s 3.5 Timer hrtimer_wakeup
413.7 µs/s 1.9 kWork pm_runtime_work
1.8 ms/s 1.1 Process [irq/36-44e0b000]
3.4 ms/s 0.00 Interrupt [16] gp_timer
2.9 ms/s 0.05 Process powertop
0.0 µs/s 0.9 kWork phy_state_machine
2.2 ms/s 0.00 Interrupt [1] timer(softirq)
2.1 ms/s 0.00 Timer OSTimerCallbackWrapper
390.4 µs/s 0.5 kWork gc_worker
35.5 µs/s 0.5 kWork vmstat_shepherd
154.2 µs/s 0.20 Process [rcu_preempt]
13.9 µs/s 0.25 Timer sched_rt_period_timer
155.9 µs/s 0.15 Process /usr/sbin/haveged --Foreground --verbo
375.4 µs/s 0.00 Interrupt [36] 44e0b000.i2c
<ESC> Exit | <TAB> / <Shift + TAB> Navigate |

Figure 15.1 – PowerTOP overview

In this screenshot, we can see that the system is quiet, with only 3.5% of CPU usage. I will show more interesting examples later, in the *Using CPUFreq* and *The CPUIdle driver* subsections of this chapter.

Now that we have a way to measure power consumption, let's look at one of the biggest knobs we have to manage power in an embedded Linux system: the clock frequency.

Scaling the clock frequency

Running for a kilometer takes more energy than walking. In a similar way, maybe running the CPU at a lower frequency can save energy. Let's see.

The power consumption of a CPU when executing code is the sum of a static component, caused by gate leakage current, among other things, and a dynamic component, caused by the switching of the gates:

$$P_{cpu} = P_{static} + P_{dyn}$$

The dynamic power component is dependent on the total capacitance of the logic gates being switched, the clock frequency, and the square of the voltage:

$$P_{dyn} = CfV^2$$

From this, we can see that changing the frequency by itself is not going to save any power because the same number of CPU cycles have to be completed in order to execute a given subroutine. If we reduce the frequency by half, it will take twice as long to complete the calculation, but the total power consumed due to the dynamic power component will be the same. In fact, reducing the frequency may actually increase the power budget because it takes longer for the CPU to enter an idle state. So, in these conditions, it is best to use the highest frequency possible so that the CPU can go back to idle quickly. This is called the **race to idle**.

> **Important note**
>
> There is another motivation to reduce frequency: **thermal management**. It may become necessary to operate at a lower frequency just to keep the temperature of the package within bounds. But that is not our focus here.

Therefore, if we want to save power, we must be able to change the voltage that the CPU core operates at. But for any given voltage, there is a maximum frequency beyond which the switching of the gates becomes unreliable. Higher frequencies need higher voltages, and so the two need to be adjusted together. Many SoCs implement such a feature: it is called **Dynamic Voltage and Frequency Scaling**, or **DVFS**. Manufacturers calculate optimum combinations of core frequency and voltage. Each combination is called **Operating Performance Point**, or **OPP**. The ACPI specification refers to them as **P-states**, with `P0` being the OPP with the highest frequency. Although an OPP is a combination of a frequency and a voltage, it is most often referred to by the frequency component alone.

A kernel driver is needed to switch between P-states. Next, we will look at that driver and the governors that control it.

The CPUFreq driver

Linux has a component named **CPUFreq** that manages the transitions between OPPs. It is part of the board support for the package for each SoC. CPUFreq consists of drivers in `drivers/cpufreq/`, which make the transition from one OPP to another, and a set of governors that implement the policy of when to switch. It is controlled per-CPU via the `/sys/devices/system/cpu/cpuN/cpufreq` directory, with `N` being the CPU number. In there, we find a number of files, the most interesting of which are as follows:

- `cpuinfo_cur_freq`, `cpuinfo_max_freq`, and `cpuinfo_min_freq`: The current frequency for this CPU, together with the maximum and minimum, measured in KHz.
- `cpuinfo_transition_latency`: The time, in nanoseconds, to switch from one OPP to another. If the value is unknown, it is set to `-1`.
- `scaling_available_frequencies`: A list of OPP frequencies available on this CPU.
- `scaling_available_governors`: A list of governors available on this CPU.
- `scaling_governor`: The CPUFreq governor currently being used.
- `scaling_max_freq` and `scaling_min_freq`: The range of frequencies available to the governor in KHz.
- `scaling_setspeed`: A file that allows you to manually set the frequency when the governor is `userspace`, which I will describe at the end of this subsection.

The governor sets the policy to change the OPP. It can set the frequency between the limits of `scaling_min_freq` and `scaling_max_freq`. The governors are named as follows:

- `powersave`: Always selects the lowest frequency.
- `performance`: Always selects the highest frequency.
- ondemand: Changes frequency based on the CPU utilization. If the CPU is idle less than 20% of the time, it sets the frequency to the maximum; if it is idle more than 30% of the time, it decrements the frequency by 5%.
- `conservative`: Like ondemand, but switches to higher frequencies in 5% steps rather than going immediately to the maximum.
- `userspace`: Frequency is set by a user space program.

The default governor when Debian starts up is `performance`:

```
$ cd /sys/devices/system/cpu/cpu0/cpufreq
$ cat scaling_governor
performance
```

To switch to the `ondemand` governor, which is the governor we should use for the exercises in this chapter, run the following command:

```
$ sudo cpupower frequency-set -g ondemand
[sudo] password for debian:
Setting cpu: 0
```

Enter `temppwd` when prompted for a password.

The parameters the `ondemand` governor uses to decide when to change OPP can be viewed and modified via `/sys/devices/system/cpu/cpufreq/ondemand/`. Both `ondemand` and `conservative` governors take into account the effort required to change frequency and voltage. This parameter is in `cpuinfo_transition_latency`. These calculations are for threads with a normal scheduling policy; if the thread is being scheduled in real time, they will both immediately select the highest OPP so that the thread can meet its scheduling deadline.

The `userspace` governor allows the logic of selecting the OPP to be performed by a user space daemon. Examples include `cpudyn` and `powernowd`, although both are orientated toward x86-based laptops rather than embedded devices.

Now that we know where the runtime details about the CPUFreq driver are located, let's look at how to define the OPPs at compile time.

Using CPUFreq

Looking at the BeagleBone Black, we find that the OPPs are coded in the device tree. Here is an extract from `am33xx.dtsi`:

```
cpu0_opp_table: opp-table {
        compatible = "operating-points-v2-ti-cpu";
        syscon = <&scm_conf>;
        [...]
        opp50-300000000 {
                opp-hz = /bits/ 64 <300000000>;
                opp-microvolt = <950000 931000 969000>;
```

```
            opp-supported-hw = <0x06 0x0010>;
            opp-suspend;
      };
      [...]
      opp100-600000000 {
            opp-hz = /bits/ 64 <600000000>;
            opp-microvolt = <1100000 1078000 1122000>;
            opp-supported-hw = <0x06 0x0040>;
      };
      [...]
      opp120-720000000 {
            opp-hz = /bits/ 64 <720000000>;
            opp-microvolt = <1200000 1176000 1224000>;
            opp-supported-hw = <0x06 0x0080>;
      };
      [...]
      oppturbo-800000000 {
            opp-hz = /bits/ 64 <800000000>;
            opp-microvolt = <1260000 1234800 1285200>;
            opp-supported-hw = <0x06 0x0100>;
      };
      oppnitro-1000000000 {
            opp-hz = /bits/ 64 <1000000000>;
            opp-microvolt = <1325000 1298500 1351500>;
            opp-supported-hw = <0x04 0x0200>;
      };
};
```

We can confirm that these are the OPPs in use at runtime by viewing the available frequencies:

```
$ cd /sys/devices/system/cpu/cpu0/cpufreq
$ cat scaling_available_frequencies
300000 600000 720000 800000 1000000
```

By selecting the `userspace` governor, we can set the frequency by writing to `scaling_setspeed`, and so we can measure the power consumed at each OPP. These measurements are not very accurate, so do not take them too seriously.

First, with an idle system, the result is 70mA @ 4.6V = 320 mW. This is independent of the frequency, which is what we would expect since this is the static component of the power consumption of this particular system.

Now, I want to know the maximum power consumed at each OPP by running a compute-bound load such as this:

```
# dd if=/dev/urandom of=/dev/null bs=1
```

The results are shown in the following table, with **Delta power** being the additional power usage above the idle system:

OPP	Freq, KHz	Power, mW	Delta power, mW
OPP50	300,000	370	50
OPP100	600,000	505	185
OPP120	720,000	600	280
Turbo	800,000	640	320
Nitro	1,000,000	780	460

These measurements show the maximum power at the various OPPs. But it is not a fair test because the CPU is running at 100%, and so it is executing more instructions at higher frequencies. If we keep the load constant but vary the frequency, then we find the following:

OPP	Freq, KHz	CPU utilization, %	Power, mW
OPP50	300,000	94	320
OPP100	600,000	48	345
OPP120	720,000	40	370
Turbo	800,000	34	370
Nitro	1,000,000	28	370

This shows a definite power saving at the lowest frequency, in the order of 15%.

Using PowerTOP, we can see the percentage of time spent in each OPP. The following screenshot shows the BeagleBone Black running a light load using the `ondemand` governor:

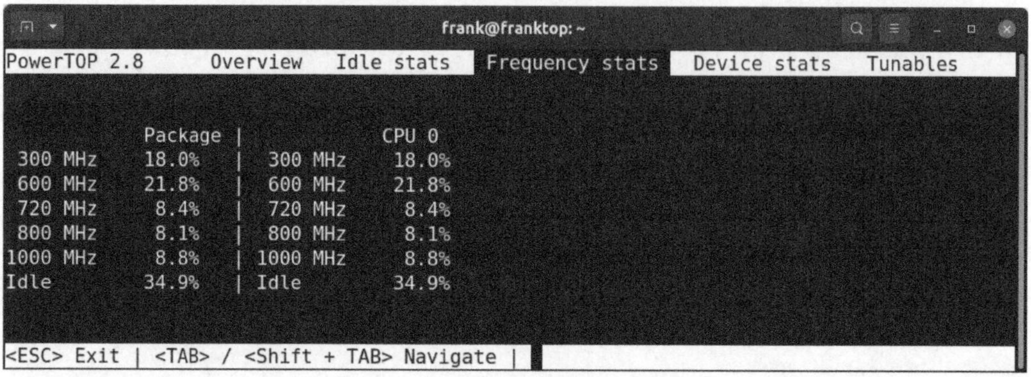
frank@franktop: ~
PowerTOP 2.8 Overview Idle stats Frequency stats Device stats Tunables
Package | CPU 0
300 MHz 18.0% | 300 MHz 18.0%
600 MHz 21.8% | 600 MHz 21.8%
720 MHz 8.4% | 720 MHz 8.4%
800 MHz 8.1% | 800 MHz 8.1%
1000 MHz 8.8% | 1000 MHz 8.8%
Idle 34.9% | Idle 34.9%
<ESC> Exit | <TAB> / <Shift + TAB> Navigate |

Figure 15.2 – PowerTOP Frequency stats

In most cases, the `ondemand` governor is the best one to use. To select a particular governor, you can either configure the kernel with a default governor, for example, `CPU_FREQ_DEFAULT_GOV_ONDEMAND`, or you can use a boot script to change the governor at boot time. There is an example System V `init` script in `MELP/Chapter15/cpufrequtils` taken from Debian.

For more information on the CPUFreq driver, take a look at files in the `Documentation/cpu-freq` directory of the Linux kernel source tree.

In this section, we were concerned about the power used when the CPU is busy. In the next section, we will look at how to save power when the CPU is idle.

Selecting the best idle state

When a processor has no more work to do, it executes a **halt instruction** and enters an idle state. While idle, the CPU uses less power. It exits the idle state when an event such as a hardware interrupt occurs. Most CPUs have multiple idle states that use varying amounts of power. Usually, there is a trade-off between the power usage and the latency, or the length of time, it takes to exit the state. In the ACPI specification, they are called **C-states**.

In the deeper C-states, more circuitry is turned off at the expense of losing some state, and so it takes longer to return to normal operation. For example, in some C-states the CPU caches may be powered off, and so when the CPU runs again, it may have to reload some information from the main memory. This is expensive, and so you only want to do this if there is a good chance that the CPU will remain in this state for some time. The number of states varies from one system to another. Each takes some time to recover from sleeping to being fully active.

The key to selecting the right idle state is to have a good idea of how long the CPU is going to be quiescent. Predicting the future is always tricky, but there are some things that can help. One is the current CPU load: if it is high now, it is likely to continue to be so in the immediate future, so a deep sleep would not be beneficial. Even if the load is low, it is worth looking to see whether there is a timer event that expires soon. If there is no load and no timer, then a deeper idle state is justified.

The part of Linux that selects the best idle state is the CPUIdle driver. There is a good deal of information about it available in the `Documentation/cpuidle` directory inside the Linux kernel source tree.

The CPUIdle driver

As with the CPUFreq subsystem, **CPUIdle** consists of a driver that is part of the BSP and a governor that determines the policy. Unlike CPUFreq, however, the governor cannot be changed at runtime and there is no interface for user space governors.

CPUIdle exposes information about each of the idle states in the `/sys/devices/system/cpu/cpu0/cpuidle` directory, in which there is a subdirectory for each of the sleep states, named `state0` to `stateN`. `state0` is the lightest sleep and `stateN` the deepest. Note that the numbering does not match that of the C-states and that CPUIdle does not have a state equivalent to `C0` (running). For each state, there are these files:

- `desc`: A short description of the state
- `disable`: An option to disable this state by writing `1` to this file
- `latency`: The time the CPU core takes to resume normal operation when exiting this state, in microseconds
- `name`: The name of this state
- `power`: The power consumed while in this idle state, in milliwatts
- `time`: The total time spent in this idle state, in microseconds
- `usage`: The count of the number of times this state was entered

In the case of the AM335x SoC on the BeagleBone Black, there are two idle states. Here is the first:

```
$ cd /sys/devices/system/cpu/cpu0/cpuidle
$ grep "" state0/*
state0/desc:ARM WFI
state0/disable:0
state0/latency:1
state0/name:WFI
state0/power:4294967295
state0/residency:1
state0/time:1023898
state0/usage:1426
```

This state is named `WFI`, which refers to the ARM halt instruction, **Wait For Interrupt**. The latency is `1` microsecond because it is just a halt instruction, and the power consumed is given as `-1`, which means that the power budget is not known (by CPUIdle at least). Now, this is the second state:

```
$ cd /sys/devices/system/cpu/cpu0/cpuidle
$ grep "" state1/*
state1/desc:mpu_gate
state1/disable:0
state1/latency:130
state1/name:mpu_gate
state1/power:0
state1/residency:300
state1/time:139156260
state1/usage:7560
```

This one is named `mpu_gate`. It has a higher latency of `130` microseconds. The idle states may be hardcoded into the CPUIdle driver or presented in the device tree. Here is an extract from `am33xx.dtsi`:

```
cpus {
     cpu@0 {
           compatible = "arm,cortex-a8";
           enable-method = "ti,am3352";
           device_type = "cpu";
```

```
            reg = <0>;
    .
    .
    .
            cpu-idle-states = <&mpu_gate>;
        };

        idle-states {
            mpu_gate: mpu_gate {
                compatible = "arm,idle-state";
                entry-latency-us = <40>;
                exit-latency-us = <90>;
                min-residency-us = <300>;
                ti,idle-wkup-m3;
            };
        };
}
```

CPUIdle has two governors:

- `ladder`: This steps idle states down or up, one at a time, depending on the time spent in the last idle period. It works well with a regular timer tick but not with a dynamic tick.
- `menu`: This selects an idle state based on the expected idle time. It works well with dynamic tick systems.

You should choose one or the other depending on your configuration of `NO_HZ`, which I will describe at the end of this section.

Once again, user interaction is via the `sysfs` filesystem. In the `/sys/devices/system/cpu/cpuidle` directory, you will find two files:

- `current_driver`: This is the name of the `cpuidle` driver.
- `current_governor_ro`: This is the name of the governor.

These show which driver and which governor are being used. The idle states can be shown in PowerTOP on the `Idle stats` tab. The following screenshot shows a BeagleBone Black using the `menu` governor:

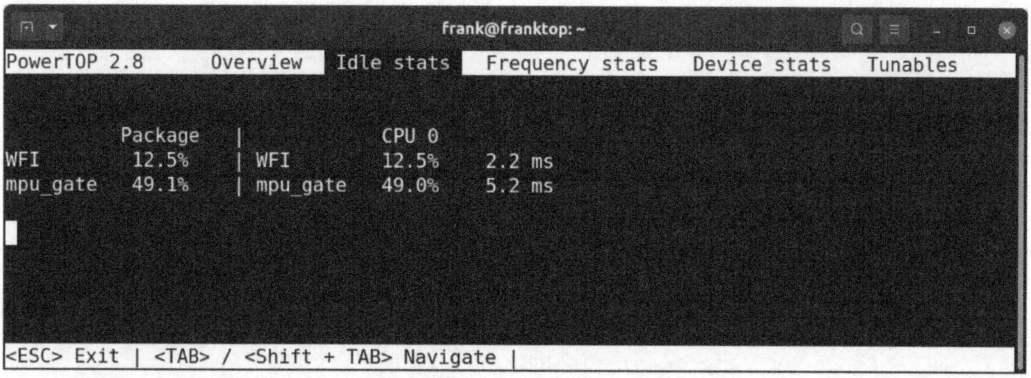

Figure 15.3 – PowerTOP Idle stats

This shows that when the system is idle, it is mostly going to the deeper `mpu_gate` idle state, which is what we would want.

Even with the CPU fully idling, most Linux systems are still configured to wake up periodically on receipt of a system timer interrupt. To save more power, we need to configure the Linux kernel for tickless operation.

Tickless operation

A related topic is the tickless, or `NO_HZ`, option. If the system is truly idle, the most likely source of interruptions will be the system timer, which is programmed to generate a regular time tick at a rate of HZ per second, where HZ is typically 100. Historically, Linux uses the timer tick as the main time base for measuring timeouts.

And yet it is plainly wasteful to wake the CPU up to process a timer interrupt if no timer events are registered for that particular moment. The dynamic tick kernel configuration option, `CONFIG_NO_HZ_IDLE`, looks at the timer queue at the end of the timer processing routine and schedules the next interruption at the time of the next event, avoiding unnecessary wake-ups and allowing the CPU to be idle for long periods. In any power-sensitive application, the kernel should be configured with this option enabled.

While the CPU consumes much of the power in an embedded Linux system, there are other components of the system that can also be powered down for energy savings.

Powering down peripherals

The discussion up to now has been about CPUs and how to reduce power consumption when they are running or idling. Now it is time to focus on other parts of the system peripherals and see whether we can achieve power savings here.

In the Linux kernel, this is managed by the **runtime power management system** or **runtime pm** for short. It works with drivers that support runtime pm, shutting down those that are not in use and waking them again when they are next needed. It is dynamic and should be transparent to user space. It is up to the device driver to implement the management of the hardware, but typically, it would include turning off the clock to the subsystem, also known as clock gating, and turning off core circuitry where possible.

The runtime power management is exposed via a `sysfs` interface. Each device has a subdirectory named `power`, in which you will find these files:

- `control`: This allows user space to determine whether runtime pm is used on this device. If it is set to `auto`, then runtime pm is enabled, but by setting it to `on`, the device is always on and does not use runtime pm.
- `runtime_enabled`: This reports that runtime pm is `enabled`, `disabled`, or, if `control` is `on`, it reports `forbidden`.
- `runtime_status`: This reports the current state of the device. It may be `active`, `suspended`, or `unsupported`.
- `autosuspend_delay_ms`: This is the time before the device is suspended. `-1` means waiting forever. Some drivers implement this if there is a significant cost to suspending the device hardware since it prevents rapid suspend/resume cycles.

To give a concrete example, I will look at the MMC driver on the BeagleBone Black:

```
$ cd /sys/devices/platform/ocp/481d8000.mmc/mmc_host/mmc1/
mmc1:0001/power
$ grep "" *
async:enabled
autosuspend_delay_ms:3000
control:auto
runtime_active_kids:0
runtime_active_time:14464
```

```
runtime_enabled:enabled
runtime_status:suspended
runtime_suspended_time:121208
runtime_usage:0
```

So, runtime pm is enabled, the device is currently suspended, and there is a delay of `3000` milliseconds after it was last used before it will be suspended again. Now I read a block from the device and see whether it has changed:

```
$ sudo dd if=/dev/mmcblk1p3 of=/dev/null count=1
1+0 records in
1+0 records out
512 bytes copied, 0.00629126 s, 81.4 kB/s
$ grep "" *
async:enabled
autosuspend_delay_ms:3000
control:auto
runtime_active_kids:0
runtime_active_time:17120
runtime_enabled:enabled
runtime_status:active
runtime_suspended_time:178520
runtime_usage:0
```

Now the MMC driver is active and the power to the board has increased from 320 mW to 500 mW. If I repeat it again after 3 seconds, it is once more suspended, and the power has returned to 320 mW.

For more information on runtime pm, look in the Linux kernel source code at `Documentation/power/runtime_pm.txt`.

Now that we know what the runtime pm is and what it does, let's see it in action.

Putting the system to sleep

There is one more power management technique to consider: putting the whole system into sleep mode with the expectation that it will not be used again for a while. In the Linux kernel, this is known as **system sleep**. It is usually user-initiated: the user decides that the device should be shut down for a while. For example, I shut the lid of my laptop and put it in my bag when it is time to go home. Much of the support for system sleep in Linux comes from the support for laptops. In the laptop world, there are usually two options:

- Suspend
- Hibernate

The first, also known as **suspend to RAM**, shuts everything down except the system memory, so the machine is still consuming a little power. When the system wakes up, the memory retains all the previous state, and my laptop is operational within a few seconds.

If I select the **hibernate** option, the contents of the memory are saved to the hard drive. The system consumes no power at all, and so it can stay in this state indefinitely, but on wake-up, it takes some time to restore the memory from disk. Hibernate is very seldom used in embedded systems, mostly because the flash storage tends to be quite slow on read/write, but also because it is intrusive to the flow of work.

For more information, look at the kernel source code in the `Documentation/power` directory.

The suspend-to-RAM and hibernate options map to two of the four sleep states supported by Linux. We'll look at these two types of system sleep and the rest of the ACPI power states next.

Power states

In the ACPI specification, the sleep states are called **S-states**. Linux supports four sleep states (`freeze`, `standby`, `mem`, and `disk`), which are shown in the following list along with the corresponding ACPI S-state ([S0], S1, S3, S4):

- `freeze` ([S0]): Stops (freezes) all activity in user space, but otherwise the CPU and memory are operating as normal.

  The power-saving results from the fact that no user space code is being run. ACPI does not have an equivalent state so S0 is the closest match. S0 is the state for a running system.

- `standby` (S1): Just like `freeze`, but additionally takes all CPUs offline except the boot CPU.
- `mem` (S3): Powers down the system and puts the memory in the self-refresh mode. Also known as **suspend to RAM**.
- `disk` (S4): Saves the memory to the hard disk and powers down. Also known as **suspend to disk**.

Not all systems have support for all states. To find out which are available, read the `/sys/power/state` file as shown:

```
# cat /sys/power/state
freeze standby mem disk
```

To enter one of the system sleep states, you just write the desired state to `/sys/power/state`.

For embedded devices, the most common need is to suspend to RAM using the `mem` option. For example, I can suspend the BeagleBone Black like this:

```
# echo mem > /sys/power/state
[ 1646.158274] PM: Syncing filesystems ...done.
[ 1646.178387] Freezing user space processes ... (elapsed 0.001
seconds) done.
[ 1646.188098] Freezing remaining freezable tasks ... (elapsed
0.001 seconds) done.
[ 1646.197017] Suspending console(s) (use no_console_suspend to
debug)
[ 1646.338657] PM: suspend of devices complete after 134.322
msecs
[ 1646.343428] PM: late suspend of devices complete after 4.716
msecs
[ 1646.348234] PM: noirq suspend of devices complete after
4.755 msecs
[ 1646.348251] Disabling non-boot CPUs ...
[ 1646.348264] PM: Successfully put all powerdomains to target
state
```

The device powers down in less than a second and then power usage drops down to below 10 milliwatts, which is the limit of measurement of my simple multimeter. But how do I wake it up again? That is the next topic.

Wakeup events

Before you suspend a device, you must have a method of waking it again. The kernel tries to help you here: if there is not at least one wakeup source, the system will refuse to suspend with the following message:

```
No sources enabled to wake-up! Sleep abort.
```

Of course, this means that some parts of the system have to remain powered on even during the deepest sleep. This usually involves the **Power Management IC** (**PMIC**), the **real-time clock** (**RTC**), and may additionally include interfaces such as GPIO, UART, and Ethernet.

Wakeup events are controlled through `sysfs`. Each device in `/sys/device` has a subdirectory named `power` containing a `wakeup` file that will contain one of these strings:

- `enabled`: This device will generate wakeup events.
- `disabled`: This device will not generate wakeup events.
- (empty): This device is not capable of generating wakeup events.

To get a list of devices that can generate wakeups, we can search for all devices where `wakeup` contains either `enabled` or `disabled`:

```
$ find /sys/devices/ -name wakeup | xargs grep "abled"
```

In the case of the BeagleBone Black, the UARTs are wakeup sources, so pressing a key on the console wakes the BeagleBone:

```
[ 1646.348264] PM: Wakeup source UART
[ 1646.368482] PM: noirq resume of devices complete after 19.963 msecs
[ 1646.372482] PM: early resume of devices complete after 3.192 msecs
[ 1646.795109] net eth0: initializing cpsw version 1.12 (0)
[ 1646.798229] net eth0: phy found : id is : 0x7c0f1
[ 1646.798447] libphy: PHY 4a101000.mdio:01 not found
[ 1646.798469] net eth0: phy 4a101000.mdio:01 not found on slave 1
[ 1646.927874] PM: resume of devices complete after 555.337 msecs
[ 1647.003829] Restarting tasks ... done.
```

We've seen how to put a device to sleep then wake it up with an event from a peripheral interface like a UART. What if we want a device to wake itself up without any outside interaction? This is where the RTC comes into play.

Timed wakeups from the real-time clock

Most systems have an RTC that can generate alarm interruptions up to 24 hours in the future. If so, the `/sys/class/rtc/rtc0` directory will exist. It should contain the `wakealarm` file. Writing a number to `wakealarm` will cause it to generate an alarm that number of seconds later. If you also enable `wakeup` events from `rtc`, the RTC will resume a suspended device.

For example, this `rtcwake` command would put the system in `standby` with the RTC waking it up after 5 seconds:

```
$ sudo su -
# rtcwake -d /dev/rtc0 -m standby -s 5
  rtcwake: assuming RTC uses UTC ...
  rtcwake: wakeup from "standby" using /dev/rtc0 at Tue Dec  1 
19:34:10 2020
[  187.345129] PM: suspend entry (shallow)
[  187.345148] PM: Syncing filesystems ... done.
[  187.346754] Freezing user space processes ... (elapsed 0.003 
seconds) done.
[  187.350688] OOM killer disabled.
[  187.350789] Freezing remaining freezable tasks ... (elapsed 
0.001 seconds) done.
[  187.352361] Suspending console(s) (use no_console_suspend to 
debug)
[  187.500906] Disabling non-boot CPUs ...
[  187.500941] pm33xx pm33xx: PM: Successfully put all 
powerdomains to target state
[  187.500941] PM: Wakeup source RTC Alarm
[  187.529729] net eth0: initializing cpsw version 1.12 (0)
[  187.605061] SMSC LAN8710/LAN8720 4a101000.mdio:00: attached 
PHY driver [SMSC LAN8710/LAN8720] (mii_bus:phy_addr=4a101000.
mdio:00, irq=POLL)
[  187.731543] OOM killer enabled.
[  187.731563] Restarting tasks ... done.
[  187.756896] PM: suspend exit
```

Since the UARTs are also a wakeup source, pressing a key on the console will wake up the BeagleBone Black before the RTC `wakealarm` expires:

```
[  255.698873] PM: suspend entry (shallow)
[  255.698894] PM: Syncing filesystems ... done.
[  255.701946] Freezing user space processes ... (elapsed 0.003 seconds) done.
[  255.705249] OOM killer disabled.
[  255.705256] Freezing remaining freezable tasks ... (elapsed 0.002 seconds) done.
[  255.707827] Suspending console(s) (use no_console_suspend to debug)
[  255.860823] Disabling non-boot CPUs ...
[  255.860857] pm33xx pm33xx: PM: Successfully put all powerdomains to target state
[  255.860857] PM: Wakeup source UART
[  255.888064] net eth0: initializing cpsw version 1.12 (0)
[  255.965045] SMSC LAN8710/LAN8720 4a101000.mdio:00: attached PHY driver [SMSC LAN8710/LAN8720] (mii_bus:phy_addr=4a101000.mdio:00, irq=POLL)
[  256.093684] OOM killer enabled.
[  256.093704] Restarting tasks ... done.
[  256.118453] PM: suspend exit
```

The Power button on the BeagleBone Black is also a wakeup source so you can use that to resume from `standby` in the absence of a serial console. Make sure to press the Power button and not the Reset button, which is next to it, otherwise the board will reboot.

This concludes our coverage of the four Linux system sleep modes. We learned how to suspend a device to the `mem` or `standby` power states then wake it up via an event from a UART, RTC, or the Power button. While the runtime pm in Linux was created mostly for laptops, we can leverage this support for embedded systems that also run on battery power.

Summary

Linux has sophisticated power management functions. I have described four main components:

- **CPUFreq** changes the OPP of each processor core to reduce power on those that are busy but have some bandwidth to spare, and so allow the opportunity to scale the frequency back. OPPs are known as P-States in the ACPI specification.
- **CPUIdle** selects deeper idle states when the CPU is not expected to be woken up for a while. Idle states are known as C-States in the ACPI specification.
- **Runtime pm** will shut down peripherals that are not needed.
- **System sleep** modes will put the whole system into a low power state. They are usually under end user control, for example, by pressing a standby button. System sleep states are known as S-States in the ACPI specification.

Most of the power management is done for you by the BSP. Your main task is to make sure that it is configured correctly for your intended use cases. Only the last component, selecting a system sleep state, requires you to write some code that will allow the end user to enter and exit the state.

The next section of the book is about writing embedded applications. We will start with packaging and deploying Python code and dig deeper into the containerization techniques that were introduced in *Chapter 10, Updating Software in the Field*, when we evaluated balena.

Further reading

- *Advanced Configuration and Power Interface Specification*, UEFI Forum, Inc.: `https://uefi.org/sites/default/files/resources/ACPI_Spec_6_4_Jan22.pdf`

Section 3: Writing Embedded Applications

Section 3 shows the reader how to use the embedded Linux platform to create a working device for their applicationw. The section starts with a survey of various Python packaging and deployment options to assist with the iterative development of your application. We then learn how to make effective use of the Linux process and threads model and how to manage memory in a resource-constrained device.

This part of the book comprises the following chapters:

- *Chapter 16, Packaging Python*
- *Chapter 17, Learning About Processes and Threads*
- *Chapter 18, Managing Memory*

16
Packaging Python

Python is the most popular programming language for machine learning. Combine that with the proliferation of machine learning in our day-to-day lives and it is no surprise that the desire to run Python on edge devices is intensifying. Even in this era of transpilers and WebAssembly, packaging Python applications for deployment remains an unsolved problem. In this chapter, you will learn what choices are out there for bundling Python modules together and when to use one method over another.

We start with a look back at the origins of today's Python packaging solutions, from the built-in standard `distutils` to its successor, `setuptools`. Next, we examine the `pip` package manager, before moving on to `venv` for Python virtual environments, followed by `conda`, the reigning general-purpose cross-platform solution. Lastly, I will show you how to use Docker to bundle Python applications along with their user space environment for rapid deployment to the cloud.

Since Python is an interpreted language, you cannot compile a program into a standalone executable like you can with a language such as Go. This makes deploying Python applications complicated. Running a Python application requires installing a Python interpreter and several runtime dependencies. These requirements need to be code-compatible for the application to work. That requires the precise versioning of software components. Solving these deployment problems is what Python packaging is all about.

In this chapter, we will cover the following main topics:

- Retracing the origins of Python packaging
- Installing Python packages with `pip`
- Managing Python virtual environments with `venv`
- Installing precompiled binaries with `conda`
- Deploying Python applications with Docker

Technical requirements

To follow along with the examples, make sure you have the following packages installed on your Linux-based host system:

- Python: Python 3 interpreter and standard library
- `pip`: Package installer for Python 3
- `venv`: Python module for creating and managing lightweight virtual environments
- Miniconda: Minimal installer for the `conda` package and virtual environment manager
- Docker: Tool for building, deploying, and running software inside containers

I recommend using Ubuntu 20.04 LTS or later for this chapter. Even though Ubuntu 20.04 LTS runs on the Raspberry Pi 4, I still prefer to develop on an x86-64 desktop PC or laptop. I choose Ubuntu for my development environment because the distribution maintainers keep Docker up to date. Ubuntu 20.04 LTS also comes with Python 3 and `pip` already installed since Python is used extensively throughout the system. Do not uninstall `python3` or you will render Ubuntu unusable. To install `venv` on Ubuntu, enter the following:

```
$ sudo apt install python3-venv
```

> **Important note**
>
> Do not install Miniconda until you get to the section on `conda` because it interferes with the earlier `pip` exercises that rely on the system Python installation.

Now, let's install Docker.

Getting Docker

To install Docker on Ubuntu 20.04 LTS, we need to do the following:

1. Update the package repositories:

```
$ sudo apt update
```

2. Install Docker:

```
$ sudo apt install docker.io
```

3. Start the Docker daemon and enable it to start at boot time:

```
$ sudo systemctl enable --now docker
```

4. Add yourself to the `docker` group:

```
$ sudo usermod -aG docker <username>
```

Replace `<username>` in that last step with your username. I recommend creating your own Ubuntu user account rather than using the default `ubuntu` user account, which is supposed to be reserved for administrative tasks.

Retracing the origins of Python packaging

The Python packaging landscape is a vast graveyard of failed attempts and abandoned tools. Best practices around dependency management change often within the Python community and the recommended solution one year may be a broken nonstarter the next. As you research this topic, remember to look at when the information was published and do not trust any advice that may be out of date.

Most Python libraries are distributed using `distutils` or `setuptools`, including all the packages found on the **Python Package Index** (**PyPI**). Both distribution methods rely on a `setup.py` project specification file that the **package installer for Python** (**pip**) uses to install a package. `pip` can also generate or *freeze* a precise list of dependencies after a project is installed. This optional `requirements.txt` file is used by `pip` in conjunction with `setup.py` to ensure that project installations are repeatable.

distutils

distutils is the original packaging system for Python. It has been included in the Python standard library since Python 2.0. `distutils` provides a Python package of the same name that can be imported by your `setup.py` script. Even though `distutils` still ships with Python, it lacks some essential features, so direct usage of `distutils` is now actively discouraged. `setuptools` has become its preferred replacement.

While `distutils` may continue to work for simple projects, the community has moved on. Today, `distutils` survives mostly for legacy reasons. Many Python libraries were first published back when `distutils` was the only game in town. Porting them to `setuptools` now would take considerable effort and could break existing users.

setuptools

setuptools extends `distutils` by adding support for complex constructs that make larger applications easier to distribute. It has become the de facto packaging system within the Python community. Like `distutils`, `setuptools` offers a Python package of the same name that you can import into your `setup.py` script. `distribute` was an ambitious fork of `setuptools` that eventually merged back into `setuptools 0.7`, cementing the status of `setuptools` as the definitive choice for Python packaging.

`setuptools` introduced a command-line utility known as `easy_install` (now deprecated) and a Python package called `pkg_resources` for runtime package discovery and access to resource files. `setuptools` can also produce packages that act as plugins for other extensible packages (for example, frameworks and applications). You do this by registering entry points in your `setup.py` script for the other overarching package to import.

The term *distribution* means something different in the context of Python. A distribution is a versioned archive of packages, modules, and other resource files used to distribute a release. A *release* is a versioned snapshot of a Python project taken at a given point in time. To make matters worse, the terms *package* and *distribution* are overloaded and often used interchangeably by Pythonistas. For our purposes, let's say that a distribution is what you download, and a package is the module[s] that gets installed and imported.

Cutting a release can result in multiple distributions, such as a source distribution and one or more built distributions. There can be different built distributions for different platforms, such as one that includes a Windows installer. The term *built distribution* means that no build step is required before installation. It does not necessarily mean precompiled. Some built distribution formats such as **Wheel** (`.whl`) exclude compiled Python files, for example. A built distribution containing compiled extensions is known as a *binary distribution*.

An **extension module** is a Python module that is written in C or C++. Every extension module compiles down to a single dynamically loaded library, such as a shared object (`.so`) on Linux and a DLL (`.pyd`) on Windows. Contrast this with pure modules, which must be written entirely in Python. The Egg (`.egg`) built distribution format introduced by `setuptools` supports both pure and extension modules. Since a Python source code (`.py`) file compiles down to a bytecode (`.pyc`) file when the Python interpreter imports a module at runtime, you can see how a built distribution format such as Wheel might exclude precompiled Python files.

setup.py

Say you are developing a small program in Python, maybe something that queries a remote REST API and saves response data to a local SQL database. How do you package your program together with its dependencies for deployment? You start by defining a **setup.py** script that `setuptools` can use to install your program. Deploying with `setuptools` is the first step toward more elaborate automated deployment schemes.

Even if your program is small enough to fit comfortably inside a single module, chances are it won't stay that way for long. Let's say that your program consists of a single file named `follower.py`, like so:

```
$ tree follower
follower
└── follower.py
```

You could then convert this module into a package by splitting `follower.py` up into three separate modules and placing them inside a nested directory also named `follower`:

```
$ tree follower/
follower/
└── follower
    ├── fetch.py
    ├── __main__.py
    └── store.py
```

The `__main__.py` module is where your program starts, so it contains mostly top-level, user-facing functionality. The `fetch.py` module contains functions for sending HTTP requests to the remote REST API and the `store.py` module contains functions for saving response data to the local SQL database. To run this package as a script, you need to pass the `-m` option to the Python interpreter as follows:

```
$ PYTHONPATH=follower python -m follower
```

The `PYTHONPATH` environment variable points to the directory where a target project's package directories are located. The `follower` argument after the `-m` option tells Python to run the `__main__.py` module belonging to the `follower` package. Nesting package directories inside a project directory like this paves the way for your program to grow into a larger application made up of multiple packages each with its own namespace.

With the pieces of your project all in their right place, we are now ready to create a minimal `setup.py` script that `setuptools` can use to package and deploy it:

```
from setuptools import setup

setup(
    name='follower',
    version='0.1',
    packages=['follower'],
    include_package_data=True,
    install_requires=['requests', 'sqlalchemy']
)
```

The `install_requires` argument is a list of external dependencies that need to be installed automatically for a project to work at runtime. Notice that I did not specify what versions of these dependencies are needed or where to fetch them from in my example. I only asked for libraries that look and act like `requests` and `sqlalchemy`. Separating policy from implementation like this allows you to easily swap out the official PyPI version of a dependency with your own in case you need to fix a bug or add a feature. Adding optional version specifiers to your dependency declarations is fine, but hardcoding distribution URLs within `setup.py` as `dependency_links` is wrong in principle.

The `packages` argument tells `setuptools` what in-tree packages to distribute with a project release. Since every package is defined inside its own subdirectory of the parent project directory, the only package being shipped in this case is `follower`. I am including data files along with my Python code in this distribution. To do that, you need to set the `include_package_data` argument to `True` so that `setuptools` looks for a `MANIFEST.in` file and installs all the files listed there. Here are the contents of the `MANIFEST.in` file:

```
include data/events.db
```

If the `data` directory contained nested directories of data we wanted to include, we could glob all of them along with their contents using `recursive-include`:

```
recursive-include data *
```

Here is the final directory layout:

```
$ tree follower
follower
├── data
│   └── events.db
├── follower
│   ├── fetch.py
│   ├── __init__.py
│   └── store.py
├── MANIFEST.in
└── setup.py
```

`setuptools` excels at building and distributing Python packages that depend on other packages. It is able to do this thanks to features such as entry points and dependency declarations, which are simply absent from `distutils`. `setuptools` works well with `pip` and new releases of `setuptools` arrive on a regular basis. The Wheel build distribution format was created to replace the Egg format that `setuptools` originated. That effort has largely succeeded with the addition of a popular `setuptools` extension for building wheels and `pip`'s great support for installing wheels.

Installing Python packages with pip

You now know how to define your project's dependencies in a `setup.py` script. But how do you install those dependencies? How do you upgrade a dependency or replace it when you find a better one? How do you decide when it is safe to delete a dependency you no longer need? Managing project dependencies is a tricky business. Luckily, Python comes with a tool called **pip** that can help, especially in the early stages of your project.

The initial 1.0 release of `pip` arrived on April 4, 2011, around the same time that Node.js and `npm` were taking off. Before it became `pip`, the tool was named `pyinstall`. `pyinstall` was created in 2008 as an alternative to `easy_install`, which came bundled with `setuptools` at the time. `easy_install` is now deprecated and `setuptools` recommends using `pip` instead.

Since `pip` is included with the Python installer and you can have multiple versions of Python installed on your system (for example, 2.7 and 3.8), it helps to know which version of `pip` you are running:

```
$ pip --version
```

If no `pip` executable is found on your system, that probably means you are on Ubuntu 20.04 LTS or later and do not have Python 2.7 installed. That is fine. We will merely substitute `pip3` for `pip` and `python3` for `python` throughout the rest of this section:

```
$ pip3 --version
```

If there is `python3` but no `pip3` executable, then install it as shown on Debian-based distributions such as Ubuntu:

```
$ sudo apt install python3-pip
```

`pip` installs packages to a directory called `site-packages`. To find the location of your `site-packages` directory, run the following command:

```
$ python3 -m site | grep ^USER_SITE
```

> **Important note**
>
> Note that the `pip3` and `python3` commands shown from here on out are only required for Ubuntu 20.04 LTS or later, which no longer comes with Python 2.7 installed. Most Linux distributions still come with `pip` and `python` executables, so use the `pip` and `python` commands if that is what your Linux system already provides.

To get a list of packages already installed on your system, use this command:

```
$ pip3 list
```

The list shows that `pip` is just another Python package, so you could use `pip` to upgrade itself, but I would advise you not to do that, at least not in the long term. I'll explain why in the next section when I introduce virtual environments.

To get a list of packages installed in your `site-packages` directory, use the following:

```
$ pip3 list --user
```

This list should be empty or much shorter than the list of system packages.

Go back to the example project from the last section. `cd` into the parent `follower` directory where `setup.py` is located. Then run the following command:

```
$ pip3 install --ignore-installed --user .
```

`pip` will use `setup.py` to fetch and install the packages declared by `install_requires` to your `site-packages` directory. The `--user` option instructs `pip` to install packages to your `site-packages` directory rather than globally. The `--ignore-installed` option forces `pip` to re-install any required packages already present on the system to `site-packages` so that no dependencies go missing. Now list all the packages in your `site-packages` directory again:

```
$ pip3 list --user
Package    Version
---------- ---------
certifi    2020.6.20
chardet    3.0.4
follower   0.1
idna       2.10
requests   2.24.0
SQLAlchemy 1.3.18
urllib3    1.25.10
```

This time, you should see that both `requests` and `SQLAlchemy` are in the package list.

To view details on the `SQLAlchemy` package you likely just installed, issue the following:

```
$ pip3 show sqlalchemy
```

The details shown contain the `Requires` and `Required-by` fields. Both are lists of related packages. You could use the values in these fields and successive calls to `pip show` to trace the dependency tree of your project. But it's probably easier to `pip install` a command-line tool called `pipdeptree` and use that instead.

When a `Required-by` field becomes empty, that is a good indicator that it is now safe to uninstall a package from your system. If no other packages depend on the packages in the deleted package's `Requires` field, then it's safe to uninstall those as well. Here is how you uninstall `sqlalchemy` using `pip`:

```
$ pip3 uninstall sqlalchemy -y
```

The trailing `-y` suppresses the confirmation prompt. To uninstall more than one package at a time, simply add more package names before the `-y`. The `--user` option is omitted here because `pip` is smart enough to uninstall from `site-packages` first when a package is also installed globally.

Sometimes you need a package that serves some purpose or utilizes a particular technology, but you don't know the name of it. You can use `pip` to perform a keyword search against PyPI from the command line but that approach often yields too many results. It is much easier to search for packages on the PyPI website (`https://pypi.org/search/`), which allows you to filter results by various classifiers.

requirements.txt

`pip install` will install the latest published version of a package, but often you want to install a specific version of a package that you know works with your project's code. Eventually, you will want to upgrade your project's dependencies. But before I show you how to do that, I first need to show you how to use `pip freeze` to fix your dependencies.

Requirements files allow you to specify exactly which packages and versions `pip` should install for your project. By convention, project **requirements files** are always named `requirements.txt`. The contents of a requirements file are just a list of `pip install` arguments enumerating your project's dependencies. These dependencies are precisely versioned so that there are no surprises when someone attempts to rebuild and deploy your project. It is good practice to add a `requirements.txt` file to your project's repo in order to ensure reproducible builds.

Returning to our `follower` project, now that we have installed all our dependencies and verified that the code works as expected, we are now ready to freeze the latest versions of the packages that `pip` installed for us. `pip` has a `freeze` command that outputs the installed packages along with their versions. You redirect the output from this command to a `requirements.txt` file:

```
$ pip3 freeze --user > requirements.txt
```

Now that you have a `requirements.txt` file, people who clone your project can install all its dependencies using the `-r` option and the name of the requirements file:

```
$ pip3 install --user -r requirements.txt
```

The autogenerated requirements file format defaults to exact version matching (==). For example, a line such as `requests==2.22.0` tells `pip` that the version of `requests` to install must be exactly 2.22.0. There are other version specifiers you can utilize in a requirements file, such as minimum version (>=), version exclusion (`!=`), and maximum version (<=). Minimum version (>=) matches any version greater than or equal to the right-hand side. Version exclusion (`!=`) matches any version except the right-hand side. Maximum version matches any version less than or equal to the right-hand side.

You can combine multiple version specifiers in a single line using commas to separate them:

```
requests >=2.22.0,<3.0
```

The default behavior when `pip` installs the packages specified in a requirements file is to fetch them all from PyPI. You can override PyPI's URL (`https://pypi.org/simple/`) with that of an alternate Python package index by adding a line such as the following to the top of your `requirements.txt` file:

```
--index-url http://pypi.mydomain.com/mirror
```

The effort required to stand up and maintain your own private PyPI mirror is not insubstantial. When all you need to do is fix a bug or add a feature to a project dependency, it makes more sense to override the package source instead of the entire package index.

> **Tip**
>
> Version 4.3 of the Jetpack SDK for the NVIDIA Jetson Nano is based on Ubuntu's 18.04 LTS distribution. The Jetpack SDK adds extensive software support for the Nano's NVIDIA Maxwell 128 CUDA cores, such as GPU drivers and other runtime components. You can use `pip` to install a GPU-accelerated wheel for TensorFlow from NVIDIA's package index:
>
> ```
> $ pip install --user --extra-index-url https://
> developer.download.nvidia.com/compute/redist/jp/
> v43 tensorflow-gpu==2.0.0+nv20.1
> ```

I mentioned earlier how hardcoding distribution URLs inside `setup.py` is wrong. You can use the `-e` argument form in a requirements file to override individual package sources:

```
-e git+https://github.com/myteam/flask.git#egg=flask
```

In this example, I am instructing `pip` to fetch the `flask` package sources from my team's GitHub fork of `pallets/flask.git`. The `-e` argument form also takes a Git branch name, commit hash, or tag name:

```
-e git+https://github.com/myteam/flask.git@master
-e git+https://github.com/myteam/flask.
git@5142930ef57e2f0ada00248bdaeb95406d18eb7c
-e git+https://github.com/myteam/flask.git@v1.0
```

Using `pip` to upgrade a project's dependencies to the latest versions published on PyPI is fairly straightforward:

```
$ pip3 install --upgrade -user -r requirements.txt
```

After you have verified installing with `pip:requirements.txt` that the latest versions of your dependencies do not break your project, you can then write them back out to the requirements file:

```
$ pip3 freeze --user > requirements.txt
```

Make sure that freezing did not overwrite any of the overrides or special version handling in your requirements file. Undo any mistakes and commit the updated `requirements.txt` file to version control.

At some point, upgrading your project dependencies will result in your code breaking. A new package release may introduce a regression or incompatibility with your project. The requirements file format provides syntax to deal with these situations. Let's say you have been using version 2.22.0 of `requests` in your project and version 3.0 is released. According to the practice of semantic versioning, incrementing the major version number indicates that version 3.0 of `requests` includes breaking changes to that library's API. You can express the new version requirements like this:

```
requests ~= 2.22.0
```

The compatible release specifier (~=) relies on semantic versioning. Compatible means greater than or equal to the right-hand side and less than the next version major number (for example, `>= 1.1` and `== 1.*`). You have already seen me express these same version requirements for `requests` less ambiguously as follows:

```
requests >=2.22.0,<3.0
```

These `pip` dependency management techniques work fine if you only develop a single Python project at a time. But chances are you use the same machine to work on several Python projects at once, each potentially requiring a different version of the Python interpreter. The biggest problem with using only `pip` for multiple projects is that it installs all packages to the same user `site-packages` directory for a particular version of Python. This makes it very hard to isolate dependencies from one project to the next.

As we'll soon see, `pip` combines well with Docker for deploying Python applications. You can add `pip` to a Buildroot- or Yocto-based Linux image but that only enables quick onboard experimentation. A Python runtime package installer such as `pip` is ill-suited for Buildroot and Yocto environments where you want to define the entire contents of your embedded Linux image at build time. `pip` works great inside containerized environments such as Docker where the line between build time and runtime is often blurry.

In *Chapter 7, Developing with Yocto*, you learned about the Python modules available to you in the `meta-python` layer and how to define a custom layer for your own application. You can use the `requirements.txt` files generated by `pip freeze` to inform the selection of dependencies from `meta-python` for your own layer recipes. Buildroot and Yocto both install Python packages in a system-wide manner, so the virtual environment techniques we are going to discuss next do not apply to embedded Linux builds. They do, however, make it easier to generate accurate `requirements.txt` files.

Managing Python virtual environments with venv

A **virtual environment** is a self-contained directory tree containing a Python interpreter for a particular version of Python, a `pip` executable for managing project dependencies, and a local `site-packages` directory. Switching between virtual environments tricks the shell into thinking that the only Python and `pip` executables available are the ones present in the active virtual environment. Best practice dictates that you create a different virtual environment for each of your projects. This form of isolation solves the problem of two projects depending on different versions of the same package.

Virtual environments are not new to Python. The system-wide nature of Python installations necessitates them. Besides enabling you to install different versions of the same package, virtual environments also provide an easy way for you to run multiple versions of the Python interpreter. Several options exist for managing Python virtual environments. A tool that was immensely popular only 2 years ago (`pipenv`) has since languished by the time of writing. Meanwhile, a new contender has arisen (`poetry`) and Python 3's built-in support for virtual environments (`venv`) is starting to see more adoption.

Venv has been shipping with Python since version 3.3 (released in 2012). Because it only comes bundled with Python 3 installations, `venv` is incompatible with projects that require Python 2.7. Now that support for Python 2.7 officially ended on January 1, 2020, this Python 3 limitation is less of a concern. `Venv` is based on the popular `virtualenv` tool, which is still maintained and available on PyPI. If you have one or more projects that still require Python 2.7 for one reason or another, then you can use `virtualenv` instead of `venv` to work on those.

By default, `venv` installs the most recent version of Python found on your system. If you have multiple versions of Python on your system, you can select a specific Python version by running `python3` or whichever version you want when creating each virtual environment (*The Python Tutorial*, `https://docs.python.org/3/tutorial/venv.html`). Developing with the most recent version of Python is usually fine for greenfield projects but unacceptable for most legacy and enterprise software. We will use the version of Python 3 that came with your Ubuntu system to create and work with a virtual environment.

To create a virtual environment, first decide where you want to put it, and then run the `venv` module as a script with the target directory path:

1. Ensure `venv` is installed on your Ubuntu system:

```
$ sudo apt install python3-venv
```

2. Create a new directory for your project:

```
$ mkdir myproject
```

3. Switch to that new directory:

```
$ cd myproject
```

4. Create the virtual environment inside a subdirectory named `venv`:

```
$ python3 -m venv ./venv
```

Now that you have created a virtual environment, here is how you activate and verify it:

1. Switch to your project directory if you haven't already:

```
$ cd myproject
```

2. Check where your system's `pip3` executable is installed:

```
$ which pip3
/usr/bin/pip3
```

3. Activate the project's virtual environment:

```
$ source ./venv/bin/activate
```

4. Check where your project's `pip3` executable is installed:

```
(venv) $ which pip3
/home/frank/myproject/venv/bin/pip3
```

5. List the packages that came installed with the virtual environment:

```
(venv) $ pip3 list
Package       Version
------------- -------
pip           20.0.2
```

```
pkg-resources 0.0.0
setuptools    44.0.0
```

If you enter the `which pip` command from within your virtual environment, you will see that `pip` now points to the same executable as `pip3`. Prior to activating the virtual environment, `pip` probably did not point to anything because Ubuntu 20.04 LTS no longer comes with Python 2.7 installed. The same can be said for `python` versus `python3`. You can now omit the `3` when running either `pip` or `python` from within your virtual environment.

Next, let's install a property-based testing library named `hypothesis` into our existing virtual environment:

1. Switch to your project directory if you haven't already:

```
$ cd myproject
```

2. Reactivate the project's virtual environment if it is not already active:

```
$ source ./venv/bin/activate
```

3. Install the `hypothesis` package:

```
(venv) $ pip install hypothesis
```

4. List the packages now installed inside the virtual environment:

```
(venv) $ pip list
Package          Version
---------------- -------
attrs            19.3.0
hypothesis       5.16.1
pip              20.0.2
pkg-resources    0.0.0
setuptools       44.0.0
sortedcontainers 2.2.2
```

Notice that two new packages were added to the list besides `hypothesis`, `attrs` and `sortedcontainers`. `hypothesis` depends on these two packages. Let's say you had another Python project that depended on version 18.2.0 instead of version 19.3.0 of `sortedcontainers`. Those two versions would be incompatible and thus conflict with each other. Virtual environments allow you to install both versions of the same package, a different version for each of the two projects.

You may have noticed that switching out of a project directory does not deactivate its virtual environment. Don't worry. Deactivating a virtual environment is as easy as this:

```
(venv) $ deactivate
$
```

This puts you back in the global system environment where you have to enter `python3` and `pip3` again. You have now seen everything you need to know to get started with Python virtual environments. Creating and switching between virtual environments is common practice now when developing in Python. Isolated environments make it easier to keep track of and manage your dependencies across multiple projects. Deploying Python virtual environments to embedded Linux devices for production makes less sense, but can still be done using a Debian packaging tool called `dh-virtualenv` (`https://github.com/spotify/dh-virtualenv`).

Installing precompiled binaries with conda

conda is a package and virtual environment management system used by the **Anaconda** distribution of software for the PyData community. The Anaconda distribution includes Python as well as binaries for several hard-to-build open source projects such as PyTorch and TensorFlow. `conda` can be installed without the full Anaconda distribution, which is very large, or the minimal **Miniconda** distribution, which is still over 256 MB.

Even though it was created for Python shortly after `pip`, `conda` has evolved into a general-purpose package manager like APT or Homebrew. Now, it can be used to package and distribute software for any language. Because `conda` downloads precompiled binaries, installing Python extension modules is a breeze. Another one of `conda`'s big selling points is that it is cross-platform, with full support for Linux, macOS, and Windows.

Besides package management, `conda` is also a full-blown virtual environment manager. `Conda` virtual environments have all the benefits we have come to expect from Python `venv` environments and more. Like `venv`, `conda` lets you use `pip` to install packages from PyPI into a project's local `site-packages` directory. If you prefer, you can use `conda`'s own package management capabilities to install packages from different channels. Channels are package feeds provided by Anaconda and other software distributions.

Environment management

Unlike venv, conda's virtual environment manager can easily juggle multiple versions of Python, including Python 2.7. You will need to have Miniconda installed on your Ubuntu system to do the following exercises. You want to use Miniconda instead of Anaconda for your virtual environments because Anaconda environments come with lots of preinstalled packages, many of which you will never need. Miniconda environments are stripped down and allow you to easily install any of Anaconda's packages should you have to.

To install and update Miniconda on Ubuntu 20.04 LTS, do the following:

1. Download Miniconda:

```
$ wget https://repo.anaconda.com/miniconda/Miniconda3-
latest-Linux-x86_64.sh
```

2. Install Miniconda:

```
$ bash Miniconda3-latest-Linux-x86_64.sh
```

3. Update all the installed packages in the root environment:

```
(base) $ conda update --all
```

Your fresh Miniconda installation comes with conda and a root environment containing a Python interpreter and some basic packages installed. By default, the python and pip executables of conda's root environment are installed into your home directory. The conda root environment is known as base. You can view its location along with the locations of any other available conda environments by issuing the following command:

```
(base) $ conda env list
```

Verify this root environment before creating your own conda environment:

1. Open a new shell after installing Miniconda.
2. Check where the root environment's python executable is installed:

```
(base) $ which python
```

3. Check the version of Python:

```
(base) $ python --version
```

4. Check where the root environment's pip executable is installed:

```
(base) $ which pip
```

5. Check the version of `pip`:

```
(base) $ pip --version
```

6. List the packages installed in the root environment:

```
(base) $ conda list
```

Next, create and work with your own `conda` environment named `py377`:

1. Create a new virtual environment named `py377`:

```
(base) $ conda create --name py377 python=3.7.7
```

2. Activate your new virtual environment:

```
(base) $ source activate py377
```

3. Check where your environment's `python` executable is installed:

```
(py377) $ which python
```

4. Check that the version of Python is 3.7.7:

```
(py377) $ python --version
```

5. List the packages installed in your environment:

```
(py377) $ conda list
```

6. Deactivate your environment:

```
(py377) $ conda deactivate
```

Using `conda` to create a virtual environment with Python 2.7 installed is as simple as the following:

```
(base) $ conda create --name py27 python=2.7.17
```

View your `conda` environments again to see whether `py377` and `py27` now appear in the list:

```
(base) $ conda env list
```

Lastly, let's delete the `py27` environment since we won't be using it:

```
(base) $ conda remove --name py27 -all
```

Now that you know how to use conda to manage virtual environments, let's use it to manage packages within those environments.

Package management

Since conda supports virtual environments, we can use pip to manage Python dependencies from one project to another in an isolated manner just like we did with venv. As a general-purpose package manager, conda has its own facilities for managing dependencies. We know that conda list lists all the packages that conda has installed in the active virtual environment. I also mentioned conda's use of package feeds, which are called channels:

1. You can get the list of channel URLs conda is configured to fetch from by entering this command:

```
(base) $ conda info
```

2. Before proceeding any further, let's reactivate the py377 virtual environment you created during the last exercise:

```
(base) $ source activate py377
(py377) $
```

3. Most Python development nowadays happens inside a Jupyter notebook, so let's install those packages first:

```
(py377) $ conda install jupyter notebook
```

4. Enter y when prompted. This will install the jupyter and notebook packages along with all their dependencies. When you enter conda list, you'll see that the list of installed packages is much longer than before. Now, let's install some more Python packages that we would need for a computer vision project:

```
(py377) $ conda install opencv matplotlib
```

5. Again, enter y when prompted. This time, the number of dependencies installed is smaller. Both opencv and matplotlib depend on numpy, so conda installs that package automatically without you having to specify it. If you want to specify an older version of opencv, you can install the desired version of the package this way:

```
(py377) $ conda install opencv=3.4.1
```

6. `conda` will then attempt to *solve* the active environment for this dependency. Since no other packages installed in this active virtual environment depend on `opencv`, the target version is easy to solve for. If they did, then you might encounter a package conflict and the reinstallation would fail. After solving, `conda` will prompt you before downgrading `opencv` and its dependencies. Enter `y` to downgrade `opencv` to version 3.4.1.
7. Now let's say you change your mind or a newer version of `opencv` is released that addresses your previous concern. This is how you would upgrade `opencv` to the latest version provided by the Anaconda distribution:

```
(py377) $ conda update opencv
```

8. This time, `conda` will prompt you to ask whether you want to update `opencv` and its dependencies for the latest version. This time, enter `n` to cancel the package update. Instead of updating packages individually, it's often easier to update all the packages installed in an active virtual environment at once:

```
(py377) $ conda update --all
```

9. Removing installed packages is also straightforward:

```
(py377) $ conda remove jupyter notebook
```

10. When `conda` removes `jupyter` and `notebook`, it removes all of their dangling dependencies as well. A dangling dependency is an installed package that no other installed packages depend on. Like most general-purpose package managers, `conda` will not remove any dependencies that other installed packages still depend on.
11. Sometimes you may not know the exact name of a package you want to install. Amazon offers an AWS SDK for Python called Boto. Like many Python libraries, there is a version of Boto for Python 2 and a newer version (Boto3) for Python 3. To search Anaconda for packages with the word `boto` in their names, enter the following command:

```
(py377) $ conda search '*boto*'
```

12. You should see `boto3` and `botocore` in the search results. At the time of writing, the most recent version of `boto3` available on Anaconda is 1.13.11. To view details on that specific version of `boto3`, enter the following command:

```
(py377) $ conda info boto3=1.13.11
```

13. The package details reveal that boto3 version 1.13.11 depends on botocore (botocore >=1.16.11,<1.17.0), so installing boto3 gets you both.

Now let's say you've installed all the packages you need to develop an OpenCV project inside a Jupyter notebook. How do you share these project requirements with someone else so that they can recreate your work environment? The answer may surprise you:

1. You export your active virtual environment to a YAML file:

```
(py377) $ conda env export > my-environment.yaml
```

2. Much like the list of requirements that pip freeze generates, the YAML that conda exports is a list of all the packages installed in your virtual environment together with their pinned versions. Creating a conda virtual environment from an environment file requires the -f option and the filename:

```
$ conda env create -f my-environment.yaml
```

3. The environment name is included in the exported YAML, so no --name option is necessary to create the environment. Whoever creates a virtual environment from my-environment.yaml will now see py377 in their list of environments when they issue conda env list.

conda is a very powerful tool in a developer's arsenal. By combining general-purpose package installation with virtual environments, it offers a compelling deployment story. conda achieves many of the same goals Docker (up next) does, but without the use of containers. It has an edge over Docker with respect to Python due to its focus on the data science community. Because the leading machine learning frameworks (such as PyTorch and TensorFlow) are largely CUDA-based, finding GPU-accelerated binaries is often difficult. conda solves this problem by providing multiple precompiled binary versions of packages.

Exporting conda virtual environments to YAML files for installation on other machines offers another deployment option. This solution is popular among the data science community, but it does not work in production for embedded Linux. conda is not one of the three package managers that Yocto supports. Even if conda was an option, the storage needed to accommodate Minconda on a Linux image is not a good fit for most embedded systems that are resource-constrained.

If your dev board has an NVIDIA GPU such as the NVIDIA Jetson series, then you really want to use `conda` for onboard development. Luckily, there is a `conda` installer named **Miniforge** (`https://github.com/conda-forge/miniforge`) that is known to work on 64-bit ARM machines like the Jetsons. With `conda` onboard, you can then install `jupyter`, `numpy`, `pandas`, `scikit-learn`, and most of the other popular Python data science libraries out there.

Deploying Python applications with Docker

Docker offers another way to bundle Python code with software written in other languages. The idea behind Docker is that instead of packaging and installing your application onto a preconfigured server environment, you build and ship a container image with your application and all its runtime dependencies. A **container image** is more like a virtual environment than a virtual machine. A **virtual machine** is a complete system image including a kernel and an operating system. A container image is a minimal user space environment that only comes with the binaries needed to run your application.

Virtual machines run on top of a **hypervisor** that emulates hardware. Containers run directly on top of the host operating system. Unlike virtual machines, containers are able to share the same operating system and kernel without the use of hardware emulation. Instead, they rely on two special features of the Linux kernel for isolation: **namespaces** and **cgroups**. Docker did not invent container technology, but they were the first to build tooling that made them easy to use. The tired excuse of *works on my machine* no longer flies now that Docker makes it so simple to build and deploy container images.

The anatomy of a Dockerfile

A **Dockerfile** describes the contents of a Docker image. Every Dockerfile contains a set of instructions specifying what environment to use and which commands to run. Instead of writing a Dockerfile from scratch, we will use an existing Dockerfile for a project template. This Dockerfile generates a Docker image for a very simple Flask web application that you can extend to fit your needs. The Docker image is built on top of an Alpine Linux, a very slim Linux distribution that is commonly used for container deployments. Besides Flask, the Docker image also includes uWSGI and Nginx for better performance.

Start by pointing your web browser at the `uwsgi-nginx-flask-docker` project on GitHub (`https://github.com/tiangolo/uwsgi-nginx-flask-docker`). Then, click on the link to the `python-3.8-alpine` Dockerfile from the `README.md` file.

Now look at the first line in that Dockerfile:

```
FROM tiangolo/uwsgi-nginx:python3.8-alpine
```

This `FROM` command tells Docker to pull an image named `uwsgi-nginx` from the `tiangolo` namespace with the `python3.8-alpine` tag from Docker Hub. Docker Hub is a public registry where people publish their Docker images for others to fetch and deploy. You can set up your own image registry using a service such as AWS ECR or Quay if you prefer. You will need to insert the name of your registry service in front of your namespace like this:

```
FROM quay.io/my-org/my-app:my-tag
```

Otherwise, Docker defaults to fetching images from Docker Hub. `FROM` is like an `include` statement in a Dockerfile. It inserts the contents of another Dockerfile into yours so that you have something to build on top of. I like to think of this approach as layering images. Alpine is the base layer, followed by Python 3.8, then uWSGI plus Nginx, and finally your Flask application. You can learn more about how image layering works by digging into the `python3.8-alpine` Dockerfile at `https://hub.docker.com/r/tiangolo/uwsgi-nginx`.

The next line of interest in the Dockerfile is the following:

```
RUN pip install flask
```

A `RUN` instruction runs a command. Docker executes the `RUN` instructions contained in the Dockerfile sequentially in order to build the resulting Docker image. This `RUN` instruction installs Flask into the system `site-packages` directory. We know that `pip` is available because the Alpine base image also includes Python 3.8.

Let's skip over Nginx's environment variables and go straight to copying:

```
COPY ./app /app
```

This particular Dockerfile is located inside a Git repo along with several other files and subdirectories. The `COPY` instruction copies a directory from the host Docker runtime environment (usually a Git clone of a repo) into the container being built.

The `python3.8-alpine.dockerfile` file you are looking at resides in a `docker-images` subdirectory of the `tiangolo/uwsgi-nginx-flask-docker` repo. Inside that `docker-images` directory is an `app` subdirectory containing a Hello World Flask web application. This `COPY` instruction copies the `app` directory from the example repo into the root directory of the Docker image:

```
WORKDIR /app
```

The `WORKDIR` instruction tells Docker which directory to work from inside the container. In this example, the `/app` directory that it just copied becomes the working directory. If the target working directory does not exist, then `WORKDIR` creates it. Any subsequent non-absolute paths that appear in this Dockerfile are hence relative to the `/app` directory.

Now let's see how an environment variable gets set inside the container:

```
ENV PYTHONPATH=/app
```

`ENV` tells Docker that what follows is an environment variable definition. `PYTHONPATH` is an environment variable that expands into a list of colon-delimited paths where the Python interpreter looks for modules and packages.

Next, let's jump a few lines down to the second `RUN` instruction:

```
RUN chmod +x /entrypoint.sh
```

The `RUN` instruction tells Docker to run a command from the shell. In this case, the command being run is `chmod`, which changes file permissions. Here it renders the `/entrypoint.sh` executable.

The next line in this Dockerfile is optional:

```
ENTRYPOINT ["/entrypoint.sh"]
```

`ENTRYPOINT` is the most interesting instruction in this Dockerfile. It exposes an executable to the Docker host command line when starting the container. This lets you pass arguments from the command line down to the executable inside the container. You can append these arguments after `docker run <image>` on the command line. If there is more than one `ENTRYPOINT` instruction in a Dockerfile, then only the last `ENTRYPOINT` is executed.

The last line in the Dockerfile is as follows:

```
CMD ["/start.sh"]
```

Like ENTRYPOINT instructions, CMD instructions execute at container start time rather than build time. When an ENTRYPOINT instruction is defined in a Dockerfile, a CMD instruction defines default arguments to be passed to that ENTRYPOINT. In this instance, the /start.sh path is the argument passed to /entrypoint.sh. The last line in /entrypoint.sh executes /start.sh:

```
exec "$@"
```

The /start.sh script comes from the uwsgi-nginx base image. /start.sh starts Nginx and uWSGI after /entrypoint.sh has configured the container runtime environment for them. When CMD is used in conjunction with ENTRYPOINT, the default arguments set by CMD can be overridden from the Docker host command line.

Most Dockerfiles do not have an ENTRYPOINT instruction, so the last line of a Dockerfile is usually a CMD instruction that runs in the foreground instead of default arguments. I use this Dockerfile trick to keep a general-purpose Docker container running for development:

```
CMD tail -f /dev/null
```

With the exception of ENTRYPOINT and CMD, all of the instructions in this example python-3.8-alpine Dockerfile only execute when the container is being built.

Building a Docker image

Before we can build a Docker image, we need a Dockerfile. You may already have some Docker images on your system. To see a list of Docker images, use the following:

```
$ docker images
```

Now, let's fetch and build the Dockerfile we just dissected:

1. Clone the repo containing the Dockerfile:

   ```
   $ git clone https://github.com/tiangolo/uwsgi-nginx-flask-docker.git
   ```

2. Switch to the docker-images subdirectory inside the repo:

   ```
   $ cd uwsgi-nginx-flask-docker/docker-images
   ```

3. Copy python3.8-alpine.dockerfile to a file named Dockerfile:

   ```
   $ cp python3.8-alpine.dockerfile Dockerfile
   ```

4. Build an image from the Dockerfile:

```
$ docker build -t my-image .
```

Once the image is done building, it will appear in your list of local Docker images:

```
$ docker images
```

A `uwsgi-nginx` base image should also appear in the list along with the newly built `my-image`. Notice that the elapsed time since the `uwsgi-nginx` base image was created is much greater than the time since `my-image` was created.

Running a Docker image

We now have a Docker image built that we can run as a container. To get a list of running containers on your system, use the following:

```
$ docker ps
```

To run a container based on `my-image`, issue the following `docker run` command:

```
$ docker run -d --name my-container -p 80:80 my-image
```

Now observe the status of your running container:

```
$ docker ps
```

You should see a container named `my-container` based on an image named `my-image` in the list. The `-p` option in the `docker run` command maps a container port to a host port. So, container port `80` maps to host port `80` in this example. This port mapping allows the Flask web server running inside the container to service HTTP requests.

To stop `my-container`, run this command:

```
$ docker stop my-container
```

Now check the status of your running container again:

```
$ docker ps
```

my-container should no longer appear in the list of running containers. Is the container gone? No, it is only stopped. You can still see my-container and its status by adding the -a option to the docker ps command:

```
$ docker ps -a
```

We'll look at how to delete containers we no longer need a bit later.

Fetching a Docker image

Earlier in this section, I touched on image registries such as Docker Hub, AWS ECR, and Quay. As it turns out, the Docker image that we built locally from a cloned GitHub repo is already published on Docker Hub. It is much quicker to fetch the prebuilt image from Docker Hub than to build it yourself on your system. The Docker images for the project can be found at https://hub.docker.com/r/tiangolo/uwsgi-nginx-flask. To pull the same Docker image that we built as my-image from Docker Hub, enter the following command:

```
$ docker pull tiangolo/uwsgi-nginx-flask:python3.8-alpine
```

Now look at your list of Docker images again:

```
$ docker images
```

You should see a new uwsgi-nginx-flask image in the list.

To run this newly fetched image, issue the following docker run command:

```
$ docker run -d --name flask-container -p 80:80 tiangolo/uwsgi-nginx-flask:python3.8-alpine
```

You can substitute the full image name (repo:tag) in the preceding docker run command with the corresponding image ID (hash) from docker images if you prefer not to type out the full image name.

Publishing a Docker image

To publish a Docker image to Docker Hub, you must first have an account and log in to it. You can create an account on Docker Hub by going to the website, https://hub.docker.com, and signing up. Once you have an account, then you can push an existing image to your Docker Hub repository:

1. Log in to the Docker Hub image registry from the command line:

```
$ docker login
```

2. Enter your Docker Hub username and password when prompted.
3. Tag an existing image with a new name that starts with the name of your repository:

```
$ docker tag my-image:latest <repository>/my-image:latest
```

   Replace <repository> in the preceding command with the name of your repository (the same as your username) on Docker Hub. You can also substitute the name of another existing image you wish to push for my-image:latest.

4. Push the image to the Docker Hub image registry:

```
$ docker push <repository>/my-image:latest
```

   Again, make the same replacements as you did for *Step 3*.

Images pushed to Docker Hub are publicly available by default. To visit the web page for your newly published image, go to https://hub.docker.com/repository/docker/<repository>/my-image. Replace <repository> in the preceding URL with the name of your repository (same as your username) on Docker Hub. You can also substitute the name of the actual image you pushed for my-image:latest if different. If you click on the **Tags** tab on that web page, you should see the docker pull command for fetching that image.

Cleaning up

We know that `docker images` lists images and `docker ps` lists containers. Before we can delete a Docker image, we must first delete any containers that reference it. To delete a Docker container, you first need to know the container's name or ID:

1. Find the target Docker container's name:

```
$ docker ps -a
```

2. Stop the container if it is running:

```
$ docker stop flask-container
```

3. Delete the Docker container:

```
$ docker rm flask-container
```

Replace `flask-container` in the two preceding commands with the container name or ID from *Step 1*. Every container that appears under `docker ps` also has an image name or ID associated with it. Once you have deleted all the containers that reference an image, you can then delete the image.

Docker image names (`repo:tag`) can get quite long (for example, `tiangolo/uwsgi-nginx-flask:python3.8-alpine`). For that reason, I find it easier to just copy and paste an image's ID (hash) when deleting:

1. Find the Docker image's ID:

```
$ docker images
```

2. Delete the Docker image:

```
$ docker rmi <image-ID>
```

Replace `<image-ID>` in the preceding command with the image ID from *Step 1*.

If you simply want to blow away all the containers and images that you are no longer using on your system, then here is the command:

```
$ docker system prune -a
```

`docker system prune` deletes all stopped containers and dangling images.

We've seen how `pip` can be used to install a Python application's dependencies. You simply add a `RUN` instruction that calls `pip install` to your Dockerfile. Because containers are sandboxed environments, they offer many of the same benefits that virtual environments do. But unlike `conda` and `venv` virtual environments, Buildroot and Yocto both have support for Docker containers. Buildroot has the `docker-engine` and `docker-cli` packages. Yocto has the `meta-virtualization` layer. If your device needs isolation because of Python package conflicts, then you can achieve that with Docker.

The `docker run` command provides options for exposing operating system resources to containers. Specifying a bind mount allows a file or directory on the host machine to be mounted inside a container for reading and writing. By default, containers publish no ports to the outside world. When you ran your `my-container` image, you used the `-p` option to publish port `80` from the container to port `80` on the host. The `--device` option adds a host device file under `/dev` to an unprivileged container. If you wish to grant access to all devices on the host, then use the `--privileged` option.

What containers excel at is deployments. Being able to push a Docker image that can then be easily pulled and run on any of the major cloud platforms has revolutionized the **DevOps** movement. Docker is also making inroads in the embedded Linux space thanks to OTA update solutions such as balena. One of the downsides of Docker is the storage footprint and memory overhead of the runtime. The Go binaries are a bit bloated, but Docker runs on quad-core 64-bit ARM SoCs such as the Raspberry Pi 4 just fine. If your target device has enough power, then run Docker on it. Your software development team will thank you.

Summary

By now, you're probably asking yourself, what does any of this Python packaging stuff have to do with embedded Linux? The answer is *not much*, but bear in mind that the word *programming* also happens to be in the title of this book. And this chapter has everything to do with modern-day programming. To succeed as a developer in this day and age, you need to be able to deploy your code to production fast, frequently, and in a repeatable manner. That means managing your dependencies carefully and automating as much of the process as possible. You have now seen what tools are available for doing that with Python.

In the next chapter, we will look in detail at the Linux process model and describe what a process really is, how it relates to threads, how they cooperate, and how they are scheduled. Understanding these things is important if you want to create a robust and maintainable embedded system.

Further reading

The following resources have more information about the topics introduced in this chapter:

- *Python Packaging User Guide*, PyPA: `https://packaging.python.org`
- *setup.py vs requirements.txt*, by Donald Stufft: `https://caremad.io/posts/2013/07/setup-vs-requirement`
- *pip User Guide*, PyPA: `https://pip.pypa.io/en/latest/user_guide/`
- *Poetry Documentation*, Poetry: `https://python-poetry.org/docs`
- *conda user guide*, Continuum Analytics: `https://docs.conda.io/projects/conda/en/latest/user-guide`
- *docker docs*, Docker Inc.: `https://docs.docker.com/engine/reference/commandline/docker`

17
Learning about Processes and Threads

In the preceding chapters, we considered the various aspects of creating an embedded Linux platform. Now, it is time to start looking at how you can use the platform to create a working device. In this chapter, I will talk about the implications of the Linux process model and how it encompasses multithreaded programs. I will look at the pros and cons of using single-threaded and multithreaded processes, as well as asynchronous message passing between processes and coroutines. Lastly, I will look at scheduling and differentiate between timeshare and real-time scheduling policies.

While these topics are not specific to embedded computing, it is important for a designer of any embedded device to have an overview of these topics. There are many good references on the subject, some of which I will list at the end of this chapter, but in general, they do not consider the embedded use cases. Due to this, I will be concentrating on the concepts and design decisions rather than on the function calls and code.

In this chapter, we will cover the following topics:

- Process or thread?
- Processes
- Threads
- ZeroMQ
- Scheduling

Let's get started!

Technical requirements

To follow along with the examples in this chapter, make sure the following software is installed on your Linux-based host system:

- Python: Python 3 interpreter and standard library
- Miniconda: Minimal installer for the `conda` package and virtual environment manager

See the section on `conda` in *Chapter 16, Packaging Python*, for directions on how to install Miniconda if you haven't already. The GCC C compiler and GNU `make` are also needed for this chapter's exercises, but these tools already come with most Linux distributions.

All the code for this chapter can be found in the `Chapter17` folder of this book's GitHub repository: `https://github.com/PacktPublishing/Mastering-Embedded-Linux-Programming-Third-Edition`.

Process or thread?

Many embedded developers who are familiar with **real-time operating systems** (**RTOS**) consider the Unix process model to be cumbersome. On the other hand, they see a similarity between an RTOS task and a Linux thread, and they have a tendency to transfer an existing design using a one-to-one mapping of RTOS tasks to threads. I have, on several occasions, seen designs in which the entire application is implemented with one process containing 40 or more threads. I want to spend some time considering whether this is a good idea or not. Let's begin with some definitions.

A **process** is a memory address space and a thread of execution, as shown in the following diagram. The address space is private to the process, so threads running in different processes cannot access it. This **memory separation** is created by the memory management subsystem in the kernel, which keeps a memory page mapping for each process and reprograms the memory management unit on each context switch. I will describe how this works in detail in *Chapter 18, Managing Memory*. Part of the address space is mapped to a file that contains the code and static data that the program is running, as shown here:

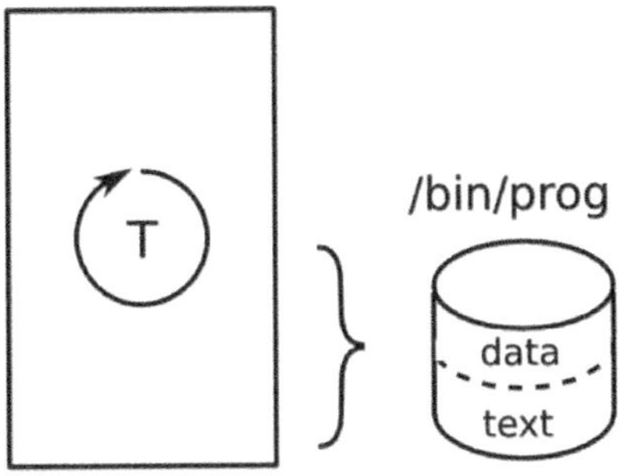

Figure 17.1 – Process

As the program runs, it will allocate resources such as stack space, heap memory, references to files, and so on. When the process terminates, these resources are reclaimed by the system: all the memory is freed up and all the file descriptors are closed.

Processes can communicate with each other using **inter-process communication** (**IPC**), such as local sockets. I will talk about IPC later on.

A **thread** is a thread of execution within a process. All processes begin with one thread that runs the `main()` function and is called the main thread. You can create additional threads, for example, using the `pthread_create(3)` POSIX function, which results in multiple threads executing in the same address space, as shown in the following diagram:

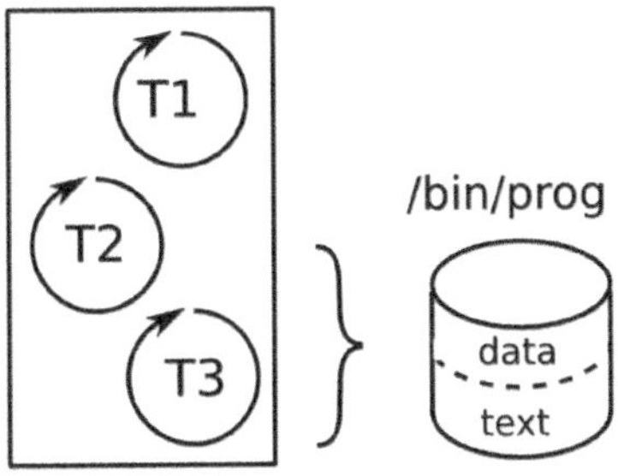

Figure 17.2 – Multiple threads

Being in the same process, the threads share resources with each other. They can read and write the same memory and use the same file descriptors. Communication between threads is easy, as long as you take care of the synchronization and locking issues.

So, based on these brief details, you can imagine two extreme designs for a hypothetical system with 40 RTOS tasks being ported to Linux.

You could map tasks to processes and have 40 individual programs communicating through IPC, for example, with messages being sent through sockets. You would greatly reduce memory corruption problems since the main thread running in each process is protected from the others, and you would reduce resource leakage since each process is cleaned up after it exits. However, the message interface between processes is quite complex and, where there is tight cooperation between a group of processes, the number of messages might be large and become a limiting factor regarding the performance of the system. Furthermore, any one of those 40 processes may terminate, perhaps because of a bug causing it to crash, leaving the other 39 to carry on. Each process would have to handle the fact that its neighbors are no longer running and recover gracefully.

At the other extreme, you could map tasks to threads and implement the system as a single process containing 40 threads. Cooperation becomes much easier because they share the same address space and file descriptors. The overhead of sending messages is reduced or eliminated, and context switches between threads are faster than between processes. The downside is that you have introduced the possibility of one task corrupting the heap or the stack of another. If any of the threads encounters a fatal bug, the whole process will terminate, taking all the threads with it. Finally, debugging a complex multithreaded process can be a nightmare.

The conclusion you should draw is that neither design is ideal and that there is a better way to do things. But before we get to that point, I will delve a little more deeply into the APIs and the behavior of processes and threads.

Processes

A process holds the environment in which threads can run: it holds the memory mappings, the file descriptors, the user and group IDs, and more. The first process is the `init` process, which is created by the kernel during boot and has a PID of one. Thereafter, processes are created by duplication in an operation known as **forking**.

Creating a new process

The POSIX function to create a process is `fork(2)`. It is an odd function because, for each successful call, there are two returns: one in the process that made the call, known as the **Parent**, and one in the newly created process, known as the **Child**, as shown in the following diagram:

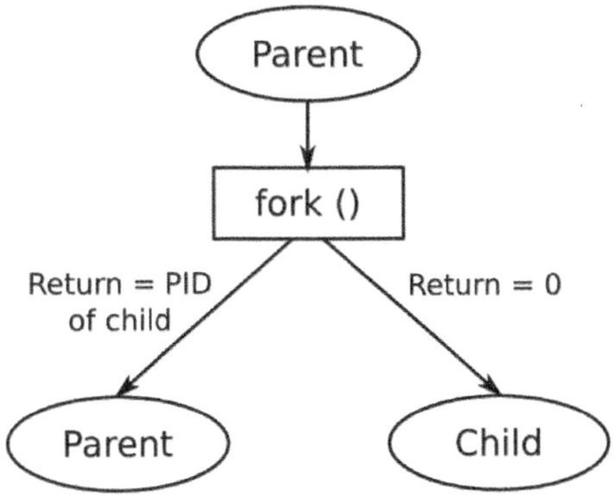

Figure 17.3 – Forking

Immediately after the call, the child is an exact copy of the parent: it has the same stack, the same heap, the same file descriptors, and it executes the same line of code – the one following `fork`. The only way the programmer can tell them apart is by looking at the return value of `fork`: it is *zero* for the child and *greater than zero* for the parent. Actually, the value that's returned to the parent is the PID of the newly created child process. There is a third possibility, which is that the return value is negative, which means that the `fork` call failed and there is still only one process.

Although the two processes are mostly identical, they are in separate address spaces. Changes that are made to a variable by one will not be seen by the other. Under the hood, the kernel does not make a physical copy of the parent's memory, which would be quite a slow operation and consume memory unnecessarily. Instead, the memory is shared but marked with a **copy-on-write** (**CoW**) flag. If either parent or child modifies this memory, the kernel makes a copy and then writes to the copy. This makes it an efficient fork function that also retains the logical separation of process address spaces. I will discuss CoW in *Chapter 18, Managing Memory*.

Now, let's learn how we can terminate a process.

Terminating a process

A process may be stopped voluntarily by calling the `exit(3)` function or, involuntarily, by receiving a signal that is not handled. One signal in particular, `SIGKILL`, cannot be handled, so it will always kill a process. In all cases, terminating the process will stop all threads, close all file descriptors, and release all memory. The system sends a signal, `SIGCHLD`, to the parent so that it knows this has happened.

Processes have a return value that is composed of either the argument to `exit`, if it terminated normally, or the signal number if it was killed. The chief use for this is in shell scripts: it allows you to test the return value from a program. By convention, `0` indicates success and any other values indicate a failure of some sort.

The parent can collect the return value with the `wait(2)` or `waitpid(2)` functions. This causes a problem: there will be a delay between a child terminating and its parent collecting the return value. In that period, the return value must be stored somewhere, and the PID number of the now dead process cannot be reused. A process in this state is known as a **zombie**, which is displayed as `state Z` in the `ps` and `top` commands. As long as the parent calls `wait` or `waitpid` whenever it is notified of a child's termination (by means of the `SIGCHLD` signal; refer to *Linux System Programming*, by Robert Love and O'Reilly Media or *The Linux Programming Interface*, by Michael Kerrisk, No Starch Press for details on handling signals). Usually, zombies exist for too short a time to show up in process listings. They will become a problem if the parent fails to collect the return value because eventually, there will not be enough resources to create any more processes.

The program in `MELP/Chapter17/fork-demo` illustrates process creation and termination:

```
#include <stdio.h>
#include <stdlib.h>
#include <unistd.h>
#include <sys/types.h>
#include <sys/wait.h>

int main(void)
{
        int pid;
        int status;
        pid = fork();
        if (pid == 0) {
```

```
        printf("I am the child, PID %d\n", getpid());
        sleep(10);
        exit(42);
    } else if (pid > 0) {
        printf("I am the parent, PID %d\n", getpid());
        wait(&status);
        printf("Child terminated, status %d\n",
WEXITSTATUS(status));
    } else
        perror("fork:");
    return 0;
}
```

The `wait` function blocks until a child process exits and stores the exit status. When you run it, you will see something like this:

```
I am the parent, PID 13851
I am the child, PID 13852
Child terminated with status 42
```

The child process inherits most of the attributes of the parent, including the user and group IDs, all open file descriptors, signal handling, and scheduling characteristics.

Running a different program

The `fork` function creates a copy of a running program, but it does not run a different program. For that, you need one of the `exec` functions:

```
int execl(const char *path, const char *arg, ...);
int execlp(const char *file, const char *arg, ...);
int execle(const char *path, const char *arg,
      ..., char * const envp[]);
int execv(const char *path, char *const argv[]);
int execvp(const char *file, char *const argv[]);
int execvpe(const char *file, char *const argv[],
      ..., char *const envp[]);
```

Each takes a path to the program file to load and run. If the function succeeds, the kernel discards all the resources of the current process, including memory and file descriptors, and allocates memory to the new program being loaded. When the thread that called `exec*` returns, it returns not to the line of code after the call but to the `main()` function of the new program. There is an example of a command launcher in `MELP/Chapter17/exec-demo`: it prompts for a command, such as `/bin/ls`, and forks and executes the string you enter. Here is the code:

```
#include <stdio.h>
#include <stdlib.h>
#include <string.h>
#include <unistd.h>
#include <sys/types.h>
#include <sys/wait.h>

int main(int argc, char *argv[])
{
        char command_str[128];
        int pid;
        int child_status;
        int wait_for = 1;

        while (1) {
            printf("sh> ");
            scanf("%s", command_str);
            pid = fork();
            if (pid == 0) {
                  /* child */
                  printf("cmd '%s'\n", command_str);
                  execl(command_str, command_str, (char *)NULL);
                  /* We should not return from execl, so only get
                    to this line if it failed */
                  perror("exec");
                  exit(1);
            }
            if (wait_for) {
                  waitpid(pid, &child_status, 0);
```

```
                printf("Done, status %d\n", child_status);
            }
        }
        return 0;
}
```

Here is what you will see when you run it:

```
# ./exec-demo
sh> /bin/ls
cmd '/bin/ls'
bin etc lost+found proc sys var
boot home media run tmp
dev lib mnt sbin usr
Done, status 0
sh>
```

You can terminate the program by typing *Ctrl* + *C*.

It might seem odd to have one function that duplicates an existing process and another that discards its resources and loads a different program into memory, especially since it is common for a fork to be followed almost immediately by one of the `exec` functions. Most operating systems combine the two actions into a single call.

There are distinct advantages to this, however. For example, it makes it very easy to implement redirection and pipes in the shell. Imagine that you want to get a directory listing. This is the sequence of events:

1. You type `ls` in the shell prompt.
2. The shell forks a copy of itself.
3. The child execs `/bin/ls`.
4. The `ls` program prints the directory listing to `stdout` (file descriptor `1`), which is attached to the terminal. You will see the directory listing.
5. The `ls` program terminates, and the shell regains control.

Now, imagine that you want the directory listing to be written to a file by redirecting the output using the > character. Now, the sequence is as follows:

1. You type `ls > listing.txt`.
2. The shell forks a copy of itself.

3. The child opens and truncates the `listing.txt` file and uses `dup2(2)` to copy the file descriptor of the file over file descriptor `1` (`stdout`).
4. The child execs `/bin/ls`.
5. The program prints the listing as it did previously, but this time, it is writing to `listing.txt`.
6. The `ls` program terminates, and the shell regains control.

> **Important Note**
>
> There was an opportunity in *step 3* to modify the environment of the child process before executing the program. The `ls` program does not need to know that it is writing to a file rather than a terminal. Instead of a file, `stdout` could be connected to a pipe so that the `ls` program, still unchanged, can send output to another program. This is part of the Unix philosophy of combining many small components that each do a job well, as described in *The Art of Unix Programming*, by Eric Steven Raymond and Addison Wesley, especially in the *Pipes, Redirection, and Filters* section.

So far, the programs we've looked at in this section all run in the foreground. But what about programs that run in the background, waiting for things to happen? Let's take a look.

Daemons

We have encountered daemons in several places already. A **daemon** is a process that runs in the background, owned by the `init` process, and not connected to a controlling terminal. The steps to create a daemon are as follows:

1. Call `fork` to create a new process, after which the parent should exit, thus creating an orphan that will be re-parented to `init`.
2. The child process calls `setsid(2)`, creating a new session and process group that it is the sole member of. The exact details do not matter here; you can simply consider this a way of isolating the process from any controlling terminal.
3. Change the working directory to the `root` directory.
4. Close all file descriptors and redirect `stdin`, `stdout`, and `stderr` (descriptors `0`, `1`, and `2`) to `/dev/null` so that there is no input, and all output is hidden.

Thankfully, all of the preceding steps can be achieved with a single function call; that is, `daemon(3)`.

Inter-process communication

Each process is an island of memory. You can pass information from one to another in two ways. Firstly, you can copy it from one address space to the other. Secondly, you can create an area of memory that both can access and share the data of.

The first is usually combined with a queue or buffer so that there is a sequence of messages passing between processes. This implies copying the message twice: first to a holding area and then to the destination. Some examples of this are sockets, pipes, and message queues.

The second way requires not only a method of creating memory that is mapped to two (or more) address spaces at once, but it is also a means of synchronizing access to that memory, for example, using semaphores or mutexes.

POSIX has functions for all of these. There is an older set of APIs known as **System V IPC**, which provides message queues, shared memory, and semaphores, but it is not as flexible as the POSIX equivalents, so I will not describe them here. The manual page on `svipc(7)` gives an overview of these facilities, and there are more details in *The Linux Programming Interface*, by Michael Kerrisk, and *Unix Network Programming, Volume 2*, by W. Richard Stevens.

Message-based protocols are usually easier to program and debug than shared memory, but are slow if the messages are large or there are many of them.

Message-based IPC

There are several options for message-based IPC, all of which I will summarize as follows. The attributes that differentiate one from the other are as follows:

- Whether the message flow is uni- or bi-directorial.
- Whether the data flow is a byte stream with no message boundary or discrete messages with boundaries preserved. In the latter case, the maximum size of a message is important.
- Whether messages are tagged with a priority.

The following table summarizes these properties for FIFOs, sockets, and message queues:

Property	**FIFO**	**Unix socket: stream**	**Unix socket: datagram**	**POSIX message queue**
Message boundary	Byte stream	Byte stream	Discrete	Discrete
Uni/bi-directional	Uni	Bi	Uni	Uni
Max message size	Unlimited	Unlimited	In the range of 100 KiB to 250 KiB	Default: 8 KiB Absolute maximum: 1 MiB
Priority levels	None	None	None	0 to 32767

The first form of message-based IPC we will look at is Unix sockets.

Unix (or local) sockets

Unix sockets fulfill most requirements and, coupled with the familiarity of the sockets API, are by far the most common mechanism.

Unix sockets are created with the `AF_UNIX` address family and bound to a pathname. Access to the socket is determined by the access permission of the socket file. As with internet sockets, the socket type can be `SOCK_STREAM` or `SOCK_DGRAM`, the former giving a bidirectional byte stream and the latter providing discrete messages with preserved boundaries. Unix socket datagrams are reliable, which means that they will not be dropped or reordered. The maximum size for a datagram is system-dependent and is available via `/proc/sys/net/core/wmem_max`. It is typically 100 KiB or more.

Unix sockets do not have a mechanism to indicate the priority of a message.

FIFOs and named pipes

FIFO and **named pipe** are just different terms for the same thing. They are an extension of the anonymous pipe that is used to communicate between parent and child processes when implementing pipes in the shell.

A FIFO is a special sort of file, created by the `mkfifo(1)` command. As with Unix sockets, the file access permissions determine who can read and write. They are unidirectional, which means that there is one reader and usually one writer, though there may be several. The data is a pure byte stream but guarantee the atomicity of messages that are smaller than the buffer associated with the pipe. In other words, writes less than this size will not be split into several smaller writes, so you will read the whole message in one go as long as the size of the buffer on your end is large enough. The default size of the FIFO buffer is 64 KiB on modern kernels and can be increased using `fcntl(2)` with `F_SETPIPE_SZ`, up to the value in `/proc/sys/fs/pipe-max-size`, which is typically 1 MiB. There is no concept of priority.

POSIX message queues

Message queues are identified by a name, which must begin with a forward slash, `/`, and contain only one `/` character: message queues are actually kept in a pseudo filesystem of the `mqueue` type. You create a queue and get a reference to an existing queue through `mq_open(3)`, which returns a file descriptor. Each message has a priority, and messages are read from the queue based on priority and then on the age order. Messages can be up to `/proc/sys/kernel/msgmax` bytes long.

The default value is 8 KiB, but you can set it to be any size in the range of 128 bytes to 1 MiB by writing the value to `/proc/sys/kernel/msgmax`. Since the reference is a file descriptor, you can use `select(2)`, `poll(2)`, and other similar functions to wait for activity in the queue.

Refer to the Linux `mq_overview(7)` man page for more details.

Summary of message-based IPC

Unix sockets are used the most often because they offer all that is needed, except perhaps message priority. They are implemented on most operating systems, so they confer maximum portability.

FIFOs are less frequently used, mostly because they lack an equivalent to a **datagram**. On the other hand, the API is very simple, since it provides the normal `open(2)`, `close(2)`, `read(2)`, and `write(2)` file calls.

Message queues are the least commonly used of this group. The code paths in the kernel are not optimized in the way that socket (network) and FIFO (filesystem) calls are.

There are also higher-level abstractions such as D-Bus, which are moving from mainstream Linux to embedded devices. D-Bus uses Unix sockets and shared memory under the surface.

Shared memory-based IPC

Sharing memory removes the need to copy data between address spaces but introduces the problem of synchronizing accesses to it. Synchronization between processes is commonly achieved using semaphores.

POSIX shared memory

To share memory between processes, you must create a new area of memory and then map it to the address space of each process that wants access to it, as shown in the following diagram:

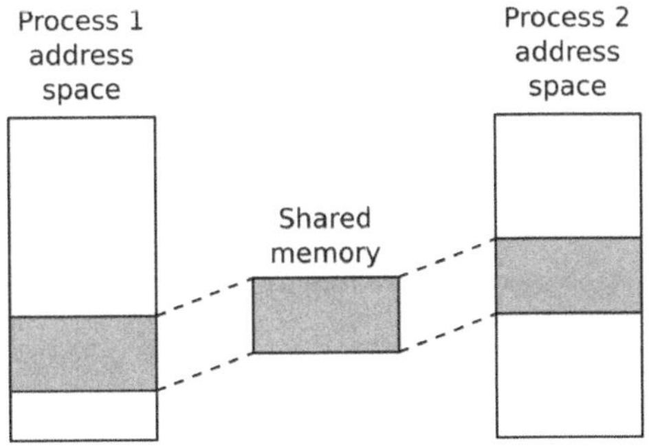

Figure 17.4 – POSIX shared memory

Naming POSIX shared memory segments follows the pattern we encountered with message queues. The segments are identified by names that begin with a / character and have exactly one such character:

```
#define SHM_SEGMENT_NAME "/demo-shm"
```

The `shm_open(3)` function takes the name and returns a file descriptor for it. If it does not exist already and the `O_CREAT` flag is set, then a new segment is created. Initially, it has a size of zero. You can use the (misleadingly named) `ftruncate(2)` function to expand it to the desired size:

```
int shm_fd;
struct shared_data *shm_p;
/* Attempt to create the shared memory segment */
shm_fd = shm_open(SHM_SEGMENT_NAME, O_CREAT | O_EXCL | O_RDWR,
0666);
if (shm_fd > 0) {
    /* succeeded: expand it to the desired size (Note: dont't
   do this every time because ftruncate fills it with zeros) */
    printf("Creating shared memory and setting size=%d\n",
            SHM_SEGMENT_SIZE);
    if (ftruncate(shm_fd, SHM_SEGMENT_SIZE) < 0) {
        perror("ftruncate");
        exit(1);
    }
    [...]
} else if (shm_fd == -1 && errno == EEXIST) {
    /* Already exists: open again without O_CREAT */
    shm_fd = shm_open(SHM_SEGMENT_NAME, O_RDWR, 0);
    [...]
}
```

Once you have a descriptor for the shared memory, you map it to the address space of the process using `mmap(2)` so that threads in different processes can access the memory:

```
/* Map the shared memory */
shm_p = mmap(NULL, SHM_SEGMENT_SIZE, PROT_READ | PROT_WRITE,
            MAP_SHARED, shm_fd, 0);
```

The program in `MELP/Chapter17/shared-mem-demo` provides an example of using a shared memory segment to communicate between processes. Here is the `main` function:

```
static sem_t *demo_sem;
[...]
int main(int argc, char *argv[])
{
        char *shm_p;
        printf("%s PID=%d\n", argv[0], getpid());
        shm_p = get_shared_memory();

        while (1) {
                printf("Press enter to see the current contents of 
shm\n");
                getchar();
                sem_wait(demo_sem);
                printf("%s\n", shm_p);
                /* Write our signature to the shared memory */
                sprintf(shm_p, "Hello from process %d\n", getpid());
                sem_post(demo_sem);
        }
        return 0;
}
```

The program uses a shared memory segment to communicate a message from one process to another. The message is `Hello from process string`, followed by its PID. The `get_shared_memory` function is responsible for creating the memory segment, if it does not exist, or getting the file descriptor for it if it does. It returns a pointer to the memory segment. Notice that there is a semaphore to synchronize access to the memory so that one process does not overwrite a message from another.

To try it out, you need two instances of the program running in separate terminal sessions. In the first terminal, you will see something like this:

```
# ./shared-mem-demo
./shared-mem-demo PID=271
Creating shared memory and setting size=65536
Press enter to see the current contents of shm

```

```
Press enter to see the current contents of shm

Hello from process 271
```

Because this is the first time the program is being run, it creates the memory segment. Initially, the message area is empty, but after one run through the loop, it contains the PID of this process, which is `271`. Now, you can run a second instance in another terminal:

```
# ./shared-mem-demo
./shared-mem-demo PID=279
Press enter to see the current contents of shm

Hello from process 271

Press enter to see the current contents of shm

Hello from process 279
```

It does not create the shared memory segment because it exists already, and it displays the message that it contains already, which is the PID of the other program. Pressing *Enter* causes it to write its own PID, which the first program would be able to see. By doing this, the two programs can communicate with each other.

The POSIX IPC functions are part of the POSIX real-time extensions, so you need to link them with `librt`. Oddly, the POSIX semaphores are implemented in the POSIX threads library, so you need to link to the pthreads library as well. Hence, the compilation arguments are as follows when you're targeting Arm Cortex-A8 SoCs:

```
$ arm-cortex_a8-linux-gnueabihf-gcc shared-mem-demo.c -lrt
-pthread \
-o arm-cortex_a8-linux-gnueabihf-gcc

```

This concludes our survey of IPC methods. We will revisit message-based IPC again when we cover ZeroMQ. Now, it is time to look at multithreaded processes.

Threads

The programming interface for threads is the POSIX threads API, which was first defined in the IEEE POSIX 1003.1c standard (1995) and is commonly known as **pthreads**. It is implemented as an additional part of the `libpthread.so` C library. There have been two implementations of pthreads over the last 15 years or so: **LinuxThreads** and **Native POSIX Thread Library** (**NPTL**). The latter is much more compliant with the specification, particularly regarding the handling of signals and process IDs. It is pretty dominant now, but you may come across some older versions of `uClibc` that use LinuxThreads.

Creating a new thread

The function you can use to create a thread is `pthread_create(3)`:

```
int pthread_create(pthread_t *thread, const pthread_attr_t
*attr,
       void *(*start_routine) (void *), void *arg);
```

It creates a new thread of execution that begins in the `start_routine` function and places a descriptor in `pthread_t`, which is pointed to by `thread`. It inherits the scheduling parameters of the calling thread, but these can be overridden by passing a pointer to the thread attributes in `attr`. The thread will start executing immediately.

`pthread_t` is the main way to refer to the thread within the program, but the thread can also be seen from outside using a command such as `ps -eLf`:

```
UID PID PPID LWP C NLWP STIME TTY TIME CMD
...
chris 6072 5648 6072 0 3 21:18 pts/0 00:00:00 ./thread-demo
chris 6072 5648 6073 0 3 21:18 pts/0 00:00:00 ./thread-demo
```

In the preceding output, the `thread-demo` program has two threads. The `PID` and `PPID` columns show that they all belong to the same process and have the same parent, as you would expect. The column marked `LWP` is interesting, though. **LWP** stands for **Light Weight Process**, which, in this context, is another name for a thread. The numbers in that column are also known as **Thread IDs** or **TIDs**. In the main thread, the TID is the same as the PID, but for the others, it is a different (higher) value. You can use a TID in places where the documentation states that you must give a PID, but be aware that this behavior is specific to Linux and is not portable. Here is a simple program that illustrates the life cycle of a thread (the code is in `MELP/Chapter17/thread-demo`):

```
#include <stdio.h>
#include <unistd.h>
```

```
#include <pthread.h>
#include <sys/syscall.h>

static void *thread_fn(void *arg)
{
        printf("New thread started, PID %d TID %d\n",
            getpid(), (pid_t)syscall(SYS_gettid));
        sleep(10);
        printf("New thread terminating\n");
        return NULL;
}

int main(int argc, char *argv[])
{
        pthread_t t;

        printf("Main thread, PID %d TID %d\n",
            getpid(), (pid_t)syscall(SYS_gettid));
        pthread_create(&t, NULL, thread_fn, NULL);
        pthread_join(t, NULL);
        return 0;
}
```

Note that, in the `thread_fn` function, I am retrieving the TID using `syscall(SYS_gettid)`. Prior to `glibc` 2.80, you had to call Linux directly through a `syscall` because there was no C library wrapper for `gettid()`.

There is a limit to the total number of threads that a given kernel can schedule. The limit scales according to the size of the system, from around 1,000 on small devices up to tens of thousands on larger embedded devices. The actual number is available in `/proc/sys/kernel/threads-max`. Once you reach this limit, fork and `pthread_create` will fail.

Terminating a thread

A thread terminates when any of the following occurs:

- It reaches the end of its `start_routine`.
- It calls `pthread_exit(3)`.

- It is canceled by another thread calling `pthread_cancel(3)`.
- The process that contains the thread terminates, for example, because of a thread calling `exit(3)`, or the process receiving a signal that is not handled, masked, or ignored.

Note that if a multithreaded program calls `fork`, only the thread that made the call will exist in the new child process. Fork does not replicate all threads.

A thread has a return value, which is a void pointer. One thread can wait for another to terminate and collect its return value by calling `pthread_join(2)`. There is an example of this in the code for `thread-demo`, as we mentioned in the preceding section. This produces a problem that is very similar to the zombie problem among processes: the resources of the thread, such as the stack, cannot be freed up until another thread has joined with it. If threads remain *unjoined*, there is a resource leak in the program.

Compiling a program with threads

The support for POSIX threads is part of the C library in the `libpthread.so` library. However, there is more to building programs with threads than linking the library: there must be changes to the way the compiler generates code to make sure that certain global variables, such as `errno`, have one instance per thread rather than one for the whole process.

> **Tip**
> When building a threaded program, you must add the `-pthread` switch to the compile and link stages. However, you don't have to also use `-lpthread` for the link stage, as you might expect if you use `-pthread`.

Inter-thread communication

The big advantage of threads is that they share the address space and can share memory variables. This is also a big disadvantage because it requires synchronization to preserve data consistency in a manner similar to memory segments shared between processes but with the provision that, with threads, all memory is shared. In fact, threads can create private memory using **thread local storage** (**TLS**), but I will not cover that here.

The `pthreads` interface provides the basics necessary to achieve synchronization: mutexes and condition variables. If you want more complex structures, you will have to build them yourself.

It is worth noting that all the IPC methods we described earlier – that is, sockets, pipes, and message queues – work equally well between threads in the same process.

Mutual exclusion

To write robust programs, you need to protect each shared resource with a mutex lock, and make sure that every code path that reads or writes the resource has locked the mutex first. If you apply this rule consistently, most of the problems should be solved. The ones that remain are associated with the fundamental behavior of mutexes. I will list them briefly here but will not go into too much detail:

- **Deadlock**: This occurs when mutexes become permanently locked. A classic situation is the **deadly embrace**, in which two threads each require two mutexes and have managed to lock one of them but not the other. Each thread blocks, waiting for the lock the other has, and so they remain as they are. One simple rule for avoiding the deadly embrace problem is to make sure that mutexes are always locked in the same order. Other solutions involve timeouts and back-off periods.
- **Priority inversion**: The delays caused by waiting for a mutex can cause a real-time thread to miss deadlines. The specific case of priority inversion happens when a high priority thread becomes blocked, waiting for a mutex locked by a low priority thread. If the low priority thread is preempted by other threads of intermediate priority, the high priority thread is forced to wait for an unbounded length of time. There are mutex protocols called **priority inheritance** and **priority ceiling** that resolve the problem at the expense of greater processing overhead in the kernel for each lock and unlock call.
- **Poor performance**: Mutexes introduce minimal overhead to the code, as long as threads don't have to block on them most of the time. If your design has a resource that is needed by a lot of threads, however, the contention ratio becomes significant. This is usually a design issue that can be resolved using finer grained locking or a different algorithm.

Mutexes are not the only way to synchronize between threads. We witnessed how two processes can use a semaphore to notify each other back when we covered POSIX shared memory. Threads have a similar construct.

Changing conditions

Cooperating threads need to be able to alert one another that something has changed and needs attention. This is called a **condition**, and the alert is sent through a **condition variable**, or **condvar**.

A condition is just something that you can test to give a `true` or `false` result. A simple example is a buffer that contains either zero or some items. One thread takes items from the buffer and sleeps when it is empty. Another thread places items into the buffer and signals the other thread that it has done so because the condition that the other thread is waiting on has changed. If it is sleeping, it needs to wake up and do something. The only complexity is that the condition is, by definition, a shared resource, so it must be protected by a mutex.

Here is a simple program with two threads. The first is the producer: it wakes every second and puts some data into a global variable before signaling that there has been a change. The second thread is the consumer: it waits on the condition variable and tests the condition (that there is a string in the buffer of nonzero length) each time it wakes up. You can find the code in `MELP/Chapter17/condvar-demo`:

```
#include <stdio.h>
#include <stdlib.h>
#include <pthread.h>
#include <unistd.h>
#include <string.h>

char g_data[128];
pthread_cond_t cv = PTHREAD_COND_INITIALIZER;
pthread_mutex_t mutx = PTHREAD_MUTEX_INITIALIZER;

void *consumer(void *arg)
{
        while (1) {
                pthread_mutex_lock(&mutx);
                while (strlen(g_data) == 0)
                        pthread_cond_wait(&cv, &mutx);

                /* Got data */
                printf("%s\n", g_data);
                /* Truncate to null string again */
                g_data[0] = 0;
                pthread_mutex_unlock(&mutx);
        }
```

```
        return NULL;
}

void *producer(void *arg)
{
        int i = 0;

        while (1) {
                sleep(1);
                pthread_mutex_lock(&mutx);
                sprintf(g_data, "Data item %d", i);
                pthread_mutex_unlock(&mutx);
                pthread_cond_signal(&cv);
                i++;
        }
        return NULL;
}
```

Note that when the consumer thread blocks on the condvar, it does so while holding a locked mutex, which would seem to be a recipe for deadlock the next time the producer thread tries to update the condition. To avoid this, `pthread_condwait(3)` unlocks the mutex after the thread is blocked, and then locks it again before waking it and returning from the wait.

Partitioning the problem

Now that we have covered the basics of processes and threads and the ways in which they communicate, it is time to see what we can do with them.

Here are some of the rules I use when building systems:

- **Rule 1**: Keep tasks that have a lot of interaction together: It is important to minimize overheads by keeping closely inter-operating threads together in one process.
- **Rule 2**: Don't put all your threads in one basket: On the other hand, try and keep components with limited interaction in separate processes, in the interests of resilience and modularity.

- **Rule 3**: Don't mix critical and noncritical threads in the same process: This is an amplification of *Rule 2*: the critical part of the system, which might be a machine control program, should be kept as simple as possible and written in a more rigorous way than other parts. It must be able to continue, even if other processes fail. If you have real-time threads, by definition, they must be critical and should go into a process by themselves.
- **Rule 4**: Threads shouldn't get too intimate: One of the temptations when writing a multithreaded program is to intermingle the code and variables between threads because it is an all-in-one program and easy to do. Keep the threads modular, with well-defined interactions.
- **Rule 5**: Don't think that threads are free: It is very easy to create additional threads, but there is a cost, not least in terms of the additional synchronization necessary to coordinate their activities.
- **Rule 6**: Threads can work in parallel: Threads can run simultaneously on a multicore processor, giving higher throughput. If you have a large computing job, you can create one thread per core and make maximum use of the hardware. There are libraries to help you do this, such as OpenMP. You should probably not be coding parallel programming algorithms from scratch.

The Android design is a good illustration. Each application is a separate Linux process that helps modularize memory management and ensures that one app crashing does not affect the whole system. The process model is also used for access control: a process can only access the files and resources that its UID and GIDs allow it to. There are a group of threads in each process. There is one to manage and update the user interface, one to handle signals from the operating system, several to manage dynamic memory allocation and freeing up Java objects, and a worker pool of at least two threads for receiving messages from other parts of the system using the Binder protocol.

To summarize, processes provide resilience because each process has a protected memory space, and when the process terminates, all resources, including memory and file descriptors, are freed up, reducing resource leaks. On the other hand, threads share resources and can communicate easily through shared variables and can cooperate by sharing access to files and other resources. Threads give parallelism through worker pools and other abstractions, which is useful in multicore processors.

ZeroMQ

Sockets, named pipes, and shared memory are the means by which inter-process communication take place. They act as the transport layers for the message passing process that makes up most non-trivial applications. Concurrency primitives such as mutexes and condition variables are used to manage shared access and coordinate work between threads running inside the same process. Multithreaded programming is notoriously difficult, and sockets and named pipes come with their own set of gotchas. A higher-level API is needed to abstract the complex details of asynchronous message passing. Enter ZeroMQ.

ZeroMQ is an asynchronous messaging library that acts like a concurrency framework. It has facilities for in-process, inter-process, TCP, and multicast transports, as well as bindings for various programming languages, including C, C++, Go, and Python. Those bindings, along with ZeroMQ's socket-based abstractions, allow teams to easily mix programming languages within the same distributed application. Support for common messaging patterns such as request/reply, publish/subscribe, and parallel pipeline is also built into the library. The *zero* in ZeroMQ stands for *zero cost*, while the *MQ* part stands for *message queue*.

We will explore both inter-process and in-process message-based communication using ZeroMQ. Let's start by installing ZeroMQ for Python.

Getting pyzmq

We are going to use ZeroMQ's official Python binding for the following exercises. I recommend installing this `pyzmq` package inside a new virtual environment. Creating a Python virtual environment is easy if you already have `conda` on your system. Here are the steps for provisioning the necessary virtual environment using `conda`:

1. Navigate to the `zeromq` directory containing the examples:

```
(base) $ cd MELP/Chapter17/zeromq
```

2. Create a new virtual environment named `zeromq`:

```
(base) $ conda create --name zeromq python=3.9 pyzmq
```

3. Activate your new virtual environment:

```
(base) $ source activate zeromq
```

4. Check that the version of Python is 3.9:

```
(zeromq) $ python --version
```

5. List the packages that have been installed in your environment:

```
(zeromq) $ conda list
```

If you see `pyzmq` and its dependencies in the list of packages, then you are now ready to run the following exercises.

Messaging between processes

We will begin our exploration of ZeroMQ with a simple echo server. The server expects a name in the form of a string from a client and replies with `Hello <name>`. The code is in `MELP/Chapter17/zeromq/server.py`:

```
import time
import zmq

context = zmq.Context()
socket = context.socket(zmq.REP)
socket.bind("tcp://*:5555")

while True:
    # Wait for next request from client
    message = socket.recv()
    print(f"Received request: {message}")

    # Do some 'work'
    time.sleep(1)

    # Send reply back to client
    socket.send(b"Hello {message}")
```

The server process creates a socket of the `REP` type for its response, binds that socket to port `5555`, and waits for messages. A 1-second sleep is used to simulate some work being done in-between the time when a request is received and a reply is sent back.

The code for the echo client is in `MELP/Chapter17/zeromq/client.py`:

```
import zmq

def main(who):
```

```
    context = zmq.Context()

    #  Socket to talk to server
    print("Connecting to hello echo server…")
    socket = context.socket(zmq.REQ)
    socket.connect("tcp://localhost:5555")

    #  Do 5 requests, waiting each time for a response
    for request in range(5):
        print(f"Sending request {request} …")
        socket.send(b"{who}")

        # Get the reply.
        message = socket.recv()
        print(f"Received reply {request} [ {message} ]")

if __name__ == '__main__':
    import sys

    if len(sys.argv) != 2:
        print("usage: client.py <username>")
        raise SystemExit
    main(sys.argv[1])
```

The client process takes a username as a command-line argument. The client creates a socket of the `REQ` type for requests, connects to the server process listening on port `5555`, and begins sending messages containing the username that was passed in. Like `socket.recv()` in the server, `socket.recv()` in the client blocks until a message arrives in the queue.

To see the echo server and client code in action, activate your `zeromq` virtual environment and run the `planets.sh` script from the `MELP/Chapter17/zeromq` directory:

```
(zeromq) $ ./planets.sh
```

The `planets.sh` script spawns three client processes called `Mars`, `Jupiter`, and `Venus`. We can see that the requests from the three clients are interleaved because each client waits for a reply from the server before sending its next request. Since each client sends five requests, we should receive a total of 15 replies from the server. Message-based IPC is remarkably easy with ZeroMQ. Now, let's use Python's built-in `asyncio` module, along with ZeroMQ, to do in-process messaging.

Messaging within processes

The `asyncio` module was introduced in version 3.4 of Python. It adds a pluggable event loop for executing single-threaded concurrent code using coroutines. **Coroutines** (also known as *green threads*) in Python are declared with the `async/await` syntax, which has been adopted from C#. They are much lighter-weight than POSIX threads and work more like resumable functions. Because coroutines operate in the single-threaded context of an event loop, we can use `pyzmq` in conjunction with `asyncio` for in-process socket-based messaging.

Here is a slightly modified version of an example of coroutines taken from the `https://github.com/zeromq/pyzmq` repository:

```
import time
import zmq
from zmq.asyncio import Context, Poller
import asyncio

url = 'inproc://#1'
ctx = Context.instance()

async def receiver():
    """receive messages with polling"""
    pull = ctx.socket(zmq.PAIR)
    pull.connect(url)
    poller = Poller()
    poller.register(pull, zmq.POLLIN)
    while True:
        events = await poller.poll()
        if pull in dict(events):
            print("recving", events)
```

```
            msg = await pull.recv_multipart()
            print('recvd', msg)

async def sender():
    """send a message every second"""
    tic = time.time()
    push = ctx.socket(zmq.PAIR)
    push.bind(url)
    while True:
        print("sending")
        await push.send_multipart([str(time.time() - tic).
encode('ascii')])
        await asyncio.sleep(1)

asyncio.get_event_loop().run_until_complete(
    asyncio.wait(
        [
            receiver(),
            sender(),
        ]
    )
)
```

Notice that the `receiver()` and `sender()` coroutines share the same context. The `inproc` transport method specified in the `url` part of the socket is meant for inter-thread communications and is much faster than the `tcp` transport we used in the previous example. The `PAIR` pattern connects two sockets exclusively. Like the `inproc` transport, this messaging pattern only works in-process and is intended for signaling between threads. Neither the `receiver()` or `sender()` coroutines returns. The `asyncio` event loop alternates between the two coroutines, suspending and resuming each on blocking or completing I/O.

To run the coroutines example from your active `zeromq` virtual environment, use the following command:

```
(zeromq) $ python coroutines.py
```

`sender()` sends timestamps to `receiver()`, which displays them. Use *Ctrl* + *C* to terminate the process. Congratulations! You have just witnessed in-process asynchronous messaging without the use of explicit threads. There is much more to say and learn about coroutines and `asyncio`. This example was only meant to give you a taste of what is now possible with Python when paired with ZeroMQ. Let's leave single-threaded event loops behind for the time being and get back to the subject of Linux.

Scheduling

The second big topic I want to cover in this chapter is scheduling. The Linux scheduler has a queue of threads that are ready to run, and its job is to schedule them on CPUs as they become available. Each thread has a scheduling policy that may be time-shared or real-time. The time-shared threads have a **niceness** value that increases or reduces their entitlement to CPU time. The real-time threads have **priority** in that a higher priority thread will preempt a lower one. The scheduler works with threads, not processes. Each thread is scheduled regardless of which process it is running in.

The scheduler runs when any of the following occurs:

- A thread is blocked by calling `sleep()` or another blocking system call
- A time-shared thread exhausts its time slice
- An interruption causes a thread to be unblocked, for example, because of I/O completing

For background information on the Linux scheduler, I recommend that you read the chapter on process scheduling in *Linux Kernel Development*, 3rd edition, by Robert Love.

Fairness versus determinism

I have grouped the scheduling policies into two categories: time-shared and real-time. Time-shared policies are based on the principal of *fairness*. They are designed to make sure that each thread gets a fair amount of processor time and that no thread can hog the system. If a thread runs for too long, it is put to the back of the queue so that others can have a go. At the same time, a fairness policy needs to adjust to threads that are doing a lot of work and give them the resources to get the job done. Time-shared scheduling is good because of the way it automatically adjusts to a wide range of workloads.

On the other hand, if you have a real-time program, fairness is not helpful. In this case, you want a policy that is **deterministic**, which will give you at least minimal guarantees that your real-time threads will be scheduled at the right time so that they don't miss their deadlines. This means that a real-time thread must preempt time-shared threads. Real-time threads also have a static priority that the scheduler can use to choose between them when there are several of them to run at once. The Linux real-time scheduler implements a fairly standard algorithm that runs the highest priority real-time thread. Most RTOS schedulers are also written in this way.

Both types of thread can coexist. Those requiring deterministic scheduling are scheduled first, and any remaining time is divided between the time-shared threads.

Time-shared policies

Time-shared policies are designed for fairness. From Linux 2.6.23 onward, the scheduler that's been used has been the **Completely Fair Scheduler** (**CFS**). It does not use timeslices in the normal sense of the word. Instead, it calculates a running tally of the length of time a thread would be entitled to run if it had its fair share of CPU time, and it balances that with the actual amount of time it has run for. If it exceeds its entitlement and there are other time-shared threads waiting to run, the scheduler will suspend the thread and run a waiting thread instead.

The time-shared policies are as follows:

- `SCHED_NORMAL` (also known as `SCHED_OTHER`): This is the default policy. The vast majority of Linux threads use this policy.
- `SCHED_BATCH`: This is similar to `SCHED_NORMAL`, except that threads are scheduled with a larger granularity; that is, they run for longer but have to wait longer until they are scheduled again. The intention is to reduce the number of context switches for background processing (batch jobs) and reduce the amount of CPU cache churn.
- `SCHED_IDLE`: These threads are run only when there are no threads from any other policy that are ready to run. It is the lowest possible priority.

There are two pairs of functions you can use to get and set the policy and priority of a thread. The first pair takes a PID as a parameter and affects the main thread in a process:

```
struct sched_param {
        ...
        int sched_priority;
        ...
```

```
};

int sched_setscheduler(pid_t pid, int policy,
        const struct sched_param *param);

int sched_getscheduler(pid_t pid);
```

The second pair operates on `pthread_t` and can change the parameters of the other threads in a process:

```
int pthread_setschedparam(pthread_t thread, int policy,
        const struct sched_param *param);

int pthread_getschedparam(pthread_t thread, int *policy,
        struct sched_param *param);
```

See the `sched(7)` man page for more on thread policies and priorities. Now that we know what time-shared policies and priorities are, let's talk about niceness.

Niceness

Some time-shared threads are more important than others. You can indicate this with the `nice` value, which multiplies a thread's CPU entitlement by a scaling factor. The name comes from the function call, `nice(2)`, which has been part of Unix since the early days. A thread becomes nice by reducing its load on the system or moving in the opposite direction by increasing it. The range of values is from `19`, which is really nice, to `-20`, which is really not nice. The default value is `0`, which is averagely nice, or so-so.

The `nice` value can be changed for `SCHED_NORMAL` and `SCHED_BATCH` threads. To reduce niceness, which increases the CPU load, you need the `CAP_SYS_NICE` capability, which is available to the `root` user. See the `capabilities(7)` man page for more information on capabilities.

Almost all the documentation for functions and commands that change the `nice` value (`nice(2)` and the `nice` and `renice` commands) talk in terms of processes. However, it really relates to threads. As we mentioned in the preceding section, you can use a TID in place of a PID to change the nice value of an individual thread. One other discrepancy in the standard descriptions of `nice` is this: the `nice` value is referred to as the priority of a thread (or sometimes, mistakenly, a process). I believe this is misleading and confuses the concept with real-time priority, which is a completely different thing.

Real-time policies

Real-time policies are intended for determinism. The real-time scheduler will always run the highest priority real-time thread that is ready to run. Real-time threads always preempt timeshare threads. In essence, by selecting a real-time policy over a timeshare policy, you are saying that you have inside knowledge of the expected scheduling of this thread and wish to override the scheduler's built-in assumptions.

There are two real-time policies:

- `SCHED_FIFO`: This is a **run to completion** algorithm, which means that once the thread starts to run, it will continue until it is preempted by a higher priority real-time thread, it is blocked in a system call, or until it terminates (completes).
- `SCHED_RR`: This a **round robin** algorithm that will cycle between threads of the same priority if they exceed their time slice, which is 100 ms by default. Since Linux 3.9, it has been possible to control the `timeslice` value through `/proc/sys/kernel/sched_rr_timeslice_ms`. Apart from this, it behaves in the same way as `SCHED_FIFO`.

Each real-time thread has a priority in the range of `1` to `99`, with `99` being the highest.

To give a thread a real-time policy, you need `CAP_SYS_NICE`, which is given only to the root user by default.

One problem with real-time scheduling, both in terms of Linux and elsewhere, is that a thread that becomes compute bound, often because a bug has caused it to loop indefinitely, will prevent real-time threads of a lower priority from running along with all the timeshare threads. In this case, the system becomes erratic and may lock up completely. There are a couple of ways to guard against this possibility.

First, since Linux 2.6.25, the scheduler has, by default, reserved 5% of its CPU time for non-real-time threads so that even a runaway real-time thread cannot completely halt the system. It is configured via two kernel controls:

- `/proc/sys/kernel/sched_rt_period_us`
- `/proc/sys/kernel/sched_rt_runtime_us`

They have default values of 1,000,000 (1 second) and 950,000 (950 ms), respectively, which means that every second, 50 ms is reserved for non-real-time processing. If you want real-time threads to be able to take 100%, then set `sched_rt_runtime_us` to `-1`.

The second option is to use a watchdog, either hardware or software, to monitor the execution of key threads and take action when they begin to miss deadlines. I mentioned watchdogs in *Chapter 13, Starting Up – The init Program*.

Choosing a policy

In practice, time-shared policies satisfy the majority of computing workloads. Threads that are I/O-bound spend a lot of time blocked and always have some spare entitlement in hand. When they are unblocked, they will be scheduled almost immediately. Meanwhile, CPU-bound threads will naturally take up any CPU cycles left over. Positive nice values can be applied to the less important threads and negative values to the more important ones.

Of course, this is only average behavior; there are no guarantees that this will always be the case. If more deterministic behavior is needed, then real-time policies will be required. The things that mark out a thread as being real time are as follows:

- It has a deadline by which it must generate an output.
- Missing the deadline would compromise the effectiveness of the system.
- It is event-driven.
- It is not compute-bound.

Examples of real-time tasks include the classic robot arm servo controller, multimedia processing, and communication processing. I will discuss real-time system design later in *Chapter 21, Real-Time Programming*.

Choosing a real-time priority

Choosing real-time priorities that work for all expected workloads is a tricky business and a good reason to avoid real-time policies in the first place.

The most widely used procedure for choosing priorities is known as **Rate Monotonic Analysis** (**RMA**), after the 1973 paper by Liu and Layland. It applies to real-time systems with periodic threads, which is a very important class. Each thread has a period and a utilization, which is the proportion of the period it will be executing. The goal is to balance the load so that all the threads can complete their execution phase before the next period. RMA states that this can be achieved if the following occur:

- The highest priorities are given to the threads with the shortest periods.
- The total utilization is less than 69%.

The total utilization is the sum of all the individual utilizations. It also makes the assumption that the interaction between threads or the time spent blocked on mutexes and the like is negligible.

Summary

The long Unix heritage that is built into Linux and the accompanying C libraries provides almost everything you need in order to write stable and resilient embedded applications. The issue is that for every job, there are at least two ways to achieve the end you desire.

In this chapter, I focused on two aspects of system design: partitioning into separate processes, each with one or more threads to get the job done, and scheduling those threads. I hope that I shed some light on this and have given you the basis to study them further.

In the next chapter, I will examine another important aspect of system design: memory management.

Further reading

The following resources provide further information about the topics that were introduced in this chapter:

- *The Art of Unix Programming*, by Eric Steven Raymond
- *Linux System Programming, 2nd edition*, by Robert Love
- *Linux Kernel Development, 3rd edition*, by Robert Love
- *The Linux Programming Interface*, by Michael Kerrisk
- *UNIX Network Programming, Volume 2: Interprocess Communications, 2nd Edition*, by W. Richard Stevens
- *Programming with POSIX Threads*, by David R. Butenhof
- *Scheduling Algorithms for Multiprogramming in a Hard-Real-Time Environment*, by C. L. Liu and James W. Layland, Journal of ACM, 1973, vol 20, no 1, pp. 46-61

18 Managing Memory

This chapter covers issues related to memory management, which is an important topic for any Linux system but especially for embedded Linux, where system memory is usually in limited supply. After a brief refresher on virtual memory, I will show you how to measure memory usage, how to detect problems with memory allocation, including memory leaks, and what happens when you run out of memory. You will have to understand the tools that are available, from simple tools such as `free` and `top`, to complex ones such as `mtrace` and Valgrind.

We will learn the difference between kernel and user space memory, and how the kernel maps physical pages of memory to the address space of a process. Then we will locate and read the memory maps for individual processes under the `proc` filesystem. We will see how the `mmap` system call can be used to map a program's memory to a file, so that it can allocate memory in bulk or share it with another process. In the second half of this chapter, we will use `ps` to measure per-process memory usage before moving on to more accurate tools such as `smem` and `ps_mem`.

In this chapter, we will cover the following topics:

- Virtual memory basics
- Kernel space memory layout
- User space memory layout
- The process memory map

- Swapping
- Mapping memory with `mmap`
- How much memory does my application use?
- Per-process memory usage
- Identifying memory leaks
- Running out of memory

Technical requirements

To follow along with the examples, make sure you have the following:

- A Linux-based host system with `gcc`, `make`, `top`, `procps`, `valgrind`, and `smem` installed

All of these tools are available on most popular Linux distributions (such as Ubuntu, Arch, and so on).

All of the code for this chapter can be found in the `Chapter18` folder in the book's GitHub repository: `https://github.com/PacktPublishing/Mastering-Embedded-Linux-Programming-Third-Edition`.

Virtual memory basics

To recap, Linux configures the **memory management unit** (**MMU**) of the CPU to present a virtual address space to a running program that begins at zero and ends at the highest address, `0xffffffff`, on a 32-bit processor. This address space is divided into pages of 4 KiB by default. If 4 KiB pages are too small for your application, then you can configure the kernel to use **HugePages**, reducing the amount of system resources needed to access page table entries and increasing the **Translation Lookaside Buffer** (**TLB**) hit ratio.

Linux divides this virtual address space into an area for applications, called **user space**, and an area for the kernel, called **kernel space**. The split between the two is set by a kernel configuration parameter named `PAGE_OFFSET`. In a typical 32-bit embedded system, `PAGE_OFFSET` is `0xc0000000`, giving the lower 3 gigabytes to user space and the top gigabyte to kernel space. The user address space is allocated per process so that each process runs in a sandbox, separated from the others. The kernel address space is the same for all processes, as there is only one kernel.

Pages in this virtual address space are mapped to physical addresses by the MMU, which uses page tables to perform the mapping.

Each page of virtual memory may be unmapped or mapped as follows:

- Unmapped, so that trying to access these addresses will result in a `SIGSEGV`.
- Mapped to a page of physical memory that is private to the process.
- Mapped to a page of physical memory that is shared with other processes.
- Mapped and shared with a **copy on write** (**CoW**) flag set: a write is trapped in the kernel, which makes a copy of the page and maps it to the process in place of the original page before allowing the write to take place.
- Mapped to a page of physical memory that is used by the kernel.

The kernel may additionally map pages to reserved memory regions, for example to access registers and memory buffers in device drivers.

An obvious question is this: why do we do it this way instead of simply referencing physical memory directly, as a typical RTOS would?

There are numerous advantages to virtual memory, some of which are described here:

- Invalid memory accesses are trapped and applications are alerted by `SIGSEGV`.
- Processes run in their own memory space, isolated from other processes.
- Efficient use of memory through the sharing of common code and data, for example, in libraries.
- The possibility of increasing the apparent amount of physical memory by adding swap files, although swapping on embedded targets is rare.

These are powerful arguments, but I have to admit that there are some disadvantages as well. It is difficult to determine the actual memory budget of an application, which is one of the main concerns of this chapter. The default allocation strategy is to over-commit, which leads to tricky out-of-memory situations, which I will also discuss later in the *Running out of memory* section. Finally, the delays introduced by the memory management code in handling exceptions—page faults—make the system less deterministic, which is important for real-time programs. I will cover this in *Chapter 21, Real-Time Programming.*

Memory management is different for kernel space and user space. The upcoming sections describe the essential differences and the things you need to know.

Kernel space memory layout

Kernel memory is managed in a fairly straightforward way. It is not demand-paged, which means that for every allocation using `kmalloc()` or similar function, there is real physical memory. Kernel memory is never discarded or paged out.

Some architectures show a summary of the memory mapping at boot time in the kernel log messages. This trace is taken from a 32-bit Arm device (a BeagleBone Black):

```
Memory: 511MB = 511MB total
Memory: 505980k/505980k available, 18308k reserved, 0K highmem
Virtual kernel memory layout:
    vector  : 0xffff0000 - 0xffff1000   (   4 kB)
    fixmap  : 0xfff00000 - 0xfffe0000   ( 896 kB)
    vmalloc : 0xe0800000 - 0xff000000   ( 488 MB)
    lowmem  : 0xc0000000 - 0xe0000000   ( 512 MB)
    pkmap   : 0xbfe00000 - 0xc0000000   (   2 MB)
    modules : 0xbf800000 - 0xbfe00000   (   6 MB)
      .text : 0xc0008000 - 0xc0763c90   (7536 kB)
      .init : 0xc0764000 - 0xc079f700   ( 238 kB)
      .data : 0xc07a0000 - 0xc0827240   ( 541 kB)
       .bss : 0xc0827240 - 0xc089e940   ( 478 kB)
```

The figure of 505,980 KiB available is the amount of free memory the kernel sees when it begins execution but before it begins making dynamic allocations.

Consumers of kernel space memory include the following:

- The kernel itself, in other words, the code and data loaded from the kernel image file at boot time. This is shown in the preceding kernel log in the `.text`, `.init`, `.data`, and `.bss`. segments The `.init` segment is freed once the kernel has completed initialization.
- Memory allocated through the slab allocator, which is used for kernel data structures of various kinds. This includes allocations made using `kmalloc()`. They come from the region marked **lowmem**.
- Memory allocated via `vmalloc()`, usually for larger chunks of memory than is available through `kmalloc()`. These are in the **vmalloc** area.

- Mapping for device drivers to access registers and memory belonging to various bits of hardware, which you can see by reading `/proc/iomem`. These also come from the **vmalloc** area, but since they are mapped to physical memory that is outside of main system memory, they do not take up any real memory.
- Kernel modules, which are loaded into the area marked **modules**.
- Other low-level allocations that are not tracked anywhere else.

Now that we know the layout of memory in kernel space, let's find out how much memory the kernel is actually using.

How much memory does the kernel use?

Unfortunately, there isn't a precise answer to the question of how much memory the kernel uses, but what follows is as close as we can get.

Firstly, you can see the memory taken up by the kernel code and data in the kernel log shown previously, or you can use the `size` command, as follows:

```
$ arm-poky-linux-gnueabi-size vmlinux
text data bss dec hex filename
9013448 796868 8428144 18238460 1164bfc vmlinux
```

Usually, the amount of memory taken by the kernel for the static code and data segments shown here is small when compared to the total amount of memory. If that is not the case, you need to look through the kernel configuration and remove the components that you don't need. An effort to allow building small kernels known as **Linux Kernel Tinification** had been making good progress until the project stalled, and Josh Triplett's patches were eventually removed from the `linux-next` tree in 2016. Now, your best bet at reducing the kernel's in-memory size is **Execute-in-Place** (**XIP**) where you trade RAM for flash (`https://lwn.net/Articles/748198/`).

You can get more information about memory usage by reading `/proc/meminfo`:

```
# cat /proc/meminfo
MemTotal: 509016 kB
MemFree: 410680 kB
Buffers: 1720 kB
Cached: 25132 kB
SwapCached: 0 kB
Active: 74880 kB
Inactive: 3224 kB
```

```
Active(anon): 51344 kB
Inactive(anon): 1372 kB
Active(file): 23536 kB
Inactive(file): 1852 kB
Unevictable: 0 kB
Mlocked: 0 kB
HighTotal: 0 kB
HighFree: 0 kB
LowTotal: 509016 kB
LowFree: 410680 kB
SwapTotal: 0 kB
SwapFree: 0 kB
Dirty: 16 kB
Writeback: 0 kB
AnonPages: 51248 kB
Mapped: 24376 kB
Shmem: 1452 kB
Slab: 11292 kB
SReclaimable: 5164 kB
SUnreclaim: 6128 kB
KernelStack: 1832 kB
PageTables: 1540 kB
NFS_Unstable: 0 kB
Bounce: 0 kB
WritebackTmp: 0 kB
CommitLimit: 254508 kB
Committed_AS: 734936 kB
VmallocTotal: 499712 kB
VmallocUsed: 29576 kB
VmallocChunk: 389116 kB
```

There is a description of each of these fields on the manual page `proc(5)`. The kernel memory usage is the sum of the following:

- `Slab`: The total memory allocated by the slab allocator
- `KernelStack`: The stack space used when executing kernel code

- `PageTables`: The memory used to store page tables
- `VmallocUsed`: The memory allocated by `vmalloc()`

In the case of slab allocations, you can get more information by reading `/proc/slabinfo`. Similarly, there is a breakdown of allocations in `/proc/vmallocinfo` for the **vmalloc** area. In both cases, you need detailed knowledge of the kernel and its subsystems in order to see exactly which subsystem is making the allocations and why, which is beyond the scope of this discussion.

With modules, you can use `lsmod` to find out the memory space taken up by the code and data:

```
# lsmod
Module Size Used by
g_multi 47670 2
libcomposite 14299 1 g_multi
mt7601Usta 601404 0
```

This leaves the low-level allocations, of which there is no record, and that prevents us from generating an accurate account of kernel space memory usage. This will appear as missing memory when we add up all the kernel and user space allocations that we know about.

Measuring kernel space memory usage is complicated. The information in `/proc/meminfo` is somewhat limited and the additional information provided by `/proc/slabinfo` and `/proc/vmallocinfo` is difficult to interpret. User space offers better visibility into memory usage by way of the process memory map.

User space memory layout

Linux employs a lazy allocation strategy for user space, only mapping physical pages of memory when the program accesses it. For example, allocating a buffer of 1 MiB using `malloc(3)` returns a pointer to a block of memory addresses but no actual physical memory. A flag is set in the page table entries such that any read or write access is trapped by the kernel. This is known as a **page fault**. Only at this point does the kernel attempt to find a page of physical memory and add it to the page table mapping for the process. It is worthwhile demonstrating this with a simple program, `MELP/Chapter18/pagefault-demo`:

```
#include <stdio.h>
#include <stdlib.h>
#include <string.h>
```

```
#include <sys/resource.h>
#define BUFFER_SIZE (1024 * 1024)

void print_pgfaults(void)
{
      int ret;
      struct rusage usage;
      ret = getrusage(RUSAGE_SELF, &usage);
      if (ret == -1) {
             perror("getrusage");
       } else {
             printf("Major page faults %ld\n", usage.ru_majflt);
             printf("Minor page faults %ld\n", usage.ru_minflt);
      }
}

int main(int argc, char *argv[])
{
      unsigned char *p;
      printf("Initial state\n");
      print_pgfaults();
      p = malloc(BUFFER_SIZE);
      printf("After malloc\n");
      print_pgfaults();
      memset(p, 0x42, BUFFER_SIZE);
      printf("After memset\n");
      print_pgfaults();
      memset(p, 0x42, BUFFER_SIZE);
      printf("After 2nd memset\n");
      print_pgfaults();
      return 0;
}
```

When you run it, you will see output like this:

```
Initial state
Major page faults 0
Minor page faults 172
After malloc
Major page faults 0
Minor page faults 186
After memset
Major page faults 0
Minor page faults 442
After 2nd memset
Major page faults 0
Minor page faults 442
```

There were 172 minor page faults encountered after initializing the program's environment and a further 14 when calling `getrusage(2)` (these numbers will vary depending on the architecture and the version of the C library you are using). The important part is the increase when filling the memory with data: 442 - 186 = 256. The buffer is 1 MiB, which is 256 pages. The second call to `memset(3)` makes no difference because all the pages are now mapped.

As you can see, a page fault is generated when the kernel traps an access to a page that has not been mapped yet. In fact, there are two kinds of page faults: `minor` and `major`. With a minor fault, the kernel just has to find a page of physical memory and map it to the process address space, as shown in the preceding code. A major page fault occurs when the virtual memory is mapped to a file, for example, using `mmap(2)`, which I will describe shortly. Reading from this memory means that the kernel not only has to find a page of memory and map it in but also has to fill it with data from the file. Consequently, major faults are much more expensive in terms of time and system resources.

While `getrusage(2)` offers useful metrics on minor and major page faults within a process, sometimes what we really want to see is an overall memory map of a process.

The process memory map

Each running process in user space has a process map that we can inspect. These memory maps tell us how a program's memory is allocated and what shared libraries it is linked to.

You can see the memory map for a process through the `proc` filesystem. As an example, here is the map for the `init` process, PID `1`:

```
# cat /proc/1/maps
00008000-0000e000 r-xp 00000000 00:0b 23281745 /sbin/init
00016000-00017000 rwxp 00006000 00:0b 23281745 /sbin/init
00017000-00038000 rwxp 00000000 00:00 0        [heap]
b6ded000-b6f1d000 r-xp 00000000 00:0b 23281695 /lib/libc-2.19.
so
b6f1d000-b6f24000 ---p 00130000 00:0b 23281695 /lib/libc-2.19.
so
b6f24000-b6f26000 r-xp 0012f000 00:0b 23281695 /lib/libc-2.19.
so
b6f26000-b6f27000 rwxp 00131000 00:0b 23281695 /lib/libc-2.19.
so
b6f27000-b6f2a000 rwxp 00000000 00:00 0
b6f2a000-b6f49000 r-xp 00000000 00:0b 23281359 /lib/ld-2.19.so
b6f4c000-b6f4e000 rwxp 00000000 00:00 0
b6f4f000-b6f50000 r-xp 00000000 00:00 0        [sigpage]
b6f50000-b6f51000 r-xp 0001e000 00:0b 23281359 /lib/ld-2.19.so
b6f51000-b6f52000 rwxp 0001f000 00:0b 23281359 /lib/ld-2.19.so
beea1000-beec2000 rw-p 00000000 00:00 0        [stack]
ffff0000-ffff1000 r-xp 00000000 00:00 0        [vectors]
```

The first two columns show the start and end virtual addresses and the permissions for each mapping. The permissions are shown here:

- `r`: Read
- `w`: Write
- `x`: Execute
- `s`: Shared
- `p`: Private (copy on write)

If the mapping is associated with a file, the filename appears in the final column, and columns three, four, and five contain the offset from the start of the file, the block device number, and the inode of the file. Most of the mappings are to the program itself and the libraries it is linked with. There are two areas where the program can allocate memory, marked `[heap]` and `[stack]`. Memory allocated using malloc comes from the former (except for very large allocations, which we will come to later); allocations on the stack come from the latter. The maximum size of both areas is controlled by the process's `ulimit`:

- **Heap**: `ulimit -d`, default unlimited
- **Stack**: `ulimit -s`, default 8 MiB

Allocations that exceed the limit are rejected by `SIGSEGV`.

When running out of memory, the kernel may decide to discard pages that are mapped to a file and are read-only. If that page is accessed again, it will cause a major page fault and be read back in from the file.

Swapping

The idea of swapping is to reserve some storage where the kernel can place pages of memory that are not mapped to a file, freeing up the memory for other uses. It increases the effective size of physical memory by the size of the swap file. It is not a panacea: there is a cost to copying pages to and from a swap file, which becomes apparent on a system that has too little real memory for the workload it is carrying and so swapping becomes the main activity. This is sometimes known as **disk thrashing**.

Swap is seldom used on embedded devices because it does not work well with flash storage, where constant writing would wear it out quickly. However, you may want to consider swapping to compressed RAM `(zram)`.

Swapping to compressed memory (zram)

The **zram** driver creates RAM-based block devices named `/dev/zram0`, `/dev/zram1`, and so on. Pages written to these devices are compressed before being stored. With compression ratios in the range of 30% to 50%, you can expect an overall increase in free memory of about 10% at the expense of more processing and a corresponding increase in power usage.

To enable zram, configure the kernel with these options:

```
CONFIG_SWAP
CONFIG_CGROUP_MEM_RES_CTLR
CONFIG_CGROUP_MEM_RES_CTLR_SWAP
CONFIG_ZRAM
```

Then, mount zram at boot time by adding this to `/etc/fstab`:

```
/dev/zram0 none swap defaults zramsize=<size in bytes>,
swapprio=<swap partition priority>
```

You can turn swap on and off using these commands:

```
# swapon /dev/zram0
# swapoff /dev/zram0
```

Swapping memory out to zram is better than swapping out to flash storage, but neither technique is a substitute for adequate physical memory.

User space processes depend on the kernel to manage virtual memory for them. Sometimes a program wants greater control over its memory map than the kernel can offer. There is a system call that lets us map memory to a file for more direct access from user space.

Mapping memory with mmap

A process begins life with a certain amount of memory mapped to the **text** (the code) and **data** segments of the program file, together with the shared libraries that it is linked with. It can allocate memory on its heap at runtime using `malloc(3)` and on the stack through locally scoped variables and memory allocated through `alloca(3)`. It may also load libraries dynamically at runtime using `dlopen(3)`. All of these mappings are taken care of by the kernel. However, a process can also manipulate its memory map in an explicit way using `mmap(2)`:

```
void *mmap(void *addr, size_t length, int prot, int flags,
int fd, off_t offset);
```

This function maps length bytes of memory from the file with the fd descriptor, starting at offset in the file, and returns a pointer to the mapping, assuming it is successful. Since the underlying hardware works in pages, length is rounded up to the nearest whole number of pages. The protection parameter, prot, is a combination of read, write, and execute permissions and the flags parameter contains at least MAP_SHARED or MAP_PRIVATE. There are many other flags, which are described in the mmap manpage.

There are many things you can do with mmap. I will show some of them in the upcoming sections.

Using mmap to allocate private memory

You can use mmap to allocate an area of private memory by setting MAP_ANONYMOUS in the flags parameter and setting the file descriptor fd to -1. This is similar to allocating memory from the heap using malloc, except that the memory is page-aligned and in multiples of pages. The memory is allocated in the same area as that used for libraries. In fact, this area is referred to by some as the mmap area for this reason.

Anonymous mappings are better for large allocations because they do not pin down the heap with chunks of memory, which would make fragmentation more likely. Interestingly, you will find that malloc (in glibc at least) stops allocating memory from the heap for requests over 128 KiB and uses mmap in this way, so in most cases, just using malloc is the right thing to do. The system will choose the best way of satisfying the request.

Using mmap to share memory

As we saw in *Chapter 17*, *Learning About Processes and Threads*, POSIX shared memory requires mmap to access the memory segment. In this case, you set the MAP_SHARED flag and use the file descriptor from shm_open():

```
int shm_fd;
char *shm_p;

shm_fd = shm_open("/myshm", O_CREAT | O_RDWR, 0666);
ftruncate(shm_fd, 65536);
shm_p = mmap(NULL, 65536, PROT_READ | PROT_WRITE,
MAP_SHARED, shm_fd, 0);
```

Another process uses the same calls, filename, length, and flags to map to that memory region for sharing. Subsequent calls to msync(2) control when updates to memory are carried through to the underlying file.

Sharing memory via mmap also offers a straightforward way to read from and write to device memory.

Using mmap to access device memory

As I mentioned in *Chapter 11, Interfacing with Device Drivers*, it is possible for a driver to allow its device node to be memory mapped and share some of the device memory with an application. The exact implementation is dependent on the driver.

One example is the Linux framebuffer, /dev/fb0. FPGAs such as the Xilinx Zynq series are also accessed as memory via mmap from Linux. The framebuffer interface is defined in /usr/include/linux/fb.h, including an ioctl function to get the size of the display and the bits per pixel. You can then use mmap to ask the video driver to share the framebuffer with the application and read and write pixels:

```
int f;
int fb_size;
unsigned char *fb_mem;

f = open("/dev/fb0", O_RDWR);
/* Use ioctl FBIOGET_VSCREENINFO to find the display
 dimensions and calculate fb_size */
fb_mem = mmap(0, fb_size, PROT_READ | PROT_WRITE, MAP_SHARED,
fd, 0);
/* read and write pixels through pointer fb_mem */
```

A second example is the streaming video interface, **Video 4 Linux, version 2**, or **V4L2**, which is defined in /usr/include/linux/videodev2.h. Each video device has a node named /dev/videoN, starting with /dev/video0. There is an ioctl function to ask the driver to allocate a number of video buffers that you can mmap into user space. Then, it is just a question of cycling the buffers and filling or emptying them with video data, depending on whether you are playing back or capturing a video stream.

Now that we have covered memory layout and mapping, let's look at memory usage starting with how to measure it.

How much memory does my application use?

As with kernel space, the different ways of allocating, mapping, and sharing user space memory make it quite difficult to answer this seemingly simple question.

To begin, you can ask the kernel how much memory it thinks is available, which you can do using the `free` command. Here is a typical example of the output:

```
    total used free shared buffers cached
Mem: 509016 504312 4704 0 26456 363860
-/+ buffers/cache: 113996 395020
Swap: 0 0 0
```

At first sight, this looks like a system that is almost out of memory with only 4,704 KiB free out of 509,016 KiB: less than 1%. However, note that 26,456 KiB is in buffers and a whopping 363,860 KiB is in caches. Linux believes that free memory is wasted memory; the kernel uses free memory for buffers and caches with the knowledge that they can be shrunk when the need arises. Removing buffers and cache from the measurement provides true free memory, which is 395,020 KiB: 77% of the total. When using `free`, the numbers on the second line marked `-/+ buffers/cache` are the important ones.

You can force the kernel to free up caches by writing a number between 1 and 3 to `/proc/sys/vm/drop_caches`:

```
# echo 3 > /proc/sys/vm/drop_caches
```

The number is actually a bitmask that determines which of the two broad types of caches you want to free: `1` for the page cache and `2` for the dentry and inode caches combined. Since `1` and `2` are different bits, writing a `3` frees both types of caches. The exact roles of these caches are not particularly important here, only that there is memory that the kernel is using but that can be reclaimed at short notice.

The `free` command tells us how much memory is being used and how much is left. It neither tells us which processes are using the unavailable memory nor in what proportions. To measure that, we need other tools.

Per-process memory usage

There are several metrics to measure the amount of memory a process is using. I will begin with the two that are easiest to obtain: the **virtual set size** (**VSS**) and the **resident memory size** (**RSS**), both of which are available in most implementations of the `ps` and `top` commands:

- **VSS**: Called VSZ in the `ps` command and VIRT in `top`, this is the total amount of memory mapped by a process. It is the sum of all the regions shown in `/proc/<PID>/map`. This number is of limited interest since only part of the virtual memory is committed to physical memory at any time.

- **RSS**: Called RSS in `ps` and RES in `top`, this is the sum of memory that is mapped to physical pages of memory. This gets closer to the actual memory budget of the process, but there is a problem: if you add the RSS of all the processes, you will get an overestimate of the memory in use because some pages will be shared.

Let's learn more about the `top` and `ps` commands.

Using top and ps

The versions of `top` and `ps` from BusyBox provide very limited information. The examples that follow use the full version from the `procps` package.

The `ps` command shows **VSS** `(VSZ)` **and RSS** `(RSS)` with the options `-Aly`, or you can use a custom format that includes `vsz` and `rss`, as shown here:

```
# ps -eo pid,tid,class,rtprio,stat,vsz,rss,comm
PID TID CLS RTPRIO STAT VSZ RSS COMMAND
1   1   TS -Ss 4496 2652 systemd
[...]
205 205 TS -Ss 4076 1296 systemd-journal
228 228 TS -Ss 2524 1396 udevd
581 581 TS -Ss 2880 1508 avahi-daemon
584 584 TS -Ss 2848 1512 dbus-daemon
590 590 TS -Ss 1332 680  acpid
594 594 TS -Ss 4600 1564 wpa_supplicant
```

Likewise, `top` shows a summary of the free memory and memory usage per process:

```
top - 21:17:52 up 10:04, 1 user, load average: 0.00, 0.01, 0.05
Tasks: 96 total, 1 running, 95 sleeping, 0 stopped, 0 zombie
%Cpu(s): 1.7 us, 2.2 sy, 0.0 ni, 95.9 id, 0.0 wa, 0.0 hi
KiB Mem: 509016 total, 278524 used, 230492 free, 25572 buffers
KiB Swap: 0 total, 0 used, 0 free, 170920 cached
PID USER PR NI VIRT RES SHR S %CPU %MEM TIME+ COMMAND
595 root 20 0 64920 9.8m 4048 S 0.0 2.0 0:01.09 node
866 root 20 0 28892 9152 3660 S 0.2 1.8 0:36.38 Xorg
[...]
```

These simple commands give you a feel of the memory usage and provide the first indication that you have a memory leak when you see that the RSS of a process keeps on increasing. However, they are not very accurate in the absolute measurements of memory usage.

Using smem

In 2009, Matt Mackall began looking at the problem of accounting for shared pages in process memory measurement and added two new metrics called **unique set size**, or **USS**, and **proportional set size**, or **PSS**:

- **USS**: This is the amount of memory that is committed to physical memory and is unique to a process; it is not shared with any others. It is the amount of memory that would be freed if the process were to terminate.
- **PSS**: This splits the accounting of shared pages that are committed to physical memory between all the processes that have them mapped. For example, if an area of library code is 12 pages long and is shared by six processes, each will accumulate two pages in PSS. Thus, if you add the PSS numbers for all processes, you will get the actual amount of memory being used by those processes. In other words, PSS is the number we have been looking for.

Information about PSS is available in `/proc/<PID>/smaps`, which contains additional information for each of the mappings shown in `/proc/<PID>/maps`. Here is a section from such a file that provides information on the mapping for the `libc` code segment:

```
b6e6d000-b6f45000 r-xp 00000000 b3:02 2444 /lib/libc-2.13.so
Size: 864 kB
Rss: 264 kB
Pss: 6 kB
Shared_Clean: 264 kB
Shared_Dirty: 0 kB
Private_Clean: 0 kB
Private_Dirty: 0 kB
Referenced: 264 kB
Anonymous: 0 kB
AnonHugePages: 0 kB
Swap: 0 kB
KernelPageSize: 4 kB
```

```
MMUPageSize: 4 kB
Locked: 0 kB
VmFlags: rd ex mr mw me
```

Note that the RSS is 264 KiB, but because it is shared between many other processes, the PSS is only 6 KiB.

There is a tool named **smem** that collates information from the `smaps` files and presents it in various ways, including as pie or bar charts. The project page for smem is `https://www.selenic.com/smem/`. It is available as a package in most desktop distributions. However, since it is written in Python, installing it on an embedded target requires a Python environment, which may be too much trouble for just one tool. To help with this, there is a small program named **smemcap** that captures the state from `/proc` on the target and saves it to a TAR file that can be analyzed later on the host computer. It is part of BusyBox, but it can also be compiled from the `smem` source.

Running `smem` natively, as `root`, you will see these results:

```
# smem -t
PID User Command Swap USS PSS RSS
610 0 /sbin/agetty -s ttyO0 11 0 128 149 720
1236 0 /sbin/agetty -s ttyGS0 1 0 128 149 720
609 0 /sbin/agetty tty1 38400 0 144 163 724
578 0 /usr/sbin/acpid 0 140 173 680
819 0 /usr/sbin/cron 0 188 201 704
634 103 avahi-daemon: chroot hel 0 112 205 500
980 0 /usr/sbin/udhcpd -S /etc 0 196 205 568
[...]
836 0 /usr/bin/X :0 -auth /var 0 7172 7746 9212
583 0 /usr/bin/node autorun.js 0 8772 9043 10076
1089 1000 /usr/bin/python -O /usr/ 0 9600 11264 16388
------------------------------------------------------------
53 6 0 65820 78251 146544
```

You can see from the last line of the output that in this case, the total PSS is about a half of the RSS.

If you don't have or don't want to install Python on your target, you can capture the state using `smemcap`, again as `root`:

```
# smemcap > smem-bbb-cap.tar
```

Then, copy the TAR file to the host and read it using `smem -S`, although this time there is no need to run as `root`:

```
$ smem -t -S smem-bbb-cap.tar
```

The output is identical to the output we get when running `smem` natively.

Other tools to consider

Another way to display PSS is via **ps_mem** (`https://github.com/pixelb/ps_mem`), which prints much the same information but in a simpler format. It is also written in Python.

Android also has a tool that displays a summary of USS and PSS for each process, named **procrank**, which can be cross-compiled for embedded Linux with a few small changes. You can get the code from `https://github.com/csimmonds/procrank_linux`.

We now know how to measure per-process memory usage. Let's say we use the tools just shown to find the process that is the memory hog in our system. How do we then drill down into that process to figure out where it is going wrong? That is the topic of the next section.

Identifying memory leaks

A memory leak occurs when memory is allocated but not freed when it is no longer needed. Memory leakage is by no means unique to embedded systems, but it becomes an issue partly because targets don't have much memory in the first place and partly because they often run for long periods of time without rebooting, allowing the leaks to become a large puddle.

You will realize that there is a leak when you run `free` or `top` and see that free memory is continually going down even if you drop caches, as shown in the preceding section. You will be able to identify the culprit (or culprits) by looking at the USS and RSS per process.

There are several tools to identify memory leaks in a program. I will look at two: `mtrace` and `valgrind`.

mtrace

mtrace is a component of `glibc` that traces calls to `malloc`, `free`, and related functions, and identifies areas of memory not freed when the program exits. You need to call the `mtrace()` function from within the program to begin tracing and then at runtime, write a path name to the `MALLOC_TRACE` environment variable in which the trace information is written. If `MALLOC_TRACE` does not exist or if the file cannot be opened, the `mtrace` hooks are not installed. While the trace information is written in ASCII, it is usual to use the `mtrace` command to view it.

Here is an example:

```
#include <mcheck.h>
#include <stdlib.h>
#include <stdio.h>


int main(int argc, char *argv[])
{
    int j;
    mtrace();
    for (j = 0; j < 2; j++)
        malloc(100); /* Never freed:a memory leak */
    calloc(16, 16); /* Never freed:a memory leak */
    exit(EXIT_SUCCESS);
}
```

Here is what you might see when running the program and looking at the trace:

```
$ export MALLOC_TRACE=mtrace.log
$ ./mtrace-example
$ mtrace mtrace-example mtrace.log

Memory not freed:
-----------------
    Address Size Caller
0x0000000001479460 0x64 at /home/chris/mtrace-example.c:11
0x00000000014794d0 0x64 at /home/chris/mtrace-example.c:11
0x0000000001479540 0x100 at /home/chris/mtrace-example.c:15
```

Unfortunately, `mtrace` does not tell you about leaked memory while the program runs. It has to terminate first.

Valgrind

Valgrind is a very powerful tool used to discover memory problems including leaks and other things. One advantage is that you don't have to recompile the programs and libraries that you want to check, although it works better if they have been compiled with the `-g` option so that they include debug symbol tables. It works by running the program in an emulated environment and trapping execution at various points. This leads to the big downside of Valgrind, which is that the program runs at a fraction of normal speed, which makes it less useful in testing anything with real-time constraints.

> **Important note**
>
> Incidentally, the name is often mispronounced: it says in the Valgrind FAQ that the grind part is pronounced with a short *i*, as in grinned (rhymes with tinned) rather than grind (rhymes with find). The FAQ, documentation, and downloads are available at `https://valgrind.org`.

Valgrind contains several diagnostic tools:

- `memcheck`: This is the default tool, and it detects memory leaks and general misuse of memory.
- `cachegrind`: This calculates the processor cache hit rate.
- `callgrind`: This calculates the cost of each function call.
- `helgrind`: This highlights the misuse of the Pthread API, including potential deadlocks, and race conditions.
- `DRD`: This is another Pthread analysis tool.
- `massif`: This profiles the usage of the heap and stack.

You can select the tool you want with the `-tool` option. Valgrind runs on the major embedded platforms: Arm (Cortex-A), PowerPC, MIPS, and x86 in 32-bit and 64-bit variants. It is available as a package in both the Yocto Project and Buildroot.

To find our memory leak, we need to use the default `memcheck` tool, with the `--leak-check=full` option to print the lines where the leak was found:

```
$ valgrind --leak-check=full ./mtrace-example
==17235== Memcheck, a memory error detector
```

```
==17235== Copyright (C) 2002-2013, and GNU GPL'd, by Julian
Seward et al.==17235==Using Valgrind-3.10.0.SVN and LibVEX;
rerun with -h for copyright info
==17235== Command: ./mtrace-example
==17235==
==17235==
==17235== HEAP SUMMARY:
==17235== in use at exit: 456 bytes in 3 blocks
==17235== total heap usage: 3 allocs, 0 frees, 456 bytes
allocated
==17235==
==17235== 200 bytes in 2 blocks are definitely lost in loss
record
1 of 2==17235== at 0x4C2AB80: malloc (in /usr/lib/valgrind/
vgpreload_memcheck-linux.so)
==17235== by 0x4005FA: main (mtrace-example.c:12)
==17235==
==17235== 256 bytes in 1 blocks are definitely lost in loss
record
2 of 2==17235== at 0x4C2CC70: calloc (in /usr/lib/valgrind/
vgpreload memcheck-linux so)
==17235== by 0x400613: main (mtrace-example.c:14)
==17235==
==17235== LEAK SUMMARY:
==17235== definitely lost: 456 bytes in 3 blocks
==17235== indirectly lost: 0 bytes in 0 blocks
==17235== possibly lost: 0 bytes in 0 blocks
==17235== still reachable: 0 bytes in 0 blocks
==17235== suppressed: 0 bytes in 0 blocks
==17235==
==17235== For counts of detected and suppressed errors, rerun
with: -v==17235== ERROR SUMMARY: 2 errors from 2 contexts
(suppressed: 0 from 0)
```

The output from Valgrind shows that two memory leaks were found in `mtrace-example.c`: a `malloc` at line 12 and a `calloc` at line 14. The subsequent calls to `free` that are supposed to accompany these two memory allocations are missing from the program. Left unchecked, memory leaks in a long-running process may eventually result in the system running out of memory.

Running out of memory

The standard memory allocation policy is to **over-commit**, which means that the kernel will allow more memory to be allocated by applications than there is physical memory. Most of the time, this works fine because it is common for applications to request more memory than they really need. This also helps in the implementation of `fork(2)`: it is safe to make a copy of a large program because the pages of memory are shared with the copy on write flag set. In the majority of cases, `fork` is followed by an `exec` function call, which unshares the memory and then loads a new program.

However, there is always the possibility that a particular workload will cause a group of processes to try to cash in on the allocations they have been promised simultaneously and so demand more than there really is. This is an **out of memory** situation, or **OOM**. At this point, there is no other alternative but to kill off processes until the problem goes away. This is the job of the **out of memory killer**.

Before we get to that, there is a tuning parameter for kernel allocations in `/proc/sys/vm/overcommit_memory`, which you can set to the following:

- `0`: Heuristic over-commit
- `1`: Always over-commit; never check
- `2`: Always check; never over-commit

Option `0` is the default and is the best choice in the majority of cases.

Option `1` is only really useful if you run programs that work with large sparse arrays and allocate large areas of memory but write to a small proportion of them. Such programs are rare in the context of embedded systems.

Option `2`, never over-commit, seems to be a good choice if you are worried about running out of memory, perhaps in a mission or safety-critical application. It will fail allocations that are greater than the commit limit, which is the size of swap space plus the total memory multiplied by the overcommit ratio. The over-commit ratio is controlled by `/proc/sys/vm/overcommit_ratio` and has a default value of 50%.

As an example, suppose you have a device with 512 MB of system RAM and you set a really conservative ratio of 25%:

```
# echo 25 > /proc/sys/vm/overcommit_ratio
# grep -e MemTotal -e CommitLimit /proc/meminfo
MemTotal: 509016 kB
CommitLimit: 127252 kB
```

There is no swap, so the commit limit is 25% of `MemTotal`, as expected.

There is another important variable in `/proc/meminfo`, called `Committed_AS`. This is the total amount of memory that is needed to fulfill all the allocations made so far. I found the following on one system:

```
# grep -e MemTotal -e Committed_AS /proc/meminfo
MemTotal: 509016 kB
Committed_AS: 741364 kB
```

In other words, the kernel had already promised more memory than the available memory. Consequently, setting `overcommit_memory` to `2` would mean that all allocations would fail regardless of `overcommit_ratio`. To get to a working system, I would have to either install double the amount of RAM or severely reduce the number of running processes, of which there were about 40.

In all cases, the final defense is `oom-killer`. It uses a heuristic method to calculate a badness score between 0 and 1,000 for each process and then terminates those with the highest score until there is enough free memory. You should see something like this in the kernel log:

```
[44510.490320] eatmem invoked oom-killer: gfp_mask=0x200da,
order=0, oom_score_adj=0
...
```

You can force an OOM event using `echo f > /proc/sysrq-trigger`.

You can influence the badness score for a process by writing an adjustment value to `/proc/<PID>/oom_score_adj`. A value of `-1000` means that the badness score can never be greater than zero and so it will never be killed; a value of `+1000` means that it will always be greater than 1,000 and so it will always be killed.

Summary

Accounting for every byte of memory used in a virtual memory system is just not possible. However, you can find a fairly accurate figure for the total amount of free memory, excluding that taken by buffers and the cache, using the `free` command. By monitoring it over a period of time and with different workloads, you should become confident that it will remain within a given limit.

When you want to tune memory usage or identify sources of unexpected allocations, there are resources that give more detailed information. For kernel space, the most useful information is in `/proc`: `meminfo`, `slabinfo`, and `vmallocinfo`.

When it comes to getting accurate measurements for user space, the best metric is PSS, as shown by `smem` and other tools. For memory debugging, you can get help from simple tracers such as `mtrace`, or you have the heavyweight option of the Valgrind `memcheck` tool.

If you have concerns about the consequence of an OOM situation, you can fine-tune the allocation mechanism via `/proc/sys/vm/overcommit_memory` and you can control the likelihood of particular processes being killed though the `oom_score_adj` parameter.

The next chapter is all about debugging user space and kernel code using the GNU debugger and the insights you can gain from watching code as it runs, including the memory management functions I have described here.

Further reading

The following resources have further information on the topics introduced in this chapter:

- *Linux Kernel Development, 3rd Edition*, by Robert Love
- *Linux System Programming, 2nd Edition*, by Robert Love
- *Understanding the Linux VM Manager* by Mel Gorman: `https://www.kernel.org/doc/gorman/pdf/understand.pdf`
- *Valgrind 3.3 - Advanced Debugging and Profiling for Gnu/Linux Applications* by J Seward, N. Nethercote, and J. Weidendorfer

Section 4: Debugging and Optimizing Performance

Section 4 teaches the reader how to make effective use of the many debug and profiling tools that Linux has to offer in order to detect problems and identify bottlenecks. *Chapter 19* focuses solely on the traditional approach of watching code execution through a debugger, which in Linux's case is the **GNU Debugger** (**GDB**). *Chapter 20* examines various profilers and tracers, beginning with `top` then moving on to `perf`, until eventually progressing all the way down to `strace`.

This part of the book comprises the following chapters:

- *Chapter 19, Debugging with GDB*
- *Chapter 20, Profiling and Tracing*
- *Chapter 21, Real-Time Programming*

19
Debugging with GDB

Bugs happen. Identifying and fixing them is part of the development process. There are many different techniques for finding and characterizing program defects, including static and dynamic analysis, code review, tracing, profiling, and interactive debugging. I will look at tracers and profilers in the next chapter, but here I want to concentrate on the traditional approach of watching code execution through a debugger, which in our case is the **GNU Project Debugger** (**GDB**). GDB is a powerful and flexible tool. You can use it to debug applications, examine the postmortem files (core files) that are created after a program crash, and even step through kernel code.

In this chapter, we will cover the following topics:

- The GNU debugger
- Preparing to debug
- Debugging applications
- Just-in-time debugging
- Debugging forks and threads
- Core files
- GDB user interfaces
- Debugging kernel code

Technical requirements

To follow along with the examples, make sure you have the following:

- Linux-based host system with a minimum of 60 GB of available disk space
- Buildroot 2020.02.9 LTS release
- Yocto 3.1 (Dunfell) LTS release
- Etcher for Linux
- MicroSD card reader and card
- USB to TTL 3.3V serial cable
- Raspberry Pi 4
- 5V 3A USB-C power supply
- Ethernet cable and port for network connectivity
- BeagleBone Black
- 5V 1A DC power supply

You should have already installed the 2020.02.9 LTS release of Buildroot for *Chapter 6, Selecting a Build System*. If you have not, then refer to the *System requirements* section of the *The Buildroot user manual* (`https://buildroot.org/downloads/manual/manual.html`) before installing Buildroot on your Linux host according to the instructions from *Chapter 6*.

You should have already installed the 3.1 (Dunfell) LTS release of Yocto for *Chapter 6, Selecting a Build System*. If you have not, then refer to the *Compatible Linux Distribution* and *Build Host Packages* sections of the *Yocto Project Quick Build* guide (`https://www.yoctoproject.org/docs/current/brief-yoctoprojectqs/brief-yoctoprojectqs.html`) before installing Yocto on your Linux host according to the instructions from *Chapter 6*.

All of the code for this chapter can be found in the `Chapter19` folder of the book's GitHub repository: `https://github.com/PacktPublishing/Mastering-Embedded-Linux-Programming-Third-Edition`.

The GNU debugger

GDB is a source-level debugger for compiled languages, primarily C and C++, although there is also support for a variety of other languages, such as Go and Objective-C. You should read the notes for the version of GDB you are using to find out the current status of support for the various languages.

The project website is `https://www.gnu.org/software/gdb/` and it contains a lot of useful information, including the GDB user manual, *Debugging with GDB*.

Out of the box, GDB has a command-line user interface that some people find off-putting, although in reality, it is easy to use with a little practice. If command-line interfaces are not to your liking, there are plenty of frontend user interfaces to GDB, and I will describe three of them later in this chapter.

Preparing to debug

You need to compile the code you want to debug with debug symbols. GCC offers two options for this: `-g` and `-ggdb`. The latter adds debug information that is specific to GDB, whereas the former generates information in an appropriate format for whichever target operating system you are using, making it the more portable option. In our particular case, the target operating system is always Linux, and it makes little difference whether you use `-g` or `-ggdb`. Of more interest is the fact that both options allow you to specify the level of debug information, from `0` to `3`:

- `0`: This produces no debug information at all and is equivalent to omitting the `-g` or `-ggdb` switch.
- `1`: This produces minimal information, but includes function names and external variables, which is enough to generate a backtrace.
- `2`: This is the default and includes information about local variables and line numbers so that you can perform source-level debugging and single-step through the code.
- `3`: This includes extra information which, among other things, means that GDB can handle macro expansions correctly.

In most cases, `-g` suffices: reserve `-g3` or `-ggdb3` if you are having problems stepping through code, especially if it contains *macros*.

The next issue to consider is the level of code optimization. Compiler optimization tends to destroy the relationship between lines of source code and machine code, which makes stepping through the source unpredictable. If you experience problems such as this, you will most likely need to compile without optimization, leaving out the `-O` compile switch, or using `-Og`, which enables optimizations that do not interfere with debugging.

A related issue is that of stack-frame pointers, which are required by GDB to generate a backtrace of function calls up to the current one. On some architectures, GCC will not generate stack-frame pointers with the higher levels of optimization (`-O2` and above). If you find yourself in a situation where you really have to compile with `-O2`, but still want backtraces, you can override the default behavior with `-fno-omit-frame-pointer`. Also look out for code that has been hand-optimized to leave out frame pointers through the addition of `-fomit-frame-pointer`: you may want to temporarily remove those bits.

Debugging applications

You can use GDB to debug applications in one of two ways: if you are developing code to run on desktops and servers, or indeed any environment where you compile and run the code on the same machine, it is natural to run GDB natively. However, most embedded development is done using a cross toolchain, and hence you want to debug code running on the device but control it from the cross-development environment, where you have the source code and the tools. I will focus on the latter case, since it is the most likely scenario for embedded developers, but I will also show you how to set up a system for native debugging. I am not going to describe the basics of using GDB here since there are many good references on that topic already, including the GDB user manual and the suggested *Further reading* section at the end of the chapter.

Remote debugging using gdbserver

The key component for remote debugging is the debug agent, `gdbserver`, which runs on the target and controls execution of the program being debugged. `gdbserver` connects to a copy of GDB running on the host machine via a network connection or a serial interface.

Debugging through `gdbserver` is almost, but not quite, the same as debugging natively. The differences are mostly centered around the fact that there are two computers involved and they have to be in the right state for debugging to take place. Here are some things to look out for:

- At the start of a debug session, you need to load the program you want to debug on the target using `gdbserver`, and then separately load GDB from your cross toolchain on the host.
- GDB and `gdbserver` need to connect to each other before a debug session can begin.
- GDB, running on the host, needs to be told where to look for debug symbols and source code, especially for shared libraries.
- The GDB `run` command does not work as expected.
- `gdbserver` will terminate when the debug session ends, and you will need to restart it if you want another debug session.
- You need debug symbols and source code for the binaries you want to debug on the host, but not on the target. Often, there is not enough storage space for them on the target, and they will need to be stripped before deploying to the target.
- The GDB/`gdbserver` combination does not support all the features of natively running GDB: for example, `gdbserver` cannot follow the child process after a `fork`, whereas native GDB can.

- Odd things can happen if GDB and `gdbserver` are from different versions of GDB, or are the same version but configured differently. Ideally, they should be built from the same source using your favorite build tool.

Debug symbols increase the size of executables dramatically, sometimes by a factor of 10. As mentioned in *Chapter 5, Building a Root Filesystem*, it can be useful to remove debug symbols without recompiling everything. The tool for the job is `strip` from the `binutils` package in your cross toolchain. You can control the strip level with these switches:

- `--strip-all`: This removes all symbols (default).
- `--strip-unneeded`: This removes symbols not required for relocation processing.
- `--strip-debug`: This removes only debug symbols.

> **Important note**
> For applications and shared libraries, `--strip-all` (the default) is fine, but when it comes to kernel modules, you will find that it will stop the module from loading. Use `--strip-unneeded` instead. I am still working on a use case for `--strip-debug`.

With that in mind, let's look at the specifics involved in debugging with the Yocto Project and Buildroot.

Setting up the Yocto Project for remote debugging

There are two things to be done to debug applications remotely when using the Yocto Project: you need to add `gdbserver` to the target image, and you need to create an SDK that includes GDB and has debug symbols for the executables that you plan to debug.

First, to include `gdbserver` in the target image, you can add the package explicitly by adding this to `conf/local.conf`:

```
IMAGE_INSTALL_append = " gdbserver"
```

In the absence of a serial console, an SSH daemon also needs to be added so that you have some way to start `gdbserver` on the target:

```
EXTRA_IMAGE_FEATURES ?= "ssh-server-openssh"
```

Alternatively, you can add `tools-debug` to `EXTRA_IMAGE_FEATURES`, which will add `gdbserver`, native `gdb`, and `strace` to the target image (I will talk about `strace` in the next chapter):

```
EXTRA_IMAGE_FEATURES ?= "tools-debug ssh-server-openssh"
```

For the second part, you just need to build an SDK as I described in *Chapter 6, Selecting a Build System*:

```
$ bitbake -c populate_sdk <image>
```

The SDK contains a copy of GDB. It also contains a `sysroot` for the target with debug symbols for all the programs and libraries that are part of the target image. Finally, the SDK contains the source code for the executables. For example, looking at an SDK built for the Raspberry Pi 4 and generated by version 3.1.5 of the Yocto Project, it is installed by default in `/opt/poky/3.1.5/`. The `sysroot` for the target is `/opt/poky/3.1.5/sysroots/aarch64-poky-linux/`. The programs are in `/bin/`, `/sbin/`, `/usr/bin/`, and `/usr/sbin/`, relative to the `sysroot`, and the libraries are in `/lib/` and `/usr/lib/`. In each of these directories, you will find a subdirectory named `.debug/` that contains the symbols for each program and library. GDB knows to look in `.debug/` when searching for symbol information. The source code for the executables is stored in `/usr/src/debug/`, relative to the `sysroot`.

Setting up Buildroot for remote debugging

Buildroot does not make a distinction between the build environment and that used for application development: there is no SDK. Assuming that you are using the Buildroot internal toolchain, you need to enable these options to build the cross GDB for the host and to build `gdbserver` for the target:

- `BR2_PACKAGE_HOST_GDB`, in **Toolchain | Build cross gdb for the host**
- `BR2_PACKAGE_GDB`, in **Target packages | Debugging, profiling and benchmark | gdb**
- `BR2_PACKAGE_GDB_SERVER`, in **Target packages | Debugging, profiling and benchmark | gdbserver**

You also need to build executables with debug symbols, for which you need to enable `BR2_ENABLE_DEBUG`, in **Build options | build packages with debugging symbols**.

This will create libraries with debug symbols in `output/host/usr/<arch>/sysroot`.

Starting to debug

Now that you have gdbserver installed on the target and a cross GDB on the host, you can start a debug session.

Connecting GDB and gdbserver

The connection between GDB and gdbserver can be through a network or serial interface. In the case of a network connection, you launch gdbserver with the TCP port number to listen on and, optionally, an IP address to accept connections from. In most cases, you don't care which IP address is going to connect, so you can just provide the port number. In this example, gdbserver waits for a connection on port 10000 from any host:

```
# gdbserver :10000 ./hello-world
Process hello-world created; pid = 103
Listening on port 10000
```

Next, start the copy of GDB from your toolchain, pointing it at an unstripped copy of the program so that GDB can load the symbol table:

```
$ aarch64-poky-linux-gdb hello-world
```

In GDB, use the target remote command to make the connection to gdbserver, giving it the IP address or hostname of the target and the port it is waiting on:

```
(gdb) target remote 192.168.1.101:10000
```

When gdbserver sees the connection from the host, it prints the following:

```
Remote debugging from host 192.168.1.1
```

The procedure is similar for a serial connection. On the target, you tell gdbserver which serial port to use:

```
# gdbserver /dev/ttyO0 ./hello-world
```

You may need to configure the port baud rate beforehand using stty(1) or a similar program. A simple example would be as follows:

```
# stty -F /dev/ttyO0 115200
```

There are many other options to stty, so read the manual page for more details. It is worthwhile noting that the port must not be being used for anything else. For example, you can't use a port that is being used as the system console.

On the host, you make the connection to gdbserver using target remote plus the serial device at the host end of the cable. In most cases, you will want to set the baud rate of the host serial port first, using the GDB command set serial baud:

```
(gdb) set serial baud 115200
(gdb) target remote /dev/ttyUSB0
```

Even though GDB and gdbserver are now connected, we are not ready to set breakpoints and start stepping through source code yet.

Setting the sysroot

GDB needs to know where to find debug information and source code for the program and shared libraries you are debugging. When debugging natively, the paths are well known and built in to GDB, but when using a cross toolchain, GDB has no way to guess where the root of the target filesystem is. You have to provide this information.

If you built your application using the Yocto Project SDK, the sysroot is within the SDK, and so you can set it in GDB like this:

```
(gdb) set sysroot /opt/poky/3.1.5/sysroots/aarch64-poky-linux
```

If you are using Buildroot, you will find that the sysroot is in output/host/usr/<toolchain>/sysroot, and that there is a symbolic link to it in output/staging. So, for Buildroot, you would set the sysroot like this:

```
(gdb) set sysroot /home/chris/buildroot/output/staging
```

GDB also needs to find the source code for the files you are debugging. GDB has a search path for source files, which you can see using the show directories command:

```
(gdb) show directories
Source directories searched: $cdir:$cwd
```

These are the defaults: $cwd is the current working directory of the GDB instance running on the host; $cdir is the directory where the source was compiled. The latter is encoded into the object files with the tag DW_AT_comp_dir. You can see these tags using objdump --dwarf, like this, for example:

```
$ aarch64-poky-linux-objdump --dwarf ./helloworld | grep DW_AT_
comp_dir
[…]
```

```
<160> DW_AT_comp_dir : (indirect string, offset: 0x244): /home/chris/helloworld
[...]
```

In most cases, the defaults, `$cdir` and `$cwd`, are sufficient, but problems arise if the directories have been moved between compilation and debugging. One such case occurs with the Yocto Project. Taking a deeper look at the `DW_AT_comp_dir` tags for a program compiled using the Yocto Project SDK, you may notice this:

```
$ aarch64-poky-linux-objdump --dwarf ./helloworld | grep DW_AT_comp_dir
<2f> DW_AT_comp_dir : /usr/src/debug/glibc/2.31-r0/git/csu
<79> DW_AT_comp_dir : (indirect string, offset: 0x139): /usr/src/debug/glibc/2.31-r0/git/csu
<116> DW_AT_comp_dir : /usr/src/debug/glibc/2.31-r0/git/csu
<160> DW_AT_comp_dir : (indirect string, offset: 0x244): /home/chris/helloworld
[...]
```

Here, you can see multiple references to the directory `/usr/src/debug/glibc/2.31-r0/git`, but where is it? The answer is that it is in the `sysroot` for the SDK, so the full path is `/opt/poky/3.1.5/sysroots/aarch64-poky-linux /usr/src/debug/glibc/2.31-r0/git`. The SDK contains source code for all of the programs and libraries that are in the target image. GDB has a simple way to cope with an entire directory tree being moved like this: `substitute-path`. So, when debugging with the Yocto Project SDK, you need to use these commands:

```
(gdb) set sysroot /opt/poky/3.1.5/sysroots/aarch64-poky-linux
(gdb) set substitute path /usr/src/debug/opt/poky/3.1.5/sysroots/aarch64-poky-linux/usr/src/debug
```

You may have additional shared libraries that are stored outside the `sysroot`. In that case, you can use `set solib-search-path`, which can contain a colon-separated list of directories to search for shared libraries. GDB searches `solib-search-path` only if it cannot find the binary in the `sysroot`.

A third way of telling GDB where to look for source code, for both libraries and programs, is to use the `directory` command:

```
(gdb) directory /home/chris/MELP/src/lib_mylib
Source directories searched: /home/chris/MELP/src/lib_mylib:$cdir:$cwd
```

Paths added in this way take precedence because they are searched *before* those from `sysroot` or `solib-search-path`.

GDB command files

There are some things that you need to do each time you run GDB, for example, setting the `sysroot`. It is convenient to put such commands into a command file and run them each time GDB is started. GDB reads commands from `$HOME/.gdbinit`, then from `.gdbinit` in the current directory, and then from files specified on the command line with the `-x` parameter. However, recent versions of GDB will refuse to load `.gdbinit` from the current directory for security reasons. You can override that behavior by adding a line such as this to `$HOME/.gdbinit`:

```
set auto-load safe-path /
```

Alternatively, if you don't want to enable auto-loading globally, you can specify a particular directory like this:

```
add-auto-load-safe-path /home/chris/myprog
```

My personal preference is to use the `-x` parameter to point to the command file, which exposes the location of the file so that I don't forget about it.

To help you set up GDB, Buildroot creates a GDB command file containing the correct `sysroot` command in `output/staging/usr/share/buildroot/gdbinit`. It will contain a line similar to this one:

```
set sysroot /home/chris/buildroot/output/host/usr/aarch64-
buildroot-linux-gnu/sysroot
```

Now that GDB is running and can find the information it needs, let's look at some of the commands we can perform with it.

Overview of GDB commands

GDB has many more commands, which are described in the online manual and in the resources mentioned in the *Further reading* section. To help you get going as quickly as possible, here is a list of the most commonly used commands. In most cases, there is a short form for the command, which is listed in the following tables.

Breakpoints

These are the commands for managing breakpoints:

Command	Short-form command	Use
`break <location>`	`b <location>`	Set a breakpoint on a function name, line number, or line. Examples of locations are `main`, `5`, and `sortbug.c:42`.
`info breakpoints`	`i b`	List breakpoints.
`delete breakpoint <N>`	`d b <N>`	Delete the breakpoint `<N>`.

Running and stepping

These are commands for controlling the execution of a program:

Command	Short-form command	Use
`run`	`r`	Load a fresh copy of the program into memory and start running it. *This does not work for remote debugging using gdbserver.*
`continue`	`c`	Continue execution from a breakpoint.
Ctrl + C	-	Stop the program being debugged.
`step`	`s`	Step one line of code, stepping *into* any function that is called.
`next`	`n`	Step one line of code, stepping *over* a function call.
`finish`	-	Run until the current function returns.

Getting information

These are commands for getting information regarding the debugger:

Command	Short-form command	Use
`backtrace`	`bt`	List the call stack
`info threads`	`i th`	Display information about the threads executing in the program.
`info sharedlibrary`	`i share`	Display information about shared libraries currently loaded by the program.
`print <variable>`	`p <variable>`	Print the value of a variable, for example, `print foo`.
`list`	`l`	List lines of code around the current program counter.

Before we can begin stepping through a program inside a debug session, we first need to set an initial breakpoint.

Running to a breakpoint

`gdbserver` loads the program into memory and sets a breakpoint at the first instruction, and then waits for a connection from GDB. When the connection is made, you enter into a debug session. However, you will find that if you try to single-step immediately, you will get this message:

```
Cannot find bounds of current function
```

This is because the program has been halted in code written in assembly, which creates the runtime environment for C/C++ programs. The first line of C/C++ code is the `main()` function. Supposing that you want to stop at `main()`, you would set a breakpoint there and then use the `continue` command (abbreviation `c`) to tell `gdbserver` to continue from the breakpoint at the start of the program and stop at `main()`:

```
(gdb) break main
Breakpoint 1, main (argc=1, argv=0xbefffe24) at helloworld.c:8
printf("Hello, world!\n");
(gdb) c
```

At this point, you may see the following:

```
Reading /lib/ld-linux.so.3 from remote target...
warning: File transfers from remote targets can be slow. Use
"set sysroot" to access files locally instead.
```

With older versions of GDB, you may instead see this:

```
warning: Could not load shared library symbols for 2 libraries,
e.g. /lib/libc.so.6.
```

In both cases, the problem is that you have forgotten to set the `sysroot`! Take another look at the earlier section on `sysroot`.

This is all very different to starting a program natively, where you just type `run`. In fact, if you try typing `run` in a remote debug session, you will either see a message saying that the remote target does not support the `run` command, or in older versions of GDB, it will just hang without any explanation.

Extending GDB with Python

We can embed a full Python interpreter into GDB to extend its functionality. This is done by configuring GDB using the `--with-python` option prior to building. GDB has an API that exposes much of its internal state as Python objects. This API allows us to define our own custom GDB commands as scripts written in Python. These extra commands may include useful debugging aids such as tracepoints and pretty printers that are not built into GDB.

Building GDB with Python support

We have already covered *Setting up Buildroot for remote debugging*. There are some additional steps needed to enable Python support inside GDB. At the time of writing, Buildroot only supports embedding Python 2.7 inside GDB, which is unfortunate, but better than no support for Python at all. We cannot use a toolchain generated by Buildroot to build GDB with Python support because it is missing some necessary thread support.

To build cross GDB for the host with Python support, perform the following steps:

1. Navigate to the directory where you installed Buildroot:

    ```
    $ cd buildroot
    ```

2. Copy the configuration file for the board you wish to build an image for:

    ```
    $ cd configs
    $ cp raspberrypi4_64_defconfig rpi4_64_gdb_defconfig
    $ cd ..
    ```

3. Clean previous build artifacts from the `output` directory:

    ```
    $ make clean
    ```

4. Activate your configuration file:

    ```
    $ make rpi4_64_gdb_defconfig
    ```

5. Begin customizing your image:

    ```
    $ make menuconfig
    ```

6. Enable use of an external toolchain by navigating to **Toolchain | Toolchain type | External toolchain** and selecting that option.

7. Back out of **External toolchain** and open the **Toolchain** submenu. Select a known working toolchain, such as **Linaro AArch64 2018.05**, as your external toolchain.
8. Select **Build cross gdb for the host** from the **Toolchain** page and enable both **TUI support** and **Python support**:

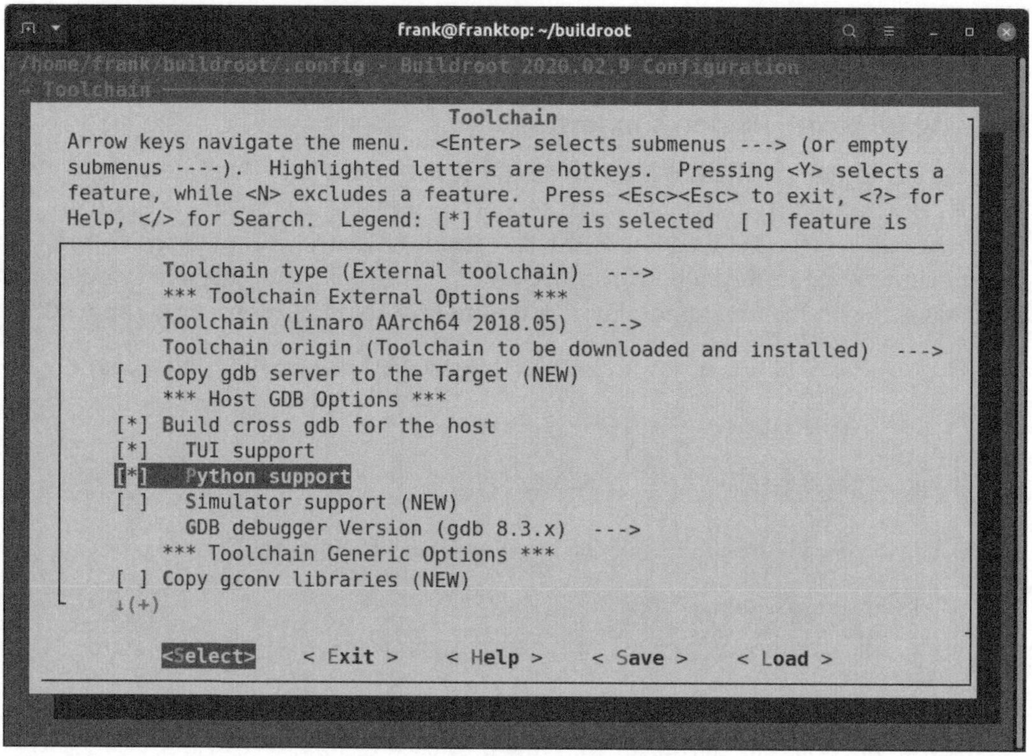

Figure 19.1 – Python support in GDB

9. Drill down into the **GDB debugger Version** submenu from the **Toolchain** page and select the newest version of GDB available in Buildroot.
10. Back out of the **Toolchain** page and drill down into **Build options**. Select **build packages with debugging symbols**.
11. Back out of the **Build options** page and drill down into **System Configuration** and select **Enable root login with password**. Open **Root password** and enter a non-empty password in the text field:

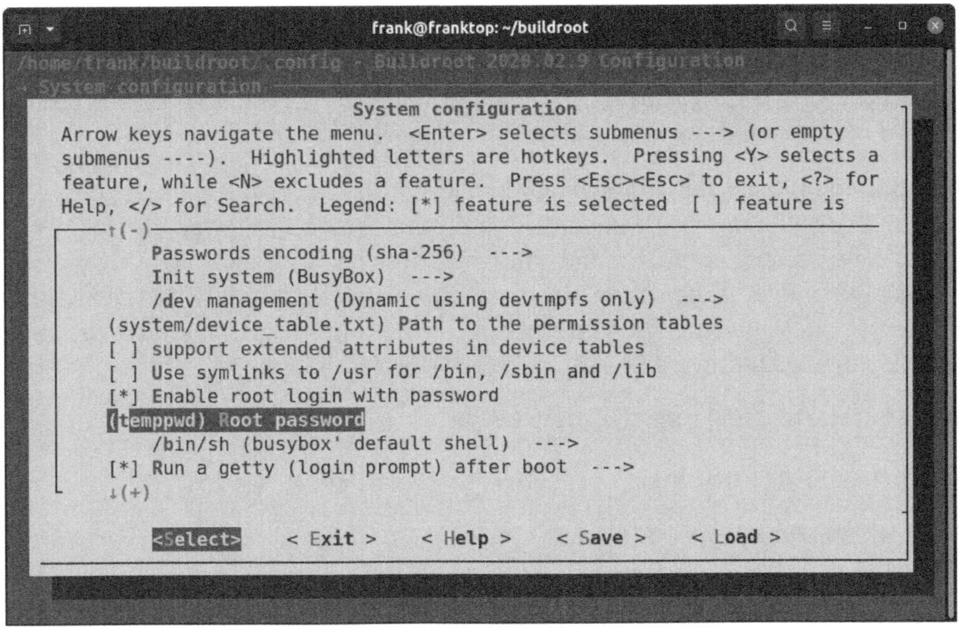

Figure 19.2 – Root password

12. Back out of the **System Configuration** page and drill down into **Target packages | Debugging, profiling and benchmark**. Select the **gdb** package to add `gdbserver` to the target image.
13. Back out of **Debugging, profiling and benchmark** and drill down into **Target packages | Networking applications**. Select the **dropbear** package to enable `scp` and `ssh` access to the target. Note that `dropbear` does not allow `root scp` and `ssh` access without a password.
14. Add the **haveged** entropy daemon, which can be found under **Target packages | Miscellaneous** so that SSH is available quicker upon booting.
15. Add another package to your image so you have something to debug. I chose the `bsdiff` binary patch/diff tool, which is written in C and can be found under **Target packages | Development tools**.
16. Save your changes and exit Buildroot's `menuconfig`.
17. Save your changes to your configuration file:

```
$ make savedefconfig
```

18. Build the image for the target:

```
$ make
```

A readymade `rpi4_64_gdb_defconfig` file for the Raspberry Pi 4 can be found in the code archive for this chapter if you wish to skip the previous `menuconfig` steps. Copy that file form `MELP/Chapter19/buildroot/configs/` to your `buildroot/configs` directory and run `make` on that if you prefer.

When the build is done, there should be a bootable `sdcard.img` file in `output/images/` that you can write to a microSD card using Etcher. Insert that microSD into your target device and boot it. Connect the target device to your local network with an Ethernet cable and locate its IP address using `arp-scan`. SSH into the device as `root` and enter the password that you set when configuring your image. I specified `temppwd` as the `root` password for my `rpi4_64_gdb_defconfig` image.

Now, let's debug `bsdiff` remotely using GDB:

1. First, navigate to the `/usr/bin` directory on the target:

```
# cd /usr/bin
```

2. Then, start `bdiff` with `gdbserver`, as we did with `helloworld` earlier:

```
# gdbserver :10000 ./bsdiff pcregrep pcretest out
Process ./bsdiff created; pid = 169
Listening on port 10000
```

3. Next, start the copy of GDB from your toolchain, pointing it at an unstripped copy of the program so that GDB can load the symbol table:

```
$ cd output/build/bsdiff-4.3
$ ~/buildroot/output/host/bin/aarch64-linux-gdb bsdiff
```

4. In GDB, set the `sysroot` like this:

```
(gdb) set sysroot ~/buildroot/output/staging
```

5. Then, use the command target remote to make the connection to `gdbserver`, giving it the IP address or hostname of the target and the port it is waiting on:

```
(gdb) target remote 192.168.1.101:10000
```

6. When `gdbserver` sees the connection from the host, it prints the following:

```
Remote debugging from host 192.168.1.1
```

7. We can now load Python command scripts such as `tp.py` into GDB from `<data-directory>/python` and use these commands like so:

```
(gdb) source tp.py
(gdb) tp search
```

   In this case, `tp` is the name of the *tracepoint* command and `search` is the name of a recursive function in `bsdiff`.

8. To show the directory where GDB searches for Python command scripts, execute the following command:

```
(gdb) show data-directory
```

The Python support in GDB can also be used to debug Python programs. GDB has visibility into CPython's internals that the standard `pdb` debugger for Python does not. It can even inject Python code into a running Python process. This enables the creation of powerful debugging tools, like this Python 3 memory analyzer (`https://github.com/facebookincubator/memory-analyzer`) from Facebook.

Native debugging

Running a native copy of GDB on the target is not as common as doing it remotely, but it is possible. As well as installing GDB in the target image, you will also need unstripped copies of the executables you want to debug and the corresponding source code installed in the target image. Both the Yocto Project and Buildroot allow you to do this.

> **Important note**
>
> While native debugging is not a common activity for embedded developers, running profile and trace tools on the target is very common. These tools usually work best if you have unstripped binaries and source code on the target, which is half of the story I am telling here. I will return to this topic in the next chapter.

The Yocto Project

To begin with, add gdb to the target image by adding this to conf/local.conf:

```
EXTRA_IMAGE_FEATURES ?= "tools-debug dbg-pkgs"
```

You need the debug information for the packages you want to debug. The Yocto Project builds debug variants of packages, which contain unstripped binaries and the source code. You can add these debug packages selectively to your target image by adding <package name>-dbg to your conf/local.conf. Or, you can simply install *all* debug packages by adding dbg-pkgs to EXTRA_IMAGE_FEATURES, as just shown. Be warned that this will increase the size of the target image dramatically, perhaps by several hundreds of megabytes.

The source code is installed in /usr/src/debug/<package name> in the target image. This means that GDB will pick it up without needing to run set substitute-path. If you don't need the source, you can prevent it from being installed by adding this to your conf/local.conf file:

```
PACKAGE_DEBUG_SPLIT_STYLE = "debug-without-src"
```

Buildroot

With Buildroot, you can tell it to install a native copy of GDB in the target image by enabling this option:

- BR2_PACKAGE_GDB_DEBUGGER in **Target packages | Debugging, profiling and benchmark | Full debugger**

Then, to build binaries with debug information and to install them in the target image without stripping, enable the first and disable the second of these two options:

- BR2_ENABLE_DEBUG in **Build options | Build packages with debugging symbols**
- BR2_STRIP_strip in **Build options | Strip target binaries**

That's all I have to say about native debugging. Again, the practice is uncommon on embedded devices because the extra source code and debug symbols add bloat to the target image. Next, let's look at another form of remote debugging.

Just-in-time debugging

Sometimes, a program will start to misbehave after it has been running for a while, and you would like to know what it is doing. The GDB *attach* feature does exactly this. I call it just-in-time debugging. It is available with both native and remote debug sessions.

In the case of remote debugging, you need to find the PID of the process to be debugged and pass it to `gdbserver` with the `--attach` option. For example, if the PID is `109`, you would type this:

```
# gdbserver --attach :10000 109
Attached; pid = 109
Listening on port 10000
```

This forces the process to stop as if it were at a breakpoint, allowing you to start your cross GDB in the normal way and connect to `gdbserver`. When you are done, you can `detach`, allowing the program to continue running without the debugger:

```
(gdb) detach
Detaching from program: /home/chris/MELP/helloworld/helloworld,
process 109
Ending remote debugging.
```

Attaching to a running process by PID is certainly handy, but what about multi-process or multithreaded programs? There are techniques for debugging those types of programs with GDB as well.

Debugging forks and threads

What happens when the program you are debugging forks? Does the debug session follow the parent process or the child? This behavior is controlled by `follow-fork-mode`, which may be `parent` or `child`, with `parent` being the default. Unfortunately, current versions (10.1) of `gdbserver` do not support this option, so it only works for native debugging. If you really need to debug the child process while using `gdbserver`, a workaround is to modify the code so that the child loops on a variable immediately after the fork, giving you the opportunity to attach a new `gdbserver` session to it and then to set the variable so that it drops out of the loop.

When a thread in a multithreaded process hits a breakpoint, the default behavior is for all threads to halt. In most cases, this is the best thing to do as it allows you to look at static variables without them being changed by the other threads. When you recommence execution of the thread, all the stopped threads start up, even if you are single-stepping, and it is especially this last case that can cause problems. There is a way to modify the way in which GDB handles stopped threads, through a parameter called `scheduler-locking`. Normally it is `off`, but if you set it to `on`, only the thread that was stopped at the breakpoint is resumed and the others remain stopped, giving you a chance to see what the thread alone does without interference. This continues to be the case until you turn `scheduler-locking` off. `gdbserver` supports this feature.

Core files

Core files capture the state of a failing program at the point that it terminates. You don't even have to be in the room with a debugger when the bug manifests itself. So, when you see `Segmentation fault (core dumped)`, don't shrug; investigate the **core file** and extract the goldmine of information in there.

The first observation is that core files are not created by default, but only when the core file resource limit for the process is non-zero. You can change it for the current shell using `ulimit -c`. To remove all limits on the size of core files, type the following command:

```
$ ulimit -c unlimited
```

By default, the core file is named `core` and is placed in the current working directory of the process, which is the one pointed to by `/proc/<PID>/cwd`. There are a number of problems with this scheme. Firstly, when looking at a device with several files named `core`, it is not obvious which program generated each one. Secondly, the current working directory of the process may well be in a read-only filesystem, there may not be enough space to store the core file, or the process may not have permissions to write to the current working directory.

There are two files that control the naming and placement of core files. The first is `/proc/sys/kernel/core_uses_pid`. Writing a `1` to it causes the PID number of the dying process to be appended to the filename, which is somewhat useful as long as you can associate the PID number with a program name from log files.

Much more useful is `/proc/sys/kernel/core_pattern`, which gives you a lot more control over core files. The default pattern is core, but you can change it to a pattern composed of these meta characters:

- `%p`: The PID
- `%u`: The real UID of the dumped process

- `%g`: The real GID of the dumped process
- `%s`: The number of the signal causing the dump
- `%t`: The time of dump, expressed as seconds since the Epoch, 1970-01-01 00:00:00 +0000 (UTC)
- `%h`: The hostname
- `%e`: The executable filename
- `%E`: The path name of the executable, with slashes (/) replaced by exclamation marks (`!`)
- `%c`: The core file size soft resource limit of the dumped process

You can also use a pattern that begins with an absolute directory name so that all core files are gathered together in one place. As an example, the following pattern puts all core files into the `/corefiles` directory and names them with the program name and the time of the crash:

```
# echo /corefiles/core.%e.%t > /proc/sys/kernel/core_pattern
```

Following a `core` dump, you would find something like this:

```
# ls /corefiles
core.sort-debug.1431425613
```

For more information, refer to the manual page, `core(5)`.

Using GDB to look at core files

Here is a sample GDB session looking at a `core` file:

```
$ arm-poky-linux-gnueabi-gdb sort-debug /home/chris/rootfs/
corefiles/core.sort-debug.1431425613
[...]
Core was generated by `./sort-debug'.
Program terminated with signal SIGSEGV, Segmentation fault.
#0 0x000085c8 in addtree (p=0x0, w=0xbeac4c60 "the") at sort-
debug.c:41
41 p->word = strdup (w);
```

This shows that the program stopped at line `41`. The list command shows the code in the vicinity:

```
(gdb) list
37 static struct tnode *addtree (struct tnode *p, char *w)
38 {
39 int cond;
40
41 p->word = strdup (w);
42 p->count = 1;
43 p->left = NULL;
44 p->right = NULL;
45
```

The `backtrace` command (shortened to `bt`) shows how we got to this point:

```
(gdb) bt
#0 0x000085c8 in addtree (p=0x0, w=0xbeac4c60 "the") at sort-
debug.c:41
#1 0x00008798 in main (argc=1, argv=0xbeac4e24) at sort-
debug.c:89
```

This is an obvious mistake: `addtree()` was called with a null pointer.

GDB began as a command-line debugger and many people still use it this way. Even though LLVM project's LLDB debugger is gaining in popularity, GCC and GDB remain the prominent compiler and debugger for Linux. So far, we have focused exclusively on GDB's command-line interface. Now we will look at some frontends to GDB with progressively more modern user interfaces.

GDB user interfaces

GDB is controlled at a low level through the GDB machine interface, GDB/MI, which can be used to wrap GDB in a user interface or as part of a larger program, and it considerably extends the range of options available to you.

In this section, I will describe three that are well suited to debugging embedded targets: the **Terminal User Interface** (**TUI**), the **Data Display Debugger** (**DDD**), and Visual Studio Code.

Terminal User Interface

Terminal User Interface (**TUI**) is an optional part of the standard GDB package. The main feature is a code window that shows the line of code about to be executed, together with any breakpoints. It is a definite improvement on the list command in command-line mode GDB.

The attraction of TUI is that it just works without any extra setup, and since it is in text mode, it is possible to use over an SSH terminal session, for example, when running `gdb` natively on a target. Most cross toolchains configure GDB with TUI. Simply add `-tui` to the command line and you will see the following:

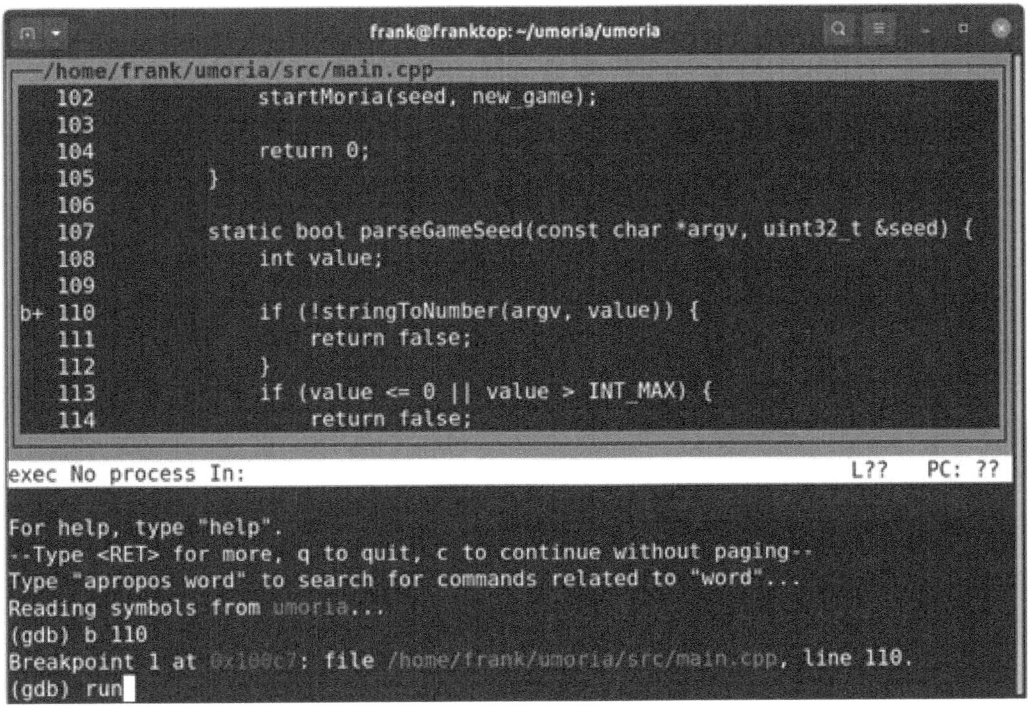

Figure 19.3 – TUI

If you still find TUI lacking and prefer a truly graphical frontend to GDB, the GNU project also offers one of those (`https://www.gnu.org/software/ddd`).

Data Display Debugger

Data Display Debugger (**DDD**) is a simple standalone program that gives you a graphical user interface to GDB with minimal fuss and bother, and although the UI controls look dated, it does everything that is necessary.

The `--debugger` option tells DDD to use GDB from your toolchain, and you can use the `-x` argument to give the path to a GDB command file:

```
$ ddd --debugger arm-poky-linux-gnueabi-gdb -x gdbinit sort-
debug
```

The following screenshot shows off one of the nicest features: the data window, which contains items in a grid that you can rearrange as you wish. If you double-click on a pointer, it is expanded into a new data item and the link is shown with an arrow:

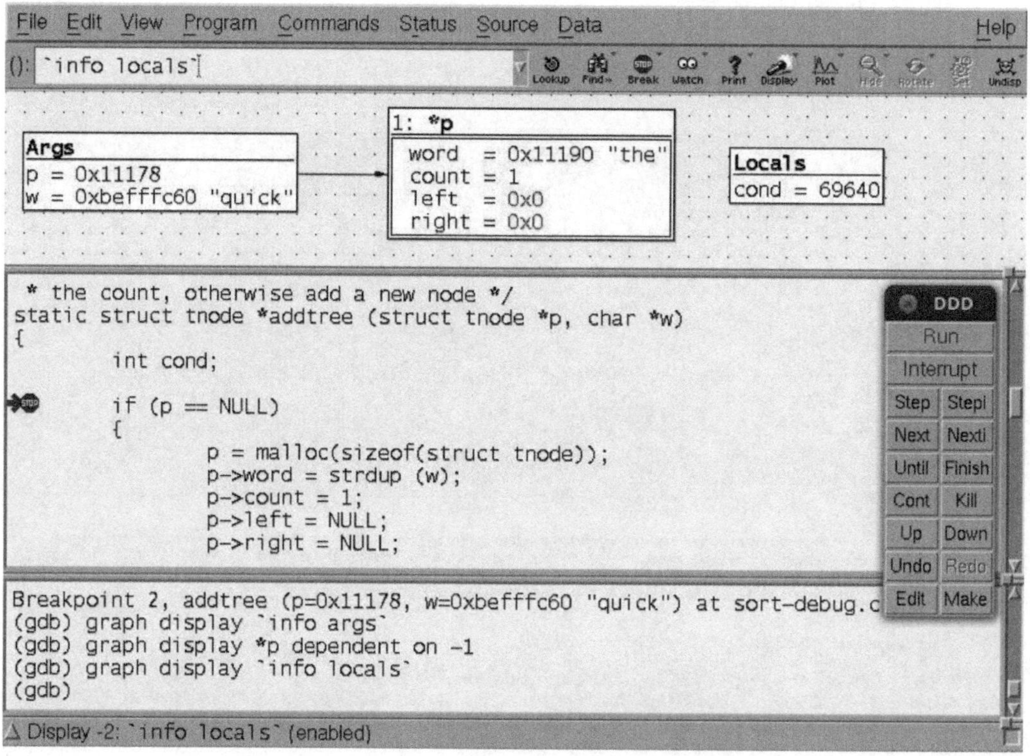

Figure 19.4 – DDD

If neither of these two GDB frontends is acceptable because you are a full stack web developer accustomed to working with the latest tools in your industry, then we still have you covered.

Visual Studio Code

Visual Studio Code is a very popular open source code editor from Microsoft. Because it is an Electron application written in TypeScript, Visual Studio Code feels more lightweight and responsive than full-blown IDEs such as Eclipse. There is rich language support (code completion, go to definition, etc.) for many languages by way of extensions contributed by its large community of users. Remote cross GDB debugging can be integrated into Visual Studio Code using extensions for CMake and C/C++.

Installing Visual Studio Code

The easiest way to install Visual Studio Code on an Ubuntu Linux system is to use `snap`:

```
$ sudo snap install --classic code
```

Before we can create a C/C++ project that we can deploy to the Raspberry Pi 4 and debug remotely, we first need a toolchain.

Installing a toolchain

We will use Yocto to build an SDK for the Raspberry Pi 4. This SDK will include a toolchain that targets the Raspberry Pi 4's 64-bit Arm cores. We already used Yocto to build a 64-bit Arm image for the Raspberry Pi 4 in the *Building an existing BSP* section of *Chapter 7, Developing with Yocto*.

Let's use that same `poky/build-rpi` output directory from that chapter to build a new `core-image-minimal-dev` image and the corresponding SDK for that image:

1. First, navigate one level above the directory where you cloned Yocto.
2. Next, source the `build-rpi` build environment:

   ```
   $ source poky/oe-init-build-env build-rpi
   ```

3. Edit `conf/local.conf` so that it includes the following:

   ```
   MACHINE ?= "raspberrypi4-64"
   IMAGE_INSTALL_append = " gdbserver"
   EXTRA_IMAGE_FEATURES ?= "ssh-server-openssh debug-tweaks"
   ```

   The `debug-tweaks` feature eliminates the need for a `root` password so that command-line tools such as `scp` and `ssh` can be used to deploy and run newly built binaries from the host to the target.

4. Then, build the development image for the Raspberry Pi 4:

```
$ bitbake core-image-minimal-dev
```

5. Use Etcher to write the resulting `core-image-minimal-dev-raspberrypi4-64.wic.bz2` image from `tmp/deploy/images/raspberrypi4-64/` to a microSD card and boot it on your Raspberry Pi 4.
6. Plug your Raspberry Pi 4 into your local network over Ethernet and use `arp-scan` to locate the IP address of your Raspberry Pi 4. We will need this IP address later when *Configuring CMake* for remote debugging.
7. Lastly, build the SDK:

```
$ bitbake -c populate_sdk core-image-minimal-dev
```

> **Important note**
>
> Never use `debug-tweaks` in production images. An automated CI/CD pipeline for OTA software updates is essential, but great care must be taken to ensure that development images do not accidentally leak out to production.

We now have a self-extracting installer named `poky-glibc-x86_64-core-image-minimal-dev-aarch64-raspberrypi4-64-toolchain-3.1.5.sh` in the `tmp/deploy/sdk` directory under `poky/build-rpi` that we can use to install this newly built SDK on any Linux development machine. Find the SDK installer in `tmp/deploy/sdk` and run it:

```
$ ./poky-glibc-x86_64-core-image-minimal-dev-aarch64-
raspberrypi4-64-toolchain-3.1.5.sh
Poky (Yocto Project Reference Distro) SDK installer version
3.1.5
================================================================
===
Enter target directory for SDK (default: /opt/poky/3.1.5):
You are about to install the SDK to "/opt/poky/3.1.5". Proceed
[Y/n]? Y
[sudo] password for frank:
Extracting SDK.................................................
.........done
Setting it up...done
SDK has been successfully set up and is ready to be used.
```

```
Each time you wish to use the SDK in a new shell session, you
need to source the environment setup script e.g.
 $ . /opt/poky/3.1.5/environment-setup-aarch64-poky-linux
```

Notice that the SDK was installed to `/opt/poky/3.1.5`. We won't source `environment-setup-aarch64-poky-linux` as instructed, but the contents of that file will be used to populate the upcoming project files for Visual Studio Code.

Installing CMake

We will use **CMake** to cross-compile the C code we will be deploying and debugging on the Raspberry Pi 4. To install CMake on Ubuntu Linux, execute the following command:

```
$ sudo apt update
$ sudo apt install cmake
```

CMake should already have been installed on your host machine as part of *Chapter 2, Learning about Toolchains.*

Creating a Visual Studio Code project

Projects built with CMake have a canonical structure that includes a `CMakeLists.txt` file and separate `src` and `build` directories.

Create a Visual Studio Code project named `hellogdb` in your home directory:

```
$ mkdir hellogdb
$ cd hellogdb
$ mkdir src build
$ code .
```

The last `code .` command will launch Visual Studio Code and open the `hellogdb` directory. A hidden `.vscode` directory containing `settings.json` and `launch.json` for a project also gets created when you launch Visual Studio Code from a directory.

Installing Visual Studio Code extensions

We need to install the following Visual Studio Code extensions to cross-compile and debug code with the toolchain from our SDK:

- C/C++ by Microsoft
- CMake by twxs
- CMake Tools by Microsoft

Click on the **Extensions** icon on the left edge of the Visual Studio Code window, search for these extensions in the marketplace, and install them. Once they are installed, your **Extensions** sidebar should look something like this:

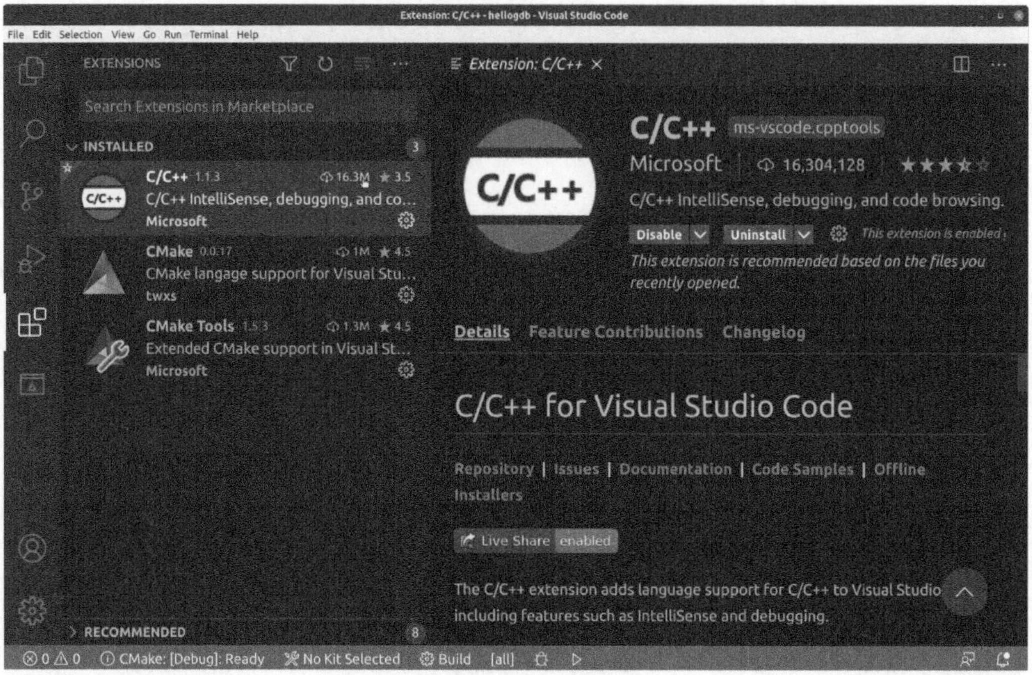

Figure 19.5 – Extensions

Now we will use CMake to integrate the toolchain that came with the SDK we built to cross-compile and debug our `hellogdb` project.

Configuring CMake

We need to populate `CMakeLists.txt` and `cross.cmake` to cross-compile the `hellogdb` project with our toolchain:

1. First, copy `MELP/Chapter19/hellogdb/CMakeLists.txt` to the `hellogdb` project folder in your home directory.
2. From inside Visual Studio Code, click on the **Explorer** icon in the upper-left corner of the Visual Studio Window to open the **Explorer** sidebar.
3. Click on `CMakeLists.txt` in the **Explorer** sidebar to view the file's contents. Notice that the project's name is defined as `HelloGDBProject` and the IP address of the target board is hardcoded as `192.168.1.128`.

4. Change that to match the IP address of your Raspberry Pi 4 and save the `CMakeLists.txt` file.
5. Expand the **src** folder and click on the **New File** icon in the **Explorer** sidebar to create a file named `main.c` inside the `hellogdb` project's `src` directory.
6. Paste the following code into that `main.c` source file and save it:

```
#include <stdio.h>

int main() {
    printf("Hello CMake\n");
    return 0;
}
```

7. Copy `MELP/Chapter19/hellogdb/cross.cmake` to the `hellogdb` project folder in your home directory.
8. Lastly, click on `cross.cmake` in the **Explorer** sidebar to view the file's contents. Notice that the `sysroot_target` and `tools` paths defined in `cross.cmake` point to the `/opt/poky/3.1.5` directory where we installed the SDK. Also notice that the values of the `CMAKE_C_COMPILE`, `CMAKE_CXX_COMPILE` and `CMAKE_CXX_FLAGS` variables were derived directly from the environment setup script included with the SDK.

With these two files in place, we are almost ready to build our `hellogdb` project.

Configuring project settings for building

Now, let's configure the `settings.json` file for the `hellogdb` project to use `CMakeLists.txt` and `cross.cmake` for building:

1. With the `hellogdb` project open in Visual Studio Code, hit *Ctrl* + *Shift* + *P* to bring up the **Command Palette** field.
2. Enter `>settings.json` in the **Command Palette** field and select **Preferences: Open Workspace Settings (JSON)** from the list of options.
3. Edit the `.vscode/settings.json` for `hellogdb` so that it looks something like this:

```
{
    "cmake.sourceDirectory": "${workspaceFolder}",
    "cmake.configureArgs": [
```

```
            "-DCMAKE_TOOLCHAIN_FILE=${workspaceFolder}/cross.
cmake"
        ],
        "C_Cpp.default.configurationProvider": "ms-vscode.
cmake-tools"
}
```

Notice the reference to `cross.cmake` in the definition of `cmake.configureArgs`.

4. Hit *Ctrl* + *Shift* + *P* to bring up the **Command Palette** field again.
5. Enter `>CMake: Delete Cache and Configuration` in the **Command Palette** field and execute it.
6. Click on the **CMake** icon on the left edge of the Visual Studio Window to open the **CMake** sidebar.
7. Click on the `HelloGDBProject` binary in the **CMake** sidebar to build it:

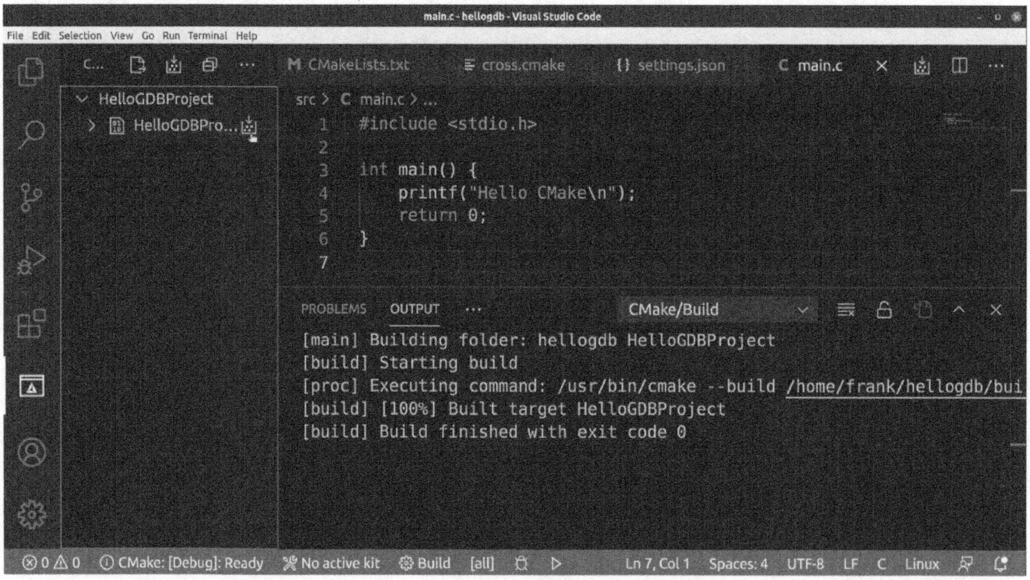

Figure 19.6 – Building HelloGDBProject

If you configured everything correctly, the contents of the **Output** pane should look like this:

```
[main] Building folder: hellogdb HelloGDBProject
[build] Starting build
[proc] Executing command: /usr/bin/cmake --build /home/frank/
hellogdb/build --config Debug --target HelloGDBProject -- -j 14
[build] [100%] Built target HelloGDBProject
[build] Build finished with exit code 0
```

Now that we've used Visual Studio Code to build an executable binary targeting 64-bit Arm, let's deploy it to the Raspberry Pi 4 for remote debugging.

Configuring launch settings for remote debugging

Now, let's create a `launch.json` file so that we can deploy the `HelloGDBProject` binary to the Raspberry Pi 4 and debug it remotely from within Visual Studio Code:

1. Click on the **Run** icon on the left edge of the Visual Studio Code window to open the **Run** sidebar.
2. Click on **Create a launch.json file** on the **Run** sidebar and select **C++ (GDB/LLDB)** for the environment.
3. Select **Default Configuration** from the list of options when prompted for a C/C++ debug configuration type.
4. Add or edit the following fields in the `"(gdb) Launch"` configuration within `.vscode/launch.json` as follows:

   ```
   "program": "${workspaceFolder}/build/HelloGDBProject",
   "miDebuggerServerAddress": "192.168.1.128:10000",
   "targetArchitecture": "aarch64",
   "miDebuggerPath": "/opt/poky/3.1.5/sysroots/x86_64-
   pokysdk-linux/usr/bin/aarch64-poky-linux/aarch64-poky-
   linux-gdb",
   ```

5. Replace the `192.168.1.128` address in `miDebuggerServerAddress` with the IP address of your Raspberry Pi 4 and save the file.
6. Set a breakpoint in `main.c` at the first line of the body of the `main()` function.
7. Click on the new **build_and_debug – Utility** in the **Run** sidebar to send the `HelloGDBProject` binary to the Raspberry Pi 4 and start it with `gdbserver`.

If the Raspberry Pi 4 and `launch.json` file were set up correctly, then the contents of the **Output** pane should look like this:

```
[main] Building folder: hellogdb build_and_debug
[build] Starting build
[proc] Executing command: /usr/bin/cmake --build /home/frank/hellogdb/build --config Debug --target build_and_debug -- -j 14
[build] [100%] Built target HelloGDBProject
[build] Process ./HelloGDBProject created; pid = 552
[build] Listening on port 10000
```

Click on the **(gdb) Launch** button in the upper-left corner of the Visual Studio Code window. GDB should hit the breakpoint we set in `main.c` and a line like the following should appear in the **Output** pane:

```
[build] Remote debugging from host 192.168.1.69, port 44936
```

This is what Visual Studio Code should look like when GDB hits the breakpoint:

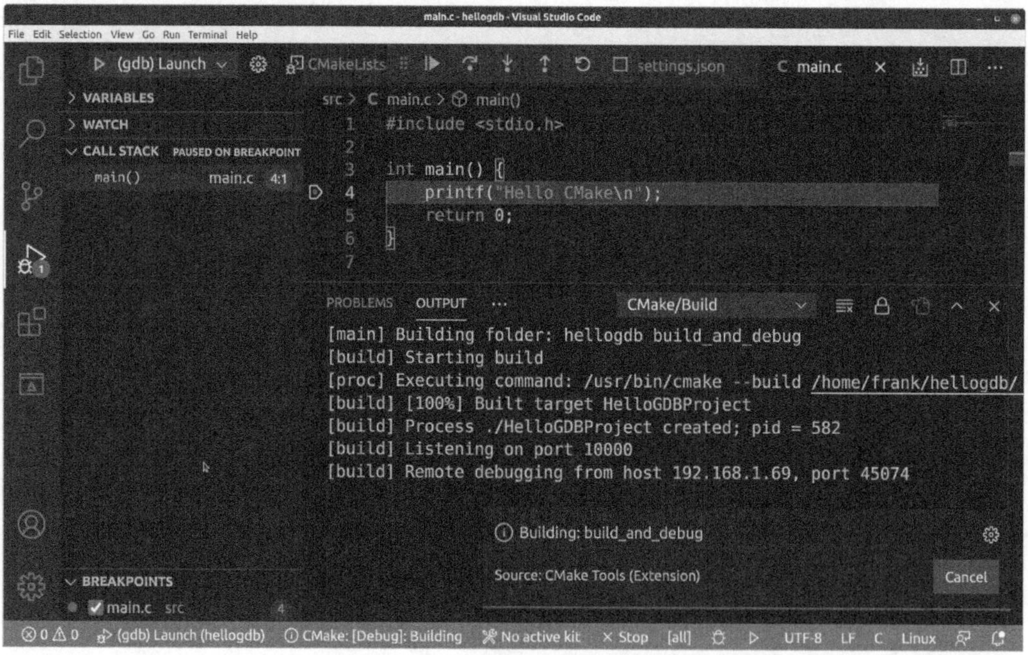

Figure 19.7 – GDB remote debugging

Hit the blue **Continue** button hovering up top, and the following lines should appear in the output pane:

```
[build] Hello CMake
[build]
[build] Child exited with status 0
[build] [100%] Built target build_and_debug
[build] Build finished with exit code 0
```

Congratulations! You have successfully integrated an SDK built with Yocto into Visual Studio Code using CMake to enable GDB remote debugging on a target device. This was no small feat, but now that you've seen how it's done, you can do the same for your own projects.

Debugging kernel code

You can use `kgdb` for source-level debugging, in a manner similar to remote debugging with `gdbserver`. There is also a self-hosted kernel debugger, `kdb`, that is handy for lighter-weight tasks such as seeing whether an instruction is executed and getting the backtrace to find out how it got there. Finally, there are kernel *Oops* messages and panics, which tell you a lot about the cause of a kernel exception.

Debugging kernel code with kgdb

When looking at kernel code using a source debugger, you must remember that the kernel is a complex system, with real-time behaviors. Don't expect debugging to be as easy as it is for applications. Stepping through code that changes the memory mapping or switches context is likely to produce odd results.

kgdb is the name given to the kernel GDB stubs that have been part of mainline Linux for many years now. There is a user manual in the kernel DocBook, and you can find an online version at `https://www.kernel.org/doc/htmldocs/kgdb/index.html`.

In most cases, you will connect to `kgdb` over the serial interface, which is usually shared with the serial console. Hence, this implementation is called **kgdboc**, which is short for **kgdb over console**. To work, it requires a platform `tty` driver that supports I/O polling instead of interrupts, since `kgdb` has to disable interrupts when communicating with GDB. A few platforms support `kgdb` over USB, and there have been versions that work over Ethernet but, unfortunately, none of those have found their way into mainline Linux.

The same caveats regarding optimization and stack frames apply to the kernel, with the limitation that the kernel is written to assume an optimization level of at least -O1. You can override the kernel compile flags by setting KCFLAGS before running make.

These, then, are the kernel configuration options you will need for kernel debugging:

- CONFIG_DEBUG_INFO is in the **Kernel hacking | Compile-time checks and compiler options | Compile the kernel with debug info** menu.
- CONFIG_FRAME_POINTER may be an option for your architecture and is in the **Kernel hacking | Compile-time checks and compiler options | Compile the kernel with frame pointers** menu.
- CONFIG_KGDB is in the **Kernel hacking | KGDB: kernel debugger** menu.
- CONFIG_KGDB_SERIAL_CONSOLE is in the **Kernel hacking | KGDB: kernel debugger | KGDB: use kgdb over the serial console** menu.

In addition to the zImage or uImage compressed kernel image, the kernel image must be in ELF object format so that GDB can load the symbols into memory. This is the file called vmlinux that is generated in the directory where Linux is built. In Yocto, you can request that a copy be included in the target image and SDK. It is built as a package named kernel-vmlinux, which you can install like any other, for example, by adding it to the IMAGE_INSTALL list.

The file is put into the sysroot boot directory, with a name such as this:

```
/opt/poky/3.1.5/sysroots/cortexa8hf-neon-poky-linux-gnueabi/
boot/vmlinux-5.4.72-yocto-standard
```

In Buildroot, you will find vmlinux in the directory where the kernel was built, which is in output/build/linux-<version string>/vmlinux.

A sample debug session

The best way to show you how it works is with a simple example.

You need to tell kgdb which serial port to use, either through the kernel command line or at runtime via sysfs. For the first option, add kgdboc=<tty>,<baud rate> to the command line, as shown here:

```
kgdboc=ttyO0,115200
```

For the second option, boot the device up and write the terminal name to the `/sys/module/kgdboc/parameters/kgdboc` file, as shown here:

```
# echo ttyO0 > /sys/module/kgdboc/parameters/kgdboc
```

Note that you cannot set the baud rate in this way. If it is the same `tty` as the console, then it is set already. If not, use `stty` or a similar program.

Now you can start GDB on the host, selecting the `vmlinux` file that matches the running kernel:

```
$ arm-poky-linux-gnueabi-gdb ~/linux/vmlinux
```

GDB loads the symbol table from `vmlinux` and waits for further input.

Next, close any terminal emulator that is attached to the console: you are about to use it for GDB, and if both are active at the same time, some of the debug strings might get corrupted.

Now, you can return to GDB and attempt to connect to `kgdb`. However, you will find that the response you get from `target remote` at this time is unhelpful:

```
(gdb) set serial baud 115200
(gdb) target remote /dev/ttyUSB0
Remote debugging using /dev/ttyUSB0
Bogus trace status reply from target: qTStatus
```

The problem is that `kgdb` is not listening for a connection at this point. You need to interrupt the kernel before you can enter into an interactive GDB session with it. Unfortunately, just typing *Ctrl* + *C* in GDB, as you would with an application, does not work. You have to force a trap into the kernel by launching another shell on the target, via SSH, for example, and writing `g` to `/proc/sysrq-trigger` on the target board:

```
# echo g > /proc/sysrq-trigger
```

The target stops dead at this point. Now you can connect to `kgdb` via the serial device at the host end of the cable:

```
(gdb) set serial baud 115200
(gdb) target remote /dev/ttyUSB0
Remote debugging using /dev/ttyUSB0
0xc009a59c in arch_kgdb_breakpoint ()
```

At last, GDB is in charge. You can set breakpoints, examine variables, look at backtraces, and so on. As an example, set a break on `sys_sync`, as follows:

```
(gdb) break sys_sync
Breakpoint 1 at 0xc0128a88: file fs/sync.c, line 103.
(gdb) c
Continuing.
```

Now the target comes back to life. Typing `sync` on the target calls `sys_sync` and hits the breakpoint:

```
[New Thread 87]
[Switching to Thread 87]

Breakpoint 1, sys_sync () at fs/sync.c:103
```

If you have finished the debug session and want to disable `kgdboc`, just set the `kgdboc` terminal to `null`:

```
# echo "" > /sys/module/kgdboc/parameters/kgdboc
```

Like attaching to a running process with GDB, this technique of trapping the kernel and connecting to `kgdb` over a serial console works once the kernel is done booting. But what if the kernel never finishes booting because of a bug?

Debugging early code

The preceding example works in cases where the code you are interested in is executed when the system is fully booted. If you need to get in early, you can tell the kernel to wait during boot by adding `kgdbwait` to the command line, after the `kgdboc` option:

```
kgdboc=ttyO0,115200 kgdbwait
```

Now, when you boot, you will see this on the console:

```
[ 1.103415] console [ttyO0] enabled
[ 1.108216] kgdb: Registered I/O driver kgdboc.
[ 1.113071] kgdb: Waiting for connection from remote gdb...
```

At this point, you can close the console and connect from GDB in the usual way.

Debugging modules

Debugging kernel modules presents an additional challenge because the code is relocated at runtime, and so you need to find out at what address it resides. The information is presented through `sysfs`. The relocation addresses for each section of the module are stored in `/sys/module/<module name>/sections`. Note that since ELF sections begin with a dot (`.`), they appear as hidden files, and you will have to use `ls -a` if you want to list them. The important ones are `.text`, `.data`, and `.bss`.

Take as an example a module named `mbx`:

```
# cat /sys/module/mbx/sections/.text
0xbf000000
# cat /sys/module/mbx/sections/.data
0xbf0003e8
# cat /sys/module/mbx/sections/.bss
0xbf0005c0
```

Now you can use these numbers in GDB to load the symbol table for the module at those addresses:

```
(gdb) add-symbol-file /home/chris/mbx-driver/mbx.ko 0xbf000000
\
-s .data 0xbf0003e8 -s .bss 0xbf0005c0
add symbol table from file "/home/chris/mbx-driver/mbx.ko" at
.text_addr = 0xbf000000
.data_addr = 0xbf0003e8
.bss_addr = 0xbf0005c0
```

Everything should now work as normal: you can set breakpoints and inspect global and local variables in the module just as you can in `vmlinux`:

```
(gdb) break mbx_write
Breakpoint 1 at 0xbf00009c: file /home/chris/mbx-driver/mbx.c,
line 93.
(gdb) c
Continuing.
```

Then, force the device driver to call `mbx_write`, and it will hit the breakpoint:

```
Breakpoint 1, mbx_write (file=0xde7a71c0, buffer=0xadf40
"hello\n\n",
length=6, offset=0xde73df80)
at /home/chris/mbx-driver/mbx.c:93
```

If you already use GDB to debug code in user space, then you should feel right at home debugging kernel code and modules with `kgdb`. Let's look at `kdb` next.

Debugging kernel code with kdb

Although **kdb** does not have the features of `kgdb` and GDB, it does have its uses, and being selfhosted, there are no external dependencies to worry about. `kdb` has a simple command-line interface that you can use on a serial console. You can use it to inspect memory, registers, process lists, and `dmesg` and even set breakpoints to stop at a certain location.

To configure your kernel so that you can call `kdb` via a serial console, enable `kgdb` as shown previously, and then enable this additional option:

- `CONFIG_KGDB_KDB`, which is in the **KGDB: Kernel hacking | kernel debugger | KGDB_KDB: Include kdb frontend for kgdb** menu

Now, when you force the kernel into a trap, instead of entering into a GDB session, you will see the `kdb` shell on the console:

```
# echo g > /proc/sysrq-trigger
[ 42.971126] SysRq : DEBUG
Entering kdb (current=0xdf36c080, pid 83) due to Keyboard Entry
kdb>
```

There are quite a few things you can do in the `kdb` shell. The `help` command will print all of the options. Here is an overview:

- **Getting information**:

  `ps`: This displays active processes.

  `ps A`: This displays all processes.

  `lsmod`: This lists modules.

  `dmesg`: This displays the kernel log buffer.

- **Breakpoints**:

  `bp`: This sets a breakpoint.

  `bl`: This lists breakpoints.

  `bc`: This clears a breakpoint.

  `bt`: This prints a backtrace.

  `go`: This continues execution.

- **Inspect memory and registers**:

  `md`: This displays memory.

  `rd`: This displays registers.

Here is a quick example of setting a breakpoint:

```
kdb> bp sys_sync
Instruction(i) BP #0 at 0xc01304ec (sys_sync)
is enabled addr at 00000000c01304ec, hardtype=0 installed=0
kdb> go
```

The kernel returns to life and the console shows the normal shell prompt. If you type `sync`, it hits the breakpoint and enters `kdb` again:

```
Entering kdb (current=0xdf388a80, pid 88) due to Breakpoint
@0xc01304ec
```

`kdb` is not a source-level debugger, so you can't see the source code or single-step. However, you can display a backtrace using the `bt` command, which is useful for getting an idea of program flow and call hierarchy.

Looking at an Oops

When the kernel performs an invalid memory access or executes an illegal instruction, a kernel **Oops** message is written to the kernel log. The most useful part of this is the backtrace, and I want to show you how to use the information there to locate the line of code that caused the fault. I will also address the problem of preserving Oops messages if they cause the system to crash.

This Oops message was generated by writing to the mailbox driver in MELP/Chapter19/mbx-driver-oops:

```
Unable to handle kernel NULL pointer dereference at virtual
address 00000004
pgd = dd064000
[00000004] *pgd=9e58a831, *pte=00000000, *ppte=00000000
Internal error: Oops: 817 [#1] PREEMPT ARM
Modules linked in: mbx(O)
CPU: 0 PID: 408 Comm: sh Tainted: G O 4.8.12-yocto-standard #1
Hardware name: Generic AM33XX (Flattened Device Tree)
task: dd2a6a00 task.stack: de596000
PC is at mbx_write+0x24/0xbc [mbx]
LR is at __vfs_write+0x28/0x48
pc : [<bf0000f0>] lr : [<c024ff40>] psr: 800e0013
sp : de597f18 ip : de597f38 fp : de597f34
r10: 00000000 r9 : de596000 r8 : 00000000
r7 : de597f80 r6 : 000fda00 r5 : 00000002 r4 : 00000000
r3 : de597f80 r2 : 00000002 r1 : 000fda00 r0 : de49ee40
Flags: Nzcv IRQs on FIQs on Mode SVC_32 ISA ARM Segment none
Control: 10c5387d Table: 9d064019 DAC: 00000051
Process sh (pid: 408, stack limit = 0xde596210)
```

The line of the Oops that reads PC is at mbx_write+0x24/0xbc [mbx] and tells you most of what you want to know: the last instruction was in the mbx_write function of a kernel module named mbx. Furthermore, it was at offset 0x24 bytes from the start of the function, which is 0xbc bytes long.

Next, take a look at the backtrace:

```
Stack: (0xde597f18 to 0xde598000)
7f00: bf0000cc 00000002
7f20: 000fda00 de597f80 de597f4c de597f38 c024ff40 bf0000d8
de49ee40 00000002
7f40: de597f7c de597f50 c0250c40 c024ff24 c026eb04 c026ea70
de49ee40 de49ee40
7f60: 000fda00 00000002 c0107908 de596000 de597fa4 de597f80
c025187c c0250b80
```

```
7f80: 00000000 00000000 00000002 000fda00 b6eecd60 00000004
00000000 de597fa8
7fa0: c0107700 c0251838 00000002 000fda00 00000001 000fda00
00000002 00000000
7fc0: 00000002 000fda00 b6eecd60 00000004 00000002 00000002
000ce80c 00000000
7fe0: 00000000 bef77944 b6e1afbc b6e73d00 600e0010 00000001
d3bbdad3 d54367bf
[<bf0000f0>] (mbx_write [mbx]) from [<c024ff40>] (__vfs_
write+0x28/0x48)
[<c024ff40>] (__vfs_write) from [<c0250c40>] (vfs_
write+0xcc/0x158)
[<c0250c40>] (vfs_write) from [<c025187c>] (SyS_
write+0x50/0x88)
[<c025187c>] (SyS_write) from [<c0107700>] (ret_fast_
syscall+0x0/0x3c)
Code: e590407c e3520b01 23a02b01 e1a05002 (e5842004)
---[ end trace edcc51b432f0ce7d ]---
```

In this case, we don't learn much more, merely that `mbx_write` was called from the virtual filesystem function, `_vfs_write`.

It would be very nice to find the line of code that relates to `mbx_write+0x24`, for which we can use the GDB command `disassemble` with the `/s` modifier so that it shows source and assembler code together. In this example, the code is in the `mbx.ko` module, so we load that into `gdb`:

```
$ arm-poky-linux-gnueabi-gdb mbx.ko
[...]
(gdb) disassemble /s mbx_write
Dump of assembler code for function mbx_write:
99 {
0x000000f0 <+0>: mov r12, sp
0x000000f4 <+4>: push {r4, r5, r6, r7, r11, r12, lr, pc}
0x000000f8 <+8>: sub r11, r12, #4
0x000000fc <+12>: push {lr} ; (str lr, [sp, #-4]!)
0x00000100 <+16>: bl 0x100 <mbx_write+16>
100 struct mbx_data *m = (struct mbx_data *)file->private_data;
0x00000104 <+20>: ldr r4, [r0, #124] ; 0x7c
```

```
0x00000108 <+24>: cmp r2, #1024 ; 0x400
0x0000010c <+28>: movcs r2, #1024 ; 0x400
101 if (length > MBX_LEN)
102 length = MBX_LEN;
103 m->mbx_len = length;
0x00000110 <+32>: mov r5, r2
0x00000114 <+36>: str r2, [r4, #4]
```

The Oops told us that the error occurred at `mbx_write+0x24`. From the disassembly, we can see that `mbx_write` is at address `0xf0`. Adding `0x24` gives `0x114`, which is generated by the code on line `103`.

> **Important note**
> You may think that I have got the wrong instruction because the listing reads `0x00000114 <+36>: str r2, [r4, #4]`. Surely, we are looking for `+24`, and not `+36`? Ah, but the authors of GDB are trying to confuse us here. The offsets are displayed in decimal, not `hex`: `36 = 0x24`, so I got the right one after all!

You can see from line `100` that `m` has the type struct `mbx_data *`. Here is the place where that structure is defined:

```
#define MBX_LEN 1024
struct mbx_data {
    char mbx[MBX_LEN];
    int mbx_len;
};
```

So, it looks like the `m` variable is a null pointer, and that is what is causing the Oops. Looking at the code where `m` is initialized, we can see that there is a line missing. With the driver modified to initialize the pointer, as shown highlighted in the following code block, it works fine, without the Oops:

```
static int mbx_open(struct inode *inode, struct file *file)
{
    if (MINOR(inode->i_rdev) >= NUM_MAILBOXES) {
        printk("Invalid mbx minor number\n");
        return -ENODEV;
    }
```

```
    file->private_data = &mailboxes[MINOR(inode->i_rdev)];
    return 0;
}
```

Not every Oops is this easy to pinpoint, especially if it occurs before the contents of the kernel log buffer can be displayed.

Preserving the Oops

Decoding an Oops is only possible if you can capture it in the first place. If the system crashes during boot before the console is enabled, or after a suspend, you won't see it. There are mechanisms to log kernel Oops and messages to an MTD partition or to persistent memory, but here is a simple technique that works in many cases and needs little prior thought.

So long as the contents of memory are not corrupted during a reset (and usually they are not), you can reboot into the bootloader and use it to display memory. You need to know the location of the kernel log buffer, remembering that it is a simple ring buffer of text messages. The symbol is `__log_buf`. Look this up in `System.map` for the kernel:

```
$ grep __log_buf System.map
c0f72428 b __log_buf
```

Then, map that kernel logical address into a physical address that U-Boot can understand by subtracting `PAGE_OFFSET` and adding the physical start of RAM. `PAGE_OFFSET` is almost always `0xc0000000`, and the start address of the RAM is `0x80000000` on a BeagleBone, so the calculation becomes `c0f72428 - 0xc0000000 + 0x80000000 = 80f72428`.

Now you can use the U-Boot `md` command to show the log:

```
U-Boot#
md 80f72428
80f72428: 00000000 00000000 00210034 c6000000 ........4.!.....
80f72438: 746f6f42 20676e69 756e694c 6e6f2078 Booting Linux on
80f72448: 79687020 61636973 5043206c 78302055 physical CPU 0x
80f72458: 00000030 00000000 00000000 00730084 0.............s.
80f72468: a6000000 756e694c 65762078 6f697372 ....Linux versio
80f72478: 2e34206e 30312e31 68632820 40736972 n 4.1.10 (chris@
80f72488: 6c697562 29726564 63672820 65762063 builder) (gcc ve
```

```
80f72498: 6f697372 2e34206e 20312e39 6f726328 rsion 4.9.1 (cro
80f724a8: 6f747373 4e2d6c6f 2e312047 302e3032 sstool-NG 1.20.0
80f724b8: 20292029 53203123 5720504d 4f206465 ) ) #1 SMP Wed O
80f724c8: 32207463 37312038 3a31353a 47203335 ct 28 17:51:53 G
```

> **Important note**
>
> From Linux 3.5 onward, there is a 16-byte binary header for each line in the kernel log buffer that encodes a timestamp, a log level, and other things. There is a discussion about it in the Linux weekly news entitled *Toward more reliable logging*, at `https://lwn.net/Articles/492125/`.

In this section, we examined how kernel code can be debugged at the source level using `kgdb`. Then we looked at setting breakpoints and printing backtraces inside the `kdb` shell. Lastly, we learned how to read kernel Oops messages either from a console using `dmesg` or the U-Boot command line.

Summary

Knowing how to use GDB for interactive debugging is a useful tool in the embedded system developer's tool chest. It is a stable, well-documented, and well-known entity. It has the ability to debug remotely by placing an agent on the target, be it `gdbserver` for applications or `kgdb` for kernel code, and although the default command-line user interface takes a while to get used to, there are many alternative frontends. The three I mentioned were TUI, DDD, and Visual Studio Code. Eclipse is another popular frontend that supports debugging with GDB by way of the CDT plugin. I will refer you to the references in the *Further reading* section for information on how to configure CDT to work with a cross toolchain and connect to a remote device.

A second and equally important way to approach debugging is to collect crash reports and analyze them offline. In this category, we looked at application core dumps and kernel Oops messages.

However, this is only one way of identifying flaws in programs. In the next chapter, I will talk about profiling and tracing as ways of analyzing and optimizing programs.

Further reading

The following resources have further information on the topics introduced in this chapter:

- *The Art of Debugging with GDB, DDD, and Eclipse*, by Norman Matloff and Peter Jay Salzman
- *GDB Pocket Reference*, by Arnold Robbins
- *Python Interpreter in GNU Debugger*, by crazyguitar: `https://www.pythonsheets.com/appendix/python-gdb.html`
- *Extending GDB with Python*, by Lisa Roach: `https://www.youtube.com/watch?v=xt9v5t4_zvE`
- *Cross-compiling with CMake and VS Code*, by Enes ÖZTÜRK: `https://enes-ozturk.medium.com/cross-compiling-with-cmake-and-vscode-9ca4976fdd1`
- *Remote Debugging with GDB*, by Enes ÖZTÜRK: `https://enes-ozturk.medium.com/remote-debugging-with-gdb-b4b0ca45b8c1`
- *Getting to grips with Eclipse: cross compiling*: `https://2net.co.uk/tutorial/eclipse-cross-compile`
- *Getting to grips with Eclipse: remote access and debugging*: `https://2net.co.uk/tutorial/eclipse-rse`

20
Profiling and Tracing

Interactive debugging using a source-level debugger, as described in the previous chapter, can give you an insight into the way a program works, but it constrains your view to a small body of code. In this chapter, we will look at the larger picture to see whether the system is performing as intended.

Programmers and system designers are notoriously bad at guessing where bottlenecks are. So if your system has performance issues, it is wise to start by looking at the full system and then work down, using more sophisticated tools as you go. In this chapter, I'll begin with the well-known `top` command as a means of getting an overview. Often the problem can be localized to a single program, which you can analyze using the Linux profiler, `perf`. If the problem is not so localized and you want to get a broader picture, `perf` can do that as well. To diagnose problems associated with the kernel, I will describe some trace tools, Ftrace, LTTng, and BPF, as a means of gathering detailed information.

I will also cover Valgrind, which, because of its sandboxed execution environment, can monitor a program and report on code as it runs. I will complete the chapter with a description of a simple trace tool, `strace`, which reveals the execution of a program by tracing the system calls it makes.

In this chapter, we will cover the following topics:

- The observer effect
- Beginning to profile
- Profiling with `top`
- The poor man's profiler
- Introducing `perf`
- Tracing events
- Introducing Ftrace
- Using LTTng
- Using BPF
- Using Valgrind
- Using `strace`

Technical requirements

To follow along with the examples, make sure you have the following:

- A Linux-based host system
- Buildroot 2020.02.9 LTS release
- Etcher for Linux
- A Micro SD card reader and card
- A Raspberry Pi 4
- A 5 V 3A USB-C power supply
- An Ethernet cable and port for network connectivity

You should have already installed the 2020.02.9 LTS release of Buildroot for *Chapter 6, Selecting a Build System*. If you have not, then refer to the *System requirements* section of *The Buildroot user manual* (`https://buildroot.org/downloads/manual/manual.html`) before installing Buildroot on your Linux host according to the instructions from *Chapter 6*.

All of the code for this chapter can be found in the `Chapter20` folder from the book's GitHub repository: `https://github.com/PacktPublishing/Mastering-Embedded-Linux-Programming-Third-Edition`.

The observer effect

Before diving into the tools, let's talk about what the tools will show you. As is the case in many fields, measuring a certain property affects the observation itself. Measuring the electric current in a power supply line requires measuring the voltage drop over a small resistor. However, the resistor itself affects the current. The same is true for profiling: every system observation has a cost in CPU cycles, and that resource is no longer spent on the application. Measurement tools also mess up caching behavior, eat memory space, and write to disk, which all make it worse. There is no measurement without overhead.

I've often heard engineers say that the results of a profiling job were totally misleading. That is usually because they were performing the measurements on something not approaching a real situation. Always try to measure on the target, using release builds of the software, with a valid dataset, using as few extra services as possible.

A release build usually implies building fully optimized binaries without debug symbols. These production requirements severely limit the functionality of most profiling tools.

Symbol tables and compile flags

Once our system is up and running, we will hit a problem right away. While it is important to observe the system in its natural state, the tools often need additional information to make sense of the events.

Some tools require special kernel options. For the tools we are examining in this chapter, this applies to `perf`, Ftrace, LTTng, and BPF. Therefore, you will probably have to build and deploy a new kernel for these tests.

Debug symbols are very helpful in translating raw program addresses into function names and lines of code. Deploying executables with debug symbols does not change the execution of the code, but it does require that you have copies of the binaries and the kernel compiled with debug information, at least for the components you want to profile. Some tools work best if you have these installed on the target system: `perf`, for example. The techniques are the same as for general debugging as I discussed in *Chapter 19, Debugging with GDB*.

If you want a tool to generate call graphs, you may have to compile with stack frames enabled. If you want the tool to attribute addresses with lines of code accurately, you may need to compile with lower levels of optimization.

Finally, some tools require instrumentation to be inserted into the program to capture samples, so you will have to recompile those components. This applies to Ftrace and LTTng for the kernel.

Be aware that the more you change the system you are observing, the harder it is to relate the measurements you make to the production system.

> **Tip**
>
> It is best to adopt a wait-and-see approach, making changes only when the need is clear, and being mindful that each time you do so, you will change what you are measuring.

Because the results of profiling can be so ambiguous, start with simple, easy-to-use tools that are readily available before reaching for more complex and invasive instruments.

Beginning to profile

When looking at the entire system, a good place to start is with a simple tool such as `top`, which gives you an overview very quickly. It shows you how much memory is being used, which processes are eating CPU cycles, and how this is spread across different cores and times.

If `top` shows that a single application is using up all the CPU cycles in user space, then you can profile that application using `perf`.

If two or more processes have a high CPU usage, there is probably something that is coupling them together, perhaps data communication. If a lot of cycles are spent on system calls or handling interrupts, then there may be an issue with the kernel configuration or with a device driver. In either case, you need to start by taking a profile of the whole system, again using `perf`.

If you want to find out more about the kernel and the sequencing of events there, use Ftrace, LTTng, or BPF.

There could be other problems that `top` will not help you with. If you have multi-threaded code and there are problems with lockups, or if you have random data corruption, then Valgrind plus the Helgrind plugin might be helpful. Memory leaks also fit into this category; I covered memory-related diagnosis in *Chapter 18, Managing Memory*.

Before we get into these more-advanced profiling tools, let start with the most rudimentary one that is found on most systems, including those in production.

Profiling with top

The **top** program is a simple tool that doesn't require any special kernel options or symbol tables. There is a basic version in BusyBox and a more functional version in the `procps` package, which is available in the Yocto Project and Buildroot. You may also want to consider using `htop`, which has functionally similar to `top` but has a nicer user interface (some people think).

To begin with, focus on the summary line of `top`, which is the second line if you are using BusyBox and the third line if you are using `top` from `procps`. Here is an example, using BusyBox's `top`:

```
Mem: 57044K used, 446172K free, 40K shrd, 3352K buff, 34452K cached
CPU: 58% usr 4% sys 0% nic 0% idle 37% io 0% irq 0% sirq
Load average: 0.24 0.06 0.02 2/51 105
PID PPID USER STAT VSZ %VSZ %CPU COMMAND
105 104 root R 27912 6% 61% ffmpeg -i track2.wav
[...]
```

The summary line shows the percentage of time spent running in various states, as shown in this table:

procps	BusyBox	Description
`us`	`usr`	User space programs with a default nice value
`sy`	`sys`	Kernel code
`ni`	`nic`	User space programs with a non-default nice value
`id`	`idle`	Idle
`wa`	`io`	I/O wait
`hi`	`irq`	Hardware interrupts
`si`	`sirq`	Software interrupts
`st`	-	Steal time: only relevant in virtual environments

In the preceding example, almost all of the time (58%) is spent in user mode, with a small amount (4%) in system mode, so this is a system that is CPU-bound in user space. The first line after the summary shows that just one application is responsible: `ffmpeg`. Any efforts toward reducing CPU usage should be directed there.

Here is another example:

```
Mem: 13128K used, 490088K free, 40K shrd, 0K buff, 2788K cached
CPU: 0% usr 99% sys 0% nic 0% idle 0% io 0% irq 0% sirq
Load average: 0.41 0.11 0.04 2/46 97
PID PPID USER STAT VSZ %VSZ %CPU COMMAND
92 82 root R 2152 0% 100% cat /dev/urandom
[...]
```

This system is spending almost all of the time in kernel space (99% `sys`), as a result of `cat` reading from `/dev/urandom`. In this artificial case, profiling `cat` by itself would not help, but profiling the kernel functions that `cat` calls might.

The default view of `top` shows only processes, so the CPU usage is the total of all the threads in the process. Press *H* to see information for each thread. Likewise, it aggregates the time across all CPUs. If you are using the `procps` version of `top`, you can see a summary per CPU by pressing the *1* key.

Once we have singled out the problem process using `top`, we can attach GDB to it.

The poor man's profiler

You can profile an application just by using **GDB** to stop it at arbitrary intervals to see what it is doing. This is the **poor man's profiler**. It is easy to set up and is one way of gathering profile data.

The procedure is simple:

1. Attach to the process using `gdbserver` (for a remote debug) or GDB (for a native debug). The process stops.
2. Observe the function it stopped in. You can use the `backtrace` GDB command to see the call stack.
3. Type `continue` so that the program resumes.
4. After a while, press *Ctrl* + *C* to stop it again, and go back to *step 2*.

If you repeat *steps 2* to *4* several times, you will quickly get an idea of whether it is looping or making progress, and if you repeat them often enough, you will get an idea of where the hotspots in the code are.

There is a whole web page dedicated to this idea at `http://poormansprofiler.org`, together with scripts that make it a little easier. I have used this technique many times over the years with various operating systems and debuggers.

This is an example of **statistical profiling**, in which you sample the program state at intervals. After a number of samples, you begin to learn the statistical likelihood of the functions being executed. It is surprising how few you really need. Other statistical profilers are `perf record`, OProfile, and `gprof`.

Sampling using a debugger is intrusive because the program is stopped for a significant period while you collect the sample. Other tools can do this with much lower overhead. One such tool is `perf`.

Introducing perf

perf is an abbreviation of the Linux **performance event counter subsystem**, `perf_events`, and also the name of the command-line tool for interacting with `perf_events`. Both have been part of the kernel since Linux 2.6.31. There is plenty of useful information in the Linux source tree in `tools/perf/Documentation` as well as at `https://perf.wiki.kernel.org`.

The initial impetus for developing `perf` was to provide a unified way to access the registers of the **performance measurement unit** (**PMU**), which is part of most modern processor cores. Once the API was defined and integrated into Linux, it became logical to extend it to cover other types of performance counters.

At its heart, `perf` is a collection of event counters with rules about when they actively collect data. By setting the rules, you can capture data from the whole system, just the kernel, or just one process and its children, and do it across all CPUs or just one CPU. It is very flexible. With this one tool, you can start by looking at the whole system, then zero in on a device driver that seems to be causing problems, an application that is running slowly, or a library function that seems to be taking longer to execute than you thought.

The code for the `perf` command-line tool is part of the kernel, in the `tools/perf` directory. The tool and the kernel subsystem are developed hand in hand, meaning that they must be from the same version of the kernel. `perf` can do a lot. In this chapter, I will examine it only as a profiler. For a description of its other capabilities, read the `perf` man pages and refer to the documentation mentioned at the start of this section.

In addition to debug symbols, there are two configuration options we need to set to fully enable `perf` in the kernel.

Configuring the kernel for perf

You need a kernel that is configured for `perf_events`, and you need the `perf` command cross-compiled to run on the target. The relevant kernel configuration is `CONFIG_PERF_EVENTS`, present in the **General setup | Kernel Performance Events and Counters** menu.

If you want to profile using tracepoints—more on this subject later—also enable the options described in the section about Ftrace. While you are there, it is worthwhile enabling `CONFIG_DEBUG_INFO` as well.

The `perf` command has many dependencies, which makes cross-compiling it quite messy. However, both the Yocto Project and Buildroot have target packages for it.

You will also need debug symbols on the target for the binaries that you are interested in profiling; otherwise, `perf` will not be able to resolve addresses to meaningful symbols. Ideally, you want debug symbols for the whole system, including the kernel. For the latter, remember that the debug symbols for the kernel are in the `vmlinux` file.

Building perf with the Yocto Project

If you are using the standard `linux-yocto` kernel, `perf_events` is enabled already, so there is nothing more to do.

To build the `perf` tool, you can add it explicitly to the target image dependencies, or you can add the `tools-profile` feature. As I mentioned previously, you will probably want debug symbols on the target image as well as the kernel `vmlinux` image. In total, this is what you will need in `conf/local.conf`:

```
EXTRA_IMAGE_FEATURES = "debug-tweaks dbg-pkgs tools-profile"
IMAGE_INSTALL_append = "kernel-vmlinux"
```

Adding `perf` to a Buildroot-based image can be more involved depending on the source of our default kernel configuration.

Building perf with Buildroot

Many Buildroot kernel configurations do not include `perf_events`, so you should begin by checking that your kernel includes the options mentioned in the preceding section.

To cross-compile `perf`, run the Buildroot `menuconfig` and select the following:

- `BR2_LINUX_KERNEL_TOOL_PERF` in **Kernel | Linux Kernel Tools**

To build packages with debug symbols and install them unstripped on the target, select these two settings:

- `BR2_ENABLE_DEBUG` in the **Build options | build packages with debugging symbols** menu
- `BR2_STRIP = none` in the **Build options | strip command for binaries on target** menu

Then, run `make clean`, followed by `make`.

Once you have built everything, you will have to copy `vmlinux` into the target image manually.

Profiling with perf

You can use `perf` to sample the state of a program using one of the event counters and accumulate samples over a period of time to create a profile. This is another example of statistical profiling. The default event counter is called `cycles`, which is a generic hardware counter that is mapped to a PMU register representing a count of cycles at the core clock frequency.

Creating a profile using `perf` is a two-stage process: the `perf record` command captures samples and writes them to a file named `perf.data` (by default), and then `perf report` analyzes the results. Both commands are run on the target. The samples being collected are filtered for the process and children of a command you specify. Here is an example of profiling a shell script that searches for the `linux` string:

```
# perf record sh -c "find /usr/share | xargs grep linux > /dev/null"
[ perf record: Woken up 2 times to write data ]
[ perf record: Captured and wrote 0.368 MB perf.data (~16057 samples) ]
# ls -l perf.data
-rw------- 1 root root 387360 Aug 25 2015 perf.data
```

Now you can show the results from `perf.data` using the `perf report` command. There are three user interfaces you can select on the command line:

- `--stdio`: This is a pure-text interface with no user interaction. You will have to launch `perf report` and `annotate` for each view of the trace.
- `--tui`: This is a simple text-based menu interface with traversal between screens.
- `--gtk`: This is a graphical interface that otherwise acts in the same way as `--tui`.

The default is TUI, as shown in this example:

```
Samples: 9K of event 'cycles', Event count (approx.): 2006177260
  11.29%  grep  libc-2.20.so         [.] re_search_internal
   8.80%  grep  busybox.nosuid       [.] bb_get_chunk_from_file
   5.55%  grep  libc-2.20.so         [.] _int_malloc
   5.40%  grep  libc-2.20.so         [.] _int_free
   3.74%  grep  libc-2.20.so         [.] realloc
   2.59%  grep  libc-2.20.so         [.] malloc
   2.51%  grep  libc-2.20.so         [.] regexec@@GLIBC_2.4
   1.64%  grep  busybox.nosuid       [.] grep_file
   1.57%  grep  libc-2.20.so         [.] malloc_consolidate
   1.33%  grep  libc-2.20.so         [.] strlen
   1.33%  grep  libc-2.20.so         [.] memset
   1.26%  grep  [kernel.kallsyms]    [k] __copy_to_user_std
   1.20%  grep  libc-2.20.so         [.] free
   1.10%  grep  libc-2.20.so         [.] _int_realloc
   0.95%  grep  libc-2.20.so         [.] re_string_reconstruct
   0.79%  grep  busybox.nosuid       [.] xrealloc
   0.75%  grep  [kernel.kallsyms]    [k] __do_softirq
   0.72%  grep  [kernel.kallsyms]    [k] preempt_count_sub
   0.68%  find  [kernel.kallsyms]    [k] __do_softirq
   0.53%  grep  [kernel.kallsyms]    [k] __dev_queue_xmit
   0.52%  grep  [kernel.kallsyms]    [k] preempt_count_add
   0.47%  grep  [kernel.kallsyms]    [k] finish_task_switch.isra.85
Press '?' for help on key bindings
```

Figure 20.1 – perf report TUI

perf is able to record the kernel functions executed on behalf of the processes because it collects samples in kernel space.

The list is ordered with the most active functions first. In this example, all but one are captured while grep is running. Some are in a library, libc-2.20, some are in a program, busybox.nosuid, and some are in the kernel. We have symbol names for program and library functions because all the binaries have been installed on the target with debug information, and kernel symbols are being read from /boot/vmlinux. If you have vmlinux in a different location, add -k <path> to the perf report command. Rather than storing samples in perf.data, you can save them to a different file using perf record -o <file name> and analyze them using perf report -i <file name>.

By default, perf record samples at a frequency of 1,000 Hz using the cycles counter.

> **Tip**
>
> A sampling frequency of 1,000 Hz may be higher than you really need and may be the cause of the observer effect. Try with lower rates; 100 Hz is enough for most cases, in my experience. You can set the sample frequency using the -F option.

This is still not really making life easy; the functions at the top of the list are mostly low-level memory operations, and you can be fairly sure that they have already been optimized. Fortunately, `perf record` also gives us the ability to crawl up the call stack and see where these functions are being invoked.

Call graphs

It would be nice to step back and see the surrounding context of these costly functions. You can do that by passing the `-g` option to `perf record` to capture the backtrace from each sample.

Now, `perf report` shows a plus sign (+) where the function is part of a call chain. You can expand the trace to see the functions lower down in the chain:

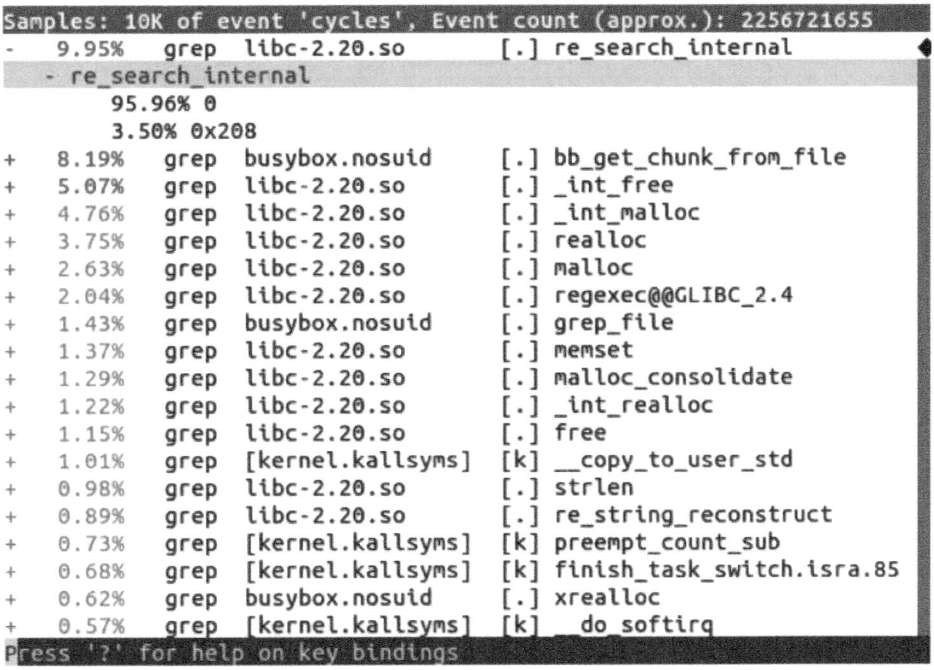

Figure 20.2 – perf report (call graphs)

> **Important note**
>
> Generating call graphs relies on the ability to extract call frames from the stack, just as is necessary for backtraces in GDB. The information needed to unwind stacks is encoded in the debug information of the executables, but not all combinations of architecture and toolchains are capable of doing so.

Backtraces are nice, but where is the assembler, or better yet, the source code, for these functions?

perf annotate

Now that you know which functions to look at, it would be nice to step inside and see the code and to have hit counts for each instruction. That is what `perf annotate` does, by calling down to a copy of `objdump` installed on the target. You just need to use `perf annotate` in place of `perf report`.

`perf annotate` requires symbol tables for the executables and `vmlinux`. Here is an example of an annotated function:

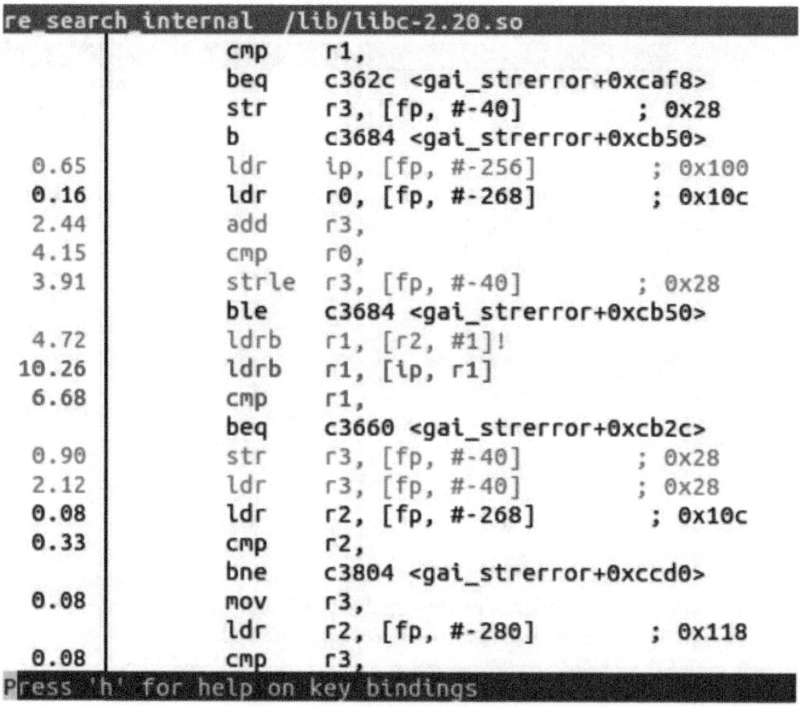

re_search_internal /lib/libc-2.20.so
cmp r1,
beq c362c <gai_strerror+0xcaf8>
str r3, [fp, #-40] ; 0x28
b c3684 <gai_strerror+0xcb50>
0.65 ldr ip, [fp, #-256] ; 0x100
0.16 ldr r0, [fp, #-268] ; 0x10c
2.44 add r3,
4.15 cmp r0,
3.91 strle r3, [fp, #-40] ; 0x28
ble c3684 <gai_strerror+0xcb50>
4.72 ldrb r1, [r2, #1]!
10.26 ldrb r1, [ip, r1]
6.68 cmp r1,
beq c3660 <gai_strerror+0xcb2c>
0.90 str r3, [fp, #-40] ; 0x28
2.12 ldr r3, [fp, #-40] ; 0x28
0.08 ldr r2, [fp, #-268] ; 0x10c
0.33 cmp r2,
bne c3804 <gai_strerror+0xccd0>
0.08 mov r3,
ldr r2, [fp, #-280] ; 0x118
0.08 cmp r3,
Press 'h' for help on key bindings

Figure 20.3 – perf annotate (assembler)

If you want to see the source code interleaved with the assembler, you can copy the relevant source files to the target device. If you are using the Yocto Project and build with the `dbg-pkgs` extra image feature, or have installed the individual `-dbg` package, then the source will have been installed for you in `/usr/src/debug`. Otherwise, you can examine the debug information to see the location of the source code:

```
$ arm-buildroot-linux-gnueabi-objdump --dwarf lib/libc-2.19.so
| grep DW_AT_comp_dir
```

```
<3f> DW_AT_comp_dir : /home/chris/buildroot/output/build/
hostgcc-initial-4.8.3/build/arm-buildroot-linux-gnueabi/libgcc
```

The path on the target should be *exactly the same* as the path you can see in `DW_AT_comp_dir`.

Here is an example of annotation with the source and assembler code:

```
re_search_internal  /lib/libc-2.20.so
       |                         ++match_first;
       |                       goto forward_match_found_start_or_reached_end;
       |
       |                     case 6:
       |                       /* Fastmap without translation, match forward.  */
       |                       while (BE (match_first < right_lim, 1)
  4.15 |          cmp    r0,
  3.91 |          strle  r3, [fp, #-40]         ; 0x28
       |          ble    c3684 <gai_strerror+0xcb50>
       |                         && !fastmap[(unsigned char) string[match_first]])
  4.72 |          ldrb   r1, [r2, #1]!
 10.26 |          ldrb   r1, [ip, r1]
  6.68 |          cmp    r1,
       |          beq    c3660 <gai_strerror+0xcb2c>
  0.90 |          str    r3, [fp, #-40]         ; 0x28
       |                         ++match_first;
       |
       |                     forward_match_found_start_or_reached_end:
       |                       if (BE (match_first == right_lim, 0))
  2.12 |          ldr    r3, [fp, #-40]         ; 0x28
  0.08 |          ldr    r2, [fp, #-268]         ; 0x10c
  0.33 |          cmp    r2,
Press 'h' for help on key bindings
```

Figure 20.4 – perf annotate (source code)

Now we can see the corresponding C source code above `cmp r0` and below the `str r3, [fp, #-40]` instruction.

This concludes our coverage of `perf`. While there are other statistical sampling profilers, such as OProfile and `gprof`, that predate `perf`, these tools have fallen out of favor in recent years, so I chose to omit them. Next, we will look at event tracers.

Tracing events

The tools we have seen so far all use statistical sampling. You often want to know more about the ordering of events so that you can see them and relate them to each other. Function tracing involves instrumenting the code with tracepoints that capture information about the event, and may include some or all of the following:

- A timestamp
- Context, such as the current PID
- Function parameters and return values
- A callstack

It is more intrusive than statistical profiling and it can generate a large amount of data. The latter problem can be mitigated by applying filters when the sample is captured and later on when viewing the trace.

I will cover three trace tools here: the kernel function tracers **Ftrace**, **LTTng**, and **BPF**.

Introducing Ftrace

The kernel function tracer **Ftrace** evolved from work done by Steven Rostedt and many others as they were tracking down the causes of high scheduling latency in real-time applications. Ftrace appeared in Linux 2.6.27 and has been actively developed since then. There are a number of documents describing kernel tracing in the kernel source in `Documentation/trace`.

Ftrace consists of a number of tracers that can log various types of activity in the kernel. Here, I am going to talk about the `function` and `function_graph` tracers and the event tracepoints. In *Chapter 21, Real-Time Programming*, I will revisit Ftrace and use it to show real-time latencies.

The `function` tracer instruments each kernel function so that calls can be recorded and timestamped. As a matter of interest, it compiles the kernel with the `-pg` switch to inject the instrumentation. The `function_graph` tracer goes further and records both the entry and exit of functions so that it can create a call graph. The event tracepoints feature also records parameters associated with the call.

Ftrace has a very embedded-friendly user interface that is entirely implemented through virtual files in the debugfs filesystem, meaning that you do not have to install any tools on the target to make it work. Nevertheless, there are other user interfaces if you prefer: trace-cmd is a command-line tool that records and views traces and is available in Buildroot (BR2_PACKAGE_TRACE_CMD) and the Yocto Project (trace-cmd). There is a graphical trace viewer named **KernelShark** that is available as a package for the Yocto Project.

Like perf, enabling Ftrace requires setting certain kernel configuration options.

Preparing to use Ftrace

Ftrace and its various options are configured in the kernel configuration menu. You will need the following as a minimum:

- CONFIG_FUNCTION_TRACER from the **Kernel hacking | Tracers | Kernel Function Tracer** menu

For reasons that will become clear later, you would be well advised to turn on these options as well:

- CONFIG_FUNCTION_GRAPH_TRACER in the **Kernel hacking | Tracers | Kernel Function Graph Tracer** menu
- CONFIG_DYNAMIC_FTRACE in the **Kernel hacking | Tracers | enable/disable function tracing dynamically** menu

Since the whole thing is hosted in the kernel, there is no user space configuration to be done.

Using Ftrace

Before you can use Ftrace, you have to mount the debugfs filesystem, which by convention goes in the /sys/kernel/debug directory:

```
# mount -t debugfs none /sys/kernel/debug
```

All the controls for Ftrace are in the /sys/kernel/debug/tracing directory; there is even a mini HOWTO in the README file there.

This is the list of tracers available in the kernel:

```
# cat /sys/kernel/debug/tracing/available_tracers
blk function_graph function nop
```

The active tracer is shown by `current_tracer`, which initially will be the null tracer, `nop`.

To capture a trace, select the tracer by writing the name of one of the `available_tracers` to `current_tracer`, and then enable tracing for a short while, as shown here:

```
# echo function > /sys/kernel/debug/tracing/current_tracer
# echo 1 > /sys/kernel/debug/tracing/tracing_on
# sleep 1
# echo 0 > /sys/kernel/debug/tracing/tracing_on
```

In that one second, the trace buffer will have been filled with the details of every function called by the kernel. The format of the trace buffer is plain text, as described in `Documentation/trace/ftrace.txt`. You can read the trace buffer from the `trace` file:

```
# cat /sys/kernel/debug/tracing/trace
# tracer: function
#
# entries-in-buffer/entries-written: 40051/40051   #P:1
#
#                          _-----=> irqs-off
#                         / _----=> need-resched
#                        | / _---=> hardirq/softirq
#                        || / _--=> preempt-depth
#                        ||| /     delay
# TASK-PID    CPU#       ||||    TIMESTAMP   FUNCTION
#    | |        |        ||||       |          |
sh-361  [000] ...1 992.990646: mutex_unlock <-rb_simple_write
sh-361  [000] ...1 992.990658: __fsnotify_parent <-vfs_write
sh-361  [000] ...1 992.990661: fsnotify <-vfs_write
sh-361  [000] ...1 992.990663: __srcu_read_lock <-fsnotify
sh-361  [000] ...1 992.990666: preempt_count_add <-__srcu_read_
lock
sh-361  [000] ...2 992.990668: preempt_count_sub <-__srcu_read_
lock
sh-361  [000] ...1 992.990670: __srcu_read_unlock <-fsnotify
sh-361  [000] ...1 992.990672: __sb_end_write <-vfs_write
```

```
sh-361 [000] ...1 992.990674: preempt_count_add <-__sb_end_
write
[...]
```

You can capture a large number of data points in just one second—in this case, over 40,000.

As with profilers, it is difficult to make sense of a flat function list like this. If you select the `function_graph` tracer, Ftrace captures call graphs like this:

```
# tracer: function_graph
#
# CPU  DURATION                  FUNCTION CALLS
# |     |   |                     |   |   |   |
 0) + 63.167 us   |              } /* cpdma_ctlr_int_ctrl */
 0) + 73.417 us   |            } /* cpsw_intr_disable */
 0)               |            disable_irq_nosync() {
 0)               |              __disable_irq_nosync() {
 0)               |                __irq_get_desc_lock() {
 0)    0.541 us   |                  irq_to_desc();
 0)    0.500 us   |                  preempt_count_add();
 0) + 16.000 us   |                }
 0)               |                __disable_irq() {
 0)    0.500 us   |                  irq_disable();
 0)    8.208 us   |                }
 0)               |                __irq_put_desc_unlock() {
 0)    0.459 us   |                  preempt_count_sub();
 0)    8.000 us   |                }
 0) + 55.625 us   |              }
 0) + 63.375 us   |            }
```

Now you can see the nesting of the function calls, delimited by braces, `{` and `}`. At the terminating brace, there is a measurement of the time taken in the function, annotated with a plus sign (`+`) if it takes more than 10 µs and an exclamation mark (`!`) if it takes more than 100 µs.

You are often only interested in the kernel activity caused by a single process or thread, in which case you can restrict the trace to the one thread by writing the thread ID to `set_ftrace_pid`.

Dynamic Ftrace and trace filters

Enabling CONFIG_DYNAMIC_FTRACE allows Ftrace to modify the function trace sites at runtime, which has a couple of benefits. Firstly, it triggers additional build-time processing of the trace function probes, which allows the Ftrace subsystem to locate them at boot time and overwrite them with NOP instructions, thus reducing the overhead of the function trace code to almost nothing. You can then enable Ftrace in production or near-production kernels with no impact on performance.

The second advantage is that you can selectively enable function trace sites rather than tracing everything. The list of functions is put into available_filter_functions; there are several tens of thousands of them. You can selectively enable function traces as you need them by copying the name from available_filter_functions to set_ftrace_filter and then stop tracing that function by writing the name to set_ftrace_notrace. You can also use wildcards and append names to the list. For example, suppose you are interested in tcp handling:

```
# cd /sys/kernel/debug/tracing
# echo "tcp*" > set_ftrace_filter
# echo function > current_tracer
# echo 1 > tracing_on
```

Run some tests and then look at trace:

```
# cat trace
# tracer: function
#
# entries-in-buffer/entries-written: 590/590   #P:1
#
#                        _-----=> irqs-off
#                       / _----=> need-resched
#                      | / _---=> hardirq/softirq
#                      || / _--=> preempt-depth
#                      ||| /     delay
#  TASK-PID   CPU#  ||||    TIMESTAMP  FUNCTION
#     | |       |   ||||       |          |
dropbear-375 [000] ...1 48545.022235: tcp_poll <-sock_poll
dropbear-375 [000] ...1 48545.022372: tcp_poll <-sock_poll
dropbear-375 [000] ...1 48545.022393: tcp_sendmsg <-inet_
sendmsg
```

```
dropbear-375 [000] ...1 48545.022398: tcp_send_mss <-tcp_
sendmsg
dropbear-375 [000] ...1 48545.022400: tcp_current_mss <-tcp_
send_mss
[...]
```

The set_ftrace_filter function can also contain commands, for example, to start and stop tracing when certain functions are executed. There isn't space to go into these details here, but if you want to find out more, read the *Filter commands* section in Documentation/trace/ftrace.txt.

Trace events

The function and function_graph tracers described in the preceding section record only the time at which the function was executed. The trace events feature also records parameters associated with the call, making the trace more readable and informative. For example, instead of just recording that the kmalloc function has been called, a trace event will record the number of bytes requested and the returned pointer. Trace events are used in perf and LTTng as well as Ftrace, but the development of the trace events subsystem was prompted by the LTTng project.

It takes effort from kernel developers to create trace events, since each one is different. They are defined in the source code using the TRACE_EVENT macro; there are over a thousand of them now. You can see the list of events available at runtime in /sys/kernel/debug/tracing/available_events. They are named subsystem:function, for example, kmem:kmalloc. Each event is also represented by a subdirectory in tracing/events/[subsystem]/[function], as demonstrated here:

```
# ls events/kmem/kmalloc
enable filter format id trigger
```

The files are as follows:

- enable: You write a 1 to this file to enable the event.
- filter: This is an expression that must evaluate to true for the event to be traced.
- format: This is the format of the event and parameters.
- id: This is a numeric identifier.
- trigger: This is a command that is executed when the event occurs using the syntax defined in the *Filter commands* section of Documentation/trace/ftrace.txt.

I will show you a simple example involving `kmalloc` and `kfree`. Event tracing does not depend on the function tracers, so begin by selecting the `nop` tracer:

```
# echo nop > current_tracer
```

Next, select the events to trace by enabling each one individually:

```
# echo 1 > events/kmem/kmalloc/enable
# echo 1 > events/kmem/kfree/enable
```

You can also write the event names to `set_event`, as shown here:

```
# echo "kmem:kmalloc kmem:kfree" > set_event
```

Now, when you read the trace, you can see the functions and their parameters:

```
# tracer: nop
#
# entries-in-buffer/entries-written: 359/359   #P:1
#
#                           _-----=> irqs-off
#                          / _----=> need-resched
#                         | / _---=> hardirq/softirq
#                         || / _--=> preempt-depth
#                         ||| /     delay
#   TASK-PID    CPU#      ||||     TIMESTAMP  FUNCTION
#      | |        |       ||||        |          |
     cat-382    [000] ...1  2935.586706: kmalloc:call_
site=c0554644 ptr=de515a00
        bytes_req=384 bytes_alloc=512
        gfp_flags=GFP_ATOMIC|GFP_NOWARN|GFP_NOMEMALLOC
     cat-382    [000] ...1  2935.586718: kfree: call_
site=c059c2d8 ptr=(null)
```

Exactly the same trace events are visible in `perf` as `tracepoint` events.

Since there is no bloated user space component to build, Ftrace is well-suited for deploying to most embedded targets. Next, we will look at another popular event tracer whose origins predate those of Ftrace.

Using LTTng

The **Linux Trace Toolkit** (**LTT**) project was started by Karim Yaghmour as a means of tracing kernel activity and was one of the first trace tools generally available for the Linux kernel. Later, Mathieu Desnoyers took up the idea and re-implemented it as a next-generation trace tool, **LTTng**. It was then expanded to cover user space traces as well as the kernel. The project website is at `https://lttng.org/` and contains a comprehensive user manual.

LTTng consists of three components:

- A core session manager
- A kernel tracer implemented as a group of kernel modules
- A user space tracer implemented as a library

In addition to those, you will need a trace viewer such as **Babeltrace** (`https://babeltrace.org`) or the **Eclipse Trace Compass** plugin to display and filter the raw trace data on the host or target.

LTTng requires a kernel configured with `CONFIG_TRACEPOINTS`, which is enabled when you select **Kernel hacking** | **Tracers** | **Kernel Function Tracer**.

The description that follows refers to LTTng version 2.5; other versions may be different.

LTTng and the Yocto Project

You need to add these packages to the target dependencies to `conf/local.conf`:

```
IMAGE_INSTALL_append = " lttng-tools lttng-modules lttng-ust"
```

If you want to run Babeltrace on the target, also append the `babeltrace` package.

LTTng and Buildroot

You need to enable the following:

- `BR2_PACKAGE_LTTNG_MODULES` in the **Target packages** | **Debugging, profiling and benchmark** | **lttng-modules** menu
- `BR2_PACKAGE_LTTNG_TOOLS` in the **Target packages** | **Debugging, profiling and benchmark** | **lttng-tools** menu

For user space trace tracing, enable this:

- BR2_PACKAGE_LTTNG_LIBUST in the **Target packages | Libraries | Other, enable lttng-libust** menu

There is a package called lttng-babletrace for the target. Buildroot builds the babeltrace host automatically and places it in output/host/usr/bin/babeltrace.

Using LTTng for kernel tracing

LTTng can use the set of ftrace events described previously as potential tracepoints. Initially, they are disabled.

The control interface for LTTng is the lttng command. You can list the kernel probes using the following:

```
# lttng list --kernel
Kernel events:
-------------
writeback_nothread (loglevel: TRACE_EMERG (0)) (type: tracepoint)
writeback_queue (loglevel: TRACE_EMERG (0)) (type: tracepoint)
writeback_exec (loglevel: TRACE_EMERG (0)) (type: tracepoint)
[...]
```

Traces are captured in the context of a session, which in this example is called test:

```
# lttng create test
Session test created.
Traces will be written in /home/root/lttng-traces/test-20150824-140942
# lttng list
Available tracing sessions:
1) test (/home/root/lttng-traces/test-20150824-140942) [inactive]
```

Now enable a few events in the current session. You can enable all kernel tracepoints using the --all option, but remember the warning about generating too much trace data. Let's start with a couple of scheduler-related trace events:

```
# lttng enable-event --kernel sched_switch,sched_process_fork
```

Check that everything is set up:

```
# lttng list test
Tracing session test: [inactive]
    Trace path: /home/root/lttng-traces/test-20150824-140942
    Live timer interval (usec): 0
 === Domain: Kernel ===
 Channels:
-------------
- channel0: [enabled]
 Attributes:
      overwrite mode: 0
      subbufers size: 26214
      number of subbufers: 4
      switch timer interval: 0
      read timer interval: 200000
      trace file count: 0
      trace file size (bytes): 0
      output: splice()
 Events:
      sched_process_fork (loglevel: TRACE_EMERG (0)) (type:
tracepoint) [enabled]
      sched_switch (loglevel: TRACE_EMERG (0)) (type:
tracepoint) [enabled]
```

Now start tracing:

```
# lttng start
```

Run the test load, and then stop tracing:

```
# lttng stop
```

Traces for the session are written to the session directory, `lttng-traces/<session>/kernel`.

You can use the Babeltrace viewer to dump the raw trace data in text format. In this case, I ran it on the host computer:

```
$ babeltrace lttng-traces/test-20150824-140942/kernel
```

The output is too verbose to fit on this page, so I will leave it as an exercise for you to capture and display a trace in this way. The text output from Babeltrace does have the advantage that it is easy to search for strings using `grep` and similar commands.

A good choice for a graphical trace viewer is the **Trace Compass** plugin for Eclipse, which is now part of the Eclipse IDE for the C/C++ developer bundle. Importing the trace data into Eclipse is characteristically fiddly. Briefly, you need to follow these steps:

1. Open the **Tracing** perspective.
2. Create a new project by selecting **File | New | Tracing project**.
3. Enter a project name and click on **Finish**.
4. Right-click on the **New Project** option in the **Project Explorer** menu and select **Import**.
5. Expand **Tracing**, and then select **Trace Import**.
6. Browse to the directory containing the traces (for example, `test-20150824-140942`), tick the box to indicate which subdirectories you want (it might be **kernel**), and click on **Finish**.
7. Expand the project and, within that, expand **Traces[1]**, and then within that, double-click on **kernel**.

Now, let's switch gears away from LTTng and jump headfirst into the latest and greatest event tracer for Linux.

Using BPF

BPF (Berkeley Packet Filter) is a technology that was first introduced in 1992 to capture, filter, and analyze network traffic. In 2013, Alexi Starovoitov undertook a rewrite of BPF with help from Daniel Borkmann. Their work, then known as **eBPF** (**extended BPF**), was merged into the kernel in 2014, where it has been available since Linux 3.15. BPF provides a sandboxed execution environment for running programs inside the Linux kernel. BPF programs are written in C and are **just-in-time** (**JIT**) compiled to native code. Before that can happen, the intermediate BPF bytecode must first pass through a series of safety checks so that a program cannot crash the kernel.

Despite its networking origins, BPF is now a general-purpose virtual machine running inside the Linux kernel. By making it easy to run small programs on specific kernel and application events, BPF has quickly emerged as the most powerful tracer for Linux. Like what cgroups did for containerized deployments, BPF has the potential to revolutionize observability by enabling users to fully instrument production systems. Netflix and Facebook make extensive use of BPF across their microservices and cloud infrastructure for performance analysis and thwarting **distributed denial of service** (**DDoS**) attacks.

The tooling around BPF is evolving, with **BPF Compiler Collection** (**BCC**) and **bpftrace** establishing themselves as the two most prominent frontends. Brendan Gregg was deeply involved in both projects and has written about BPF extensively in his book *BPF Performance Tools: Linux System and Application Observability, Addison-Wesley*. With so many possibilities covering such a vast scope, new technology such as BPF can seem overwhelming. But much like cgroups, we don't need to understand how BPF works to start making use of it. BCC comes with several ready-made tools and examples that we can simply run from the command line.

Configuring the kernel for BPF

BCC requires a Linux kernel version of 4.1 or newer. At the time of writing, BCC only supports a few 64-bit CPU architectures, severely limiting the use of BPF in embedded systems. Fortunately, one of those 64-bit architectures is `aarch64`, so we can still run BCC on a Raspberry Pi 4. Let's begin by configuring a BPF-enabled kernel for that image:

```
$ cd buildroot
$ make clean
$ make raspberrypi4_64_defconfig
$ make menuconfig
```

BCC uses LLVM to compile BPF programs. LLVM is a very large C++ project, so it needs a toolchain with wchar, threads, and other features to build.

> Tip
>
> A package named `ply` (`https://github.com/iovisor/ply`) was merged into Buildroot on January 23, 2021, and should be included in the 2021.02 LTS release of Buildroot. `ply` is a lightweight, dynamic tracer for Linux that leverages BPF so that probes can be attached to arbitrary points in the kernel. Unlike BCC, `ply` does not rely on LLVM and has no required external dependencies aside from `libc`. This makes it much easier to port to embedded CPU architectures such as `arm` and `powerpc`.

Before configuring our kernel for BPF, let's select an external toolchain and modify `raspberrypi4_64_defconfig` to accommodate BCC:

1. Enable use of an external toolchain by navigating to **Toolchain | Toolchain type | External toolchain** and selecting that option.
2. Back out of **External toolchain** and open the **Toolchain** submenu. Select the most recent ARM AArch64 toolchain as your external toolchain.
3. Back out of the **Toolchain** page and drill down into **System configuration | /dev management**. Select **Dynamic using devtmpfs + eudev**.
4. Back out of **/dev management** and select **Enable root login with password**. Open **Root password** and enter a non-empty password in the text field.
5. Back out of the **System configuration** page and drill down into **Filesystem images**. Increase the **exact size** value to `2G` so that there is enough space for the kernel source code.
6. Back out of **Filesystem images** and drill down into **Target packages | Networking applications**. Select the **dropbear** package to enable `scp` and `ssh` access to the target. Note that `dropbear` does not allow `root scp` and `ssh` access without a password.
7. Back out of **Network applications** and drill down into **Miscellaneous** target packages. Select the **haveged** package so programs don't block waiting for `/dev/urandom` to initialize on the target.
8. Save your changes and exit `menuconfig`.

Now, overwrite `configs/raspberrypi4_64_defconfig` with your `menuconfig` changes and prepare the Linux kernel source for configuration:

```
$ make savedefconfig
$ make linux-configure
```

The `make linux-configure` command will download and install the external toolchain and build some host tools before fetching, extracting, and configuring the kernel source code. At the time of writing, the `raspberrypi4_64_defconfig` from the 2020.02.9 LTS release of Buildroot still points to a custom 4.19 kernel source tarball from the Raspberry Pi Foundation's GitHub fork. Inspect the contents of your `raspberrypi4_64_defconfig` to determine what version of the kernel you are on. Once `make linux-configure` is done configuring the kernel, we can reconfigure it for BPF:

```
$ make linux-menuconfig
```

To search for a specific kernel configuration option from the interactive menu, hit / and enter a search string. The search should return a numbered list of matches. Entering a given number takes you directly to that configuration option.

At a minimum, we need to select the following to enable kernel support for BPF:

```
CONFIG_BPF=y
CONFIG_BPF_SYSCALL=y
```

We also need to add the following for BCC:

```
CONFIG_NET_CLS_BPF=m
CONFIG_NET_ACT_BPF=m
CONFIG_BPF_JIT=y
```

Linux kernel versions 4.1 to 4.6 need the following flag:

```
CONFIG_HAVE_BPF_JIT=y
```

Linux kernel versions 4.7 and later need this flag instead:

```
CONFIG_HAVE_EBPF_JIT=y
```

From Linux kernel version 4.7 onward, add the following so that users can attach BPF programs to `kprobe`, `uprobe`, and tracepoint events:

```
CONFIG_BPF_EVENTS=y
```

From Linux kernel version 5.2 onward, add the following for the kernel headers:

```
CONFIG_IKHEADERS=m
```

BCC needs to read the kernel headers to compile BPF programs, so selecting `CONFIG_IKHEADERS` makes them accessible by loading a `kheaders.ko` module.

To run the BCC networking examples, we also need the following modules:

```
CONFIG_NET_SCH_SFQ=m
CONFIG_NET_ACT_POLICE=m
CONFIG_NET_ACT_GACT=m
CONFIG_DUMMY=m
CONFIG_VXLAN=m
```

Make sure to save your changes when exiting `make linux-menuconfig` so that they get applied to `output/build/linux-custom/.config` before building your BPF-enabled kernel.

Building a BCC toolkit with Buildroot

With the necessary kernel support for BPF now in place, let's add the user space libraries and tools to our image. At the time of writing, Jugurtha Belkalem and others have been working diligently to integrate BCC into Buildroot but their patches have yet to be merged. While an LLVM package has already been incorporated into Buildroot, there is no option to select the BPF backend needed by BCC for compilation. The new `bcc` and updated `llvm` package configuration files can be found in the `MELP/Chapter20/` directory. To copy them over to your 2020.02.09 LTS installation of Buildroot, do the following:

```
$ cp -a MELP/Chapter20/buildroot/* buildroot
```

Now let's add the `bcc` and `llvm` packages to `raspberrypi4_64_defconfig`:

```
$ cd buildroot
$ make menuconfig
```

If your version of Buildroot is 2020.02.09 LTS and you copied the `buildroot` overlay from `MELP/Chapter20` correctly, then there should now be a `bcc` package available under **Debugging, profiling and benchmark**. To add the `bcc` package to your system image, perform the following steps:

1. Navigate to **Target packages** | **Debugging, profiling and benchmark** and select **bcc**.
2. Back out of **Debugging, profiling and benchmark** and drill down into **Libraries** | **Other**. Verify that **clang**, **llvm**, and LLVM's **BPF backend** are all selected.
3. Back out of **Libraries** | **Other** and drill down into **Interpreter languages and scripting**. Verify that **python3** is selected so that you can run the various tools and examples that come bundled with BCC.
4. Back out of **Interpreter languages and scripting** and select **Show packages that are also provided by busybox** under BusyBox from the **Target packages** page.
5. Drill down into **System tools** and verify that **tar** is selected for extracting the kernel headers.
6. Save your changes and exit `menuconfig`.

Overwrite configs/raspberrypi4_64_defconfig with your menuconfig changes again and build the image:

```
$ make savedefconfig
$ make
```

LLVM and Clang will take a long time to compile. Once the image is done building, use Etcher to write the resulting output/images/sdcard.img file to a micro SD card. Lastly, copy the kernel sources from output/build/linux-custom to a new /lib/modules/<kernel version>/build directory on the root partition of the micro SD card. This last step is critical because BCC needs access to the kernel source code to compile BPF programs.

Insert the finished micro SD into your Raspberry Pi 4, plug it into your local network with an Ethernet cable, and power the device up. Use arp-scan to locate your Raspberry Pi 4's IP address and SSH into it as root using the password you set in the previous section. I used temppwd for the root password in the configs/rpi4_64_bcc_defconfig that I included with my MELP/Chapter20/buildroot overlay. Now, we are ready to gain some firsthand experience of experimenting with BPF.

Using BPF tracing tools

Doing almost anything with BPF, including running the BCC tools and examples, requires root privileges, which is why we enabled root login via SSH. Another prerequisite is mounting debugfs as follows:

```
# mount -t debugfs none /sys/kernel/debug
```

The directory where the BCC tools are located is not in the PATH environment, so navigate there for easier execution:

```
# cd /usr/share/bcc/tools
```

Let's start with a tool that displays the task on-CPU time as a histogram:

```
# ./cpudist
```

`cpudist` shows how long tasks spent on the CPU before being descheduled:

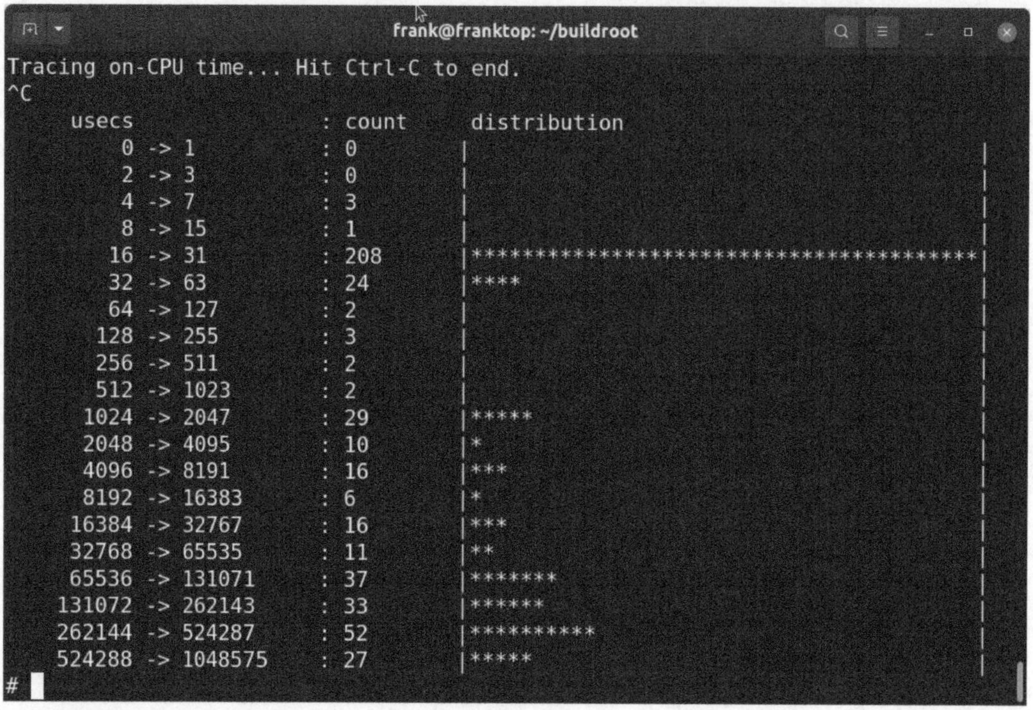
frank@franktop: ~/buildroot
Tracing on-CPU time... Hit Ctrl-C to end.
^C
usecs : count distribution
0 -> 1 : 0 |
2 -> 3 : 0 |
4 -> 7 : 3 |
8 -> 15 : 1 |
16 -> 31 : 208 |**|
32 -> 63 : 24 |****
64 -> 127 : 2 |
128 -> 255 : 3 |
256 -> 511 : 2 |
512 -> 1023 : 2 |
1024 -> 2047 : 29 |*****
2048 -> 4095 : 10 |*
4096 -> 8191 : 16 |***
8192 -> 16383 : 6 |*
16384 -> 32767 : 16 |***
32768 -> 65535 : 11 |**
65536 -> 131071 : 37 |*******
131072 -> 262143 : 33 |******
262144 -> 524287 : 52 |**********
524288 -> 1048575 : 27 |*****
#

Figure 20.5 – cpudist

If instead of a histogram you see the following error, then you forgot to copy the kernel sources to the micro SD card:

```
modprobe: module kheaders not found in modules.dep
Unable to find kernel headers. Try rebuilding kernel with
CONFIG_IKHEADERS=m (module) or installing the kernel
development package for your running kernel version.
chdir(/lib/modules/4.19.97-v8/build): No such file or directory
[...]
Exception: Failed to compile BPF module <text>
```

Another useful system-wide tool is `llcstat`, which traces cache reference and cache miss events and summarizes them by PID and CPU:

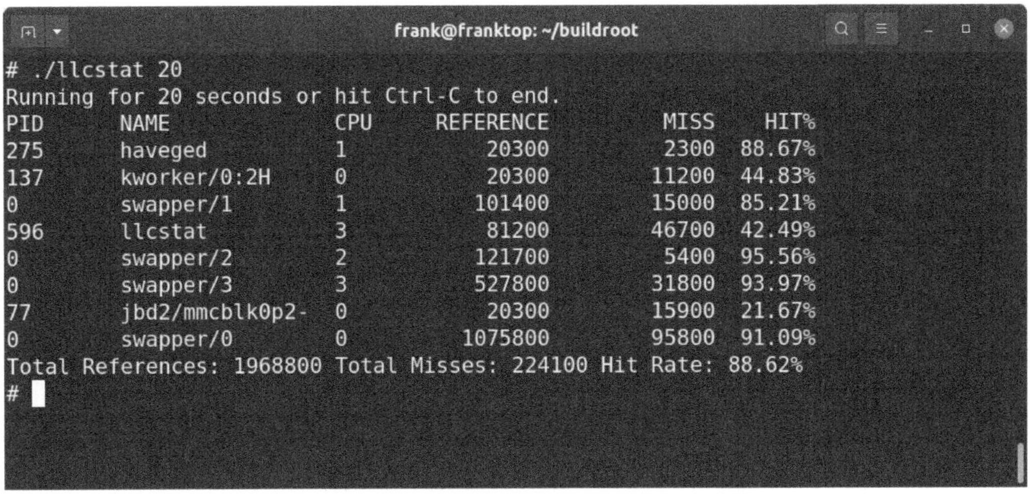

Figure 20.6 – llcstat

Not all BCC tools require us to hit *Ctrl* + *C* to end. Some such as `llcstat` take a sample period as a command-line argument.

We can get more specific and zoom in on specific functions using tools such as `funccount`, which takes a pattern as a command-line argument:

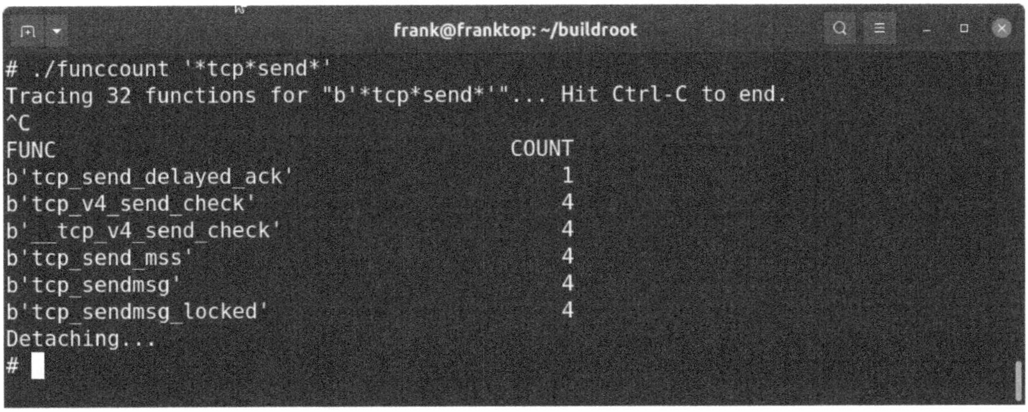

Figure 20.7 – funccount

In this instance, we are tracing all kernel functions containing `tcp` followed by `send` in their names. Many BCC tools can also be used to trace functions in user space. That requires either debug symbols or instrumenting the source code with **user statically defined tracepoint** (USDT) probes.

Of special interest to embedded developers are the `hardirqs` tools, which measure the time spent in the kernel servicing hard interrupts:

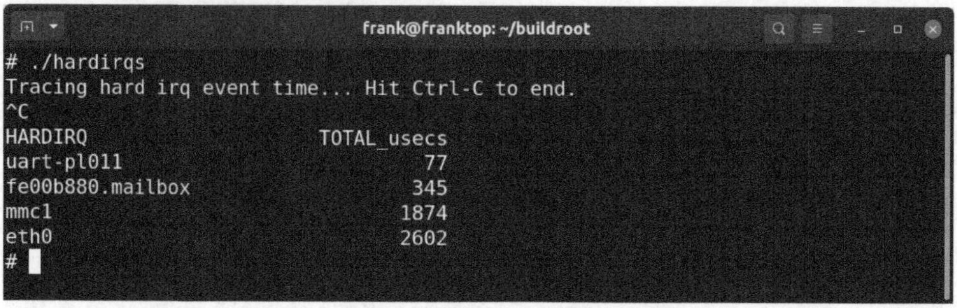
frank@franktop: ~/buildroot
./hardirqs
Tracing hard irq event time... Hit Ctrl-C to end.
^C
HARDIRQ TOTAL_usecs
uart-pl011 77
fe00b880.mailbox 345
mmc1 1874
eth0 2602
#

Figure 20.8 – hardirqs

Writing your own general-purpose or custom BCC tracing tools in Python is easier than you might expect. You can find several examples to read and fiddle with in the `/usr/share/bcc/examples/tracing` directory that comes with BCC.

This concludes our coverage of Linux event tracing tools: Ftrace, LTTng, and BPF. All of them require at least some kernel configuration to work. Valgrind offers more profiling tools that operate entirely from the comfort of user space.

Using Valgrind

I introduced Valgrind in *Chapter 18, Managing Memory*, as a tool for identifying memory problems using the `memcheck` tool. Valgrind has other useful tools for application profiling. The two I am going to look at here are Callgrind and Helgrind. Since Valgrind works by running the code in a sandbox, it can check the code as it runs and report certain behaviors, which native tracers and profilers cannot do.

Callgrind

Callgrind is a call graph-generating profiler that also collects information about processor cache hit rate and branch prediction. Callgrind is only useful if your bottleneck is CPU-bound. It's not useful if heavy I/O or multiple processes are involved.

Valgrind does not require kernel configuration, but it does need debug symbols. It is available as a target package in both the Yocto Project and Buildroot (`BR2_PACKAGE_VALGRIND`).

You run Callgrind in Valgrind on the target like so:

```
# valgrind --tool=callgrind <program>
```

This produces a file called `callgrind.out.<PID>`, which you can copy to the host and analyze with `callgrind_annotate`.

The default is to capture data for all the threads together in a single file. If you add the `--separate-threads=yes` option when capturing, there will be profiles for each of the threads in files named `callgrind.out.<PID>-<thread id>`, for example, `callgrind.out.122-01` and `callgrind.out.122-02`.

Callgrind can simulate the processor L1/L2 cache and report on cache misses. Capture the trace with the `--simulate-cache=yes` option. L2 misses are much more expensive than L1 misses, so pay attention to code with high `D2mr` or `D2mw` counts.

The raw output from Callgrind can be overwhelming and difficult to untangle. A visualizer such as **KCachegrind** (`https://kcachegrind.github.io/html/Home.html`) can help you navigate the mountains of data Callgrind collects.

Helgrind

Helgrind is a thread-error detector for detecting synchronization errors in C, C++, and Fortran programs that include POSIX threads.

Helgrind can detect three classes of errors. Firstly, it can detect the incorrect use of the API. Some examples are unlocking a mutex that is already unlocked, unlocking a mutex that was locked by a different thread, or not checking the return value of certain `pthread` functions. Secondly, it monitors the order in which threads acquire locks to detect cycles that may result in deadlocks (also known as the deadly embrace). Finally, it detects data races, which can happen when two threads access a shared memory location without using suitable locks or other synchronization to ensure single-threaded access.

Using Helgrind is simple; you just need this command:

```
# valgrind --tool=helgrind <program>
```

It prints problems and potential problems as it finds them. You can direct these messages to a file by adding `--log-file=<filename>`.

Callgrind and Helgrind rely on Valgrind's virtualization for their profiling and deadlock detection. This heavyweight approach slows down the execution of your programs, increasing the likelihood of the observer effect.

Sometimes the bugs in our programs are so reproducible and easy to isolate that a simpler, less invasive tool is enough to quickly debug them. That tool more often than not is `strace`.

Using strace

I started the chapter with a simple and ubiquitous tool, `top`, and I will finish with another: **strace**. It is a very simple tracer that captures system calls made by a program and, optionally, its children. You can use it to do the following:

- Learn which system calls a program makes.
- Find those system calls that fail, together with the error code. I find this useful if a program fails to start but doesn't print an error message or if the message is too general.
- Find which files a program opens.
- Find out which `syscalls` a running program is making, for example, to see whether it is stuck in a loop.

There are many more examples online; just search for *strace tips and tricks*. Everybody has their own favorite story, for example, `https://alexbilson.dev/posts/strace-debug/`.

`strace` uses the `ptrace(2)` function to hook calls as they are made from user space to the kernel. If you want to know more about how `ptrace` works, the manual page is detailed and surprisingly readable.

The simplest way to get a trace is to run the command as a parameter to `strace`, as shown here (the listing has been edited to make it clearer):

```
# strace ./helloworld
execve("./helloworld", ["./helloworld"], [/* 14 vars */]) = 0
brk(0)                                       = 0x11000
uname({sys="Linux", node="beaglebone", ...}) = 0
mmap2(NULL, 4096, PROT_READ|PROT_WRITE, MAP_PRIVATE|MAP_
ANONYMOUS, -1, 0) = 0xb6f40000
access("/etc/ld.so.preload", R_OK)          = -1 ENOENT (No such
file or directory)
open("/etc/ld.so.cache", O_RDONLY|O_CLOEXEC) = 3
fstat64(3, {st_mode=S_IFREG|0644, st_size=8100, ...}) = 0
mmap2(NULL, 8100, PROT_READ, MAP_PRIVATE, 3, 0) = 0xb6f3e000
close(3)                                     = 0
open("/lib/tls/v7l/neon/vfp/libc.so.6", O_RDONLY|O_CLOEXEC) =
-1
 ENOENT (No such file or directory)
```

```
[...]
open("/lib/libc.so.6", O_RDONLY|O_CLOEXEC) = 3
read(3,
"\177ELF\1\1\1\0\0\0\0\0\0\0\0\0\3\0(\0\1\0\0\0$`\1\0004\0\0\
0"...,
512) = 512
fstat64(3, {st_mode=S_IFREG|0755, st_size=1291884, ...}) = 0
mmap2(NULL, 1328520, PROT_READ|PROT_EXEC, MAP_PRIVATE|MAP_
DENYWRITE,
3, 0) = 0xb6df9000
mprotect(0xb6f30000, 32768, PROT_NONE)  = 0
mmap2(0xb6f38000, 12288, PROT_READ|PROT_WRITE,
MAP_PRIVATE|MAP_FIXED|MAP_DENYWRITE, 3, 0x137000) = 0xb6f38000
mmap2(0xb6f3b000, 9608, PROT_READ|PROT_WRITE,
MAP_PRIVATE|MAP_FIXED|MAP_ANONYMOUS, -1, 0) = 0xb6f3b000
close(3)
[...]
write(1, "Hello, world!\n", 14Hello, world!
)          = 14
exit_group(0)                           = ?
+++ exited with 0 +++
```

Most of the trace shows how the runtime environment is created. In particular, you can see how the library loader hunts for `libc.so.6`, eventually finding it in `/lib`. Finally, it gets to running the `main()` function of the program, which prints its message and exits.

If you want `strace` to follow any child processes or threads created by the original process, add the `-f` option.

> **Tip**
>
> If you are using `strace` to trace a program that creates threads, you almost certainly want to use the `-f` option. Better still, use `-ff` and `-o <file name>` so that the output for each child process or thread is written to a separate file named `<filename>.<PID | TID>`.

A common use of `strace` is to discover which files a program tries to open at startup. You can restrict the system calls that are traced through the `-e` option, and you can write the trace to a file instead of `stdout` using the `-o` option:

```
# strace -e open -o ssh-strace.txt ssh localhost
```

This shows the libraries and configuration files `ssh` opens when it is setting up a connection.

You can even use `strace` as a basic profile tool. If you use the `-c` option, it accumulates the time spent in system calls and prints out a summary like this:

```
# strace -c grep linux /usr/lib/* > /dev/null
% time     seconds  usecs/call     calls    errors syscall
------ ----------- ----------- --------- --------- ----------
 78.68    0.012825           1     11098        18    read
 11.03    0.001798           1      3551              write
 10.02    0.001634           8       216        15    open
  0.26    0.000043           0       202              fstat64
  0.00    0.000000           0       201              close
  0.00    0.000000           0         1              execve
  0.00    0.000000           0         1         1    access
  0.00    0.000000           0         3              brk
  0.00    0.000000           0       199              munmap
  0.00    0.000000           0         1              uname
  0.00    0.000000           0         5              mprotect
  0.00    0.000000           0       207              mmap2
  0.00    0.000000           0        15        15    stat64
  0.00    0.000000           0         1              getuid32
  0.00    0.000000           0         1              set_tls
------ ----------- ----------- --------- --------- -----------
100.00    0.016300                 15702        49 total
```

`strace` is extremely versatile. We have only scratched the surface of what the tool can do. I recommend downloading *Spying on your programs with strace*, a free zine by Julia Evans available at `https://wizardzines.com/zines/strace/`.

Summary

Nobody can complain that Linux lacks options for profiling and tracing. This chapter has given you an overview of some of the most common ones.

When faced with a system that is not performing as well as you would like, start with `top` and try to identify the problem. If it proves to be a single application, then you can use `perf record/report` to profile it, bearing in mind that you will have to configure the kernel to enable `perf` and you will need debug symbols for the binaries and kernel. If the problem is not so well localized, use `perf` or BCC tools to get a system-wide view.

Ftrace comes into its own when you have specific questions about the behavior of the kernel. The `function` and `function_graph` tracers provide a detailed view of the relationship and sequence of function calls. The event tracers allow you to extract more information about functions, including the parameters and return values. LTTng performs a similar role, making use of the event trace mechanism, and adds high-speed ring buffers to extract large quantities of data from the kernel. Valgrind has the advantage of running code in a sandbox and can report on errors that are hard to track down in other ways. Using the Callgrind tool, it can generate call graphs and report on processor cache usage, and with Helgrind, it can report on thread-related problems.

Finally, don't forget `strace`. It is a good standby for finding out which system calls a program is making, from tracking file open calls to finding file pathnames and checking for system wake-ups and incoming signals.

All the while, be aware of, and try to avoid, the observer effect; make sure that the measurements you are making are valid for a production system. In the next chapter, I will continue with this theme as we delve into the latency tracers that help us quantify the real-time performance of a target system.

Further reading

I highly recommend *Systems Performance: Enterprise and the Cloud, Second Edition*, and *BPF Performance Tools: Linux System and Application Observability*, both by Brendan Gregg.

21
Real-Time Programming

Much of the interaction between a computer system and the real world happens in real time, and so this is an important topic for developers of embedded systems. I have touched on real-time programming in several places so far: in *Chapter 17, Learning About Processes and Threads*, we looked at scheduling policies and priority inversion, and in *Chapter 18, Managing Memory*, I described the problems with page faults and the need for memory locking. Now it is time to bring these topics together and look at real-time programming in some depth.

In this chapter, I will begin with a discussion about the characteristics of real-time systems, and then consider the implications for system design, at both the application and kernel levels. I will describe the real-time `PREEMPT_RT` kernel patch, and show how to get it and apply it to a mainline kernel. The final sections will describe how to characterize system latencies using two tools: **cyclictest** and **Ftrace**.

There are other ways to achieve real-time behavior on an embedded Linux device, for instance, using a dedicated microcontroller or a separate real-time kernel alongside the Linux kernel in the way that Xenomai and RTAI do. I am not going to discuss these here because the focus of this book is on using Linux as the core for embedded systems.

In this chapter, we will cover the following topics:

- What is real time?
- Identifying sources of non-determinism
- Understanding scheduling latency
- Kernel preemption
- The real-time Linux kernel (`PREEMPT_RT`)
- Preemptible kernel locks
- High-resolution timers
- Avoiding page faults
- Interrupt shielding
- Measuring scheduling latencies

Technical requirements

To follow along with the examples, make sure you have the following:

- A Linux-based host system with a minimum of 60 GB of available disk space
- Buildroot 2020.02.9 LTS release
- Yocto 3.1 (Dunfell) LTS release
- Etcher for Linux
- A microSD card reader and card
- BeagleBone Black
- A 5 V 1 A DC power supply
- An Ethernet cable and port for network connectivity

You should have already installed the 2020.02.9 LTS release of Buildroot for *Chapter 6, Selecting a Build System*. If you have not, then refer to the *System requirements* section of *The Buildroot user manual* (`https://buildroot.org/downloads/manual/manual.html`) before installing Buildroot on your Linux host according to the instructions from *Chapter 6*.

You should have already installed the 3.1 (Dunfell) LTS release of Yocto for *Chapter 6, Selecting a Build System*. If you have not, then refer to the *Compatible Linux Distribution* and *Build Host Packages* sections of the *Yocto Project Quick Build* guide (`https://www.yoctoproject.org/docs/current/briefyoctoprojectqs/brief-yoctoprojectqs.html`) before installing Yocto on your Linux host according to the instructions from *Chapter 6*.

What is real time?

The nature of real-time programming is one of the subjects that software engineers love to discuss at length, often giving a range of contradictory definitions. I will begin by setting out what I think is important about real time.

A task is a real-time task if it has to complete before a certain point in time, known as the **deadline**. The distinction between real-time and non-real-time tasks is shown by considering what happens when you play an audio stream on your computer while compiling the Linux kernel. The first is a real-time task because there is a constant stream of data arriving at the audio driver, and blocks of audio samples have to be written to the audio interface at the playback rate. Meanwhile, the compilation is not real-time because there is no deadline. You simply want it to complete as soon as possible; whether it takes 10 seconds or 10 minutes does not affect the quality of the kernel binaries.

The other important thing to consider is the consequence of missing the deadline, which can range from mild annoyance through to system failure or, in the most extreme cases, injury or death. Here are some examples:

- **Playing an audio stream**: There is a deadline in the order of tens of milliseconds. If the audio buffer underruns, you will hear a click, which is annoying but you will get over it.
- **Moving and clicking a mouse**: The deadline is also in the order of tens of milliseconds. If it is missed, the mouse moves erratically and button clicks will be lost. If the problem persists, the system will become unusable.
- **Printing a piece of paper**: The deadlines for the paper feed are in the millisecond range, which if missed may cause the printer to jam, and somebody will have to go and fix it. Occasional jams are acceptable, but nobody is going to buy a printer that keeps on jamming.
- **Printing sell-by dates on bottles on a production line**: If one bottle is not printed, the whole production line has to be halted, the bottle removed, and the line restarted, which is expensive.

- **Baking a cake**: There is a deadline of 30 minutes or so. If you miss it by a few minutes, the cake might be ruined. If you miss it by a lot, the house may burn down.
- **A power-surge detection system**: If the system detects a surge, a circuit breaker has to be triggered within 2 milliseconds. Failing to do so causes damage to the equipment and may injure or kill someone.

In other words, there are many consequences to missed deadlines. We often talk about these different categories:

- **Soft real-time**: The deadline is desirable but is sometimes missed without the system being considered a failure. The first two examples in the previous list are examples of this.
- **Hard real-time**: Here, missing a deadline has a serious effect. We can further subdivide hard real-time into mission-critical systems, in which there is a cost to missing the deadline, such as the fourth example, and safety-critical systems, in which there is a danger to life and limb, such as the last two examples. I put in the baking example to show that not all hard real-time systems have deadlines measured in milliseconds or microseconds.

Software written for safety-critical systems has to conform to various standards that seek to ensure that it is capable of performing reliably. It is very difficult for a complex operating system such as Linux to meet those requirements.

When it comes to mission-critical systems, it is possible, and common, for Linux to be used for a wide range of control systems. The requirements of the software depend on the combination of the deadline and the confidence level, which can usually be determined through extensive testing.

Therefore, to say that a system is real-time, you have to measure its response times under the maximum anticipated load and show that it meets the deadline for an agreed proportion of the time. As a rule of thumb, a well-configured Linux system using a mainline kernel is good for soft real-time tasks with deadlines down to tens of milliseconds, and a kernel with the `PREEMPT_RT` patch is good for soft and hard real-time mission-critical systems with deadlines down to several hundreds of microseconds.

The key to creating a real-time system is to reduce the variability in response times so that you have greater confidence that the deadlines will not be missed; in other words, you need to make the system more deterministic. Often, this is done at the expense of performance. For example, caches make systems run faster by making the average time to access an item of data shorter, but the maximum time is longer in the case of a cache miss. Caches make a system faster but less deterministic, which is the opposite of what we want.

> **Tip**
>
> It is a myth of real-time computing that it is fast. This is not so; the more deterministic a system is, the lower the maximum throughput.

The remainder of this chapter is concerned with identifying the causes of latency and the things you can do to reduce it.

Identifying sources of non-determinism

Fundamentally, real-time programming is about making sure that the threads controlling the output in real time are scheduled when needed and so can complete the job before the deadline. Anything that prevents this is a problem. Here are some problem areas:

- **Scheduling**: Real-time threads must be scheduled before others, and so they must have a real-time policy, `SCHED_FIFO` or `SCHED_RR`. Additionally, they should have priorities assigned in descending order, starting with the one with the shortest deadline, according to the theory of rate monotonic analysis that I described in *Chapter 17, Learning About Processes and Threads*.
- **Scheduling latency**: The kernel must be able to reschedule as soon as an event such as an interrupt or timer occurs, and not be subject to unbounded delays. Reducing scheduling latency is a key topic later on in this chapter.
- **Priority inversion**: This is a consequence of priority-based scheduling, which leads to unbounded delays when a high-priority thread is blocked on a mutex held by a low-priority thread, as I described in *Chapter 17, Learning About Processes and Threads*. User space has priority inheritance and priority ceiling mutexes; in kernel space, we have RT-mutexes, which implement priority inheritance, and I will talk about them in the section on the real-time kernel.
- **Accurate timers**: If you want to manage deadlines in the region of low milliseconds or microseconds, you need timers that match. High-resolution timers are crucial and are a configuration option on almost all kernels.
- **Page faults**: A page fault while executing a critical section of code will upset all timing estimates. You can avoid them by locking memory, as I shall describe later on.
- **Interrupts**: They occur at unpredictable times and can result in an unexpected processing overhead if there is a sudden flood of them. There are two ways to avoid this. One is to run interrupts as kernel threads, and the other, on multi-core devices, is to shield one or more CPUs from interrupt handling. I will discuss both possibilities later.

- **Processor caches**: These provide a buffer between the CPU and the main memory and, like all caches, are a source of non-determinism, especially on multi-core devices. Unfortunately, this is beyond the scope of this book, but you may want to refer to the references at the end of the chapter for more details.
- **Memory bus contention**: When peripherals access memory directly through a DMA channel, they use up a slice of memory bus bandwidth, which slows down access from the CPU core (or cores) and so contributes to non-deterministic execution of the program. However, this is a hardware issue and is also beyond the scope of this book.

I will expand on the most important problems and see what can be done about them in the next sections.

Understanding scheduling latency

Real-time threads need to be scheduled as soon as they have something to do. However, even if there are no other threads of the same or higher priority, there is always a delay from the point at which the wake-up event occurs—an interrupt or system timer—to the time that the thread starts to run. This is called **scheduling latency**. It can be broken down into several components, as shown in the following diagram:

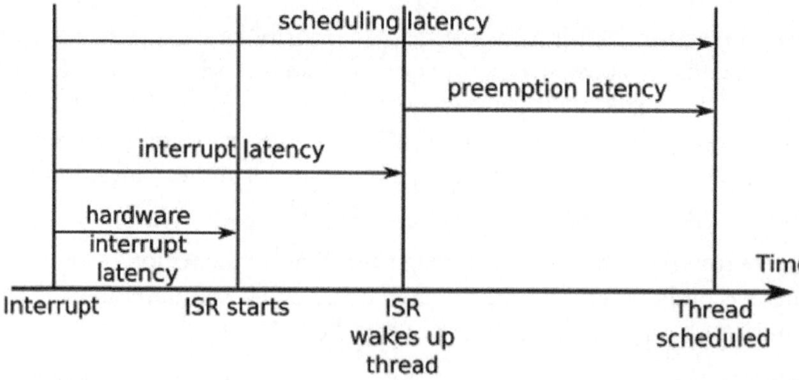

Figure 21.1 – Scheduling latency

Firstly, there is the hardware interrupt latency from the point at which an interrupt is asserted until the **interrupt service routine** (**ISR**) begins to run. A small part of this is the delay in the interrupt hardware itself, but the biggest problem is due to interrupts being disabled in software. Minimizing this *IRQ off time* is important.

The next is interrupt latency, which is the length of time until the ISR has serviced the interrupt and woken up any threads waiting on this event. It is mostly dependent on the way the ISR was written. Normally, it should take only a short time, measured in microseconds.

The final delay is the preemption latency, which is the time from the point that the kernel is notified that a thread is ready to run to that at which the scheduler actually runs the thread. It is determined by whether the kernel can be preempted or not. If it is running code in a critical section, then the rescheduling will have to wait. The length of the delay is dependent on the configuration of kernel preemption.

Kernel preemption

Preemption latency occurs because it is not always safe or desirable to preempt the current thread of execution and call the scheduler. Mainline Linux has three settings for preemption, selected via the **Kernel Features | Preemption Model** menu:

- `CONFIG_PREEMPT_NONE`: No preemption.
- `CONFIG_PREEMPT_VOLUNTARY`: This enables additional checks for requests for preemption.
- `CONFIG_PREEMPT`: This allows the kernel to be preempted.

With preemption set to `none`, kernel code will continue without rescheduling until it either returns via a `syscall` back to user space, where preemption is always allowed, or it encounters a sleeping wait that stops the current thread. Since it reduces the number of transitions between the kernel and user space and may reduce the total number of context switches, this option results in the highest throughput at the expense of large preemption latencies. It is the default for servers and some desktop kernels where throughput is more important than responsiveness.

The second option enables explicit preemption points, where the scheduler is called if the `need_resched` flag is set, which reduces the worst-case preemption latencies at the expense of slightly lower throughput. Some distributions set this option on desktops.

The third option makes the kernel preemptible, meaning that an interrupt can result in an immediate reschedule so long as the kernel is not executing in an atomic context, which I will describe in the following section. This reduces worst-case preemption latencies and, therefore, overall scheduling latencies to something in the order of a few milliseconds on typical embedded hardware.

This is often described as a soft real-time option, and most embedded kernels are configured in this way. Of course, there is a small reduction in overall throughput, but that is usually less important than having more deterministic scheduling for embedded devices.

The real-time Linux kernel (PREEMPT_RT)

There is a long-standing effort to reduce latencies even further that goes by the name of the kernel configuration option for these features, **PREEMPT_RT**. The project was started by Ingo Molnar, Thomas Gleixner, and Steven Rostedt and has had contributions from many more developers over the years. The kernel patches are at `https://www.kernel.org/pub/linux/kernel/projects/rt`, and there is a wiki at `https://wiki.linuxfoundation.org/realtime/start`. An FAQ, albeit out of date, can also be found at `https://rt.wiki.kernel.org/index.php/Frequently_Asked_Questions`.

Many parts of the project have been incorporated into mainline Linux over the years, including high-resolution timers, kernel mutexes, and threaded interrupt handlers. However, the core patches remain outside of the mainline because they are rather intrusive and (some claim) only benefit a small percentage of the total Linux user base. Maybe one day the whole patch set will be merged upstream.

The central plan is to reduce the amount of time the kernel spends running in an **atomic context**, which is where it is not safe to call the scheduler and switch to a different thread. Typical atomic contexts are when the kernel is in the following states:

- Running an interrupt or trap handler.
- Holding a spin lock or is in an RCU-critical section. Spin locks and RCU are kernel-locking primitives, the details of which are not relevant here.
- Between calls to `preempt_disable()` and `preempt_enable()`.
- Hardware interrupts are disabled (**IRQs off**).

The changes that are part of `PREEMPT_RT` fall into two main areas: one is to reduce the impact of interrupt handlers by turning them into kernel threads, and the other is to make locks preemptible so that a thread can sleep while holding one. It is obvious that there is a large overhead in these changes, which makes average-case interrupt handling slower but much more deterministic, which is what we are striving for.

Threaded interrupt handlers

Not all interrupts are triggers for real-time tasks, but all interrupts steal cycles from real-time tasks. Threaded interrupt handlers allow a priority to be associated with the interrupt and for it to be scheduled at an appropriate time, as shown in the following diagram:

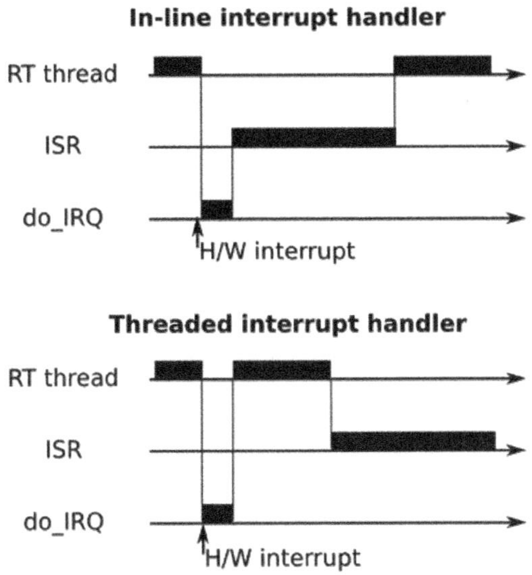

Figure 21.2 – In-line versus threaded interrupt handlers

If the interrupt handler code is run as a kernel thread, there is no reason why it cannot be preempted by a user space thread of higher priority, and so the interrupt handler does not contribute toward scheduling latency of the user space thread. Threaded interrupt handlers have been a feature of mainline Linux since 2.6.30. You can request that an individual interrupt handler be threaded by registering it with `request_threaded_irq()` in place of the normal `request_irq()`. You can make threaded IRQs the default by configuring the kernel with `CONFIG_IRQ_FORCED_THREADING=y`, which makes all handlers into threads unless they have explicitly prevented this by setting the `IRQF_NO_THREAD` flag. When you apply the `PREEMPT_RT` patches, interrupts are, by default, configured as threads in this way. Here is an example of what you might see:

```
# ps -Leo pid,tid,class,rtprio,stat,comm,wchan | grep FF
PID TID CLS RTPRIO STAT COMMAND WCHAN
3 3 FF 1 S ksoftirqd/0 smpboot_th
7 7 FF 99 S posixcputmr/0 posix_cpu_
19 19 FF 50 S irq/28-edma irq_thread
20 20 FF 50 S irq/30-edma_err irq_thread
42 42 FF 50 S irq/91-rtc0 irq_thread
43 43 FF 50 S irq/92-rtc0 irq_thread
44 44 FF 50 S irq/80-mmc0 irq_thread
45 45 FF 50 S irq/150-mmc0 irq_thread
```

```
47 47 FF 50 S irq/44-mmc1 irq_thread
52 52 FF 50 S irq/86-44e0b000 irq_thread
59 59 FF 50 S irq/52-tilcdc irq_thread
65 65 FF 50 S irq/56-4a100000 irq_thread
66 66 FF 50 S irq/57-4a100000 irq_thread
67 67 FF 50 S irq/58-4a100000 irq_thread
68 68 FF 50 S irq/59-4a100000 irq_thread
76 76 FF 50 S irq/88-OMAP UAR irq_thread
```

In this case, which is a BeagleBone running `linux-yocto-rt`, only the `gp_timer` interrupt was not threaded. It is normal that the timer interrupt handler is run inline.

> **Important note**
>
> The interrupt threads have all been given the default `SCHED_FIFO` policy and a priority of `50`. It doesn't make sense to leave them at the defaults, however; now is your chance to assign priorities according to the importance of the interrupts compared to real-time user space threads.

Here is a suggested order of descending thread priorities:

- The POSIX timers thread, `posixcputmr`, should always have the highest priority.
- Hardware interrupts associated with the highest-priority real-time thread.
- The highest-priority real-time thread.
- Hardware interrupts for the progressively lower-priority real-time threads, followed by the thread itself.
- The next highest priority real-time thread.
- Hardware interrupts for non-real-time interfaces.
- The soft IRQ daemon, `ksoftirqd`, which on RT kernels is responsible for running delayed interrupt routines and, prior to Linux 3.6, was responsible for running the network stack, the block I/O layer, and other things. You may need to experiment with different priority levels to achieve a balance.

You can change the priorities using the `chrt` command as part of the boot script, using a command such as this:

```
# chrt -f -p 90 `pgrep irq/28-edma`
```

The `pgrep` command is part of the `procps` package.

Now that we've been introduced to the real-time Linux kernel by way of threaded interrupt handlers, let's dig deeper into its implementation.

Preemptible kernel locks

Making the majority of kernel locks preemptible is the most intrusive change that `PREEMPT_RT` makes, and this code remains outside of the mainline kernel.

The problem occurs with spin locks, which are used for much of the kernel locking. A spin lock is a busy-wait mutex that does not require a context switch in the contended case, and so it is very efficient as long as the lock is held for a short time. Ideally, they should be locked for less than the time it would take to reschedule twice. The following diagram shows threads running on two different CPUs contending the same spin lock. **CPU 0** gets it first, forcing **CPU 1** to spin, waiting until it is unlocked:

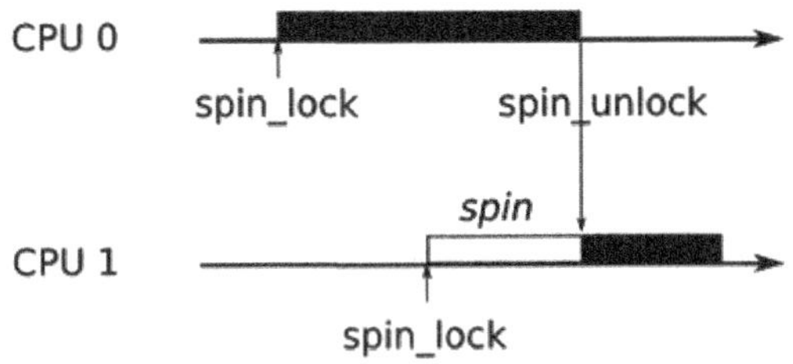

Figure 21.3 – Spin lock

The thread that holds the spin lock cannot be preempted since doing so may make the new thread enter the same code and deadlock when it tries to lock the same spin lock. Consequently, in mainline Linux, locking a spin lock disables kernel preemption, creating an atomic context. This means that a low-priority thread that holds a spin lock can prevent a high-priority thread from being scheduled, a condition otherwise known as *priority inversion*.

> **Important note**
>
> The solution adopted by `PREEMPT_RT` is to replace almost all spin locks with RT-mutexes. A mutex is slower than a spin lock, but it is fully preemptible. Not only that, but RT-mutexes implement priority inheritance and so are not susceptible to priority inversion.

We now have an idea of what's in the `PREEMPT_RT` patches. So, how do we go about getting them?

Getting the PREEMPT_RT patches

The RT developers do not create patch sets for every kernel version because of the amount of porting effort involved. On average, they create patches for every other kernel. The most recent kernels that are supported at the time of writing are as follows:

- 5.10-rt
- 5.9-rt
- 5.6-rt
- 5.4-rt
- 5.2-rt
- 5.0-rt
- 4.19-rt
- 4.18-rt
- 4.16-rt
- 4.14-rt
- 4.13-rt
- 4.11-rt

> **Important note**
>
> The patches are available at `https://www.kernel.org/pub/linux/kernel/projects/rt`.

If you are using the Yocto Project, there is an `rt` version of the kernel already. Otherwise, it is possible that the place you got your kernel from already has the `PREEMPT_RT` patch applied. If not, you will have to apply the patch yourself. Firstly, make sure that the `PREEMPT_RT` patch version and your kernel version match exactly; otherwise, you will not be able to apply the patches cleanly. Then, you apply it in the normal way, as shown in the following command lines. You will then be able to configure the kernel with `CONFIG_PREEMPT_RT_FULL`:

```
$ cd linux-5.4.93
$ zcat patch-5.4.93-rt51.patch.gz | patch -p1
```

There is a problem in the previous paragraph. The RT patch will only apply if you are using a compatible mainline kernel. You are probably not, because that is the nature of embedded Linux kernels. Therefore, you will have to spend some time looking at failed patches and fixing them, and then analyzing the board support for your target and adding any real-time support that is missing. These details are, once again, outside the scope of this book. If you are not sure what to do, you should request support from the kernel vendor that you are using and on kernel developer forums.

The Yocto Project and PREEMPT_RT

The Yocto Project supplies two standard kernel recipes: `linux-yocto` and the latter having the real-time patches already applied. Assuming that your target is supported by the Yocto kernels, you just need to select `linux-yocto-rt` as your preferred kernel and declare that your machine is compatible, for example, by adding lines similar to these to your `conf/local.conf`:

```
PREFERRED_PROVIDER_virtual/kernel = "linux-yocto-rt"
COMPATIBLE_MACHINE_beaglebone = "beaglebone"
```

So, now that we know where to get a real-time Linux kernel, let's switch gears and talk about timing.

High-resolution timers

Timer resolution is important if you have precise timing requirements, which is typical for real-time applications. The default timer in Linux is a clock that runs at a configurable rate, typically 100 Hz for embedded systems and 250 Hz for servers and desktops. The interval between two timer ticks is known as a **jiffy** and, in the examples given previously, is 10 milliseconds on an embedded SoC and 4 milliseconds on a server.

Linux gained more accurate timers from the real-time kernel project in version 2.6.18, and now they are available on all platforms, provided that there is a high-resolution timer source and device driver for it—which is almost always the case. You need to configure the kernel with `CONFIG_HIGH_RES_TIMERS=y`.

With this enabled, all the kernel and user space clocks will be accurate down to the granularity of the underlying hardware. Finding the actual clock granularity is difficult. The obvious answer is the value provided by `clock_getres(2)`, but that always claims a resolution of 1 nanosecond. The `cyclictest` tool that I will describe later has an option to analyze the times reported by the clock to guess the resolution:

```
# cyclictest -R
# /dev/cpu_dma_latency set to 0us
WARN: reported clock resolution: 1 nsec
WARN: measured clock resolution approximately: 708 nsec
```

You can also look at the kernel log messages for strings like this:

```
# dmesg | grep clock
OMAP clockevent source: timer2 at 24000000 Hz
sched_clock: 32 bits at 24MHz, resolution 41ns, wraps every
178956969942ns
OMAP clocksource: timer1 at 24000000 Hz
Switched to clocksource timer1
```

The two methods provide rather different numbers, for which I have no good explanation, but since both are below 1 microsecond, I am happy.

High-resolution timers can measure variations in latency with sufficient accuracy. Now, let's look at a couple of ways to mitigate such non-determinism.

Avoiding page faults

A **page fault** occurs when an application reads or writes to memory that is not committed to physical memory. It is impossible (or very hard) to predict when a page fault will happen, so they are another source of non-determinism in computers.

Fortunately, there is a function that allows you to commit all the memory used by the process and lock it down so that it cannot cause a page fault. It is `mlockall(2)`. These are its two flags:

- `MCL_CURRENT`: This locks all pages currently mapped.
- `MCL_FUTURE`: This locks pages that are mapped in later.

You usually call `mlockall` during the startup of the application with both flags set to lock all current and future memory mappings.

> **Tip**
>
> MCL_FUTURE is not magic, in that there will still be a non-deterministic delay when allocating or freeing heap memory using malloc()/free() or mmap(). Such operations are best done at startup and not in the main control loops.

Memory allocated on the stack is trickier because it is done automatically, and if you call a function that makes the stack deeper than before, you will encounter more memory-management delays. A simple fix is to grow the stack to a size larger than you think you will ever need at startup. The code would look like this:

```
#define MAX_STACK (512*1024)
static void stack_grow (void)
{
        char dummy[MAX_STACK];
        memset(dummy, 0, MAX_STACK);
        return;
}

int main(int argc, char* argv[])
{
        [...]
        stack_grow ();
        mlockall(MCL_CURRENT | MCL_FUTURE);
        [...]
```

The stack_grow() function allocates a large variable on the stack and then zeroes it out to force those pages of memory to be committed to this process.

Interrupts are another source of non-determinism we should guard against.

Interrupt shielding

Using threaded interrupt handlers helps mitigate interrupt overhead by running some threads at a higher priority than interrupt handlers that do not impact real-time tasks. If you are using a multi-core processor, you can take a different approach and shield one or more cores from processing interrupts completely, allowing them to be dedicated to real-time tasks instead. This works either with a normal Linux kernel or a PREEMPT_RT kernel.

Achieving this is a question of pinning the real-time threads to one CPU and the interrupt handlers to a different one. You can set the CPU affinity of a thread or process using the `taskset` command-line tool, or you can use the `sched_setaffinity(2)` and `pthread_setaffinity_np(3)` functions.

To set the affinity of an interrupt, first note that there is a subdirectory for each interrupt number in `/proc/irq/<IRQ number>`. The control files for the interrupt are in there, including a CPU mask in `smp_affinity`. Write a bitmask to that file with a bit set for each CPU that is allowed to handle that IRQ.

Stack growing and interrupt shielding are nifty techniques for improving responsiveness, but how can you tell whether they are actually working?

Measuring scheduling latencies

All the configuration and tuning you may do will be pointless if you cannot show that your device meets the deadlines. You will need your own benchmarks for the final testing, but I will describe here two important measurement tools: `cyclictest` and Ftrace.

cyclictest

`cyclictest` was originally written by Thomas Gleixner and is now available on most platforms in a package named `rt-tests`. If you are using the Yocto Project, you can create a target image that includes `rt-tests` by building the real-time image recipe like this:

```
$ bitbake core-image-rt
```

If you are using Buildroot, you need to add the `BR2_PACKAGE_RT_TESTS` package in the **Target packages | Debugging, profiling and benchmark | rt-tests** menu.

`cyclictest` measures scheduling latencies by comparing the actual time taken for sleeping to the requested time. If there was no latency, they would be the same, and the reported latency would be 0. `cyclictest` assumes a timer resolution of less than 1 microsecond.

It has a large number of command-line options. To start with, you might try running this command as `root` on the target:

```
# cyclictest -l 100000 -m -n -p 99
# /dev/cpu_dma_latency set to 0us
policy: fifo: loadavg: 1.14 1.06 1.00 1/49 320
T: 0 ( 320) P:99 I:1000 C: 100000 Min: 9 Act: 13 Avg: 15 Max:
134
```

The options selected are as follows:

- `-l N`: This loops `N` times (the default is unlimited).
- `-m`: This locks memory with `mlockall`.
- `-n`: This uses `clock_nanosleep(2)` instead of `nanosleep(2)`.
- `-p N`: This uses the real-time priority `N`.

The result line shows the following, reading from left to right:

- `T: 0`: This was thread `0`, the only thread in this run. You can set the number of threads with parameter `-t`.
- `(320)`: This was PID `320`.
- `P:99`: The priority was `99`.
- `I:1000`: The interval between loops was 1,000 microseconds. You can set the interval with the `-i N` parameter.
- `C:100000`: The final loop count for this thread was 100,000.
- `Min: 9`: The minimum latency was 9 microseconds.
- `Act:13`: The actual latency was 13 microseconds. The *actual latency* is the most recent latency measurement, which only makes sense if you are watching `cyclictest` as it runs.
- `Avg:15`: The average latency was 15 microseconds.
- `Max:134`: The maximum latency was 134 microseconds.

This was obtained on an idle system running an unmodified `linux-yocto` kernel as a quick demonstration of the tool. To be of real use, you would run tests over a 24-hour period or longer while running a load representative of the maximum you expect.

Of the numbers produced by `cyclictest`, the maximum latency is the most interesting, but it would be nice to get an idea of the spread of the values. You can get that by adding `-h <N>` to obtain a histogram of samples that are up to `N` microseconds late. Using this technique, I obtained three traces for the same target board running kernels with no preemption, with standard preemption, and with RT preemption while being loaded with Ethernet traffic from a **flood ping**. The command line was as shown here:

```
# cyclictest -p 99 -m -n -l 100000 -q -h 500 > cyclictest.data
```

Then, I used `gnuplot` to create the three graphs that follow. If you are curious, the data files and the `gnuplot` command script are in the code archive, in `MELP/Chapter21/plot`.

The following is the output generated with no preemption:

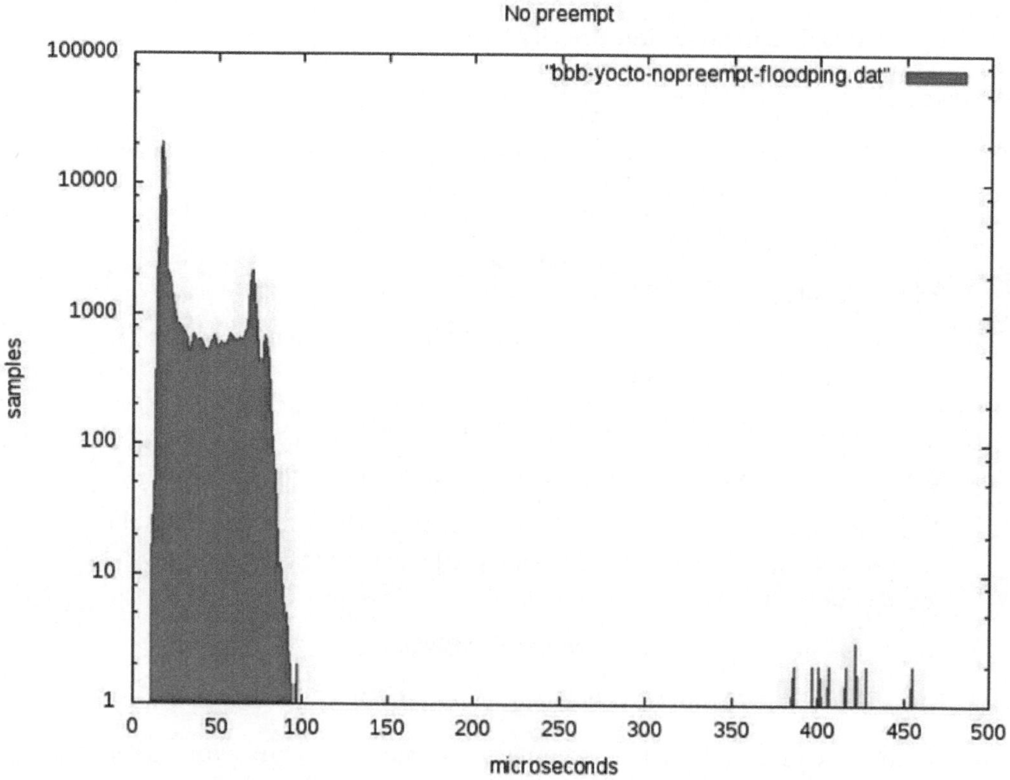

Figure 21.4 – No preemption

Without preemption, most samples are within 100 microseconds of the deadline, but there are some outliers of up to *500 microseconds*, which is pretty much what you would expect.

This is the output generated with standard preemption:

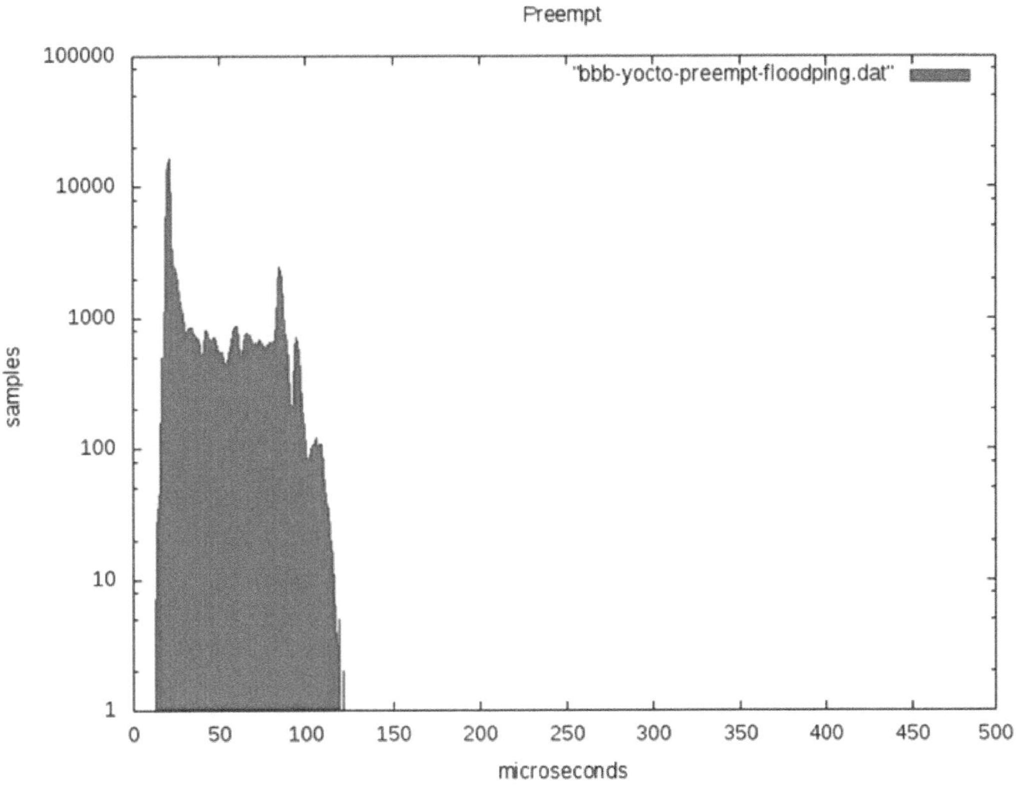

Figure 21.5 – Standard preemption

With preemption, the samples are spread out at the lower end, but there is nothing beyond 120 microseconds.

Here is the output generated with RT preemption:

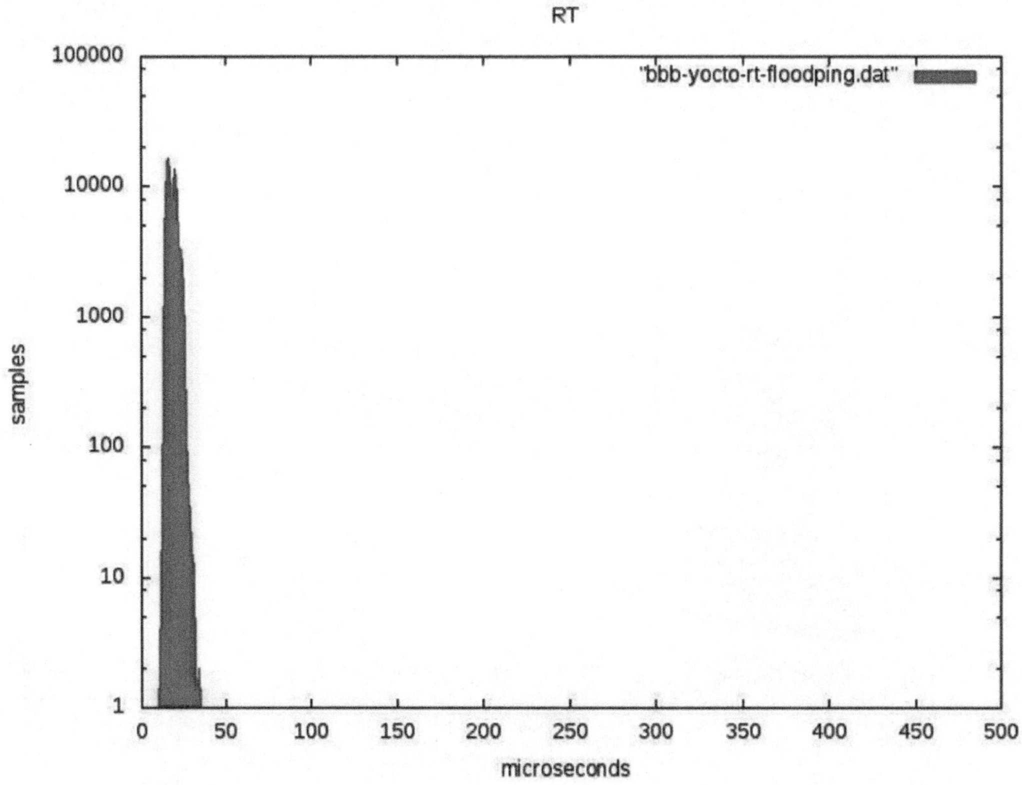

Figure 21.6 – RT preemption

The RT kernel is a clear winner because everything is tightly bunched around the 20-microsecond mark, and there is nothing later than 35 microseconds.

`cyclictest`, then, is a standard metric for scheduling latencies. However, it cannot help you identify and resolve specific problems with kernel latency. To do that, you need Ftrace.

Using Ftrace

The kernel function tracer has tracers to help track down kernel latencies—that is what it was originally written for, after all. These tracers capture the trace for the worst-case latency detected during a run, showing the functions that caused the delay.

The tracers of interest, together with the kernel configuration parameters, are as follows:

- `irqsoff`: `CONFIG_IRQSOFF_TRACER` traces code that disables interrupts, recording the worst case.

- `preemptoff`: `CONFIG_PREEMPT_TRACER` is similar to `irqsoff`, but traces the longest time that kernel preemption is disabled (only available on preemptible kernels).
- `preemptirqsoff`: Combines the previous two traces to record the longest time either `irqs` and/or preemption are disabled for.
- `wakeup`: Traces and records the maximum latency that it takes for the highest-priority task to get scheduled after it has been woken up.
- `wakeup_rt`: This is the same as `wakeup` but only for real-time threads with the `SCHED_FIFO`, `SCHED_RR`, or `SCHED_DEADLINE` policies.
- `wakeup_dl`: This is the same but only for deadline-scheduled threads with the `SCHED_DEADLINE` policy.

Be aware that running Ftrace adds a lot of latency, in the order of tens of milliseconds, every time it captures a new maximum, which Ftrace itself can ignore. However, it skews the results of user space tracers such as `cyclictest`. In other words, ignore the results of `cyclictest` if you run it while capturing traces.

Selecting the tracer is the same as for the function tracer we looked at in *Chapter 20, Profiling and Tracing*. Here is an example of capturing a trace for the maximum period with preemption disabled for a period of `60` seconds:

```
# echo preemptoff > /sys/kernel/debug/tracing/current_tracer
# echo 0 > /sys/kernel/debug/tracing/tracing_max_latency
# echo 1 > /sys/kernel/debug/tracing/tracing_on
# sleep 60
# echo 0 > /sys/kernel/debug/tracing/tracing_on
```

The resulting trace, heavily edited, looks like this:

```
# cat /sys/kernel/debug/tracing/trace
# tracer: preemptoff
#
# preemptoff latency trace v1.1.5 on 3.14.19-yocto-standard
# --------------------------------------------------------------------
# latency: 1160 us, #384/384, CPU#0 | (M:preempt VP:0, KP:0,
SP:0 HP:0)
# -----------------
# | task: init-1 (uid:0 nice:0 policy:0 rt_prio:0)
# -----------------
```

```
# => started at: ip_finish_output
# => ended at: __local_bh_enable_ip
#
#
#      _------=> CPU#
#     / _-----=> irqs-off
#     | / _----=> need-resched
#     || / _---=> hardirq/softirq
#     ||| / _--=> preempt-depth
#     |||| / delay
# cmd pid ||||| time | caller
# \ / ||||| \ | /
init-1 0..s. 1us+: ip_finish_output
init-1 0d.s2 27us+: preempt_count_add <-cpdma_chan_submit
init-1 0d.s3 30us+: preempt_count_add <-cpdma_chan_submit
init-1 0d.s4 37us+: preempt_count_sub <-cpdma_chan_submit
[...]
init-1 0d.s2 1152us+: preempt_count_sub <-__local_bh_enable
init-1 0d..2 1155us+: preempt_count_sub <-__local_bh_enable_ip
init-1 0d..1 1158us+: __local_bh_enable_ip
init-1 0d..1 1162us!: trace_preempt_on <-__local_bh_enable_ip
init-1 0d..1 1340us : <stack trace>
```

Here, you can see that the longest period with kernel preemption disabled while running the trace was `1160` microseconds. This simple fact is available by reading `/sys/kernel/debug/tracing/tracing_max_latency`, but the previous trace goes further and gives you the sequence of kernel function calls that led up to that measurement. The column marked `delay` shows the point on the trail where each function was called, ending with the call to `trace_preempt_on()` at `1162us`, at which point kernel preemption is once again enabled. With this information, you can look back through the call chain and (hopefully) work out whether this is a problem or not.

The other tracers mentioned work in the same way.

Combining cyclictest and Ftrace

If `cyclictest` reports unexpectedly long latencies, you can use the `breaktrace` option to abort the program and trigger Ftrace to obtain more information.

You invoke breaktrace using -b<N> or --breaktrace=<N>, where N is the number of microseconds of latency that will trigger the trace. You select the Ftrace tracer using -T [tracer name] or one of the following:

- -C: Context switch
- -E: Event
- -f: Function
- -w: Wakeup
- -W: Wakeup-RT

For example, this will trigger the Ftrace function tracer when a latency greater than 100 microseconds is measured:

```
# cyclictest -a -t -n -p99 -f -b100
```

We now have two complementary tools for debugging latency issues. cyclictest detects the pauses and Ftrace provides the details.

Summary

The term *real-time* is meaningless unless you qualify it with a deadline and an acceptable miss rate. When you have these two pieces of information, you can determine whether or not Linux is a suitable candidate for the operating system and, if so, begin to tune your system to meet the requirements. Tuning Linux and your application to handle real-time events means making it more deterministic so that the real-time threads can meet their deadlines reliably. Determinism usually comes at the price of total throughput, so a real-time system is not going to be able to process as much data as a non-real-time system.

It is not possible to provide mathematical proof that a complex operating system such as Linux will always meet a given deadline, so the only approach is through extensive testing using tools such as cyclictest and Ftrace and, more importantly, using your own benchmarks for your own application.

To improve determinism, you need to consider both the application and the kernel. When writing real-time applications, you should follow the guidelines given in this chapter about scheduling, locking, and memory.

The kernel has a large impact on the determinism of your system. Thankfully, there has been a lot of work on this over the years. Enabling kernel preemption is a good first step. If you still find that it is missing deadlines more often than you would like, then you might want to consider the `PREEMPT_RT` kernel patches. They can certainly produce low latencies, but the fact that they are not in the mainline yet means that you may have problems integrating them with the vendor kernel for your particular board. You may instead, or in addition, need to embark on the exercise of finding the cause of the latencies using Ftrace and similar tools.

That brings me to the end of this dissection of embedded Linux. Being an engineer of embedded systems requires a very wide range of skills, which includes a low-level knowledge of hardware and how the kernel interacts with it. You need to be an excellent system engineer who is able to configure user applications and tune them to work in an efficient manner. All of this has to be done with hardware that is, often, only just capable of carrying out the task. There is a quotation that sums this up: *An engineer can do for a dollar what anyone else can do for two.* I hope that you will be able to achieve this with the information I have presented during the course of this book.

Further reading

The following resources have further information about the topics introduced in this chapter:

- *Hard Real-Time Computing Systems: Predictable Scheduling Algorithms and Applications* by Giorgio Buttazzo
- *Multicore Application Programming* by Darryl Gove

Other Books You May Enjoy

If you enjoyed this book, you may be interested in these other books by Packt:

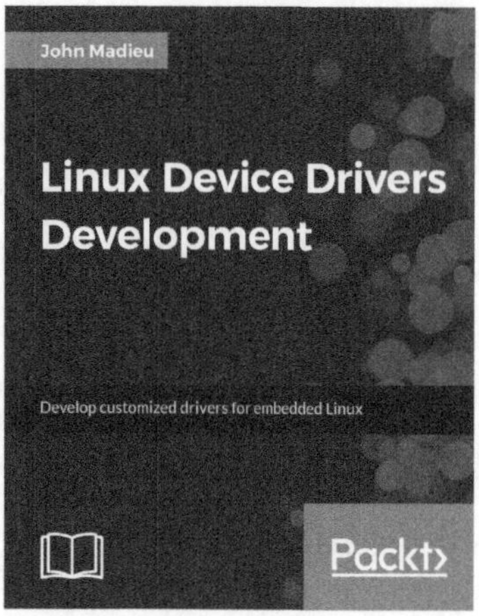

Linux Device Drivers Development

John Madieu

ISBN: 978-1-78528-000-9

- Use kernel facilities to develop powerful drivers
- Develop drivers for widely used I2C and SPI devices and use the regmap API
- Write and support devicetree from within your drivers
- Program advanced drivers for network and frame buffer devices
- Delve into the Linux irqdomain API and write interrupt controller drivers
- Enhance your skills with regulator and PWM frameworks
- Develop measurement system drivers with IIO framework
- Get the best from memory management and the DMA subsystem
- Access and manage GPIO subsystems and develop GPIO controller drivers

Hands-On RTOS with Microcontrollers

Brian Amos

ISBN: 978-1-83882-673-4

- Understand when to use an RTOS for a project
- Explore RTOS concepts such as tasks, mutexes, semaphores, and queues
- Discover different microcontroller units (MCUs) and choose the best one for your project
- Evaluate and select the best IDE and middleware stack for your project
- Use professional-grade tools for analyzing and debugging your application
- Get FreeRTOS-based applications up and running on an STM32 board

Packt is searching for authors like you

If you're interested in becoming an author for Packt, please visit `authors.packtpub.com` and apply today. We have worked with thousands of developers and tech professionals, just like you, to help them share their insight with the global tech community. You can make a general application, apply for a specific hot topic that we are recruiting an author for, or submit your own idea.

Leave a review - let other readers know what you think

Please share your thoughts on this book with others by leaving a review on the site that you bought it from. If you purchased the book from Amazon, please leave us an honest review on this book's Amazon page. This is vital so that other potential readers can see and use your unbiased opinion to make purchasing decisions, we can understand what our customers think about our products, and our authors can see your feedback on the title that they have worked with Packt to create. It will only take a few minutes of your time, but is valuable to other potential customers, our authors, and Packt. Thank you!

Index

A

B

C

D

E

G

H

I

L

M

N

O

P

T

U

V

Printed in France by Amazon
Brétigny-sur-Orge, FR

10271682R00437